Handbook of the Philosophy of Medicine

Thomas Schramme • Steven Edwards
Editors

Handbook of the Philosophy of Medicine

Volume 2

With 14 Figures and 8 Tables

 Springer

Editors
Thomas Schramme
Department of Philosophy
University of Liverpool
Liverpool, UK

Steven Edwards
Philosophy, History and Law
Swansea University
Swansea, UK

ISBN 978-94-017-8687-4   ISBN 978-94-017-8688-1 (eBook)
ISBN 978-94-017-8689-8 (print and electronic bundle)
DOI 10.1007/978-94-017-8688-1

Library of Congress Control Number: 2016950589

Printed on acid-free paper

This Springer imprint is published by Springer Nature
The registered company is Springer Science+Business Media B.V.
The registered company address is: Van Godewijckstraat 30, 3311 GX Dordrecht, The Netherlands

Preface

Philosophy of medicine is a subject that has been around since the beginning of medicine but has only fairly recently, roughly in the last 40 years, been professionally developed into a discipline in its own right. It has gained a stronger status in relation to medical ethics or bioethics, which focuses on moral issues in medicine, whereas philosophy of medicine has a broader and less applied remit, addressing metaphysical, epistemological, and other philosophical issues in medicine.

There are now dedicated societies and academic centers dealing with different topics in philosophy of medicine. This interest is continuously increasing, not least because it has become obvious that several issues in bioethics are based on more theoretical problems of medicine.

The *Handbook of the Philosophy of Medicine* is offered as an all-embracing reference work that analyzes and discusses philosophical issues in relation to medicine and health care. It does not directly focus on ethical issues in health care, which have been thoroughly discussed in the last few decades, but centers around the basic concepts and methodological problems in medicine, which often underlie the ethical debates in health care.

This is the first wide-ranging, multiauthored handbook in the field. It introduces and develops dozens of topics, concepts, and issues and is written by distinguished specialists from multiple disciplines. The *Handbook of the Philosophy of Medicine* aims to be the most thorough book of its kind, covering all major topics that have been discussed in this vibrant area. It provides a single source of information for this far-ranging and still developing field. The chapters also advance these debates and aim at setting the agenda for years to come. The handbook will provide essential reading for anyone who wishes to develop an in-depth understanding of the philosophy of medicine or any of its subfields. It will be an invaluable source for laypeople, academics with an interest in medicine, and health care specialists who want to be informed and up to date with the relevant discussions.

A book project of this scale is very much a team effort. We are immensely grateful for the support of so many friends and colleagues. Most importantly, our authors have been fantastic to work with. Their enthusiasm for the project and their desire to advance the discipline, as well as their level of scholarship in the relevant areas, have made our task very easy. The members of the Advisory Board, Ruth Chadwick, Wim Dekkers, Martyn Evans, Elselijn Kingma, Lennart Nordenfelt, and Pekka Louhiala, were extremely supportive and helped us enormously in identifying relevant topics and suitable authors. Finally, editorial staff at Springer, Alexa Singh, Navjeet Kaur, and Abhijit Baroi, were a pleasure to work with. They diligently and speedily produced the submitted chapters. In addition, Mike Hermann at the New York office supervised the project from beginning to end and provided invaluable advice.

Department of Philosophy, University of   Thomas Schramme
Liverpool, Liverpool, UK
Philosophy, History and Law, Swansea   Steven Edwards
University, Swansea, UK

Contents

Volume 2

About the Editors

Thomas Schramme is Chair in Philosophy at the University of Liverpool. He was Professor of Philosophy at the University of Hamburg from 2009 to 2016. He had affiliations with Swansea University (2005–2009) and the University of Mannheim (1998–2004). He earned his Ph.D. at Free University Berlin with a thesis on the concept of mental illness. His main research interests are in philosophy of medicine, political philosophy, and moral philosophy. He has published in journals such as *Bioethics*, *Ethical Theory and Moral Practice*, *International Journal of Law and Psychiatry*, and *Theoretical Medicine and Bioethics*. He edited several special issues and sections: "Expanding the normative framework of public health ethics: Some results from an interdisciplinary research group," *Public Health Ethics* 1/2015 (with Stefan Huster); "Christopher Boorse and the Philosophy of Medicine," *Journal of Medicine and Philosophy* 39 (6), 2014; "New Trends in Philosophy of Psychiatry," *Theoretical Medicine and Bioethics* 31 (1), 2010; "Lennart Nordenfelt's theory of health," *Medicine, Health Care and Philosophy: A European Journal* 10 (1), 2007. In addition, Schramme published several edited collections: *New Perspectives on Paternalism and Health Care* (Springer 2015), *Being Amoral: Psychopathy and Moral Incapacity* (MIT Press), and *Philosophy and Psychiatry* (de Gruyter Verlag 2004; with Johannes Thome).

Prof. Steven D. Edwards After working in the fields of intellectual disability and psychiatric nursing in the 1970s and 1980s, Prof. Edwards left nursing to study philosophy at the University of Manchester, UK. From there he obtained degrees in philosophy at the levels of undergraduate, masters (M.Phil.) (Relativism), and Ph.D. (Philosophy of Mind). After studying and teaching in the Department of Philosophy at the University of Manchester, he worked as a Senior Lecturer in Philosophy at Buckinghamshire Chilterns University, before moving to join the Centre for Philosophy and Healthcare at University of Wales, Swansea, in 1995. He obtained a University of Wales Personal Chair in Philosophy of Healthcare in 2004. His academic interests are varied and he has published in a wide range of areas of philosophy, but over the past 20 years he has specialized in ethics and philosophy in the context of healthcare. He was founding coeditor of the journal *Nursing Philosophy* and has published books in philosophy of nursing, nursing ethics, philosophy of disability, philosophy of mind, and relativism. In addition to these books, he has published approximately 70 academic papers in scholarly journals. With respect to course leadership, for several years he was Director of Swansea University's MA Ethics of Health Care, and also Program Director of the BSc Medical Science and Humanities. He has been actively involved in the establishment of Clinical Ethics Committees in South Wales and is currently Chair of ABMU Health Board Clinical Ethics Committee. His current research is focussed on linguistic rights in healthcare, as well as ethical issues regarding the treatment of extremely premature neonates.

Contributors

Peter Allmark Centre for Health and Social Care Research, Sheffield Hallam University, Sheffield, UK

Mahesh Ananth Department of Philosophy, Indiana University South Bend, South Bend, IN, USA

Nicanor Pier Giorgio Austriaco O.P. Department of Biology, Providence College, Providence, RI, USA

Kristine Bærøe University of Bergen, Bergen, Norway

Jerome Bickenbach Human Functioning Sciences, Swiss Paraplegic Research, Nottwil, Switzerland

Andrew Bloodworth Department of Inter-Professional Studies, College of Human and Health Sciences, Swansea University, Swansea, UK

Kenneth Boyd Biomedical Teaching Organisation, Edinburgh University Medical School, Edinburgh, Scotland, UK

Hillel D. Braude The Mifne Center, Rosh Pinna, Israel

Matthias Braun Department of Theology, Friedrich-Alexander-University Erlangen-Nuremberg, Erlangen, Germany

Alena Buyx Institute of Experimental Medicine, Christian Albrechts University of Kiel, Kiel, Germany

Silvia Camporesi Department of Global Health and Social Medicine, King's College London, London, UK

Arthur Caplan NYU Langone Medical Center and School of Medicine, New York, NY, USA

Havi Carel Department of Philosophy, University of Bristol, Bristol, UK

Ruth Chadwick University of Manchester, Manchester, UK

Angus Clarke Institute of Medical Genetics Building, Cardiff University School of Medicine, Cardiff, UK

Clare Clement College of Medicine, Institute of Life Sciences 2, Swansea University, Swansea, Wales, UK

Peter Dabrock Department of Theology, Friedrich-Alexander-University Erlangen-Nuremberg, Erlangen, Germany

Catherine Dekeuwer Jean Moulin University Lyon III, Lyon, France

Wim Dekkers IQ Healthcare, Radboud University Medical Center, Nijmegen, The Netherlands

Marcus Doel College of Science, Department of Geography, Wallace Building, Swansea University, Swansea, Wales, UK

Andrew Edgar Cardiff University, Cardiff, UK

Steven Edwards Philosophy, History and Law, Swansea University, Swansea, Wales, UK

Ashley Frawley Department of Public Health, Policy and Social Sciences, Swansea University, Swansea, UK

Eva Friedel Klinik für Psychiatrie und Psychotherapie Campus Charité Mitte, Charité-Universitätsmedizin Berlin, Berlin, Germany

KWM Fulford Faculty of Philosophy, University of Oxford, Oxford, UK

S. Nassir Ghaemi Department of Psychiatry, Tufts University School of Medicine, Boston, MA, USA

Mood Disorders Program, Tufts Medical Center, Boston, USA

Cambridge Health Alliance, Harvard Medical School, Boston, USA

Jan-Christoph Heilinger University of Munich, Munich Center for Ethics, Munich, Germany

Andreas Heinz Klinik für Psychiatrie und Psychotherapie Campus Charité Mitte, Charité-Universitätsmedizin Berlin, Berlin, Germany

Jeanette Hewitt Centre for Philosophy, History, and Law, Swansea University, Swansea, UK

Martin Hoffmann Philosophisches Seminar, Universität Hamburg, Hamburg, Germany

Bjørn Hofmann The Norwegian University of Science and Technology, Gjøvik, Norway

Centre for Medical Ethics, University of Oslo, Oslo, Norway

Stephen Holland Departments of Philosophy and Health Sciences, University of York, Heslington, York, UK

Søren Holm School of Law, The University of Manchester, Manchester, UK
Center for Medical Ethics, HELSAM, University of Oslo, Oslo, Norway
Department of Health Science and Technology, Aalborg University, Aalborg, Denmark

Jeremy Howick Nuffield Department of Primary Care Health Sciences, University of Oxford, Oxford, UK

Peter Hucklenbroich Institut für Ethik, Geschichte und Theorie der Medizin, Westfälische Wilhelms-Universität Münster, Münster, Germany

David Hughes Department of Public Health and Policy Studies, Swansea University, Swansea, UK

Katrina Hutchison Department of Philosophy, Macquarie University, Sydney, NSW, Australia

Ashrafunnesa Khanom College of Medicine, Institute of Life Sciences 2, Swansea University, Swansea, Wales, UK

Elselijn Kingma University of Southampton, Southampton, UK

Hans-Peter Krüger Institut für Politische Philosophie und Philosophische Anthropologie, Universität Potsdam, Potsdam, Germany

Martin Langanke Faculty of Theology, Systematic Theology, Ernst Moritz Arndt University of Greifswald, Greifswald, Germany
Institute for Ethics and History of Medicine, University Medicine Greifswald, Greifswald, Germany

Vic Larcher Honorary Consultant in Paediatrics and Ethics, Great Ormond Street Hospital, London, UK

Keekok Lee Faculty of Humanities, University of Manchester, Manchester, UK

Dorothée Legrand Archives Husserl, CNRS, Ecole normale supérieure, Paris Sciences et Lettres Research University, Paris, France

Christian Lenk Ulm University, Institute for History, Theory and Ethics of Medicine, Ulm, Germany

Henrik Lerner Department of Health Care Sciences, Ersta Sköndal University College, Stockholm, Sweden

Wenke Liedtke Faculty of Theology, Systematic Theology, Ernst Moritz Arndt University of Greifswald, Greifswald, Germany

Pekka Louhiala Department of Public Health, University of Helsinki, Finland

Heidi Maibom University of Cincinnati, Cincinnati, OH, USA

James A. Marcum Department of Philosophy, Baylor University, Waco, TX, USA

Eric Matthews The School of Divinity, History and Philosophy, University of Aberdeen, Aberdeen, UK

John McMillan Bioethics Centre, University of Otago, Dunedin, New Zealand

Mike McNamee College of Engineering, Swansea University, Swansea, UK

Alexander Mebius Royal Institute of Technology (KTH), Stockholm, Sweden
Nuffield Department of Primary Care Health Sciences, University of Oxford, Oxford, UK

Oliver Müller University of Freiburg, Department of Philosophy and BrainLinks-BrainTools, Freiburg, Germany

Lennart Nordenfelt Ersta Sköndal University College, Stockholm, Sweden

John Paley Sheffield Hallam University, Sheffield, UK

Raimo Puustinen Medical School, University of Tampere, Tampere, Finland

Frances Rapport Centre for Healthcare Resilience and Implementation Science, Macquarie University, Sydney, NSW, Australia

Jens Ried Department of Theology, Friedrich-Alexander-University Erlangen-Nuremberg, Erlangen, Germany

Wendy Rogers Department of Philosophy and Department of Clinical Medicine, Macquarie University, Sydney, NSW, Australia

Federica Russo Department of Philosophy, Faculty of Humanities, University of Amsterdam, Amsterdam, The Netherlands

Matthew Sample University of Washington, Department of Philosophy, Seattle, WA, USA

John Saunders College of Human and Health Sciences, Swansea University, Swansea, UK

Jan Schildmann Faculty of Medicine, Institute for Medical Ethics and History of Medicine, Ruhr-Universität Bochum, Bochum, Germany

Jann E. Schlimme Department of Psychiatry and Psychotherapy, Charité University Medicine, Berlin, Germany

Thomas Schramme Department of Philosophy, University of Liverpool, Liverpool, UK

Derek Sellman Faculty of Nursing, Edmonton Clinic Health Academy, University of Alberta, Edmonton, AB, Canada

James Stacey Taylor Philosophy, Religion, and Classical Studies, The College of New Jersey, Ewing, NJ, USA

William E. Stempsey Department of Philosophy, College of the Holy Cross, Worcester, MA, USA

Melanie Storey College of Medicine, Institute of Life Sciences 2, Swansea University, Swansea, Wales, UK

Dorota Szawarska Warsaw, Poland

Tim Thornton College of Health and Wellbeing, University of Central Lancashire, Preston, Lancashire, UK

Hugh Upton College of Human and Health Sciences, Swansea University, Swansea, Wales, UK

Sridhar Venkatapuram Global Health and Social Medicine, King's College London, London, UK

Jochen Vollmann Faculty of Medicine, Institute for Medical Ethics and History of Medicine, Ruhr-Universität Bochum, Bochum, Germany

Carolin Wackerhagen Klinik für Psychiatrie und Psychotherapie Campus Charité Mitte, Charité-Universitätsmedizin Berlin, Berlin, Germany

Jerome C. Wakefield Silver School of Social Work and Department of Psychiatry, School of Medicine, New York University, New York, NY, USA

Simon Walker Bioethics Centre/Te Pokapū Matatika Koiora, University of Otago, Dunedin, New Zealand

Simon Woods PEALS (Policy, Ethics and Life Sciences) Research Centre, Newcastle University, Newcastle upon Tyne, UK

Sarah Wright College of Medicine, Institute of Life Sciences 2, Swansea University, Swansea, Wales, UK

Peter Zachar Department of Psychology, Auburn University Montgomery, Montgomery, AL, USA

Part IV

Clinical Settings and Healthcare Personnel

Applying Medical Knowledge: Diagnosing Disease

39

William E. Stempsey

Contents

Abstract

The term "diagnosis" can refer to the name of a disease that afflicts a person or to the process of determining a diagnosis in the first sense. Complex philosophical, metaphysical, epistemological, normative, and logical issues permeate all aspects of diagnosis, beginning with the question of what is being diagnosed. The nature of disease is philosophically controverted. Both ontological and physiological conceptions of disease continue to influence thinking about disease and hence how to diagnose it. The question of whether the concept of disease is essentially value laden remains open. Diagnosis presupposes some classification of diseases, known as a nosology, in order to distinguish one disease from another. There are many possible ways to classify diseases, and nosologies can have different goals, e.g., providing a basis for rational treatment and prognosis, enabling statistical

W.E. Stempsey (✉)
Department of Philosophy, College of the Holy Cross, Worcester, MA, USA
e-mail: wstempse@holycross.edu

© Springer Science+Business Media Dordrecht 2017
T. Schramme, S. Edwards (eds.), *Handbook of the Philosophy of Medicine*,
DOI 10.1007/978-94-017-8688-1_31

reporting, fostering research, and for administrative aspects of health care. The major elements of the diagnostic process include the history of the illness, the physical examination, and various kinds of laboratory and clinical testing. Each of these elements requires interpretation and is influenced by philosophical presuppositions. Diagnostic reasoning makes use of probabilistic, causal, and deterministic models. It is fundamentally a process of hypothesis formation about possible diagnoses (differential diagnosis) and the systematic confirmation and ruling out of possibilities until one diagnosis is judged best to explain all the data. Diagnosing disease is important for a broad array of medical and social reasons.

Introduction

The term "diagnosis" can refer to the name of a disease or biomedical problem afflicting a person or to the process of determining the presence and nature of the disease. Although the process of diagnosis has been extensively studied and there is general agreement on basic aspects, the complexity of many real-life situations makes it difficult to formulate a universal description of the diagnostic process. One reason for this is that complex philosophical issues permeate all facets of diagnosing disease, including the question of just what disease itself is. This chapter addresses metaphysical, epistemological, normative, and logical issues in three aspects of diagnosing disease: the nature of disease, nosology or the classification of diseases, and the diagnostic process and logical models of diagnostic reasoning.

Disease

If diagnosis is a search for the presence and nature of disease, the nature of diagnosis will depend upon conceptions of disease and how diseases are classified. This section deals with the concept of disease and the following one with classification. The word "disease" can refer to the class of all diseases or to various subsets of that class, such as pneumonia, diabetes mellitus, arthritis, etc., and further subsets, such as bacterial pneumonia, viral pneumonia, rheumatoid arthritis, septic arthritis, etc. "Disease" can also be used to refer to a single instance of one of the above. Other related terms, such as illness and sickness, are often used in common discourse as synonyms but can also have precise meanings and relationships that vary in different theories of health and disease. This chapter focuses on disease as distinguished from related terms such as illness and sickness in the standard biomedical model. Disease refers to a set of biological phenomena that are said to be the cause of a person's experience of illness, which is feeling unwell. The social ramifications of disease and illness are described by the term "sickness."

The metaphysics of disease remains controversial. Historically, there have been two fundamental conceptions of the nature of disease qua disease: physiological and ontological (Temkin 1963, p. 631; Engelhardt 1975, pp. 125–141). The classic physiological conception of disease is the humoral theory that goes back to the time of Hippocrates and dominated for centuries. It presupposes a biologically conceived teleology. When the body is functioning in accord with its nature, there is a proper balance of the four humors: blood, phlegm, black bile, and yellow bile. Disease is deviation from the normal healthy state, that is, an imbalance of the humors (Temkin 1973, p. 398). Even though the classical humoral theory has been long abandoned, the physiological theory of disease has remained influential in concepts such as homeostasis and the idea of disease as deviation from the state of normality called health.

While physiological conceptions take diseases to be deviations from some normal state, ontological conceptions take diseases to be things in themselves. This does not necessarily mean that diseases are concrete things. For example, Thomas Sydenham (1624–1689) held that diseases are observable clusters of signs and symptoms but that they cannot be localized to any particular organ in the body. Still, these clusters display regularity from individual to individual and were conceived as unchanging abstract objects similar to species of plants (Nordenfelt 1995, pp. 152–153). Other ontologists take disease to be actual physical entities. With the discovery of the association of bacteria, parasites, and the like, with certain clusters of symptoms, some ontologists identified these invading organisms as the disease. Another ontological view is that of Rudolf Virchow (1821–1902), the early champion of cellular pathology. Virchow at first repudiated the ontological conception of disease in favor of a physiological one. In 1847, he wrote that diseases were only physiological phenomena under altered conditions, but by 1895 he was calling himself a "thoroughgoing ontologist," regarding pathological cells within the body as the disease itself and not merely the cause of the disease (Virchow 1958, pp. 26, 192; Stempsey 2000, p. 72).

While the physiological and ontological conceptions of disease continue to influence certain aspects of contemporary diagnosis, current thinking is more focused on historical development of concepts of disease. Disease today is more likely to be seen as a process, influenced by current scientific thinking and cultural influences, emphasizing cause, the bearer of the disease, and the set of manifestations (Nordenfelt 1995, pp. 172–173). For example, since the completion of the mapping of the human genome, the concept of genetic disease has seen great emphasis.

One of the major issues philosophers of medicine have explored is the question of whether the concept of disease is essentially value laden. Two opposing positions are often referred to as naturalism and normativism. Naturalists, most prominently Christopher Boorse (1997) in his influential biostatistical theory, believe that the concept of disease is purely descriptive; disease is a value-free scientific concept. Normativists, who have proposed a diverse set of theories, take various kinds of values to be essential components of the concept of disease (Engelhardt 1975; Nordenfelt 1995; Stempsey 2000).

In short, contemporary thinking about the concept of disease can only be described as complex (Hofmann 2001). It is being reframed contextually, based on metaphysical, epistemological, and axiological commitments, to reflect the pathological processes that afflict human beings, bring them to the attention of medical professionals, and serve as warrants for treatment (Cutter 2003).

Nosology

If diagnosis is about explaining a set of symptoms (subjective experiences of feeling unwell) and signs (objectively observable phenomena) in terms of some particular disease, then the question of how one disease is differentiated from another is foundational for diagnosis. The classification of diseases is known as nosology. A fundamental philosophical question for nosology is whether disease classifications mirror independently existing diseases in the realist sense or whether classifications are constructed for various purposes and values. Whether the class of diseases constitutes a natural kind is still debated; Reznek (1987) has denied this. However, even if disease were a natural kind, it is clear from an examination of various existing nosological systems that disease classifications aim at much more than simply trying to map entities that exist in a realist sense.

There are several desirable characteristics for any nosology (Murphy 1997, pp. 122–126): (1) Disease categories should correspond to naturally occurring sets of characteristics seen in particular diseases. (2) A classification ought to be exhaustive, i.e., it should include all the conditions for which people seek medical help. (3) Categories should be disjoint. That is, no particular case should fall into more than one category. (4) The classification should be useful for understanding disease mechanisms, categorizing descriptive features, fostering effective treatment or management, and determining a prognosis and for purposes of such matters as administration, law, and education. (5) The classification should be as simple as possible and still achieve its goals. (6) The classification ought to be constructible, in the sense of allowing both exhaustiveness and disjointness. It is clear that these are ideal characteristics; they cannot all be achieved simultaneously. For instance, complete exhaustiveness and disjointness are in practice impossible to achieve. Most diseases can be classified in several ways, e.g., according to etiology, symptoms, or anatomical location. Exhaustive classifications will necessarily fail to be disjoint. Decisions about which ideals should take priority will have to be made according to usefulness for the particular intended purposes of the nosology.

Thomas Sydenham (1979), in the seventeenth century, and François Boissier de Sauvages (1768), in the eighteenth, constructed nosologies that sought explicitly to be exhaustive in scope. Assuming that diseases were ontological kinds, they relied on empirical observation over rationalistic systems, believing that this would provide a basis for rational treatment. René Laennec (1982), in the late eighteenth century, advocated an anatomico-clinical approach, showing that a nosology based purely on symptoms would not be exhaustive. He conceived of the human organism as consisting of three parts: solids, liquids, and the *principe vital*, an animating force. All diseases were classified as lesions in one of these parts. (Stempsey 2000, pp. 109–110).

Such nosologies are of interest today primarily for historical reasons, but they do reflect the ongoing interest in classifying diseases according to a set of ideals and also emphasizing the practical usefulness of a nosology for rational treatment. An examination of contemporary disease classifications shows a commitment to the same sorts of ideals but with a greatly expanded set of particular purposes.

The International Statistical Classification of Diseases and Related Health Problems (ICD) is one of a family of international classifications of health, disease, disability, and health interventions produced by the World Health Organization. The current, tenth revision (ICD-10), is intended to assist in the "systematic recording, analysis and interpretation and comparison of morbidity and mortality data" across time and place (WHO 2010, v.2, sec. 2.1). Thus, its primary purpose is to facilitate statistical reporting of morbidity and mortality. The classification is divided into 21 chapters. Chapters I–XVII cover local diseases, arranged by the main systems of the body. Chapter XVIII includes symptoms, signs, and abnormal clinical and laboratory findings that are not elsewhere classified. Chapter XIX covers injuries, poisoning, and other consequences of certain external causes. Chapter XX includes other external causes of morbidity and mortality. Chapter XXI classifies data explaining reasons for contact with health services by a person not currently sick, or circumstances in which a person is receiving care.

The Systematized Nomenclature of Medicine (SNOMED) is a comprehensive, multilingual collection of clinical health-care terminology. It is owned and maintained by the International Health Terminology Standards Development Organisation (IHTSDO), a not-for-profit association governed by its national members, twenty-seven countries as of April 2014, and headquartered in Denmark (IHTSDO 2014a). The current version, SNOMED CT (Clinical Terms) is a computer-based terminological system. Terminological systems provide terms denoting concepts and their relations from a specific domain and can be used to describe information in a structured and standardized way. SNOMED CT enables consistency in indexing, storing, retrieving, and aggregating clinical data across specialties and health-care venues. It enables computerizing medical records, thus providing consistency in the way data is stored, encoded, and used for clinical care and research (Cornet and deKeiser 2008). Thus, it serves primarily a clinical purpose: it brings consistency to the way patient data is stored.

SNOMED grew out of the Systematized Nomenclature of Pathology (SNOP), developed by the College of American Pathologists (CAP) in 1965 and later extended to other medical fields as SNOMED. In 2007, the intellectual property rights for SNOMED CT and previous versions of SNOMED and SNOP were transferred from the CAP to the IHTSDO (IHTSDO 2014b).

SNOP was intended to assist pathologists in standardizing terminology in the cataloguing of specimens. SNOP presumes an anatomico-clinical model of disease, in which all diseases can be described by some anatomical change. Although SNOP did not claim to be clinically oriented, it did provide an exhaustive classification of disease, if disease is understood in that particular anatomico-clinical model. Diseases are described with respect to four fields: topography (the part of the body affected), morphology (the structural changes produced in the disease), etiology (the etiologic agent responsible for the disease), and function (the manifestations of the disease). Within each field, terms are given a number up to four digits, the number of digits reflecting increasing specificity. For example, if a small bowel specimen shows ulceration (M4003) in the ileum (T65) with recovery of *Salmonella typhi* (E1361), and the patient shows clinical manifestations of disease (F9497), the specimen is coded as T65-M4003-E1361-F9497 (Stempsey 2000, pp. 112–114). SNOMED in 1979 expanded the "SNOP concept" with three additional fields: a disease field was added to record discharge diagnoses for statistical reporting purposes; a procedure field to record administrative, diagnostic, and therapeutic and preventative procedures; and an occupation field to formally report a patient's work for purposes of specialties like industrial medicine (Stempsey 2000, pp. 114–115). Thus, even early versions of SNOMED have already moved beyond simple classification.

The current version, SNOMED CT, refines the primary purpose of this family of classifications with its emphasis on making health records accessible electronically and meaningful for clinical and administrative uses. Content is presented using three components: concepts, descriptions, and relationships. Concepts are arranged into hierarchies (clinical findings, procedures, body structures, organisms, physical objects, physical forces, events, social context, etc.) from the general to the more detailed; each concept has a unique numeric identifier. Descriptions link other appropriate terms to concepts. A concept can have several associated terms that describe the same clinical concept. Every description has a unique numeric description identifier. Relationships link concepts to other concepts. One example is the "is-a" relationship, which can be used to relate a concept to more general concepts. For instance, the concept "infective pneumonia" bears the "is-a" relationship to the more general concept "pneumonia," and both "bacterial pneumonia" and "viral pneumonia" bear the "is-a" relationship to the more general "infective pneumonia." SNOMED CT thus allows retrieval of information about many elements of disease and its clinical management with a high degree of complexity. This enables a wide range of clinical meanings to be captured in a record, without requiring the terminology to include a separate concept for every detailed combination of ideas that may be relevant to a particular case (IHTSDO 2014c).

The entire question of disease and nosology in psychiatry is more controverted and will only briefly be considered here. The fifth chapter of ICD-10 is devoted to mental disorders and serves as a worldwide standard, but the American Psychiatric Association's Diagnostic and Statistical Manual of Mental Disorders (DSM) is perhaps more influential and has received more notoriety for its sometimes very significant revisions. The current, fifth major revision (DSM-5) was published in 2013. Successive revisions of the DSM have increasingly moved away from Freudian understandings of psychiatry to a more scientific, or at least evidence based, approach to understanding psychiatric disease and its classification. A major problem, however, is that the etiology of a great number of mental disorders is inadequately understood and so cannot serve as the basis for nosology as is increasingly the case with somatic disease. Furthermore, the obvious social dimensions of mental disorders and the difficulty in standardizing such dimensions create problems in trying to establish precise disease categories for mental disorders. Social norms change, and this raises the question of whether psychiatric diagnostic categories simply reflect current norms or are naturally occurring entities more like somatic disease entities. The inclusion and then removal of homosexuality as a mental disorder, for example, has led some to suggest that psychiatric diseases are simply reflections of current social mores and defined by committee fiat. The situation is far more complex, however, and will not be further considered here. It is simply noted that the purpose of psychiatric nosology remains oriented toward the same practical goals as other types of nosologies (Jablensky 2012, pp. 77–94).

Current nosology thus is oriented toward very different goals than were the first attempts to categorize all diseases centuries ago. Current classifications are primarily reporting mechanisms. Although they still recognize the practical import of nosology as facilitating effective care of those who suffer, they make no claims at offering frameworks for choosing treatments. Rather, they serve primarily as means for categorizing disease for purposes of research that will foster public health and for administrative assistance in health-care management and payments.

Diagnosis

The process of diagnosis includes three basic elements: the history of the illness, the physical examination, and laboratory and other sorts of clinical tests. In a typical case, a physician "takes a history" from the patient; develops hypotheses about the diagnosis; performs a physical examination; generates a differential diagnosis, a list of possible diagnoses that fit the hypotheses; tests the hypotheses by laboratory and other sorts of clinical tests such as x-ray examinations; modifies the differential diagnosis; and repeats these various steps until a diagnosis is arrived at (LeBlond et al. 2009, pp. 11–12). This section first considers the three elements and then turns to the logic of diagnosis and the process of reasoning that physicians follow.

History of the Illness

"Taking the history" refers to the initial conversation of physician and patient in which the physician listens to the patient's relating of why he or she is seeking medical help and asks questions to help clarify the information provided by the patient. Some have recommended that the term "taking a history" is misleading and should be replaced because it puts the patient in a merely passive state (Lazare et al. 1995, p. 18), but "taking the history" is still most widely used.

Patient assessments, which include the history and other elements of diagnosis, can be comprehensive or focused. Comprehensive assessments are appropriate for new patients, whether in the hospital or in an outpatient setting. A comprehensive health history can provide fundamental and personalized knowledge about the patient and strengthen the clinician-patient relationship. Comprehensive initial assessments can also provide baselines for future assessments. Focused assessments are more appropriate for established patients, especially during routine or urgent care visits. They address particular concerns or symptoms, often restricted to a specific body system (Bickley and Szilagyi 2013, pp. 4–6).

The comprehensive adult health history seeks both subjective information, such as the patient's experience of pain, and objective information, such as age and family history. The history should include identifying data such as age, gender, occupation, marital status, and an assessment of reliability, which may vary according to the patient's memory, trust of the physician, and other social factors. The initial focus is on the chief complaint or complaints, what it is that brought the patient to seek medical care. Several aspects of the patient's history are then sought. The history of the present illness includes the symptoms, how and when each symptom developed, and the patient's thoughts and feelings about the illness. The physician's questioning may seek to identify pertinent positives and negatives to aid hypothesis formation and to find out about the patient's medications, allergies, and history of smoking and alcohol use. The past history includes childhood illnesses; adult illnesses, whether medical, surgical, obstetric/gynecological, or psychiatric; and health maintenance practices such as immunizations, screening tests, and lifestyle issues. Family history includes age and health or cause of death of siblings, parents, and grandparents and the presence of any genetic diseases or other diseases that are disposed to run in families. Personal and social history includes educational level, family of origin, current household, and personal interests and lifestyle. These elements can provide important clues in the diagnostic process. The final part is the review of systems, in which the physician systematically asks about the presence or absence of common symptoms related to each major body system (Bickley and Szilagyi 2013, pp. 6–13).

The medical interview has three functions (Lazare et al. 1995, pp. 3–19). The first is determining and monitoring the nature of the patient's problem with the objective of enabling the clinician to establish a diagnosis, recommend further diagnostic procedures, suggest a course of treatments, and predict the nature of the illness. The medical interview enables a physician to generate multiple hypotheses during the course of the interview and elicit additional data to refute or confirm them. The history is estimated to contribute 60–80 % of data for diagnosis. The second function is focused on developing, maintaining, and concluding the therapeutic relationship. It helps to define the nature of the physician-patient relationship; communicate professional expertise, interest, respect, support, and empathy; and elicit the patient's perspective on the problem and the methods and goals of treatment. This may indirectly help the physician to glean effective diagnostic data from the interview. The third function is patient education and implementation of treatment plans with the objective of fostering consensus, patient satisfaction, cooperation, and improved treatment outcome. The importance of each function of the interview varies according to the nature of the interview, but the three functions are often interdependent. This functional analysis calls attention to the dynamics and complexity of the medical interview. The medical interview, or taking the history, has multiple purposes that go beyond mere diagnosis. The diagnostic process is ultimately carried out as a means for providing the most effective treatment for the patient and enabling the physician to offer a prognosis. Treatment involves providing drugs, surgery, and the like, but also developing a healing relationship between doctor and patient.

Kathryn Montgomery Hunter (1991, p. 5) sees all of medicine as fundamentally narrative, but most important are the opening stories that patients tell their physicians. She is representative of the school of thought that holds the nature of medicine to be better explained by the methodological analogue of literature than by the natural or social sciences. Even if one does not accept this narrative analysis for all aspects of medicine, it does seem apt for certain activities, especially the medical interview. In this type of literary analysis, patients are seen as texts. While patients are ordinary readers of their texts, physicians are more like sophisticated interpreters. Physicians make sense of signs using a "diagnostic circle" very much like the hermeneutic circle, whereby parts of a text can be understood only with reference to the whole, and the whole can be understood only with reference to the parts (Hunter 1991, p. 9). Thus, with both patient and physician as readers, there is "one illness, two stories" (Hunter 1991, pp. 13–15). The patient's account of illness and the medical version of that account are fundamentally, irreducibly different narratives, and this difference is essential to the work of medical care. The "medical plot," the narrative organization of the case, is fundamentally shaped by the search for a diagnosis and an answer to the question of what is the best treatment for this particular patient (Hunter 1991, p. 65). The patient's story is itself given a sort of medical treatment, being retold in light of the physical examination and clinical tests; in the process, it becomes a fundamentally different story (Hunter 1991, pp. 128–130). The rewriting of the patient's story becomes part of the healing process (Hunter 1991, pp. 138–141). This sort of analysis reinforces the importance of seeing diagnosis in the context of a larger therapeutic relationship. It also highlights the importance that interpretation has in all aspects of diagnosis.

Physical Examination

The physical examination is the second major element that contributes data to the diagnostic process. A comprehensive presentation of the goals and processes of carrying out the physical examination can be found in well-established texts on physical diagnosis such as LeBlond et al. (2009) and Bickley and Szilagyi (2013); a detailed description of them will not be given here. The physical examination is often considered to be a purely scientific matter of observation and a source of objective data, opposed to the subjective data that patients report during the medical interview. However, there are several conceptual issues underlying the physical examination that influence how physical findings are perceived and interpreted. First, the observations made by clinicians during a physical examination are first of all perceptions of the examiner. As such, they are inherently subjective. As has been generally recognized by philosophers of science, all observations are fashioned by the underlying theories that are brought to the observations. To take one classic example, Koplik's spots are considered to be pathognomonic for measles. These are small, bluish-white specks on an irregular red background in the buccal mucosa and occur early in the course of measles. Whether particular bluish-white specks should be considered Koplik's spots is a judgment that depends on the subjective perceptions and judgments of the diagnostician. Such judgments already depend on conceptual commitments about the nosological entity of measles (Engelhardt 1981, pp. 305–306). Psychological factors, such as assumed probabilities and distortions due to expectations, are also known to influence perceptions of what is and what is not observed (Kahneman and Tversky 1982, pp. 144–146).

Diagnostic Testing

The third element of diagnosis consists of the many sorts of laboratory and other clinical tests carried out for the purpose of confirming or ruling out the hypotheses arrived at during the history and physical examination. In light of the ambiguity that can result from the perceptual issues inherent in the physical examination, laboratory and other clinical test results are often preferred and considered to be more objective. Many of the same conceptual issues, and even more complex ones, enter into the interpretation of test results, however.

Clinical tests can include laboratory testing of blood and body fluids such as urine, surgical biopsies of tissues, and clinical examinations such as x-ray studies, computerized tomography, echocardiography, sonography, and other types of procedures.

There are several purposes for which such testing might be done. First, laboratory and clinical tests can be a way to mitigate problems of interobserver variability in both the medical interview and the physical examination. Second, testing allows physicians to extend their medical examinations below the surface of the body. Third, quantitative assessment of levels of bodily constituents can give insight into the physiological processes occurring within the body. Fourth, testing such as bacterial and fungal culturing or toxicological screening can identify the etiological agents responsible for disease. Fifth, laboratory testing of body components can identify markers that might indicate risk for future development of disease. With the rapid development of biotechnology focused on the gene, this last purpose is assuming increasing importance (Stempsey 2000, pp. 149–150).

Two aspects of philosophical importance in laboratory and clinical testing are the choice of tests and the interpretation of tests. Choice of whether to do a test at all and choice of the particular tests to be done involve normative elements, which can be understood in terms of a complex cost-benefit analysis. First, the value of the test for confirming or excluding the particular diagnosis must be considered. Second, the consequences for the patient of including or excluding the diagnosis must be considered. Some diagnoses may be of little importance for the patient, but others, such as being HIV positive, bring serious social consequences. Reducing uncertainty or identifying risk may be important to some patients but not to others. Third, the risk of the diagnostic procedure itself to the patient has moral import. Tests bring discomfort and risk of harm to the patients. The importance of gaining information must be balanced against the potential harm of the test. Many routinely done tests expose patients to radiation, for example. Even a routine blood draw exposes a patient to a very small chance of bruising and infection. To take a more serious case, it is hard to see how one could justify exposing a patient to the dangers of a brain biopsy if the information that would be obtained could have no influence on decisions about treatment or prognosis. Fourth, testing incurs economic costs including wages to health-care personnel, cost of instruments and equipment, and possibly costs of hospitalization and loss of income to the patients. Fifth, if enough tests are performed, it is likely that conflicting results will be obtained. This is usually resolved by getting more tests, which might resolve the conflict but might also exacerbate it (Wulff 1976, pp. 109–110).

The second important philosophical aspect of laboratory and clinical testing is the interpretation of test results. As already mentioned, test results can conflict with one another. This problem is made worse by the easy availability of technology, such as automated machines that can produce many test results from one very small blood sample. Even when there is no conflict of data, results must still be interpreted for significance. Quantified data present particular problems. Precise numbers can suggest a degree of certainty that should not be presumed. In addition, establishing a range of values that is considered to be normal presents the difficulty of correlating population data and drawing inferences from that data for individual patients. These issues are further addressed in the next section.

Diagnostic Reasoning

The data obtained from the three elements of history, physical examination, and diagnostic testing must be gathered and interpreted to formulate a diagnosis, i.e., a name of a disease that best explains the data. This process is diagnostic reasoning. Diagnostic reasoning proceeds from effect to cause, the opposite logical direction used in explaining pathogenesis. Its process cannot be depicted by any one simple logical scheme for several reasons: because nosologies differ and change over time, because diagnosis has different end goals that vary in different clinical situations, and because many patients have multiple diseases rather than just one (Feinstein 1973a, pp. 212–232). For simplicity, "data" here refers to the evidence gleaned from the history, physical examination, and various clinical tests. The diagnostician must authenticate data, decide whether the data deviate from some designated state of normality, and consider the pertinence of the data for the goal of the particular diagnosis. Inferential reasoning then proceeds toward the goal of a diagnostic category and ends when the ultimate end goal, whether it is the ability to make a prognosis or to render a rational treatment, is reached (Feinstein 1973b, pp. 264–283).

It has been shown that physicians use many different strategies and make extensive use of heuristics in order to reach the end goal (Elstein et al. 1978, pp. 252–272; Tversky and Kahneman 1982, pp. 3–20). The process of diagnosis focuses on one diagnostic hypothesis or perhaps more than one. Hypotheses might be general or specific. Reasoning proceeds by progressive modification and refinement of the hypotheses. The arrived at diagnosis is then assessed for coherency, adequacy, and parsimony (Kassirer 1989, p. 894).

Psychologists have carried out extensive studies of how diagnosticians reason. Expert diagnosticians generate diagnostic hypotheses early. The hypotheses they consider are limited in number, rarely exceeding five. Physicians vary considerably in diagnostic effectiveness, depending on the nature of the problem at hand. Hence, diagnostic competence is not simply a characteristic of an individual diagnostician but is case dependent. Experience is also found to be a basic element of competence. Expert diagnosticians have knowledge of how findings relate to diseases or conditions, the relative frequency of the possible conditions in the population, and the particular characteristics of those conditions that carry severe risk, even if their occurrence is low. Effective diagnosticians are able to retain all this information and use it correctly when needed. This capacity has been shown to be an outcome of repetitive practice (Elstein et al. 1978).

Although it is probably impossible to give an exact description of a precise reasoning process for every expert diagnostician in every case, three types of diagnostic reasoning are commonly used (Kassirer 1989, p. 894). First, probabilistic reasoning focuses on the probability of a particular diagnosis given the evidence. Assessment using only terms such as "likely," "common," and "rare" is problematic because such terms are vague and have no standard meaning. Probabilistic diagnostic reasoning turns to quantitative methods as more satisfactory. An ideal test would give an unequivocal answer that confirms or rules out a diagnostic hypothesis, but this is a rare occurrence except in cases where a disease is defined by a test result. Ascertaining the probability of a diagnosis given a positive or negative test result is covered by a rule formulated by Thomas Bayes in the eighteenth century. According to Bayes's theorem, the probability of a diagnosis in a particular patient depends on other probabilities: the prevalence of the diagnosis in the population from which the patient comes, the sensitivity of the test (the proportion of positive test results in people who have the disease), and the specificity of the test (the proportion of negative test results in people who do not have the disease). Thus, test results can be interpreted according to mathematical principles that are easily derived from the most fundamental laws of probability. This approach can be valuable for the diagnostic process, but its limitations must also be recognized. For example, suppose a test to detect a particular cancer has a false-positive rate of just 1 % (specificity $= 0.99$). Suppose, further, that the prevalence of the cancer in the adult population is known to be 100 per 100,000. Thus, of 100,000 people, 99,900 do not have cancer. If the test were administered to those without cancer, 1 % or 999 would have a false-positive test result (Bradley 1993, pp. 70–90). This alone shows the problem of relying on test results at face value and the need for understanding their statistical basis to allow proper interpretation. But there are also other limitations in this sort of probabilistic reasoning. The prevalence of a disease in a population is not always known; when this is the case, it must be subjectively estimated. In addition, many results cannot be described simply as positive or negative; continuous variables must be broken into discrete intervals to use in calculations. Bayesian calculation also depends on the assumption that diseases are mutually exclusive, which is problematic in many cases. In addition, certain diseases manifest themselves in stages and cannot be considered simply as present or absent (Kassirer 1989, p. 895).

The second type of diagnostic reasoning is causal reasoning, which is especially valuable for its explanatory power. Causal reasoning relies on the common sense notion of cause-and-effect relations between variables. In diagnostic reasoning, it focuses on describing anatomical, physiological, and biochemical mechanisms of the normally functioning human body, the body's pathophysiological behavior in disease, and idiosyncrasies of individual patients. Causal models (e.g., fluid-electrolyte equilibrium) are generated, usually relating stimuli and responses. The process of testing, verifying, and falsifying hypothetical causal connections is a fundamental aspect of diagnosis. Causal reasoning can also be useful in setting the context for future data gathering in the diagnostic process. It can help in verifying a diagnosis and assessing its coherency. Major benefits of causal reasoning in diagnosis are its explanatory power and its ability to provide a rational basis for therapeutic interventions (Kassirer 1989, pp. 896–897).

The third type of reasoning is deterministic or categorical reasoning. Deterministic reasoning uses predominantly compiled knowledge that may arise from probabilistic or causal associations between clinical findings. It requires the identification of rules that describe routine practices. The rules can have many purposes, such as describing therapeutic approaches or making prognoses. They might also recommend further diagnostic tests given certain already ascertained data. The rules are in the form of conditionals: If x obtains, then do y; if x does not obtain, then do z. They are represented by branching algorithms, ordered sets of instructions in a flow chart. The flow chart contains a diagram of graphic symbols for each act of reasoning. Two main types of "boxes," often referred to as "nodes," are used to indicate logical activities. A decision box contains a statement of a question to be answered; an execution box contains a statement of a procedure to be performed. A decision box is followed by a branching pathway of at least two possibilities; the reasoning pathway takes a direction indicated by the answer to the question. Arrows are used to indicate the exits and pathways leading from one decision or execution box to the next (Feinstein 1974, pp. 6–7). Typically, each nonterminal node requires unequivocal answers, which then serve as the matter of the branches leaving that node. The terminal nodes represent precise outcomes, answering to the questions the algorithm was designed to answer.

Algorithms are particularly useful in relatively straightforward cases where the logic of the diagnostic process can be precisely defined. Another advantage is that with a well-defined and explicit procedure, it is difficult to omit important questions or tests. Deterministic reasoning, however, depends on the quality of the data that serve as input and does not deal effectively with uncertainty. It may also yield bad answers if the algorithm is applied in a context sufficiently different from the one for which it was designed. Finally, the need to formulate all the rules necessary for even moderately complex diagnostic tasks is a challenge. In complex cases, the branching algorithm can become unwieldy (Kassirer 1989, pp. 897–898).

Each of these three approaches has benefits and limitations, but the limitations can sometimes be ameliorated by the concurrent use of other approaches. Hence, the three approaches are complementary. Probabilistic models can be useful for triggering hypotheses but are dependent on knowing the prevalence of disease in the population from which the patient comes. Causal models, on the other hand, are specific to disease entities and independent of the patient population. They are dependent on fundamental knowledge of physiological function and dysfunction. Once a hypothesis proposes a particular cause, causal reasoning is useful for verification of the cause and for explaining the observations. Causal reasoning can also identify circumstances in which the assumption of independence between diseases required by probabilistic models does not hold. When a knowledge base is built from these models, deterministic models may be constructed to aid in future diagnosis and even serve as bases for computer-assisted diagnosis (Kassirer 1989, p. 898).

Diagnostic Goals and Context

From a semantic standpoint, there are several different kinds of diagnoses. Nosological diagnosis purports to identify a disease or diseases from which a patient suffers. This, however, cannot completely describe diagnosis. It would require that every aspect of the diagnosis is the name of some disease and this does not reflect actual medical practice. Some diagnoses, for instance, are abnormality diagnoses; they include disease but also other disorders, injuries, wounds, lesions, defects, deformities, disabilities, etc. Other diagnoses are causal diagnoses; they give accounts or explanations of the data obtained in the diagnostic process. The category of diagnosis itself may not have clear boundaries, but may be "fuzzy" (Sadegh-Zadeh 2012, pp. 328–335).

The diagnostic context includes the patient, the physician, the physician's practice, the hospital, the patient's family, medical knowledge, and other factors; it produces a diagnosis as one of its outputs. Although a diagnosis is commonly purported to be a statement of some truth, it is perhaps better described as a performative utterance, a speech act, which generates truth and triggers individual, group, and even organizational behavior. A diagnosis imposes a social status on a person. It can exempt people from normal obligations, provide special financial compensation, and cause people who have committed crimes to be found non-culpable by reason of insanity. Thus, diagnosis is also essentially a social act. Diagnosis is, in this sense, a social construct (Sadegh-Zadeh 2012, pp. 335–339). While it may be the case that a diagnosis is constructed from facts, taken in a realist sense, the process of diagnosis depends on conceptual commitments and value judgments at every stage (Stempsey 2000). Diagnosing disease is important not only as a basis for effective treatment, but for a much broader array of medical and social reasons.

Definitions of Key Terms

Disease	(1) a set of biological phenomena that are said to be the cause of a person's experience of illness, which is feeling unwell; (2) the class of all diseases or various subsets of that class; and (3) a single instance of (2)
Diagnosis	(1) the name of a disease that afflicts a person; (2) the process of determining (1)
Differential diagnosis	(1) a set of diagnostic hypotheses that fit the data obtained from the diagnostic process; (2) the process of formulating (1)
Nosology	Classification of diseases

Probabilistic model of diagnostic reasoning	Ascertaining the probability of a diagnosis given particular data using standard mathematical models of probability such as Bayes's theorem
Causal model of diagnostic reasoning	The process of testing, verifying, and falsifying hypothetical cause-effect relationships that explain anatomical, physiological, and biochemical mechanisms of the body's pathophysiological behavior in disease
Deterministic model of diagnostic reasoning	Formulating rules that describe routine diagnostic practices based on compiled knowledge that may arise from probabilistic or causal associations. Rules are typically represented by branching algorithms in a flow chart containing decision points about possible ways to proceed given some determined answer

Summary Points

- "Diagnosis" can refer to the name of a disease or the process of determining a disease present in an individual.
- The concept of disease is philosophically controverted, and it influences judgments about diagnosis.
- Diagnosis presupposes nosology, which can take many forms depending on the goal or goals judged to be most important.
- The history of a patient's illness, the physical examination, and various kinds of laboratory and clinical tests all provide data for diagnosis.
- The process of diagnosis requires interpretation of all elements that disclose data and depends on conceptual and value commitments.
- Diagnostic reasoning includes various strategies and uses probabilistic, causal, and deterministic models in a complementary way.
- Diagnosis is essentially a social act and carries important social implications.

References

Bickley LS, Szilagyi PG (2013) Bates' guide to physical examination and history taking, 11th edn. Wolters Kluwer/Lippincott William and Wilkins, Philadelphia

Boorse C (1997) A rebuttal on health. In: Humber JM, Almeder RF (eds) What is disease? Humana Press, Totowa, pp 3–143

Bradley GW (1993) Disease, diagnosis and decisions. Wiley, Chichester

Cornet R, deKeiser N (2008) Forty years of SNOMED: a literature review. BMC Med Inform Decis Mak 8(suppl 1):S2. Available via http://www.biomedcentral.com/1472-6947/8/S1/S2. Accessed 24 June 2014

Cutter MAG (2003) Reframing disease contextually. Kluwer Academic, Dordrecht

de la Croix B, de Sauvages F (1768) Nosologia methodica sistens morborum classes juxta Sydenhami mentem et botanicorum ordinem. Fratrum de Tournes, Amsterdam

Elstein AS, Shulman L, Sprafka SA (1978) Medical problem solving: an analysis of clinical reasoning. Harvard University Press, Cambridge

Engelhardt HT Jr (1975) The concepts of health and disease. In: Engelhardt HT, Spicker SF (eds) Evaluation and explanation in the biomedical sciences. Reidel, Dordrecht, pp 125–141

Engelhardt HT Jr (1981) Clinical judgment. Metamedicine 2:301–317

Feinstein AR (1973a) An analysis of diagnostic reasoning. I. The domains and disorders of clinical macrobiology. Yale J Biol Med 46:212–232

Feinstein AR (1973b) An analysis of diagnostic reasoning. II. The strategy of intermediate decisions. Yale J Biol Med 46:264–283

Feinstein AR (1974) An analysis of diagnostic reasoning. III. The construction of clinical algorithms. Yale J Biol Med 47:5–32

Hofmann B (2001) Complexity of the concept of disease as shown through rival theoretical frameworks. Theor Med Bioeth 22:211–236

Hunter KM (1991) Doctor's stories: the narrative structure of medical knowledge. Princeton University Press, Princeton

IHTSDO (2014a) Welcome to IHTSDO. Available via http://www.ihtsdo.org. Accessed 25 June 2014

IHTSDO (2014b) History of SNOMED CT. Available via http://www.ihtsdo.org/snomed-ct/history0. Accessed 25 June 2014

IHTSDO (2014c) Introducing SNOMED CT, the global clinical terminology. Available via http://ihtsdo.org/fileadmin/user_upload/doc/download/doc_StarterGuide_Current-en-US_INT_20140222.pdf. Accessed 25 June 2014

Jablensky A (2012) The nosological entity in psychiatry: a historical illusion or a moving target? In: Kendler KS, Parnas J (eds) Philosophical issues in psychiatry II: nosology. Oxford University Press, Oxford, pp 77–94

Kahneman D, Tversky A (1982) Variants of uncertainty. Cognition 11:143–157

Kassirer JP (1989) Diagnostic reasoning. Ann Intern Med 110:893–900

Laennec R (1982) Traite d'anatomie patholigique. In: Boulle L, Grmek MD, Lupovici C, Samion-Contet J (eds) Laennec: catalogue des manuscrits scientifiques. Masson et Fondation Singer-Polignac, Paris, ms 2186 (III)

Lazare A, Putnam SM, Lipkin M (1995) Three functions of the medical interview. In: Lipkin M, Putnam SM, Lazare A (eds) The medical interview: clinical care, education, and research. Springer, New York, pp 3–19

LeBlond RF, Brown DD, DeGowin RL (2009) DeGowin's diagnostic examination, 9th edn. McGraw Hill, New York

Murphy E (1997) The logic of medicine, 2nd edn. Johns Hopkins University Press, Baltimore

Nordenfelt L (1995) On the nature of health: an action-theoretic approach, 2nd rev and enlarged ed. Kluwer, Dordrecht

Reznek L (1987) The nature of disease. Routledge & Kegan Paul, London

Sadegh-Zadeh K (2012) Handbook of analytic philosophy of medicine. Springer, Dordrecht

Stempsey WE (2000) Disease and diagnosis: value-dependent realism. Kluwer, Dordrecht

Sydenham T (1979) The works of Thomas Sydenham, MD, from the Latin edition of Dr. Greenhill, with a life of the author by Latham, RG, facsimile of the Sydenham Society's two-volume edition of 1848–1850, Classics of Medicine Library, Birmingham

Temkin O (1963) The scientific approach to disease: specific entity and individual sickness. In: Crombie AC (ed) Scientific change: historical studies in the intellectual, social and technical conditions for scientific discovery and technical invention, from antiquity to the present. Basic Books, New York, pp 629–647

Temkin O (1973) Health and disease. In: Wiener P (ed) Dictionary of the history of ideas: studies of selected pivotal ideas, vol 2. Scribner's, New York, pp 395–407

Tversky A, Kahneman D (1982) Judgment under uncertainty. In: Kahneman D, Slovic P, Tversky A (eds) Judgment under uncertainty: heuristics and biases. Cambridge University Press, Cambridge, pp 3–20

Virchow RLK (1958) Disease, life, and man: selected essays. Stanford University Press, Stanford

WHO (2010) International statistical classification of disease and related health problems, 10th rev, 2010 ed, 3 vols. World Health Organization, Geneva

Wulff HR (1976) Rational diagnosis and treatment. Blackwell Scientific, Oxford

Technology and Dehumanization of Medicine

Keekok Lee

Contents

Abstract

As the subject matter raised by the title is extremely large, this chapter can only focus on a few aspects for some detailed examination. The nature of technology in general would have to be looked at in order to set the scene for a later discussion of medical technology. Technology cannot be understood except as part of the philosophy of Modernism which involves the ontological *volte-face* of holding that all organisms, including the human organism are machines. This means that Modern Medicine not merely treats patients as machine but also uses machines to treat patients. Machines are intended to be cost-effective in the long run by increasing productivity; as such they necessarily replace human labor. In which medical contexts, then, would replacing human beings by machines constitute the highest level of dehumanization?

K. Lee (✉)
Faculty of Humanities, University of Manchester, Manchester, UK
e-mail: keekok.lee@manchester.ac.uk

© Springer Science+Business Media Dordrecht 2017
T. Schramme, S. Edwards (eds.), *Handbook of the Philosophy of Medicine*,
DOI 10.1007/978-94-017-8688-1_69

Introduction

This essay would address the following aspects of the subject set out in its title:

1. The nature of technology; the history of technology in terms of different types of technologies, their respective relationships to basic/theoretical science; the values embedded in technology; the economics of technology.
2. The implications of above for medicine (which in this context includes aspects of healthcare), especially, in terms of (a) the doctor-patient relationship, (b) the nurse-patient relationship, (c) the relationship between (a) and (b) on the one hand and medical technology of the near future, and (d) the de-skilling, in one crucial aspect, of health professionals (doctors and nurses) with the advent of high-tech. The de-humanization of medicine would be explored within these contexts.
3. The essay would show that 2 is but the outcome of the logic of Modernity, since its inception in Western Europe from the seventeenth century – standing behind the Scientific Revolution, which ushered in Modernity, is a philosophical revolution involving the profound ontological *volte-face* of transforming the universe (including organisms and, therefore, human beings in it) to become machine. This constitutes the radical change to the artifactual mode in the perception and understanding of Nature and ourselves under Modernity.

Relationship Between Technology and Basic Science at the Empirical Level

What is technology? Put very simply and simplistically, technology is nothing but the tools which we humans use to enable us to accomplish certain ends, what we cannot achieve relying only on our four limbs as well as our sensory organs, such as our eyes. In the long history of human-kind, our early ancestors deployed what is called "found" technology or "prototechnology" (Ihde 1993, p. 48), that is to say, whatever object they happened to come across which could do the job they had in mind, such as, the fallen branch of a tree which could be used to reach for ripe fruit or nuts high up a tree, as a walking stick to help those limping with a bruised foot. In a similar manner, a rock with a sharp edge – an adze – was used to cut up meat or scrape clean an animal's hide. With the minimum amount of tinkering, the object could be made to become an instant tool. This type of tool use is certainly also found in other primates, such as chimpanzees.

"Found" technology is, however, not what pre-occupies the scholars of technology in general who are more interested in the history which followed that very early phase. For instance, those who study European technological civilisation have suggested dividing it up into various phases. Mumford (1946) proposes a threefold division (whose edges are meant to be overlapping) in terms of the type of energy and characteristic materials used. The eotechnic phase is a water-wind-and-wood complex; the paleotechnic phase is a steam-coal-and-iron complex; the neotechnic phase is an electricity-and-alloy (as well as synthetic compounds) complex. The first, for him, stretches roughly from 1000 AD to 1750, the second, from 1750 to 1850s, and the third, from the 1850s to the present. Mumford's classification is heuristically enlightening in general but, perhaps, less helpful from the standpoint of this essay which is concerned with medical technology. So a different division is proposed, not based so much on the conjoint variables of energy and material, but on whether the technology is craft or science based. In the case of the latter, it shows that what is significant is the relationship between the technology and the kind of science it is based on. The more basic the theoretical discovery the more powerful, in general, is the technology generated – for instance, technology in medicine and agriculture based on Mendelian genetics (at the level of chromosomes) is less powerful than biotechnology based on DNA genetics and molecular biology – see Lee (2005). The suggested classification in the context of European technological history is as follows (however, bearing in mind that the boundaries between them are not meant to be neat and tidy, but overlapping):

Phase I: Relatively autonomous craft-based technology.
    A: Roughly equivalent to Mumford's eotechnic phase.
    B: Roughly equivalent to Mumford's paleotechnic phase.
Phase II: Science-theory-led technology.
    A: Roughly equivalent to Mumford's neotechnic phase, but ending by the 1940s.
    B: From the 1940s to the present.

Note that this division fails to superimpose neatly upon that which obtains in the history of science itself. There, the radical cleavage is between pre-modern science (up to the seventeenth century) and the rise of modern science (from the seventeenth century onwards). Phase IA falls clearly into the pre-modern scientific era, but Phase IB (roughly up to 1830s) falls clearly into the modern scientific period. In other words, the major cleavage has been drawn between the kind of technology which is theory led and inspired, in contrast to that which is relatively autonomous of basic scientific theories and discoveries themselves. Although Phase IB, in terms of temporal location, coincided with the rise of modern science, the technology it represented was, nevertheless, by and large, not a spin-off of theoretical advances.

On the contrary, during IB, it often happened that technology inspired theoretical research rather than that theoretical advances led the way to new technologies. For instance, this relationship of technology preceding theory is true in the case of the invention of the steam engine, which first appeared in the form of the steam pump, as a response to the demands of the coal mining industry to mine seams at deeper levels where flooding occurred. It later made railway transportation possible as the steam locomotive, and replaced sailing ships on the high seas in the form of the steamer. Attempts to improve its efficiency eventually led to the establishment of the abstract, fundamental science of thermodynamics by Sadi Carnot, a French army officer and engineer, and worked on later by famous scientists like Joule, Kelvin, Clausius and Boltzmann, Atkins 1984, p. 7 writes:

The aims adopted and the attitudes struck by Carnot and by Boltzmann epitomize thermodynamics. Carnot traveled toward thermodynamics from the direction of the engine, then the
symbol of industrialized society: his aim was to improve its efficiency. Boltzmann traveled to
thermodynamics from the atom, the symbol of emerging scientific fundamentalism: his aim was
to increase our comprehension of the world at the deepest levels then conceived. Thermodynamics still has both aspects, and reflects complementary aims, attitudes, and applications. It
grew out of the coarse machinery: yet it has been refined to an instrument of great delicacy. It
spans the whole range of human enterprise, covering the organization and deployment of both
resources and ideas about the nature of change in the world around us. Few contributions to
human understanding are richer than this child of the steam engine and the atom.

Even more remarkably, during IB, technological discoveries, which formed the
very basis of the Industrial Revolution (at least in Britain), were made by people who
knew no science, had no formal education and, indeed, in some cases, could not even
read or write. The most famous of these apprentices and craft-based mechanics is
George Stephenson. Later in life, when he became famous and rich, he was only
partially successful in overcoming his illiteracy. What is now called the Davy Lamp
– the safety lamp for miners, which first appeared in 1815 – was also an invention by
Stephenson. But because of his humble background, illiteracy and ignorance of
physics and chemistry, Humphrey Davy – Fellow and later President of the Royal
Society on whom a baronetcy was eventually conferred – could not credit Stephenson as a fellow inventor. See Davies (1980, pp. 19–32).

Phase I, A and B, in spite of differences between them, share the essential
similarity of being craft-based and relatively autonomous of explicit scientific/
theoretical input. In other words, both IA and IB displayed a split between science
and technology – either science was pursued relatively autonomously of technology
or that technology led the way to scientific theorizing. The causal direction the other
way round, of theory inducing technology, by and large, did not occur until much
later under Phase II when the major technological innovations are theory led or
induced. With regard to Phase IIA, on the theoretical side, by 1850, many of the
fundamental scientific discoveries had already been made. Regarding electro-
magnetism, Faraday, in 1831, found that a conductor cutting the lines of force of a
magnet created a difference in potential. This, together with the work done by Volta,
Galvani, Oersted, Ohm, Ampere and Henry, provided the theoretical foundation for
the conversion and distribution of energy as well as for such significant inventions
like the electric cell, the storage cell, the dynamo, the motor, the electric lamp.
During the last quarter of the nineteenth century, these were spectacularly translated
into industrial terms in the form of the electric power station, the telephone, the radio
telegraph. Augmenting these were the phonograph, the moving picture, the steam
turbine, the airplane. That was on the physics front. On the chemistry front, equiv-
alently spectacular developments followed theoretical advances. Mumford (1946,
pp. 217–218) again has aptly written:

In (this) phase, the main initiative comes, not from the ingenious inventor, but from the
scientist who establishes the general law: the invention is a derivative product. It was Henry
who in essentials invented the telegraph, not Morse; it was Faraday who invented the
dynamo, not Siemens; it was Oersted who invented the electric motor, not Jacobi; it was

Clerk-Maxwell and Hertz who invented the radio telegraph, not Marconi and De Forest. The translation of the scientific knowledge into practical instruments was a mere incident in the process of invention. While distinguished individual inventors like Edison, Baekeland and Sperry remained, the new inventive genius worked on the materials provided by science.

In other words, it was only roughly from 1850 onwards that modern society began to reap the material benefits promised by modern science, its method, its philosophy and its ideological goal of controlling Nature. That promise took more than two centuries to materialise when the paths of pure (theoretical) science and technology no longer diverged acting, by and large, independently of each other, but began to be harnessed to work as joint forces. However, at least on one level of understanding, the team may be said to be led by pure science, the senior partner, whilst technology follows. (Yet at a deeper level, this may be an over-simplification – for qualifications, see what follows.) In Phase I when each was relatively autonomous, technology, sometimes, led the way to theoretical advance – witness the relationship between the steam engine and the fundamental science of thermodynamics. However, under the new settlement, technology has lost that causal initiative and now becomes, much more so than before, the executive arm, so to speak, of pure science. Bear in mind what has already been observed, namely, that as technology becomes basic science led, it becomes more and more powerful as shown in the very history of medical technology recounted below.

As far as medical technology is concerned the phase called "found" technology in the history of (Western) modern medicine is neither here nor there. However, the phase of craft-based technology is relevant to its history. One instance which springs immediately to mind is the stethoscope whose life began when René Laennec (in 1819) invented it by rolling up a piece of paper, putting one end on the chest of the patient, the other end to his ear. He resorted to such a device because the patient in question happened to be an obese lady, making it difficult for him to listen to her lungs without such a make-shift medium. The scalpel in early surgery could be another instance, as it was basically a knife. However, do not forget that the crucial distinction between Phase I and Phase II is not the dates but that the former is craft-based technology and the latter is (basic/theoretical) science–induced. Just one example will be cited to illustrate this point, namely, the first kidney dialysis machine which appeared was a Heath Robinson contraption. The Dutch doctor, Willem J Kolff built an "artificial kidney" for his dying patient, made out of wooden drums, some cellophane tubing and laundry tubs. In this make-shift fashion, he was successful in draining the blood from the patient, removing impurities from it and then pumping the clean blood back into the patient. The date was as late as 1945, but the technology was purely craft-based – see Healthtechnologies timeline (2014).

Medical technology, since the seventeenth century, first came under Phase I, A and B. An example with some basic science input is the thermometer, an instrument with a history of several centuries; however, the modern user-friendly version was not available until Fahrenheit in 1724 constructed the Fahrenheit scale, with the freezing point of water at the lower end and the boiling point at the higher, and then manufactured a tool using such a scale and mercury (a material with a high coefficient of expansion) to measure the fluctuations in temperature of the human body. The compound microscope, based on the discovery of the lens, was made by two Dutch spectacle makers, Zacharias Jansen and his father as early as 1590. However, it existed more as a novelty rather than as a serious tool for scientific research. It was left to van Leeuwenhoek, a Dutch draper turned scientist, to perfect it to advance biological knowledge, being the first to see and describe bacteria, yeast plants, the circulation of blood corpuscles in capillaries. Eventually, it enabled medical research to usher in the age of bacteriology with Robert Koch's discovery, first, of the anthrax bacillus in 1876, and even more importantly of the tubercle bacillus in 1882, and even later, the age of antibiotics (post-1945). Antibiotics became available to the general public when these were produced industrially after the Second World War made possible via the work of Howard Florey and Ernst Chase, who isolated the bacteria-killing substance found in the mould a decade after Alexander Fleming accidentally chanced to come upon some on one of the glass plates in his laboratory in 1928, which he had at an earlier date coated with staphylococcus bacteria as part of his research. Furthermore, Florey got an American drug company to mass produce the penicillin just in time to treat all the cases of bacterial infections amongst the Western troops on D-Day (6 June 1944). In 1945, Fleming, Chain, and Florey were awarded the Nobel Prize in medicine – see Lee (2012).

However, disease is not only caused by certain bacteria but also by certain viruses, with which the compound microscope cannot cope. Further progress was only made when the electron microscope was invented in the late 1930s. In other words, the history of the microscope covers both Phase I as well as Phase IIA, as the invention of the compound microscope is primarily a craft-based technological product, using the lens and grinding it, whereas the electron microscope could not have been invented without the discovery of basic science, that is, of quantum physics as pioneered by Bohr (1885–1962), Einstein (1979–1955), and others. More than the electron microscope, the invention of the X-ray machine and other later even more high-tech machines (under Phase IIB) illustrate excellently the indispensable role played by basic scientific discoveries such as radium and radiation through the pioneering work of Marie and Pierre Curie (1897–1904). In 1895, the physicist Wilhelm C. Roentgen discovered a form of electromagnetic radiation which could pass through the body, leaving on a photographic plate an image of the bones or organs, thereby enabling the doctor to see the human interior for the first time in medical history, trailing in its wake a whole suite of high-tech diagnostic tools, such as the electrocardiograph (1903) developed by the Dutch physician and physiologist Wilhelm Einthoven which involved a "string" galvanometer suspended in a magnetic field, measuring small changes in electrical potential as the heart contracts and relaxes. By strapping the device to the arms and left leg of the patient, Einthoven could record the heart's wave patterns – the string, by moving, obstructed a beam of light whose shadow was then recorded on paper or a photographic plate. For the invention of this machine, he was awarded the Nobel Prize in medicine in 1924. The CAT scan (computerised axial tomography) invented in 1972 goes beyond X-rays combining them with a computer to create very detailed images of the inside of the body, with the X-ray tube rotating around the body and the computer producing an image of the scan. Unlike standard X-rays, a CAT scan can show up structures of blood vessels, tumours as well as bones – see "CAT scan (2014)." For this invention, the British engineer, Godfrey Hounsfield and the South African-born physicist Allan Cormack were awarded the Nobel Peace in medicine in 1979. On the other hand, magnetic resonance imaging (MRI) relies on magnetic fields and radio waves to produce also very detailed images of the inside of the body, including the brain and spinal cord as well as bones/joints, heart and blood vessels, soft tissues such as breasts, internal organs including the womb or prostate gland; indeed it is capable of doing a whole-body scan. As this diagnostic tool does not use X-rays, it eliminates the fear of radiation and also makes it possible to scan people with certain types of medical implants, such as a pacemaker operated by a battery. The first such equipment entered medical service in 1981. Paul Lauterbur and Peter Mansfield were awarded the Nobel Prize in medicine in 2003 for this diagnostic tool, although not without provoking a controversy. (See "MRI" (2014), Dreizen (2004)).

Technology and Economics

Technology, as tool, is meant to help us gain better control of Nature, to realise our own ends and projects. However, executing our goals and intentions requires the use of resources, whether these are taken directly from Nature (such as wood, titanium, fossil-fuel/solar/wind energy) or indirectly derived from Nature (such as plastic, brass or bronze). This means that technology and economics necessarily cross paths, as economics in general is concerned with the efficient allocation of resources, which in turn is linked with the notion of productivity. Productivity is generally defined as the amount of output per unit of input; furthermore, it is also regarded as a basic yardstick to measure the health of an economy. "It can be said without exaggeration that in the long run probably nothing is as important for economic welfare as the rate of productivity growth" (Baumol et al. 1989; see also Field 2008). However, for the purpose of this essay, the remit of the concept of productivity may be made much narrower, confining it only to that more familiar aspect which involves labor productivity in the economic system. Labor productivity simply means output divided by the number of workers, or the number of hours worked. Take the following hypothetical, though historically based, example: in the eighteenth century, in England, when weaving was a cottage industry, a worker, working 8 h a day, was able to weave, say, a foot of cloth. In the nineteenth century, a weaving machine, first powered by water and later by steam with one worker, working the machine 8 h a day, could produce a 100 f. of cloth. Labor productivity gain (or economic growth) would then be a 100 %. Machines replacing human labor historically were, and still, are a major means of increasing productivity (or growth), although sometimes, the increase could be obtained through a change in the technique of production (the software side of production, so to speak) rather than directly in replacing humans by machines (the hardware side of production), such as in the famous example cited by Adam Smith about the division of labor in the manufacture of pins. If one worker were to manufacture a pin from the beginning of the process to the end, then that worker would produce, say, one pin a day, whereas if "(o)ne man draws out the wire, another straights it, a third cuts it, a fourth points it, a fifth grinds it at the top for receiving the head; to make the head requires two or three distinct operations... to whiten the pin is another . . .. in this manner, into about eighteen distinct operations . . .." If these operations were shared between ten persons, between them, they could produce "upwards of forty-eight thousand pins in a day. Each person, therefore, making a tenth part of forty-eight thousand pins, might be considered as making four thousand eight hundred pins in a day. But if they had all wrought separately and independently, and without any of them having been educated to this peculiar business, they certainly could not each of them have made twenty, perhaps not one pin in day..." (Smith 1776, Book I, Chap. 1).

In similar spirit, Henry Ford combined the innovations above when he is said to have pioneered mass production in the motor car industry through automation – this meant that machines made large quantities of the parts needed which were then assembled together to make up the car as fast as the parts were produced by the machines – see "The evolution of mass production" (2014).

However, labor productivity as a concept is Janus-faced – on the one hand, it increases productivity in general, but on the other, it necessarily renders the workers it displaces at least, temporarily, if not permanently, out of work, their skills having been rendered superfluous. Historically, this trend has not been worrying, for the simple reason that another sector of the economy would open up to offer opportunities for employment – for instance, as labor productivity in agriculture improved, making farm workers redundant, many of these workers would become factory operatives as the manufacturing sector began to grow; when labor productivity in turn occurred in manufacture, many displaced (or younger) workers turned to the growing service sector of the economy. However, digital technology of late has (even ignoring the impact of robotic technology which will be looked at a little later) greatly improved labor productivity in all sectors of the economy including service sectors such as banking and retailing. Is there yet another sector of the economy waiting to absorb workers thus displaced by digital technology? As none so far has appeared on the horizon, this leads some to postulate that the near future will not be like the past, and some economists, such as Erik Brynjolfsson (a professor at the MIT Sloan School of management, as cited by Rotman 2013), to say: "It's one of the dirty secrets of economics: technology progress does grow the economy and create wealth, but there is no economic law that says everyone will benefit." (See also Brynjolfsson and McAfee 2011; Rifkind 2005). Hence, there is both gain and loss involved; in other words, although some would gain, many may well lose as the race against machines intensifies especially in the near and further future.

Technology, Economics, and Medicine

In today's society, medicine is an important part of any economy and may be considered to be an industry, whether the medicine practised is primarily state or privately funded. As such, the laws of economics involving the notion of labor productivity would apply to it as relentlessly as they would apply to any other industry. What exactly then is the impact of economics upon the practice and theory of medicine? This section will look at the former.

By and large, in a state-funded health service, the onus on those operating it is to reduce the cost to the public purse; in a privately funded service, it is to return as much profit as possible to the shareholders of the corporation involved. (The issue is further complicated by the requirements of internal accountancy which demands each part of the health service to operate in the black). Inevitably, the health service has no choice but to opt for labor productivity, as labor costs are a standing item of expenditure, whereas if a machine could replace labor, although the initial invest-ment (what is called fixed capital) may be great, it is a one-off investment of capital, such that in the longer term, gain rather than loss will show up in the accounting spread sheets.

Before this aspect of the impact on the practice of medicine will be explored in greater detail, one must straightaway point out that one should distinguish between machines and machines. For instance, the justification for some machines in med-icine lies, it is said, primarily, to improve success rate in diagnosis and treatment. The CAT, the MRI scans, for instance, would fall into this category; so would a machine such as the laparoscope which permits keyhole surgery which is considered as less invasive than the older method, thereby permitting less pain and bleeding post operation, reduced less scarring, a shorter hospital stay, and a faster recovery time. (See "Laparoscopy" (2014) for a brief description of the instrument and other accompanying devices, under the specific conditions of their use for instance in removing a damaged or diseased organ in the patient.) The *raison d'être* of such machines is to improve the quality of the medical intervention, not to render the surgical/nursing team redundant (See Ballantyne (2002)). However, although this is a crucial matter not to be overlooked, this does not mean that all forms of machinery involved in medicine would be so positive in their impact upon the medical team/ patient relationship.

This is because, as already shown in the preceding section, machines are the standard method of procuring labor productivity. In other words, the more fixed capital per worker is used, the more productive the worker will be (other things being equal) – for example, if one nurse sitting in the ward office could monitor on screen the data coming in from one or more machines attached to a dozen or more patients, indicating the condition of each patient lying in the adjacent ward, then the hospital would have gained on the cost of hiring, say, only one nurse to monitor the progress of 12 or more patients, every month, every year of the life span of the said machine (s). Furthermore, if the machines are designed with the capability of flashing up warning visual and sound signals about the condition of a patient as it is about to turn critical, then this would also enable the nurse on duty to sit in the office doing other administrative tasks while keeping an eye and an ear open regarding the monitoring system. This high-tech form of nursing would in the end alter the very nature of nursing itself – nursing would be less about looking after patients in an intimate, personal manner but more about occupying a monitoring role of their purely medical conditions, as an adjunct to doctors. In other words, the original Florence

Nightingale model of nursing which was about providing comfort, succour, and compassion to the suffering would attenuate, if not be totally superseded.

The above sort of consideration leads to the crux of this essay, namely, the link between high-tech in particular and dehumanization of medicine in the practice of medicine. Low-tech or craft-based technology, as previously shown, is more labor-intensive while high-tech is *ex hypothesi* less labor but more capital intensive. This means that in the context of running a hospital, a patient admitted to a modern hospital is more likely to encounter fewer human-contact/interaction moments, if not actually fewer human beings than if admitted to a "backward", less well-equipped establishment. Imagine the following: on arrival, the main door is operated automatically (quite unlike the scenario at a five-star hotel where a commissionaire stands at the porch, rushing forward to open the door of the car or taxi bearing the customer to its portals, with a bell-boy or two following immediately to take care of the luggage). In other words, if the front door of a hospital (whether automated or not) had a porter standing by to help open the door, carry the case to the reception, to say a cheerful hello and so on, the patient would feel more welcome than if such a worker had been dispensed with on the ground of saving cost. Take another scenario: instead of a human being (in the role of a nurse or administrator) taking the history of the patient and the illness, the patient in some establishments would be given a specially designed small computer and told to tick the right boxes to the various matters as presented by the electronic questionnaire. Only the literally illiterate or the computer-illiterate would be exempt from this impersonal mode of communication, the rest would have to struggle as best they can to make sense of it. The data inputted could then be said to be standardized and objective but the downside is that it denies the patient yet another occasion of making contact with a fellow human being who is in the position of an expert to help them negotiate their way through the process and procedure of seeking medical attention for their predicament.

If one were to peep into the near future of care of both the sick and/or the elderly (in advanced economies), the following scenario emerges in which robotics appears to play an increasingly prominent part. Japan plays the lead role in this evolution – see Dethlefs and Martin (2006). In terms of demographics, Japanese society is fast becoming one with an increasingly large elderly population; in terms of industrial manufacturing, it has pioneered the use of robots. So obviously, the robotic solution to the matter of caring for the sick but especially the elderly is an obvious option. In 2013, the Japanese government allocated 2.39bn yen to develop such robots. The really sophisticated ones are expected to replace human beings even to the extent of offering companionship; one such belonging to an older generation of machines is Paro who is regarded as a friend by the residents in a Japanese care home – see Hudson (2013), Kelly (2013). Furthermore, there is one version in the shape of a baby seal which can respond to its name; its interactions with the user make it seem as if it is alive, moving its head and legs, and it can learn to respond in ways the user prefers. The user can stroke it, it "feels" being stroked via its tactile sensor – see "Paro therapeutic robot" (2014). This version is acknowledged to have a wholesome psychological effect on the patients, enabling them to relax, by providing stimulation and motivation in very much the same way as a sympathetic fellow human carer can do. In other words, such a robot appears to be able to replace a human being even in terms of providing companionship and fellowship. Technically, scientists/engineers could aim to combine such "psychological" capabilities with the physical ones of lifting the patient from one position to another, moving the patient from one location to another, helping the patient to dress and undress, to keep proper personal hygiene, to remind and jolly her to take the right pills at the right time, fetching and carrying, heating up a prepared meal in a microwave, vacuuming the floor, alerting the hospital when the elderly person takes a turn for the worst, (the elderly could live and be cared for in her own home looked after by if not one, then two, or a suite of robots). This futuristic scenario would then raise the question: if the robots are equivalent in function and performance to a human, then surely this kind of development in elderly care would not amount to dehumanization of medicine in the straightforward understanding of the term? However, it would be beyond the remit of this essay to further address this set of issues.

As for the doctor–patient relationship, one must distinguish between two different things: (a) the pressures on the time of the doctor (let us say) given the rising numbers of patients passing through the surgery means that no more than a few minutes could be given to each patient; (b) high-tech medical diagnosis which is the order today. Both contexts may make the patient feel the impact of the so-called dehumanization of medicine (the impact is said to be less in the private health system); however, here, the second context will only be considered. In days of yore, the doctor personally put the stethoscope against the patient's chest (today, while the stethoscope may still hang around the neck of the doctor, it is no longer used as a serious diagnostic tool but more perhaps as a trade icon), would feel the pulse, would palpate an organ or two, would look even at the condition of the tongue, the complexion, and so on, apart from asking questions about the onset and subsequent development of the illness – at the end of the consultation, the doctor would give the patient a diagnosis. However, today, diagnosis depends on the results of tests, involving blood, urine samples, tissue samples in biopsies and so on (see Pillinger (2014), Green (2005), Rull (2012)). Samples once taken from the patient are forwarded to specialist labs for analysis by experts such as a hematologist who would not have met and examined the patient; the doctor (s) would not (or would not dare to) pronounce until the results of all these tests become available and deciphered, no matter how sure she is in her mind about the condition of the patient. Impersonal tests mediate between the patient and the doctor; as a result, the patient may feel that her medical fate, for better or for worse, is sealed not so much by the doctor(s) but by machines and experts which carry out the analysis of these tests in a distant laboratory, who necessarily are faceless and nameless and have no immediate knowledge of their personal suffering and pain.

Another dimension of the dehumanization of medicine in the context of the doctor–patient relationship is even more radical as it involves in principle (though not in practice yet) of rendering the individual doctor superfluous. This is machine diagnosis; in one sense, it is already part of today's medical culture. The project had long been on the horizon but today with information technology in the ascendant, it looks as if a medical diagnostic software has successfully been designed and created.

It is called Isabel. The story began in 1999 when a young girl called Isabel was struck down by chickenpox; however, the doctor(s) in charge had overlooked two rare but well-known complications of chickenpox, namely toxic shock syndrome and necrotizing fasciitis. As a result, the raging effects of the latter are still with the patient, even today. Her father, Jason Maude, started that same year Isabel Healthcare, establishing a Web-based checklist system aimed at helping doctors uncertain about their diagnosis. It is not marketed as a replacement of doctors but as a backup tool in case of uncertainties, as well as a teaching tool in medical education. In other words, this mode of presentation, though user-friendly to the medical profession, nevertheless, logically implies that (at least in the majority of, if not necessarily, in all cases), Isabel is more reliable than the averagely competent doctor the patient may encounter in the average surgery and average hospital – see Nash (2010) and Hafner (2012). The target market of Isabel is, therefore, the medical profession rather than the ordinary individuals who may prefer Isabel to diagnose their conditions and who can afford to buy a license for its use. However, today, there is a poor man's equivalent of Isabel; people use the internet to access information about their conditions and to self-diagnose in the light of such knowledge – see Kluwer (2014), which shows that individuals who use this mode believes that "collectively," the information yielded via the internet is greater than that held by any one individual practitioner of medicine. It appears that their line of reasoning is no different from that of those professionals who use Isabel. In turn, this raises the question: does machine diagnosis invariably dehumanize medicine or can it, under certain appropriate circumstances, empower the individual to redress to an extent the imbalance which has traditionally existed between the all-knowing professional and the, by and large, ignorant patient?

Division of Labor, Ontological *Volte Face* and Dehumanization of Medicine

Adam Smith's account of the division of labor is not confined merely to economics but has been extrapolated under Modernity to apply in the intellectual domain. In medicine, part of the tremendous growth in knowledge must be laid at the door of specialization which is the intellectual equivalent of the division of labor in manufacturing. Smith, while applauding the benefits such a technique undoubtedly would bring to economic growth, was also well aware of its downside, namely, to use the terminology of this essay, to dehumanize the worker. To quote him again, Smith 1776, Book V, Chap. I:

> The man whose whole life is spent in performing a few simple operations, of which the effects are perhaps always the same, or very nearly the same, has no occasion to exert his understanding or to exercise his invention in finding out expedients for removing difficulties which never occur. He naturally loses, therefore, the habit of such exertion, and generally becomes as stupid and ignorant as it is possible for a human creature to become. … in every improved and civilized society this is the state into which the labouring poor, that is, the great body of the people, must necessarily fall, unless government takes some pains to prevent it.

The downside of the division of labor in the manufacturing sector upon the laboring poor, as spelt out above by Smith, of course, simply does not obtain in the same fashion in the knowledge sector of the economy, (such as in medicine) as in the lower rungs of the manufacturing sector. However, the spirit of Smith's critique may be said to obtain, all the same, as intellectual specialisms, in principle, while permitting the expert to be an authority of his specialism, nevertheless, has the unfortunate effect of excluding him from knowledge in related, neighboring domains of knowledge, thereby forcibly making him ignorant about such fields. In other words, the human body is divided into parts, the study of each part falling into the domain of its own particular specialism – the hematologist is the expert on blood, the brain surgeon on the brain, the orthopedic surgeon on bones and fractures, the psychiatrist on the mental aspects of the individual, and so on. The hematologist has neither knowledge nor a professional view about the brain and vice versa – in the language of trade unions, everyone respects work boundaries. This fragmentation of knowledge means that often a patient might have to be passed along from one specialist to another, undergoing one test and another, before the patient would finally, with luck, arrive at the door of the right specialist for a proper diagnosis – this, indeed, is one argument for the relevance of machine diagnosis as performed by a sophisticated software such as Isabel, as Isabel does not have to respect such work and knowledge boundaries.

Furthermore, this proliferation of specialisms necessarily entails fragmentation of the human being, such that wholeness of the person is lost (Reiser 1978). In analyzing modern medicine or biomedicine today, division of labor and fragmentation must be understood at, at least, two levels, namely, the epistemological and the ontological as well as the relationship between them. Epistemological fragmentation has already been briefly referred to just above. But closely entwined with that is the fragmentation involved when the human being, since the beginning of modern science/medicine, was no longer regarded as organism but as machine – this is the ontological *volte face* which underpins the Scientific Revolution itself – see Lee (2005, 2012).

A machine is a human artifact, made up of parts, specifically designed, constructed, and put together in order to help its creator to achieve a certain goal. A car is paradigmatically such a machine. It is the ontological contrast of organism, as organisms (in the history of their evolution in Nature) are simply the end results of Natural Selection involving a long and complicated process of the interaction between the organism with its genetic inheritance and the environment. A machine is peculiarly unproblematic both from the epistemological and ontological points of view – as it is a human creation, we humans, necessarily know precisely how to construct and deconstruct it in a straightforward manner. When we dismantle a watch into its parts, we are dismantling a whole into its parts, such that it is obvious, a whole is no more than the sum of its parts; we may then put the parts together again, and nonmysteriously, the whole appears again in front of our very eyes. If the universe and everything it contains is nothing but machine, then the universe no longer poses mysteries for us humans, which, we, over time and with assiduity, could not unravel and deconstruct at will. In this way, we, moderns, can leave the obscurantist philosophy of Aristotle about organisms behind, as organisms have now been revealed to be *au fond* nothing but machines.

When this kind of world-view is then applied in the domain of medicine, illness is perceived to be mal-functioning of one or sometimes more than one of its parts, in the same way that when a watch today stops working, we diagnose that its battery has run out, we then open it up, we remove the exhausted battery and put in a new one, and we can immediately see that the watch starts to tick again. When a scan or two, reveal that it is the kidneys which are diseased and therefore not functioning, we then do a kidney transplant, and the patient, to all intents and purposes, starts to live a normal life again. In theory, one can conceive of a patient surviving with all the major organs being transplanted organs, although in practice, as far as one knows such a feat of re-engineering has not yet been accomplished. Bones could be replaced, such as in the case of hip replacements. The research programme in medicine behind which stands the ontological view that the human organism is machine, remains, today, a fruitful one, holding out further promises of success, especially with the help of more recent technologies such as IT, nanotechnology, biotechnology, and others. Success is sweet for all parties concerned, practitioners and clients alike. However, it remains fair to observe that the recipients, grateful though they undoubtedly are, know that the rest of their lives is dependent on drugs, some of which can have some disturbing side effects.

Conclusion

The subject matter raised by the title of this essay is immensely large and complicated; as one cannot do justice, here, to all aspects, one has been highly selective and focussed on only a few for limited discussion. From that discussion, several points appear to have emerged:

1. The trend of machines replacing humans in medicine and the health system will continue as such a cost-saving imperative is axiomatic to the dominant model of economics and accountancy prevailing today.
2. Machine diagnosis of illness is already a part of medical culture, although it has not so far entirely diminished nor rendered superfluous the role of doctors in the actual practice of medicine. However, in principle, there appear no inherent difficulties in developing in this direction. As the cost of training a doctor is high, the logic of economics and accounting may well point to the day when fewer doctors worldwide might be considered to be required to keep up with the same level of health care.
3. The ordinary person in the street and potential/actual patient appear not to be too concerned with 2 as far as machine diagnosis is concerned provided the diagnosis yielded is as good if not better than that provided by the average doctor in the average surgery or hospital. In other words, although machine diagnosis in the abstract may appear to constitute a threat to the individual in depersonalized

context, nevertheless, in practice, it may not be perceived to be so threatening, as the patient is primarily interested in a correct diagnosis and as quickly as possible.

4. The ordinary person may turn out not to be too concerned, if at all, with the existential threat involved in the ontological *volte face* that human beings are nothing but machines, as long as they can survive with the aid of a medicine based on such a *volte face*, and be able to lead an existence with sufficient quality of life to it.

5. However, the ordinary person does not or may not find congenial the dehumanizing effects of machines displacing humans in the larger context (not the narrower/restrictive one of diagnosis) of the doctor–patient relationship and the nurse–patient relationship, especially in the latter domain, when patients expect a human-to-human relationship where care and compassion may obtain which can console, comfort, and ameliorate the suffering of the sick. In other words, the patient is not simply a diseased organ, a fractured leg, a dicey heart, a ropey kidney, a peptic ulcer, but a person with emotions, feeling pain and so on, not a malfunctioning machine whose defective parts could be technologically replaced or repaired.

6. The trend in the care of the elderly appears to be pointing in the direction of robotics. The sick or the elderly are psychological/social beings who happen not to be well and/or frail. If robots are to replace human carers, then it is imperative that robots become humanized, as Paro, the baby seal appears to demonstrate. However, this recognition is telling as it is nothing but the recognition that technology/machine is in principle dehumanizing in the context of medicine and health system.

References

Atkins FW (1984) The second law. Scientific American Books, New York

Ballantyne GH (2002) Review of early clinical results of telerobotic surgery. http://cmaps. cmappers.net/rid=1HZ2RWKZY-1Y1GHF0-G08/ResearchPaper6.pdf

Baumol WJ, Blackman SAB, Wolff EN (1989) Productivity and American leadership: the long view. MIT Press, Cambridge, MA

Brynjolfsson E, McAfee A (2011) Race against the machine: how the digital revolution is accelerating innovation, driving productivity, and irreversibly transforming the employment and the economy. The MIT Center for Digital Business, Cambridge, MA

CAT scan (2014) http://www.nhs.uk/conditions/ct-scan/pages/introduction.aspx. Accessed 21 Aug 2014

Davies H (1980) George Stephenson. Hamlyn Paperbacks, Middlesex

Dethlefs N, Martin B (2006) Japanese technology policy for aged care. Sci Public Policy 33 (1):47–57. https://www.uow.edu.au/~bmartin/pubs/06spp.html

Dreizen P (2004) The Nobel Prize for MRI: a wonderful discovery and a sad controversy. Lancet 363(9402):78. Accessed 21 Aug 2014

Evolution of mass production (2014) Ford Motor Company. DIALOG. http://www.ford.co.uk/experience-ford/heritage/evolutionof mass production

Field A (2008) Productivity. The Concise Encyclopedia of Economics. Available via DIALOG. http://www.econlib.org/library/Enc/Productivity.html#abouttheauthor. Accessed 21 Sept 2014

Green R (2005) Blood tests. http://www.netdoctor.co.uk/liver_kidney_urinary_system/examina tions/bloodsamples.htm

Hafner K (2012) For second opinion, consult a computer? http://www.nytimes.com/2012/12/04/ health/quest-to-eliminate-diagnostic-lapses.html?pagewanted=all&_r=0

High technologies timeline (2014) Greatest engineering achievements of the 20th century. National Academy of Engineering. DIALOG. http://www.greatachievements.org/?id=3824. Accessed 21 Aug 2014

Hudson A (2013) A robot is my friend: can machines care for elderly? BBC News. http://www.bbc. co.uk/news/technology-24949081

Ihde D (1993) Philosophy of technology: an introduction. Paragon House, New York

Kelly H (2013). Robots: the future of elder care? http://whatsnext.blogs.cnn.com/2013/07/19/ robots-the-future-of-elder-care/

Kluwer W (2014) Wolters Kluwer Health Q1 Poll: Self-Diagnosis. http://www.raredisease.org.uk/ documents/RDUK-Family-Report.pdf

Laparoscopy (keyhole surgery) (2014) http://www.nhs.uk/Conditions/laparoscopy/Pages/introduc tion.aspx

Lee K (2005) Philosophy and revolutions in genetics: deep science and deep technology, 2nd edn. Palgrave Macmillan, Basingstoke

Lee K (2012) The philosophical foundations of modern medicine. Palgrave Macmillan, Basingstoke

MRI (2014) http://inventors.about.com/od/mstartinventions/a/MRI.htm. Accessed 21 Aug 2014

Mumford L (1946) Technics and civilization. George Routledge & Sons, London

Nash DB (2010) Isabel, a new diagnostic aid for the 21st century. Pharm Ther 35(12):651. http:// www.ncbi.nlm.nih.gov/pmc/articles/PMC3008375/

Paro therapeutic robot (2014) http://www.parorobots.com/

Pillinger J (2014) Urine test. http://www.netdoctor.co.uk/health_advice/examinations/urinesample. htm

Reiser SJ (1978) Medicine and the reign of technology. Cambridge University Press, Cambridge

Rifkind J (2005) The end of work. http://www.foet.org/press/interviews/Spiegel-%20August% 203%202005.pdf

Rotman R (2013) Destroying jobs. http://www.technologyreview.com/featuredstory/515926/how-technology-is-destroying-jobs/

Rull G (2012) Biopsy. http://www.patient.co.uk/health/biopsy

Smith A (1776/1976) Of the Division of Labour. In: Campbell RH, Skinner AS, Todd WB (eds) An inquiry into the nature and causes of the wealth of nations. Clarendon Press, Oxford

Professionalism in Health Care

41

Andrew Edgar

Contents

Abstract

This chapter will explore professionalism historically, from the work of Gregory and Percival in the eighteenth century to contemporary "new professionalism." The chapter will identify how the core traditional values of professionalism, in particular commitments to an other-regarding social ethic and to maintaining high levels of scientifically informed expertise, alongside the defense of professional self-regulation, have been articulated and challenged. Classic accounts of professionalism are found in the work of Durkheim, Tawney, and Parsons. Critics have argued professionalism is in practice self-serving, particularly insofar as a professional ethic has justified the autonomous self-regulation of the profession. Over the last 30 years, responses to the perceived crisis of professionalism – due to the loss of broad public trust in the professions, changes in the nature of professional expertise, and increased demands for external regulation – have precipitated a series of more or less radical responses.

A. Edgar (✉)
Cardiff University, Cardiff, UK
e-mail: edgar@cardiff.ac.uk

T. Schramme, S. Edwards (eds.), *Handbook of the Philosophy of Medicine*,
DOI 10.1007/978-94-017-8688-1_30

New professionalism has now begun to question the desirability of professional autonomy and self-regulation and to articulate a professionalism committed to public engagement and the acceptance of external regulation.

Introduction

"Professionalism" may be understood as the set of competences or virtues that a practitioner is expected to manifest insofar as they are a member of a profession. Such virtues would typically be thought to include an altruistic concern for the best interests of the patient or client over and above those of the professional him- or herself and a commitment to maintaining high levels of training, expertise, and competency in the exercise of professional skills. Broadly, "professionalism" is then the quality of being a good professional, where goodness is understood both, morally, in terms of the professional's relationship to their clients and to a wider public and in terms of the sustaining of appropriate expertise and technical competence. As such, understandings of professionalism will have important consequences for the education and training of the professional and for the regulation of professional practice, being articulated in codes of conduct.

Within this broad definition, there is considerable scope for debating its substantial content. The precise interpretation of what professionalism entails will vary from profession to profession and even within a profession such as medicine, between such subdisciplines as general practice, nursing, and psychiatry. The substantial understanding of professionalism changes as professions face diverse pressures, both from without, for example, as legal and political environments change, the assertiveness of clients develops, or as markets intrude upon professional practices, and from within – as professional practices themselves develop and diversify. This chapter will therefore explore diverse interpretations of professionalism by using the framework of a historical review of the development of the medical profession, recognizing how this history is itself entwined with reflection, by both practitioners and academics, on the nature of the profession and processes of professionalization.

Eighteenth-Century Origins of Professionalism

In eighteenth-century Britain, medicine, alongside the law and the church, may be seen to have already established itself as professions. As such, the physician had a relatively high social status in a highly stratified society. Crucially, to be recognized as a practitioner of a profession raised one above the mere status of trade or craft. The professional was a member of "polite society" and thus the social equal of their middle-class clientele. As Leake characterizes the situation, the eighteenth-century physician "disdained work [and] condescended to help sick people," taking no fee, although a guinea would be left for them "as they withdrew" (1970, p. 68).

Thus, in contrast to trade, which is pursued instrumentally in order to earn one's living, pursuing a profession implied some notion of vocation or calling.

A professional was distinguished from a mere craft or trade by both the more theoretical nature of the professional's expertise and by the requirement for the professional to exercise judgment in applying that expertise. While craft or trade might presuppose considerable manual skill, professional practice required theory and phronesis. Thus, physicians received a university education (preeminently then in Leiden or Edinburgh) embracing chemistry, surgery, anatomy, medical theory, and clinical practice. The eighteenth-century medical education also incorporated the pedagogical technique of "walking the wards" (Lindemann 2008). That is to say that the physician learned their profession, not merely from theory nor like the craft worker through application of learned rules of practice, but rather through exposure to diverse examples of real patients. Such exposure developed a subtle and contextually sensitive clinical judgment. In contrast, apothecaries, surgeons, and barber surgeons, as trades, continued to be trained through apprenticeships, within the remnants of the medieval guild system (Lindemann 2008).

The complexity of professional knowledge and practice, even in the eighteenth century, is already such that the lay person is not readily able to assess the success or efficacy of professional practice. While the efficacy of a trade or craft worker can typically be assessed by anyone – for the potter's cup will hold liquid, the carpenter's chair will be strong and comfortable, and the wheelwright's spokes are sturdy enough for the dirt road – that a patient is not cured may not be evidence of the failure or incompetence of the physician, and the accuracy of a diagnosis is not readily judged by any but other physicians (see Edgar 2011). The patient is thus required to trust the physician in a way that they do not trust the potter, carpenter, or wheelwright.

While the distinction between professions and trades begins to articulate the epistemological grounding of professionalism, it is in the social status of the profession, and in the social relationship of the professional to their client, that the moral dimension of professionalism emerges. Even though the eighteenth-century professional is already aspiring to a degree of knowledge that is largely incomprehensible to their lay clientele, the physician does not stand above their patient as a man of science. The scientific authority of the professional is not yet so universally accepted as to command, on its own, the attention and obedience of the client. Indeed, to assert scientific superiority would be to violate the etiquette and mores of "polite" middle-class society. Rather, in acquiring middle-class status, the professional is placed in a precarious equality with their clientele (see Porter 1997, pp. 255–258 and 281–287). It is precisely this social equality, and not science, that secures a relationship of trust between the physician and the patient, and thus the patient's obedience to the physician's instructions.

The first overt guidance on medical ethics in the modern literature, Thomas Percival's *Medical Ethics*, was published in 1803 (Percival 1849). This may be understood in some part as a response to this issue of patient trust. The Hippocratic Oath had served as a basis for medical ethics and the moral self-understanding of physicians since the fifth century BCE. Percival is concerned with the situation of the modern physician. He thus reinterprets the spirit of the Hippocratic Oath in terms of the medical profession as a modern guild, where the profession is in a compact with the general public. "Every man who enters into a fraternity engages by a tacit compact not only to submit to the laws, but to promote the honour and interest, of the association, so far as they are consistent with morality and the general good of mankind" (Percival 1849, part I §22). As such, an ethos of self-regulation is already placed at the core of professionalism, with the individual practitioner under an obligation to maintain the public reputation of the profession as a whole. *Medical Ethics*, in consequence, outlines the knowledge and awareness that the physician should have that goes beyond mere biomedical training. While issues such as the law (including the physician's responsibilities with respect to dueling) and religious sensibilities are discussed at some length, Percival's primary focus is on matters of etiquette, in the physician's relationship both to patients and to fellow practitioners. (The book's original motivation was to clarify the relationship between physicians, surgeons, and apothecaries in his own Manchester hospital – where the latter were struggling for professional recognition.) It is thus in the observance of professional etiquette that the patient's trust is secured, rather than in the assertion of scientific competence. The concern with etiquette does indeed allow Percival to begin to articulate issues of genuine ethical concern, such as patient confidentiality, albeit that critics suggest that he fails effectively to separate the two and thus fails to recognize the greater importance of ethics over etiquette (see Leake 1927, pp. 2–3).

John Gregory's *Lectures on the Duties and Qualifications of a Physician* was delivered, while he was chair of physic at Edinburgh between 1766 and 1773 (Gregory 1817). Gregory is more overtly concerned than is Percival with medical malpractice and incompetence. While celebrating the breadth of knowledge, and indeed genius, required of the physician, he recognizes the uncertainty of the judgment of the individual physician. He argues that there is "no established authority to which [physicians] can refer in doubtful cases. Every physician must rest on his own judgment, which appeals for its rectitude to nature and experience alone" (Gregory 1817, p. 17). In response to this, Gregory stresses the urgent need to establish objective criteria for the assessment of medical practice and the mechanisms of scrutiny that will enforce compliance with them. The problem lies, in part, precisely in the exclusion of the lay person from any understanding of medical science. "The science of medicine alone is kept so carefully concealed from the world, and the art must necessarily be practised in so private a manner, as renders it difficult for the public to form a just estimate of a physician's knowledge from the success of his practice" (Gregory 1817, p. 210). Gregory's solution to this problem is not merely to strengthen the rigorous scientific basis of medicine, thereby anticipating modern appeals to the importance of epidemiology and evidence-based medicine, but also to ensure that physicians are open about their mistakes and failings with the public and crucially to educate that lay public in medicine, so that they may fairly judge medical practice (see Boyd 2005). Part of the ethics of the physician thus lies in their obligation to communicate clearly, honestly, and effectively beyond the narrow limits of the profession itself (see Gregory 1817, pp. 187–188).

In summary, the eighteenth century sees not merely the modern profession taking shape but also the outline of disputes over the nature of professionalism that is still current. Percival's ethics begins to articulate the ideology of professional self-regulation. While Percival focuses on the personal relationship between the physician and patient as guarantor of trust, Gregory begins to pose critical questions about the actual self-serving nature of such autonomy and the potential that the ideology of professionalism might have to conceal malpractice. The trust that the profession requires from the public is thus grounded, neither in ethics nor in an authoritarian appeal to arcane knowledge, but rather in public engagement and dialogue.

Civic Professionalism

The British Medical Association (BMA) was founded in 1832 (initially as the Provincial Medical and Surgical Association) and the General Medical Council (GMC), which has responsibility for maintaining a register of doctors and for education and training, in 1858. In 1847 the American Medical Association (AMA) was founded. These institutions may be seen to consolidate the paternalism and autonomy of the profession; precisely insofar the professional association takes over, from the state, the legal responsibility for regulating practitioners. In the USA, this regulation was, from the first, grounded in the adoption by the AMA of a code of ethics. This code was based upon Percival's *Medical Ethics* and covered the duties of the physician to the patient, to other professionals, and to the public (wherein the physician has a role as a "good citizen," using their medical expertise to advise on matters of public health) and also the duties of patients and the public to physicians (see Baker 1995, pp. 75–87). The GMC, while responsible for disciplining doctors found guilty of improper conduct, actively resisted the adoption of a code of ethics, turning instead to jurisprudence, and as such an approach grounded in common law. The limits of acceptable practice, in the British context, thus came to be established through case law (see Crowther 1995).

The AMA exemplifies the profession's moral responsibility for safeguarding the interests of patients and a wider public when, in the early twentieth century, it critically investigates and transforms medical education. Crucially, the early regulation of the medical profession, and thus the emerging definition of professionalism, rests not merely on the moral behavior (or even etiquette) of the practitioner but also upon the scientific rigor of their expertise. Percival had railed against quackery (1849, ch. 2 §21), as had Gregory (1817, p. 124). The professional medical bodies thus sought to undermine the claim of "irregulars," such as homeopaths, to the title of doctor or physician, as well as ensuring that those legitimately claiming the title were properly educated. In the second half of the nineteenth century, the AMA worked to consolidate medical education as grounded in laboratory work, clinical instruction, and an extensive program of lectures, so that medical training would cease to be a mere apprenticeship (Baker 1995, pp. 14–15). In the face of continuing evidence of widespread quackery and poorly or even uneducated doctors, the AMA created the Council for Medical Education in

1904 with the objectives of establishing minimal standards for acceptance into medical schools and determining medical school curricula. Abraham Flexner's survey of medical school, *Medical Education in the United States and Canada*, was published in 1910. This led to the eventual closure of proprietary schools that existed merely to provide profits to their owners (frequently awarding "honorary" medical degrees) and to the integration of medical schools into universities. In addition, a medical curriculum based upon 2 years of scientific study and 2 years in teaching hospitals (reflecting the practice of "walking the wards") was established and state licensing of physicians negotiated. The regulatory bodies of the medical profession may thus be seen to be protecting patients from failures in the medical market. Lacking the necessary expertise to judge between good and bad physicians or indeed physicians and quacks, the professional body steps in, paternalistically, to control the market in physicians.

The philosophical articulation of this development of civic professionalization – specifically a view that sees the profession as occupying a crucial place in civil society and thus inculcating a sense of public service into the practitioner – may be found in work of sociologist Emile Durkheim (1992) and historian R. H. Tawney (1921). Both present professionalism as a solution to social ills arising from the advance of liberal capitalism. For Durkheim, this is the anomie, the loss of moral values and meaning, brought about by an advanced division of labor. For Tawney, it is the mistaken sense that the acquisition of property is a good in itself, rather than something to be judged by the benefit that it offers to society as a whole.

Durkheim's lectures on "Professional Ethics," originally delivered between 1890 and 1900, develop themes already explored in his *The Division of Labour* (1984). *The Division of Labour* argues that while the advanced division of labor character-istic of modern industrial societies was necessary and advantageous to economic prosperity, it had the disadvantage of fragmenting social solidarity, leaving the individual member of society increasingly isolated, with little or no sense of communal belonging or moral orientation. Individual self-interest trumps collective morality. The modern state is seen as too large and bureaucratically impersonal a body to instill communal identity in its citizens. Occupational groupings, akin to Roman and medieval guilds, are thus proposed as a check against both the imper-sonal and distant state and the individualism and self-interest of the market. While the economic exchanges and the practice of business encourage the individual to think only of what is in their own interest, professions offer to their practitioners the pursuit of purposes – social functions – that have merit beyond individual gain. As such, membership of an occupation restores a sense of purpose and collective identity in the face of anomie. While each occupation has a particular social function and thus, Durkheim argues, its own morality, membership of the occupational group will not merely inculcate a sense of internal group solidarity, but will have ramifi-cations for the practitioner's relationships with those outside the group. The virtues learned within the occupational group blossom in a general sense of social solidarity.

Durkheim here articulates an ideal of professionalism whereby the profession stands as a bulwark against the alienating encroachment of both market and state. The professional pursues their occupation not for pecuniary reward, but rather from a motivation, or indeed a calling, to serve society. The implication is that professional bodies, such as the AMA or BMA, should constitute themselves as modern guilds. However, it may be noted that Durkheim is not strictly theorizing "professions" in the English sense of the term. The French term refers to any occupation and not merely to the *professions liberals* (Freidson 2001, p. 53). Durkheim's call is for a fundamental reorganization of all occupational groups.

Tawney takes the profession, in the English sense of the term and as exemplified in medicine and law, as a model for occupational organization. All occupations benefit from professionalization. The profession is not merely an aggregate of workers all pursuing the same occupation nor even a trade union, protecting its members' economic interests, but rather it "is a body of men who carry on their work in accordance with rules designed to enforce certain standards both for the better protection of its members and for the better service of the public" (1921, p. 106). The profession meets a social function, but as such gives its members a sense of purpose beyond mere pecuniary gain. To practice a profession is to know that one is responsible to some "higher authority" (p. 14). Members within a profession compete with each other, not for financial or material reward, but rather for honor and reputation. So the professional will not perform certain acts (such as the sale of patent medicines (p. 109)), harmful to the client or wider public, no matter the potential financial reward. Public and professional service is thus put before personal interest.

The model of professionalism that emerges from Durkheim and Tawney may also be seen in the work of pragmatists and reformers such as John Dewey, Jane Addams, and Herbert Croly. The civic professional becomes a new type of hero, providing a model of selfless civic service to ordinary people. The professions use their scientific knowledge in improving social life, but not for the amoral and pecuniary ends encouraged by capitalist markets (see Light 2010, pp. 273–274). The model receives a more complex articulation in Talcott Parsons' structural-functionalist sociology. Parsons is specifically concerned with the medical profession, taking it as paradigmatic of modern professionalism (1951, pp. 288–323). His analysis, while highly theoretical, is grounded both in empirical study and in a significant degree of personal sympathy with medicine as a vocation. (He originally had some intention to follow the example of his brother and to train as a physician.) At the core of his analysis lies the assumption that professions fulfill core functions for a modern society. All societies, within Parsonian theory, require certain functions to be fulfilled in order to stabilize and reproduce themselves (such as the production of the means of subsistence, the education or socialization of children, and the maintenance of political and legal order). Illness and disease pose fundamental problems both to the individual and to society as a whole. The ill person cannot continue their everyday activities and, as such, cannot fulfill the functions (or "social roles") that society expects of them. Illness is thus a form of social deviance which the medical profession controls and corrects (Parsons 1951, pp. 288–289). The professionalism that is expressed in scientific expertise and certain standards of public and private morality facilitates the realization of this function.

The bold outline of Parsons' structural functionalism omits much of the subtlety of his analysis and not least his sensitivity to illness as a culturally embedded and interpreted phenomenon, emotionally affecting and meaningful to both the patient and the physician. The patient is vulnerable and frequently fearful (Parsons 1951, p. 300). Medical examination and treatment requires intrusions into aspects of the patient's life that are usually kept private, including the eliciting of personal information and intimate physical contact, both of which contemporary Western culture treats as potentially embarrassing or compromising (p. 309). The patient's lack of knowledge of medical science and the uncertainties of their diagnosis and potential recovery may lead to seemingly irrational behavior and magical beliefs (of which the physician may have to be tolerant, if such beliefs aid recovery) (p. 315). Equally physicians themselves are potentially affected by the emotional strain of treating certain patients (and Parsons gives the example of a surgeon's relationship to a 9-year-old (p. 308)) and must protect themselves from this exposure. Further, while rigorously trained, the physician is still confronted by the frustrations of uncertainty in diagnosis, treatment, and prognosis and thus in the limitations of medical science (p. 302). Finally, appreciative of the insights of psychoanalysis and other forms of psychotherapy, Parsons highlights the complex dependencies and vulnerabilities that lie in the relationship between patient and physician (see pp. 304–305).

Society responds to the need to develop an effective means to cope with illness, in the face of these cultural and emotional pressures, through the institution of the sick role and the physician role. Social roles may be understood as patterns of behavior, bound up with certain obligations and privileges. In adopting the "sick role" of the patient is permitted to relinquish many of the activities and duties they normally must pursue, such as work, but with the reciprocal obligation to strive for recovery. The complementary role of the physician entails an obligation to do their best to aid the patient and not to exploit the patient's vulnerability. In return the physician enjoys significant social status and prestige. The physician thereby exemplifies a set of qualities that characterize "the "professional" pattern in our society, namely, achievement, universalism, functional specificity, affective neutrality and collectivity-orientation, in that order" (p. 305). It is precisely the practice of these professional qualities that allows the physician to fulfill their social function. In explicating what Parsons means by these terms, his ideal type of the professional will become clear.

The achievement orientation of the professional entails the grounding of their practice in a rigorous scientific knowledge base. To claim that professionalism is universalistic, rather than particularistic, is in part to acknowledge the universality of legitimate scientific inquiry. Parsons notes the initial rejection of Pasteur's discoveries by the medical profession, for he was a mere chemist, as a clear violation of such universalism (1951, p. 306). The recruitment and registration of professionals is similarly universalistic in being meritocratic, thus avoiding the particularism of, say, nepotism. Parsons notes that particularistic forms of recruitment may strengthen group solidarity but will weaken social solidarity, as in-groups are set against each other (p. 306). While this may be taken as a comment on and reinforcement of Durkheim's account of solidarity, it also highlights the need for the profession to be oriented to the needs of society as a whole and not to its particular interests. Universalism does not however entail that professionals are generalists or "wise men" (pp. 292 and 306). This may be seen in the legitimation of the obligations attendant on the sick role. The patient must follow the instructions of the physician. Yet the physician lacks any formal sanction by which they can enforce compliance. The specificity of their expertise is thus significant precisely in that it legitimates the physician's claims upon the patient. The physician acquires not a generalized authority over the patient but an authority to ask specific things of the patient, in the interests of their health (p. 307). A specific expertise is thus part of the grounding of the patient's trust in the physician, not least insofar as it clearly articulates the nature and degree of the physician's legitimate intrusion across emotional and symbolically sensitive boundaries of personal privacy and decorum. The affective neutrality of the professional develops upon this, as the professional distances their practice from their personal feeling, treating patients irrespective of personal preferences, likes or dislikes, or moral judgments. In addition, this entails that the trust of the patient is further secured in that the profession is overtly working for the patient's interests and not their own (p. 308).

It may be noted that Parsons explicitly places "collectivity-orientation," which is to say the sense of civic duty of the professional, suppressing their self-interest in favor of patient and public interests, last. This orientation differentiates the professional from the commercial entrepreneur. The social role of entrepreneur positively sanctions self-interested behavior. In medicine this differentiation from commercialism is, Parsons suggests, of fundamental importance. In other professions, such as law and engineering, the relationship of the professional to commercial activity may be significantly more ambiguous (Parsons 1939, p. 458). Not so medicine. Parsons observes that US physicians at the time of writing were prohibited from various forms of commercial activity, such as advertising. Similarly the physician cannot refuse a patient on the grounds that they are a poor credit risk. The implication is that these are, as much as anything, symbolic legal prohibitions, expressing something fundamental about the nature of professionalism (Parsons 1951, p. 312). The functional importance of an overt "collectivity-orientation" lies in the vulnerability of the patient. Ignorant of their own condition and of its effective treatment and given the severity of the consequences of a mistake in choosing appropriate medical care, the typical advice offered to a consumer of "caveat emptor" cannot apply. The physician is in a dominant position and potentially able to exploit the patient. This potential must be suppressed in order to secure the relationship of trust between physician and patient (pp. 311–312).

The collectivity-orientation suggests the civic ethic with which Durkheim and Tawney characterize professionalism. However, while they tended to see this precisely as an ethic and thus as a moral culture inherent to professionalism, Parsons is more skeptical. While he entertains the possibility that people of a generally altruistic motivation are attracted to medicine and repelled by business, it is more important that the institutional structures of the medical profession negatively sanction self-interested behavior and reward altruistic behavior (Parsons

1951, p. 318, 1939, pp. 465–466). Thus, an institutionally well-ordered profession, which socializes students appropriately and, perhaps more importantly, that refuses to reward dishonest, self-serving, and otherwise unprofessional behavior, forces its members to behave as if they are altruistic, regardless of their personal and psychological motivation.

In summary, the work of Durkheim, Tawney, and Parsons may be seen to articulate the medical profession's self-understanding in a "golden age" of professionalism. Trust is sustained between the professional and their client, grounded in the professional's commitment to both sustaining the scientific expertise that informs their practice and maintaining high standards of other-regarding moral behavior. Professionals are responsible enough to regulate themselves and thus ensure that standards of expertise and morality are maintained. Parsons' model of the professional is presented as an ideal type and as such a heuristic to guide sociological research. This highlights a certain ambiguity in the literature as to whether the type is a normative ideal to which the professions ought to aspire or an empirical description of current professional practice. Parsons observes that: "It is true that medical associations do have committees on ethics and disciplinary procedures. But it is exceedingly rare for cases to be brought into that formal disciplinary procedure" (1951, p. 316). In part this suggests that individual professionals are self-regulating and that the institutional sanctions work effectively. More subtly and problematically, however, Parsons notes that the strict enforcement of professional standards by formal disciplinary committees would introduce significant strains and conflicts into the profession. Professionals would, for example, be required to testify against each other, and to expose their failings to the public. The implication of Parsons' argument appears to be that it is better – or more functional – for professional misdemeanors to be dealt with informally and out of public view than to risk public trust through formal disclosure. It is here that skepticism over the role of professions, and indeed the ethos of professionalism, begins to emerge.

Professional Dominance Theory and Deprofessionalization

In Act 1 of his 1906 play, *The Doctor's Dilemma*, George Bernard Shaw's character Sir Patrick Cullen – an aging doctor and teacher, "not yet quite at the end of his tether" – remarks that: "All professions are conspiracies against the laity." Shaw himself remarks in the substantial preface to the play that the "medical profession [is] a conspiracy to hide its own shortcomings" (Shaw 1909). Shaw offers a vigorous attack on the medical profession, questioning its overt altruism as being little more than a convenient veil that prevents the public from recognizing a multitude of professional shortcomings – including the performance of unnecessary operations for the sake of the fee. Significantly Shaw is not launching an attack on the personal morality of physicians but rather upon institutional factors, such as low pay, that encourage, or indeed necessitate, immortal practices. Shaw thereby anticipates the core of the critical approach to professionalism that was to emerge in the 1970s, when the Parsonian assumption that the professional is collectivity-orientated comes to be questioned by both sociologists and historians. This period also begins to mark the decline in public trust in the professions, and academic research may be seen both to stimulate and to give voice to that growing distrust.

Eliot Freidson's *Profession of Medicine* (1970) argues that professionalization is a fundamentally political process. Freidson's professional dominance perspective argues that professionalization is the political process through which a high degree of autonomy is secured for the profession. Autonomy allows the profession to regulate itself, identify and discipline malpractice, and determine the most appropriate form that the provision of its services should take. While the Parsonian perspective suggests that the legitimacy of this autonomy is largely self-evident, given the functional value of the profession to contemporary society, for Freidson "[a] profession attains and maintains its position by virtue of the protection and patronage of some elite segment of society which has been persuaded that there is some special value in its work" (Freidson 1970, p. 72). The profession must make its case, not least to the state and the general public. The trappings of professionalism, including the appeal to expert knowledge and ethics, serve to make this case. Insofar as the complexity of the knowledge base is comprehensible only to the trained physician, no one outside the profession is in a position to criticize its practice. More subtly, if the codes of conduct that govern professional practice are more than just etiquette – more than the maintenance of a polite and financially lucrative relationship to the patient, alongside stable relationships within the profession – being rather genuine ethics, grounded in an ethos of public service, then again external legal regulation of the profession is unnecessary. The skeptic, in making their critical argument against professional autonomy, will question both of these assumptions, reducing professionalism to a rhetoric.

For the skeptic, professional autonomy in medicine is not seen as the necessary facilitation of benevolent and paternalistic action toward patients and the general public but rather as a means of securing market dominance over health-care provision. Autonomy works ultimately in the self-interest of the profession, not the general public, by securing the profession a more or less monopolistic position within the health-care market (Berlant 1975; Bledstein 1976; Larson 1978). Autonomy thus gives the profession an economic advantage in that it can exclude competing occupations from entering the health-care market, thereby increasing the power of the profession to determine fees (Elston 1991). In the nineteenth century, the AMA is seen to work, actively, to exclude alternative or "irregular" practitioners such as homeopaths, from the market (Starr 1982). It may be noted, as a problem with such an argument, that much contemporary sociology of medicine tends, unlike Parsons, to affect an agnosticism toward issues of medical efficacy. If homeopathy and other alternative medicines are genuinely ineffective, and potentially harmful if prescribed for serious conditions, as contemporary evidence-based medicine strongly suggests, then the appeal to medical expertise made by the AMA is more than simply a matter of monopolizing a market. It has a genuine ethical dimension in protecting the public from harm. A stronger case is made by critics of professionalism with respect to the relation between medical subdisciplines:

disciplines such as nursing may be denied full professional status as the medical division of labor is controlled by physicians (Freidson 1970, pp. 57–63). It can be also argued that medical autonomy has restricted the forms of effective medicine being made available. Autonomous and self-regulating professionals come to be suspected of providing the services they want to provide, rather than those that patients need. As gatekeepers to medical services, they are criticized as being nonaccountable. Profitable curative approaches, for example, have been promoted over and above preventative medicine (see Light 2010, p. 276). More subtly, a monopolistic medical profession can have undue influence in determining public understandings of health and health care. The sick role itself is thereby revealed as a site of political negotiation, as the legitimacy of the state of a particular condition, such as chronic fatigue syndrome or degrees of mental health, as illness is contested and constructed.

Freidson summarizes the problems of professionalization by claiming that: "While the profession's autonomy seems to have facilitated the improvement of scientific knowledge about disease and its treatment, it seems to have impeded the improvement of the social modes of applying that knowledge" (1970, p. 371). Freidson acknowledges that, historically, the medical profession did need protection from "the urgent ignorance of its clientele [and] the mischief of low-class competitors" (ibid), but that autonomy has now led to a destructive degree of complacency in the profession as it isolates itself from external criticism. Crucially, it loses sight of the patient's perspective. Most fundamentally this is expressed in a failure to identify poor and negligent practice. In the UK, in the 1970s, evidence of medical malpractice and poor standards was becoming more public (RCGP 1974) and yet was receiving no official response from the GMC and other professional bodies. The Merrison Inquiry into the regulation of the medical profession, commissioned by the Secretary of State for Social Services in 1972, made no reference to the evidence that had been presented to it concerning poor standards of practice (Secretary of State for Social Services 1975). Self-regulation was failing to protect the patient or public. Freidson argues that this failure is rooted in a reluctance by professions to criticize each other, thereby mirroring Parsons' analysis. Mistakes are regarded as inevitable in complex practices, and while self-criticism may be encouraged, the open criticism of others violates a requirement for mutual charity. It may after all be the critic's turn to be the subject of criticism next (Freidson 1970, p. 179). This suggests that the institutions to which Parsons appealed in order to secure the altruistic behavior of professions are actually fundamentally flawed and work against the interests of patients and public.

For some (Light 2010, p. 272), an irony of Freidson's argument lies in its publication occurring just as the dominance of the medical profession is in decline. While, as Freidson readily admits, the medical profession's autonomy was never absolute, it has been argued that changes within the provision of medicine and the organization of the medical subdisciplines as well as changes in wider society have begun to erode the power that the medical profession exercised during its "golden age" (roughly 1945–1965). At the extreme, this has been argued to constitute a deprofessionalization of medicine (Reed and Evans 1987). Critical changes include the intrusion of profit-making organizations into the medical market in the 1980s (e.g., in the USA an increase in for-profit health care and more stringent financial management of health-care provision and the introduction of quasi-markets into the organization and ethos of the UK National Health Service), whereby decisions on the provision of health care are shifted away from the physician. Internal changes within medicine have compounded or been entwined with this shift. These include the successful struggles of nursing and other "professions allied to medicine," such as physiotherapy, to assert their own professional identity. For Freidson (1994), the rise of the professional manager, and thus the development of more finely structured hierarchies within medicine, similarly undermines the physicians' autonomy, as decision making over policy and even prescribing shifts to the managerial profession. Perhaps more fundamentally, the development of evidence-based medicine (and organizations such as the UK's National Institute for Health and Care Excellence (NICE) that offer guidance to governments and the medical profession on the efficacy of treatments), alongside the use of clinical governance and even clinical targets, has begun to challenge traditional notions of clinical judgment. The autonomy, not merely of the profession but more specifically of the individual practitioner, is compromised insofar as compliance with nationally agreed clinical guidelines for treatment reduces the need for phronesis, and the erstwhile professional becomes a mere technician.

There has been a significant loss of patient trust in the profession, aligned with an increasingly consumerist attitude on behalf of patients, thus leading to increased litigation and external investigation and regulation. The model of a passive and ignorant patient used by Parsons has been challenged. In part this is due to a general rise in levels of public education, so that the physician is more likely to be confronted by patients who are as well-educated and as articulate as themselves. Patient groups, supporting either sufferers of particular conditions or defending patients' rights in general, have demanded a voice for the patient in negotiating their treatment. Significantly, Parsons argued that a function of the medical profession was to keep patients isolated, in order, given the deviant nature of illness, to inhibit the formation of groups of deviants (1951, pp. 320–321). Such groups now play an important role in checking abuses of professional power. Talbot argues that the loss of public trust is as much rooted in a crisis over the behavior of physicians toward patients, including an increasing business orientation and loss of effective communication skills, as in a direct experience of poor practice (Talbot 2011, p. 127). This would suggest either a decline in the physician's standards of professionalism (expressed in less demonstrable respect for patients) or higher expectations of professional behavior from the public. With respect to a wider public, a number of well-publicized instances of malpractice in the UK and elsewhere, since the 1990s, including those of individual practitioners such as Harold Shipman, Richard Neale, and Rodney Ledward or institutional failings at Bristol Royal Infirmary, Alder Hey in Liverpool, and most recently the Mid-Staffordshire NHS Trust, have served to underline a public perception of the failings of professional self-regulation.

In summary, professional dominance perspectives share sociology's earlier assumption that the medical profession does have autonomy and considerable power. They differ from early perspectives in questioning the supposed altruism and public service ethos of the profession. Professionalism, expressed in a commitment to public service and the maintenance of a scientifically grounded expertise, is challenged as a mere rhetoric or ideology that conceals, consciously or otherwise, the self-serving nature of the profession. Growing public awareness of failures in self-regulation, alongside structural and cultural changes in the provision of health care, has led to the establishment of mechanisms of external regulation. Debates that began in the eighteenth century, with the concerns of Gregory over standards of professional practice and Percival's defense of a medical ethic, thus reemerge and pose a new challenge to develop a viable contemporary conception of professionalism.

New Professionalism

Hafferty (2006) suggests that initial responses, in the 1980s, to the perceived crisis in professionalism were restricted to a largely polemical defense of professionalism in the face of increasing commercialism. In the early 1990s, renewed attempts to define and operationalize "professionalism" arise, integrating notions of professionalism as a competence into physician training and accountability. This in turn leads to attempts to measure professionalism (see Arnold et al. 1998; Epstein and Hundert 2002). Understandings of professionalism are nonetheless diverse. Indeed, it may be argued that the values espoused by professionals continued, well beyond this period, to be highly ambiguous and contested (Pattison and Pill 2004). A continuum of responses may nonetheless be identified, running from a conservative reassertion of the traditional values of professionalism to a more reform-oriented "new professionalism," variously rethinking the demands of civic professionalism, embracing the need for external regulation and guidance, and thus abandoning professional autonomy as a defining characteristic of professionalism.

Conservative responses to the crisis presuppose the continuing need for professional autonomy. This is argued for, somewhat surprisingly, by Freidson in his final work, *Professionalism: The Third Logic* (2001). Reconsidering the golden age of professionalism and thus something closely akin to the Parsonian ideal type of a profession, Freidson places the logic of professional practice between that of the market, on one side, and bureaucratic planning on the other. He thus, in effect, restates familiar arguments that defend professionalism in the face of both the corrupting influence of commercialism (which would place self-interest above public service) and state regulation (which would undermine professional judgment). At the core of his argument lies a reassertion of the specialist and complex nature of professional expertise, characterized as it is by uncertainty and contingency. The nonprofessional, be this either the consumer in the marketplace or the civil servant, is then assumed to be unable to understand and judge good professional practice. Monopoly and self-regulation are thus essential if professions are to continue to serve the public. While Freidson's argument has been rigorously challenged (see Hafferty et al. 2003), not least in that it fails to take account of the very institutional failures documented in his earlier work, similar restatements of traditional arguments abound.

Cruess et al. (2004), for example, articulates the familiar view of professionals using expertise to the good of society – governed by codes of ethics that commit them to traditional values of "competence, integrity and morality, altruism, and the promotion of public good" – in return for status and financial rewards, as a social contract. Swick (2000) similarly offers a normative definition of "professionalism" in terms of nine behaviors, focusing around the need to subordinate person interests to those of the patient, thus to act ethically and to demonstrate humanistic values such as compassion and integrity; professionals thereby respect the social contract between the profession and the public; they are committed to maintain high levels of technical excellence and to reflect upon their practice and be accountable to peers. Such behaviors would, Swick argues, restore public trust in the profession.

The conservative arguments perhaps do little other than repackage old ideals of professionalism. The debate does, nonetheless, lead to strategies for reinforcing and policing the ethical grounding of professionalism and thus strategies to make professional autonomy workable. Two prominent examples may be briefly reviewed. The American Board of Internal Medicine (ABIM), through its Medical Professionalism Project, developed the "Physician Charter" (ABIM Foundation et al. 2002). This widely adopted code of conduct articulates professional ethics by promoting "physician responsibilities" that include commitments to professional competence and scientific knowledge, honesty, and confidentiality. Further, patient autonomy and social justice are included in the governing principles of the charter. This is indicative of an awareness of the rise of the patient's rights movement and the implications that a social contract has in the context of debates over the rationing and prioritization of health care. Corresponding responsibilities thus include commitment to the quality of care, access to care, and just distribution of finite resources. Crucially the charter makes explicit issues that challenge or undermine professionalism. These include the abuse of power, arrogance, greed, misrepresentation, lack of conscientiousness, and conflicts of interest (ABIM 1995). At the very least, this suggests that professionalism may be as much recognized in its absence as in its presence but also entails responsibilities to managing conflicts of interest and a (perhaps somewhat vaguer) commitment to professional responsibilities.

The Accreditation Council for Graduate Medical Education (ACGME) takes the debate a step further by including "professionalism" as one of the six core competences that a physician requires and through which training and revalidation can be oriented. Professionalism requires the demonstration of respect, compassion, and integrity; responsiveness to patient needs superseding self-interest; accountability to patients, society, and the profession; excellence and ongoing professional development; adherence to ethical principles; sensitivity and responsiveness to diverse patient population; and respect for patient privacy and autonomy (Swing 2007). "Professionalism" by this operationalization is complemented by competences in "medical knowledge" and "practice-based learning and improvement" – and thus the traditional commitments to maintaining scientific expertise – and by a competence in patient care, which includes effective communication, caring, and respectful behavior (ibid). The increased recognition of the importance of communication skills suggests that etiquette toward the patient, if not adopted cynically, has become an important aspect of professional conduct.

A number of concerns may be expressed with these traditional responses and in particular with the integration of professionalism into education and validation. Firstly, it may be noted that the treatment of professionalism as a measurable competence sees resistance from the likes of Wear and Aultman (2006), not least in their argument that professionalism may be reduced to that which is measurable, expressive of a fear that the phronetic, contextual, and reflexive competences of the professional may be marginalized in favor of a largely mechanic rule following. Secondly, research into the experiences and attitudes of medical students suggests that traditional values such as altruism no longer resonate with them. The superseding of personal interest disrupts a desirable work-life balance and may be seen to leave students vulnerable to exploitation by their teachers and physicians vulnerable to exploitation by patients (Hafferty 2002). This unease with selflessness may be even more strongly felt in traditionally subordinate medical subdisciplines and particularly in nursing. Finally, where traditional approaches see respect for codes of conduct as an integral part of professionalism, it may be asked whether an ethics, not dissimilar in its outline to that advocated by Durkheim, has the power to check the abuses and failings of professional autonomy (see Freidson 2001, p. 215). Traditional approaches to professionalism tend thereby to take for granted the assumption that professions can autonomously regulate their own practitioners. This assertion of a code of conduct may, nonetheless, be interpreted critically as a political move, consciously or unconsciously, to safeguard a self-interested autonomy, rather than a genuine response to the problem.

Hafferty's review of the more reformist "new professionalism" suggests two issues (2006, p. 198f). One rests upon the individual disciplines of the practitioner him- or herself; the other on the practitioner's place in wider society. The former develops the idea of the reflective practitioner (Schön 1983) and as such grounds the integration of professionalism into education, specifically in practice-based learning. For Epstein, critical self-reflection facilitates professionalism, in that it "enables physicians to listen attentively to patients' distress, recognize their own errors, refine their technical skills, make evidence-based decisions, and clarify their values so that they can act with compassion, technical competence, presence, and insight." Indeed, the lack of such reflection is blamed "for some deviations from professionalism and errors in judgment and technique" (1999, p. 833). In part, this approach may be seen to reassert the autonomy and indeed phronesis of the individual practitioner, thereby defending them against further regulation. Epstein's approach also suggests that professional reflection is a largely tacit competence, to be learned not through the following of explicit rules but rather through the examples and guidance provided by mentors (ibid). As such, it may be seen to reproduce the distinction that has held since the eighteenth century between a craft, as the mere mechanical application of a rule of practice, and a profession, requiring a phronetic capacity to understand the relevance of theoretical knowledge contextually and particularistically.

Epstein's approach may renew the ethical commitment of the professional but continues to be potentially self-serving if it lacks rigorous enforcement. The rethinking of civic professionalism by the likes of Sullivan (1999, 2004), Mechanic (2000), and Frankford and Konrad (1998) begins to respond to this challenge. The altruism that is fundamental to traditional notions of professionalism is reinterpreted as civic engagement and thus as a professional commitment to civic equality and social justice. Echoing the calls of Gregory in the eighteenth century, the patient and public are brought into dialogue with the professional within a "body politic." Trust is restored in the profession, not simply through the institution of more rigorous or inventive codes of conduct but rather through the profession leading discussion with the public as to what the nature and role of the profession should be (Sullivan 2000). This leads Frankford and others to reject the traditional commitment to medical autonomy (Frankford et al. 2000). The rise of evidence-based medicine and the quality-of-care movement, not least insofar as the "patient experience," is placed centrally to any judgment of good treatment and confronts the profession with external standards for assessing and regulating their practice. More precisely, the responsibility for such assessment may not lie most effectively with the profession's own regulative bodies. NICE and the Care Quality Commission in England play such a role. New professionalism may then be understood as embracing external regulation and the imposition of clinical guidelines. Such acceptance need not, as some fear, reduce the practitioner to a mere technical expert. Rather, as Light defends "accountability-based" professionalism, there is a shift from a variable quality of care, due to its individual determination by the autonomous practitioner, to the use of "guidelines, protocols, and care pathways" to ensure outcomes grounded in clinical research. A new clinical research elite sets evidence-based standards, which would for Light emphasize primary care, prevention, and the management of illness over and above the curative interventions that have been the tradition sources of professional prestige. This would in turn require teamwork and cooperation between the medical subdisciplines (including managers and specialists in evidence-based medicine and epidemiology), disrupting the traditional hierarchy that allows physicians to control and delegate (Light 2010, p. 279).

Within the UK, Irvine's conception of "patient-centered care" offers a model of such new professionalism. Patient-centered care recognizes that the modern age is one of patient autonomy, not professional autonomy. Patients have better advocacy from charitable and support groups and are given a clear voice in legal actions against inadequate care but are also increasingly expert in their own conditions – so throwing into question the model of the patient found in say Parsons and later Freidson. For Irvine, the patient is the final arbiter of what is right for them, and:

> [T]hey equate professionalism with consistently good doctoring. For them 'good doctors' are up to date, competent, respectful, courteous, kind, empathetic and honest; people who will listen to them, relate to them, do their best to find out promptly what is wrong with them, prescribe the right treatment and care for them in a manner which makes them feel that their interests come first. Patients want their doctors to be good team players when teamwork is needed. (Irvine 2014, p. 7)

Crucially, this model is not presented as mere personal motivation and ethic but as something that must be regulated and enforced. Irvine sees this in the development of the GMC in the 1990s and beyond, as its code "Good Medical Practice" was instituted, not merely as advice but as the framework within which education, regulation, and all importantly the ongoing revalidation of the physician's fitness to practice proceed.

In summary, new professionalism has responded to the crisis in public trust by rethinking codes of conduct and thus the image of what "good doctoring" is, integrating such codes rigorously into education and validation but more radically questioning the traditional value of autonomy. Professionalism thereby ceases to be a mere ethic and comes to embrace the acceptance of regulation and cooperation with other professional disciplines; professional altruism is transformed into the acceptance that the patient lies at the center of health-care provision and has a fundamental right to consistent, high-quality care.

Definition of Key Terms

Civic professionalism	Approach to professionalism that focuses on the professional's participation in civil society.
Deprofessionalization	Thesis that professions are losing their distinctive status, due to the loss of autonomy and increased routinization of the application of expertise.
Dominance theory	A sociological theory developed by Eliot Freidson and others, critically analyzing the power exercised by professions, as a dominant position working in the profession's own interests.
New professionalism	Response to the perceived crisis in professional, due to a loss of public trust and increase regulation. New professionalism challenges traditional professional characteristics and in particular professional autonomy.
Professionalism	Set of values traditionally associated with professional performance, focusing on an altruistic and other-regarding ethic, alongside commitment to maintaining professional expertise.

Summary Points

- Professionalism is traditionally characterized as entailing an other-regarding ethic and a commitment to the maintenance of high standards of scientifically based expertise.
- The "golden age" of professionalism, between approximately 1945 and 1965, sees high levels of public trust in the professions, allowing profession to be self-regulating and autonomous.
- The self-regulation of professions is challenged in the 1970s, as it is increasingly recognized that self-regulation serves the interests of professionals and fails to deliver high standards of care to patients and society as a whole.
- A crisis of professionalism occurs in the 1970s and 1980s, as professional self-regulation is seen to fail patients and the general public and as public trust in professions declines.
- Developments such as the emergence of new professions within medicine, evidence-based medicine, and a renewed emphasis on patient-centered care and patient rights undermine traditional defenses of professional autonomy.
- New professionalism responds to the crisis in professionalism, most fundamentally by rejecting the ideal of professional autonomy, in favor of evidence-based external regulation and the imposition of practice guidelines.

References

ABIM Foundation. American Board of Internal Medicine, ACP-ASIM Foundation. American College of Physicians-American Society of Internal Medicine, European Federation of Internal Medicine (2002) Medical professionalism in the new millennium: a physician charter. Ann Intern Med 136(3):243–246

American Board of Internal Medicine (1995) Project professionalism. American Board of Internal Medicine, Philadelphia

Arnold EL, Blank LL, Race KE, Cipparrone N (1998) Can professionalism be measured? The development of a scale for use in the medical environment. Acad Med 73:1119–1121

Baker R (1995) The codification of medical morality: historical and philosophical studies of the formalization of Western medical morality in the eighteenth and nineteenth centuries volume two: Anglo-American medical ethics and medical jurisprudence in the nineteenth century. Kluwer, Dordrecht

Berlant JL (1975) The profession and monopoly. University of Californian Press, Berkeley

Bledstein B (1976) The culture of professionalism. W. W. Norton, New York

Boyd KM (2005) Medical ethics: principles, persons, and perspectives: from controversy to conversation. J Med Ethics 31:481–486

Crowther MA (1995) Forensic medicine and medical ethics in nineteenth-century Britain. In: Baker R (ed) The codification of medical morality. Kluwer, Dordrecht, pp 173–190

Cruess SR, Johnston S, Cruess RL (2004) Profession: a working definition for medical educators. Teach Learn Med 16:74–76

Durkheim E (1984) Division of labour in society. Macmillan, London

Durkheim E (1992) Professional ethics and civic morals. Routledge, London

Edgar A (2011) Professional values, aesthetic values, and the ends of trade. Med Health Care Philos 14(2):195–201

Elston MA (1991) The politics of professional power. In: Gabe J, Calnan M, Bury M (eds) The politics of professional power. Routledge, London, pp 58–98

Epstein RM (1999) Mindful practice. JAMA 282:833–839

Epstein RM, Hundert EM (2002) Defining and assessing professional competence. JAMA 287:227–235

Flexner A (1910) Medical education in the United States and Canada: a report to the Carnegie foundation for the advancement of teaching, vol 4, Bulletin. The Carnegie Foundation for the Advancement of Teaching, New York

Frankford DM, Konrad TR (1998) Responsive medical professionalism: integrating education, practice, and community in a market-driven era. Acad Med 73:138–145

Frankford DM, Patterson M, Konrad TR (2000) Transforming practice organizations to foster lifelong learning and commitment to medical professionalism. Acad Med 75:708–717

Freidson E (1970) Profession of medicine: a study of the sociology of applied knowledge. Harper & Row, New York

Freidson E (1994) Professionalism reborn: theory, prophecy and policy. University of Chicago Press, Chicago

Freidson E (2001) Professionalism: the third logic. University of Chicago Press, Chicago

Gregory J (1817) Lectures on the duties and qualifications of a physician. Carey and Son, Philadelphia

Hafferty FW (2002) What medical students know about professionalism. Mt Sinai J Med 69:385–397

Hafferty FW (2006) Definitions of professionalism: a search for meaning and identity. Clin Orthop Relat Res 449:183–204

Hafferty FW, Havighurst CC, Relman AS, Freidson E (2003) Review symposium on Eliot Freidson's professionalism: the third logic. J Health Polit Policy Law 28(1):133–172

Irvine D (2014) Patients, their doctors and the politics of medical professionalism: address to members of the American Osler Society. Available from http://www.pickereurope.org/individual-clinician-feedback-is-vital/. Accessed 14 Aug 2014

Larson MS (1977) The rise of professionalism: a sociological analysis. University of Californian Press, London

Leake CD (1927) Percival's medical ethics. Williams and Wilkins, Baltimore

Leake CD (1970) Percival's medical ethics: promise and problems. Ann N Y Acad Sci 169:388–396

Light DW (2010) Health-care professions, markets, and countervailing powers. In: Bird CE, Peter C, Fremont AM, Stefan T (eds) Handbook of medical sociology, 6th edn. Vanderbilt University Press, Nashville

Lindemann M (2008) Medicine, medical practice, and public health. In: Wilson PH (ed) A companion to eighteenth-century Europe. Blackwell Reference Online, Oxford. http://www.blackwellreference.com/subscriber/tocnode?id=g9781405139472_chunk_g978140513947212. Accessed 1 Aug 2014

Mechanic D (2000) Managed care and the imperative for a new professional ethic: a plan to address the growing misfit between traditional medical professionalism and emerging health care structures. Health Aff 19:100–111

Parsons T (1939) The professions and social structure. Soc Forces 17:457–467

Parsons T (1951) The social system. Routledge, London

Pattison S, Pill R (eds) (2004) Values in professional practice: lessons for health, social care and other professionals. Radcliffe, Oxford

Percival J (1849) Medical ethics, 2nd edn. Shrimpton, Oxford

Porter R (1997) The greatest benefit of mankind: a medical history of humanity from antiquity to the present. Harper Collins, London

RCGP (1977) Evidence to the Royal Commission on the NHS, Journal of the RCGP 27:197–206

Reed RR, Evans D (1987) The Deprofessionalization of Medicine: Causes, Effects and Responsibiltieis. JAMA 258:3279–3282

Schön D (1983) The reflective practitioner, how professionals think in act. Basic Books, New York

Secretary of State for Social Services (1975) Report of the Committee of Inquiry into the regulation of the medical profession. Chairman Dr A.W. Merrison. Cmnd 6018. Stationery Office, London

Shaw GB (1909) Preface to 'The Doctor's Dilemma. Available http://www.gutenberg.org/files/5069/5069-h/5069-h.htm. Accessed 14 Aug 2014

Starr P (1982) The social transformation of American medicine. Basic Books, New York

Sullivan WM (1999) What is left of professionalism after managed care? Hastings Cent Rep 29:7–13

Sullivan WM (2000) Medicine under threat: professionalism and professional identity. Can Med Assoc J 162:673–675

Sullivan WM (2004) Can professionalism still be a viable ethic? Good Soc 31:15–20

Swick HM (2000) Toward a normative definition of medical professionalism. Acad Med 75:612–616

Swing SR (2007) The ACGME outcome project: retrospective and prospective. Med Teach 29:648–654

Talbot JA (2011) Medical professionalism in the new century: accomplishments and challenges in the future for an American medical school. In: Bhugra D, Malik A (eds) Professionalism in mental healthcare: experts, expertise and expectations. Cambridge University Press, Cambridge, pp 126–138

Tawney RH (1921) The acquisitive society. Bell and Sons, London

Wear D, Aultman JM (2006) Introduction. In: Delese W, Aultman JM (eds) Professionalism in medicine: critical perspectives. Springer, New York, pp. vii–xi

Skilled Know-How, Virtuosity, and Expertise in Clinical Practice

42

Hillel D. Braude

Contents

Abstract

The terms "skilled know-how," "virtuosity," and "expertise" all denote forms of technical mastery. Applied to medicine they refer to different aspects of medical expertise. Yet, what exactly is medical expertise? Is it a kind of cognition, or action, or a combination of both? Additionally, what aspects of clinical practice does technical expertise refer to? In this chapter technical expertise in clinical practice is analyzed in terms of three identified components: cognition, motoric action, and interpersonal relations. Furthermore, the three components of technical mastery are related to Aristotle's concept of practical wisdom, or *phronesis*. In his *Nicomachean Ethics*, Aristotle differentiated between two different forms of human action: *techné* and *phronesis*. In broad terms *techné* refers to an action that results in the production of external objects, while *phronesis* refers to an action that has its end in itself. This distinction provides the architectonic keystone of this analysis of expertise in clinical practice. This approach presents an alternative to the predominant cognitive conception

H.D. Braude (✉)
The Mifne Center, Rosh Pinna, Israel
e-mail: hillel.braude@mcgill.ca

© Springer Science+Business Media Dordrecht 2017
T. Schramme, S. Edwards (eds.), *Handbook of the Philosophy of Medicine*,
DOI 10.1007/978-94-017-8688-1_68

699

of technical expertise in clinical practice. A full understanding of technical expertise, skilled know-how, and virtuosity is not possible without highlighting the important role of intentionality in action and other forms of pre-reflective knowing in clinical practice.

Introduction

The terms "skilled know-how," "virtuosity," and "expertise" all denote forms of technical mastery. Applied to medicine they refer to different aspects of medical expertise. Yet, what exactly is medical expertise? (Despite the subtle differences of meaning, the terms skilled know-how, virtuosity, and expertise will be referred to more or less synonymously under the rubric of medical expertise.) Is it a kind of cognition, or action, or a combination of both? Additionally, what aspects of clinical practice does technical expertise refer to? Geoffrey Norman et al. note that, "Expertise in medicine requires mastery of a diversity of knowledge and skills – motor, cognitive, and interpersonal ..." (2006, 339). These three elements pertain to each stage of clinical practice, i.e., patient diagnosis, evaluation of possible therapies, and deciding the best course of action in the particular circumstance (Pellegrino and Thomasma 1981). The development of this chapter will provide a discursive analysis of technical expertise in clinical practice in terms of these three components of motoric action, cognition, and interpersonal relations. Furthermore, these three components of technical mastery will be related to Aristotle's concept of practical wisdom, or *phronesis*. In his *Nicomachean Ethics*, Aristotle (1925) differentiated between two different forms of human action: *techné* and *phronesis*. In broad terms *techné* refers to an action that results in the production of external objects, while *phronesis* refers to an action that has its end in itself. This distinction provides the architectonic keystone for this analysis of expertise in clinical practice. Additionally, where it is helpful for elucidation, this analytic review of expertise in clinical practice will draw on evidence from the neurosciences. This approach presents a critique of the predominant conception of technical expertise primarily in terms of cognition, which arguably has obstructed the development of comprehensive literature around skilled know-how in clinical practice beyond a primary level. A full understanding of technical expertise, skilled know-how, and virtuosity is not possible without highlighting the important role of intentionality in action and other forms of pre-reflective knowing in clinical practice.

Clinical Practice as *Phronesis* or *Techné*

A number of authors have argued that clinical reasoning is best understood as a form of Aristotelian *phronesis* (see, e.g., Pellegrino and Thomasma 1981; Gatens Robinson 1986; Widdershoven-Heerding 1987; Beresford 1996; McGee 1996; Montgomery 2000; Braude 2012b). In the *Nicomachean Ethics*, Aristotle (1925) lists *phronesis* as one of the intellectual virtues alongside philosophic wisdom, or *sophia*, and understanding, or *nous* (1103a6). Aristotle notes that practical reasoning requires means of verification that are appropriate for the subject matter at hand: "For it is the mark of an educated man to look for precision in each class of things just so far as the nature of the subject admits; it is evidently equally foolish to accept probable reasoning from a mathematician and to demand from a rhetorician scientific proofs" (1094b). In this statement, Aristotle presents the radical idea that certain kinds of practical knowing are justified primarily through calculating the ends of their actions in the real world, not in terms of mathematical or other kinds of theoretical abstraction.

Clinical practice is an exemplary form of *phronesis* because of its perennial concern for what is temporally in flux. Aristotle (1925) notes that a key aspect of *phronesis* is its association with what is variable:

> No one deliberates about things that are invariable, nor about things that it is impossible for him to do. Therefore, since scientific knowledge involves demonstration, but there is no demonstration of things whose first principles are variable (for all such things might actually be otherwise), and since it is impossible to deliberate about things that are of necessity, practical wisdom cannot be scientific knowledge nor art; not science because that which can be done is capable of being otherwise, not art because action and making are different kinds of thing. The remaining alternative, then, is that it is a true and reasoned state of capacity to act with regard to the things that are good or bad for man. (1140a)

Arguably clinical medicine is the exemplary science of the contingent. All clinicians, not only expert ones, necessarily are faced with individual variability in their everyday practice. Similar diseases present differently due to biological variability and the influence of patient subjectivity on the experience of illness. Human biology presents a multileveled complexity than can be accounted for purely by the physical sciences (Schaffner 1994). The epistemological attempt to define clinical reasoning needs to take account of this inherent variability in the human condition, best accounted for through the Aristotelian virtue of *phronesis*.

Is it not a category error, however, to describe clinical practice as a form of practical wisdom, and not rather a kind of technical expertise? In the Hippocratic tradition, medicine was considered to be a form of craft (*techné*) (Edelstein 1967). Techniques of all sorts characterize modern clinical practice, from auscultation to conducting an autopsy on a cadaver. Is not this sense of technical mastery associated with craftsmanship more suitable to describe clinical practice, especially in relation to skilled know-how, virtuosity, and expertise? Aristotle (1925) distinguished *phronesis* from *techné* in one essential sense: the end of *phronesis* is the action itself (1140b5–7). On the other hand, *techné* is defined by being an action that has an end other than itself (1140b6–7). Furthermore, *phronesis* and *techné* can also be understood in terms of their relation to two further categories of human activity, *poiesis* and *praxis* (Heidegger 1997. See also the discussion on *phronesis* informed by this distinction by Hans Georg Gadamer 1975; and Robert Bernasconi 1989). Thus, *phronesis* can be distinguished further as a form of *praxis* and *techné* as a form of *poiesis*. *Praxis* is a form of practical activity that is intended to further human well-being or the good and is not associated with any particular end product external to the act. *Poiesis* refers to any human activity that results in a product external to the human activity itself. The act of making associated with crafts (*techné*) is associated, therefore, with *poiesis*.

Aristotle (1925) conceived of the end of medicine being health (1094a). If curing disease or health is considered to be separate from medical action, then indeed, medicine should be considered a form of *techné*. This is the position taken by Barbara Hofmann (2002), in her insightful critique of medicine as practical wisdom. If, on the other hand, clinical practice is concerned with intermediary steps in order to achieve personal well-being, then it is akin to *phronesis*. As argued, however, medicine through clinical reasoning is unusual in sharing aspects of *techné* and *phronesis* (Braude 2012a). Or rather, clinical practice modeled on *phronesis* explicitly incorporates aspects of *techné* without contradiction. As has been observed, "*Phronesis* demonstrates this dual quality by being concerned with both technical issues and intermediary steps towards the end of action" (Braude 2016). Yet, what differentiates a specific act in the world as being one of *phronesis* or *techné* depends on the constitutive variables concerning the agent, the intention, and the outcome. This point will become more apparent through the analysis of medical expertise in this chapter.

Aristotle uses the metaphor of medicine as exemplary for the dual nature of *phronesis*. Thus, in the *Nicomachean Ethics*, Aristotle argues that medicine is a form of practical wisdom whose end is the health of the individual. "Medicine," Aristotle writes, "does not govern health, but is for the sake of health" (1925, 1145a11). Medicine is an exemplary form of practical wisdom, since in determining what is best for a particular individual, technical know-how is necessary but not sufficient. "Medicine," as Kathryn Montgomery writes, "is neither a science nor a technical skill (although it puts both to use) but the ability to work out how general rules – scientific principles, clinical guidelines – apply to one particular patient" (2006, 5). Medicine as a form of practical wisdom lies close to the determination of *poiesis* in requiring technical expertise to achieve the ends of clinical action. At the same time, this knowledge can never be divorced from the self-knowing associated with *phronesis*. Clinical practice shares with *phronesis* an inherent structure of moral agency (Gallagher 2007). As philosopher Stephen Toulmin elegantly states, "Once brought to the bedside, so to say, applied ethics and clinical medicine use just the same Aristotelian kinds of "practical reasoning," and a correct choice of therapeutic procedure in medicine is the right treatment to pursue, not just as a matter of medical technique but for ethical reasons also" (Toulmin 1982).

Cognitive Expertise

Cognition is the first component of medical expertise mentioned by Norman et al. (2006). Cognition refers to all mental processes related to knowledge, including but not limited to memory, attention, perception, representational schemas, consciousness, and language. Norman et al. also note that, "much of what

we call medical expertise is really closer to medical diagnostic expertise …"
(2006, 340). In other words, clinical expertise is often conflated with processes
associated with clinical reasoning, which in turn is most often assessed in terms of
cognition. It is worth pondering the reasons for this cognitive emphasis in the
literature around medical expertise, and how this cognitive bias influences the
understanding of clinical expertise. For the moment, however, this analysis will
focus on clinical reasoning itself as a form of "skilled know-how" conceptualized in
terms of cognition. (For a fuller analysis of clinical reasoning and cognitive
knowing, see Braude, 2016).

The influential hypothetico-deductive model conceives of clinical reasoning as a
form of cognition applied to evaluating and managing a patient's medical problem
(Barrows and Tamblyn 1980). According to this model, a clinician creates working
hypotheses inferred from the patient's presenting symptoms. The clinician then
refines these hypotheses through a gradual process of elimination, until the most
compelling hypothesis is chosen, which best fits with the primary clinical diagnosis
(Barrows and Feltovich 1987). In its cognitive approach to clinical reasoning, the
hypothetico-deductive model only accounts for explicit analytic inferences. Its
intellectual and methodological basis is derived from the psychological heuristics
and biases approach developed a number of decades previously by Daniel Kahneman and Amos Tversky (1974). (For a review of the application of the discipline of
cognitive psychology to evaluate clinical decision-making, see Elstein 2000, 2009).

Physician Pat Croskerry, among others, has championed applying the tools of
cognitive science in order to examine our inherent cognitive biases involved in
clinical reasoning. Croskerry cites more than 40 different kinds of cognitive and
affective biases that together may contribute to impaired clinical judgment
(Croskerry 2008; Croskerry et al. 2008). The kinds of cognitive impediments
affecting effective clinical decision include those relating to the structure of cognition, psychological ego defenses of the decision-maker, and the neurophysiological
state of the decision-maker at the moment of decision. Despite their different
nuances and variations, these are all cognitive; however, their influence and impact
are to a great extent unknown to the decision-maker at the time of the decision.
While skeptical toward the inherent biases, Croskerry's cognitive program is ultimately amelioristic in providing a means of improving cognitive decision-making.
Thus, Croskerry conceives that these largely unconscious cognitive biases can be
made explicit through processes of self-reflection, introspection, and metacognition.

Metacognition refers to the processes involved in thinking about one's own
thinking. It may also refer to the activity of monitoring and controlling one's own
cognitive activity (Proust 2013). Applied to clinical reasoning, metacognition provides a cognitive mechanism enabling a clinician to validate or reject a diagnostic
or therapeutic decision (Marcum 2012). Faced with a set of clinical symptoms that
do not fit a recognized picture, or a patient reacting adversely to a specific
treatment, the clinician is forced to reflect more explicitly on the clinical presentation and her diagnostic reasoning. The cognitive processes whereby diagnostic
reasoning may be improved through metacognition facilitate the development of
clinical expertise. The master clinician is differentiated from the average clinician

by his/her conscious ability to reflect on inherent cognitive biases and change them during the normal course of medical practice.

While the cognitivist approach to clinical reasoning attempts to render implicit biases into explicit knowing, it only mediates processes of clinical reasoning that may be rendered into explicit inferences. The cognitivist approach does not attempt to account for tacit knowing as an essential element of diagnostic reasoning. The model of tacit knowing posited by philosopher Michael Polanyi (1962, 1966) includes nonanalytic or non-inferential forms of knowing. Tacit knowing refers to knowledge that functions at the periphery of attention and makes explicit knowledge possible. Stephen Henry (2010) argues that there are two features of tacit knowing that are especially relevant to clinical medicine. Firstly, explicit knowledge could not exist without the prior existence of a "tacit background." For example, Henry observes that tacit knowing occurs when a physician who is explicitly listening to a patient's story is simultaneously aware, but in a qualitatively different way, of the patient's tone of voice, facial expression, and choice of words. Moreover, these tacit particulars are crucial to informing the physicians' processes of clinical judgment. Secondly, the mechanism of how "tacit particulars give rise to explicit knowledge cannot be fully captured in formal models or discrete steps; the relationship is ultimately inarticulable" (Henry 2010, 293). This theory of tacit knowing fits in well with theories of clinical reasoning based on gestalt perception, which provides evidence that perception of a given object exhibits intrinsic qualities that cannot be completely reduced to its constitutive sensible components (Cervellin et al. 2014). Theories of tacit knowing help explain the clinical reliance on pattern recognition, a critical component of diagnostic expertise. In summary, models of clinical reasoning based in terms of tacit knowing presents an alternative model of clinical rationality. A complete model of clinical reasoning needs to include both cognitive and tacit forms of knowing (Marcum 2012).

Tacit knowing is non-inferential. Yet, since it improves with experience, it too can be considered a form of technical skill or mastery. This intuitive skill is privileged in (the mathematician) Stuart and (philosopher) Hubert Dreyfus' influential schema of adult skill acquisition, which has also been applied as a model for the development of medical expertise (Dreyfus and Dreyfus 1988; Dreyfus 2004). They conceive five levels of developing expertise from that of novice to advanced beginner, to competence, to proficiency, to expertise. The development from novice to real expert is characterized by the movement from rule-based decision-making to situational discriminations, whereby the expert demonstrates flexibility, wisdom, and improvisational ability. For Dreyfus and Dreyfus, learning how to play the game of chess provides the exemplary form of human skill acquisition and cognitive mastery. For example, in reference to stage five, that of proficiency, they write:

> The proficient chess player, who is classed a master, can recognize almost immediately a large repertoire of types of positions. He or she then deliberates to determine the move that will best achieve his or her goal. One may know, for example, that he or she should attack, but he or she must calculate how best to do so. (Dreyfus 2004, 179)

Increased proficiency includes the ability for gestalt pattern recognition, as well as the technical ability to devise instrumental means to achieve one's aims. Stage five – that of expertise – is similar to the stage of proficiency, but even that much more refined. The real expert possesses a "vast repertoire of situational discriminations" as well as the ability to see "immediately how to achieve this goal." The expert possesses the ability to distinguish between apparently similar situations requiring different responses.

This model is similar to others whereby developing expertise passes through a cognitive rule based, to an autonomous phase (Fitts and Posner 1967). In the autonomous phase, knowledge is characterized by being implicit and non-verbalizable (Masters 1992). What most defines this conception of expertise is the ability to rely on immediate intuition. As Stuart Dreyfus describes, "The brain of the expert gradually decomposes ... situations into subclasses, each of which requires a specific response. This allows the immediate intuitive situational response that is characteristic of expertise" (Dreyfus 2004, 180).

The sense of expertise as immediately intuitive is synonymous with Hubert Dreyfus' understanding of Aristotelian *phronesis*, informed by the interpretation provided by the German philosopher Martin Heidegger. This understanding of *phronesis* has two main aspects. Firstly, *phronesis* is akin to a form of "pure perceiving." Secondly, arising from this *phronesis* is completely nonconceptual. In Heidegger's terms, *phronesis* "no longer falls within the domain of the logos" (1997, 112). This intuitive certainty is derived from the combination of great training and skill, together with an embodied immersion in the life-world in which expertise functions.

Dreyfus and Dreyfus's conception of expertise has been proliferative, generating further analysis and secondary discussion, particularly in its application to medicine (see, e.g., Benner 1984; Thornton 2010). The correctness of their schema is not examined here. Rather, for the present purposes it is important to consider its application in relation to the two types of diagnostic expertise so far discussed. For the most part, the cognitive model of clinical reasoning has been privileged as more rational than that of tacit reasoning, because it fits in with the cognitive science model of rationality (Stanovich 2011). Yet, clinicians themselves continue to argue for the validity of gestalt recognition and intuition in their day-to-day clinical practice (see, e.g., Woolley and Kostopolou 2013). Interestingly Hubert Dreyfus (2006) suggests that the cognitive model occurs prior to and becomes superseded by intuitive expertise that is essentially nonconceptual. However, as others have noted, when a breakdown in diagnostic reflection occurs, the clinician necessarily reverts back to more explicit cognitive reflection (Marcum 2012). Thus, there is a dialectic relation between cognitive and intuitive processes of diagnostic reasoning.

Whether *phronesis* is absolutely nonconceptual is a matter of philosophical speculation that cannot be settled here. As previously argued, *phronesis* does have an intuitive component, more akin to pre-reflective consciousness, than explicit conception (Braude 2012b, 2013). Additionally, *phronesis* has an integrative function that can unite the two main forms of clinical reasoning. *Phronesis* is a particularly apt and useful model for clinical reasoning because it allows for the possibility of linking and integrating different cognitive processes according to the context and need of the moment. Different forms of cognition, such as affect, emotion, executive attention, rational cognition, and intuition may all constitute components of practical wisdom. Additionally, *phronesis* links the moral, ontological, and epistemological components of clinical medicine into a single framework. As has been observed, "Modelling clinical reasoning on *phronesis* succeeds in providing a means of integrating the different cognitive components of clinical reasoning, while maintaining respect for the gestalt of clinical reasoning as a particular form of conscious experience" (Braude 2012a, 947–948). Analyzing medical expertise needs to take account of these different levels of clinical reasoning. However, there still remains to be addressed the technical component of medical expertise, albeit in relation to the conception of clinical practice as a form of *phronesis*. This will be addressed in the second element of medical expertise, i.e., motoric activity and its relation to intentionality.

Motoric Expertise

In discussing technical expertise in clinical practice, it is obvious that medicine encompasses so many different kinds of skills and situations that it is impossible to define a single kind of "virtuosity." The skills necessary for a psychiatrist are obviously very different from that of family physician, and in turn very different from a cardiac surgeon. However, clinical practice as a form of *phronesis* unites very different kinds of clinical action. The nature of a clinical action then may be evaluated in terms of the relation between technical action and practical wisdom of its constitutive parts. While it is true that developing expert cognition, for example, in terms of diagnostic reasoning, is obviously a critical skill for clinical practice, technical skill refers arguably pre-eminently to motoric action. The virtuosity of a skilled hand surgeon is more explicitly embodied than the psychiatrist skilled in taking an expert history. However, as mentioned, the literature on technical mastery emphasizes processes of cognition at the expense of motoric action. While diagnostic reasoning is more cognitive than motoric, it is not more mental. Thus, motoric action can similarly be mapped in terms of cortical and subcortical function and the neural networks between them, as well as cortical structures directly involved in action planning (Jeannerod and Frak 1999). The question that then arises is why has motoric action not been adequately taken account of in the literature on technical expertise? Secondly, is motoric action fundamentally different from mental processes of diagnostic processing in terms of inherent conceptuality? In short, is motoric action closer to Aristotelian *phronesis* or *techné*? In order to avoid the emphasis on conceptual processes, Tim Thornton (2010) discusses anesthesia as exemplary for clinical expertise, with its emphasis on both manual and mental dexterity. All forms of surgical practice requiring technical skill fit this picture of technical expertise. Yet, does manual dexterity constitute an essentially different kind of clinical expertise to diagnostic reasoning?

This discussion on motoric activity will focus initially on one component of manual dexterity that is, perhaps, metonymic for clinical dexterity more generally, i.e., visuospatial ability. In his bestselling volume "How Doctors Think," Jerome Groopman (2007) quotes the expert cardiologist James Lock describing the visuospatial skills necessary to insert a cardiac catheter through a child's blood vessels and then into his heart:

> The catheter appears as a thin white line on a flat monitor screen next to the table. It can be difficult in such a two-dimensional projection to know the catheter's position. "The combination of how your hand moves and what the image looks like will tell you whether the catheter is pointed toward you or away. I can tell where it is even if my hand is off the catheter. Knowing in which direction you are going shouldn't be something you need to think about."... "You need to process what you see very quickly and act on the information in a split second," Lock said, "because the heart is beating. It's not like you can stop the child's heart and ponder. Once you are inside of a kid's heart with a catheter, you have an enormous amount you have to accomplish, and there is a great deal of risk if what you do is not done quickly and well." (Groopman 2007, 141)

Groopman observes that this visuospatial ability may be more paramount in determining surgical skill than nimbleness of hands, or straightforward manual dexterity. Additionally, like other kinds of technical skill, it is acquired through a combination of formal learning and repeated practice (Norman et al. 2006). This aspect of motoric skill makes it analogous to other kinds of cognitive expertise. Additionally, what is perhaps most emblematic of motoric skill, i.e., its automaticity makes it exemplary for Dreyfus' model of expertise. As William James first noted, (1890), well-practiced tasks can be performed with little effort or cognitive control, as opposed to novice performances of the same task. In terms of visuospatial ability, researchers have demonstrated that subjects "can adjust their movements in response to a change in the location of a visual target of which they are perceptually unaware" (Haggard and Johnson 2003, 76). This kind of automatic motoric skill, bypassing higher cortical control, fits in well with the Dreyfus' five stage schema of technical expertise. What they refer to as intuition is synonymous with automaticity of skilled motoric action. Indeed, the notion that intuition is a form of practical wisdom that is inherently nonconceptual seems to fit in best with the model of motoric action.

Is the motoric component of a clinical action best assessed in terms of *phronesis* or *techné*? Motoric action at first glance appears closer to technical expertise considered in terms of crafthood, or *techné*, than other forms of clinical practice, since it produces an externally visible result. However, differentiating between *phronesis* and *techné* in motoric action in clinical practice requires a closer analysis in terms of phenomenology of action. In this regard, an action can be defined as a "movement of the body, resulting from specific mental preparation, and aimed at some goal that the agent desires to achieve" (Haggard and Johnson 2003, 73). Action in the clinical context is no different. A clinician will initiate a specific motoric action resulting from a process of cognitive reflection in order to achieve a therapeutic effect. This might include, for example, taking a blood sample for a pathological investigation, writing a prescription on a pad of paper, or inserting a scalpel in the skin to drain an abscess. Technical expertise or skill can focus on each of these three elements, however, the middle component – movement of the body – is strictly speaking the only truly motoric component of action.

Haggard and Johnson's (2003) analysis of the phenomenology of action highlights the following paradox: a phenomenology of action demonstrates that we have minimal conscious experience of many of our motoric activities, especially those which are automatic, such as breathing and walking. On the other hand, we are able to report in considerable detail the processes of preparation and execution of our actions. Thus, we are able to provide a richer phenomenological description of the mental processes reflecting on an action prior to its occurrence, and the results of a specific action, rather than the action itself, which consists of unconscious microcomponents. This fact helps explain the relative lack of literature on motoric expertise in clinical practice, as opposed to processes of diagnostic reasoning. It also helps to differentiate motoric action in terms of the relation between *phronesis* and *techné*.

In her incisive book on *Intention*, philosopher Elizabeth Anscombe (1963) puts forward the thesis that an agent's knowledge of what he or she is doing is not characteristically based on observation. For Anscombe, practical action is characterized by a kind of intentionality that is not observable in terms either of the physical preparation of action nor of its measurable outcomes. This does not mean that these two aspects, prior to and post action, are not associated with practical action. Rather, they are not what is essential about practical action. As Anscombe states, "That what one knows as intentional is only the intention, or possibly also the bodily movement; and that the rest is known by observation to be the result, which was also willed in the intention." (1963, 51–52). In other words, it is the embodied action itself that is associated with practical knowledge. It is this, as Haggard and Johnson emphasize, that most resists direct observation.

Anscombe's conception that practical knowledge is non-observational is motivated by the idea that practical knowledge is "the cause of what it understands," rather than being derived from "objects known" (1963, 87–8). Without going into a detailed comparison, Anscombe's insight restates the central understanding that the end of *phronesis* is the action itself, in contradistinction to *techné*, which produces a result external to the action. For Anscombe, what characterizes a practical action is that it is motivated by an intention that is non-observable. An action might outwardly be the same, but is differentiated by its motivating intentionality. This insight differentiates between an action that might be associated with *techné*, such as a sculptor hammering a statue, and an act of practical knowledge, such as an orthopedic surgeon doing a similar action while inserting a hip replacement. Another key difference between these two kinds of action is that practical knowledge is self-reflexive, whereas *techné* is not necessarily so. In other words, an act resulting from practical knowledge will necessarily impact self-referentially on the doer, as well as result in an external product of the action. This introduces an ethical dimension into practical knowledge – although this was not explicitly addressed by Anscombe in her work on *Intention* – that is especially pertinent for clinical action involving a vulnerable other – the individual patient. Thus, when a physician performs a clinical act, it is self-reflexive, even when it is primarily other-directed. A clinical act should always include self-knowledge on the part of the clinician. For this reason, Eric Cassell cites approvingly the two essential habits of mind essential for clinicians posited by the great Canadian physician Sir William Osler (1848–1919), i.e., imperturbability and equanimity. "Imperturbability means coolness and presence of mind under all circumstances, calmness amid storm, clearness of judgments in moments of grave peril and impassiveness." (Osler 1905, 3ff). Equanimity is, "an evenness of mind or temper. The ability not to be disturbed or upset by the foolishness around you, the temper or fits of emotion or agitation of others (your patients above all)" (Cassell 2015, 231).

As stressed in this chapter and elsewhere (Braude 2012a, 2013), this kind of self-awareness is not simply the ability for metacognition, but the ability to become self-aware of the presence and importance of pre-reflective states of consciousness. This includes the kind of non-observable kinesthetic awareness that Anscombe associates with *phronesis*. Touching themes very close to the ones developed in this chapter, philosopher Shaun Gallagher observes in an important essay on "Moral Agency, Self-Wisdom and Practical Agency" that the phenomenological conception of intentional action is always accompanied by a pre-reflective self-consciousness. Gallagher continues that, "the person with *phronesis* knows what they are doing on an implicit level which is best expressed not by reflective or theoretically abstract propositions, but by descriptions on the highest pragmatic level of discourse . . ." (2007, 217).

In summary, clinical action is a kind of *techné* in being associated with an external outcome, e.g., draining an abscess. At the same time, it is always a form of *phronesis* impacting on the doer. This insight central to medical practice is exemplified in the Doctrine of Double Effect, which gives moral legitimacy to an equivocal action provided that the good and not harmful effect is intended, even though the unintended harmful effect may be foreseen (Mangan 1949). In medicine, the application of the Doctrine of Double Effect allows physicians to administer adequate palliative care to patients, even if it may lead to their death. It also provides support for the moral argument against physician-assisted suicide and euthanasia (Sulmasy and Pellegrino 1999). Intentionality is important because of the effect of an act on the self of the physician and may not be assessed purely in terms of the actual outcome.

Interpersonal Expertise

The third and final component of medical expertise referred to by Norman et al. (2006) is that of interpersonal relations. This component relates both to the quality of a particular medical action and its purpose or end. As such, the intersubjective context of a particular action might not explicitly inform the processes of diagnostic reflection or the therapeutic action directed toward an individual patient, but nevertheless provides an overarching structure that influences every component of clinical practice. A clinician may be particularly skilled in personally relating to patients and in conveying information. At the same time, this medical action is laden with moral responsibility. Clinical practice reduced to its most simple equation as the intersubjective relationship between an individual physician and patient for the latter's physical and mental well-being necessarily introduces an ethical dimension into the discussion about medical expertise. This ethical dimension undergirds the question whether technical expertise in medicine can ever be "value-free" or is always embedded with moral values arising from the clinical encounter. (The relation between technical mastery and ethics is exemplified in the word "virtuosity." With roots in Post-Classical Latin and Middle French and referring to an exceptional performative ability, especially in the realm of musical instrumentation, virtuosity highlights the intimate relation between exceptional technical skill and moral virtue.) That a clinical action always needs to be related to the well-being of the individual patient firmly grounds clinical reasoning as a form of *phronesis*. Like the other two components of clinical expertise, cognition and motoric activity discussed in the earlier section of this chapter, focusing on interpersonal relations, forces one to brush against the issue of *phronesis* and its relation to *techné*.

Knowledge of the physician is intersubjective. In other words, the knowledge is never purely objective but is possessed by one subjectivity about another. This requires a shift in the traditional medical focus from objective disease to subjective categories, such as personal goals and function. Thus, Eric Cassell, observes that:

> Clinicians and clinical medicine require an alternative definition of sickness that does not diminish the importance of pathophysiology and the effects of disease but encompasses the impact of sickness on the patient's life and the impress of the patient on the sickness . . . . The goal of the clinician and clinical medicine is to restore the sick person to function so that goals and purposes can be achieved and well-being restored. (2015, 22)

Determining what constitutes the correct clinical goals and purposes is an inherently intersubjective process that requires the empathic ability of the clinician to feel and understand something of one patient's experience of pain, vulnerability, and suffering and express appropriate concern (Braude 2016). Here too *phronesis* is necessary to provide a clinician with the means to achieve the appropriate balance between clinical distance and empathic concern. Phenomenologists consider empathy to be a *sui generis* form of intentionality directed at other experiencing subjects (Zahavi and Overgaard 2012). Moreover, according to the phenomenological account provided by Edith Stein (1989), empathy is direct, unmediated, and non-inferential. Another key phenomenological aspect of empathy is the fact that empathy is always both self- and other-relating. In other words, intersubjectivity in clinical practice is always as much about the subjectivity of the clinician, as it is about the patient. A good clinician needs constantly to be assessing his/her motives/ biases in relation to that of his patient. Yet, the direction of the intersubjective reflection should always ultimately be directed toward the well-being of the patient, even during a moment of personal self-reflection.

Medical empathy is a cognitive and affective phenomenon that mediates the internal aspects of clinical reasoning processes, with outer worldly directed motoric action. As with other aspects of clinical practice that incorporate tacit, intuitive dimensions, it is questionable how empathic expertise can be formally taught and developed. Nonetheless, it is certain that technological advances in brain imaging techniques, together with second- and third-person observational methods will increasingly inform the social neuroscientific understanding into the nature of medical empathy (Schilbach et al. 2013). For example, studies on the empathy of pain primarily demonstrate significant action in regions involved in the affective aspects of the pain-processing network. These include the anterior cingulate cortex, the anterior insula, the cerebellum, and the brainstem (Singer et al. 2004). A number of functional MRI and MEG investigations of participants observing facial expression and stimuli depicting trauma to body parts have reported significant signal change in both the affective dimension of pain as well as the somatosensory cortex and posterior insula involved in the sensory discrimination of pain (Decety and Svetlova 2012). Jean Decety argues that physicians are able to downregulate their own pain response to observing the pain of others through managing and controlling their own higher cortical response (Decety Forthcoming). Management of their "negative arousal" enables physicians to liberate their cognitive resources necessary for effective therapeutic action and empathic concern. Through "feeling less," or having less affectivity, physicians are able to provide more effective care. This brief description of medical empathy presents just a hint of the relevance of social neuroscience for the development of interpersonal expertise in clinical practice. To translate into clinically relevant information, these second- and third-person-based neuroscience studies will need to be combined with first-person experience. Translated into formal techniques, processes of introspection, i.e., the perception of internal physical or physiological states (Wiens 2005), can help bring to conscious awareness the cognitive and affective bases of empathy and other physiological manifestations of intersubjectivity. It is predictable that affective introspection will become as valuable a tool for self-reflection on clinical reasoning as the use of metacognition to evaluate the cognitive foundations of clinical reasoning. Introspection is also an important component of narrative competence, defined as "the set of skills required to absorb, interpret, and be moved by the stories one hears or reads" in order to achieve "the genuine intersubjective contact required for an effective therapeutic alliance" (Charon 2004, 862–863).

In summary, as with the other two components of clinical practice, clinical empathy can be assessed in terms of both *phronesis* and *techné*. Considering clinical empathy as a teachable ability that can be objectified through neuroscientific techniques situates it on the side of *techné*. In this way, clinicians will be able to ratchet up or down their empathic concerns, based on the clinical needs of the moment. Considering empathy as an embodied phenomenon existing between two corporeal beings, that is, both self-other related, as well as being direct, unmediated, and non-inferential, empathy is situated firmly on the side of *phronesis*. Thus, empathy is akin with the intersubjectivity that Gallagher claims "is endogenous to the embodied practices that constitute practical knowledge" (2007, 206).

Conclusion

This chapter has provided an analysis of skilled know-how, virtuosity, and expertise in clinical practice. Specifically, the three identified components of clinical expertise, i.e., cognitive, motoric, and interpersonal, have been related to Aristotelian *phronesis*, in particular the tension that arises in each of these three elements between *phronesis* and *techné*. As emphasized, whether technical expertise is closer to *phronesis* or *techné* is determined through evaluating the ends of a specific action. If a clinical action has an end in itself that is self-referential, involving the moral virtue of the person doing the action, then the clinical action is most likely a form of practical wisdom. If the action results in a product external to the action then it is associated on the spectrum of *techné*. Expert clinical reasoning is associated with *phronesis* in not being able to be simply reduced to a form of cognition. Similarly, a motoric action can be considered *phronetic* in relation to the intentionality possessed by the actor. Finally, empathy exemplifies the interpersonal dimension of clinical practice, also associated with *phronesis*.

While *techné* and *phronesis* have been distinguished throughout this chapter, the purpose was not to establish an irresolvable dichotomy between these two fundamental forms of human action. Rather, this analysis suggests that the relation between *techné* and *phronesis* in clinical practice is fluid. A clinical action that may be considered at one moment as a form of *techné* may be considered a form of *phronesis* in another context, particularly if performed with another intention. Moreover, the sense of moral agency that is most associated with *phronesis* may also pertain to a lesser extent in more purely technical actions. As Gallagher observes, the "secondary contextualization of action in pragmatic and social settings ... is necessary for both the development of expertise and the acquisition of *phronesis*" (2007, 210). Particularly, in medicine, it is not possible to ultimately separate purely technical actions from their moral ends (Braude 2012b).

Finally, in considering clinical expertise equally in terms of cognition, motoric activity, and interpersonal relations, this analysis has moved away from the theoretical conception privileging cognition in clinical reasoning. Elucidating pre-reflective categories such as affect and intentionality plays an important role in determining the nature of clinical expertise. Reconsidering cognition as an "essentially unitary phenomenon" (Cosmelli and Ibánẽz 2008, 235) implies the need to reconsider cognition in cognitive science, as well as in the uniquely particular context of clinical practice. Arguably, the emphasis on cognition in the literature around medical expertise has prevented the full understanding of its noncognitive and nonconceptual dimensions, especially in terms of motor activity and intentionality. A key motivation behind this chapter review of skilled know-how, virtuosity, and expertise in clinical practice has been to address this "cognitive" deficit.

Definition of Key Terms

Action	A movement of the body, resulting from specific mental preparation and aimed at some goal that the agent desires to achieve.
Cognition	All mental processes related to knowledge, including but not limited to memory, attention, perception, representational schemas, consciousness, and language.
Doctrine of double effect	Ethical principle that gives moral legitimacy to an equivocal action provided that the good and not harmful effect is intended, even though the unintended harmful effect may be foreseen.
Metacognition	The processes involved in thinking about and monitoring one's own cognitive activity.
Phenomenological introspection	Philosophical method to become self-aware of prereflective states of consciousness.
Praxis	Practical activity that is intended to further human well-being or the good and is not associated with any particular end product external to the act.
Poiesis	Any human activity that results in a product external to the human activity itself.
Phronesis	The moral capability to evaluate the means and ends of a particular action. In clinical reasoning phronesis affords the means of linking and integrating different cognitive processes.
Tacit Knowing	Knowledge that functions at the periphery of attention and makes explicit knowledge possible.
Techné	An action associated with craftsmanship, resulting in the production of external objects.

Summary Points

- This chapter analyzes skilled know-how, virtuosity, and expertise in clinical practice in terms of its three components, i.e., cognitive, motoric, and interpersonal expertise.
- These three identified components of clinical expertise are related to Aristotle's conception of practical wisdom, phronesis, and techné.

- Whether technical expertise is closer to phronesis or techné is determined through evaluating the ends of a specific action.
- If a clinical action has an end in itself that is self-referential, involving the moral virtue of the person doing the action, then the clinical action is most likely a form of practical wisdom.
- Analyzing clinical expertise equally in terms of cognition, motoric activity, and interpersonal relations makes a break from the theoretical conception of clinical expertise primarily in terms of cognition.

References

Anscombe GEM (1963) Intention. Cornell University Press, New York

Aristotle (1925) Nicomachean ethics (trans: Ross WD). Clarendon Press, Oxford

Barrows HS, Feltovich PJ (1987) The clinical reasoning process. Med Educ 21:86–91

Barrows HS, Tamblyn RM (1980) Problem based learning: an approach to medical education. Springer, New York

Benner P (1984) From novice to expert: excellence and power in clinical nursing practice. Addison-Wesley, Reading

Beresford EB (1996) Can phronesis save the life of medical ethics? Theor Med 17:209–224

Bernasconi R (1989) Heidegger's destruction of phronesis. South J Philos XXVIII(S1):127–147

Braude HD (2016) Clinical reasoning and knowing. In: Marcum J (ed) The Bloomsbury companion to philosophy of medicine. Bloomsbury Academic Press, London

Braude HD (2016) The affective limits of medical empathy. In: Bustan S (ed) Fundamental transdisciplinary questions on suffering and pain. Springer, New York

Braude HD (2012a) Conciliating cognition and consciousness: the perceptual foundations of clinical reasoning. J Eval Clin Pract 18:945–950

Braude HD (2012b) Intuition in medicine: a philosophical defense of clinical reasoning. The University of Chicago Press, Chicago

Braude HD (2013) Human all too human reasoning: comparing clinical and phenomenological intuition. J Med Philos 38(2):173–189

Cassell EJ (2015) The nature of clinical medicine: the return of the clinician. Oxford University Press, Oxford

Cervellin G, Borghi L, Lipps G (2014) Do clinicians decide relying primarily on Bayesian principles or on Gestalt perception? Some pearls and pitfalls of Gestalt perception in medicine. Intern Emerg Med 9:513–519

Charon R (2004) Narrative and medicine. N Engl J Med 350(9):862–864

Cosmelli D, Ibáñez A (2008) Human cognition in context: on the biologic, cognitive and social reconsideration of meaning as making sense of action. Integr Psychol Behav Sci 42:233–244

Croskerry P (2008) Cognitive and affective dispositions to respond. In: Croskerry P, Cosby K, Schenkel S, Wears R (eds) Patient safety in emergency medicine. Lippincott, Williams and Wilkins, Philadelphia, pp 219–227

Croskerry P, Abbass A, Wu A (2008) How doctors feel: affective issues in patient safety. Lancet 372:1205–1206

Decety J (Forthcoming) Empathy in medical practice: challenges and opportunities. In: Bustan S (ed) Fundamental transdisciplinary questions on suffering and pain. Springer, New York

Decety J, Svetlova M (2012) Putting together phylogenetic and ontogenetic perspectives in empathy. Dev Cogn Neurosci 2:1–24

Dreyfus SE (2004) The five stage model of skill-acquisition. Bull Sci Technol Soc 24(3):177–181

Dreyfus HL (2006) Overcoming the myth of the mental. Topoi 25:43–49

Dreyfus HL, Dreyfus SE (1988) Mind over machine: the power of human intuition and expertise in the era of the computer, 2nd edn. Free Press, New York

Edelstein L (1967) Ancient medicine. The Johns Hopkins University Press, Baltimore/London

Elstein AS (2000) Clinical problem solving and decision psychology. Acad Med 75(10): S134–S136

Elstein AS (2009) Thinking about diagnostic thinking: a 30 year perspective. Adv Health Sci Educ Theory Pract 14:7–18

Fitts P, Posner M (1967) Human performance. Brooke/Cole, Belmont

Gadamer HG (1975) Truth and method. Seabury Press, New York

Gallagher S (2007) Moral agency, self-consciousness, and practical wisdom. J Conscious Stud 14 (5–6):199–223

Gatens Robinson E (1986) Clinical judgement and the rationality of the human sciences. J Med Philos 11:167–178

Groopman J (2007) How doctors think. Houghton Mifflin Company, Boston/New York

Haggard P, Johnson H (2003) Experiences of voluntary action. J Conscious Stud 10(9–10):72–84

Heidegger M (1997) Plato's Sophist (trans: Rojcewicz R, Schuwer A). Indiana University Press, Bloomington/Indianapolis

Henry SG (2010) Polanyi's tacit knowing and the relevance of epistemology to clinical medicine. J Eval Clin Pract 16(2):292–297

Hofmann B (2002) Medicine as practical wisdom (*phronesis*). Poiesis Prax 1:135–149

James W (1890) Principles of psychology. Henry Holt, New York

Jeannerod M, Frak V (1999) Mental imaging of motor activity in humans. Curr Opin Neurobiol 9:735–739

Kahneman D, Tversky A (1974) Judgment under uncertainty: heuristics and biases. Science 185:1124–1131

Mangan J (1949) An historical analysis of the principle of double effect. Theol Stud 10:41–61

Marcum JA (2012) An integrated model of clinical reasoning: dual-process theory of cognition and metacognition. J Eval Clin Pract 18:954–961

Masters RSW (1992) Knowledge, knerves and know-how: the role of explicit versus implicit knowledge in the breakdown of a complex motor skill under pressure. Br J Psychol 83:343–358

McGee G (1996) Phronesis in clinical ethics. Theor Med 17(4):317–328

Montgomery K (2000) Phronesis and the misdescription of medicine. In: Kuczewski MG, Polansky R (eds) Bioethics: ancient themes in contemporary issues. The MIT Press, Cambridge, MA, pp 57–66

Montgomery K (2006) How doctors think: clinical judgment and the practice of medicine. Oxford University Press, Oxford

Norman G, Eva K, Brooks L, Hamstra S (2006) Expertise in medicine and surgery. In: Ericcson KA, Charness N, Feltovich PJ, Hoffman R (eds) The Cambridge handbook of expertise and expert performance. Cambridge University Press, Cambridge, pp 339–354

Osler W (1905) Aequinimatas. P. Blakiston, Philadelphia

Pellegrino E, Thomasma DC (1981) A philosophical basis of medical practice. Oxford University Press, New York

Polanyi M (1962) Personal knowledge: towards a post-critical philosophy. Routledge and Kegan Paul, London

Polanyi M (1966) The tacit dimension. Doubleday & Company, Garden City, New York

Proust J (2013) The philosophy of metacognition: mental agency and self-awareness. Oxford University Press, Oxford

Singer T, Seymour B, O'Doherty J, Kaube H, Dolan RJ, Frith CD (2004) Empathy for pain involves the affective but not the sensory components of pain. Science 303:1157–1161

Schaffner K (1994) Discovery and explanation in biology and medicine. University of Chicago Press, Chicago

Schilbach L, Timmermans B, Reddy V, Costall A, Bente G, Schilcht T, Vogeley K (2013) Toward a second-person neuroscience. Behav Brain Sci 36:393–462

Stanovich KE (2011) Rationality and the reflective mind. Oxford University Press, New York

Stein E (1989) On the problem of empathy. ICS Publishers, Washington, DC

Sulmasy D, Pellegrino E (1999) The rule of double effect: clearing up the double talk. Arch Intern Med 159:545–550

Thornton T (2010) Clinical judgement, expertise and skilled coping. J Eval Clin Pract 16:284–291

Toulmin S (1982) How medicine saved the life of ethics. Perspect Biol Med 25(4):736–750

Widdershoven-Heerding I (1987) Medicine as a form of practical understanding. Theor Med 8:179–185

Wiens S (2005) Interoception in emotional experience. Curr Opin Neurol 18:442–447

Woolley A, Kostopolou O (2013) Clinical intuition in family medicine: more than first impressions. Ann Fam Med 11(1):60–66

Zahavi D, Overgaard S (2012) Empathy without isomorphism: a phenomenological account. In: Decety J (ed) Empathy: from bench to bedside. The MIT Press, Cambridge, MA, pp 3–20

Meaning and Use of Placebo: Philosophical Considerations

43

Pekka Louhiala and Raimo Puustinen

Contents

Abstract

Confusion around the concept placebo and its derivatives is widespread, and the aim of this chapter is to elaborate the nature of these concepts in medicine. The historical development is first described. The current understandings and conceptual problems related to placebo are then examined. Finally, ways to clarify the ongoing conceptual disarray are proposed.

P. Louhiala (✉)
Department of Public Health, University of Helsinki, Finland
e-mail: pekka.louhiala@helsinki.fi

R. Puustinen
Medical School, University of Tampere, Tampere, Finland
e-mail: raimo.puustinen@uta.fi

© Springer Science+Business Media Dordrecht 2017
T. Schramme, S. Edwards (eds.), *Handbook of the Philosophy of Medicine*,
DOI 10.1007/978-94-017-8688-1_34

...placebo effect, probably the most fascinating and misunderstood aspect of human healing, which goes far beyond a mere sugar pill: it is counterintuitive, it is strange, it is the true story of mind-body healing, and it is far more interesting than any made-up nonsense about therapeutic quantum energy patterns. (Goldacre 2009, p. xi)

Introduction

In clinical treatment of patients, the knowing prescription of placebos has not been used in medicine for many years. (Shapiro and Shapiro 1997)

Placebos are commonly used in UK primary care. (Howick et al. 2013)

It is suggested that in select cases, use of placebo may even be morally imperative. (Lichtenberg et al. 2004)

Clinical placebo interventions are unethical, unnecessary, and unprofessional. (Hróbjartsson 2008)

As the quotations from recent medical literature indicate, there is fundamental disagreement both about the prevalence of the use of placebos in clinical medicine and the ethics of such practice. The disagreement is at least partly due to the ambiguous nature of the concept placebo and its derivatives. That is, when the authors of the above quotations use the word placebo, they mean different things. Confusion around these concepts is indeed widespread, and the situation seems not to be any better today than three decades ago when Grünbaum (1986, p. 19) wrote: "...the medical and psychiatric literature on placebos and their effects is conceptually bewildering, to the point of being a veritable Tower of Babel."

The aim of this chapter is to elaborate the nature of the concept placebo and its derivatives in medicine. The historical development of the concepts is first described. Then, the current understandings and conceptual problems related to them are examined. Finally, ways to clarify the ongoing conceptual disarray are proposed.

From an Everyday Word to a Medical Concept

In the placebo literature, the first appearance of the word placebo has been generally attributed to *Vulgate*, the fourth-century Latin translation of the Old Testament by St Jerome, where, in the Psalm 116:19, we find the expression "Placebo Domino in regione vivorum" ("I shall please the Lord in the land of the living"). Since the word placebo is a common Latin expression, the first-person future indicative of the verb *placeo* (to please), this attribution is not historically plausible. The expression must have been in general use since the birth of the Latin language, and the word placebo can, indeed, be found in several Latin texts predating St Jerome for centuries, such as Petronius' Satyricon, Seneca's De Consolatione, and Martial's Epigrammata, to name a few (see References for internet sources).

In the Medieval Catholic church, especially in France, the word placebo was associated to the tradition of singing the Psalm 116 during funerals, "Singing the Placebo." That practice was commercialized when professional mourners started to attend the ceremonies and charge a fee for their performance. Placebo gained thus a profane meaning as a cunning flatterer, as vividly expressed in a fourteenth-century Merchant's Story by Chaucer (2001), where a character in the story was named Placebo.

With its profane meaning, the word placebo found its way also to the medical literature in the wake of the eighteenth-century enlightened scientific acumen. For example, in a text published in 1763, a British physician wrote about a local charlatan how "Placebo never saw a professor in his chair, nor never made up a Doctor's prescription. Without knowledge chemical or practical, he was said to understand the waters better *than them all*" (italics original) (Sutherland 1763 p. xxiii–xxiv).

In medicine the meaning of the concept placebo was extended from indicating charlatans to the use of ineffective treatments in an attempt to merely please the patient. In 1776, a Scottish physician W. Robertson wrote in his book *Observationes Miscellaneae Inaugurales de Vino Praecipue* how "Ex modo et quantitate quibus administratur, nihil nisi placebo effe conludere volo" (the medication given had nothing but pleasing effect to his patient) (Robertson 1776).

A rather modern definition of placebo as an ineffective medication or treatment was given by another Scottish physician Andrew Duncan in 1752: "Where a *placebo* merely is wanted, the purpose may be answered by means, which, although perhaps reduced under the *materia medica*, do not, however, deserve the name of medicines. When a class of medicines, then, is said to be indifferent with regard to a morbid affection, nothing further is meant, than that is has no peculiar tendency to increase the evil; while, at the same time, no peculiar benefit can be expected from its employment" (italics original) (Duncan 1770).

The established use of the term placebo in the late eighteenth-century medical parlance is indicated, at least in the Anglophone world, with the term's entry to medical dictionaries. The first edition of the Motherby's New Medical Dictionary from 1785, for example, does not mention placebo, but in the third edition 1791 we find an entry "Placebo: A common place method or medicine" (Motherby 1785, 1791).

Similarly, Hooper's Medical Dictionary from 1798 does not include the term placebo, but it appears in the 1811 edition as "Placebo. I will please: an epithet given to any medicine adapted more to please than benefit the patient" (Hooper 1798, 1811). The explanation is identical with the one given in Coxe's Philadelphia Medical Dictionary in 1808 (Coxe 1808).

By the early nineteenth century, the term placebo seems to have been a part of physicians' everyday clinical vocabulary, as indicated in a scene in Sir Walter Scott's novel *St Ronan's Well*, published in 1823: "You mistake the matter entirely, my dear Mrs. Blower," said the doctor; "there is nothing serious intended – a mere placebo – just a divertisement to cheer the spirits, and assist the effect of the waters – cheerfulness is a great promoter of health" (Scott 1824).

The term placebo gained also pejorative meanings as can be seen in an Editorial of the Edinburgh medical and surgical journal in 1834 "...it would appear that the homoeopathic plan of treating diseases is totally inert, and can be useful only as a placebo to hypochondriacs and nervous women, by relieving them from swallowing the manifold drugs which they think is their duty to burden their stomachs" (Editorial 1834).

The term "placebo effect" has also long roots as can be seen in the 1776 quotation above. By the early twentieth century, the expression seems to have been in common use when discussing the outcome of treatments. An anonymous writer, for example, ponders in The International Journal of Surgery in 1900, how in the course of the assisted delivery "My rule is to prohibit all pulling in the first stage, and dispense with chloroform entirely, unless it be a little for its placebo effect – not enough to arrest contractions"(Anonymous 1900). Oswald, in turn, wrote in *The Sanitarian* in 1902, when discussing indigenous healing methods among Africans, that "there may have been a mere placebo effect about the procedure...where a victim of serpent bites was dosed with a decoction of boiled ants..." (Oswald 1902). In 1920 Graves published a case report of a 15-year-old boy with delayed puberty and epileptic seizures (Graves 1920). Various drugs had been given without a marked effect. Finally, Graves decided to try testicular extract in tablet form, and the boy's symptoms declined gradually, which, according to Graves, might have been related to the "placebo effects of the drugs given prior to admission."

The term "placebo effect" was made popular beyond medical circles in 1955 when Henry Beecher published his article "The powerful placebo" (Beecher 1955). Beecher was a strong supporter of randomized controlled trials (RCTs) designed with two arms, one receiving the active drug under investigation and one receiving some inert substance that was called placebo. His paper was both a review of the topic and a meta-analysis of 15 studies covering a wide variety of conditions. Beecher found a "relatively constant" therapeutic effectiveness of 35 % for placebos and concluded that it suggested "a fundamental mechanism in common" for placebos. That estimate became a standard reference to placebo effect both in subsequent trials and medicine in general. While in the 1950s RCTs developed rapidly to a "golden standard" in clinical research, placebo "changed from what was called the 'humble humbug' to an entity with occult-like powers that could mimic potent drugs" (Kaptchuk 1998). Since then, there has been a tendency to regard the placebo effect in the research context as a necessary background "noise" that must be subtracted from the results of a trial (Hunter 2007).

More recent derivatives of the term placebo entering into medical vocabulary are "pure" and "impure" placebo. The concepts were introduced in the 1940s at a Cornell Conference on Therapy, the proceedings of which were published in 1947 (Gold et al. 1947). In that publication, DuBois divided placebos into three classes: (1) pure placebos (e.g., bread pills or lactose tablets with no significant physiological effects), (2) impure placebos ("adulterated with a drug that might have some pharmacological action, such as tincture of gentian or a very small dose of nux vomica"), and (3) "the universal pleasing element which accompanies every prescription."

Current Understandings of the Concepts

Placebo

In November 2014 The *Wiktionary* defines placebo as "a dummy medicine containing no active ingredients; an inert treatment." This short definition seems to represent the overall current understanding of the concept placebo among both the lay people and the medical profession. The latter has, however, suggested wider and more complicated definitions for the concept placebo and its derivatives.

Chaput de Saintonge and Herxheimer (1994), for example, expand the realm of placebo "to the causes of the aggregated non-specific effects of treatments when specific effects have been segregated." This characterization seems to cover practically all elements of therapeutic encounter, except a specific pharmacological or other physiological mechanism. A table in the paper classifies placebos into eight main classes: (1) scars; (2) pills, tablets, and injections; (3) appliances; (4) touch; (5) words; (6) gestures; (7) local ambience; and (8) social interventions.

More recently, Benedetti (2009) has included the context of treatment into the definition of placebo:

> ...a placebo would be better defined as an inert treatment plus the context that tells the patient a therapeutic act is being performed.

The American Medical Association brings the beliefs of the physician into the definition, when it defines placebo as "a substance provided to a patient that the physician believes has no specific pharmacological effect upon the condition being treated" (AMA 2007).

The concepts pure and impure placebo were hardly ever mentioned in medical literature for decades after their introduction, and even in the context of empirical placebo research, the concept has been used only recently (Fässler et al. 2009; Howick et al. 2013). According to Howick et al. (2013), "Pure placebos are interventions such as sugar pills ... or saline injections without direct pharmacologically active ingredients for the condition being treated. Impure placebos are substances, interventions or 'therapeutic' methods which have known pharmacological, clinical or physical value for some ailments but lack specific therapeutic effects or value for the condition for which they have been prescribed."

Placebo Effect

Also for the notion "placebo effect," several different definitions have been proposed.

Shapiro and Shapiro (1997), for example, define placebo effect as "primarily the nonspecific psychological or psychophysiological therapeutic effect produced by a placebo, but may be the effect of spontaneous improvement attributed to the placebo."

Miller and Kaptchuk (2008) have suggested that the placebo effect should be reconceptualized as "contextual healing." By this they refer to the context of the clinical encounter, as distinct from the specific treatment interventions containing factors such as the environment of the clinical setting, the communication between patient and clinician, and the rituals of treatment.

Also Moerman (2002) has referred to the context when he has suggested that much of what is called the placebo effect is a special case of the "meaning response," which is defined as the physiological or psychological effect of meaning in the origins or treatment of illness. When such effects are positive, they include most of the things that have been called the placebo effect, and, when they are negative, they include most of what has been called the nocebo effect. Meaning response is attached to the prescription of active as well as inert medications and treatments.

Louhiala and Puustinen (2008) have suggested that "placebo effect" should be replaced with "care effect" to address the outcome of a therapeutic encounter that cannot be attributed to the specific physiological response to the treatment given.

Conceptual Problems in Placebo Literature

To be scientifically useful, theoretical concepts used in scientific enquiry need to be clearly defined and unambiguous. Yet, as can be seen in the examples above, there is no consensus within the scientific community on the definitions of placebo and its derivatives pure placebo, impure placebo, and placebo effect. In addition to the lack of consensus, some of the current definitions of those terms are internally incoherent.

When, for example, The American Medical Association (2007) defines placebo as "a substance provided to a patient that the physician believes has no specific pharmacological effect upon the condition being treated," it can be concluded that a substance (or method) may be a placebo today but not tomorrow (or vice versa), depending on the beliefs of the physician. Equally, a substance (or method) is a placebo when given by Dr. A (who believes it to be ineffective) but not when given by Dr. B (who believes the contrary).

On the other hand, if the Wiktionary definition of placebo as an inert treatment is agreed upon, the logical problem with using the term placebo effect is obvious. If placebo has, by definition, no effect, how could a placebo effect exist? This logical fallacy can be found even in a standard textbook *The Powerful Placebo* (Shapiro and Shapiro 1997), where placebo is defined as:

> any treatment . . . that is used for its ameliorative effect on a symptom or disease but that actually is ineffective or is not specifically effective for the condition being treated.

Further on, placebo effect is defined as:

> primarily the nonspecific psychological or psychophysiological therapeutic effect produced by a placebo, but may be the effect of spontaneous improvement attributed to the placebo.

If the word placebo in the latter definition is replaced with its definition above, the following "definition" of placebo effect is obtained:

> ...therapeutic effect produced by [a treatment] ... that actually is ineffective or is not specifically effective for the condition being treated...but may be the effect of spontaneous improvement attributed to the [treatment].

The first part is not meaningful and the second part limits the therapeutic effect to spontaneous improvement only (Moerman 2002; Puustinen and Louhiala 2014). Shapiro and Shapiro, like many other authors, use the term "nonspecific" referring to the alleged result of the placebo effect. This, however, refers only to the fact that we do not know what takes place in a therapeutic encounter when a patient feels better even he or she has not received any biologically plausible treatment.

The same confusion resides in using terms pure and impure placebo. From the practical point of view, the concept "pure placebo" is usually clear and meaningful. Technically, however, "pure" placebos are not without *any* effects since biological substances are never completely inert. Saline as such, for example, is practically inert when administered in small doses, but in intramuscular dosing the *procedure itself* is far from inert. Vitamin C and lactose have been used as "placebos" although they certainly have meaningful biological effects in many circumstances.

The category of "impure placebos" is more ambiguous and, in fact, extremely problematic. The list of treatments that have been categorized as impure placebos is long (Howick et al. 2013), but only three examples are enough to demonstrate the problematic nature of the concept: antibiotics for suspected viral infections, non-essential physical examinations, and positive suggestions. All these have been mentioned as examples of impure placebos in several empirical studies during recent years.

Antibiotics for suspected viral infections. If a physician *knows* that an infection is caused by a virus, prescribing antibiotics is clearly unethical. In real life, however, it is practically impossible to be certain about the cause of an infection. Medical decision-making is always based on probabilities, and in individual cases the physician weighs the potential gains and harms of the prescribed treatment (Louhiala 2009).

Nonessential physical examinations and nonessential technical examinations of a patient. The spectrum of physical or technical examinations that are "essential" for a particular patient is highly dependent on the context. The experience of the physician and the setting of the consultation, for example, define the variety of examinations, and there is no clear line between "essential" and "nonessential" examinations.

Positive suggestions. The role of a physician is to inform, comfort, and give hope to the patient, and positive suggestions are an essential element of this activity. It is not meaningful to describe it as a "'therapeutic' method" which lacks "specific therapeutic effects or value for the condition for which they have been prescribed."

As the category of impure placebos is highly ambiguous, we may ask whether dividing the concept placebo into categories "impure" and "pure" placebos is relevant in any scientifically fruitful way. While clinical practitioners may prescribe, give, or recommend treatments that can be considered ineffective, labeling all such treatments as impure placebos paints a simplistic picture of clinical reality.

Placebos in Clinical Practice

Several studies have suggested that the deliberate use of placebos is a common and widely accepted practice among physicians. The lowest and highest reported proportions of doctors who have prescribed or administered placebos in their clinical practice have been 20 % and 97.5 %, respectively (Louhiala 2012; Howick et al. 2013).

A closer look at these studies shows, however, that the conclusion about the popularity of the use of placebos is false or at least seriously misleading. Some of the studies have not provided a definition for placebo and it was thus up to the respondents to interpret what they considered to be a placebo in their practice. In an oft-cited questionnaire survey from Israel, for example, 53 % of the physicians reported using a placebo (Nitzan and Lichtenberg 2004). Because the key concept was not defined, the respondents may have understood placebo in at least four different ways: "First, placebo may have meant deliberate deception through the administration of an inert substance. Second, it may have meant giving an inert substance openly. Third, some may have thought of a situation in which the doctor or nurse believes that the drug works even though there is no supporting scientific evidence. Fourth, some respondents may have thought more about the placebo effect than the nature of the substance given" (Louhiala 2009).

Furthermore, studies that have defined placebo show a large variation in their definitions. In a questionnaire survey among internists in Chicago (Sherman and Hickner 2008), for example, the respondents were given several alternatives for the definition of a placebo. They could either give their own definition or choose between an intervention that is not expected to have an effect through a known physiologic mechanism, or an intervention not considered to have a "specific" effect on the condition treated, but with a possible "unspecific" effect, or an intervention that is inert or innocuous. The main finding of the study was that 45 % of the respondents reported that they had used a placebo in clinical practice. Given this broad variety of definitions and interpretations of the basic concept, the finding is not informative.

A neglected aspect in all of the empirical studies addressing the use of the placebo has been the clinical prescription or administration process. The choice of words is not trivial here: "administering," "prescribing," "recommending," and "ordering" are different issues.

Given the conceptual confusion in defining the concept placebo, it is not surprising that opposite views have been presented also about the acceptability of the use of placebos in clinical practice. Walter Brown, an American psychiatrist, wrote in 1998 that "we should respect the benefits of placebos – their safety, effectiveness and low cost – and bring the full advantage of these benefits into our everyday practices" (Brown 1998). Asbjorn Hróbjartsson, a Danish clinical epidemiologist, concluded in his paper that "Clinical placebo interventions are unethical, unnecessary, and unprofessional" (Hróbjartsson 2008). Liechtenberg et al. (2004) have suggested that "in select cases, use of the placebo may even be morally imperative." Howick et al. (2013) have proposed further investigations to develop "ethical and cost-effective placebos."

The arguments in support of the use of placebos can be summarized as follows: "they work in clinical trials, are cheap, and have no side effects." This statement is not only an ethical argument but demonstrates also the conceptual problem that is so common: "they" work and "they" do not have side effects, even though "they" are supposed to be, by definition, inert.

It is widely believed that a beneficial response to placebo treatment requires deception or at least some kind of a "white lie" to the patient. Lying to the patient is, however, ethically problematic, to say the least. For example, if the patient later finds out that the physician has not told the whole truth about the treatment, there may be serious consequences not only for the present physician-patient relationship but also for future relationships with other health-care professionals.

Some recent studies examining open-label use of placebos have suggested that a beneficial response to placebo treatment is not necessarily limited to settings where the patients have been deceived. As our knowledge on this topic is thus far very limited and an open-label use of pure placebos remains anyway a special case, no general recommendations can be given on such use.

Clarifying the Conceptual Confusion

The conceptual problems related to placebo and its derivatives have been acknowledged, and different solutions have been proposed to resolve the confusion.

On one hand, it has been suggested that the concept of placebo should be discarded altogether (Götzsche 1995) or that it should be limited to research context only (Louhiala and Puustinen 2008). In the latter case the term would refer only to the procedures and substances that are used as biologically inert controls to active treatments in medical research. If inert treatments are used in clinical practice, they should not be called placebos but ineffective treatments.

As reported earlier, several alternative concepts have been proposed to replace "placebo effect." Miller and Kaptchuk's *contextual healing* and Moerman's *meaning response* avoid the logical problem within the term placebo effect. Contextual healing refers to the therapeutic encounter on the whole which is, by necessity, always contextual in one way or another. Meaning response goes even further in addressing the essence of therapeutic encounter as a process attempting to create meaning to understand and solve the patient's problem. These concepts have not, to our reading, been analyzed in depth nor adopted for wider use in medical writing (Puustinen and Louhiala 2014).

Care effect refers to the phenomena that take place within both research settings and clinical consultations leading to beneficial therapeutic outcomes in cases when the medical treatment given cannot explain those outcomes in full (Puustinen and Louhiala 2014). "Care" and "caring" carry positive connotations (Tudor Hart and Dieppe 1996), but not the burden "placebo" has obtained as referring to something unreal or negative ("dummy," "sham," "inert"). The patient's experience of having been cared for is always real. A care effect may be evoked in a clinical trial, too, but clinical practice and research are fundamentally different settings. In a trial, care effect may be considered a confounding factor, in clinical medicine an ally.

Definitions of Key Terms

Placebo	Is commonly defined as an inert treatment. However, it is often understood more broadly, even to cover practically all elements of therapeutic encounter except a specific pharmacological or other physiological mechanism.
Placebo effect	Also has several different definitions. In the research context, it may refer to the change in a placebo group. In the clinical context, it usually refers to the changes in the patient's condition that cannot be explained by a specific pharmacological or physiological mechanism.
Contextual healing	Refers to the context of the clinical encounter, as distinct from the specific treatment interventions containing factors such as the environment of the clinical setting, the communication between patient and clinician, and the rituals of treatment.
Meaning response	Is the physiological or psychological effect of meaning in the origins or treatment of illness.
Care effect	Is the outcome of a therapeutic encounter that cannot be attributed to the specific physiological response to the treatment given.

Summary Points

- A placebo is commonly understood as a dummy medicine or an inert treatment.
- Within medicine, however, much wider and complex definitions have been provided.
- The so-called placebo effect is a complex phenomenon, and the use of a placebo is not a necessary condition for a placebo effect.
- Because of the problematic nature of the concept placebo effect, several alternatives have been suggested to replace it (e.g., contextual healing, meaning response, and care effect)
- The category of "impure placebos" is highly ambiguous, and dividing the concept placebo into categories "impure" and "pure" is not meaningful.

- Although several studies seem to suggest that the deliberate use of placebos is a common and widely accepted practice among physicians, a closer look at these studies shows, however, that the conclusion about the popularity of the use of placebos is false or at least seriously misleading.
- The deliberate use of placebos – understood as inert treatments – in clinical practice is not ethically justified.

References

American Medical Association Council on Ethical and Judicial Affairs (2007) Placebo use in clinical practice. http://www.ama-assn.org/ama/pub/physician-resources/medical-ethics/code-medical-ethics/opinion8083.page. Accessed 19 Nov 2014

Anonymous (1900) Int J Surg 9:238

Beecher H (1955) The powerful placebo. JAMA 159:1602–1606

Benedetti F (2009) Placebo effects – understanding the mechanisms in health and disease. Oxford University Press, Oxford

Brown WA (1998) The placebo effect. Sci Am 278(1):90–95

Chaput de Saintonge DM, Herxheimer A (1994) Harnessing placebo effects in health care. Lancet 344:995–998

Chaucer G (2001) The merchant's prologue and tale. Cambridge University Press, Cambridge

Coxe J (1808) The Philadelphia medical dictionary. Thomas Dobson, Philadelphia

Duncan A (1770) Elements of therapeutics. Drummond, Edinburgh

Editorial (1834) Edinb Med Surg J 42:483

Fässler M, Gnadinger M, Rosemann T et al (2009) Use of placebo interventions among Swiss primary care providers. BMC Health Serv Res 9:144

Gold H, Barr DB, Cattell M et al (eds) (1947) Cornell conferences on therapy: use of placebos in therapy. Macmillan, New York

Goldacre B (2009) Bad science. Fourth Estate, London

Götzsche P (1995) Concept of placebo should be discarded. BMJ 311:1640

Graves TC (1920) Commentary on a case of hystero-epilepsy with delayed puberty. Lancet 196:1134–1135

Grünbaum A (1986) The placebo concept in medicine and psychiatry. Psychol Med 16(1):19–38

Hooper R (1798) A compendious medical dictionary. Myrray and Highley, London

Hooper R (1811) A compendious medical dictionary. Longman, London

Howick J, Bishop FL, Heneghan C et al (2013) Placebo use in the United Kingdom: results from a national survey of primary care practitioners. PLoS One 8(3), e58247

Hróbjartsson A (2008) Clinical placebo interventions are unethical, unnecessary and unprofessional. J Clin Ethics 19:66–69

Hunter P (2007) A question of faith. EMBO Rep 8:125–128

Kaptchuk T (1998) Powerful placebo: the dark side of the randomised controlled trial. Lancet 351:1722–1725

Lichtenberg P, Heresco-Levy U, Nitzan U (2004) The ethics of the placebo in clinical practice. J Med Ethics 30:551–554

Louhiala P (2009) The ethics of the placebo in clinical practice revisited. J Med Ethics 35:407–409

Louhiala P (2012) What do we really know about the deliberate use of placebos in clinical practice? J Med Ethics 38:403–405

Louhiala P, Puustinen R (2008) Rethinking the placebo effect. Med Humanit 34:107–109

Martial. Epigrammata. http://www.perseus.tufts.edu/hopper/text?doc=Perseus:text:2008.01.0506:book=3:poem=51&highlight=placebo. Accessed September 12, 2015

Miller F, Kaptchuk T (2008) The power of context: reconceptualizing the placebo effect. J R Soc Med 101:222–225

Moerman DE (2002) Meaning, medicine and the 'placebo effect'. Cambridge University Press, Cambridge

Motherby G (1785) A new medical dictionary or general repository of physic. Containing an explanation of the terms and a description of the various particulars relating to anatomy, physiology, physic, surgery, materia medica, pharmacy &c. &c. &c. Printed for J. Johnson, London

Motherby G (1791) A new medical dictionary or general repository of physic. Containing an explanation of the terms and a description of the various particulars relating to anatomy, physiology, physic, surgery, materia medica, pharmacy &c. &c. &c. Printed for J. Johnson, London

Nitzan U, Lichtenberg P (2004) Questionnaire survey on use of placebo. BMJ 329:944–946

Oswald FL (1902) Cosmopolitan health studies. Sanitarian 49:500–505

Petronius. Satyricon. http://sacred-texts.com/cla/petro/satyrlat/satl130.htm. Accessed September 12, 2015

Puustinen R, Louhiala P (2014) The paradox of placebo – real and sham in medicine. In: Louhiala P, Heath I, Saunders J (eds) The medical humanities companion, vol 3, Treatment. Radcliffe, Oxford

Robertson W (1776) Observationes miscellaneae inaugurales De vino praecipue. Balfour et Smellie, Edinburgi, p 56

Scott W (1824) St Ronan's Well. Archibald Constable, Edinburgh, p 210

Seneca. De Consolatione ad Helvium. http://www.perseus.tufts.edu/hopper/text?doc=Perseus:text:2007.01.0017:book=11:chapter=4&highlight=placebo. Accessed September 12, 2015

Shapiro AK, Shapiro E (1997) The powerful placebo – from ancient priest to modern physician. The Johns Hopkins University Press, Baltimore

Sherman R, Hickner J (2008) Academic physicians use placebos in clinical practice and believe in the mind–body connection. J Gen Intern Med 23:7–10

Sutherland A (1763) Attempts to revive ancient medical doctrines. A Millar, London, pp xxiii–xxiv

TudorHart J, Dieppe P (1996) Caring effects. Lancet 347:1606–1608

Philosophical Issues in Nanomedicine

44

Christian Lenk

Contents

Abstract

In this chapter, the emerging field of nanomedicine is examined from a philosophical point of view. Firstly, the introduction works out the broader context of nanotechnology in today's scientific culture and shows some utopian undertones in the public discourse on nanotechnology. Secondly, in the following section on practical applications, some examples for research activities in nanomedicine are described and discussed. The third section gives a short introduction into the discussion on language and metaphors in nanobiotechnology. In the following section, the ethical issues in the context

C. Lenk (✉)
Ulm University, Institute for History, Theory and Ethics of Medicine, Ulm, Germany
e-mail: christian.lenk@uni-ulm.de

© Springer Science+Business Media Dordrecht 2017
T. Schramme, S. Edwards (eds.), *Handbook of the Philosophy of Medicine*,
DOI 10.1007/978-94-017-8688-1_32

729

of nanomedicine are outlined. These selected issues are (1) risk assessment, (2) personal and human identity, (3) human enhancement, and (4) distribution of benefits and risks in the context of the implementation of innovative applications in medicine. Finally, some conclusions sum up the discussion on nanomedicine in philosophy and deal with characteristic hopes found in the public in the context of this biotechnology.

Introduction

In the late 1990s, an influential report of the US National Science and Technology Council (NSTC) was published with the title "Nanotechnology: Shaping the World Atom by Atom." The subtitle especially can be seen as characteristic for the report's line of argumentation. Referring to biological and molecular mechanisms in nature, the project is sketched out, to gain technological advances by following the example of nature for human purposes in the nano-area (nanometer, one billionth part of a meter). In the words of the Nobel laureate Horst Störmer, who is cited as follows in the report: "Nanotechnology has given us the tools ... to play with the ultimate toy box of nature – atoms and molecules. Everything is made from it ... The possibilities to create new things appear limitless" (NSTC 1999, p. 1). From the philosopher's point of view, this seems to be, at first glance, simply the vision or dream of an engineer; the expert on science and technology studies may regard this as mere speculation. However, beyond such rather negative associations, there are maybe some echoes of the beginnings of Western philosophy, namely, pre-Socratic natural philosophy (or speculation) with the two famous representatives of atomism, Leukipp and Democritus. In reading the hopes and ideas in the NSTC paper, one senses a similar spirit of speculation regarding the inner forces of matter and a similar enthusiasm about the enigmas of the world in some subsequent scholars influenced by these early thinkers.

However, the *motifs* of "shaping the world" or "to play with the toy box of nature" also point to human (or expert) control over nature or indeed over other human beings. Perhaps, this is the reason why a wider audience, especially those in nongovernmental organizations (e.g., the German *Bund für Umwelt und Naturschutz* or *Friends of the Earth*), regards the abovementioned visions rather with suspicion than with sympathy. However, especially in the field of nanomedicine, there seems to be a considerable gap between the original and lofty visions of nanotechnology at the conceptual level and concrete projects in the medical area, which do not aim at shaping humans or organs de novo "atom by atom" but rather aim at pragmatic translations of technological ideas into applied projects. Certainly, this does not mean that nanotechnology in medicine is per se a harmless endeavor. But at least one can say that it is obviously an endeavor which has similar aims to medicine, i.e., the healing of patients and the fighting of diseases, and has therefore to be evaluated in a similar way, for example, regarding proper risk-benefit assessment.

Examples of Practical Applications

The philosophical analysis of new technologies and scientific approaches must certainly take into account the visions, goals, and projects which are described by the protagonists of nanomedicine themselves. However, beneath the explanations of the actors, it is also necessary to examine the practical endeavors and concrete applications which result from research in nanomedicine. Like in other cases, such a double perspective will typically reveal a number of similarities between practice and theory but also a number of important differences. The difference between the visions and goals of nanotechnology in general and the practical applications of nanomedicine in particular may be considerable due to the strict demands which are normally presented to medical applications in human beings. This typically includes the pharmacological and medical proof that the risks of using the new application are acceptable in relation to the medical goals sought and that the relevant medical device or active agent is indeed effective in a specified and verifiable way. In this sense, in the following, a number of examples will be presented of new inventions in the field of nanomedicine. As the examples show, all these approaches depend on the special characteristics of the tiny, i.e., nano, particles used. On the other hand, the examples show a broad range of different approaches. These differences will probably lead to heterogeneous results of risk analysis.

A first example is the use of magnetic nanoparticles for tumor therapy. In the course of this therapy, a huge number of these nanoparticles are injected into the tumor tissue. Subsequently, the particles inside the tumor are heated by an alternating magnetic field. The aim is here to achieve a particular method of tumor treatment which is superior to conventional surgery. Due to this aim, the new method was tested in patients with glioblastoma, a kind of brain tumor (Müller-Jung 2009). Another approach based on the use of magnetic particles is their combination with modified viruses. These so-called *Lentiviruses* are equipped with modified genes for therapeutic purposes, dependent on the patients' pathology. In animal experimentation, researchers have tried to navigate such genetic "taxicabs" into the coronary heart arteries of mice, where the genes would be incorporated by the target cells and then develop their therapeutic function (Müller-Jung 2009).

The regeneration of body tissue and cells is a general theme of nanomedicine. For example, researchers developed a gel, based on nanotechnology, for the regeneration and the growth of the cartilage in the human body. Such active agents could be important in order to cure degenerative diseases in the aging populations of industrial states. A comparable approach involves the artificial building of protein structures for the regeneration of blood vessels and angiogenesis, i.e., the building and growth of new capillaries or blood vessels. In this context, researchers speak of "protein imitation for medicine and biotechnology," the production of body-like nanostructures which can serve as a starting point for the regeneration of body structures of vital importance (Kurz 2011). An example of the practical application of such an approach is research on the therapy of patients with paraplegia (currently also on the stage of animal experimentation). In the experiment, an active agent was transported by newly developed nanomolecules to the paraplegic lesions (in the spinal marrow) of dogs to alleviate the symptoms the researchers had previously induced by toxic chemicals (DÄ 2009; Shi et al. 2010).

From a research ethics point of view, this overview already illustrates a number of ethical problems such as, for example, experimentation with vulnerable patients (patients with brain tumors); the first-in-human use of newly developed substances; animal experimentation for basic research; the possible risk of growth stimulus for body tissues, which can also result in uncontrolled cancer growth of tissue and cells; and finally the possible risk of allergic and rejection reactions of the human body (cf., e.g., the dramatic Gelsinger case, where a patient died due to the infusion of a huge number of genetically modified viruses (Kimmelman 2008)).

After this short introduction into the field of nanomedicine, the following philosophical analysis will be structured in two main parts. Firstly, how can the language and descriptions of nanotechnology be classified from the perspective of the humanities? What developments in terms of the history of ideas can be identified? Secondly, how does the approach of nanomedicine need to be evaluated from an ethical point of view, and what ethical presumptions and principles are involved in such an evaluation? Both areas are permeated by anthropological issues, for example, whether the human body can be seen as a machine or whether a possible "improvement" of human beings is seen as ethically acceptable.

Some Considerations on the Language of Nanotechnology and the Theory of Science

As Köchy points out in his article on the *Conceptualisation of living systems in nanobiotechnology*, the presentation of nanotechnology in scientific and popular scientific contributions strongly follows the traditional machine model (or metaphor) of life. The decisive references in classical philosophy in this regard are, for example, René Descartes and Julien Offray de La Mettrie in the seventeenth and eighteenth centuries. In the famous passage in the *Discourse de la méthode*, Descartes argues as follows:

> This will not seem strange to those who know how many different automata or moving machines can be devised by human ingenuity, by using only very few pieces in comparison with the larger number of bones, muscles, nerves, arteries, veins and all the other parts in the body of every animal. They will think of this body like a machine which, having been made by the hand of God, is incomparably better structured than any machine that could be invented by human beings, and contains many more admirable movements. Descartes 1999 [1637], 39 f

The human and animal body is here compared with a machine, and the body parts and organs appear as a *comparandum* to the "pieces" which are the constitutive elements of the machine. The imagined thinkers or observers ("those who know," "they") "will think of this body *like a machine*" (emphasis by the author), but this body machine is far more perfect than the everyday machines produced by human craftsman, due to the far more perfect constitution of its creator (i.e., God). However, as this is conceived by Descartes, it seems to be rather a distinction of degree than of quality. It is therefore perhaps not surprising to come to the conclusion that such a model or metaphor in the end is closer to an identification as opposed to a comparison. This is suggested in the following passage by George Tombs: "For Descartes, the metaphor became an abstract *equation*, linking the human body and the machine. And that equation became one of the pillars of an entire philosophical system. [. . .] Expressed another way, metaphor as analogy *likens* one thing to another; metaphor as equation affirms that one thing *is* another" (Tombs 2002, p. 168; emphasis by the author). The result is then a kind of confusion between the heuristic/didactic function of the mere model and the ontological function of an identification of two different categories of objects (the human body and the machine).

Similarly, Köchy draws the conclusion in his text that "The old debate concerning the relationship of machine and organism gets a new topicality and meaning in the context of nanobiotechnology. At the same time, the content of the previous machine conception changes" (Köchy 2008, S. 186 f., translation by the author). However, as he (Köchy) shows in a number of examples, the model is used in a rather unclear and undefined way which points maybe to the fact that it is used by the authors in an unconscious manner. A lack of awareness regarding linguistic and metaphorical distinctions seems also to be a problem in the description of concepts of nanotechnology in high-ranking international publications, as the following citations show:

> That biological motors perform work and are engaged in well-defined mechanical tasks such as muscle contraction or the transport of objects is apparent in all living systems. Controlling motion using molecular switches is particularly attractive for the construction of nanomechanical valves.

> The exquisite solutions nature has found to control molecular motion, evident in the fascinating biological linear and rotary motors, has served as a major source of inspiration for scientists to conceptualize, design and build – using a bottom-up approach – entirely synthetic molecular machines. Browne and Feringa 2006, pp. 32 f

In the first citation, it is not clearly recognizable, whether the text refers to muscle fibers of the human body, to which the metaphor of the engine is applied, or whether the topic is the molecular engine, which takes on the task of muscle fibers. Both subjects appear in principle exchangeable or identical.

In the second citation, nature appears virtually as an engineer, an agent who controls molecular motion and is therefore a prototype for the scientists who want to construct molecular machines. What Descartes initially insinuated of the human body (the metaphor of the machine) is in this citation an inherent part of the body and firmly fixed in its perspective of bodily functioning. "Nature" here takes on the teleological function, which was occupied by God in the seventeenth-century conception of the world (see Descartes' citation above, "They will think of this body like a machine which, having been made by the hand of God, . . .").

When the message of the traditional machine model of the human body in philosophy was "The human body is also a kind of machine and has therefore to be analyzed and understood as such," the message of nanobiotechnology seems to be twofold. Firstly (according to the classic Cartesian premise), "natural entities are also a kind of machines," but then secondly "molecular machines can also be transformed in natural entities." The subtext is in the second case not so much the ambitious, presupposed possibilities of nanotechnology but the very possibility of exchange between nature and technology. One of the implications of such a conceptualization is therefore the tendency to blur the line between the traditional concepts of *physis* and *techne*, i.e., things from nature and artificial products. In the science literature, this is then frequently phrased as a quasi-ontological statement, where special qualities are ascribed to the products of nanobiotechnology.

Ethical Considerations

In a previous review article on the ethical aspects of nanomedicine, four main points were identified: (1) the problem of an adequate risk assessment in the case of innovative and first-in-human nanotechnology applications; (2) the area of personal and human identity; (3) a possible enhancement of human beings by nanomedicine; and (4) the distribution of benefits and risks which might result during the course of the introduction of nanotechnology into medicine (Lenk and Biller-Andorno 2007). The four topics seem still to be essential components in the understanding of the ethical analysis of nanomedicine and will be described in the following with reference to recent developments.

Risk Assessment

The description of risks and attempts to control adverse effects has a long tradition in medical research. However, different possibilities and foci in the ethical analysis of risk are conceivable. In medicine, the risk of a new drug's application is usually described as a pharmacological side effect. For example, the consequence of testing a new pharmaceutical drug for the patient could be that her cancer is cured or the disease progression is stopped but she will lose her fertility. Such consequences are then described according to the pharmacological paradigm and analyzed biostatistically for the whole patient population. However, the significance and meaning of loss of fertility for the patient from the familial, social, and psychological point of view are not described. Although it is increasingly the case that questionnaires concerning the quality of life of patients are used in medical research, this is not a sufficient clarification of patient risk from the ethical point of view. In fact, the mere medical-pharmacological risk analysis obscures crucial dimensions of harm and has therefore to be complemented by further ethical considerations. Such an approach should also be integrated into research in nanomedicine.

In the area of nanotechnology, it is also known that nanoparticles can pass into the environment. This will probably not lead to the so-called gray goo scenario (cf. Drexler 1986, the worry that nanotechnology-based little organisms or replicators could convert the biosphere in an uncontrollable way into dust or "gray goo") but could nevertheless cause further pollution of the environment or the impairment of other organisms.

A further difficulty in the area of nanomedicine is the combination of risks in medical applications in the human body, as in the case of gene therapy, whereby the gene drug is supposed to reach the body cells encapsulated in nanostructures or so-called gene ferries (cf. Lenk and Biller-Andorno 2007). Gene therapy is connected with a number of severe risks (Kimmelman 2008), so that such an approach leads to the combination of two innovative applications, whereby yet unknown side effects could occur in interrelation. Therefore, some commentators and science journalists see the issue of adequate risk evaluation of nanotechnology in medicine as the decisive problem for the further development of this form of research (Müller-Jung 2009).

This assessment is further highlighted by the fact that insurance companies partly exclude nanotechnology from their insured risks. As an insurance expert for risk assessment explained in a recent interview, from the perspective of insurances (who have for the sake of risk calculation a major interest in the proper determination of possible damages), the risk assessment for nanotechnology lags behind the technological innovation at the present point of time (Allianz Global Corporate & Specialty 2013). In the interview, it is also pointed out that the structure of some nanotubes resembles asbestos fibers, and it was demonstrated that some nanoparticles pose a danger for the health of water organisms. Therefore, the risk assessment of nanotechnology (understood as an interdisciplinary endeavor between the respective scientific disciplines and ethics) has to be developed further to keep pace with the technological development.

Personal and Human Identity

New applications from nanotechnology in medicine could also alter our perception of the natural human body. These considerations have to be seen in the context of the first part of this chapter, where the natural body was addressed as a kind of machine. This also has some ethical implications, for example, when the body as a machine is changed or complemented by applications from nanotechnology. There are a wide range of implants for different organs and functions which are currently already applied in the human body. To mention only two examples: for patients who have lost a knee and lower leg, these body parts can be replaced by a computerized and motorized so-called C-leg. Another example of modern implants is the subcutaneous defibrillator which automatically gives an electric shock to the patient's heart in case of cardiac arrhythmia. These are only two examples of cases where modern prostheses have the ability to react semi-autonomously and according to internal steering algorithms regarding bodily movements or dysfunctions. However, these examples show the accuracy of the machine metaphor because obviously the body machine is here complemented by other (helpful) real machines. It depends on the individual patient's ability to adapt to these implants whether he or she will feel that his identity has changed as a result of these prostheses and implants.

In the case of nanomedicine, changes in the human body will be probably less obvious and clear-cut. However, this does not mean that they could not have an impact regarding personal and human identity. How will patients react on the possibility of infusing small nanomachines into their blood system with the aim of clearing blood vessels and capillaries? Is this substantially different from conventional drugs against plaque deposits in the blood vessels? The US National Science and Technology Council's report mentions the following possible applications in this regard:

> Nanotechnology will lead to new generations of prosthetic and medical implants whose surfaces are molecularly designed to interact with the body. Some of these even will help attract and assemble raw materials in bodily fluids to regenerate bone, skin or other missing or damaged tissues. New nanostructured vaccines could eliminate hazards of conventional vaccine development and use, which rely on viruses and bacteria. Nanotubules that act like tiny straws could conceivably take up drug molecules and release them slowly over time. A slew of chip-sized home diagnostic devices with nanoscale detection and processing components could fundamentally alter patient-doctor relationships, the management of illnesses, and medical culture in general. (NSTC 1999, p. 8)

These scenarios already point to the next ethical theme, namely, a possible enhancement of the human body (over and above mere therapeutic medical goals). Positively interpreted, some of the applications mentioned in the NSTC report (automatic and steady regeneration of body tissue, artificial drug secretion) could be seen as a kind of integration of therapeutic mechanisms into the human body which perhaps leads to a new form of "gentle" medicine. Other ideas, for example, the automatic monitoring of body functions and transfer of medical measurements to a physician or control center, could clearly change conventional ways of human living and could also have an impact on human identity. Surely, in the context of today's modern societies, this would be a voluntary decision of the person or patient her- or himself. However, there are, in the context of health care, a number of developments which show a societal dynamic of their own, where the individual person has to conform for not being excluded from the societal "fabric" or to be disadvantaged in the access to health-care services. In any case, a steady and automatic monitoring of body functions would lead to the situation that the concerned persons are permanently "accompanied" by a medical surveillance team. When the right to privacy also includes a "right to be let alone," this might lead to the abandonment of such a right and a decisive change in human living (cf. Hall et al. 2012, p. 769).

Human Enhancement

Ideas and doubts concerning the possibility of human enhancement by nanotechnology might be the area where there is the largest gap between a science-fiction description of enhancement and currently existing applications of nanomedicine (cf. Lenk and Biller-Andorno 2007, p. 179). One has also to consider that nontherapeutic or enhancement activities in medicine exist independently of the possibilities of nanomedicine. The extension of biomedicine from the therapeutic occupation with existing diseases toward the improvement of bodily and mental qualities and functions is not initiated or fostered by nanomedicine as such. However, as was also mentioned in the last paragraph, there are a number of imaginable but yet not existing applications of nanomedicine which have to be classified not as a therapy but as an enhancement (for a further distinction between the two areas, cf. Lenk 2002). A number of applications of nanotechnology are described particularly in the field of rehabilitative medicine; they include, for example, the reconstruction of human tissue or body material which has deteriorated or disappeared due to degenerative or aging processes. In this medical field, nanotechnology applications could well lead to an "enhancement" of the human body, when regenerative mechanisms are strengthened or complemented. However, such a form of enhancement would probably not be seen as ethically problematic, although it could change, very gradually, important qualities of the "conditio humana" such as the normal process of human aging.

Distribution of Benefits and Risks

There are several points to consider in relation to justice in the introduction of new medical interventions, which are also relevant for nanotechnology in medicine. Firstly, international documents on research ethics such as the Declaration of Helsinki (cf. Art. 34) foresee that patients who take part in medical research studies should also profit from this participation and get a kind of reward for the connected risk and harm they might suffer. The authorization process of drugs in contemporary industrialized countries seeks to ensure that only verifiably efficient and safe drugs get to the drug market. However, this evidence does not exist in the case of early study phases in medical research studies. Therefore, patients in such research studies sometimes run a considerable risk of suffering from unexpected side effects. A well-known example is the so-called Gelsinger case for gene therapy, where a young volunteer with a slight disease, due to an idealistic motivation, took part in an experimental study and died because of a dramatic conjunction of scientific ambition, a problematic study design, and preclinical studies which were not significant enough. This shows, on the one hand, the urgent need to minimize risk for participants in such studies by appropriate measurements and, on the other hand, the need for an effective political regulation. Research promotion by laissez-faire deregulation can in such cases be extremely harmful for the patients concerned and study participants. Unfortunately, it is not always an advantage to be part of the scientific or medical avant-garde.

Secondly, some authors argue that the development of nanomedicine could contribute to widening the gap of medical supply between the industrialized and developing countries (Hall et al. 2012, p. 775). From the ethical point of view, such a claim makes sense if there is a general right to adequate health care and participation in medical progress. From the medical point of view, such a claim for participation in medical progress is only reasonable when new applications bring a significant improvement in health care and the concrete health circumstances of patients. The authors of the named article give the example of a new medical device ("optical colposcope"), based on nanotechnology, which could enhance the diagnosis of cervical cancer (ibid.). In this context, they formulate the idea that the demand for justice in health care could be extended to include the research process itself (i.e., the selection and promotion of projects which focus on the health demands of the population in developing countries). Such an endeavor could then be integrated into national or international research funding, for example, on the part of the European Union. On the other hand, it seems to be rather unrealistic at the present point of time to expect that existing medical commercial companies would make such a commitment.

Conclusion

To draw some conclusions, one has firstly to see that all kinds of ethics and technology assessments are based on considerations concerning societal and technical developments in the future. The majority of the scenarios described in the literature will probably prove inaccurate because they are not based on a sound data basis, are more visionary than accurate from a methodological point of view, and are biased by the hopes and expectations of their authors and protagonists. If, for example, philosophers are invited to express a view of how the application of philosophy in education programs could change our society and make the world a better place, they would probably also draft visionary and mainly positive ideas. A comparable phenomenon occurs in nanotechnology, when protagonists as stakeholders of technology and possible recipients of research funding and investment present their technical plans and ideas.

This shows at the same time the importance of a proper, systematic, and interdisciplinary methodology of technology assessment, which also focuses on the broader societal implications and consequences. Because the real impact of a new technology can in most cases be revealed only in a broader perspective (this is also impressively demonstrated by the way the digital revolution and the internet change today's society and economy), a narrow approach which exclusively focuses on persons directly involved will probably not adequately describe the truly significant changes. Misguided expectations in regard to nanotechnology lead to what Wiesing and Clausen call in a recent article the "three dubious hopes in the context of nanomedicine":

- Firstly, that "[n]anobiotechnology will individualize therapy" (a dubious hope because also with nanomedicine it will be too costly to develop a drug for a single person or a small group),
- Secondly, that an "intervention [based on nanotechnology] is causal and therefore successful at the nanolevel" (a dubious hope because other therapeutic approaches

like for example the administration of insulin for diabetes patients are equally "causal", but hence not unproblematic or without unintended side-effects),

- and thirdly, interventions based on nanomedicine are "carried out with precision at the nano-level" (a dubious hope because such a promise is always brought forward with the introduction of any new medical technology, but this can only be evaluated after practical proving of a new approach). (Wiesing and Clausen 2014, p. 21)

This leads then, as Wiesing and Clausen explain, to the frequent doom and gloom scenarios for new technologies (ibid., 22). As was demonstrated in this chapter, for a comprehensive understanding of nanotechnology and its ethical implications, an interdisciplinary approach is necessary which in principle has to start from a linguistic perspective. The citations and remarks on the human-machine metaphor also show that the currently existing language in nanotechnology runs risk to confuse the metaphorical and the factual level and makes it difficult to distinguish existing scientific progresses from metaphorical and conceptual considerations.

Definitions of Key Terms

Nanomedicine	Medical applications which are based on mechanisms in the nanosphere (10 exp −9 m).
Scientific language	The specific language used in science in contrast to everyday language.
Risk assessment	A systematic assessment of an action's or project's negative side effects.
Applied ethics	Branch of ethics which is devoted to the analysis of ethical problems in practical circumstances, mostly in specific societal spheres (economy, medicine, science, trade, etc.).
Techno-utopianism	Ideology or system of belief which postulates the accessibility of utopian aims by technological means.

Summary Points

- Nanomedicine and nanotechnology did raise a number of fundamental questions in philosophy, ethics, and theory of science in the last 15 years.
- Characteristics are a metaphorical language of nanoscience, utopian undertones in the formulation of scientific goals, and especially comprehensive therapeutic hopes in the context of nanomedicine.
- An overview about current practical applications shows the arrival of nanomedicine in clinical applications with concrete patient groups.
- Among the ethical fields of discussion and analysis in the context of nanomedicine are risk assessment, personal and human identity, human enhancement, and the distribution of benefits and risks.

- Due to the evolutionary development of nanotechnology, a final ethical assessment of nanomedicine altogether is not possible at the present point of time, but a consolidated and comprehensive ethical assessment is carried out in this chapter.

References

Allianz Global Corporate & Specialty (2013) Die Nanotechnologie ist aus unserer Welt nicht mehr wegzudenken. [We cannot imagine our world without nanotechnology] Interview with Michael Bruch. Munich. www.allianz.com/de/presse/news/geschaeftsfelder/versicherung/news_2013-01-30.html. Accessed 16 Sept 2014

Browne FR, Feringa BL (2006) Making molecular machines work. Nat Nanotechnol 1:25–35

DÄ (2009) Nanomedizin: Heilung von Querschnittsgelähmten oder unkalkulierbares Risiko? [Nanomedicine: healing of paraplegics or incalculable risk?] DeutschesÄrzteblatt

Descartes R (1999 [1637]) Discourse on method [Discourse de la method]. In: Discourse on method and related writings. Penguin Books, London, pp 1–54

Drexler E (1986) Engines of creation: the coming era of nanotechnology. Anchor Press/Doubleday, New York

Hall RM, Sun T, Ferrari M (2012) A portrait of nanomedicine and its bioethical implications. J Law Med Ethics 40(4):763–779

Kimmelman J (2008) The ethics of human gene transfer. Nat Rev Genet 9:239–244

Köchy K (2008) Konzeptualisierung lebender Systeme in den Nanobiotechnologien [Conceptualisation of living systems in nanobiotechnology]. In: Köchy K, Norwig M, Hofmeister G (eds) Nanobiotechnologien Philosophische, anthropologische und ethische Fragen [Nanobiotechnologies. Philosophical, anthropological and ethical questions]. Verlag Karl Alber, Freiburg/München, pp 175–201

Kurz S (2011) Neue Blutgefäße mit Nanomedizin. Knorpelheilung, Tumortherapie und Wirkstofftaxis: Winzigste Partikel werden zu Helfern [New blood vessels with nanomedicine. Cartilage healing, tumour therapy and taxicabs for active agents: tiny particles become helpers]. Die Welt

Lenk C (2002) Therapie und Enhancement. Ziele und Grenzen der modernen Medizin [Therapy and enhancement. Aims and limits of modern medicine]. Lit Verlag, Münster

Lenk C, Biller-Andorno N (2007) Nanomedicine – emerging or re-emerging ethical issues? A discussion of four ethical themes. Med Health Care Philos 10(2):173–184

Müller-Jung J (2009) Heiler im Schattenreich [Healers in the realm of shades]. Frankfurter Allgemeine Zeitung

National Science and Technology Council (NSTC) (1999) Nanotechnology: shaping the world atom by atom. Washington, DC. http://www.wtec.org/loyola/nano/IWGN.Public.Brochure/

Shi Y, Kim S, Huff TB et al (2010) Effective repair of traumatically injured spinal cord by nanoscale block copolymer micelles. Nat Nanotechnol 5:80–87

Tombs G (2002) Man the machine: a history of a metaphor from Leonardo da Vinci to H.G. Wells. Doctoral thesis, McGill University, Montreal

Wiesing U, Clausen J (2014) The clinical research of nanomedicine: a new ethical challenge? Nanoethics 8(1):19–28

Philosophy of Sports Medicine

45

Silvia Camporesi and Mike McNamee

Contents

Abstract

The focus of this chapter is on the philosophy of Sports Medicine, that is, the practice of medicine in the context of sport. The chapter begins by examining ways in which a distinction in kind can be claimed between Sports Medicine and medicine per se. It does this by focussing first on the goals of medicine. This strategy proves to be indecisive, and it is concluded that a difference in degree only, rather than in kind, can be claimed for Sports Medicine. However, when the focus is directed to the normative aspects of medicine per se, in comparison with Sports Medicine, important differences can be identified. These differences

S. Camporesi
Department of Global Health and Social Medicine, King's College London, London, UK
e-mail: silvia.1.camporesi@kcl.ac.uk

M. McNamee (✉)
College of Engineering, Swansea University, Swansea, UK
e-mail: m.j.mcnamee@swansea.ac.uk

© Springer Science+Business Media Dordrecht 2017
T. Schramme, S. Edwards (eds.), *Handbook of the Philosophy of Medicine*,
DOI 10.1007/978-94-017-8688-1_33

concern, especially, the way in which normative concepts central to medicine per se are operationalized in Sports Medicine. It is shown how norms regarding privacy, confidentiality, autonomy, and paternalism all apply in significantly different ways in the sporting context. Parallel differences are also identified in relation to the therapy/enhancement distinction. The problem of balancing current sporting goals against long-term health is also discussed.

Introduction

Sports Medicine is something of a paradox. On the one hand, a sufficiently similar practice to that which we now call Sports Medicine was practiced in the ancient cultures of Greece and Rome (Berryman 1992; Heggie 2011; Carter 2012). On the other hand, despite these venerable roots, it is fair to say that only during the latter half of the twentieth century that it started to seriously establish its professional credentials. Many sports and even some professional sports, even until very recently, had the most limited medical and healthcare resources (Howe 2004). What might have been called "Sports Medicine" in the highest football (soccer) leagues in Europe until the 1970s often consisted of a masseur and a trainer who carried on a bucket of cold water and sponge with (possibly) an analgesic spray. Team physicians were a much later advent.

Precisely who falls under the phrase sports medic is far from clear. The term sports physician is adopted here as the standard. This will typically refer to a medical doctor with some specialism in sports. Across the globe, there are a variety of standards and qualities of preparation, and some countries do not have a designated specialism with national standards and nomenclature. Thus, Sports Medicine more generally conceived and understood as the name of a community need not be restricted to registered medical practitioners but can also include physiotherapists (physical therapists), healthcare practitioners, dentists, and in some cases athletic trainers. Each of these occupations is likely to have varying professional standards, norms, codes of conduct, and other regulatory frameworks and goals. The focus in this chapter is on sports physicians, medically registered professionals, in order to bring some order and specificity to the discussion.

Merely being members of the medical professions brings a certain coherence and identity to the notion of Sports Medicine, but one cannot expect a high degree of overlap in aims and processes. The goals of medicine are, of course, contested (Allert et al. 1996; Callahan and Hanson 1999). Brulde's (2001) account of the goals of medicine is revealing. Surveying a range of institutions and policy frameworks, he identifies seven different and mutually irreducible goals. It is hardly surprising, then, that there is no agreement as to the nature and purposes of Sports Medicine. Some of the claims made on behalf of Sports Medicine range from political slogans to bloated commercial claims. Perhaps most bewildering of all is the claim that "exercise is medicine" (http://www.exerciseismedicine.org/support_page.php?p=113). This is of course a patently absurd idea. But it begs questions about the conceptual borders of Sports Medicine that are rarely discussed since they are either taken for granted as unproblematic or relegated in priority by clinicians in order of a concentration on the main business of clinical work. Where sports physicians and scholars have made claims regarding the ethics of Sports Medicine, they have asserted that the ethics of Sports Medicine are "distinct" Green (2004) or "unique" (Johnson 2004; Testoni et al. 2013). The nature and ethics of Sports Medicine are critically discussed here, largely as a direct challenge to the unsubstantiated claims. A more modest proposal about the fiduciary obligations of sports physicians to their athletes and players (hereafter "athlete[s]") is presented and defended.

The Nature and Goals of Medicine and Sports Medicine

Although there is no uncontested essence to the concept, there is no good reason to think that is essentially contested. It is likely that there would be widespread agreement on very general ideas that the relief of suffering (Cassell 1982), or that the return to normal species functioning (Boorse 1975), are enduring features of the practice of medicine. The concept of medicine appears to have somewhat blurred and historically changing contours. Of course, even riverbeds shift – though very slowly.

Brulde notes seven independent goals: (i) to promote functioning; (ii) to maintain/restore normal structure/functioning; (iii) to promote quality of life; (iv) to save and prolong life; (v) to assist patients' coping with pathological conditions; (vi) to improve living conditions; and (vii) to promote children's growth and development (Brulde 2001). Each of these goals has something to recommend it as a claim to the nature of medicine as it is practiced today across the globe. Some appear more central than others; certainly much of Western medicine is in keeping with Boorse's general idea that health is to be understood as biostatistically normal functioning and that it is the job of medicine to secure and/or maintain this goal with and for the patient. Others, such as "improving living conditions" or "assisting patients coping with pathological conditions," might arguably fall more readily to associated branches of healthcare or welfare, respectively.

Some scholars, like Hoberman (2014) argue that we are witnessing the exportation of norms of Sports Medicine (enhancement) into mainstream medicine. Hoberman writes that "physician-assisted doping" has transformed high-performance sport into a "chronically overmedicated subculture" (Hoberman 2014, p. 572) that has been exported elsewhere ("the doping doctors of the sports world have pioneered 'entrepreneurial' medical practices that are now available to enormous numbers of people in search of hormonal rejuvenation").

This is not the place to substantively pursue the questions arising from the conceptual vagueness of medicine or Sports Medicine. It is just to note that there is no knockdown argument that we can employ about Sports Medicine's nature and ethics, without recourse to some nonneutral conception of medicine itself (Edwards and McNamee 2006). What can and should be done is to examine the claims made by the various constituencies of Sports Medicine on behalf of its medical status and its ethics.

Perhaps the boldest of all claims from within Sports Medicine is that exercise is itself a form of medicine, with or without physician assistance or intervention. But what, if any, sense is to be made of the slogan "exercise is medicine"? It can hardly be seen as some self-evident truth. First, it is noteworthy that the assertion is made not only by highly regarded professionals working in Sports Medicine in equally highly regarded scientific journals (e.g., Lobelo et al. 2014) on behalf of an international movement with a registered trademark "Exercise is Medicine®." So, perhaps it is best understood as nothing more than a slogan that captures a particularly modern set of pathological conditions that arise from sedentary lifestyles. Yet it should be noted, secondly, that the claim on the Exercise is Medicine (EIM) website, which has global policy and professional support, appears not merely to be that exercise is therapeutic or preventative of pathological conditions but that it is medicine in itself. Their mix of marketing and biomedical science appears to give the impression that exercise supplants traditional medicine in responding to the catalog of pathologies consequent upon inactivity. They continue, citing Robert N. Butler, MD, Former Director, National Institute on Aging, to the effect that "If exercise could be packed in a pill, it would be the single most widely prescribed and beneficial medicine in the nation." (EIM public presentation, slide 2, 20.3.15 http://www.exerciseismedicine. org/support_page.php?p=113). Thirdly, it is important to note that they propose implicitly, and explicitly on occasion, in their website pictures of physicians, and in publications, the idea that assessment and exercise referral is the province of the physician who is the legitimate mediator between the inactive (ergo pathological) populations and their exercise medicine. This of course is a highly contestable idea, one which physical educators, yoga practitioners, and health promotion officers might readily contest.

On more philosophical grounds one may query whether this colonization of leisure time is normatively justified or not. Though the idea of an obesity epidemic is questioned by some (e.g., Gard and Wright 2005; Gard 2010) there is widespread agreement that global health is indeed compromised by sedentary lifestyles. From this fact, if fact it is, the conclusion that exercise, presumably mediated by sports physicians, is the best or only response is of course highly contentious.

There is a further conceptual problem to consider. In the UK, and elsewhere, Sports Medicine as a profession has taken this turn towards exercise more generally rather than focusing exclusively on sport as a particular form of exercise. There may be excellent professional and political reasons for the adoption of this wider frame of reference. For example, a broader community of sport *and* exercise professionals could draw down greater funding from the state keen to keep individuals out of hospitals thus minimizing public expenditure; medical insurers in privately funded schemes might want to support this conceptual inflation because it is cheaper for them, and the fee-paying customer, to prescribe exercise over, for example, surgical intervention; by expanding their focus, the Sports Medicine community might acquire greater power over the lifestyles of citizens; and so on. This last benefit to the medical community has been more generally challenged under the construct of medicalization: the colonization of our lives by the medical profession (Parens 2013). Still, there are reasons pro and contra such conceptual inflation.

Nevertheless, the issues that arise from the adoption of a public health perspective into Sports Medicine are so heterogeneous that it is difficult to bring them into a singular conceptual framework. This heterogeneity brings further challenges in the context of ethical issues, since it would require an examination of public health ethics. In order to restrict the discussion, focus in the remainder of this chapter is on the medical issues arising from the more limited focus of Sports Medicine. In particular, it addresses the claims made regarding the distinctness or uniqueness of Sports Medicine among the family of medical professions.

Is There Anything Unique or Distinct About Sports Medicine?

The medical professions are many and varied. Nevertheless, it would be widely agreed that some of the occupations more readily claim to be at the center of medicine while others were more peripheral. For example, consider the contrast between general practitioners with cosmetic surgery. Bearing this in mind, few outside of Sports Medicine would not agree that it has enjoyed a kind of marginal existence and status. It is probably to be understood as undergoing what Habermas (1975) (albeit in a political context) called a "crisis of legitimation." In such a crisis, it is unclear how effective sports physicians might be in advancing their legitimacy claims. On the one hand, they might adopt a conservative strategy by advancing arguments that established their commonality with undisputed branches of medicine. On the other hand, sports physicians might formulate more ambitious claims regarding the distinctness or uniqueness of their clinical practice. If defensible, a claim regarding the "distinctness" or "uniqueness" (Dunn et al. 2007; Green 2004; Johnson 2004; Testoni et al. 2013) might be supposed to mitigate against the marginalization of Sports Medicine and the issue of its allegedly lowly status among the medical professions.

While the literature on the philosophy and ethics of Sports Medicine is not voluminous, there is widespread agreement on the central topics. A review of such a plethora of, largely spurious, claims includes: (i) treating pediatric athletes; (ii) medical advertising; (iii) innovative treatment; (iv) limits to patient confidentiality; (v) conflicting healthcare goals; (vi) enabling dangerous behavior; (vii) the physician-athlete relationship; (viii) privacy issues; (ix) concerns of autonomy; (x) informed consent; (xi) short-term gain, long-term risk; (xii) medical means to nonmedical ends; (xiii) drugs and the conflict of interest of the team physician; (xiv) effects of the cost of Sports Medicine care; and (xv) role of advertising in Sports Medicine. Time and space do not permit comment on all these claims, but a consideration of the more plausible contenders is presented below.

It will also be argued below that the claims of distinctness or uniqueness are overblown; what really exist are merely differences of degree, not differences of kind. Nevertheless, indeed *a fortiori*, a kind of transcendental argument can be used even before one considers these issues in detail. Suppose the claims to distinctness/ uniqueness were true. One might reasonably ask how the proposers of the distinctness/ uniqueness claim knew that the issues were then to be *bona fide* medical ones. Would it not be the case, rather, that in virtue of being distinct or unique they would not be shared with other branches of medicine? And if that were the case, how could we vouch for their being *medical* at all? The claim to distinctness/ uniqueness thus turns out to be self-defeating. Indeed, a hope to solve the conundrums of Sports Medicine by analyzing the norms of Sports Medicine would be self-defeating as we would end up challenging the norms itself of medicine. By successfully demonstrating their difference, they must rescind claims to being medical. In any event, it would be worthwhile eschewing these claims and, after Wittgenstein (1953), considering the senses in which Sports Medicine shares family resemblances with others medical professions, displaying the degrees to which those resemblances are nuanced in particular cases.

Issues of Privacy and Confidentiality in Sports Medicine

It has been claimed that the physician-athlete relationship is a highly personalized one where the clinician must take the athlete patient's needs and goals seriously. On the one hand, the entire shift towards personalized medicine (chimerical or not) might undermine this bold claim. More prosaically, many general practitioners will say that their success or failure as a general practitioner may well hinge on the extent to which they treat the individual in front of them, and not the condition they present with, as the well-known saying goes. Moreover, certain parts of occupational medicine (such as might be enjoyed by pilots or chief executive officers in global businesses) would be predicated on their "personalized" approach. And of course the harrowing case of Conrad Murray, Michael Jackson's personal physician, regarding the claim to medicine's being personalized might well be framed as a professional failing. Part of a claim to highly personalized medicine will entail a consideration of the kinds of information that a physician may hold in relation to their patient.

Privacy issues are unique to Sports Medicine. On the face of it, this has little to commend this idea since privacy (or confidentiality to use a standard currency) is a widely shared norm across medical professions. But in Sports Medicine, like in many other branches of medicine, privacy is a nuanced issue. In some cases, the right of individual athletes is waived by contract, while in other cases it is breached by everyday norms of media reporting. So, in the first instance, National Football League players in the USA have – as part of their contract – waivers regarding privacy of data concerning injury status and treatment. This enables the media circus that attends most professionally commercialized sports to expose their product to the market in a variety of ways. And even where there is no contractual provision, such as in English Premiership Football, coaches, physiotherapists, and players discuss injuries and speculate all the time in public via radio or television (Ribbans et al. 2013). None of this is so different to discussions of politicians' health status or the fitness to perform in any given number of public roles. The claim qua personalized health seems unsustainable as a unique aspect of Sports Medicine.

There will also be occasions, similar to those experienced in occupational medicine or elsewhere, where a physician will divulge confidential health data to protect others. While cases such as sexually transmitted diseases are frequently used as exemplars, team sports reveal a less discussed case in the light of athletes who have communicable diseases and ought not to share, for example, showers with other teammates or even simply sharing the field of play/court/ring and so forth.

Autonomy and Consent in Sports Medicine

A fairly counterintuitive claim has been made that concerns of autonomy generate uniqueness in Sports Medicine (Johnson 2004). Most medical ethicists or philosophers of medicine would think such a claim scarcely worthy of comment given the very widespread acceptance of the principle of respect for the autonomy of the patient. Now that seems almost trite were it not for the fact that many have queried athletes' desire to be autonomous in the face of complex, medically relevant, questions about their health and injury status; recovery times to training and participation in sports competitions; return to play decision (e.g., after concussions); and so on. Many athletes simply respond to their clinician when faced with a diagnosis and alternative treatment plans that they will go with whatever the "doc" recommends. And, of course, they are hardly unique in offering heteronymous responses. But if and insofar as athletes do want to be active and to have the final say in, for example, treatment interventions, then they will be aligned with general conceptions of best practice – at least within the mainstream of western medical ethics, where respect for autonomy is thought one of the foundational principles (Beauchamp and Childress 2012) and by some the first among those principles (e.g., Gillon 2003).

What may be present to an unusual degree in Sports Medicine is the extent to which individual athletes and players defer to their team doctors on treatment decisions. This should hardly surprise anyone since there is a considerable mutuality in their respective interests: the athlete/player wants to be at their fittest to compete, while the physician wants to enable optimal participation for the individual and/or their team. Nevertheless, two issues remain. First, the palpable existence of heteronymous athletes will trigger the well-known problem (Seedhouse 2008) of whether, or to what extent, it is the job of the physician not merely to respect autonomy but to foster it in their patients. Again, the problem is not unique to Sports Medicine but familiar. Secondly, in the increasingly globalized market for sports labor, it is interesting how issues of multiculturalism will affect the paternalistic-autonomy respectful dyad. Issues of linguistic competence (on behalf of the physician to explain and the patient to understand), wildly differing belief systems about causal efficacy from western pharmacology to witchcraft, and systems of authority and deference, combine to present sport physicians with exceptional challenges. Yet medical professionals working in general practice within multicultural societies will report sufficiently similar problems to undermine claims to uniqueness here.

What the increasingly multicultural nature of sports workforces highlights is the difficulties of gaining informed consent from their athlete patients. While informed consent reifies respect for autonomy, it may be overridden in conditions of incompetence. Incompetence (i.e., incapacity with respect to decision-making) in sports is likely to arise in a number of cases. Take just two: competence compromised temporarily by head injury (McNamee and Partridge 2013; McNamee et al. 2015) and incompetence by virtue of immature reasoning powers. And of course there can be cases of the two (Webborn et al. 2015) but this does not generate new considerations, merely conjoining the two. In the first instance, there has been a surge in concern about concussion prevalence in contact sports (Clay et al. 2013) and the specific ethical issues that arise because of it.

Where paternalism might be thought obligatory in Sports Medicine is in the development of talent identification and development programs (Baker et al. 2013). Recent decades have witnessed the increasingly early specialization of athletic talents, at periods of life where children's life plans are both unformed and uninformed (Tymowski 2001). Given the complexity of the decision to focus or specialize on just one sport to the exclusion of other activities (including, but not limited to, other sports), the child or adolescent is likely to be thought incompetent in relation to the choice at hand. Can an average 8-year-old really tell that they want to become the next Andre Agassi or that they would prefer to specialize in gymnastics or playing a musical instrument where the choice is exclusive because of early specialization (Camporesi 2013; Camporesi and McNamee 2016)? This increasing problem is likely to be exacerbated by the claims of direct to consumer genetic testing in Sports Medicine (Webborn et al. 2015), which may attract "tiger parenting" in an attempt to secure the greatest marginal benefits for one's athletically gifted offspring.

Trading Present Sports Participation Against Long-Term Health

An issue that is likely to be found at the elite end of sports and Sports Medicine is the consideration of whether short-term gains are justifiable in terms of long-term risks. In his felicific calculus, Jeremy Bentham (1879) argued that ceteris paribus the nearness in time a pleasure was to be had – its propinquity – was a rational criterion for preference of one thing over another. But it seems that in the case of Sports Medicine there are different "goods" at play that become ranked in the utilitarian calculus of discounting future health for nearness of probability of winning. Cases like these abound because high-performance athletes are focused more on their athletic achievements now than their future health status. Therefore, they adopt a "win-at-all-costs attitude" as described by Krumer et al. (2011) that discounts future health for current athletic success.

Despite its ethical provenance, it is less easy, although not impossible, to find examples beyond Sports Medicine for this form of intervention that discounts future health for another nearer in time type good. Thus, for example, women may choose early IVF treatments with large doses of hormones that may compromise their health more generally conceived. In this case, the future health of their body is compromised for a different type of good, having a child. Moreover, self-harming behaviors such as smoking and alcohol consumption also harm the long-term health of the individual for the nearness of a different kind of good. Of course, though medically relevant, these are not interventions. Less mainstream examples might be drawn from cosmetic surgery where individuals seek interventions to satisfy temporal desires for a particular physical appearance. Gender realignment surgeries and hormonal therapies may also harm the long-term health of the individual at the discount at a nearer in time kind of good viz sexual identity. A particularly challenging example might be elective amputation both in the context of Sports Medicine and outside. In the former context, it has been argued that some would elect to have transtibial surgery in order to become a paralympic athlete (McNamee et al. 2014). Outside the context of Sports Medicine, individuals also request for an otherwise limb amputation out of requests of "identity," under the umbrella of body identity integrity disorder (Müller 2009; Ryan 2009). The nature of the condition as a "genuine" medical disorder or not is currently under discussion (Giummarra et al. 2011). Uniqueness notwithstanding, it is certainly true that Sports Medicine more readily throws up cases where present high functioning is traded off against future good health. This risk-taking phenomenon is evident beyond sports in wider society of course. The extent to which famous, role model, athletes are driving this trend in cases of extreme sports, BASE jumping, solo mountaineering, as well as more prosaic activities such as football and rugby is a moot point, and certainly impinges upon questions of resources and public health. Equally uncertain is the role of Sports Medicine in facilitating risky endeavors.

Therapy, Enhancement, and the Use of Medical Means to Nonmedical Ends

The use of medical means to nonmedical ends in general philosophy of medicine raises again some particular status issues of the role of (sports) medicine in human enhancement (Edwards and McNamee 2006; Savulescu et al. 2011). It raises important questions about whether the traditional goals of medicine are therapeutic in nature (understood to include prevention) or whether they embrace nontherapeutic ends (Boorse 2015; Pellegrino 1999). A significant body of literature has arisen in the last decade concerning this issue generally and the normative force (or not) of the therapy/enhancement distinction.

Briefly, the therapy/enhancement distinction as referenced in the President's Council on Bioethics "Beyond Therapy Report" (2003) is based on Christopher Boorse's (1975, p. 77) definition of health as "normal species functioning," which defined enhancement beyond species typical functioning. According to Boorse's biostatistical theory of health (BST), health is "normal species functioning," which is the statistically typical contribution of all the organism's parts and processes to the organism's overall goals of survival and reproduction. Christopher Boorse argues that to be healthy is to function normally and that health is value-free.

Nevertheless, as demonstrated by many scholars including Scully and Rehmann-Sutter (2001), Kingma (2007), and Mills (2011), social and biological norms are inextricably linked and the biostatistical theory of species functioning cannot be not a value-free account of health, as the "norm" in a particular context contains social judgments together with biological facts. The concept of the "normal" which is considered to be value-neutral in Boorse's "normal species functioning" is not actually value-free, as it has both descriptive and normative implications. The etymology itself of the word "normal" from the latin "normalis" is telling, as "normalis" was the word used to refer to "standing at a right angle," where "norma" was the carpenter's square. Indeed, in mathematics the word "normal" can still be used to mean "perpendicular." As argued by Catherine Mills (2011, 2013) building on Canguilhem (1978), biological and social norms are inseparable and irreducible, and the reference point for normal species functioning is not to be "deduced from nature" but it is a choice that includes social norms. In other words, the concept of the "normal" is a value judgment that cannot be grounded only in descriptive statements about nature. Hence, the therapy-enhancement distinction referencing to the normal species functioning as the demarcating axis implies a normative connotation and the "existence of a directed axis along which different human embodiments can be arranged in a proper order from "worse" to "better"" (Scully and Rehmann-Sutter 2001, p. 90).

The notion of how precisely "normal" is to be understood warrants a more extensive discussion that cannot be pursued here. For present purposes, however, it is worth considering the role the distinction plays in sport medicine. If we accept the definition of enhancement as going beyond normal species typical functioning (as in the *Beyond Therapy* Report), we could say that elite athlete serve as a benchmark for normal species functioning. By pushing the species boundaries to the limit in elite performance thanks to "physician-assisted doping," some scholars like John Hoberman (2014) argue that the benchmark for normal species functioning gets pushed too. Consider an example in which the therapy-enhancement distinction in Sports Medicine is challenged. Drugs prescribed for return to play such as cortisol are considered part of therapeutic use exemption and referred to as "recovery drug." But they actually represent a very good example of a drug that although used to "restore" a previous state of health (the state of health previous to the injury) confers a performance advantage which can be compared to the advantage conferred by a performance enhancing drug (e.g., testosterone, which is rarely if ever given a Therapeutic Use Exemption (TUE) certificate according to the protocol of the World Anti-Doping Code), even though its anabolic steroid effects are very similar to the one produced by cortisol, with the only exceptions being some sports such as power lifting and bodybuilding that have World Anti-Doping Agency compliant federations.

Hamilton and Dimeo (2015) provide a recent example of recovery drug that crosses the therapy/enhancement distinction. This is cortisol, a steroid that is used to enable a return to play after shoulder injury by baseball player Ryan Zimmerman. After injuring his shoulder in the summer of 2012, Zimmerman was able to go from "being one of baseball's worst hitters to one of its best" thanks to cortisol injections whose use was considered ethically justifiable as part of a recovery drug due to a therapeutic use exemption (in times of stress it allows the body to use stored energy in the muscles, liver, and fat tissue; it does not heal the injury but simply allows the athlete to play through it). The use of a recovery drug like cortisol under a TUE not only does not restore the body to a previous health state (as it simply allows the body to play through the injury without healing) but on the contrary has long-term implications for the health of the athlete. It has been demonstrated that athletes often adopt a risky approach according to which they would sacrifice long-term health for short-term goal (Krumer et al. 2011), as highlighted above. The normative justification for this is far from straightforward. Indeed this is the conundrum of the Sports Medicine physician when confronted with the difficult decision of whether to prescribe or not cortisol (or similar "recovery drugs") to athletes who request it for a swifter return to play or training.

It should be born in mind that the T/E distinction, which is based on a biostatistical theory of health which itself presupposes a value-free concept of "normal species functioning", is in reality informed by social norms too. However, medicine and sports are two separate contexts, with different values at play. Douglas (2007) has highlighted that a drug which could confer performance advantage could be ethically justified in one context (outside of sport) but not in another (sport) because of the inherent values of the practice. Camporesi and McNamee (2012) argue along similar lines in reference to gene transfer to raise the tolerance to pain in the context of a clinical trial and of sports competition.

Returning to the testosterone case, we can see that in the context of sport it is allowed under guide of TUE (under the form of cortisol, which is an analogous of testosterone), but not for performance enhancement, because of the supposed validity of the T/E distinction. Outside the context of sport, testosterone is prescribed for supposedly "real" medical conditions such as hypogonadism where it functions as a recovery drug that also enhances performance. It is also increasingly prescribed as an "anti-aging" drug (Madrigal 2015). This second kind of prescription falls beyond the goals of medicine understood as restoration or preservation of health but presupposes a continuum between health and well-being as proper goals of medicine. This would lead us to discuss the goals of medicine and Sports Medicine and whether the traditional goals of medicine are therapeutic in nature (understood to include prevention) or whether they embrace nontherapeutic. According to Scripko (2010), the arguments that enhancement technologies do not belong to the proper scope of doctor's profession are historically inaccurate. Perhaps it will be best to follow Scully and Rehmann-Sutter (2001) who suggest abandoning the T/E as a global distinction and arguing on a case-by-case direct evaluation of the moral relevance of the distinction. So, for example, in the case of gene transfer to raise the tolerance to pain (Camporesi and McNamee 2012) one will have to evaluate the details of the biomedical technologies under discussion alongside the contextual values that inform the particular sporting practice that will form the basis of our ethical evaluation of each case (e.g., Green 2009; Murray 2009).

The Sports Physician and Their Fiduciary Relationship with Athlete Patients

In a notorious case of medical collusion with the team coach in order to help secure victory in a high profile European Cup rugby match, a British doctor once made an incision into the mouth of a player (at his request) in order to make it appear to third parties that his removal from the play had been for a legitimate blood injury. This had allowed the team to make an apparently legal substitution of a specialist kicker who might win them the match in the dying minutes (Holm and McNamee 2009). The opposing team doctor, suspecting unfair play, followed them into the dressing room soon after the player's withdrawal and the plot was uncovered. Thereafter the scandal became known as "Bloodgate." The doctor attempting to cheat the officials was subsequently reprimanded, while the team physiotherapist who colluded in the deception was struck off the professional register of physiotherapists but reinstated on appeal. Interestingly, he vowed never to return to Sports Medicine and be confronted with pressures antithetical to the Hippocratic Oath.

Sohn and Steiner (2014) argue that the sports physician has an obligation arising from the Hippocratic Oath of nonmaleficence, and cases of assisted doping or return to play break this obligation as they harm the health of the athlete. But does a nonmaleficence obligation trump the other obligations that a sports physician may have (that arise out of the contract with the athlete/team), such as beneficence? This may need to be understood in the context of Sports Medicine as an obligation to optimize the athlete performance (make the athlete as fit as possible to compete). It could be argued that a broader understand of "benefit" needs also to be specified in this context which goes beyond the health to include other "goods" such as being as fit as possible to play.

Nevertheless, it raised the ire of the British Sports Medicine community many of whom had found themselves caught in the middle of the pressures to assist team performance (at any cost) and their traditional role to act as a fiduciary to their (athlete) patient. It even prompted the quoting of Shakespeare's Macbeth: "I am in blood, stepped so far ..." wrote two physicians (Devitt and McCarthy 2010) acknowledging – after that the profession had been implicated in wrongdoing for so long that it could not see its way back.

Many of the problems that face Sports Medicine are highlighted in professional sports and perhaps exaggerated there under the influence of considerable sums of money. The issues that arise here, in addition to others concerning confidentiality and disclosure, license to practice and insurance cover for international sporting events beyond their registered jurisdiction, trustworthiness in the face of competing conflicts owed to players and their employers, are also exacerbated when the sport physician has no clear fiduciary duty to the best interests of their patient (Holm et al. 2011). Committing their services to the athlete patient will be the best means to assuage, though not necessarily to remove, the kinds of conflicts that arise when the sports physician serves two masters at the same time. But this too begs questions as to sports physicians' self-identity and vocation. To what extent should they be seen as a branch of occupational medicine, serving the welfare of co-employees for the employer, or acting as an independent fiduciary irrespective of the source of payment for their services (Holm et al. 2011).

Conclusion

The very nature of medicine and the role that health, illness and injury play in the lives of patients, means that ethical problems are likely to arise. Sports Medicine frequently resides in contested terrain because of the role that the body plays in athletic performance, and the extremes of motivation to win with more or less attention to the welfare of players. Thus sports physicians must consider very general moral considerations that apply to all persons, but also how these are heightened in terms of the knowledge they have of the particular bodies of their athlete patients and because of the things they are allowed or requested to do *by* and *on* athlete patients. These problems are ethical but fundamentally conceptual too. It seems that it is precisely due to the lack of coherent self-understanding of the nature and goals of Sports Medicine that the ethical problems appear particularly, though not uniquely or distinctly, to be found there. Instead it has been shown here that the goals of Sports Medicine are no less contested than those of medicine itself.

Definitions of Key Terms

Sports Medicine	Medicine as practiced in the context of sport
Goals of medicine	That which medical practice hopes to achieve
Sports medic/physician	Medical doctor with some specialism in sports
Therapy/enhancement distinction	Referencing to the normal species functioning based on Boorse's biostatistical theory of health and used in applied ethics not without controversies to demarcate between ethically permissible and ethically impermissible application of a technology

Summary Points

- When focussing on the goals of medicine, no distinction in kind between medicine per se and Sports Medicine can be discerned; all that can be claimed is a difference of degree.
- But key norms in medical practice are operationalized differently in Sports Medicine.
- These include respect for patients' privacy and confidentiality for example.
- In Sports Medicine, these norms are standardly overridden and information regarding an athlete's health status may be given to third parties, for example, the sports media.
- Also, in Sports Medicine the relationship between achievement of current sporting goals is also controversial since athletes may compromise health status in later life by prioritizing short-term sporting success.
- The relationship between the doctor and the athlete also generates particular problems for the sports physician.

References

Allert G, Blasszauer B, Boyd K, Callahan D (1996) The goals of medicine: setting new priorities. Hastings Cent Rep 26(6):S1

Baker J, Cobley S, Schorer J (eds) (2013) Talent identification and development in sport: international perspectives. Routledge

Beauchamp TL, Childress JF (2012) Principles of biomedical ethics, 7th edn. Oxford University Press, New York

Bentham J (1879) An introduction to the principles of morals and legislation. Clarendon, Oxford

Berryman JW (1992) Sport and exercise science: essays in the history of sports medicine. University of Illinois Press, Urbana

Boorse C (1975) On the distinction between disease and illness. Philos Public Aff 49–68

Brülde B (2001) The goals of medicine. Towards a unified theory. Health Care Anal 9(1):1–13

Callahan D, Hanson MJ (eds) (1999) The goals of medicine: the forgotten issue in health care reform. Georgetown University Press

Camporesi S (2013) Bend it like Beckham! The ethics of genetically testing children for athletic potential. Sport Ethics Philos 7(2):175–185

Camporesi S, McNamee MJ (2012) Gene transfer for pain: a tool to cope with the intractable, or an unethical endurance enhancing technology? Life Sci Soc Policy 8(1):20

Camporesi S, McNamee MJ (2016) Ethics, genetic testing, and athletic talent: children's best interests, and the right to an open (athletic) future. Physiol Genomics 48(3):191–195. doi:10.1152/physiolgenomics.00104.2015

Canguilhem G (1978) On the normal and the pathological, vol 3. Springer

Carter N (2012) Medicine, sport and the body: a historical perspective. A & C Black

Cassel EJ (1982) The nature of suffering and the goals of medicine. N Engl J Med 306(11):639–645

Clay MB, Glover KL, Lowe DT (2013) Epidemiology of concussion in sport: a literature review. J Chiropractic Med 12(4):230–251. doi:10.1016/j.jcm.2012.11.005

Devitt BM, McCarthy C (2010) "I am in blood Stepp'd in so far…": ethical dilemmas and the sports team doctor. Br J Sports Med 44(3):175–178

Douglas T (2007) Enhancement in sport, and enhancement outside sport. Stud Ethics Law Technol 1(1)

Dunn WR, George MS, Churchill L et al (2007) Ethics in sports medicine. Am J Sports Med 35 (5):840–844

Edwards SD, McNamee M (2006) Why sports medicine is not medicine. Health Care Anal 14 (2):103–109

Gard M (2010) The end of the obesity epidemic. Routledge, Abingdon

Gard M, Wright J (2005) The obesity epidemic. Routledge, Abingdon

Gillon R (2003) Ethics needs principles – four can encompass the rest – and respect for autonomy should be "first among equals". J Med Ethics 29(5):307–312

Giummarra MJ, Bradshaw JL, Nicholls MER, Hilti LM, Brugger P (2011) Body integrity identity disorder: deranged body processing, right fronto-parietal dysfunction, and phenomenological experience of body incongruity. Neuropsychol Rev 21(4):320–333

Green SK (2004) Practice makes perfect? Ideal standards and practice norms in sports medicine. Virtual Mentor 6(7)

Green GA (2009) The role of physicians, scientists, trainers, coaches and other nonathletes in athletes' drug use. In: Murray TH, Maschke KJ, Wasunna AA (eds) Performance-enhancing technologies in sports. John Hopkins University Press, Baltimore, pp 81–96

Habermas J (1975) Legitimation crisis (trans: McCarthy T). Beacon Press, Boston

Hamilton L, Dimeo P (2015) Steroids in sport: zero tolerance to testosterone needs to change. The Conversation. https://theconversation.com/steroids-in-sport-zero-tolerance-to-testosterone-needs-to-change-48774. Accessed 13 Oct 2015

Heggie V (2011) A history of British sports medicine. Manchester University Press, Manchester/New York

Hoberman J (2014) Physicians and the sports doping epidemic. AMA J Ethics Virtual Mentor 16(7):570–574. http://journalofethics.ama-assn.org/2014/07/oped1-1407.html

Holm S, McNamee M (2009) Ethics in sports medicine. BMJ 339:b3898

Holm S, McNamee MJ, Pigozzi F (2011) Ethical practice and sports physician protection: a proposal. Br J Sports Med 45(15):1170–1173

Johnson R (2004) The unique ethics of sports medicine. Clin Sports Med 23(2):175–182

Kingma E (2007) What is it to be healthy? Analysis 67(2):128–133

Krumer A, Shavit T, Rosenboim M (2011) Why do professional athletes have different time preferences than non-athletes? Judgment Decis Mak 6:542–551

Lobelo F, Stoutenberg M, Hutber A (2014) The exercise is medicine global health initiative: a 2014 update. Br J Sports Med. doi:10.1136/bjsports-2013-093080

Madrigal AC (2015) Why testosterone is the drug of the future. Fusion. http://fusion.net/story/42619/why-testosterone-is-the-drug-of-the-future/. Accessed 3 Feb

McNamee M, Partridge B (2013) Concussion in sports medicine ethics: policy, epistemic and ethical problems. Am J Bioeth 13(10):15–17

McNamee M, Savulescu J, Willick S (2014) Ethical considerations in Paralympic sport: when are elective treatments allowable to improve sports performance? PM&R 6(8):S66–S75

McNamee M, Partridge B, Anderson L (2015) Concussion ethics and sports medicine. Clin Sports Med

Mills C (2011) Futures of reproduction: bioethics and biopolitics, vol 49. Springer

Mills C (2013) Reproductive autonomy as self-making: procreative liberty and the practice of ethical subjectivity. J Med Philos 38(6):639–656

Müller S (2009) Body integrity identity disorder (BIID)—is the amputation of healthy limbs ethically justified? Am J Bioethics 9(1):36–43

Murray T (2009) Ethics and endurance-enhancing technologies in sport. In: Maschke K et al (eds) Performance-enhancing technologies in sports. Ethical, conceptual, and scientific issues, pp 141–159

Parens E (2013) On good and bad forms of medicalization. Bioethics 27(1):28–35

Pellegrino ED (1999) The goals and ends of medicine: how are they to be defined?

Ribbans B, Ribbans H, Nightingale C, McNamee M (2013) Sports medicine, confidentiality and the press. Brit J Sports Med 47(1):40–43

Ryan CJ (2009) Out on a limb: the ethical management of body integrity identity disorder. Neuroethics 2(1):21–33

Savulescu J, ter Meulen R, Kahane G (eds) (2011) Enhancing human capacities. Wiley, Oxford

Scripko PD (2010) Enhancement's place in medicine. J Med Ethics 36(5):293–296

Scully JL, Rehmann-Sutter C (2001) When norms normalize: the case of genetic "enhancement". Hum Gene Ther 12(1):87–95

Seedhouse D (2008) Ethics: the heart of health care. Wiley, Oxford

Sohn DH, Steiner R (2014) Nonmaleficence in sports medicine. Virtual Mentor 16(7):539–541. http://journalofethics.ama-assn.org/2014/07/ecas3-1407.html

Testoni D, Hornik CP, Smith PB, Benjamin DK Jr, McKinney RE Jr (2013) Sports medicine and ethics. Am J Bioeth 13(10):4–12

Tymowski G (2001) Rights and wrongs: children's participation in high-performance sports. In: Berson IR, Berson MJ, Cruz BC (eds) Cross cultural perspectives in child advocacy. pp 55–93

Webborn N, Williams A, McNamee M, Bouchard C, Pitsiladis Y, Ahmetov I, Ashley E et al (2015) Direct-to-consumer genetic testing for predicting sports performance and talent identification: consensus statement. Brit J Sports Med 49(23):1486–1491

Wittgenstein L (1953) Philosophical investigations. 1967. Blackwell, Oxford

Part V

Medical Knowledge

Medicine as Art and Science

46

Kristine Bærøe

Contents

Abstract

Conceptual understanding of the essence of medical practice is important for many reasons. For example, it is crucial for how doctors interpret their role and effectuate it in practice, to help societies regulate and organize adequate provision of health care, and to enable critique of ongoing practice and identification of improved solutions for the future. Also, it is of importance to the medical

K. Bærøe (✉)
University of Bergen, Bergen, Norway
e-mail: kristine.baroe@igs.uib.no

© Springer Science+Business Media Dordrecht 2017
T. Schramme, S. Edwards (eds.), *Handbook of the Philosophy of Medicine*,
DOI 10.1007/978-94-017-8688-1_35

profession itself as it helps distinguish medical practice from other healthcare practices as a way of supporting medical professionalism. Accounts of the essence of medical practice have extensively used the terms "art" and "science." However, the conceptual meanings of these terms are not obvious, and neither is it evident how one should perceive the relation between them. In this entry, various meanings of these terms will be addressed and their suggested internal relations in medical practice described. Finally, some practical and political challenges connected to one of the more comprehensive accounts are pointed out. In this way, the relevance of getting a firmer conceptual grip on the normative essence of medical practice is illustrated.

Introduction

Historically, discussions of medicine in terms of art and science are based on a conceptual understanding of medicine as *medical practice*. Thus, medical practice will also be the focus of this presentation. So what is the essence of practicing medicine? This question can be reformulated as both a descriptive and a normative question: What is the essence of medicine as it is in fact practiced? How should medicine ideally be practiced? The first question cannot be answered in isolation from descriptive accounts of how practicing medicine is actually organized and divided in real-world healthcare systems, and the latter question cannot be answered in isolation from normative accounts of what is considered to be the overall aim of medicine.

There is no direct access to the epistemological processes that support medical practice. Since one cannot gain knowledge of these processes by simply observing clinical work, one's understanding of them has to be based on conceptual analysis. Descriptively, one can try to account for what is actually going on in doctors' minds when they are practicing medicine. Normatively, one can discuss what should – ideally – be going on in their minds during this work. Importantly, these different perspectives must be kept apart to avoid the mistaken presumption that all doctors' medical practices coincide with ideal standards. (This assumption might be true but has to be explored empirically before being justified as an assumption.) Fortunately, much work has been carried out to elaborate accurate descriptions of processes of medical reasoning and normative ideals of medical practice. Central to many approaches are the concepts of "science" and "art" and elaborations on how these conceptualizations capture the essence of medical practice. The heading of this entry might invite one to think of these alternatives as apparent counterparts, but the general tendency in the literature is to acknowledge both categories as necessary parts of medical practice. Still, approaches may differ in how art and science in medical practice relate – or should relate – to each other.

Discussions of how to conceptualize medical practice on these terms are important for several reasons. The discussions have a bearing on how the role of being a physician is understood in general and more specifically on how doctors themselves interpret their role and effectuate it in practice. Conceptual clarification of medical practice is important for how society regulates and organizes the provision of healthcare; this can only be done adequately insofar as it corresponds with a reasonable conceptualization of the ideal content of clinical work. Also, conceptual clarity of medical practice enables one to scrutinize and criticize the impacts of external organizational arrangements on real-world practice and, in turn, enable one to identify better organizational solutions. Furthermore, conceptual clarity is called for to delimit medical practice against other kinds of healthcare activities. It also enables decisions on relevant methods for developing and improving ongoing future practices. Conceptual clarification is also increasingly important for the medical profession itself in order to justify the privileged position it occupies in organized societies. It helps the professionals to be accountable to authorities and citizens and may support trust in that the medical profession handles its societal task of providing good medical care.

This entry is structured as follows: In the first section, a general epistemological framework for clarification of the fundamental conditions for the different approaches is presented. In the second section, meanings of "medicine as art" and "medicine as science" in relation to modern medical practice are presented. Next, versions of conceptual relations between art and science in medicine are described according to assumptions that the art and the science dimensions of medical practice are (a) independent of each other, (b) integrated with each other, or (c) the art dimension encompasses essentially different knowledge bases (including science) that supplement or complement each other. In the final section, philosophical and practical challenges involved in the art of balancing different knowledge bases in medical practice are described.

Epistemological Frame

Conceptualization of medicine as art and science gives associations to two basically different scientific traditions: science of humanities and science of nature. Since the Renaissance, humanistic disciplines have been concerned with disclosing and understanding the meaning of products created by humans through hermeneutical approaches, while science of nature traditionally has been taken to disclose and explain hidden facts about nature by experimental research. More recently, the social sciences have emerged as independent disciplines. Social sciences concern societies, human behavior, and social human relations and draw upon both methods of sciences of humanities and nature. These fundamentally different objects of scientific concerns imply different methods for reaching knowledge that is justified as scientifically valid. Depending on how the core tasks of medical practice are defined, seeking to establish knowledge within medical practice has the potential of calling on all of these traditions.

The Hippocratic Oath has for thousands of years served as a conceptual frame for defining the core tasks of practicing doctors. In the original version of the Oath translated into English, medical practice is basically referred to as "art." In the modern version of the Oath, the following statement is included: "I will remember that there is art to medicine as well as science, and that warmth, sympathy, and understanding may outweigh the surgeon's knife or the chemist's drug" (Hippocratic Oath). In the old version, art refers to the whole practice of medicine considered as all-needed-capacities-included (Original Version Hippocratic Oath). However, it is described as art that can be taught to others. It is thus presumed that this art has some character of being *reproducible,* which is a criterion acknowledged for establishing knowledge within the science of nature rather than within knowledge production in the humanities. In the modern version of the Oath, art is basically related to the dimension of promoting understanding while science connects to actions involving the patient's body and that are based on knowledge that can be theoretically explained. Thus, historically, conceptualization of medicine as art within the medical profession's own constitutive declaration seems to differ with respect to its substantial meaning. In the following, medicine as art and science is basically understood according to modern medicine and existing tensions between conceptions of art and science.

Practicing medicine according to the ideal description of the modern Oath requires doctors to seek medically relevant knowledge along two different axes. They have to relate to nature in terms of seeking to identify and explain relevant features of the body in light of theoretical explanations. At the same time, they must seek to understand human products of meaning in terms of interpretations and explanations of patients' communication, reactions, and actions.

Most conspicuously, there is a fundamental epistemological gap between relating medicine to art – and by implication to the soft discipline of human science – on the one side and to science understood as the hard science of nature on the other (Snow 1998). Although the ideal description of modern medicine (the Oath) assumes that doctors base their knowledge on both, this gap allows for a different emphasis on these epistemologies and uncertainty with respect to how they should be taken to relate to each other. Empirically, emphasis on either dimension might depend on where in the medical process of identifying illness, treating or caring – and consequently, where in a specialized healthcare system – the practice to be described or assessed is found. The closer to the treatment of the bodily malfunction that medicine is practiced, the more the focus has to be on the explainable relations between intervention and expected outcome. When striving for identification of the medical issue or in providing nonphysical interhuman care, the more a focus on obtaining knowledge in terms of understanding is called for. However, one cannot conclude that in the first case medicine should be understood as science while in the latter case it is a matter of art. As the following sections will show, the science and art dimensions of practicing modern medicine have various interpretations, and the relation between them might be a bit less straightforward than suggested in the modern Hippocratic Oath.

Medicine as Science

In what sense is medical practice understood as science? One way to preliminarily clarify this dimension is to say that medical practitioners strive to be scientific and base their practice on scientific foundation (Sassower and Grodin 1987) or that medical practice is scientific (Munson 1981). Another way of putting this is to say that medical practice requires the application of science (Munson 1981; Saunders 2000). In this sense, medicine is not taken to be a science itself; medicine is rather seen as an activity being based on translation of scientific knowledge into practice.

The question, then, is: what has been considered *relevant science* for medical practice? Again, descriptive and normative perspectives must be kept apart. For the following descriptive perspective on medicine as science, the focus is on what has been considered relevant science for medicine and thus has largely shaped the development of this practice. From a normative point of view, however, this historic perspective on medical science has been contested as representing an inadequate scope of scientific concerns (Malterud 1995).

Science Versus Nonscience

Scientific knowledge should be conceptually distinguished from nonscientific knowledge. Different criteria have been suggested (e.g., scientific knowledge must be empirically testable, explanatory, predictive (Sassower and Grodin 1987). However, as the history of science shows, criteria that qualify knowledge as science are not written in stone. So, from a normative point of view, some precaution is required when it comes to claiming absolute universal distinctions between science and nonscience in general and within disciplines, like medicine, in particular. From a general point of view, however, it might be uncontroversial to say that the aim to produce articulated and systematically justified knowledge is essential in science while it is not in nonscience.

In order to claim knowledge about a state of affairs, three criteria have been considered central since being discussed in Plato's dialogue *Theaetetus*: A proposition has to be true, one has to believe it, and one has to be able to justify it. Intuitively, these claims seem reasonable. From a philosophical point of view, however, the actual meanings of these criteria can all be scrutinized and discussed (What is truth? What is it to believe? What is it to justify?). This gives rise to various theories of science, which in turn base different methodological approaches to what is considered valid knowledge. Thus, in terms of science, modern medicine can descriptively be accounted for according to the dominating scientific view on how to reach valid knowledge in the field.

Medical science in modern times has unquestionably been dominated by biomedical science (Foss 1989). Thereby, the essence of medicine understood as science in this entry basically relates to biomedical knowledge and the criteria defining the scientific activity within this area. This approach can be traced back to Descartes and his dualistic account of the human mind as something distinct from the human body (Foss 1989). Hence, the human body and the mind were subjected to different fields of study. The concept of science applied on the body remained tightly connected with what can be derived from the laws of nature. The science of nature expanded into organic disciplines, like anatomy, biology, and physiology, and these approaches proved to be a helpful and effective means to understand and develop tools to cure illness. Hence, science involved in medicine in modern times has basically been explained and practiced within a biomedical paradigm. (This applies to somatic medicine as the status of psychiatry as a science has been more contested.) At the same time, criteria defining scientific activity within this particular paradigm have also constrained the scope of what is considered valid knowledge on which to base medicine considered as a scientific medical practice.

Based on consensus, the medical community has broadly accepted the standards for evidence-based medicine (EBM). The ideal of EBM is to search for well-justified knowledge about efficacy and effectiveness of medical interventions based on experimental approaches within patient populations (Cochrane 1999). A basic principle of these clinical experiments is to strive for objectivity. For the results of the studies to be as objective as possible, one has to control for biases that might arise with respect to patient selection and outcome observations (and inherent interpretations). Therefore, participants are divided randomly into treatment and control groups. Also, the trials are double or triple blinded. In the first case, neither participants nor investigators know who receive the interventions being tested or who are in the control group. In the latter case, the groups of treatment assignments are also concealed for the team that analyzes the data. This approach is called a randomized controlled trial (RCT) and is referred to as the gold standard for medical research on clinical treatment; it tops the hierarchy of methodological approaches to knowledge ranked by the strength of evidence they produce. Scientific knowledge on which to base medicine correlates with research outcomes produced at the highest obtainable level of evidence. However, for pragmatic or ethical reasons, not all kinds of clinical research can be carried out as RCTs. Scientific knowledge can then be obtained by studies producing weaker evidence (e.g., controlled studies without randomization and observational, cohort, and case–control studies). At the bottom of the evidence hierarchy, and with very low scientific status, one finds expert opinion (e.g., expert reports of expert committees and experienced clinicians) (Essential Evidence Plus 2014).

The justification for the monopoly that the biomedical paradigm seemed to enjoy for a while has been contested (DiMatteo 1979; McWhinney 1986; Wulff 1986; Foss 1989; Malterud 1995; Saunders 2000). For instance, the recognition that medicine involves encounters between human subjects and not merely human bodies calls for a different kind of scientific approach than the one vindicated on the quantifiable conditions characterizing biomedical research alone (Malterud 1995). Human interaction is taken to be an essential part of medical practice. Thus, interpretive qualitative approaches developed within the tradition of humanities are called upon to inform medical practice. This acknowledgment also implies the need for including not only quantitative but also qualitative research approaches in the EBM framework.

From Science to Practice

Scientific results do not present themselves with a manual of how they should be used in medical practice. There is a gap between medical scientific research (broadly construed) and medical practice that needs to be bridged. At least two fundamental challenges arise, and these are both connected to epistemic uncertainty. For one, how can practitioners be expected to gather all information and make use of the best available evidence in the myriad of published research? There is, of course, a practical side to this issue that has to do with time allocation. Philosophically, the core of this problem has to do with feasible expectations concerning individual assessments of strength of evidence. Proponents of basing medical practice on evidence have found a solution to the first challenge. Frameworks for systematically synthesizing knowledge and evidence assessment within medical research into guidelines have been developed (Woolf et al. 2012). The development of guidelines aims to reduce the messiness of the field of published research and provide healthcare personnel with tools for smoother and more feasible implementation of evidence in practice. It is worth noticing that the process of gathering and assessing knowledge cannot be considered as an objective and value-neutral activity in itself; clinical guidelines represent recommended policies for shaping practice and involve value trade-offs and judgment (Opel et al. 2013). Nevertheless, guidelines provide doctors with helpful manuals to handle the uncertainty related to the assessment of evidence. However, at the end of the day it is left to the doctors – and their clinical judgment – to choose whether to rely on these tools in their daily medical practice.

Proponents of EBM have been careful in pointing out that simply complying with evidence-based guidelines will not necessarily amount to adequate healthcare (Sackett et al. 1996). The evidence is based on population studies, and individual patients might present themselves with atypical conditions, comorbidity, and various personal preferences. Ultimately, this translational process has to lean upon an individual healthcare worker's judgment. It has to do so both to judge which recommending (synthesized) guideline is relevant in a particular case and then to assess whether this guideline actually covers the situation of the patient in question. Within this translational work bridging between general knowledge and particular cases, the art dimension of clinical work – or at least part of it – is located (Saunders 2000). This is independent of whether science is understood specifically according to an EBM framework or to a less specific knowledge concept. I will elaborate on this interpretation of medicine as art below. For now it is worth noting that art understood in the broad sense of representing a kind of translational judgment is also considered a crucial condition for adequately realizing science in successful evidence-based practice.

Medicine as Art: General

Attempts to grasp the content of medicine in terms of art can be a challenge. A reason for this is that medicine as art has, to a large extent, merely been negatively defined by pointing out what medicine as science does not cover. It has succinctly summed up how the art of medicine is often described by contrasts – being concerned with the particular rather than the general, practical knowledge rather than theoretical; it includes the soul and is not merely focused on the body; it pays attention to mental processes and the unspecified effects of treatment (the doctor as a scientist tries to exclude the placebo effect; as an artist he/she makes use of it); it is concerned with values and not only facts; it concerns intuitions and affections and not merely rationality and knowledge; it provides courage and not merely medicine; it listens and not merely hears; it aims to restore rather than construes or generates; it integrates diagnosing and treatment (as science has separated) (Hofmann 2001).

The art of medicine is also accounted for independently of science. The art dimension has been described to encompass interpretations stemming from interhuman action (Malterud 1995); it can be taken to include tacit know-how based on experience (Malterud 1995), as well as any heuristics used to bring about practical conclusions under uncertainty (McDonald 1996). Moreover, it has been associated with the skill of bringing about a healthy outcome by technical interventions (i.e., according to the antique term *techne* (Hofmann 2003)) and the intellectual virtue *phronesis* (Gatens-Robinson 1986; Widdershoven-Heerding 1987; Davis 1997).

These ways of defining medicine as art can meaningfully be cataloged across two different accounts of how art comes into play in clinical care. This can happen, as already mentioned, within the work carried out by the judgment in translating general knowledge (broadly construed) into particular cases by practical reasoning and more specifically by involving and combining both nonmedical and biomedical knowledge in clinical care in order to bring about health.

Medicine as Art: Translating General Knowledge into Particular Cases

The process of translating theoretical knowledge into clinical practice cannot itself be labeled a scientific activity. From an epistemic point of view, particular clinical assessments are always subjected to some extent of uncertainty in knowing whether all relevant symptoms are uncovered, knowing which guideline – if any- to apply and in knowing how a particular body will react to treatment. In this translational process where the individual patient does not present him- or herself in any predefined manner, human reasoning cannot purposively work in a predefined automatic manner if the goal is to reach a certain health outcome. The literature describes heuristics available to the doctor's reasoning like rules of thumb and extrapolation (McDonald 1996). In sum, clinical judgment can encompass any ad hoc strategy or heuristic the individual doctor actual makes use of in order to bring the particular clinical situation of uncertainty to a practical conclusion. Thus, judgment can address issues concerning the patient's emotions; it can strategically produce health effects by comforting and not merely by medical theories (e.g., by actively alleviating fear and by downplaying the significance of observed anomalies); it can be based on values, experience-based intuitions, affections, and interpretative listening to what the patient – consciously or not – is communicating; it can encourage rather than provide medical fixes.

It is important not to confuse medicine as art with the idea that it represents a gift or some kind of esoteric knowledge. Strategies and heuristics can be learned through experiences (Malterud 1995). When they work automatically in experienced doctors, their clinical perceptions and conclusions may occur as being intuitive. This, however, does not necessarily make the emerging knowledge about the particular case tacit in the sense that it is impossible to articulate. Nevertheless, the translational reasoning process required to bridge between general knowledge and particular cases under uncertainty is not objectively controllable in the way scientific processes are required to be. The process is both context driven by features of the situation in question and personal in the way that trade-offs invoke a doctor's personal values. Thus, exercised clinical judgment does not follow any detectable systematic patterns that can be picked up, described, and reproduced in an objective scientific matter. In this sense, associations to uncontrollable, unforeseen reasoning processes supposed to be part of making art an aesthetic activity explain the labeling. But this alone does not promote any reasons to disregard the reasoning activity as something mysterious – it might simply represent another kind of rationality than the one presumed by the biomedical paradigm (Malterud 1995). The art of making clinical judgment along these lines can logically result in both failures and successes depending on the outcome. This is important to remember since one might be inclined to associate the art characteristic of medicine merely to clinical success stories.

Medicine as Art: Combining Contributions of Both Nonmedical and Biomedical Knowledge

As just pointed out, judgment is inevitably called for, even when translating science into practice. However, the interpretation of medicine as art is also distinguished from the interpretation of medicine as science in yet another way. In this version, the essence of medical practice considered as art is seen as being based on substantive contributions of knowledge coming from outside the biomedical domain. This conceptualization of medicine as art comes in at least two versions. On the one side, this conceptualization of medicine as art can be seen as referring to merely moral aspects of interhuman interaction (Saunders 2000). That is, the art elements refer to elements required for a morally justified medical practice where respectful treatment of the patient is emphasized.

In the other version, the elements involved in art are basically understood as everything involved in clinical encounters, including biomedical knowledge. Patients are fully recognized as human beings with lives and contextualized worries; they present themselves with both physical and mental attributes that must be taken into account in order for doctors to be able to respond with good and effective care. Malterud (1995) specified capacities that stem from interhuman encounters and that are considered crucial in order to adequately handle a patient's need together with biomedical knowledge. These capacities are not compatible with the construed rationality of the traditional biomedical perspective on medicine.

Malterud noted that these capacities should also be acknowledged for producing core knowledge for an ideal medical practice and as a consequence should be included in clinical epistemology.

Conceptual Relationships Between Medicine as Art and Medicine as Science

How is the conceptual relation between art and science in medicine described? Based on the literature, it seems apt to distinguish between three different versions of how art and science might relate conceptually in medical practice:

(a) *The art and the science dimensions of medical practice are independent of each other.*

The perspective reflected in the modern version of the Oath indicates some separateness between "art" and "science": Art is associated with promoting interrelational understanding while "science" is associated with skills required for technical interventions. Also, if art is basically considered as skillful treatment of patients merely in a moral sense, then art and science can be considered as distinct and independent elements in medical practice.

(b) *The art and science dimensions of medical practice are integrated with each other.*

When art captures the sense of translating general knowledge into particular cases, art is at the same time considered as an intrinsic part of practicing medicine on line with applying science. This would be the case independently of how successful the translation is according to any evaluative perspectives on medical performance. Analytically, any perspectives on medical practice that claim the inseparable nature of art and science, or claims that practical reasoning in principle can be broken down to such elements being inextricably bound together (like in conceptualizations of techne and phronesis), present the relationship between art and science as an matter of integration.

(c) *The art dimension encompasses essentially a different knowledge basis that supplements or complements the science dimension.*

The view that both biomedical and nonmedical constructions of knowledge are needed for *adequate* care and thus an adequate clinical epistemology presumes that knowledge emerging from interhuman encounters either supplements or complements scientific knowledge (i.e., biomedical science) in medical practice. In the first case, art will supplement biomedical knowledge if it provides nonbiomedical information that justifies nonstandardized interventions (e.g., a lack of a social network might justify a longer hospital stay or a patient's preference on intervention alternatives is taken into account). In the second case, art will complement biomedical knowledge if it is crucial in identifying what is at stake and what intervention is called for in order to achieve a beneficial outcome (e.g., when burdening social relations create physical symptoms). In both these cases different "types of knowledge construction are intimately interwoven in dialectic interplay" (Malterud 1995).

Synthesizing Approaches to the Role of Art and Science in Medicine

Exercising medicine as an art requires interpretive capacities which are called for in the translation of general scientific biomedical knowledge into particular cases; in acting as moral agents in encounters with patients; in establishing nonbiomedical knowledge with relevance for providing adequate care; and in the overall activity of combining all of these elements, including biomedical science, in the practice of medicine. This latter version of an all-things-considered art might very well equate with a broadly construed conception of practical, medical reasoning.

Concluding Remarks

Empirically, in medical practice all of the conceptually different relationships between art and science might very well be played out in a single clinical consultation. There are no logical bars to that. In that case, the conceptualization of art in the original version of the Hippocratic Oath as a comprehensive all-things-considered kind of art might in fact be closer to real-world medical practice than the more specified art concept presented in the modern version of the Oath.

In version (c) above, when the art dimension encompasses differently construed knowledge bases that either complement or supplement each other, careful balancing between the two categories is required. Structurally, evaluations of such a balancing process depend on what the aim of the medical practice is considered to be. This aim is rarely clearly stated in other than very general terms (like in legal regulations of provided healthcare). For instance, the aim of medical practice can be described as providing healthcare of high quality or healthcare according to the patient's best interest. In their clinical practice, doctors must both give this aim a substantive interpretation on a case-to-case basis and balance the concerns to emphasize accordingly. Uncertainty with respect to how balancing between different knowledge bases should be carried out within medical practice gives rise to various philosophical and practical issues. The list is not exhaustive but points to the fact that conceptualizations of medicine as art and science have relevance for the shaping of real-world healthcare provision and politics.

Epistemological Challenges

Malterud's account of a more adequate clinical epistemology requires supplementing/complementing qualitative research on premises of the tradition of the humanities. Still, the fundamental question concerning the normative limits of what to include/exclude in medical practice remains to be answered. Moreover, who decides on where to put the limits, i.e., what are relevant concerns and what are not?

Challenges in Organized Healthcare and Medical Education

The aim of medical practice may differ across different departments of a healthcare system, e.g., between primary and secondary healthcare. In primary care, diagnostic work may require doctors to take on a very broad perspective on what might be at stake before eventually referring the patient to the specialized care, i.e., for less broad approaches to specific domains of somatic or mental care. To correctly view the overall picture, GPs might be required to take more nonbiomedical information into account than their colleagues in secondary care specialities. Thus, adequate care might require unequal stress on the art dimension versus the scientific dimension depending on where in the system the healthcare is provided. How can this be handled by educational training?

Political Challenges

With a lack of clear instructions on how to balance the art and science dimensions of medical practice, unequal performance among clinicians is to be expected. For instance, clinicians might differ in what scope of nonmedical social concerns they find reasonable to include in their medical practice. This will, for one, lead to inequality in healthcare provided to patients with equal conditions and equal circumstances by different doctors. From certain positions on the social justice of healthcare, this will be unfair. Secondly, within public healthcare systems, doctors are given decisive discretionary power on distributional matters that ideally should be up to those with democratic powers to decide (Eriksen 2001). Should something be done to counter these "black holes" of democracy?

Challenges for the Medical Professionalism

The indeterminate nature of the overall goal of medical practice and its uncertain implications for how individual medical doctors should balance different knowledge bases in their practice also creates challenges for professional accountability. If there is no way to hold doctors accountable for the way they stress core elements in clinical epistemology relative to each other, there is nothing to support patients' trust in the professional's judgment in this regard.

Definition of Key Terms

Descriptive	Describes how something *is* without evaluating.
Normative	Describes how something *should be/should not be*, i.e., what would be ideal, good, right, fair, bad, wrong, unfair, etc.

Epistemology	Philosophical approaches concerned with the nature and scope of knowledge.
Biomedical paradigm	Set of broadly accepted premises structuring biomedical research.
Heuristics	Experience-based strategies for problem-solving and inquiries.

Summary Points

- Medical practice is often described in terms of "art" and "science."
- It is not obvious how these terms should be understood, neither how the relation between them should be described.
- Various meanings of medicine as science and medicine as art and the relation between them are presented.
- Medicine as science tends to refer to biomedical sciences, but an adequate clinical epistemology calls for supplementing/complementing this research with interpretive, qualitative research on phenomena occurring in interhuman encounters between doctor and patient.
- Exercising medicine as an art requires interpretive capacities, which is called for in the translation of general scientific biomedical knowledge into particular cases; in acting as moral agents in encounters with patients; in establishing nonbiomedical knowledge with relevance for providing adequate care; and in the overall activity of combining all of these elements, including biomedical science, in the practice of medicine.

References

Cochrane AL (1999) Effectiveness & efficiency: random reflections on health services. Royal Society of Medicine Press Limited, London

Davis FD (1997) Phronesis, clinical reasoning, and Pellegrino's philosophy of medicine. Theor Med Bioeth 18(1–2):173–195

DiMatteo MR (1979) A Social-psychological analysis of physician-patient rapport: toward a science of the art of medicine. J Soc Issues 35(1):12–33

Eriksen EO (2001) Demokratiets sorte hull - om spenningen mellom fag og politikk i veldferdstaten. Abstrakt Forlag, Oslo

Essential Evidence Plus. Available via http://www.essentialevidenceplus.com/product/ebm_loe.cfm?show=grade. Accessed 31 Aug 2014

Foss L (1989) The challenge to biomedicine: a foundations perspective. J Med Philos 14(2):165–191

Gatens-Robinson E (1986) Clinical judgment and the rationality of the human sciences. J Med Philos 11(2):167–178

Hippocratic Oath. Available via http://guides.library.jhu.edu/content.php?pid=23699&sid=190964. Accessed 31 Aug 2014

Hofmann B (2001) Legen som kroppstekniker. Tidsskr Nor Laegeforen 121(10):1266–1269

Hofmann B (2003) Medicine as techne – a perspective from antiquity. J Med Philos 28(4):403–425

Malterud K (1995) The legitimacy of clinical knowledge: towards a medical epistemology embracing the art of medicine. Theor Med Bioeth 16(2):183–198

McDonald CJ (1996) Medical heuristics: the silent adjudicators of clinical practice. Ann Intern Med 124(1_Part_1):56–62

McWhinney IR (1986) Are we on the brink of a major transformation of clinical method? CMAJ Can Med Assoc J 135(8):873

Munson R (1981) Why medicine cannot be a science. J Med Philos 6(2):183–208

Opel DJ, Taylor JA, Phillipi CA, Diekema DS (2013) The intersection of evidence and values in clinical guidelines: who decides what constitutes acceptable risk in the care of children? Hosp Pediatr 3(2):87–91

Original Version Hippocratic Oath. The Internet Classics Archive. Available via http://classics.mit.edu/Hippocrates/hippooath.html. Accessed 31 Aug 1014

Sackett D, Rosenberg WMC, Gray JAM, Haynes RB, Richardson WS (1996) Evidence based medicine: what it is and what it isn't. BMJ 312(7023):71–72

Sassower R, Grodin MA (1987) Scientific uncertainty and medical responsibility. Theor Med Bioeth 8(2):221–234

Saunders J (2000) The practice of clinical medicine as an art and as a science. Med Humanit 26(1):18–22

Snow CP (1998) The two cultures. Cambridge University Press, Cambridge/New York

Widdershoven-Heerding I (1987) Medicine as a form of practical understanding. Theor Med Bioeth 8(2):179–185

Woolf S, Schunemann H, Eccles M, Grimshaw J, Shekelle P (2012) Developing clinical practice guidelines: types of evidence and outcomes; values and economics, synthesis, grading, and presentation and deriving recommendations. Implement Sci 7(1):61

Wulff HR (1986) Rational diagnosis and treatment. J Med Philos 11(2):123–134

Biomedical Reductionist, Humanist, and Biopsychosocial Models in Medicine

47

S. Nassir Ghaemi

Contents

Abstract

In this chapter, three basic approaches to medicine are examined. The biological reductionistic model is criticized commonly but it is found to have important merits. The biopsychosocial (BPS) model is praised commonly but it is found to

S.N. Ghaemi (✉)
Department of Psychiatry, Tufts University School of Medicine, Boston, MA, USA

Mood Disorders Program, Tufts Medical Center, Boston, USA

Cambridge Health Alliance, Harvard Medical School, Boston, USA
e-mail: nghaemi@tuftsmedicalcenter.org

© Springer Science+Business Media Dordrecht 2017
T. Schramme, S. Edwards (eds.), *Handbook of the Philosophy of Medicine*,
DOI 10.1007/978-94-017-8688-1_38

have many limitations. The BPS model is seen as representing eclecticism, which in turn represents a relativism about truth which is part of current cultural mores. Both perspectives are examined in the context of the history of medicine, where two basic tendencies are identified: the Galenic and Hippocratic approaches. The Galenic approach is based on biological speculation and is holistic and individualized to the patient. It held sway for most of recorded human history but caused much suffering through its false ideology. The Hippocratic approach is parroted but little understood: it is based on clinical observation, refusal to treat symptoms, and a commitment to identifying diseases. It is biologically reductionistic but humanistic. The evolution of modern medical breakthroughs, such as the antibiotic revolution, is seen as reflecting a rejection of Galenic models for Hippocratic ones. The BPS model is seen as a return to Galenic assumptions. A medical humanist model for the future, based on Hippocratic foundations and revised by awareness of the strengths and limitations of biological reductionism, is proposed.

Introduction

Three major approaches to a basic philosophy of medicine can be defined as follows:

Biomedical reductionist models take the view that all disease can be reduced to biological causes in the body; typically, treatments of those diseases are also biological in character, such as surgery or medications.

Humanist models take the view that illnesses sometimes may reflect diseases of the body, but sometimes they reflect problems between human beings of a non-biological nature, such as psychological or personal concerns. Treatment can be biological, but it often is not, entailing psychological or personal interventions such as counseling or self-help programs.

Biopsychosocial models take the view that all disease consists of an interaction between biological, psychological, and social causes; typically treatments of those diseases are also multiple, with biological (medications or surgery), psychological (counseling or self-help), and social (public health policy) interventions.

These three basic approaches to medicine have historical roots. This essay explores those historical roots and examines the concepts that evolved over time; it also will critique how those concepts have fared in medical practice.

Historical Background: Galenic Versus Hippocratic Approaches

The largest themes in the philosophy of medicine can be traced in historical sources to two basic lines of thinking: Galenic versus Hippocratic approaches. This claim is simplified necessarily, but simplification may help to clarify basic differences that matter more to the general reader than smaller and more nuanced distinctions that matter more to specialists in the history of medicine. In this description, those nuances are being minimized not because they do not exist, but because they do not matter for the purposes of this chapter. There will be some combining of perspectives of different thinkers in one or the other of these basic philosophies of medicine, and the use of Hippocrates and Galen as the primary leaders in these schools of thought is based on their historical influence, with an awareness of the importance of other individuals before and after them in advancing or revising or clarifying their actual viewpoints. There also is awareness of the limits of historical documentation: As relates to Hippocratic writings, there is awareness of the fact that they mostly represent lecture notes, with lack of clarity at times of the exact identify of the lecturer; and they are incomplete. As relates to Galenic writings, they are extensive, but have passed through centuries of translation and revision. Basic sources exist for the overview below, to which the reader is directed (Jones 1931; Temkin 1973, 2002; Jouanna 1999; Porter 1999; Nutton 2001; McHugh 2006; Wootton 2007; Ghaemi 2008), as opposed to many repeated references after each statement made in the following summary.

With these scholarly caveats, the two basic trends of thinking in the history of medicine will be described.

Hippocratic Approaches

Hippocrates lived in the late fifth century BC, a contemporary of Socrates and Plato in a very exciting time of ancient Greek culture. His school of medicine, from the island of Kos, was set up as an alternative to the already prominent views of the school of Knidos. Both schools were influenced by the Egyptian tradition in medicine, centered in the city of Alexandria, as well as ancient sources from the Middle East (Mesopotamia). The school of Knidos, established around 700 BC, was the oldest and original source of the teaching of medicine in ancient Greece. Hippocrates was a successor to other teachers from Kos who revised and evolved ideas from Knidos, combined with new ideas influenced by the classic philosophers of Athens such as Socrates.

Most physicians pay lip service to Hippocrates and, if asked, will associate the man with the Hippocratic oath and the maxim "first do no harm." In fact, Hippocrates never said this; the phrase was invented in the mid-nineteenth century and falsely attributed to the Greek physician (Wootton 2007). Despite its historical falsehood, if we ask what this maxim means, most physicians, never having taken a history of medicine course, will tend to reply that it means that one should not harm the patient, first and foremost. Or perhaps they will translate it into standard risk-benefit analysis, where the benefits of treatment should outweigh the harm. This is all superficial. It would be like physicists saying that Newton sat under a tree and taught us that things fall. There was much more to Newton than the law of gravity; there is much more to Hippocrates than the Hippocratic oath.

There is a general misunderstanding of the term "Hippocratic," often associated with the ethical maxims of the Hippocratic oath, such as "first do no harm," later Latinized as *Primum non nocere*. A false claim, as noted, the full original quote was in the maxim of Epidemics I: "As to diseases, make a habit of two things – to help, or at least to do no harm" (Jones 1931). The Hippocratic tradition in medicine is thus identified simply with a conservative approach to treatment. While partly true, this popular simplification fails to capture the deeper genius of Hippocratic thinking, for its ethical maxims were not abstract opinions but rather grew out of its theory of disease.

The *basic* Hippocratic belief is that nature is the source of healing, and the job of the physician is to aid nature in the healing process. A non-Hippocratic view is that nature is the source of disease and that the physician (and surgeon) needs to fight nature to effect cure. Even in ancient Greece, physicians had many potions and pills to cure ailments; Hippocrates resisted that interventionistic medicine, and his treatment recommendations often involved diet, exercise, and wine – all designed to strengthen natural forces in recovery. If nature will cure, then the job of the physician is to hasten nature's work carefully and to avoid adding to the burden of illness.

Based on this philosophy of disease, the Hippocratics divided diseases into three types: *curable*, *incurable*, and *self-limiting*. *Curable* diseases require intervention, aimed at aiding the natural healing process. *Incurable* diseases generally were best left untreated, since treatments didn't improve illness and, due to side effects, would only add to suffering. *Self-limiting* diseases also didn't require treatment, since they improved spontaneously; by the time any benefits of treatment would occur, the illness would resolve by itself, again leaving only an unnecessary side-effect burden.

The Hippocratic approach emphasized clinical observation. Although the four humor theory was accepted, the presence or absence of disease was based on clinical sign and symptoms, not just speculation based on the four humors. This was another great breakthrough in Hippocratic thinking, an approach which would be submerged for over a millennium: base your thinking on observable clinical facts, not on your theories.

The basic Hippocratic insight into treatment was that the practice of medicine meant knowing when *not* to treat, not just assuming that one should always treat all symptoms or all patients.

Galenic Approaches

Galen came along in ancient Rome in the second century AD, over half a millennium after Hippocrates. But his influence would last almost two millennia, and in many ways, he can be seen as the most influential figure in the history of medicine. This is because Galen's approach surpassed Hippocrates' thinking and remained influential until the present day and, in fact, can be seen as still the most preeminent approach to medical practice today.

Although Galen wrote respectfully of Hippocrates and cloaked himself in the mantle of Hippocrates' reputation, he diverged remarkably from Hippocrates on the key topic of treatment. Galen loved drugs; Hippocrates distrusted them. They agreed on the humoral theory, because there was no other conception of disease in ancient times. But they differed on everything else, with key differences on three matters: (a) the relative importance of clinical observation as opposed to biological theory, (b) the relative importance of natural history, and (c) the basic attitude of the physician toward treatment.

As noted above, the Hippocratic approach emphasized clinical observation as the most important aspect of medical knowledge. Galen's approach was quite different (Temkin 1973). He emphasized biological theory. Galen took the four humor theory very seriously, and inferred biological causes for the humors (the heart, for instance, heated the blood), and then would make treatment decisions on the basis of his biological theories (almost always some variant of bleeding). Galen was a theorizer, in contrast to Hippocrates who was an observer. The Hippocratic approach also emphasized the natural history of illness; nature was not seen as the enemy, and in fact it was noted that many illnesses resolved on their own, meaning naturally. Nature itself healed those illnesses. For Galen, nature was the enemy. Only the doctor healed. The doctor went to war against nature, whereas the Hippocratic doctor, seeing nature as a friend, was not going to war at all against anything. The attitude of the Galenic doctor then was aggressive: many treatments were given, and the patient suffered so the disease could be cured. This way of thinking is behind the old medical joke: The disease was cured, but unfortunately the patient died. The Hippocratic doctor would let a disease live, even for decades, as long as the patient survived. Hence the humorous comment from the nineteenth-century Hippocratic physician Oliver Wendell Holmes who remarked that the secret to longevity is to have a chronic illness and take good care of it (Holmes 1891).

An interesting aspect of Galenic medicine is that it was, in modern terms, "holistic" and "individualized to the patient." This is because the modern concept of disease was not present in ancient times. For Galen, there was only one "disease": an imbalance of the four humors. This imbalance could happen in an infinity of combinations in each individual person. So in a way, there was an infinity of diseases, one for each human being. Thus, he emphasized individualizing treatment to each patient: You get bleeding of this amount, this way, for this long; another person gets bleeding that amount, that way, for that long. You could add one of a thousand chemicals or herbs in varied combinations, and each person gets his or her own treatment – all based on pure speculation (Temkin 1973).

Galen wrote a great deal, and persuasively, and many of his writings survived. Hippocrates wrote little if at all; his ideas were recorded mostly as lecture notes, and most of them did not survive into the Middle Ages. Galen's ideas would take over the philosophy of medicine for a millennium.

The Evolution of Medical Thinking in the Middle Ages

From the fall of Rome until the Renaissance, a millennium of timespan represented the gradual explanation and transmittal of Galenic philosophy throughout the world. The main source of transmission was the Islamic world, and there the most prominent medical thinker was Ibn Sina (Avicenna, eleventh century AD). (Much that follows can be sourced in a current text (Pormann and Savage-Smith 2007)). His main work, the Canon, which consisted of 14 volumes, would be taught as the primary medical text for over 500 years, not only in the Middle East but also throughout Christian Europe well into the seventeenth century. Although Ibn Sina has been held in high regard in the Islamic world, his basic philosophy of medicine is Galenic and not original to him. Ibn Sina expounded the four humor theory in detail and supported bleeding as a basic approach to treating many supposed illnesses; he also wrote extensively about over a thousand herbal or medicinal treatments, most of which was based on biological speculation rather than on clinical observation. He did make some clinical observations that stood the test of time, such as the sexual transmission of some diseases. By and large, though, the effect of Ibn Sina's work was to cement the influence of Galenic thinking throughout the Middle Ages.

In contrast to the powerful impact of Ibn Sina, some other Islamic physicians took up the basic philosophy of Hippocrates and tried to oppose Galenic orthodoxy. Among these, al-Razi (Rhazes, ninth century AD) and Ibn Rushd (Averroes, twelfth century AD) are prominent. Razi was the only medieval physician to directly attack Galen, in a book titled "Doubts about Galen." He directly attacked the legitimacy of the humoral theory and based his writing on disease purely on clinical observation, as in the Hippocratic tradition. In so doing, he described measles and smallpox. Like the Hippocratics, he emphasized the importance of *not* treating many patients and the need to avoid intervening in incurable diseases. Galen's influence was so profound that Razi couched his criticisms in the context of expressing great appreciation for the "master" Galen. Nonetheless, Razi was attacked widely for his temerity in criticizing the great Galen. Razi's long-term influence in the Islamic world may have been also limited due to his free-thinking and secular philosophy, as opposed to Ibn Sina's more mainstream religious orthodoxy.

Three centuries after Razi, Ibn Rushd would arise in Islamic Spain and have more influence. Ibn Rushd also was a liberal thinker, but this was not a problem in liberal Spain, where Islamic rulers were more tolerant than in the Persia of Razi or the Iraq of Ibn Sina. Ibn Rushd returned, like Razi, to Hippocrates and opposed the Galenic aggressiveness of Ibn Sina's philosophy. He did so through a Commentary on the Canon of Ibn Sina. Again, he emphasized clinical observation over the humoral theory, and he noted the importance of avoiding treatment in many patients. Like Razi, Ibn Rushd was more secular than Ibn Sina and more liberal in his political and social philosophy. His work was translated into Christian Europe from Islamic Spain, and thus he had longer-standing influence in the late Middle Ages.

The Seventeenth-Century Breakthrough

The Enlightenment did not occur out of the blue. It was an outgrowth of the impact in Christian Europe of more liberal elements of Islamic thought, combined with a rediscovery of ancient Greek and Roman texts. The key figure in modern

Enlightenment philosophy, its founder, was Descartes (sixteenth century), and he was influenced by the philosophical writings of thinkers like Ibn Rushd.

In medical thinking, the beginning of a change was heralded by the controversial Paracelsus (sixteenth century AD) of Switzerland. He picked up the mantle of Razi, without realizing it, when he became famous for rejecting Galen's authority and insisting on clinical observation. Like Razi, he was attacked widely and became quite embittered. A contemporary of Martin Luther, Paracelsus can be seen as a medical reformer who failed in his own time, but whose efforts represented the beginning of the end of the millennium-long reign of Galen. He rejected the humoral theory, arguing that many diseases were caused by outside causes, not by internal changes in the body. He strongly opposed bleeding, still by far the most prominent treatment in medicine in his era. He proposed many different minerals and medicines instead. He argued for cleanliness in managing wounds as opposed to the classic Galenic approach of frequent debridement.

Three major thinkers would soon follow in the seventeenth century, all contemporaries of each other, and together, they would succeed where Paracelsus had failed: they would kill Galen as the tyrant of medicine. These three men were Thomas Sydenham, William Harvey, and Giovanni Morgagni (Porter 1999; Wootton 2007).

Sydenham was an active support of the English revolutionaries and also was revolutionary in his medical thinking. Known as the English Hippocrates (Low 1999), he overtly returned to the basic Hippocratic idea of clinical observation and laid forth the general concept of clinical "syndromes" representing "signs and symptoms," a perspective now standard in clinical medicine, but quite radical in his age, since it rejected any reliance on the biological theorizing of Galen.

Where Sydenham rejected the whole concept of biological theorizing, Harvey replaced Galen's biological theorizing with a new approach of observation-based biological experiment. In so doing, Harvey famously identified the circulation of the blood. Sydenham opposed Harvey's biological theories, emphasizing the need for clinical observation, but both men together had the final impact of killing Galen, at least in the philosophy of medicine. If one was to be biological, then it would have to be based on experiment in the here and now, not based on what theories one might speculate about without testing them in experiment. Further, where biological knowledge was limited, clinical observation was seen as more scientifically valid than any other biological speculation.

Morgagni was Italian, unlike the other two English physicians. Morgagni became famous for his new concept of disease, described in his classic book "The seats and causes of disease." Morgagni made the radical claim, again now seen as commonplace, that diseases were caused by abnormalities in organs of the body. When combined with Sydenham's syndrome theory, it was a minor step to connect clinical syndromes identified through careful observation to abnormalities in organs of the body.

Finally, after more than a thousand years, Enlightenment medicine had a new explanation for diseases that could replace the four humor theory. It is important to note that this modern, radical, scientifically sound new approach was *not* holistic or individualized to the patient, as in Galen's theory. All patients with the same abnormalities of the same organ would have the same clinical syndromes. Morgagni and Sydenham were identifying the group nature of disease and the fact that human beings were not individually different when it came to many diseases. Similarly, Harvey's discovery of the circulation of the blood was not different in one individual versus another: this expression of human biology was the same in everyone.

Statistics

Following these basic clinical and biological breakthroughs of the seventeenth century, the medical profession began to be influenced gradually by the birth of the new field of statistics in the eighteenth century. As exemplified by the French revolutionary thinker Pierre-Simon Laplace, the basic philosophy of modern statistics was founded on the view that mathematical methods would now be used to quantify, rather than ignore, error. Overlapping with Laplace in the late eighteenth century, and living well into the nineteenth century, the figure who founded medical statistics, and first applied those new mathematical approaches to medicine, was Pierre Charles Alexandre Louis, who introduced "the numerical method" to clinical medicine and applied it most famously to the first experimental study of the two-millennium-long practice of bleeding (Stigler 1986).

In 1828, he published the research study which has had, in my estimation, the most profound impact in the international medical practice. He examined the outcomes of bleeding for pneumonia in 77 patients in Paris (Yankauer 1996). Since it was considered unethical to withhold medical treatment that was thought to be effective, he did not try to see what happened in pneumonia with versus without bleeding; instead he compared outcomes in those who received more versus less bleeding. In some subjects bleeding was given early in the course of pneumonia, in others later. He observed that the longer one waited to bleed patients, the greater the percentage of those who survived.

The medical world was shocked. Even Louis did not try to make his claim straightforwardly. Like Razi a thousand years earlier, Louis was apologetic in his challenge to Galenic doctrine. In his paper, he stated that his study did not mean that bleeding was never effective, but rather that it might be delayed and used in later stages of pneumonia. For his cautious interpretation, Louis was pilloried in the letters to the editor of the French medical journal in which his study was published. Many physicians were enraged that Louis would place individual patients into a numerical test and that he would treat human beings as numbers. His methods were seen as unhumanistic and illiberal.

These critics were faced with the reality of the numbers, though. Louis attracted young physicians from around the world, bred in democratic nations, like the great Oliver Wendell Holmes, who, from his base as a Harvard professor of medicine, would go on to be a leading figure in American medicine. Holmes was a democrat and a humanist, and he saw that Louis' medical statistics, like science in general, was consistent with a humanistic outlook (Holmes 1891). If science could prove that bleeding was not effective, then so much the worse for bleeding.

Louis' work was the beginning of the end of bleeding. In about a decade, the importation of leeches to Paris declined from the millions to the thousands. It would still take half a century, until around the turn of the twentieth century, until the practice of bleeding ended.

What had begun back before the fifth century BC, when Hippocrates and his students roamed the island of Cos, would last until about 1900, when steam engines and electricity and large industrial factories existed. Galen's favorite treatment finally was let go by the world's physicians after more than 2,000 years.

The Impact of Pathology

Along with the development of medical statistics, the nineteenth century saw another new method in medicine that would prove to be the final step in leaving ancient methods behind and beginning the era of modern science: postmortem pathology. Morgagni's theory that diseases were due to abnormalities of organs was finally proven true when postmortem pathology evolved as a common medical practice in the late nineteenth century. One of the leaders in the pathology movement was the Canadian physician William Osler (Bliss 1999). Osler conducted tens of thousands of postmortem autopsies and carefully recorded the pathological findings of his patients. At the same time, he had examined those patients while living, applying Sydenham's method of meticulous clinical evaluation of signs and symptoms. He went back and forth between the two approaches: clinical syndrome observations were confirmed or rejected based on pathological findings at autopsy, and vice versa, autopsy findings were informed by prior clinical syndrome observations. Gradually, Osler and his colleagues and disciples evolved the "clinicopathological" method which has become the standard approach of modern scientific medicine. The development of the microscope in prior centuries, and its increasing use in histology in the nineteenth century, also facilitated the effectiveness of the clinicopathological method, as gross evaluation of organs was augmented by histological study of organ tissues.

Osler augmented his clinicopathological skills with an appreciation for the medical statistics of Louis, and the field of clinical research, with statistical evaluation of clinical and pathological findings, had begun. Osler's extensive knowledge of the history of medicine was added to the mix as he overtly taught a return to the basic Hippocratic philosophy of medicine and a rejection of the Galenic thinking that had led to so much bleeding for so long.

His ideas had a major influence on twentieth-century medicine through his professional role as the first chairman of the new department of medicine of the first modern medical school in the United States at Johns Hopkins University in Baltimore and later through his final position as Regius Professor of Medicine at Oxford. As importantly, he wrote a modern Canon of Medicine, as influential for a brief time as Ibn Sina's work had been for much longer: *The Principles and Practice of Medicine* (Osler 1912). Osler's textbook would be the last prominent textbook of medicine written by a single thinker. In it, he captured in detail the most careful clinical syndrome observations and the most recent pathological evidence. He provided cautious, Hippocratic treatment recommendations, which were so sparse that he was accused of "therapeutic nihilism." From the late 1890s when he published his text, past his death in 1920, his textbook was the preeminent source for medical practice in the Anglo-American world. It would remain so into the 1940s, until the introduction of antibiotics, the next great revolution in medical practice.

A final impact on Osler was the influence of his literary and religious background in the Victorian late nineteenth-century period. He brought the humanistic ideals of the Enlightenment into the very core of modern medicine and showed how it could be applied along with rigorous scientific clinical and pathological methods (Osler 1932). Osler was both a biological reductionist and a humanist.

The Revolution of Randomization

Oslerian medicine focused on diagnosis, not treatment, because it was scientifically honest about the fact that there were not many effective treatments. Louis' methods had proven this fact. In the 1920s, Louis' numerical method was taken forward hugely through the development of the concept of "randomization" by Ronald Fisher, a statistician and geneticist. Fisher applied his idea initially in agriculture, but it didn't take long before it was picked up in medicine and applied for the first time by the British medical epidemiologist, A. Bradford Hill, in 1948. The first randomized clinical trial was conducted to prove the efficacy of an early antibiotic, streptomycin, in miliary tuberculosis (Hill 1971).

Antibiotics had been discovered before the Second World War, but began to be used widely after the war, into the 1950s. The work of Fisher and Hill was central in proving their efficacy, and the new statistical methods began to be used for many different medications in medicine.

None proved so effective and radical as the antibiotic class. These medications transformed the practice of medicine and saved millions of lives that for millennia were lost to infections.

We have lost historical memory of that period, what was only known in the memory of lost generations, of the grandparents and great-grandparents of the readers of this chapter. Readers can find a sense of the amazing impact of antibiotics in reading works of physicians from the mid-twentieth century, like Lewis Thomas in his classic book *The Youngest Science* (Thomas 1995). Thomas describes being a medical intern in the most prestigious Boston hospitals in the 1930s, just before the introduction of antibiotics. He describes how a young child would come to the emergency room with an infected cut of the hand; sepsis would ensue and the child would die. A decade later, no child would die of that cause, easily cured with penicillin. Tuberculosis was cured with streptomycin. Syphilis, which in its neurological effects caused the equivalent of schizophrenia in 1 % of the world's population, was cured (Shorter 1997). Addison's disease, which produced an expected lifespan of 30 years due to uncontrolled infections, became a chronic condition that could be managed for a lifetime with steroids and penicillin. Thus could a young man like John F. Kennedy survive to become president in his 40s. Diabetes also was transformed, with the discovery of insulin, from a death sentence to a chronic manageable illness. Heart attacks and strokes, so commonly the cause of sudden death, became less common with the treatment of hypertension and, in later years, the reduction of cholesterol.

Clinical medicine was finally transformed by having biological treatments that actually cured diseases, unlike the thousands of treatments of Galen and Ibn Sina and their disciples. The Hippocratic method of careful clinical evaluation, modified by Sydenham and Harvey and Morgagni and Osler, could now be tested through the new statistical methods to identify truly effective treatments for real diseases. Speculation and theory were put in their rightful place of generating hypotheses, to be tested and possibly rejected based on experiment and clinical observation, rather than the reverse.

This modern neo-Hippocratic medicine proved immensely effective, and, for the first time in human history, physicians could save lives based on true knowledge, rather than guessing or, worse, harming based on false beliefs.

The Biopsychosocial Model: Late Twentieth-Century Dissatisfaction

It would be inconsistent with human history for this story to end here. By the late twentieth century, a new dissatisfaction arose with the mid-twentieth-century scientific transformation of modern medicine. We continue to live today with a backlash against these medical successes.

Along with the biological advances of antibiotics and other new treatments like steroids and insulin, there was a parallel development in medicine: Sigmund Freud's psychoanalysis. Freud discovered that certain apparent neurological problems did not have a biological cause in the body, but rather were produced in the body through purely psychological influences. He began his work with "hysteria," which related often to physical manifestations for which neurologists like Freud could find no brain basis. These included seizures and bodily paralysis. Some had found that hypnosis could produce or improve such hysterical symptoms, and Freud showed that a "talking cure" could produce the same benefit. Simply talking in what is now called psychotherapy had medical benefits.

Freud's work was taken in many directions, but in clinical medicine the main impact was in the field of "psychosomatic medicine" (Shorter 1997). Many internal medicine physicians became interested in how the mind might affect the body, especially for those medical conditions for whom physical causes were difficult to identify. Those physicians often obtained formal training in Freudian psychoanalysis and then would become specialists in psychosomatic medicine. One such person was the gastrointestinal specialist George Engel, who would later found the biopsychosocial model (Engel 1977). Engel specialized in ulcerative colitis and peptic ulcer disease. Both conditions were thought to be of largely psychological origin for much of Engel's career, in the early to mid-twentieth century. By his later years, though, new work was discovering genetic causes for ulcerative colitis and infectious causes for peptic ulcers. The medical profession also began to become more interested in the biological mechanisms of inflammation that underlie those conditions. In other fields, an increasing use of testing of various kinds – x-rays, blood tests, and other machine-based measurements – was leading away from the clinical bedside observation that had characterized most medical diagnosis in prior centuries.

By the 1970s, toward the end of his career, Engel became disturbed by these trends (Ghaemi 2010) and wrote his classic paper contrasting a biopsychosocial model against what he called the bioreductionist model of medicine. Engel's critique struck a cultural nerve and became the standard approach taught in American medical schools in the end of the twentieth century and into the present time.

Definitions of the Biopsychosocial Model

The proposal made by Engel is that there are two basic models of medicine, the biological reductionist and the biopsychosocial (BPS). The former only looks at biological causes of disease; the latter argues that most (or all) disease is multifactorial, with psychological and social causes, not just biological ones. Engel came to this conclusion on the basis of his interest in psychosomatic medicine and functional bowel disorders and peptic ulcer disease. At the time he made this claim, it had been widely held that such conditions had important psychological causes.

It is important to keep in mind that by psychological causes, Engel was thinking in the Freudian/psychoanalytic paradigm. He meant unconscious mental states, often dating back to childhood, that produced physical symptoms (Ghaemi 2010).

It is also important to note that he hardly expanded on social causes in any of his writing, and he certainly was not thinking about the profession of social work in his theory, even though the BPS model has now become the mantra of the social work profession.

A typical case which Engel would present in lectures and writings is of a man with heart problems, who goes to the emergency room with chest pain (Engel 1980). There he is met by an inexperienced medical intern who does a terrible job with a needle trying to get an arterial blood gas in the patient's wrist. The patient becomes very anxious and is in pain and then has a ventricular arrhythmia. A code is called and he is given intravenous medications and electrical defibrillation such that he is resuscitated. Engel's point is that one could look at the whole story from the viewpoint of the physical and biological interventions, but the key to the story is the psychological impact of the intern's painful incompetence, which triggered the arrhythmia.

By the late 1970s, when Engel began speaking about these ideas, evidence began to accumulate both for and against his model. On the one hand, the new field of social epidemiology was identifying important social and psychological factors that predisposed to some illnesses, such as diabetes and heart diseases. On the other hand, the illnesses closest to Engel's interest, like peptic ulcer disease, were found not to be biopsychosocial at all. An infectious agent, H. Pylori, was found to be more important than the most complex psychosocial speculations about ulcers. Irritable bowel syndrome was found to be importantly genetic, with a complex immunological pathophysiology; psychological and social factors were not confirmed as being central to those bowel conditions (Ghaemi 2010).

Evolution of the Biopsychosocial Model

Three groups latched onto the BPS model and continue to hold to it very strongly today: (1) primary care physicians, (2) psychiatrists, and (3) social workers.

Primary care physicians see many patients with many symptom complaints that often do not, after medical workup, have a physical basis in the body. Hence, the interest in psychological and social factors in the lives of patients that may bring them to the doctor (Weiss 1980).

Psychiatrists and social workers do counseling with many patients for life problems, like unhappiness after divorce or grief after the death of a loved one, that may not have any relation to a physical problem in the brain causing psychological symptoms (like manic-depressive disease or schizophrenia). At the time of Engel's cri de coeur, psychiatry was moving to more use of medications; this biological approach was met with much resistance by the psychoanalytic core of the profession. The BPS model has become the mantra which many psychiatrists use to push back against using medications or thinking about psychiatric symptoms as related to diseases of the brain or body (Gabbard and Kay 2001).

The social work profession sees its raison d'etre as tied to the BPS model; the word "social" in the phrase gives the social work profession a claim to relevance in medical care (Kerson 1987). This need not be the case, since social work as a profession predates the BPS model by over half a century. Further, as noted, Engel more or less ignored the social aspect of the BPS model.

Claims and Critiques of the BPS Model

The BPS model is attractive for professional reasons as given above, but its basic claims do not stand up to conceptual or scientific scrutiny. At times, it is hard to even clearly understand what the basic BPS theory is. This suggests that it is more a slogan than anything else, a label used by those who wish to maintain a humanistic attitude toward patients. But the latter wish, humanism, is not inherently in conflict with biological reductionism or inherently consistent with the BPS ideology. (The following critiques have been previously published by me in more detail at book length (Ghaemi 2010).)

Regarding the veracity of BPS claims, it is false to claim that *all* medical diseases have psychological and social factors in their etiologies. Many are purely biological; one can cite many purely genetic conditions, like trisomy 21 or phenylketonuria. Those conditions are 100 % genetic and biological in etiology; there are no psychological or social factors in their causation. Biological reductionism is correct in those diseases.

So the BPS claim would have to be weakened: One could claim that *most* illnesses are multifactorial in etiology. This also is a false claim. There are hundreds, if not thousands, of purely genetic or purely biological diseases of various kinds (infections, cancers, autoimmune diseases). Many of them may be rare, but they abound.

The BPS claim can be weakened further: One could claim that most chronic illnesses are multifactorial in etiology, like coronary vascular disease and diabetes and depressive conditions. This claim would be more defensible, but then many acute medical diseases would have to be excluded from the BPS model. Further, the influence of psychological and social factors in these illnesses still is exerted by a biological mechanism. For instance, social isolation is associated with diabetes; the mechanism may involve overeating and lack of activity leading to insulin resistance in the pancreas. Social factors are in the causal pathway but they always have to exert their effects through the biological mechanism, insulin resistance. The biological component is essential to the disease; the social components are not. One could get the insulin resistance by nonsocial means, such as genetic transmission of insulin resistance or a medication side effect. So even on this claim, though one can claim multifactorial etiology, not all the factors are equal in importance, and the biological factor still seems most important.

The BPS claim might be restated so as to move away from etiology altogether. The claim could be that all or most illnesses, whatever their etiologies, are affected by psychological and social factors. If you have a purely genetic disease, the course of your illness will still be impacted by your psychological state or your social condition. This is the most defensible version of the BPS approach to illness, but it cedes a great deal. It accepts biological reductionism in relation to cause for many illnesses, and it makes claims only regarding pathogenesis, or amelioration of the course of the biological illness. Though this claim is more defensible, it is rarely made in this limited way. Usually BPS advocates make etiological claims, as Engel did. The above critiques would then apply.

The Essence of the BPS Model

The above critiques bring out the vagueness and limitations of the BPS model as put forward by many of its advocates. In my analysis of this literature (Ghaemi 2010), I have come to the conclusion that there is one essence and core to the BPS model that is more central than any of the claims above. *The essence of the BPS model is eclecticism.* By eclecticism, I mean that the BPS model wishes to avoid any definitive assertion of causation or importance of any one of the three factors. It not only wishes to avoid biological reductionism, it wishes to avoid psychological and social reductionism. It wishes not to make definitive claims of any kind, except the claim that one can never be definitive.

This is what attracts clinicians, especially psychiatrists and social workers and some primary care physicians. One can always use the BPS model to criticize anyone else's claims about biological or psychological or social causation, and then one can defend whatever claims one wishes to defend with the same model. Essentially, it allows clinicians to do whatever they want, under the cover of being "holistic" and biopsychosocial. The slogan of "individualizing care to the patient" is then brought out to further defend the clinician's wish to be free. All these attitudes are tied into the wish to be humanistic, to treat the patient as an individual human being who is unique and has feelings and a certain social context. All this can be true, but none of it proves or disproves a biological reductionist etiology to any putative disease.

Readers will note from the interpretation of the history of Galenic versus Hippocratic approaches to medicine that the BPS model is revisiting some very old territory. Galenic medicine, for two millennia, was holistic and individualized to the patient – but it was far from humanistic. Bleeding and purging for millennia only tortured many poor human beings who suffered from the biological ignorance of their physicians.

The BPS model can be quite anti-humanistic and dehumanizing (Ghaemi 2010). If you have purely biological disease, which has a biological cure, such as *H. Pylori*-related peptic ulcer disease, your clinician is harming your humanity by not diagnosing or treating it. He or she might be the most pleasant and humane person in the world, with the best of intentions, providing the best of counseling, and attuned to your personal life quite well. But your ulcer pain will persist until you get the right antibiotic.

In psychiatry, the same problem exists with dismissive BPS (Mojtabai and Olfson 2010) attitudes about the concept of disease. For instance, it is known that bipolar illness is almost completely genetic in etiology. And there is a treatment that essentially cures: lithium can produce complete remission in about one-third of persons with that condition. Yet it is only prescribed to about 10 % of diagnosed patients in the United States, and most patients receive instead symptomatic treatments with medications for depressive or anxiety or sleep symptoms, along with counseling. The latter approach is biopsychosocial, but it is ineffective, and patients continue to suffer needlessly while a much more effective cure is ignored because it entails thinking about treating an underlying biological disease, as opposed to seeing biological factors as limited in importance.

Postmodernism and Medical "Narrative"

Another aspect of the eclecticism of the BPS model is that it merges with an extreme skepticism about scientific truth. This is reflected in postmodernist attitudes in the past half century in Western culture, inaugurated by the 1960s counterculture (Ghaemi 2013). In this thinking, science is just another "narrative," not any more right or wrong than other ideologies, whether literary or political or cultural. There is no truth, only claims to truth which really reflect social and cultural interest groups. Science is what scientists say is true, but that is no more true than what theologians say is true. Michel Foucault and other postmodernists made trenchant critiques of the history of medicine on this basis (Foucault 2001). Their views have become very popular in modern culture. Even among those who have not read them, these postmodernist views have become part of the Weltanschauung of the current age. In medicine and psychiatry, they get played out through an attraction to extreme eclecticism, with a dismissive attitude toward "the" truth, and a consequent adherence to an eclectic interpretation of the BPS theory.

Some also now speak of the importance of "narrative" in understanding medical illnesses. The professions of history of science and medical anthropology are now thoroughly postmodernist. Any history of medicine which seeks to claim eternal truth for any fact is dismissed *tout court*. The concept of progress is *verboten*. Nothing is allowed but the relativistic and at times nihilistic attitudes of those who wish to dissolve all medicine and science into a soup of eclecticism.

Even those who see themselves as scientifically oriented persons often succumb to the unconscious influences of the postmodernist spirit of our age. In medicine, the genetic revolution has led to the current mania for "personalized" medicine. This idea promises to succeed in achieving the Galenic goal: all illness will finally be individualized on biological grounds, just as Galen always wished. The genetic work is an empirical claim, and we can wait to judge it on empirical grounds. As epigenetics becomes incorporated, and the influence of environment on genes is better understood, it may provide another means to support some BPS intuitions. We will have to wait to judge these claims on empirical grounds. I would only comment that the history of medicine argues for caution against these claims, as they were strongly believed for 2,000 years and caused terrible harm. Future advocates of these ideas should keep in mind the errors of the past.

A Medical Humanism for the Future

While we await the playing out of the genomic revolution, I would suggest that if it fails to achieve its most grandiose goals, which it may, then we should have a more realistic alternative. I would like to propose here another perspective, not one that takes sides on these debates but one that seeks to learn from them (Ghaemi 2010).

I would suggest that future physicians and clinicians would do well to realize that the BPS model, as stated eclectically and forcefully, is false. So too is any strong formulation of biological reductionism. There are many diseases that can be understood reductionistically as being biological in etiology. There are also important chronic medical illnesses that have key social and psychological aspects, both to etiology and to course of illness. We all agree that humanism is important and that whatever the etiology of a person's disease or absence of disease, it is the person who either has the disease or does not. We still have to deal with a human being, with all her psychological and social and individual traits.

It is true that many patients who see primary care doctors and psychiatrists and social workers do not have any medical disease at all, but some do, and some even have purely biological diseases. Some persons even have purely social problems, or purely psychological problems, with no relevant biological component at all. How can we tell which is which?

I suggest that the main culprit here is eclecticism and underneath it the postmodernist relativism that is our current unconscious philosophy of life. We need to become conscious of the importance of the scientific attitude, in the straight

Enlightenment tradition, the notion that there are truths, that some facts are better proven than others. We need to be willing to commit to biological reductionism as true when the scientific proof is present for it and similarly for social and psychological reductionism and similarly for some cases where the scientific proof is antireductionistic and supports the importance of multiple factors.

In other words, we should not prejudge these matters, but let scientific methods tell us what to believe. We should believe in science and nothing else. But we should really believe, more so than in other ideologies, including the comfortable eclecticisms of the departments of literature and medical anthropology.

No matter what our science tells us, we also should be committed to the reality that dates back to Hippocrates, the fact that the individual patient as a human being must be understood as a human being. In this feature we are all individual, although even here, as the great psychoanalyst Harry Stack Sullivan once said, we are all much more alike than otherwise.

Definition of Key Terms

Biomedical reductionist models	Take the view that all disease can be reduced to biological causes in the body; typically, treatments of those diseases are also biological in character, such as surgery or medications.
Humanist models	Take the view that illnesses sometimes may reflect diseases of the body, but sometimes they reflect problems between human beings of a non-biological nature, such as psychological or personal concerns. Treatment can be biological, but it often is not, entailing psychological or personal interventions such as counseling or self-help programs.
Biopsychosocial models	Take the view that all disease consists of an interaction between biological, psychological, and social causes; typically treatments of those diseases are also multiple, with biological (medications or surgery), psychological (counseling or self-help), and social (public health policy) interventions.
Hippocratic approaches	To medicine emphasize clinical observation and not treating symptoms. Rather only some symptoms which are caused by diseases should be treated. Hippocratic approaches are disease oriented, not symptom oriented, and clinical observation based not biological speculation based.
Galenic approaches	To medicine emphasize biological theory and treating symptoms. Disease concepts are neglected, and all illnesses are seen as individualized to each person based on the specific combination of the four humors in that

person. Galenic approaches are symptom oriented, not disease oriented, and biological speculation based not clinical observation based.

Medical humanism   Medical humanism is a biological reductionist approach to disease that recognizes the importance of also understanding each human being as a human being, not only based on psychological and social aspects but also based on existential aspects of the human condition.

Summary Points

- The history of medicine involves two basic currents of thinking, Galenic and Hippocratic, the former being biologically speculative and holistic but unhumanistic, the latter being clinically observational and disease based but more humanistic.
- Biological reductionism, though commonly criticized, is valid for many diseases.
- The biopsychosocial model, though commonly praised, is false for many diseases.
- The biopsychosocial model represents, in essence, eclecticism.
- Medical humanism is not incompatible with biological reductionism.

References

Bliss M (1999) William Osler: a life in medicine. Oxford University Press, New York

Engel GL (1977) The need for a new medical model: a challenge for biomedicine. Science 196 (80):129–136

Engel GL (1980) The clinical application of the biopsychosocial model. Am J Psychiatry 137:535–544

Foucault M (2001) Madness and civilization: a history of insanity in the age of reason. Routledge, London

Gabbard GO, Kay J (2001) The fate of integrated treatment: whatever happened to the biopsychosocial psychiatrist? Am J Psychiatry 158:1956–1963

Ghaemi SN (2008) Toward a Hippocratic psychopharmacology. Can J Psychiatry 53:189–196

Ghaemi SN (2010) The rise and fall of the biopsychosocial model: reconciling art and science in psychiatry. Johns Hopkins Press, Baltimore

Ghaemi N (2013) On depression: diagnosis, drugs and despair in the modern world. Johns Hopkins Press, Baltimore

Hill AB (1971) Principles of medical statistics, 9th edn. Oxford University Press, New York

Holmes OW (1891) Currents and counter-currents in medical science. Medical essays 1842–1882. Houghton-Mifflin, Boston

Jones WHS (1931) The works of Hippocrates

Jouanna J (1999) Hippocrates. Johns Hopkins University Press, Baltimore

Kerson TS (1987) Clinical social work in health care: new biopsychosocial approaches. Health Soc Work 12:77–78

Low G (1999) Thomas Sydenham: the English Hippocrates. Aust N Z J Surg 69:258–262

McHugh PR (2006) Hippocrates a la mode. In: The mind has mountains. Johns Hopkins Press, Baltimore

Mojtabai R, Olfson M (2010) National trends in psychotropic medication polypharmacy in office-based psychiatry. Arch Gen Psychiatry 67:26–36

Nutton V (2001) Hippocrates of Cos. In: Encyclopedia of life sciences. John Wiley and Sons. http://dx.doi.org/10.1038/npg.els.0002519

Osler W (1912) The principles and practice of medicine. D. Appleton and Company, New York

Osler W (1932) Aequanimitas, 3rd edn. The Blakiston Company, Philadelphia

Pormann P, Savage-Smith E (2007) Medieval Islamic medicine. Georgetown University Press, Washington, DC

Porter R (1999) The greatest benefit to mankind: a medical history of humanity. Norton, New York

Shorter E (1997) A history of psychiatry. Wiley, New York

Stigler S (1986) A history of statistics. Harvard University Press, Cambridge, MA

Temkin O (1973) Galenism: rise and decline of a medical philosophy. Cornell University Press, Ithaca

Temkin O (2002) On second thought and other essays in the history of medicine and science. Johns Hopkins University Press, Baltimore

Thomas L (1995) The youngest science. Penguin, New York

Weiss RJ (1980) The biopsychosocial model and primary care. Psychosom Med 42:123–130

Wootton D (2007) Bad medicine: doctors doing harm since Hippocrates. Oxford University Press, Oxford

Yankauer A (1996) Pierre Charles-Alexandre Louis: the impact of a clinical trial. Pharos Alpha Omega Alpha Honor Med Soc 59:15–19

Medical Theory and Its Notions of Definition and Explanation

48

Peter Hucklenbroich

Contents

Abstract

This chapter elucidates several special features of the usage of the notions *definition* and *explanation* in medicine and medical theory. As these special features are intimately connected to the key concept of d*isease entity*, the first section gives a short reconstruction of this concept. The second section presents three methods of defining disease entities, supplemented by a fourth, logically unsound method found in many medical textbooks. The third section shows that there are two senses of explaining symptoms and pathological conditions by referring to disease entities, i.e., a part-whole kind of explanation and a causal one. The relationship between *explanation* and *diagnosis* of diseases is analyzed by comparing their logical structure. In the last section, the very special kind of explanation found exclusively in medicine, viz., explaining *why* some condition is a disease or is pathological, is clarified by elucidating the concept of *pathologicity* and its criteria.

P. Hucklenbroich (✉)
Institut für Ethik, Geschichte und Theorie der Medizin, Westfälische Wilhelms-Universität Münster, Münster, Germany
e-mail: hucklen@ukmuenster.de

© Springer Science+Business Media Dordrecht 2017
T. Schramme, S. Edwards (eds.), *Handbook of the Philosophy of Medicine*,
DOI 10.1007/978-94-017-8688-1_44

Introduction

Definitions and explanations are important conceptual tools in all scientific disciplines that contain full-fledged, well-articulated theories – hence, also in medicine and medical science. However, usage of these concepts in medicine exhibits several special features that are consequences of the conceptual structure of medical theory of disease (general pathology) and the logic and methodology of clinical reasoning. In particular, these special features play an essential role in the conceptual clarification and explication of the notions of *disease* and *diagnosis* and have a decisive impact on the handling of definitions and explanations. Hence, the following discussion consists of four sections: first, some basic concepts and principles of general pathology and theory of disease are outlined in order to improve understanding of the following sections (section "Some Concepts and Principles of General Medical Pathology"). Subsequently, the forms and characteristics of definitions of disease entities are presented and analyzed (section "The Definition of Disease Entities"). After this, the relationship between the concepts of *diagnosis* and *explanation* is elucidated (section "Explanation and Diagnosis"). Finally, the particular linguistic usage of explaining *why a particular medical condition is abnormal or pathological*, respectively, *why it is a disease*, is conceptually analyzed and reconstructed (section "Explanation of Pathologicity").

Some Concepts and Principles of General Medical Pathology

The expression *general pathology* (German: *Krankheitslehre*) is taken to refer here to the whole body of medical theories that refer to states and processes of health and disease as occurrences within an individual human life span. General pathology in this medical sense incorporates anatomical, functional, behavioral, mental, and subjectively experienced states and processes. Knowledge of all these conditions is spread over the whole body of medical theories and their representations in handbooks and textbooks. There are, however, very few attempts at giving a unified, systematic, and comprehensible overview and account of general pathology in this sense; hence, it has to be obtained from multiple sources (e.g., Büchner et al. 1969; Sandritter and Beneke 1974; Riede 2004; Siegenthaler 2007; Bickley and Szilagyi 2013; Hammer and McPhee 2014).

Even in everyday, prescientific discourse, some states and processes of life are characterized as pathological ones. Scientific pathology systematizes this knowledge and constructs a systematic nosology, entailing that all pathological conditions are parts and manifestations of particular diseases or, more precisely, of particular kinds of diseases called *disease entities*: every case of falling ill, every illness or sickness, and every disorder or malady are, in the view of medical science, a case of a disease entity. Disease entities comprise not only the "diseases" of lay understanding, such as infectious or metabolic disorders, but also congenital or acquired disfigurements, malformations and mutilations, wounds, burns and injuries, intoxications, cancer, addiction and dependency, and mental disorders like schizophrenia – to mention only some of the broad varieties of disease entities. Currently, the number of disease entities known to medical science totals, at least, a five-digit figure. These disease entities are *kinds* or *types* of diseases, terminologically designated by *disease entity, unit of disease, nosological unit*, or *disease pattern*. As *types*, they must be conceptually distinguished from the individual cases of disease that form their instances (*token*).

Every individual case of falling ill is a case of at least one disease entity that is at its bottom and forms its basis. Particularly, all subjectively and objectively perceptible and observable pathological signs, symptoms, and findings are *manifestations*, hence *parts* of one disease entity (or concomitantly occurring disease entities). The term *disease entity* should not be misinterpreted as designating something like a physical object or body or a *kind* of physical objects or organisms. As Caroline Whitbeck puts it, "[...] a disease, in the sense of a *disease entity* (or *disease type*) could not be [...] very much like a body [...] Diseases are not particular physical objects, but this does not prevent their existence being as objective as types of rock or species of trees" (Whitbeck 1977, p. 623).

At the present time, the entirety of all existing disease entities is not yet completely known and discovered. Hence, it is possible that certain symptoms, or constellations of symptoms, are already known to medical science but the disease entity (or disease entities) of which they are manifestations is unknown or not yet ascertained. In the history of medicine and medical science, a typical pattern of discovery takes its course from primarily observing some single, isolated *symptoms* or clusters of symptoms, to secondarily lumping them together to typical constellations of symptoms called *syndromes*, to eventually identifying one *disease entity* by discovering the *causal connection* between them and thus identifying the consistent, unifying basis of all observed symptoms and findings in that syndrome. This typical course in history of medicine, together with the definitions of *disease entity* and of *syndrome*, was put forward in the handbook *Die klinischen Syndrome* by Leiber and Olbrich, founded in 1957. This huge handbook was an attempt at collecting all known syndromes of medicine and was continued unto the eighth edition in 1996; at present, it is transformed into an electronic resource and database (Leiber and Olbrich 1957; Burg et al. 1996).

On account of these structural properties, *identification* and *definition* of disease entities depend essentially on identification and recognition of its *primary cause*. As a first approximation to an explanation, the *presence* of a certain disease entity *explains* the *occurrence* of all symptoms and findings that form its parts and manifestations. From these two statements, guidelines regarding the explication of the notions of definition and explanation in the context of medical pathology are derived (Engelhardt 1975; Gifford 2011; Schramme 2012; Wulff et al. 1990).

The Definition of Disease Entities

Disease entities are kinds of processes in the course of individual human lives that exhibit a beginning (onset) and an end (outcome) in time and, consequently, a definite temporal extension (duration). In borderline cases, the onset may coincide with the onset of individual life itself, viz., the time of procreation or of formation of a zygote. Likewise, the outcome of a disease may coincide with the end of life itself, viz., in the case of a lethal outcome. With the exception of congenital disease, the onset of a disease forms a *transition* within individual life, viz., the transition from the state when the disease is *not* (*yet*) present (= "relative health") to the state when it is (= "diseasedness"). In the case of congenital disease, the onset is not a transition *inside* individual life but a transition *identical* with the *onset* of individual life. The process or event that brings about this transition is designated by *primary cause, first cause, etiological factor*, or *primary lesion* and is taken to be a *unique* event (*the* cause or *the* etiological factor). From the viewpoint of causal analysis, the primary cause of a disease is a *necessary* condition that is *specific* for this disease entity. The primary cause of a disease is followed by a specific, typical chain or cascade of pathological events inside the affected individual. This specific chain or cascade of events forms a temporal pattern that is called *natural course, natural history*, or *pathogenesis*. Generally, pathogenesis takes place simultaneously on multiple, diverse levels of the patient organism. Pathological phenomena and changes may occur on the levels of biochemistry and molecular biology; of morphology and function of cells, tissues, and organs; of function and development of whole systems of the organism; and of the perceptible and observable phenomena of behavior and experience of the ill person. Because all these levels are causally connected and intertwined, there is no sharp distinction between "clinical" and "pathological" levels, though for pragmatic reasons this distinction is retained. Even the subjectively experienced *illness* of the patient is, in the view of medicine, only a small part of the entire course of the disease (therefore, disease and illness are *in medicine* not mutually exclusive concepts, as they are in some *philosophical* theories of medicine). At the present time, there are only very few attempts to analyze and reconstruct the concept of disease entity from a philosophical point of view (Whitbeck 1977; Reznek 1987; Hucklenbroich and Buyx 2013; Hucklenbroich 2014a; 2016a, b).

The identification of a novel disease entity presupposes a comparison of its cause and course with the whole system of known disease entities – the medical *nosology*. It presupposes (i) identification of a novel, so far unknown, etiological factor, which (ii) causes a novel natural course of disease or pathogenesis that is not identical with and cannot be subsumed under an already known pathogenesis.

In the case of identified, well-established disease entities, there are, principally, three different ways to define them:

(i)   Definition by its unique etiological factor
(ii) Definition by its typical, specific pathogenesis
(iii) Definition by parts or manifestations that form necessary and sufficient conditions (= obligatory and pathognomonic symptoms) of it

The account of disease entities in medical textbooks usually combines methods (i) and (ii), by describing its etiological factor as well as its typical natural course. Although this description is usually presented as the "definition" of the disease, this is not a correct method of defining the concept in the logical and philosophical sense of definition, because definitions must not be *creative*, i.e., they ought not entail *empirical* consequences (Essler 1970, p. 71). But the statement – entailed by the "textbook method" of definition – that a definite etiological factor causes a definite natural course of disease *is* an empirical statement derivable from it. Hence, the textbook definitions are not definitions in the logical sense but are *empirical theories* about causal connections between etiological factors and their effects, constituting a definite disease entity (Gøtzsche 2007). As Henrik Wulff puts it:

> In order to define a disease, it is necessary to fix a set of criteria *which are fulfilled by all patients said to be suffering from the disease and by no patients not said to be suffering from the disease*. In some textbooks the description of a disease begins with a 'definition' but on closer examination it is usually found not to be a logically satisfactory definition but only an ultrashort description. (Wulff 1976, p. 50)

The third method of defining a disease entity, by specifying necessary and sufficient conditions, must not be confused with a similar but logically different method of presenting disease entities found in medical textbooks, namely, "defining" by specifying *diagnostic criteria*. The difference may be characterized as follows: diagnostic criteria of a disease comprise conditions that are conclusive evidence for its presence but are not necessary conditions; hence, they are not bound to be present in every instance of it and are not usable as defining criteria. Defining criteria, vice versa, may be but are not bound to be employable for diagnostic purposes, because they may be remote in time or practically inaccessible for diagnostic techniques. Diagnosis of a particular disease entity is proven or ascertained by so-called *pathognomonic* findings. A pathognomonic finding of a disease entity, or a set of findings that are, taken together, pathognomonic of it, is a finding or a set that forms a sufficient condition of it – thus the diagnosis is established. But these sufficient conditions need not be necessary conditions. Necessary conditions of a disease entity are called *obligatory* symptoms or findings that play a different role in diagnostics: They are useful for the *exclusion* of a diagnosis, if they are missing. Therefore, positive diagnostic criteria for a disease are not identical with a definition, unless they are, at the same time, obligatory findings.

To sum up, it may be stated that the meaning and usage of *definition* in medicine deviates from strict logical conventions (i) by calling characterizations of diseases (disease entities) *definitions* that are, in fact, *empirical theories* and (ii) by calling diagnostic criteria for diseases (disease entities) *definitions* that are, in fact, only *sufficient conditions* but need not be necessary conditions, as required for a proper, genuine definition.

Explanation and Diagnosis

It is common in medical communication to state that a particular symptom or finding S, or a particular set of symptoms and findings S in a patient, is *explained* by a certain disease (disease entity) D or, better, by the presence of D. This manner of speaking may be reconstructed in the following way: as shown above (section "Some Concepts and Principles of General Medical Pathology"), all symptoms and pathological findings in a case of disease entity D are manifestations of D and, hence, *parts* of D. In the same sense, as the presence of a part is explained by the presence of its whole, the presence of S is explained by the presence of D ("part-whole explanation"). Furthermore, as shown above, all symptoms and findings of a disease entity D are *causally* connected by a causal chain or cascade that starts from the primary cause or etiological factor. Thus, it is possible to explain a symptom or finding S by antecedent members of the chain, ultimately by the primary cause. This kind of explanation is not a part-whole explanation but a *causal* explanation of S. These two kinds of explanations of S are not inconsistent with one another but are complementary, because they operate on different levels of description and conceptual resolution of the same unitary and consistent process.

The statement that, in a particular patient X, a case of disease entity D is present is called a *diagnosis* or diagnostic statement D(X). Therefore, it is possible to say that a part-whole explanation of S by D represents an "explanation *by diagnosis*," because the symptom S(X) that is to be explained (*explanandum*) is logically derived from the statement that D is present in X (diagnosis D(X)) and the theoretical description of disease entity D (together forming the *explanans*).

This way of explaining symptoms may be called "explanation by diagnosis," because diagnosis D(X) forms part of the explanans. But this *explanation by diagnosis* must be distinguished sharply from *inference to diagnosis*: inference to diagnosis D(X) is identical with *proof of diagnosis* (i.e., proof of statement D(X)), as sketched above (section "The Definition of Disease Entities"). Proof of diagnosis uses pathognomonic findings (sufficient conditions), and its logical direction runs inversely to explanation, viz., from statements S(X) and theoretical knowledge about D to diagnosis D(X). Thus, in *explanation* we infer from an established, known diagnosis D(X) to established, known symptoms S(X), whereas in *proof* we infer from established, known symptoms S(X) to a hitherto unknown particular diagnosis D(X) (Nordenfelt and Lindahl 1984; Schaffner 1985; Schaffner 1993; Stegmüller 1983; Wieland 2004.

Explanation of Pathologicity

A special case of explanation in medicine is formed by answering the question as to *why a particular condition C is a disease* or *why it is pathological*. To answer this question, what is required is not the concept of disease or disease entity but the concept of *pathologicity*, a technical term of medical science. A more common term for the same purpose is the term *disease value* (German: *Krankheitswert*). But the term *disease value* is seductive and may mistakenly lead to the opinion that the question of pathologicity is an evaluative question, in the sense of subjective, sociocultural, or ethical values and is dependent on cultural and historical variations and changes, thus forming a culturally relative notion. However, for medical theory and medical understanding, it is an essential precondition that any judgment of pathologicity does not resort to evaluations of the kind mentioned above (Hucklenbroich 2016a). Instead, medical judgments of pathologicity refer to criteria that rely on objective or at least objectifiable facts. For example, one main criterion of pathologicity refers to the question whether condition C will cause a *premature*, early death of the person X affected by C: will X under condition C suffer death earlier than under condition non-C?

A second criterion of pathologicity, or better a second set of criteria of this sort, refers to the question of whether condition C implies or causes the presence of definite, certain natural signs (symptoms, complaints) that indicate a state of disease. The most prominent sign of this sort is *pain*, but there are lots of other signs such as nausea, dyspnea, dizziness, blackout (syncope), tremor, insomnia, hallucinations, etc. These natural, objectively identifiable signs of pathologicity are deeply entrenched in the psychosomatic nature of human beings; they are not due to any subjective or sociocultural values or norms but are universally valid in mankind. The complete, systematic account of all criteria of pathologicity forms an essential part of *general pathology* and *symptomatology*, as components of medical theory (Hucklenbroich 2014a, b, 2016a, b).

The whole system of disease entities recognized by contemporary medicine relies, in the last instance, on the system of criteria of pathologicity. Thus, the general question as to why a particular condition C is pathological, or is a disease, or possesses disease value, may be answered by a statement of the following form:

> Condition C is a disease, or is pathological, or possesses disease value, *because C falls within the scope of at least one criterion of pathologicity.*

Statements of this form constitute a unique kind of explanation that is specific to theoretical medicine.

Definitions of Key Terms

Disease entity	Kind of disease
Pathologicity	Property of being pathological
Etiological factor	The (unique) primary cause (of a disease)
Pathogenesis	Natural course (of a disease)
Diagnosis of a disease D	Statement "D(X)" (referring to a patient X)
Illness	The parts of a disease process that are subjectively experienced and evaluated by the patient
General pathology	Complete body of medical theories concerning general features of normal and pathological conditions (or concerning states and processes of health and disease)

Summary Points

- Diseases are instances (or cases) of disease entities.
- An illness is the part of a disease that is subjectively experienced and evaluated by the affected person.
- Disease entities may be defined:
  - By their unique, specific etiological factor
  - By their specific pathogenesis
  - By any subset of their symptoms and pathological findings that are necessary and sufficient conditions of their presence
- Symptoms and pathological findings S of a disease D may be explained:
  - By the presence of the disease D (part-whole explanation)
  - As a causal effect of the etiological factor E of D or of some subsequent pathological process in the pathogenesis of D that causes S (causal explanation)
- Explanation of S by (presence of) D must be distinguished from diagnostic proof of D by S.
- Pathologicity is established by a system of criteria that are made explicit in general pathology.
- Explaining why condition C is a disease, or why C is pathological, is proving that C falls within the scope of at least one criterion of pathologicity.

References

Bickley LS, Szilagyi PG (2016) Bates' guide to physical examination and history taking, 12th edn. Walters Kluwer, Philadelphia

Büchner F, Letterer E, Roulet F (eds) (1969) Prolegomena einer Allgemeinen Pathologie. Springer, Berlin

Burg G et al (eds) (1996) Leiber – Die klinischen Syndrome, 8th edn. Urban & Schwarzenberg, München

Engelhardt HT Jr, Spicker SF (eds) (1975) Evaluation and explanation in the biomedical sciences. Reidel, Dordrecht

Essler WK (1970) Wissenschaftstheorie I. Definition und Reduktion. Alber, Freiburg

Gifford F (ed) (2011) Philosophy of medicine. Elsevier, Amsterdam

Gøtzsche P (2007) Rational diagnosis and treatment. Evidence-based clinical decision-making, 4th edn. Chichester, Wiley

Hammer GD, McPhee SJ (eds) (2014) Pathophysiology of disease, 7th edn. McGraw Hill, New York

Hucklenbroich P (2014a) "Disease entity" as the key theoretical concept of medicine. J Med Philos 39:609–633

Hucklenbroich P (2014b) Medical criteria of pathologicity and their role in scientific psychiatry – comments on the articles of Henrik Walter and Marco Stier. Front Psychol 5:128. doi:10.3389/fpsyg.2014.00128

Hucklenbroich P (2016a) Die Normativität des Krankheitsbegriffs: Zur Genese und Geltung von Kriterien der Krankhaftigkeit. Analyse & Kritik 38:1–38

Hucklenbroich P (2016b) Disease entities and the borderline between health and disease: where is the place of gradations? In: Keil G, Keuck L, Hauswald R (eds) Vagueness in Psychiatry. Oxford University Press, Oxford, pp. 75–92

Hucklenbroich P, Buyx A (eds) (2013) Wissenschaftstheoretische Aspekte des Krankheitsbegriffs. Mentis, Münster

Leiber B, Olbrich G (1957) Wörterbuch der klinischen Syndrome. Urban & Schwarzenberg, München

Nordenfelt L, Lindahl BIB (eds) (1984) Health, disease, and causal explanation in medicine. Reidel, Dordrecht

Reznek L (1987) The nature of disease. Routledge, London

Riede U (2004) Color atlas of pathology. Pathologic principles, associated diseases, sequelae. Thieme, Stuttgart/New York

Sandritter W, Beneke G (eds) (1974) Allgemeine Pathologie. Schattauer, Stuttgart

Schaffner KF (ed) (1985) Logic of discovery and diagnosis in medicine. University of California Press, Berkeley

Schaffner KF (1993) Discovery and explanation in biology and medicine, 2nd edn. University of Chicago Press, Chicago

Schramme T (ed) (2012) Krankheitstheorien. Suhrkamp, Berlin

Siegenthaler W (ed) (2007) Siegenthaler's differential diagnosis in internal medicine. From symptom to diagnosis. Thieme, Stuttgart/New York

Stegmüller W (1983) Erklärung – Begründung – Kausalität. Springer, Berlin

Whitbeck C (1977) Causation in medicine: the disease entity model. Philos Sci 44(4):619–631

Wieland W (2004) Diagnose, 2nd edn. Hoof, Warendorf

Wulff HR (1976) Rational diagnosis and treatment. Blackwell, Oxford

Wulff HR, Andur Pedersen S, Rosenberg R (1990) Philosophy of medicine. An introduction, 2nd edn. Oxford, Blackwell

Cultural Influences on Medical Knowledge 49

David Hughes

Contents

Abstract

This chapter examines how culture influences the content and practical application of medical knowledge. The current state of knowledge about pathology and treatment is not simply the outcome of a neutral process of scientific investigation and discovery, but is shaped by changing theoretical frameworks affected by more general cultural perspectives. Just as the disease classification systems utilized by doctors emerge in a social context, so lay health beliefs reflect local cultural perspectives, and medical practice involves mediating between expert and lay belief systems. Moreover, medical practice is itself conditioned by the subcultural perspectives associated with the medical profession, its constituent specialisms, and the diverse hospital and community settings where healthcare is provided. The dual nature of medicine as both a scientific and practice-based discipline has resulted in tensions between the art and science of practice, with some doctors putting more weight on clinical judgment based on experience

D. Hughes (✉)
Department of Public Health and Policy Studies, Swansea University, Swansea, UK
e-mail: d.hughes@swansea.ac.uk

© Springer Science+Business Media Dordrecht 2017
T. Schramme, S. Edwards (eds.), *Handbook of the Philosophy of Medicine*,
DOI 10.1007/978-94-017-8688-1_73

rather than the standardized application of codified knowledge. More generally there remains a divide between practitioners and laboratory-based medical research which reflects the history of medicine in Western countries.

Introduction

Culture powerfully shapes human understandings of the world, including knowledge about health and illness. "We seldom realize," wrote the popularizing philosopher Alan Wilson Watts (1989: 53–54), "that our most private thoughts and emotions are not actually our own. For we think in terms of languages and images which we did not invent, but which were given to us by our society." Culture provides the conceptual scaffolding via which people make sense of the objects and events around them. Members of different cultural groups see the world in different ways and cultural perspectives change over time, so that time and place crucially affect expert "knowledge."

Culture as understood by most scholars encompasses language and its associated classificatory taxonomies, social norms, customs, moral precepts, and other symbolic resources such as visual art, music, and dance. For the purposes of this chapter, we adopt a wide definition in which the ideational aspect of a culture includes its modes of analysis, its characteristic forms of problem solving, and its technologies for generating new knowledge. This rests on the proposition that the constellation of beliefs and values found in a given social group influences the search techniques and tools of discovery that it uses.

Cultural influences affect the domains of expert as well as commonsense knowledge and shape the behavior of professionals as much as the laity. This chapter considers medical knowledge from both expert and lay perspectives and examines how it is shaped by wider social and professional influences. It starts by considering the conventional image of medical knowledge as a progressive unfolding of scientific discovery and a contrary view from social science and philosophy that argues that such knowledge must be seen in a social and cultural context. Later sections deal with the changing nature of disease classifications; the complicated linkages between scientific advance, technology, and culture; patient cultures and illness behavior; the culture of medical practice; and the relationship between medicine and science.

Medical Knowledge and the Narrative of Scientific Discovery

A key question in considering cultural influences on medical knowledge is whether the latter emerges from a direct engagement with the facts of the natural world or must be regarded, at least in part, as a human product influenced by the wider society. From the perspective of mainstream Western medicine, understandings of disease are characterized by a progressive accumulation of knowledge over time.

Diseases are conceptualized as distinct entities that present a recurrent signature or natural history associated with known signs and symptoms and may be managed (more or less successfully) with a repertoire of treatments shown to be effective by evidence concerning past outcomes. According to conventional histories of medicine, science discovers better ways of treating known diseases and finds new diseases. With the discovery of effective treatments, the incidence of "old" diseases, such as smallpox, polio, mumps, and dracunculiasis, has reduced dramatically. As knowledge advances, medical scientists may find that what was considered to be a single disease has more than one variant or discover new diseases. Since the mid-twentieth century new conditions as diverse as AIDS (acquired immune deficiency syndrome), SARS (severe acute respiratory syndrome), Ebola fever, Marburg hemorrhagic fever, hantavirus pulmonary syndrome, post-traumatic stress disorder, and chronic fatigue syndrome have found their way into medical textbooks.

Yet even within the ranks of the medical profession, some observers questioned whether the image of step-by-step discovery of an obdurate, external reality told the whole story. While medical knowledge was undoubtedly advancing, some raised doubts about the conceptualization of diseases as stable entities that had existed even before science discovered them. Lester King (1954: 199), a former editor of the *Journal of the American Medical Association* (JAMA) and president of the American Association for the History of Medicine, observed that:

> We are faced with the problem whether certain relational patterns, like diseases, "exist in nature", while other patterns, like a melody or a poem, we can create arbitrarily by our own skill and ingenuity. The question becomes, does a disease, whatever it is, have real existence, somehow, in its own right, in the same way as the continent of Australia? Such real existence would be independent of its discovery by explorer or investigator. A disease exists whether we know it or not. The contrasting point of view would hold, that a disease is created by an inquiring intellect, carved out by the very process of classification, in the same way that a statue is carved out of a block of marble by the chisel strokes of the sculptor.

King was not arguing the case for nominalism over realism, but rather pointing to the difficulty of grasping an underlying reality in which the precise nature of disease – the patterns observed by physicians – varied over time and between individual patients. Not only, in his view, did systems of classification shift over time, but the disease entities themselves might change as humans interacted in different ways with their changing physical and social environments.

The uncertain relationship between causes identified by scientific medicine and the effects produced in particular individuals, as well as the constantly evolving nature of diseases, were central themes in René Dubos' (1959) celebrated work, *Mirage of Health*. Dubos described how humans provide a habitat for microbes that can easily transform into virulent pathogens and highlighted medicine's inability to explain why the presence of indigenous microbial flora led to infection and disease in one person but not another. For Dubos, human and bacterial populations are part of the same evolving biosphere, and a world in which drugs remove all bacteriological threats is an unattainable goal. Just as humans change to cope with the threat posed by microbes, both via the discovery of new treatments and natural adoptive mechanisms such as immunity, so microbes mutate to exploit weaknesses in biological defenses and develop resistance to previously effective antimicrobial drugs. Thus in place of the image of linear scientific advance, Dubos articulated a vision of changing patterns of interaction between human hosts and evolving microorganisms in which previously eradicated diseases might reappear and established drug therapies might become ineffective. Given that humans share a biosphere with other living organisms, and that interactions may be mutually harmful, some scholars argue that it becomes hard to distinguish diseases from other natural processes.

It can be argued that a similar picture of progress counterbalanced by new challenges (or the return of old ones) is visible in many other areas of medical practice. Advances in the treatment of infectious and other acute diseases need to be weighed against a rising incidence of heart disease, cancers, Alzheimer's disease, and other chronic conditions, which is affecting many advanced countries because of factors such as increasing life expectancy, changes in lifestyle and diet, and growing social inequality (Nordenfelt 1990). Moreover many of the treatments that are developed offer incremental rather than "big step" health gain, so that skeptics write of "halfway technologies" and point to the high cost of interventions that may at best buy a few more months of life (Thomas 1971).

In the philosophy of science, the notion of linear scientific advance was challenged by Kuhn's (1962) seminal work *The Structure of Scientific Revolutions*. Rather than steady, cumulative progress, Kuhn identified discontinuities that arose as periods of "normal science" were punctuated by moments of revolutionary change, when one dominant scientific paradigm was displaced by another. In the "normal" phase a community of scientists who share a general perspective and a set of associated theories – a paradigm or "disciplinary matrix" – seek to fill gaps or resolve anomalies revealed by observations which do not fit with the existing paradigm. Generally this results in incremental modifications to theory or revision of faulty evidence. However, Kuhn points to a pattern where over time changing search technologies and new directions of inquiry throw up an accumulation of observations that do not fit with existing theory. This leads to increasing "debate over fundamentals" and a search for a new conceptual framework – a new world view. After a period of turmoil and controversy, an older paradigm such as Newtonian mechanics is replaced by its successor, quantum physics.

Although Kuhn himself did not use examples from medical science to advance his argument, many later scholars have taken up the idea of changing paradigms in medicine. Medical scientists working in a specialty such as cardiology can be seen as a community of specialists who share a "disciplinary matrix," in the sense of frequent ongoing communication between in-group members and relatively high consensus about the current state of disciplinary knowledge (Hai 2009). Over time major shifts in knowledge occur, such as the transition from Galenic theory to the theory of blood circulation or the emergence of germ theory, often with considerable social resistance from interest groups with a stake in the existing paradigm

(Stern 1927). In our own time advances in genomics and regenerative medicine (stem cell research) suggest that a radical transformation of disciplinary theories and therapies is on the horizon (Perpich 2004; Latimer 2013). One controversial issue in Kuhnian analysis as applied to medicine has been whether changes that may be highly significant for practice in particular specialties really amount to paradigmatic change or are better seen as modifications of middle-level theory that leave existing paradigms intact. Developments in ulcer treatment following the discovery of *Helicobacter pylori* (see below) sparked controversy about what constitutes paradigm shift and whether medicine is a special case.

There is a family resemblance between Kuhnian approaches and the approach of scholars in social history and sociology who write of the social framing of diseases (Rosenberg 1989). Just as Kuhnian analysis directs attention to the dominant modes of reasoning within the scientific community and how the paradigmatic glasses through which it views data reflect its norms and culture, so the idea of framing recognizes that medical knowledge must be seen in a social and cultural context. Rosenberg (1989: 4) is interested in "the nexus between biological event, its perception by patient and practitioner, and the collective effort to make cognitive and policy sense out of those perceptions." The choice of the language of framing is a deliberate attempt to distance this approach from that of social constructivist writers, who in Rosenberg's view have tended to underplay the materiality of disease and exaggerate the degree of arbitrariness in scientific disease classifications, with the consequence that many case studies focus on "socially resonant diseases" such as hysteria, chlorosis, and neurasthenia. Actually this may misrepresent the position of constructivists who acknowledge that real biological pathology exists (see Wright and Treacher 1982; Nicolson and McLaughlin 1987), but, compared with the idea of "construction," the more neutral concept of "framing" sits more easily with the approaches of many social scientists and historians studying disease classifications and their social and cultural connections.

Culture, Disease, and Classification

The concept of classification refers to the idea that human knowledge is not merely an ensemble of facts, but a complex system of categories and ideas about category relations. To know the important attributes of some given phenomenon, it will be enough to place it in a category which shares its general characteristics, and human actors need only memorize those unique features that distinguish it from other items in that category. Health and illness are also understood via a process of classification and categorization (Bowker and Star 1999). It can be argued that the classification system employed by medical professionals overlaps with and is influenced by the systems of classification used in other scientific domains and indeed with general cultural knowledge concerning matters such as practical reasoning, problem solving, political interest, and morality (White 1991). Moreover, it is evident that classificatory schemata used in medicine evolve over time and may differ somewhat from place to place, even among Western countries (Fabrega 1974; Helman 2007; Payer 1988).

It is obvious that disease classifications change over time, but perhaps more difficult to separate simple medical progress from changing understandings shaped by prevailing social mores and cultural perspectives. Many scholars argue that culture, conceived in broad terms, shapes the explanatory frameworks that emerge within the science of the time, as well as the search procedures, instruments of discovery, and modes of problem solving that are deployed.

The way that changing understandings of etiology and treatment shape disease labels, as well as the nature of the condition and the patient experience, is vividly illustrated by Peitzman's (1989) study of the changing framing of renal disease between the eighteenth and twentieth centuries. Peitzman shows how physicians trying to make sense of observed signs and symptoms moved through a succession of explanatory theories and disease classifications. In the late eighteenth century, "dropsy" was a general diagnosis for patients suffering from bodily swelling through an excess of fluid – what medicine today calls edema – which was understood in terms of existing humoral theories of illness. Although dropsy was a familiar malady encountered regularly by physicians, the clinical skills of the day were unable to differentiate edemas arising from different causes. It was only in the 1820s that doctors began to understand these symptoms in a different way, after Richard Bright distinguished that subset attributable to kidney dysfunction. Bright was able to construct a disease entity out of the association between the clinical picture in life, postmortem findings, and chemical changes in urine. Later in the century clinicians redefined and refined the characteristics of Bright's disease using such techniques as microscopic examination of tissue and urinary sediment.

The essence of Bright's disease was that patients got sick through their kidneys, but in the twentieth century this same conceptual space came to be occupied not by one disease but several. A new generation of doctors looked to physiology rather than the older lesion-based anatomical knowledge and searched for functional indicators using laboratory methods. Techniques applied to the stomach and the heart were applied by analogy to the kidney. As doctors began to perform tests for such things as dye excretion and urea loads, new terms such as renal insufficiency and renal failure entered the medical vocabulary. Renal failure meant retention of urea and other substances normally discharged by the healthy kidney. Gradually it became clear that patients might progress to renal failure without showing all the characteristics attributed to Bright's disease. Peitzman outlines a complicated succession of, sometimes competing, pathologic classification frameworks put forward by physicians and clinical scientists as they tried to identify subtypes of renal disease.

Peitzman's analysis concludes with an examination of a common diagnostic category applied to many renal disease patients from the late twentieth century to the present time, end-stage renal failure. Many dropsy sufferers would probably fall into that category if transported forward in time, and yet the experience of illness is completely different for the ESRF patient. Most are treated long before they become "dropsical," so that the bloated bodies characterizing eighteenth-century sufferers would not be encountered by modern physicians. Nephrologists are now unlikely to come across the severe edema and uremia that characterized dropsy, and indeed much of their time is spent managing problems of the "cure" – dialysis – rather than the underlying pathology. The specialist rarely sees a kidney. The renal doctor is only likely to see kidneys as shadows on an ultrasound image or, microscopically, biopsied a small slice at a time.

The history of renal disease illustrates how a basic clinical picture is defined and redefined over time using a succession of differently focused explanatory frameworks. It is not merely that new disease labels are applied to constant physical phenomena, but one overarching conceptual scheme displaces another. Moreover this change is not simply a reflection of the state of a cumulatively developing corpus of medical knowledge, but depends on changing technologies, social practices, and professional and societal world views. Peitzman (1989: 21) argues that the shift of frame from dropsy to Bright's disease is not merely a new diagnosis based on new data, but represents a change in the way that doctors name diseases – "a new, nineteenth-century way of thinking about and defining disease." The focus shifts from the patient history and experiences reported to the physician to laboratory investigations that only the physician can perform. Anatomical observations are replaced by "functional diagnosis," and emerging nineteenth-century technologies yielded up new clinical parameters that helped to define the disease entity. When the explanatory limitations of Bright's disease become apparent, no single disease category emerged to cover the spectrum of diffuse renal disease. The term that came into widespread use – end-stage renal failure – had its origins in a 1972 Act of Congress, which outlined a practical threshold for public financial support for Americans requiring chronic dialysis treatment. ESRF is an administrative category bound up inextricably with twentieth-century US social policy and societal attitudes toward disabled people, but it became a shorthand diagnostic label commonly used by clinicians. As Peitzman states, each of the disease labels examined "has had its use, its particular reality, and its message," and each is closely related to the way of seeing of the time.

Peitzman tells us that the transition between frames takes time and is not accepted by all practitioners but says little about the conflict and micro-political struggles sometimes associated with scientific advances – something that is emphasized in the Kuhnian approach. The social anthropologist Bernhard Stern (1927, 1941), an early critic of the conventional history of medicine, focuses more on opposition to scientific advances and the social and cultural factors that retard the diffusion of innovation. In a classic text that still remains relevant today, Stern (1927) shows that almost all the major medical advances of the eighteenth and nineteenth centuries – from Harvey's theory of blood circulation to Jenner's work on vaccination and the breakthroughs of Semmelweis and Pasteur – met with resistance at the time of their discovery. Forces that impede change operate at the individual, group, and institutional levels. Individuals resist change because it can mean personal inconvenience, temporary pain, more work, and an end to old comfortable habits. For the group it can lead to disruption of existing routines and customs that disturb the status quo. At the institutional level, existing patterns of tradition and authority tend to protect established practices. Stern highlights the brakes on change applied when a new theory conflicts with established cultural ideas and also the self-protective behavior of professionals or powerful interest groups who regard innovation as a threat to their economic interests. He argues that scientific advances are often intertwined with political struggles, and technical knowledge may be redefined to suit the profession's interest. Thus Stern (1941: 216) maintains that "medicine cannot develop and never has developed in isolation, that the nature of its role and its achievements are circumscribed by the soil in which it is rooted."

Scientific Progress and the Social and Cultural Context

How far, the reader may ask, is opposition to scientific progress a facet of medical history that is now firmly in the past? A more recent case that suggests its continued relevance concerns the discovery of the *Helicobacter pylori* bacterium and the resultant shift from the excess acid theory of peptic ulcers to the bacterial infection theory. The case illustrates how reluctance to accept new evidence may be related to issues of both culture and power.

In the 1960s the view emerged that ulcers were the product of stress resulting in an excess of acid damaging the surface of the stomach or duodenum. It was assumed that high acidic concentrations in these organs made it impossible for bacteria to survive, but this was challenged in 1979 when the Australian pathologist Warren observed spiral bacteria in microscopic slides prepared from endoscopy tissue biopsies. Further work over several years by a team led by Warren and the gastroenterologist Marshall established the existence of a previously unknown bacterium that they named *Helicobacter pylori*.

The *H. pylori* case has come to be associated with debates about the nature of scientific and medical paradigms and possible refinements of the Kuhnian position that are beyond the scope of this discussion (Thagard 1998; Gillies 2005; Hutton 2012). However, scholars on both sides of this debate acknowledge that Warren and Marshall's discovery was met with skepticism and resistance from the scientific community. Even though the theory of bacteriological infection was well established in other domains, it was some years before the causal role of *H. pylori* in peptic ulcers was widely accepted by practitioners, so that treatments based on the acid excess theory continued to be prescribed.

Collyer (1996) suggests that the new theory ran counter to the interests of large pharmaceutical companies, such as GlaxoSmithKline, which had invested heavily in profitable H2-antagonist drugs. The new treatment approach did not initially involve a purpose-designed antibiotic that might have had commercial appeal and so failed to gain corporate sponsorship for research and dissemination that the drug industry could have provided. It was only when Procter & Gamble realized that one of their patented products had anti-bacteriological as well as acid-reducing effects that the company began to support the ongoing research.

Nor was there much support for the new theory in the medical profession. Collyer (1996) argues that the new infection theory encountered resistance because it suggested that physicians' existing ideas about the importance of stress, lifestyle, and individual responsibility for behavioral change had been flawed. The older approach aligned with prevailing cultural stereotypes about the association between overeating and poor diet with stomach disease, but the new one suggested that, rather than being a matter of individual responsibility, high rates of recurrence of ulcers among treated patients reflected the limitations of present medical knowledge.

Commentators skeptical about the importance of cultural influences point out that several recent studies of new diseases (e.g., Richman and Jason 2001; Young 1997) involve psychological symptoms, in which the nature of underlying pathology is difficult to identify. The argument is that ideas about social construction or cultural framing are easier to apply when no physical disease exists. However, this criticism cannot be applied to Greaves' (1998) study of acute myocardial infarction, a leading cause of death in Western countries, which surprisingly did not emerge as a recognized disease entity until the twentieth century. It was only in the 1920s that the "new" heart conditions found their way into medical textbooks, and Greaves reviews the competing theories about why "heart attacks" had not been recognized earlier, including failure of diagnosis and the non-appearance of a disease of affluence in advance of the "epidemiological transition" to modern lifestyles. He finds both explanations unconvincing but is also dissatisfied with social constructivist accounts that portray the discovery of myocardial infarction as the result of a new disease classification connected with the emerging specialism of cardiology and its need to establish an expert knowledge base. Greaves instead argues that material changes in lifestyles and risk came into play at the same time that doctors were moving toward new theories of heart disease and patients toward new ways of understanding their illnesses. There was a "looping effect" (see also Hacking 1996) whereby medical and lay definitions comingled in shaping societal perceptions of the new condition. This was reinforced by "a cultural climate and expectation which is conducive to and sustains part of the epidemic of these heart disorders" (Greaves 1998: 139). Greaves' analysis thus involves a complex composite of objective and subjective and individual and social factors, in which there is an overlap between science and the wider corpus of cultural knowledge.

Lay Health Beliefs

Greaves' mention of the interplay between professional and patient definitions suggests that disease classification systems need to be considered in conjunction with lay understandings of illness. Physicians are familiar with a range of disease entities and their characteristic manifestations but also have firsthand knowledge of how patients understand and respond to their experiences of illness. Medical practice involves taking account of these lay perspectives and finding ways to mediate between professional and patient understandings of health and illness.

Illness refers to a person's subjective experience of ill health. As Fabrega (1974: 120) writes, "People don't feel X-ray shadows, blood chemistries, or auscultatory findings. Rather, people feel or report weakness, coughing, and excessive urination." Thus illness refers to the individual's perception of feeling unwell – pain, discomfort, and so on – and any modification of normal behavior that results. This is heavily shaped by culture, as well as social position and personality. Like disease classification systems, lay health beliefs and illness behavior vary according to place and time.

The example of depressive disorders is often used to make this point. Early studies suggested that patients from certain non-Western cultures reported fewer symptoms related to internal mood states and more relating to physical symptoms. Arthur Kleinman (1980) studied depression and neurasthenia in Taiwan and mainland China and found that patients used terms referring or relating to the body while utilizing few categories corresponding to Western psychological states. This supported the notion that somatization, the physical presentation of psychological distress, was more common among non-Western populations, an idea that has been challenged in more recent debates. Contemporary scholars regard somatization as a worldwide phenomenon but argue that different groups present somatic symptoms in different ways related to wider patterns of cultural meanings and the various psychological and social functions that somatization serves (Kirmayer and Young 1998; Kohrt 2014).

Differences between lay belief systems and Western medicine are not confined to distant cultures. Chrisman (1977) suggested a framework for the cross-cultural analysis of folk ideas about illness, setting out some of the basic modes of thought about illness – what he calls "thought logics" – that apply in many countries. He identifies a logic of degeneration or the running down of the body, a mechanical logic concerned with blockages or damage to bodily structures, a logic of balance linked to the disruption of bodily harmony, and a logic of invasion involving germ theory and material intrusions.

These logics are readily apparent in the findings of some of the important British research in this area. A classic study by Blaxter (1983) interviewed a sample of middle-aged, working-class women in Scotland about their ideas on health and illness. When questioned about the causes of illnesses, most women gave explanations which bore only a loose resemblance to those of medical science. Infection was the most commonly cited cause, followed by heredity, then by environmental hazards, and then other factors such as the secondary effects of other diseases, stress, and childbearing. Another seminal study carried out by Pill and Stott (1982) in South Wales looked at women in their early 30s who came from skilled manual backgrounds. Again infection (or "germs") was the most commonly mentioned cause of illness, followed by lifestyle, heredity, and stress. About half the women in the sample utilized concepts of causality that implied that illness was associated with choices about behavior and a degree of individual responsibility. These women were more likely to be homeowners and to have had more education than the women in Blaxter's sample, and their feeling of greater control over their lives may account for the different emphasis.

The logic of invasion can be seen as the cultural result of the theories of microbiology that are central to mainstream medicine. But heredity seems to come up more in lay belief systems than in conventional medicine, and lay beliefs which emphasize "stress," worry, and tension seem closer to holistic approaches than to the mainstream biomedical model, which emphasizes physical processes.

One important point is that although lay beliefs often appear to contain illogical ideas or inconsistencies, they can be part of a wider system of beliefs that makes sense to participants. This is illustrated by Helman's (1978) study of patterns of belief about infectious diseases in a North London community. Helman argues that some common infectious diseases that involve raised body temperature are understood in terms of a folk belief system which is quite distinct from medical science. Patients distinguish the subjectively "hot" diseases that are usually thought of as fevers from the cold diseases that are classified as colds or chills. Each of these two categories is associated with a set of ideas about cause, the course of the illness, treatment, and the degree of blame attaching to the sufferer. Colds and chills are seen as a result of the interaction between the individual and unfavorable environmental conditions, particularly low temperatures, which through dampness, cold winds, and drafts penetrate vulnerable surfaces of the body such as the head and feet. Transitions such as moving into a cold room after a hot bath are believed to make the individual particularly vulnerable. Treatment involves restoring temperature balance by hot drinks or a warm bed. Individuals often believe themselves to be to blame for getting a cold because of irresponsible actions like going outside with wet hair and the like. Fevers on the other hand are due to invisible entities – germs or bugs – transmitted from individual to individual. One important treatment is fluid that flushes out germs. The individual carries less personal blame for fevers because they are unavoidably transmitted through contact with other people. Helman points to the similarities between the way people in Britain talk about germs and people in simple agricultural societies talk about spirits – from the point of view of folk beliefs, both are intangible and hypothetical and strike in mysterious ways.

These early studies have been supplemented by a corpus of later research that confirms variation in health beliefs and behavior among men and women from different social classes, geographical areas, and ethnic groups (for reviews see Lupton 2003; Stainton-Rogers 1991; Blaxter 2010). However, scholars differ in their views about whether divergent lay perspectives on illness are entirely a cultural phenomenon, depending on beliefs and attitudes passed from generation to generation. Sociologists in particular have often argued against the proposition that a culture of poverty, in which successive generations in disadvantaged populations engage in unhealthy behaviors, is the primary explanation for social class differences in morbidity and mortality. They have instead argued that material differences in the living conditions and life chances of richer or poorer social groups affect the resources available and everyday experiences of health and illness.

From the point of view of doctors and other healthcare professionals, understanding such differences is important for good practice. Sensitivity to these matters pays off even in narrow terms of clinical effectiveness. For example, Iniu et al. (1976) examined how far patients treated for hypertension cooperated with treatment. Doctors who had received training about patients' health beliefs were encouraged to discuss patients' ideas more fully before explaining the diagnosis and arranging treatment. When these patients were compared with a control group who had not had the benefit of such a discussion, they were found to comply better with the prescribed drug regime and to achieve better blood pressure control. Harwood (1971) gives another example in a culture contact situation. Puerto Ricans in New York retain a belief system in which all illnesses, medicines, and foods are hot or cold. Vitamin supplements prescribed for pregnant women were frequently not taken because they were believed to be "hot" and to cause rashes and irritations to babies. However, there was no difficulty if supplements were taken with fruit juice – which is classified as cold. Other important studies show how, in areas as diverse as the implementation of Ebola control policies (Hewlett and Hewlett 2008), HIV/AIDS education programs (Lyttleton 1993), and the treatment of immigrant populations in developed countries (Fadiman 1997), the successful application of ideas from Western medical science depends on awareness of, and sensitivity to, local or migrant cultures.

Medical Culture

The practical application of medical knowledge involves interaction with other healthcare professionals in a range of clinical sites, typically associated with distinctive organizational subcultures. The culture of medicine, or more specifically the subcultural beliefs and practices of the specialism or healthcare locale in which the individual doctor is practicing, is an important factor that affects how expert knowledge is mobilized in real-world situations.

Medical culture is shaped by convergent influences such as medical school but also affected by the different career trajectories and work environments of practitioners. Professional cultures are transmitted both through the formal training process and the bedside experience of speciality work. Career advancement may be more dependent on normative compliance rather than technical excellence, and the literature suggests the importance of sponsorship and the existence of an influential patronage system (Bosk 1979; Atkinson 1981). Nor is the single hospital or clinic necessarily the unit of analysis; cultures may cut across organizational boundaries, as when medical consultants hold appointments or admitting rights in more than one facility. In cultural terms hospitals are becoming more rather than less complex entities as they adjust to an increasingly complex division of labor, a proliferation of special locales, and a range of new occupational categories. This has been associated by some scholars with "tribalism" and conflict, not just between different occupational groups such as doctors and managers, but within the medical profession itself. For example, sociologists argue that the medical profession has adjusted to oversight by general managers by "re-stratifying" itself to create a group of management-oriented doctors who act as mediators between clinicians and hospital administration and may sometimes support rationalized policies opposed by professional colleagues (Numerato et al. 2012).

Interactions between doctors are guided by in-group norms and tacit rules. Both talk in medical consultations with patients and the language of case presentation among colleagues take a stylized form that serves to legitimize the expertise and authority of professionals (Atkinson 1995). Generally medical talk communicates the objective nature of decision making and the uniform competence of the practitioners. However, hierarchy and disciplinary rivalries also enter the picture. Thus, Atkinson (1995) found that the hematologists he studied erected subtle "us/we" and "them/they" distinctions when they considered the evidence assembled by the team compared with other more distant colleagues, weaving into their case narratives delicate attributions of differential credibility and sometimes blame.

Ethnographic studies suggest that a gap exists between the version of medical practice presented in public forums, or in consultations with patients, and the version communicated between colleagues behind the scenes. The discrepancy between public and private accounts may be especially clear when error is involved. A number of researchers describe how doctors distinguish between different types of error and determine what constitutes an error in particular circumstances. Clinical uncertainty and the unpredictability of treatment mean that what constitutes a mistake may be a highly contested matter. Bosk (1979) enumerates four types of error recognized by doctors. "Technical errors" occur when a surgeon is performing his role conscientiously, but his skill falls short of what the task requires. "Judgmental errors" occur when an incorrect strategy of treatment is chosen. "Normative errors" occur when a surgeon (usually a subordinate) fails in the eyes of others to discharge his/her role obligations conscientiously. "Quasi-normative errors" occur when subordinates fail to follow the practices or techniques favored by individual senior surgeons ("attendings"). Bosk found that the first two categories were usually seen as involving honest mistakes that were an accepted cost of training. But the last two types of error breached moral rules, specifically the etiquette governing role relations between senior surgeons and house staff, and were regarded in more serious light. Where a junior made repeated technical errors, he or she might still be regarded as a conscientious professional who could pursue a career in another branch of medicine, but repeated normative errors were taken to indicate unsuitability for the profession. Bosk describes how peer surveillance of performance takes place through a series of rounds, reviews, and conferences in which the moral meanings surrounding surgical error are reinforced. While colleagues take a supportive stance toward technical errors and perceive them as occasions for learning lessons, they are unforgiving and intolerant of moral errors.

For example, professional self-protection has been blamed for continuing high rates of iatrogenesis and several recent scandals about care in British NHS hospitals. After the discovery of high mortality rates in a pediatric cardiac surgery unit, the 2001 Bristol Royal Infirmary Inquiry Report suggested that professional culture has played a significant part in hiding and amplifying bad practices. It mentioned factors such as a mind-set of "professional hubris" in a teaching hospital, a "club culture" with insiders and outsiders, professional rivalries, the unwillingness of senior doctors to engage with interdisciplinary teams except as team leaders, the covering up of patient deaths on the basis that surgeons were on a "learning curve," and the discouragement of "whistle-blowing." A decade or so later, similar issues were laid bare by the Francis Inquiry Report following revelations about poor patient outcomes at the Mid Staffordshire NHS Trust. The Inquiry wrote of lack of engagement between management and senior doctors, an over-preoccupation with targets, a tendency to "close ranks" to hide problems, and a "culture of fear" preventing disclosure of adverse incidents (Holmes 2013). These were perhaps the two most prominent in a string of recent British scandals that highlight how medical practice within modern multidisciplinary healthcare settings, subject to financial pressures and increasingly rationalized management regimes, is affected by social factors that influence how medical knowledge is applied in the treatment of individual patients.

Science and Art in Medical Culture

A final point for consideration is how medicine fits into the wider domain of science. Different cultures segment and organize their corpus of expert knowledge in different ways, including how they map domains such as religion, magic, philosophy and science, and the relations between them (Fabrega 1974). In Western Europe medicine did not always align itself with science, and indeed there is a degree of continuing ambivalence about the relationship among medical practitioners.

Before the 1840s Western medicine was practice based and mixed a romantic philosophy of nature with mystical ideas about spirituality and machine metaphors of the body (Verwey 1990). It was only in the mid-nineteenth century that medically trained researchers in German universities incorporated the new physiology into the medical curriculum and some years later before the British universities followed suit (Jewson 1976). The growth of the research laboratories depended on the institutional support of the medical schools. The rise of scientific medicine provides a new source of legitimation for the previously diverse and individualistic craft of healing. It was "a powerful and compelling means of conferring "expert status" on medicine, thereby consolidating its position as an "autonomous" learned profession" (Austoker 1988: 31). William Osler pioneered "science at the bedside" practice based on the growing body of laboratory-derived knowledge and brought about striking advances in the treatment of vitamin deficiencies and pernicious anemia (Beeson 1980).

However, within the medical profession there remained an undercurrent of resistance to a purely technical medicine that has persisted into the modern era. Thus the rise of scientific rationality led to a defensive counteraction through the reaffirmation of an older clinical tradition, which emphasized the individuality of patients and the indeterminacy of the practitioner's experiential knowledge and skills (Jamous and Peloille 1970). French hospital doctors responded to growing "technicality" by appealing to the mystery of clinical experience, a body of knowledge not susceptible to precise codification. Over time a clinical tradition that had originally developed in eighteenth-century France had a continuing influence on physicians in Europe and North America and finds its voice in opposition to modern developments such as standardization and the application of clinical decision theory. This is manifest in the continuing tension between healthcare managers and medical professionals mentioned earlier and highlighted in events such as the scandal concerning patient care in the Mid Staffordshire NHS Trust.

The uneasy relationship between medicine and science reflects the fact that science is not fully under the medical profession's control. Clinical researchers do not enjoy clear superiority over nonclinical scientists working in chemistry, physiology, pharmacology, or genetics, who are often based in the research institute rather than the medical school (Strong 1984). The basic medical education is not a sufficient preparation for advanced bioscience research. Generally speaking medical graduates in Western countries learn only enough to be able to mediate between science and practice. This mediation effectively comes to mean controlling patients' access to the products of scientific research. For example, physicians function as "gatekeepers" to a variety of high-cost interventions or drugs. The medical profession's close contacts with the pharmaceutical industry and its legal monopoly in many countries over prescribing ensure that it does not share this strategic position with other occupations.

Definitions of Key Terms

Culture	Is the system of language, belief, and knowledge that shapes a given social group's understanding of the world; for the purposes of this chapter, this includes the group's characteristic modes of problem solving and the techniques via which it generates new knowledge.
Medical knowledge	Is the corpus of empirical observations, evidence, and theory transmitted via published literature, databases, and oral communications between medical practitioners and researchers and commanding significant support within the profession at a given time.
The medical profession	Consists of the persons formally licensed or registered by authoritative national bodies to engage in medical practice; generally speaking governments grant the profession authority to define what counts as legitimate medical knowledge and to regulate the conduct of its members.
Lay health beliefs	Are the beliefs that people hold about the health, illness, and disease; they are shaped by culture, social position, and individual biographies.

| Medical culture | Refers to the language, thought processes, styles of communication, customs, and beliefs observable in medical education and practice; it is transmitted both in the medical school and via informal socialization in clinical settings. |
| The art and science of medicine | Refers to two strands within medical opinion that respectively emphasize the experience and intuitive clinical skills of individual doctors and the value of systematic scientific evidence and standardization and rationalization in medical decision making. |

Summary Points

- Culture, the system of symbols and beliefs through which a group understands its world, influences the content of expert as well as everyday knowledge.
- Although medical knowledge may be seen as the product of scientific discovery involving direct engagement with the facts of the natural world, it has been built up within social and cultural contexts that influence its development.
- Rather than seeing medical advance as a linear process of progressive discovery, many philosophers and social scientists have argued that one theoretical paradigm will over time replace another and that these changing conceptual frameworks reflect the wider societal culture and prevailing modes of thought.
- Examples such as those presented in this chapter show that disease classifications and understandings of etiology are closely connected with other aspects of contemporary culture.
- Doctors are experts in the body of theory, evidence, and experience that comprises Western medical knowledge but must apply that knowledge in interaction with patients whose lay health beliefs about illness and its causes may not align with professional perspectives; thus the practice of medicine involves mediating between expert knowledge and lay belief systems influenced by local cultures.
- Medical knowledge is applied within the context of medical culture and the particular subcultural contexts of the clinical specialties and variegated locales in which practice takes place; studies have shown that sociocultural factors such as hierarchy, professional rivalry, and self-protective behavior impact upon medical practice.
- Medicine is both an art and a science and medical knowledge has both experiential and scientific components; professionals differ in their views about the relative importance of the clinical judgment of the individual doctor (rooted in traditional medical culture) and standardization based on codified, evidence-based knowledge.
- More generally there is a continuing tension between medicine as a practice-based discipline and medical science in the research laboratory, something which is the outcome of history and the way Western cultures segment domains of knowledge.

References

Atkinson P (1981) The clinical experience: the construction and reconstruction of medical reality. Gower, London

Atkinson P (1995) Medical talk and medical work. Sage, London

Austoker J (1988) A history of the Imperial Cancer Research Fund, 1902–1986. Oxford University Press, Oxford

Beeson P (1980) Changes in medical therapy during the past half century. Medicine 59:79–99

Blaxter M (1983) The causes of disease: women talking. Soc Sci Med 17:59–69

Blaxter M (2010) Health, 2nd edn. Polity, Cambridge

Bosk C (1979) Forgive and remember: managing medical failure. Chicago University Press, Chicago

Bowker GC, Star SL (1999) Sorting things out: classification and its consequences. MIT Press, Cambridge, MA

Chrisman NJ (1977) The health seeking process: An approach to the natural history of illness. Culture, Medicine and Psychiatry 1:351–377

Collyer FM (1996) Understanding ulcers: medical knowledge, social constructionism and helicobacter pylori. Ann Rev Health Soc Sci 6:1–39

Dubos R (1987) Mirage of health: utopias, progress and biological change (1st edn. 1959). Rutgers University Press, New Brunswick

Fabrega H (1974) Disease and social behavior: an interdisciplinary perspective. MIT Press, Cambridge, MA

Fadiman A (1997) The spirit catches you and you fall down: a Hmong child, her American doctors, and the collision of two cultures. Farrar, Straus and Giroux, New York

Gillies D (2005) Hempelian and Kuhnian approaches in the philosophy of medicine: the Semmelweis case. Stud Hist Philos Biol Biomed Sci 36:159–181

Greaves D (1998) What are heart attacks? Rethinking some aspects of medical knowledge. Med Healthc Philos 1:133–141

Hacking I (1996) The looping effects of human kinds. In: Sperber D, Premack D, Premack AJ (eds) Causal cognition: a multidisciplinary debate. Clarendon, Oxford, pp 351–383

Hai H (2009) Kuhn and the two cultures of Western and Chinese medicine. J Camb Stud 4:10–36

Harwood A (1971) The hot-cold theory of disease: implications for treatment of Puerto Rican patients. JAMA 216:1153–1158

Helman CG (1978) "Feed a cold, starve a fever" – folk models of infection in an English suburban community, and their relation to medical treatment. Cult Med Psychiatry 2:107–137

Helman CG (2007) Culture, health and illness, 5th edn. Hodder Arnold, London

Hewlett BS, Hewlett BL (2008) Ebola, culture, and politics: the anthropology of an emerging disease. Wadsworth, Belmont

Holmes D (2013) Mid Staffordshire scandal highlights NHS cultural crisis. Lancet 381:521–522

Hutton J (2012) Composite paradigms in medicine: analysing Gillies' claim of reclassification of disease without paradigm shift in the case of Helicobacter pylori. Stud Hist Philos Biol Biomed Sci 43:643–654

Inui TS, Yourtree EL, Williamson JW (1976) Improved outcomes in hypertension after physician tutorials: a controlled trial. Ann Intern Med 84:646–651

Jamous H, Peloille B (1970) Professions as self-perpetuating systems? Changes in the French university hospital system. In: Jackson JA (ed) Professions and professionalization: sociological studies 3. Cambridge University Press, Cambridge, pp 109–152

Jewson N (1976) The disappearance of the sick man from medical cosmology, 1770–1870. Sociology 10:225–244

King LS (1954) What is disease? Philos Sci 21:193–203

Kirmayer L, Young A (1998) Culture and somatization: clinical, epidemiological, and ethnographic perspectives. Psychosom Med 60:420–430

Kleinman A (1980) Patients and healers in the context of culture: an exploration of the borderland between anthropology, medicine, and psychiatry. University of California Press, Berkeley

Kohrt BA (2014) Somatization. In: Cockerham WC, Dingwall R, Quay S (eds) The Wiley-Blackwell encyclopedia of health, illness, behavior and society. Wiley, New York, pp 2248–2251

Kuhn TS (1962) The structure of scientific revolutions. University of Chicago Press, Chicago

Latimer J (2013) The gene, the clinic, and the family: diagnosing dysmorphology, reviving medical dominance. Routledge, London.

Lupton D (2003) Medicine as culture: illness, disease and the body, 2nd edn. Sage, London

Lyttleton C (1993) Knowledge and meaning: the AIDS education campaign in rural northeast Thailand. Soc Sci Med 38:135–146

Nicolson M, McLaughlin C (1987) Social constructionism and medical sociology: a reply to M.R. Bury. Sociol Health Illn 9:107–126

Nordenfelt L (1990) Comments on Wulff's, Thung's and Lindahl's essays on the growth of medical knowledge, pp 121–130. In: ten Have H, Kimsma G, Spicker SF (eds) The growth of medical knowledge. Kluwer, Dordrecht, pp 121–130

Numerato D, Salvatore D, Fattor G (2012) The impact of management on medical professionalism: a review. Sociol Health Illn 34:626–644

Payer L (1988) Medicine and culture: varieties of treatment in the United States, England, West Germany, and France. Holt, New York

Peitzman SJ (1989) From dropsy to Bright's disease to end-stage renal disease. Milbank Q 67 (Suppl 1):16–32

Perpich JG (2004) The dawn of genomic and regenerative medicine: new paradigms for medicine, the public's health, and society. Technol Soc 26:405–414

Pill R, Stott NCH (1982) Concepts of illness causation and responsibility: some preliminary data from a sample of working class mothers. Soc Sci Med 16:43–52.

Richman JA, Jason LA (2001) Gender biases underlying the social construction of illness states: the case of chronic fatigue syndrome. Curr Sociol 49:15–29

Rosenberg CE (1989) Disease in history: frames and framers. Milbank Q 67(Suppl 1):1–15

Stainton Rogers W (1991) Explaining health and illness: an exploration of diversity. Wheatsheaf, London

Stern B (1941) Society and medical progress. Princeton University Press, Princeton

Stern B (1968) Social factors in medical progress (1st edn. 1927). AMS Publishers, New York

Strong PM (1984) Viewpoint: the academic encirclement of medicine. Sociol Health Illn 6:339–358

Thagard P (1998) Ulcers and bacteria I: discovery and acceptance. Stud Hist Philos Sci Part C Biol Biomed Sci 29:107–136

Thomas L (1971) The technology of medicine. NEJM 285:1366–1368

Verwey G (1990) Medicine, anthropology, and the human body. In: ten Have H, Kimsma G, Spicker SF (eds) The growth of medical knowledge. Kluwer, Dordrecht, pp 133–162

Watts AW (1989) The book: on the taboo against knowing who you are. Vintage Books, New York

White K (1991) The sociology of health and illness, trend report. Curr Sociol 39:1–40

Wright P, Treacher A (eds) (1982) The problem of medical knowledge: examining the social construction of medicine. Edinburgh University Press, Edinburgh

Young A (1997) The harmony of illusions: inventing post-traumatic stress disorder. Princeton University Press, Princeton

Hippocrates and the Hippocratic Tradition: Impact on Development of Medical Knowledge and Practice?

50

James A. Marcum

Contents

Abstract

What impact, if any, did Hippocrates and the Hippocratic tradition have on the development of medical knowledge and practice? For some, Hippocrates is the "Father of (Western or Modern) Medicine," and the Hippocratic tradition provides a framework for the development of contemporary medicine – especially a rational, scientific medicine. Hippocrates and the Hippocratic tradition are not only important in terms of the development of medical knowledge but also its practice, as exemplified by the Hippocratic oath. For others, modern medicine represents a rejection not so much of Hippocrates but only of the Hippocratic tradition, especially its vitalism and humoral theory of health and disease. In this chapter, the impact of Hippocrates and the Hippocratic tradition on the development of medical knowledge is explored first, followed by an examination of how they, especially the oath, shaped medical practice. The chapter concludes with a discussion of the lessons this exploration into Hippocrates and the Hippocratic tradition teach about the future of medical knowledge and practice.

J.A. Marcum (✉)
Department of Philosophy, Baylor University, Waco, TX, USA
e-mail: James_Marcum@baylor.edu

© Springer Science+Business Media Dordrecht 2017
T. Schramme, S. Edwards (eds.), *Handbook of the Philosophy of Medicine*,
DOI 10.1007/978-94-017-8688-1_82

Introduction

In this introductory section, it is briefly discussed who Hippocrates is and what the Hippocratic tradition is in order to provide the historical background necessary for the two main sections of the chapter. In the first section, it is explored what kind of impact Hippocrates' theory of medicine – especially as articulated in the Hippocratic tradition in terms of vitalism and humoralism – had on the development of medical knowledge. The impact's trajectory for that development is examined with respect to such diverse medical specialties, ranging from cardiology to spine surgery. In the second section, the impact of Hippocrates and the Hippocratic tradition on medical practice is explored, especially in terms of the Hippocratic oath. In a concluding section, the lessons this exploration into Hippocrates and the Hippocratic tradition teach about the future of medical knowledge and practice are discussed.

Who was Hippocrates? This question is difficult to answer, at best, because of limited resources on Hippocrates' personal life, medical practice, and literary output, especially by his peers. Unfortunately, the earliest extant biography of Hippocrates was not written until almost five centuries after his death by Soranus of Ephesus. Several other brief biographical works date from the tenth and twelfth centuries CE. "The material about Hippocrates was invented," claims Jody Pinault, "growing slowly during the Hellenistic period" (1992, 1). Indeed, the consensus today is that little is known about the historical Hippocrates in terms of his life, career, and writings (Jouanna 1999; King 2001; Levine 1971; Nutton 2013; Scarborough 1997; Schiefsky 2005; Smith 1990; Temkin 1991). "The commingling of legend, myth, and hagiography in the biography of Hippocrates attests to the fact," concludes Steven Miles, "that almost nothing is known about him" (2004, 28).

Traditionally, the birth of Hippocrates is assigned to the year 460 BCE, during the 80th Olympiad, on the Greek island of Cos. Hippocrates' father was Heraclides, who was also a physician and whose lineage is reputed to include Asclepius – the divine Greek physician. Hippocrates' mother was Phaenarete, who was supposedly a descendent of Hercules. Hippocrates lived during the classical or golden period of Greek culture under the aegis of the "first citizen of Athens," Pericles. Hippocrates' father was responsible for his early medical education, but, after his parent's death, he left Cos to further his medical education. According to Soranus of Cos, Hippocrates first traveled to Thessaly in obedience to a command given in a dream. When the plague that infested Athens erupted during the second year of the Peloponnesian war (430 BCE), Pericles invited Hippocrates to save the city's inhabitants from it. Hippocrates was successful, and a golden wreath was bestowed upon him, and he was made a citizen of Athens. He eventually returned to Cos where he was influential in the Coan school of medicine. He is alleged to have died in Larissa, although the exact date is uncertain.

The historical fact of Hippocrates' existence, however, is not in contention among scholars. Indeed, such contemporaries as Plato, Aristotle, and Aristotle's student Menon refer to him in their writings (Longrigg 1998). For example, Plato informs the reader that Hippocrates, a "member of the Asclepiadae," collected fees from students for instruction in the medical arts (*Protagoras* 311b-c) and also discusses Hippocrates' clinical method in terms of assessing the "nature of the whole" with respect to a phenomenon's simplicity or complexity (*Phaedrus* 270c-d). Aristotle called him a great physician, although he found him small in stature (*Politics* 1326a13-16). Finally, Menon discusses Hippocrates' medical theory concerning the etiology of disease in terms of breaths or *physai* (*Anonymus Londinensis* 5.35–7.40). What is in contention among scholars, however, is the myth surrounding Hippocrates' personal and professional life, especially when the literary works attributed to him began to escalate during the Hellenistic period while the medical literary works were being compiled in Alexandria – , which leads to the next question.

What is the Hippocratic tradition? Briefly, the tradition represents the impact of Hippocrates on the development of medical knowledge and practice (Joly 1983; Mansfeld 1983; Michell 2010; Smith 1979). As Wesley Smith (1979) demonstrates in an analysis of the historical trajectory of the tradition, medical communities from every age – since Hippocrates practiced medicine – have been influenced by him. An example from the modern Hippocratic tradition is Thomas Sydenham, who is known as the "English Hippocrates." Sydenham championed Hippocratic observation to cure disease in contrast to theoretical constructs to explain it. Of course, Galen is an important figure in the development of the Hippocratic tradition, as are other ancient personages – especially from the Hellenistic period when the Hippocratic corpus was initially being collected in the fourth century BCE. Smith (1979) points in particular to the pseudepigrapha, a collection of letters and speeches, as chiefly responsible for establishing the mythical dimensions of the Hippocratic tradition. Throughout medical history, Hippocrates has been used to justify the current approach to medical knowledge and practice, and no single Hippocratic tradition captures its nature, but rather there are multiple traditions based on a particular historical era and country.

A major problem associated with the Hippocratic tradition – often called the Hippocratic question – is determining which, if any, of the books forming the Hippocratic corpus were genuinely written by Hippocrates. To date, over 60 volumes comprise the corpus (Corpus Medicorum Graecorum 2015). In a critical analysis of the question, Geoffrey Lloyd (1975) tackles both the external and internal evidence concerning various attempts to ascribe Hippocratic authorship to selected works in the corpus. With respect to external evidence, Lloyd concludes that it is simply too self-serving for the author citing Hippocrates as author to provide a standard by which to evaluate whether a book from the corpus was indeed authored by Hippocrates. Moreover, he acknowledges that a collection of medical treatises is extant by the early third century BCE but that the commentaries forming the corpus obfuscate rather than clarify Hippocratic authorship. With respect to the internal evidence, Lloyd concludes that it too cannot supply a standard by which to judge the authenticity of a book's Hippocratic authorship because of the "heterogeneity" of the doctrines expounded in the corpus – to the extent that even contradictions surface within it. "It may be that some of Hippocrates' work has come down to us in the Corpus," concludes Lloyd, "but we cannot now prove this, nor determine which his work is" (1975, 189). This is certainly a sober warning to keep in mind as the impact of Hippocrates and the Hippocratic tradition on the development of medical knowledge and practice is explored in the next two sections.

The Development of Medical Knowledge

In this section, the impact of Hippocrates and the Hippocratic tradition on the development of medical knowledge is discussed. To that end, the notion of the nature of medicine from a Hippocratic perspective is examined initially – especially as that notion diverges from a traditional or pre-Hippocratic understanding of medicine in terms of the role of religion and the supernatural. Next, the commitment of Hippocratic medicine to the notions of holism and vitalism, which it shared to some extent with pre-Hippocratic medicine, is examined. Then, the commitment of Hippocratic medicine to a rationalistic and naturalistic approach to medical knowledge is discussed, especially with respect to pre-Socratic philosophy and the notion of humoralism. Finally, the section concludes with a brief overview of the impact of Hippocratic medicine on contemporary medical specialties and terminology, ranging from cardiology to spine surgery.

What is medicine, from a Hippocratic perspective? To answer that question requires a brief discussion of pre-Hippocratic or traditional Greek medicine. Pre-Hippocratic medicine was intimately linked to religion with respect to the etiology and treatment of illness (Jouanna 2012; Longrigg 1993). The classic example is the sacred disease, epilepsy. According to traditional Greek medicine, the cause of epilepsy was divine in origin as was the treatment, especially in terms of incantations and purifications. In contrast, the author of the Hippocratic text, *On the Sacred Disease*, claims that epilepsy is not divinely caused, but rather its cause was the result of blood flow blocked within the brain via the accumulation of phlegm within the vessels. The author goes on to chide those who claim a divine cause for the disease because they are ignorant of the disease's etiology. However, Hippocratic medicine was not inimical to religion, and it incorporated religion into the care and treatment of the patient. What it excluded from medical practice was the magic and superstition (Hankinson 1998; Martin 2004).

Although pre-Hippocratic medicine differs significantly from Hippocratic medicine vis-à-vis religious influence on medical knowledge and practice, they both shared a commitment to a notion of the whole – or what is contemporarily called holism (Smuts 1926) – in terms of understanding health and illness (Nutton 2013; Pitman 2006). This commitment to holism involves imaging the body as a whole (*holon*) or, as Jacques Jouanna articulates it, "a copy of the Whole" (1999, 276). Besides the wholeness of the body, the patient is also embedded within an environmental context. For example, the author of *On Airs, Waters, and Places* counsels the physician to take note of changes in the seasons and stars, when considering a disease's etiology. In other words, the patient is a microcosm functioning within a macrocosm, and changes within that macrocosm can adversely affect the micro-cosm. As James Gordon explains,

> Hippocrates and the tradition out of which modern biomedicine has grown emphasized the environmental causes and treatment of illness; the etiological and therapeutic importance of psychological factors, nutrition and life-style; the interdependence of mind, body and spirit, and the need for harmony between an individual and his social milieu and natural environment. (1982, 547)

Thus, Hippocratic holism – especially as it is used to justify contemporary holistic medicine – is comprehensive in terms of embedding the whole patient within social and environmental contexts to address illness.

In addition, both pre-Hippocratic and Hippocratic medicine also shared a commitment to a vital principle or to a notion of vitalism for understanding life and living processes, especially health and illness. Although the term vitalism is not introduced until the late eighteenth century, the notion itself is prevalent throughout its complex history (Myers 1900; Wheeler 1939). Within the Hippocratic corpus, the vital principle is articulated with respect to a variety of terms for air, such as *aer*, *anemos*, *phusa*, and *pneuma*, with *pneuma* emerging as the chief term for the principle that animates the body (Frixione 2012; Lloyd 2007). According to the author of *On Breaths*, for instance, the breath of life involves the transformation of the breathed air or *aer* into the wind or *pneuma* that blows or circulates throughout the body and thereby animates it. Health and disease, then, depend upon the quality of this vital principle. As Charles Cumston summarizes Hippocratic vitalism, "Hippocrates admits without hesitation that life is a principle unknown to man, the necessity of which imposes itself as soon as one considers the unity, finality and harmonious plan of the vital phenomena" (1904, 314–315). It is the principle or *archeus* that organizes and makes life possible and that is at root of both health and illness. Finally, although the Hippocratic vital principle is not fully developed – or "incomplete" as Cumston acknowledges – it is often referenced with respect to further historical development of vitalism and neovitalism (Normandin and Wolfe 2013).

As Hippocratic medicine matured, especially in terms of its apex in Hellenistic medicine, it takes what is often called a revolutionary turn in terms of rationalism and naturalism (Boylan 2005; Heidel 1941; Langholf 1990; Longrigg 1998; Scarborough 2002; Schiefsky 2005; Sullivan 1996). As James Longrigg summarizes this turn of ancient Greek medicine,

> One of the most impressive contributions of the ancient Greeks to Western culture was their invention of rational medicine. It was the Greeks who first evolved rational systems of medicine for the most part free from magical and religious elements and based upon natural causes. (1993, 1)

Although Longrigg admits that incorrect rationalistic theories are no better than irrational religious superstitions, he argues that the former can correct itself while the latter cannot. Longrigg goes on to explain that Hippocratic medicine was dependent on Ionian rationalism, which endeavored to explain phenomena in naturalistic terms. For example, Empedocles proposed the elements of earth, water, fire, and air to account for the composition of complex phenomena like life and tissue (Solmsen 1950). Besides the four elements, four qualities – heat, cold, dry, and wet – were also invoked in early Greek natural philosophy to explain phenomena, including health and disease. Hippocratic medicine qua rational, then, sought to identify the invisible causes of health and disease, and no better theory represented that approach than humoralism.

Within the Hippocratic corpus, there are a variety of humoral theories to account for health and disease, both in terms of the number and types of humors. For example, the author of *On the Sacred Disease* posited two humors – phlegm and bile. Eventually, the mature Hippocratic humoral theory, especially as Galen developed it later, posited four humors – blood, phlegm, yellow bile, and black bile (Balzer and Eleftheriadis 1991; Lonie 1981; Nutton 1993). The balance of these humors is responsible for a person's health, while an imbalance in them results in disease (Fig. 1). Moreover, the four humors were also associated with other approaches for explaining natural phenomena. The author of *On the Nature of Man*, for instance, correlated the humors with the four qualities, as well as with the four seasons. It was these correlations, as Vivian Nutton explains, that made the Hippocratic humoral theory attractive such that it "became the dominant medical philosophy" (1993, 287). Indeed, the theory dominated medical knowledge and practice for over a millennium. Finally, the origin of the contemporary notion of homeostasis is often located to the Hippocratic humoral theory in terms of the balance of humors (Bujalkova et al. 2001; Kontopoulou and Marketos 2002).

Besides homeostasis, many current medical specialties claim Hippocratic origins. For example, Hippocrates is called the "Father of clinical nephrology" (Eknoyan 1988), and he is credited with the foundations of modern cardiology and championed as the "Father of circulation" in contrast to Harvey (Cheng 2000, 2001). Moreover, Hippocratic origins are claimed for various surgical specialties,

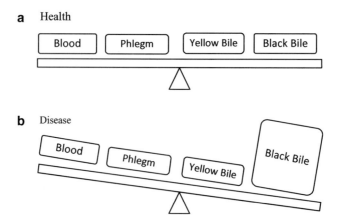

Fig. 1 Humoral pathology (**a**) health (**b**) disease

such as neurosurgery (Chang et al. 2007) and spinal surgery (Marketos and Skiadas 1999a). Interestingly, Hippocratic medicine has also been recognized as foundational for the emergence of genomic medicine:

> Genomic medicine's viewpoints on the biological foundations of human nature, the conceptualization of health and disease, the determinants of individuality in disease predisposition, and the personalized approach to diagnosis, prognosis, and treatment represent a revival of methodological and humanitarian Hippocratic principles. (Sykiotis et al. 2006, 181)

Finally, many contemporary medical terms, such as edema, ileus, and thorax; diseases, such as arthritis, eclampsia, and pneumonia; and notions, such as anesthesia and analgesia, are traced to their Hippocratic roots (Astyrakaki et al. 2010; Marketos and Skiadas 1999b; Yapijakis 2009).

The Development of Medical Practice

Besides medical knowledge, the Hippocratic tradition has had a major impact on the practice of medicine – particularly in terms of its clinical and ethical dimensions. With respect to clinical practice, the author of *Epidemics I* (▶ Chap. 9, "Goals of Medicine") identifies three components to the practice of medicine. The first is the disease, which can be explained in naturalistic terms; the second is the patient, who has the disease and represents a psychosomatic whole; and, the third is the physician, who endeavors to assist nature in helping the patient recover from the disease. These three components form the Hippocratic triangle (Fig. 2; Duffin 2005; Marketos and Skiadas 1999b). Although knowledge of the disease and its etiology is important in treating the patient, so is knowledge of the patient, which has a direct impact on how the physician treats the patient and which is vital for understanding the nature of medicine itself and its goals. For the Hippocratic physician, as well as for physicians throughout history, the Hippocratic oath provides an unsurpassed ethical means – the Hippocratic ethic – for discharging the duties of the profession associated with the interactions among the triangle's components, as well as for defining the profession and its duties to patients and society.

Fig. 2 The Hippocratic triangle

If the Hippocratic corpus is contentious among scholars, the Hippocratic oath is even more so – especially in terms of the oath's origins and authorship (Davey 2001; Miles 2004). For example, the date for the oath's composition varies from the sixth century BCE to the first century CE – although there appears to be consensus that it was composed in the fifth century BCE. Moreover, even though it is part of the Hippocratic corpus, Hippocrates is not considered its author. In fact, Ludwig Edelstein (1967), based on an analysis of the oath's textual content and its historical context, claimed that the oath represents a Pythagorean document. In "On Second Thoughts" on Edelstein's thesis, however, Owsei Temkin challenged Edelstein's analysis and thesis, although he conceded "Pythagorean influences might well have played a role behind the oath" (2002, 4). Finally, Plinio Prioreschi (1995) charged that many of the prohibitions Edelstein found in the oath, which Edelstein claimed were associated with the Pythagoreans, are also found elsewhere in ancient Greek culture and not necessarily unique to the Pythagoreans.

The Hippocratic oath consists of two main parts, after invoking the gods (Apollo and Asclepius) and goddesses (Hygeia and Panacea) associated with medicine as witnesses (Edelstein 1967; Nutton 2013). The first part concerns the duties of the physician to the profession, particularly in terms of honoring one's teachers, and the transmission of medical knowledge between generations. Specifically, the oath demands the inductee

> [t]o hold him who has taught me this art as equal to my parents and to live my life in partnership with him, and if he is in need of money to give him a share of mine, and to regard his offspring as equal to my brothers in male lineage and to teach them this art—if they desire to learn it—without fee and covenant; to give a share of precepts and oral instruction and all the other learning to my sons and to the sons of him who has instructed me and to pupils who have signed the covenant and have taken an oath according to the medical law, but no one else. (Edelstein 1967, 6)

Thus, "the Oath," as Lisa Keränen summarizes this part, "works to unite members of the profession into a tight-knit community" (2001, 59). In other words, as some commentators observe, it serves to demarcate the genuine physician from quacks and charlatans.

The second part of the Hippocratic oath concerns the covenant of the physician with the patient and contains at least half-dozen injunctions and consequences. The first pertains to a therapeutic injunction, "I will apply dietetic measures for the benefit of the sick according to my ability and judgment," which is associated with an ethical standard of patient non-maleficence, "I will keep them from harm and injustice" (Edelstein 1967, 6). The next involves a deep regard for human life in terms of prohibiting suicide or euthanasia, "I will neither give a deadly drug to anybody if asked for it, nor will I make a suggestion to this effect," and abortion, "I will not give to a woman an abortive remedy" (Edelstein 1967, 6). These injunctions are important for the Hippocratic physician, who in "purity and holiness" endeavors to "guard my life and my art" (Edelstein 1967, 6). As for surgery, "I will not use the knife, not even on sufferers from stone, but will withdraw in favor of such men as are engaged in this work" (Edelstein 1967, 6). In other words, as some commentators have noted, Hippocratic physicians do not presume to practice what they have not been trained to do.

Again, the Hippocratic oath returns to an injunction concerning patient non-maleficence, in terms of not taking advantage of the patient's vulnerability:

> Whatever houses I may visit, I will come for the benefit of the sick, remaining free of all intentional injustice, of all mischief and in particular of sexual relations with both female and male persons, be they free or slaves. (Edelstein 1967, 6)

The following injunction concerns confidentiality, "What I may see or hear in the course of the treatment or even outside of the treatment in regard to the life of men, which on no account one must spread abroad, I will keep to myself holding such things shameful to be spoken about" (Edelstein 1967, 6). Finally, the oath concludes with the consequences of fulfilling or transgressing the oath:

> If I fulfill this oath and do not violate it, may it be granted to me to enjoy life and art, being honored with fame among all men for all time to come; if I transgress it and swear falsely, may the opposite of all this be my lot. (Edelstein 1967, 6)

In sum, the oath for many physicians has functioned "as a powerful reminder and declaration that we are all part of something infinitely larger, older, and more important than a particular era, specialty, or institution" (Markel 2014, 29).

The Hippocratic oath contains many injunctions and statements, however, which are considered problematic vis-à-vis contemporary medical values and practice (Morgenstern 2008). For example, swearing to Greek gods is certainly awkward to those who believe in other religions. Another problematic part of the oath is teaching the art of medicine only to males and excluding females, even though two goddesses are invoked as witnesses. Other challenging parts of the oath include prohibition of suicide or euthanasia and abortion, albeit only for pessary. Moreover, the prohibition of the knife or surgery appears problematic, even though others defend it as physicians recognizing their limitations (Antoniou et al. 2010). In sum, Eugene Robin and Robert McCauley (1995) argue that the oath represents a "cultural lag" in which the contemporary medical community has failed to incorporate current changes in society, especially with respect to values and scientific innovations, into the oath.

Robert Veatch (1984) identifies another serious problem with the Hippocratic oath, which leads him to pronounce the death of any possible ethic based on it. The problem stems from the Hippocratic principle concerning the physician's promise to labor "for the benefit of the sick according to my ability and judgment" and to "keep them from harm or injustice." Although Veatch acknowledges the principle that appears praiseworthy prima facie, upon further reflection, it is problematic with respect to three points. The first is paternalism in that the patient's perspective of what is beneficial vis-à-vis therapeutic options is not taken into consideration. The next is individualism in that only the benefit of the individual patient is considered and not that of the larger community in which both the patient and physician reside.

And, the final is consequentialism in that the oath is only concerned with the consequences of a physician's actions and not with their inherent morality. Veatch then argues for a shift from a Hippocratic ethic based on paternalism, individualism, and consequentialism to an ethic based on "principles such as autonomy, truth-telling, avoiding killing and justice" (1984, 48).

Given these problematic injunctions and statements of the Hippocratic oath, the contemporary response to it is often controversial and ranges along a spectrum of those who dismiss it and propose revised or alternative oaths to those who defend and champion it. For those who dismiss and replace it with a revised or an alternative oath, the Hippocratic oath represents an archaic and irrelevant document, especially in terms of contemporary medical values (Hurwitz and Richardson 1997; Meffert 2009; Robin and McCauley 1995; Rosalki 1993; Wagley 1987). Louis Lasagna (1964), dean of Tufts Medical College, introduced one of the more well-known alternative oaths. In it, Lasagna stresses the humanity not only of the patient but also of the physician, without compromising the advances of scientific medicine. For example, one statement claims, "I will remember that there is art to medicine as well as science, and that warmth, sympathy, and understanding may outweigh the surgeon's knife or the chemist's drug." Finally, Keränen (2001) argues that such drastic revision of the oath is warranted since the oath represents an Aristotelian epideictic rhetoric, which operates ceremonially to construct especially a moral community. Incorporating contemporary moral and social values into a revised Hippocratic oath, then, is critical for the "long-term function of moving its audience from core values rooted in the past to principled action in the future" (Keränen 2001, 67).

For others who defend the Hippocratic oath and champion it, the oath is still relevant vis-à-vis contemporary medical values and practice, and it represents a means particularly for defining medical professionalism (Heubel 2015; Kravitz 1984; Markel 2014). For example, Spyros Marketos and colleagues criticize the revised and alternative oaths as often too legalistic and argue that the original oath's "true meaning, overall respect for the patient, can be accommodated in different cultures and historical periods" (Marketos et al. 1996, 101). Indeed, Lycurgus Davey goes so far as to argue that

> Hippocrates' oath is as fitting an ideal today as it was 2500 years ago. Let not the quaintness of its language nor the terseness of its terms obscure or distract from the highly principled guidance offered by the oath of Hippocrates. Only with his guidance can we hope to restore American medicine's golden age. (2001, 564)

Indeed, for some, the oath also serves as the basis for a robust medical ethics – in spite of Veatch's pronouncement of the Hippocratic ethic's demise (Orr et al. 1997). For example, Edmund Pellegrino claims that the Hippocratic ethic "is marked by a unique combination of humanistic concern and practical wisdom admirably suited to the physician's tasks in society" (2000, 42). Based on this characteristic of the ethic, Pellegrino then expands it in terms of its axiology to include ethical issues that face contemporary medicine, such as patient participation in treatment, physician competence and duties, and the institutionalization of medicine. In sum, the oath serves as an ideal of who the physician is and of how the medical profession should provide the best possible healthcare.

Hippocratic Lessons for Contemporary Medicine

The present exploration of Hippocrates and the Hippocratic tradition teaches several important lessons not only about the development of medical knowledge and practice but also about their future advancement. Although there are a number of important lessons that can be derived from them, especially for contemporary medicine (Fabre 1997; Marketos 1993), only four are discussed in this final section. The first concerns medical knowledge and its rational approach to explaining disease as well as its relationship to alternative epistemic approaches of medicine; the second relates to medical practice particularly in a highly technologized medicine and the suffering associated with the patient illness experience; the third involves medical professionalism with respect to the duties required of the physician; and, the fourth pertains to medical philosophy in terms of the ethical challenges facing contemporary medical care and the role of virtue theory in addressing those challenges. The section concludes with a brief discussion concerning the role of the Hippocratic spirit for medicine in the twenty-first century (Daikos 2003; Helidonis and Prokopakis 2001).

With respect to medical knowledge, the Hippocratic tradition of explaining disease rationally, particularly in terms of their natural causes, is certainly an important lesson for contemporary medicine. Religion and spirituality may be important dimensions of a patient's illness experience and certainly need to be addressed (Koenig et al. 2012). However, the material and physical mechanisms underlying the etiology of disease often – but not always – demand priority. Although medicine should be based on the best empirical evidence available at the time, the Hippocratic tradition teaches a certain level of humility concerning the veracity or uncertainty of medical knowledge. After all, both vital spirits and humors are no longer viable for explaining health and disease or for treating patients. But, on the other hand, the epistemic humility that Hippocratic medicine teaches should provide sufficient motivation to support and continue the biomedical research needed to develop the medical knowledge required to provide the best technical care for treating patients. Moreover, medical research should be open-minded, what Grant Gillett (2004) calls a Hippocratic attitude, toward alternative epistemic approaches to investigating and explaining disease. Finally, Hippocratic medicine teaches contemporary practitioners how the limits to medical knowledge and its application to the clinic can help to avoid medical futility (Jecker 1991).

With respect to medical practice, the Hippocratic tradition teaches that the emphasis should be not simply on the disease but on the patient who is experiencing the disease. In other words, medical practice involves the patient and the disease, as well as the efforts of the medical professional to treat the patient, i.e., the Hippocratic triangle (Fig. 2). It also teaches that medical professionals must be fastidious in their integrity toward the goal of relieving or attenuating suffering associated with illness. Unfortunately, a triumphal, positivist perspective of medical progress in which disease can be cured – either through pharmaceutical or surgical therapeutics – or even prevented, through genomic counseling or engineering, often blinds the healthcare professional to outcomes of greater patient harm and suffering and of a poorer quality of life for the patient. In other words, the treatment is often more painful and injurious than the disease – even to the extent of death. Progressive metaphysics with a verisimilitude epistemology – or what is generally called scientism – can be detrimental to the medicine's goal of reducing patient suffering and not adding to it (Cassell 2004). Moreover, the lesson that Hippocratic medicine teaches is a holism in terms of treating the whole patient within a given context. The patient does not simply have a disease but is living with it, and the medical professional must take into consideration not only the patient but also the context in which the patient is living with the disease.

With respect to medical professionalism, the Hippocratic tradition, especially in terms of its oath, teaches that to define medical professionalism requires a moral sense of duties and obligations not only to its patients but also to the profession itself (Coulehan 2006). As Daniel Sulmasy (1999) argues, an oath in general involves performative statements that carry considerable moral weight and consequences, compared to promises or codes. Given the drastic changes in the medical profession since the origination of the oath, however, whether the oath can serve any role in framing contemporary medical professionalism is questionable. For example, Friedrich Heubel (2015) argues that the "Charter on Medical Professionalism" represents a better means for defining contemporary medical professionalism than the Hippocratic oath. Moreover, as Fabrice Jotterand argues,

> the resources for a better understanding of medical professionalism lie not in the Hippocratic Oath, tradition, or ethos in and of themselves. Rather, it must be found in a philosophy of medicine that explores the values internal to medicine, thus providing a medical-moral philosophy so as to be able to resist the deformation of medical professionalism by bioethics, biopolitics, and governmental regulation. (2005, 108–109)

Although the Hippocratic oath cannot define contemporary medical professionalism, it can serve as a heuristic guide – according to Jotterand – toward that end. Ultimately, what is needed is not a return to Hippocratic medicine but rather a contemporary medical philosophy to define clinical medicine and its professionalism with respect to medical knowledge and practice.

With respect to medical philosophy, the Hippocratic oath and tradition teach that the virtues are important for performing medical duties and obligations, especially when faced with ethical challenges, and that they can provide the basis for a robust medical philosophy to guide contemporary medicine, when confronted with ethical challenges. Although virtue ethics waned historically, there has been a resurgence in its impact especially on medical practice and professionalism:

As it stands, the Hippocratic Oath can no longer be viewed as *the* action-guiding inspiration of current medical practice. However, the last word has not yet been said...To only apply the rules—bottom-line ethics—is not a solid ethical foundation. What is needed is to focus on the integrity, consistency, and excellence of character in the physician-patient relationship. Virtue ethics is appealing for its ability to provide a normative basis to the values internal to medicine. (Ogunbanjo and van Bogaert 2009, 31)

Although the Hippocratic oath might not be "*the* action-guiding inspiration" for a contemporary medical ethics, it still provides motivation and inspiration to develop a robust medical philosophy, especially with respect to the Hippocratic virtues. The Hippocratic virtues can be divided into two major sets (Berry 1997). The first pertains to "the virtues of expertise and skill necessary to accomplish curing – the fundamental purpose of the healing art – including the virtues of diligence, carefulness, conscientiousness, and the like" (Berry 1997, 412). The other set involves "virtues necessary to caring for the patient – kindness, sympathy, loyalty, and the like" (Berry 1997, 412).

For contemporary medicine, Pellegrino (1995) has identified several virtues representing both sets of Hippocratic virtues, such as benevolence, compassion and caring, justice, and prudence, which could assist in constituting a comprehensive and normative foundation for medical ethics. But, he claims that although necessary, these virtues are insufficient for the task. In addition, Pellegrino embeds these virtues within a broader moral framework to generate a robust medical philosophy to guide contemporary medical practice. Specifically, he distinguishes four elements involved in a moral act – the agent performing the act, the act itself, the circumstances under which the act is performed, and the act's consequences. In this framework, he locates various modern moral theories. Thus, virtue theory is associated with the moral agent; deontology with the act; "particularizing theories," such as situational ethics, with the circumstances surrounding the act; and teleological theories with the act's consequences. He argues that such a framework bodes well for medicine, especially in terms with the telos or goal of providing quality medical care. He concludes, however:

Today's challenge is not how to demonstrate the superiority of one normative theory over the other, but rather how to relate each to the other in a matrix that does justice to each and assigns to each its proper normative force. (Pellegrino 1995, 273)

Unfortunately, this challenge still confronts contemporary medicine.

In conclusion, Hippocrates and the Hippocratic tradition have served as an ideal or symbol for both the practicing physician and for the institution of medicine as a profession, especially in terms of motivating medicine to provide the patient with the best medical care possible (Cantor 2002; Scarborough 2002; Tullis 2004). As John Fabre notes:

The very nature of medicine is such that, unless it is firmly based on idealistic foundations, on notions of altruism, love, and so on, it can rapidly degenerate into a squalid business.

The Hippocratic doctors recognized this and they were not shy, as we are today, to preach idealism. (1998, 162)

Indeed, the way toward resolving many of the issues facing modern medicine, from ethical to political to practical, would benefit from the Hippocratic ideal of a healthcare system that truly cares for the patient. In other words, the Hippocratic spirit continues to animate efforts to develop medicine as authentically human. As George Daikos concludes concerning this spirit, "The humane spirit is one of our great Hippocratic heritages" (2003, 188).

Definitions of Key Terms

Hippocratic corpus	A collection of over 60 treatises on various medical topics that were written by Hippocrates' followers and assembled in Alexandria.
Hippocratic oath	A vow consisting of assurances made concerning the behavior of physicians toward benefiting and not harming one another and their patients.
Hippocratic question	The question concerning which treatises, if any, within the Hippocratic corpus were written by Hippocrates.
Hippocratic tradition	The impact of Hippocrates and his followers on the development of medical knowledge and practice throughout history.
Holism	The notion that the properties of the whole are greater than the arithmetic sum of the properties of the parts making up the whole.
Humoralism	A theory of health and disease based on the balance of the four humors, blood, phlegm, yellow bile, and black bile.
Vitalism	The notion that life is the result of an external force that animates the body.

Summary Points

- Hippocrates lived and practiced medicine during the golden age of ancient Greece.
- The Hippocratic corpus is a collection of medical treatises written by Hippocrates' followers and compiled in Alexandria during the Hellenistic period.
- Hippocratic medicine involved a shift from the religious and superstitious approach to health and disease to the rational and natural explanation of them.
- Hippocratic vitalism pertains to the pneuma that circulates throughout the body, thereby animating it.
- Hippocratic humoralism is the medical theory to describe health and disease in terms of the balance of four humors: blood, phlegm, yellow bile, and black bile (Fig. 1).

- The Hippocratic triangle of medical practice comprises the interaction of the patient, the disease, and the physician (Fig. 2).
- The Hippocratic oath consists of two main parts describing the obligation of physicians to the welfare of both the medical profession and its patients.
- The Hippocratic spirit represents the inspiration and motivation for developing a competent and caring healthcare system throughout history.

References

Antoniou SA, Antoniou GA, Granderath FA, Mavroforou A, Giannoukas AD, Antoniou AI (2010) Reflections of the Hippocratic oath in modern medicine. World J Surg 34:3075–3079

Astyrakaki E, Papaioannou A, Askitopoulou H (2010) References to anesthesia, pain, and analgesia in the Hippocratic Collection. Anesth Analg 110:188–194

Balzer W, Eleftheriadis A (1991) A reconstruction of the Hippocratic humoral theory of health. J Gen Phil Sci 22:207–227

Berry RM (1997) The genetic revolution and the physician's duty of confidentiality: the role of the old Hippocratic virtues in the regulation of the new genetic intimacy. J Leg Med 18:401–441

Boylan M (2005) Hippocrates (c. 450-c. 380 B.C.E.). In: Internet encyclopedia of philosophy. Available via DIALOG. http://www.iep.utm.edu/hippocra/. Accessed 05 July 2015

Bujalkova M, Straka S, Jureckova A (2001) Hippocrates' humoral pathology in nowaday's reflections. Bratisl Lek Listy 102:489–492

Cantor D (ed) (2002) Reinventing Hippocrates. Ashgate, Burlington

Cassell EJ (2004) The nature of suffering and the goals of medicine, 2nd edn. Oxford University Press, New York

Chang A, Lad EM, Lad SP (2007) Hippocrates' influence on the origins of neurosurgery. Neurosurg Focus 23:E9

Cheng TO (2000) Hippocrates and cardiology. Am Heart J 141:173–183

Cheng TO (2001) The true father of circulation: Harvey or Hippocrates? Ann Thorac Surg 71:1399–1404

Corpus Medicorum Graecorum (2015) Available via DIALOG. http://cmg.bbaw.de/. Accessed 07 July 2015

Coulehan J (2006) You say self-interest, I say altruism. In: Wear D, Aultman JM (eds) Professionalism in medicine. Springer, New York, pp 103–127

Cumston CG (1904) The phenomenism of Hippocrates. Med Lib Hist J 2:307–317

Daikos GK (2003) The Hippocratic spirit. Hormones (Athens) 2:186–188

Davey LM (2001) The oath of Hippocrates: an historical review. Neurosurgery 49:554–566

Duffin J (2005) Lovers and livers: disease concepts in history. University of Toronto Press, Toronto

Edelstein L (1967) Ancient medicine. Johns Hopkins University Press, Baltimore

Eknoyan G (1988) Origins of nephrology: Hippocrates, the father of clinical nephrology. Am J Nephrol 8:498–507

Fabre JW (1997) The Hippocratic doctor: ancient lessons for the modern world. Royal Society of Medicine Press, London

Fabre J (1998) Modern medicine and the Hippocratic doctors of ancient Greece. J R Soc Med 91:161–163

Frixione E (2012) Pneuma – fire interactions in Hippocratic physiology. J Hist Med Allied Sci 68:505–528

Gillett G (2004) Clinical medicine and the quest for certainty. Soc Sci Med 58:727–738

Gordon JS (1982) Holistic medicine: advances and shortcomings. West J Med 136:546–551

Hankinson RJ (1998) Magic, religion and science: divine and human in the Hippocratic corpus. Apeiron 31:1–34

Heidel AW (1941) Hippocratic medicine. Its spirit and method. Columbia University Press, New York

Helidonis ES, Prokopakis EP (2001) The contribution of Hippocratic oath in third millennium medical practice. Am J Otolaryngol 22:303–305

Heubel F (2015) The "soul of professionalism" in the Hippocratic oath and today. Med Health Care Philos 18:185–194

Hurwitz B, Richardson R (1997) Swearing to care: the resurgence in medical oaths. BMJ 315:1671–1674

Jecker NS (1991) Knowing when to stop: the limits of medicine. Hastings Cent Rep 21:5–8

Joly R (1983) Hippocrates and the school of Cos. In: Ruse M (ed) Nature animated. Springer, New York, pp 29–47

Jotterand F (2005) The Hippocratic oath and contemporary medicine: dialectic between past ideals and present reality? J Med Phil 30:107–128

Jouanna J (1999) Hippocrates (trans: DeBevoise MB). Johns Hopkins University Press, Baltimore

Jouanna J (2012) Greek medicine from Hippocrates to Galen (trans: Allies N). Brill, Leiden

Keränen L (2001) The Hippocratic oath as epideictic rhetoric: reanimating medicine's past for its future. J Med Hum 22:55–68

King H (2001) Greek and Roman medicine. Bristol Classical Press, London

Koenig H, King D, Carson VB (eds) (2012) Handbook of religion and health, 2nd edn. Oxford University Press, New York

Kontopoulou TD, Marketos SG (2002) Homeostasis: the ancient Greek origin of a modern scientific principle. Hormones 1:124–125

Kravitz R (1984) Why the Hippocratic oath is worth preserving. Pharos Alpha Omega Alpha Honor Med Soc 47:37–39

Langholf V (1990) Medical theories in Hippocrates. De Gruyter, Berlin

Lasagna L (1964) Would Hippocrates rewrite his oath? N Y Times Mag 11:40–43

Levine EB (1971) Hippocrates. Twayne, New York

Lloyd GER (1975) The Hippocratic question. Classical Quart (ns) 25:171–192

Lloyd G (2007) Pneuma between body and soul. J Roy Soc Anthro Inst (ns) 13:S135–S146

Longrigg J (1993) Greek rational medicine: philosophy and medicine from Alcmaeon to the Alexandrians. Routledge, New York

Longrigg J (1998) Greek medicine from the hero to the Hellenistic age: a source book. Routledge, New York

Lonie IM (1981) The Hippocratic treatises "On generation", "On the nature of the child", "Diseases IV": a commentary. Walter de Gruyter, Berlin

Mansfeld J (1983) The historical Hippocrates and the origins of scientific medicine. In: Ruse M (ed) Nature animated. Springer, New York, pp 49–76

Markel H (2014) The Hippocratic oath as an example of professional conduct. In: De Angelis CD (ed) Patient care and professionalism. Oxford University Press, New York, pp 19–30

Marketos S (1993) Medicine is an aspect of civilization: lessons from the Hippocratic medicine. Microsurgery 14:4–5

Marketos SG, Skiadas P (1999a) Hippocrates: the father of spine surgery. Spine 24:1381–1387

Marketos SG, Skiadas P (1999b) The modern Hippocratic tradition: some messages for contemporary medicine. Spine 24:1159–1163

Marketos SG, Diamandopoulos AA, Bartsocas CS, Poulakou-Rebelakou E, Koutras DA (1996) The Hippocratic oath. Lancet 347:101–102

Martin DB (2004) Inventing superstition: from the Hippocratic to the Christians. Harvard University Press, Cambridge, MA

Meffert JJ (2009) "I swear!" Physician oaths and their current relevance. Clin Dermatol 27:411–415

Miles SH (2004) The Hippocratic oath and the ethics of medicine. Oxford University Press, New York

Michell CB (2010) The Christian Hippocratic tradition in medicine. Ethics Med 26:69–70

Morgenstern J (2008) The medical oath: honorable tradition or ancient ritual? UWOMJ 78:P27–P29

Myers CS (1900) IV. – vitalism: a brief historical and critical review (I.). Mind 9:218–233

Normandin S, Wolfe CT (eds) (2013) Vitalism and the scientific image in post-enlightenment life science, 1800–2010. Springer, New York

Nutton V (1993) Humoralism. In: Bynum W, Porter R (eds) Companion encyclopedia of the history of medicine. Routledge, London, pp 281–291

Nutton V (2013) Ancient medicine, 2nd edn. Routledge, New York

Ogunbanjo GA, van Bogaert KD (2009) The Hippocratic oath: revisited. SA Fam Pract 51:30–31

Orr RD, Pang N, Pellegrino ED, Siegler M (1997) Use of the Hippocratic oath: a review of twentieth century practice and a content analysis of oaths administered in medical schools in the US and Canada in 1993. J Clin Ethics 8:377–388

Pellegrino ED (1995) Toward a virtue-based normative ethics for the health professions. Kennedy Inst Ethics J 5:253–277

Pellegrino ED (2000) Toward an expanded medical ethics: the Hippocratic ethic revisited. In: Veatch RM (ed) Cross cultural perspectives in medical ethics, 2nd edn. Jones and Bartlett, Boston, pp 41–53

Pinault JR (1992) Hippocratic lives and legends. Brill, Leiden

Pitman V (2006) The nature of the whole: Holism in ancient Greek and Indian medicine. Motilal Banarsidass, Delhi

Prioreschi P (1995) The Hippocratic oath: a code for physicians, not a Pythagorean manifesto. Med Hypoth 44:447–462

Robin ED, McCauley RF (1995) Cultural lag and the Hippocratic oath. Lancet 345:1422–1424

Rosalki J (1993) The Hippocratic contract. J Med Ethics 19:154–156

Scarborough J (1997) Hippocrates of Cos. Anc Greek Authors 176:199–219

Scarborough J (2002) Hippocrates and the Hippocratic ideal in modern medicine: a review essay. Int J Class Tradit 9:287–297

Schiefsky MJ (2005) Hippocrates on ancient medicine. Brill, Leiden

Smith WD (1979) The Hippocratic tradition. Cornell University Press, Ithaca

Smith WD (ed) (1990) Hippocrates pseudepigraphic writings. Brill, Leiden

Smuts JC (1926) Holism and evolution. Little and Ives, New York

Solmsen F (1950) Tissues and the soul: philosophical contributions to physiology. Philos Rev 59:435–468

Sullivan R (1996) Thales to Galen: a brief journey through rational medical philosophy in ancient Greece. Part I: pre-Hippocratic medicine. Proc R Coll Physicians Edinb 26:135–142

Sulmasy DP (1999) What is an oath and why should a physician swear one? Theor Med Bioeth 20:329–346

Sykiotis GP, Kalliolias GD, Papavassiliou AG (2006) Hippocrates and genomic medicine. Arch Med Res 37:181–183

Temkin O (1991) Hippocrates in a world of pagans and Christians. Johns Hopkins University Press, Baltimore

Temkin O (2002) "On second thought" and other essays in the history of medicine and science. Johns Hopkins University Press, Baltimore

Tullis R (2004) Hippocratic oaths. Medicine and its discontents. Atlantic Books, London

Veatch RM (1984) The Hippocratic ethic is dead. New Physician 48:41–42, 48

Wagley PF (1987) The Hippocratic oath. Hum Med 3:110–114

Wheeler LR (1939) Vitalism: its history and validity. Witherby, London

Yapijakis C (2009) Hippocrates of Kos, the father of clinical medicine, and Asclepiades of Bithynia, the father of molecular medicine. In Vivo 23:507–514

Causation and Correlation in Medical Science: Theoretical Problems

Federica Russo

Contents

Abstract

Establishing causal relations is a core enterprise of the medical sciences. Understanding the etiology of diseases, and the treatments to reduce the burden of disease, is in fact an instantiation of the very many activities related to causal analysis and causal assessment in medical science. In medicine, correlations have a "Janus" character. On the one hand, we should beware of correlations as they do not *imply* causation – a well-established "mantra" in statistics and in the philosophy of causality. On the other hand, correlations are a very important and useful piece of *evidence* in order to establish causal relations – a line of argument that is currently debated in the philosophical and medical literature. Understanding the limits and potentialities of correlations in medicine is all the more important if we consider the emergence of a "data-intensive science" when the search for correlations in big data sets is becoming key in the medical sciences.

F. Russo (✉)
Department of Philosophy, Faculty of Humanities, University of Amsterdam, Amsterdam,
The Netherlands
e-mail: f.russo@uva.nl

© Springer Science+Business Media Dordrecht 2017
T. Schramme, S. Edwards (eds.), *Handbook of the Philosophy of Medicine*,
DOI 10.1007/978-94-017-8688-1_46

Introduction: Causation in the Medical Sciences

The medical sciences are interested in describing, explaining, and intervening on causes and effects of health and disease. This is a very broad characterization that allows us to be as inclusive as possible when discussing causal issues in medicine.

On the one hand, "medical sciences" is an umbrella term that includes various strands of research, of health care, and, possibly, of alternative or complementary approaches to medicine. Thus, under "medical sciences" we might include clinical medicine, basic health care, epidemiology, gender medicine, or any other approach that engages with the causes and effects of health and disease from a scientific point of view. On the other hand, "causation" is also an umbrella term that includes various ways in which causes and effects are involved in the phenomena of health and disease. Thus, for instance, causation in medicine includes questions about the biochemical mechanisms of disease causation, or about the social inequalities connected to health inequalities, or with the design and implementation of preventative interventions at the individual or population level.

"Causation in the medical sciences" thus refers to a conceptual and methodological complexity that extends far beyond the scope of this chapter. Here, specifically, the focus is on the perennial question about the relation between correlation and causation. More precisely, this question amounts to asking to what extent or under what conditions can one infer causation from correlation – a question that has preoccupied philosophers of causality since the "probabilistic turn" in the 1960s and 1970s. The seminal works of I. J. Good (1961a, b) and Patrick Suppes (1970) paved the way for a probabilistic characterization and analysis of causal relations that is still of relevance today in the natural, social, and medical sciences.

In the medical sciences, the question arises mainly with respect to those research methods and scientific practices that involve substantial use of statistics for the analyses of data. Paradigmatic examples include (various strands of) epidemiology, evidence-based medicine, or data-driven approaches.

In order to grasp what the problem with correlations is, it is vital to understand its methodological basis. Medical research done in labs (e.g., oncological biomedicine) or in randomized controlled trials generates and collects data that have to be analyzed using statistical models. These models establish correlations, and the question is whether – and under what conditions – these correlations can be interpreted as *causal* relations.

Most often, these correlations are *quantitatively* expressed in the language of probability theory and statistics, in which case we talk about *statistical generalizations*. Typical examples are epidemiological claims about the risks of developing a disease given a certain exposure, or of not developing a disease given some preventative interventions. It is no accident, in fact, that the very concept of "risk" in the medical sciences is related to that of "causation," albeit no consensus has been reached about the precise terms of their relationships. But sometimes correlations may take the form of *qualitative* statements about difference-making relations. Further research is needed to spell out the form and use of qualitative difference-making claims in, e.g., the experimental reasoning as put forward by

Claude Bernard (1856) or in the narratives of case reports (on narratives, see, for instance, Goyal 2013, and on the controversial status of case reports in medicine, see, e.g., Nissen and Wynn 2012). Thus the discussion is confined here to correlations expressed in the quantitative language of probability and statistics.

So, given the long-standing discussion in epidemiology and germane areas (e.g., econometrics, quantitative sociology, or demography), it is a legitimate question to ask: What good are correlations in medicine? While it is widely agreed that "correlation is not causation," in the last decade or so, the debate has been shifting from the question of *What is the extra X that makes correlations causal?* (which, admittedly, has a metaphysical flavor) to a question about the import of correlations as *evidence* to establish causal claims (in the medical sciences, but also elsewhere). This shift also means that the question about correlation and causation is now approached from an epistemological and methodological point view, from which metaphysical consequences can be addressed.

Correlation Is Not Causation

It is widely agreed that "correlation is not causation." That this amounts to *nearly* an accepted truth is clear from the way the debate developed in the medical sciences and in the philosophy of causality.

On the one hand, the medical sciences – and especially epidemiology – have been investigating what concept cashes out causation in this context. Mark Parascandola and Douglas L. Weed offer an overview of the various possibilities, showing that none of the available concepts (e.g., counterfactual, INUS, probabilistic, etc.) capture all cases of "medical causation" (Parascandola and Weed 2001). These authors admit that the probabilistic concept of causation is the one that fares better than others, and yet it faces challenges. One reason is that there are cases where causes are necessary and/or sufficient for their effects; another reason is that, admittedly, probabilities (or correlations) do not guarantee causation. Analyses like the one of Parascandola and Weed (2001) typically lead to "precautionary" (and even skeptical) stances about the plausibility and use of an explicit causal talk (see also Lipton and Ødegaard 2005).

On the other hand, the philosophy of causality, since the "probabilistic turn" initiated by authors like Good and Suppes, identified the potential of probabilistic analyses, as well as problems and challenges thereof. Simply put, probabilistic analyses of causality hold that causes make a difference in the probability (of the occurrence) of the effect: $P(E) \neq P(E|C)$. This inequality can be read in two ways. Some causes *raise* the probability of the effect – for instance, consumption of fat food raises the probability of cardiovascular diseases. Some causes, instead, *lower* the probability of the effect – for instance, regular exercise *prevents* cardiovascular diseases. It is worth noting that the requirement of "difference-making" was originally stated only in terms of probability *raising*, thus questioning the status of preventatives as proper "causes" (for a discussion, see Illari and Russo 2014,

Chap. 8). This, however, is not the main conceptual challenge concerning "correlation and causation."

Two conceptual challenges can be identified. The first has to do with the "generic versus single-case" problem. The second has to do with the "third variable" problem.

The first problem – generic versus single-case – has been debated at length in the philosophical literature, and it is also known as the "population versus individual" or "type versus token" problem (for a discussion about terminological distinctions and similarities, see Illari and Russo 2014, Chap. 5). Simply put, philosophers soon realized that probabilistic inequalities valid at the population level do not guarantee causal inference to the individual level. Let's illustrate with a simplified medical example. The medical sciences have established, with a significant degree of confidence, that smoking causes (in the sense of *raising the probability of*) lung cancer. Yet, it is well known that some cases of lung cancer are not due to smoking and that not all smokers develop lung cancer. Situations like this raise at least two theoretical questions. One question concerns the status of (statistical) generalizations that purportedly have *causal* meaning: What does it mean that smoking causes cancer *at the population level*? Another question, also related to the previous one, concerns the "metaphysical priority" of population- or individual-level causal relations. Are causal relations *generic* (or type-level) and from these we have to derive single-case (or token-level) ones? Or, instead, are causal relations *single-case* and generic claims are mere (statistical) aggregates of those? Federica Russo and Jon Williamson analyze the relation between generic and single-case causal relations in medicine and suggest that one level has no metaphysical priority over the other (Russo and Williamson 2011b). Rather, from an epistemological and methodological point of view, there is a mutual dependence between the two levels.

The second problem – third variable – has been studied at length in statistics (with applications to medicine, social science, or others). To understand what the problem of the third variable amounts to, it is useful to recall the main steps involved into establishing correlational claims through statistical modeling. Briefly and simply put, once data are collected, scientists organize them according to variables and then study the dependencies and independences between these variables using statistical models. Each of these steps involves conceptual, methodological, and practical challenges that will not be discussed here. The point at stake is that, given the correlation between variables X and Y, it is possible to find a *third variable Z*, which, when included in the model, questions the validity of the correlation between X and Y. This may happen for a number of reasons. Let's illustrate with the aid of toy examples.

Consider a case where variable "yellow fingers" is correlated with variable "lung cancer"; however, once we introduce the variable "cigarette smoking," the correlation disappears because "cigarette smoking" causes *both* "yellow fingers" and "lung cancer" (cases like this are also discussed as instantiations of the common cause principle and cigarette smoking is said to *screen off* "yellow fingers" from "lung cancer"). A different case concerns the correlation between variables "coffee drinking" and "cardiovascular disease." This correlation may, or may not, disappear when we introduce variable "cigarette smoking." In fact, "cigarette smoking" may be a common cause of both "coffee drinking" and "cardiovascular disease" – in this case the correlation would disappear. But it is also possible that "coffee drinking" has its own effect on "cardiovascular disease." In this case we should study the effects on "cardiovascular disease" due to "coffee drinking," those due to "smoking," and those due to possible interactions between the two. In cases like this, we have to *control* for possible *confounding variables*. Available statistical techniques for control include conditioning on specific values of variables, stratification ex ante or ex post, etc.

Generally speaking, a main theoretical challenge with correlations is their validity, whether internal or external. Thomas D. Cook and Donald T. Campbell introduced the terms internal and external validity, in the area of quasi-experimental methods (Cook and Campbell 1979). Internal validity refers to the confidence with which we deem the correlation between variables X and Y causal, in the population of reference. External validity refers instead to the possibility of establishing the same correlation also *outside* the population of reference. Thus, for instance, in the medical sciences we might be interested in establishing the efficacy of a drug for a specific population of reference and also for *other* populations. The same holds for the efficacy of public health interventions.

Another important aspect of correlations in the medical sciences concerns the fact that correlational claims are *generic*. One reason why we are interested in establishing (and validating) generic claims is that they contribute to building medical knowledge (population level) *and* to serve as a basis for diagnosis and prognosis (individual level). The challenge here concerns the kind of information that correlations provide for the purpose of establishing causal claims. It is worth noting that, thus formulated, the focus is shifted from the question *Why should we beware of correlations?* to the question *What good are correlations in the medical sciences?*. This latter question is examined next.

Correlation as Evidence

In the philosophy of causality, part of the debate has been devoted to explicating the very concepts of "cause" or "causality." Several accounts have been proposed, for instance, analyzing the concept of cause/causality in terms of counterfactuals, necessary and sufficient components, invariance relations, probabilities, etc. (for systematic presentation of such attempts, see Illari and Russo 2014). As mentioned above, the applicability of these concepts to the medical sciences, and to epidemiology in particular, has also been examined by Parascandola and Weed (2001). A different line of argument, however, has been introduced in the debate since the paper by Russo and Williamson (2007).

Russo and Williamson argue that the *concept* of causality should not be confused with the *evidence* needed to establish causal claims. Most accounts of causality can be reinterpreted as offering an account of the type of evidence to support causal claims. The thesis, now customarily referred to in the literature as "Russo-Williamson thesis"

(RWT), states that, typically, causal claims in medicine are established on the basis of *evidence* of difference-making and of mechanisms. This emphasis on the *evidence* needed to establish a causal claim makes RWT epistemological and methodological in character. A corollary of RWT is *evidential pluralism*, namely, the position according to which causal claims are established on the basis of multifarious evidence. Thus correlations are an important *evidential component* to establish causal claim, but causality is *not reduced* in any way to correlations (nor to mechanisms). RWT sparked lively debates and a new stream of research. Let us examine the core of the thesis, some of the prospective developments, and objections.

To begin with, it is worth clarifying the status of the thesis. RWT is an *epistemological* thesis about how to establish causal knowledge (in medicine). In particular, it is a thesis about the evidence that supports causal claims. RTW is *not* a metaphysical thesis about the *nature* of causality. In particular, the thesis does not state that causality is *constituted by* difference-making (correlations) and mechanisms. RWT can of course be discussed in its metaphysical implications, but that is an orthogonal issue. In some papers, Russo and Williamson (2011a) couple evidential pluralism with the epistemic theory of causality (for details, see Williamson 2005): Difference-making and mechanisms are evidential components, and the concept of causality is provided by the epistemic theory, according to which causality is the ultimate belief of an omniscient agent. Here, an epistemology for causal relations (RWT) is combined with a metaphysical theory about causation (the epistemic theory). However, not everyone embracing RWT also endorses this metaphysical position (see, e.g., Gillies 2011; Clarke et al. 2014).

Let's now go into the details of the thesis. Phyllis Illari (2011) points out that RTW should not be read as saying that there are different *types* of evidence (difference-making and mechanisms), but that difference-making and mechanisms capture the *object* of evidence, i.e., what we have (or need) evidence *of*. The difference is subtle but fundamental. In the first case, we are interpreting "difference-making" and "mechanisms" rigidly, as if these were fixed categories, and causal claims were established by ticking both boxes. In the second case, instead, "difference-making" and "mechanisms" refer to the type of information that we examine in establishing causal claims. Under this reading, evidential components become highly intertwined and interdependent, which is actually the case in the scientific practice. For instance, suppose a scientist is observing the modes of transmission of a bacterium, say, *Vibrio cholerae*. These observations may provide evidence of the mechanisms underlying the transmission; the same observations may also provide evidence that the bacterium makes a difference to the occurrence of the disease. Two things are worth noting. First, read this way, RWT does not imply that we must have full or complete knowledge of disease mechanisms – a point also made by Donald Gillies (2011). Second, difference-making can be quantitatively expressed in terms of (statistical) correlations but can also be expressed using qualitative statements, for instance, about counterfactuals.

It is now possible to explain more clearly the import and meaning of difference-making and of mechanisms. Evidence of difference-making is useful in order to establish *change-relating* relations or to make predictions – to do so we need to know *that* C causes E. Evidence of mechanisms is useful in order to explain disease or to design intervention to reduce the burden of disease – to do so we need to know *how* C causes E. Thus, the term "evidence of production" better grasps what is at stake, as mechanisms are just one way in which causes produce effects – processes, information transfer, and the action of capacities are other ways in which we can grasp how causes produce effects (for a discussion see Illari and Russo 2014, Chap. 6).

Evidence of difference-making must be also considered as complementary to evidence of production. In fact, while evidence of production helps with *confounding* (one variant of the "third variable" problem mentioned above), evidence of difference-making helps with *masking*. Masking is the problem of establishing which mechanism "wins," when competing mechanisms are simultaneously active. For instance, exercising makes you burn calories and thus lose weight; but, at the same time, exercising makes you hungry and eat more. It is difficult to say which out of the two mechanisms will "win." So confounding and masking are in fact the two sides of the same coin. Evidence of production helps us decide what variables to include, exclude, or control in the statistical model. Evidence of difference-making helps us disentangle the different effects when multiple causal paths are simultaneously at work.

Rethinking correlations as an evidential component for establishing causal claims is also interesting in the light of Bradford Hill's viewpoints on causal inference (Hill 1965). In this famous paper, Hill formulated nine aspects to consider when making a judgment about a correlation between two variables. Howard Frumkin (2006) summarizes them thus:

1. **Strength of association**. The stronger the relationship between the independent variable and the dependent variable, the less likely it is that the relationship is due to an extraneous variable.
2. **Temporality**. It is logically necessary for a cause to precede an effect in time.
3. **Consistency**. Multiple observations, of an association, with different people under different circumstances and with different measurement instruments increase the credibility of a finding.
4. **Theoretical plausibility**. It is easier to accept an association as causal when there is a rational and theoretical basis for such a conclusion.
5. **Coherence**. A cause-and-effect interpretation for an association is clearest when it does not conflict with what is known about the variables under study and when there are no plausible competing theories or rival hypotheses. In other words, the association must be coherent with other knowledge.
6. **Specificity in the causes**. In the ideal situation, the effect has only one cause. In other words, showing that an outcome is best predicted by one primary factor adds credibility to a causal claim.
7. **Dose-response relationship**. There should be a direct relationship between the risk factor (i.e., the independent variable) and people's status on the disease variable (i.e., the dependent variable).

8. **Experimental evidence.** Any related research that is based on experiments will make a causal inference more plausible.
9. **Analogy.** Sometimes a commonly accepted phenomenon in one area can be applied to another area.

Viewpoints 1, 3, 7, and 8 are about difference-making, while viewpoints 2, 4, 5, 8, and 9 are about production or mechanisms. This is interesting because if the scientific community by and large accepts Hill's viewpoints, then RWT-like arguments are a good candidate for a philosophical conceptualization of the importance of correlations and of their complementarity to considerations about the mechanisms of disease causation. But the interest in Hill's viewpoints is not confined to RWT-like arguments. In fact, inferential approaches such as the one developed by Julian Reiss (2015) also appeal to these different aspects of causal relations. As Reiss himself puts it:

> The [inferentialist theory of causality] maintains that the meaning of causal claims is given by their inferential connections with other claims. In particular, causal claims are infer-entially related to evidential claims—the claims from which a causal claim can be inferred—as well as to claims about future events, explanatory claims, claims attributing responsibility, and counterfactual claims (claims predicting 'what would happen if')—the claims that can be inferred from a causal claim.

This opens up new spaces for philosophical investigations in order to understand the role and use of correlations in causal inference.

So far, the discussion about evidential pluralism has not made clear whether this position is normative or descriptive – a worry expressed by, e.g., Alex Broadbent (2011). On the one hand, a descriptive reading of evidential pluralism would simply testify the use of multifarious evidence in the medical sciences (and elsewhere). Of course, no description is totally neutral, and the account should explain how (historical accounts of) scientific practices are analyzed. On the other hand, a normative reading of evidential pluralism would prescribe current and future scientific practices to adhere to it. This is an attractive option, but one that should be handled with care. In fact, there is no simple way in which philosophy can tell science what to do, in a simple top-down way. The debate on the role and use of correlation should seen as an opportunity to foster a dialogue between philosophy and medicine, philosophers and medical scientists.

Stakes are high for two reasons. One reason is that the philosophy underlying evidential pluralism is in much need of input coming from the medical sciences. Another reason is that it is controversial whether evidential pluralism fits different scientific practices in the medical sciences. This is related to the problem, mentioned in the opening of this contribution, of defining the medical sciences. Some accounts aim at being as inclusive as possible, and they have to provide an account of evidential pluralism (and, for the matter, of the meaning, role, and use of correlations) in practices as diverse as randomized controlled trials, case reports, cohort studies, diagnosis, etc. In turn, this is related to questions about methodological pluralism. In fact, under those accounts embracing the view of "medical sciences" as an umbrella term for different scientific practices, one should also accept, albeit implicitly, that causal relations are established using different methods, depending on the context. Thus, for instance, it is one thing to establish the efficacy of a drug or a treatment, for which a randomized controlled trial is perfectly appropriate, and it is another thing to establish what disease is causing such and such symptoms in a particular patient, for which *other* methods are appropriate.

Correlation and Data-Intensive Science

The problem of inferring causation from correlation should also be discussed in the context of *data-intensive science*. Medicine and epidemiology are increasingly using bigger and bigger data sets. Examples of research projects where big data sets are customarily created, analyzed, and used abound. One such example is the "EPIC" cohort. EPIC (European Prospective Investigation into Cancer and Nutrition) is a project jointly coordinated by IARC (International Agency for Research on Cancer) and Imperial College London. Initially, the project investigated the relation between (different types of) cancer and nutrition; later, the study also investigated several chronic diseases such as diabetes and included also genetic and environmental factors. Only between 1992 and 2000, the study examined data about some 520,000 individuals. Another study is the European consortium working on the "EXPOsOMICS" project. This project aims at developing novel methods to study environmental exposures, such as air pollution and water contamination, on selected diseases. A peculiarity of this project is the use of "omics technologies" that allow scientists to study changes in our bodies at the molecular level. The project also uses data from the EPIC cohort as well as many others. In spite of the hope of being able to establish meaningful (and even causal) correlations in big data, there are a number of delicate issues that the scientific and philosophical communities are currently debating.

One aspect relates to the "size" of these data sets: Is it really the *size* making the novelty, or is it something else? It might be argued that the use of emerging technologies, such as the omics technologies, is what allows us to produce data sets of unprecedented size. But, in turn, the use of technology for the production and analysis of data raises several methodological and epistemological issues. Some concern the very conceptualization of data (simply put, in spite of the name, data are not *given*, but rather constructed – for one account see, e.g., Leonelli 2015), while others concern the techniques for data analysis (statistics and data mining – see, e.g., discussion in a special issue (Merelli et al. 2014)).

In sum, providing an understanding of the role and use of correlations in causal inference raises important questions about the nature of causation itself but also about evidence and methods. These topics add up to the well-known, and much discussed, issues related to common cause structures or confounding that occupied much of the debate in statistics and in the philosophy of causality so far. The recent emphasis on data-intensive science, while opening up opportunities for studying correlations on even larger data sets, urges philosophical analyses about their conceptual underpinnings.

Definition of Key Terms

Correlation	The relation between two variables indicating that they are statistically dependent.
Causation	The relation between variables or events, indicated the relations of dependence and production between them.
Evidence	The information, input, or observation used to assess and support scientific claims about causation, explanation, or prediction.
Evidential pluralism	The position according to which evidence is multifarious.
Evidence of production	Information gathered from lab experiments, statistical studies, or other types of studies indicating how a cause produces its effect(s).
Evidence of difference-making	Information gathered from lab experiments, statistical studies, or other types of studies indicating that a case makes a difference to the occurrence of its effect(s).

Summary Points

- Large part of contemporary medicine is concerned with establishing causal relations with the aid of statistics.
- Studies using statistics have to consider carefully that "correlation is not causation," just as any other discipline that relies on quantitative analyses of data.
- Statistical tools used in medicine raise problems that are akin to those raised in other disciplines, for instance, the problem of confounding and control and the choice of variables, of the models, and of data in the first place.
- Despite all these warnings, correlations remain very useful to establish causal relations, as they are *evidence* for causal relations.
- Conceiving of correlations as evidence is part of a larger view of causation, according to which causal relations are established, based on various sources of evidence.
- Understanding the status of correlations for causal assessment in medicine is vital; data-driven approaches – where the search of correlation is a pillar – are more and more widespread.

References

Bernard C (1856) An introduction to the study of experimental medicine, 1927th edn. Macmillan, New York

Brendan C, Gillies D, Illari P, Russo F, Williamson J (2014) Mechanisms and the evidence hierarchy. Topoi 33:339–360. doi:10.1007/s11245-013-9220-9, Online first

Broadbent A (2011) Inferring causation in epidemiology: mechanisms, black boxes, and contrasts. In: Illari PMK, Russo F, Williamson J (eds) Causality in the sciences. Oxford University Press, Oxford, pp 45–69

Cook TD, Campbell DT (1979) Quasi-experimentation. Design and analysis issues for field settings. Rand MacNally, Chicago

Frumkin Howard (2006) Causation in medicine. http://www.aoec.org/CEEM/methods/emory2.html

Gillies D (2011) The Russo-Williamson thesis and the question of whether smoking causes heart disease. In: Illari PMK, Russo F, Williamson J (eds) Causality in the sciences. Oxford University Press, Oxford, pp 110–125

Good IJ (1961a) A causal calculus I. Br J Philos Sci 11:305–318

Good IJ (1961b) A causal calculus II. Br J Philos Sci 12:43–51

Goyal R (2013) Narration in medicine. In: Pier J, Schmid W, Hühn P, Meister JC (eds) The living handbook of narratology. Hamburg University, Hamburg, http://www.lhn.uni-hamburg.de/article/narration-medicine

Hill BA (1965) The environment of disease: association or causation? Proc R Soc Med 58:295–300

Illari PMK (2011) Mechanistic evidence: disambiguating the Russo-Williamson thesis. Int Stud Philos Sci 25(2):139–157

Illari P, Russo F (2014) Causality: philosophical theory meets scientific practice. Oxford University Press, Oxford

Leonelli S (2015) What counts as scientific data? A relational framework. Philos Sci 82:1–12

Lipton R, Ødegaard T (2005) Causal thinking and causal language in epidemiology. Epidemiol Perspect Innovat 2:8, http://www.epi-perspectives.com/content/2/1/8

Merelli I, Pérez-Sánchez H, Gesing S, D'Agostino D (2014) High-performance computing and big data in omics-based medicine. BioMed Res Int 825649. doi:10.1155/2014/825649

Nissen T, Wynn R (2012) The recent history of the clinical case report: a narrative review. RSM Short Rep 3(12):87. doi:10.1258/shorts.2012.012046

Parascandola M, Weed DL (2001) Causation in epidemiology. J Epidemiol Community Health 55:905–912

Reiss J (2015) Causation, evidence, and inference. Routledge, New York

Russo F, Williamson J (2007) Interpreting causality in the health sciences. Int Stud Philos Sci 21(2):157–170

Russo F, Williamson J (2011a) Epistemic causality and evidence-based medicine. Hist Philos Life Sci 33:563–582, http://philsci-archive.pitt.edu/id/eprint/8351

Russo F, Williamson J (2011b) Generic vs. single-case causal knowledge. The case of autopsy. Eur J Philos Sci 1(1):47–69

Suppes P (1970) A probabilistic theory of causality. North-Holland, Amsterdam

Williamson J (2005) Bayesian nets and causality: philosophical and computational foundations. Oxford University Press, Oxford

Evidence-Based Medicine in Theory and Practice: Epistemological and Normative Issues

52

Wendy Rogers and Katrina Hutchison

Contents

Abstract

Evidence-based medicine (EBM) emerged during the 1990s, with the aim of improving clinical practice by increasing the extent to which clinical care was informed by medical research, particularly randomized controlled trials (RCTs) and systematic reviews of RCTs. This chapter gives an account of EBM, followed by examination of epistemological and ethical justifications and critiques of EBM. EBM relies upon epistemological claims about the ability of RCTs to eliminate certain forms of bias and to establish whether or not there is a causal

W. Rogers (✉)
Department of Philosophy and Department of Clinical Medicine, Macquarie University, Sydney, NSW, Australia
e-mail: wendy.rogers@mq.edu.au

K. Hutchison
Department of Philosophy, Macquarie University, Sydney, NSW, Australia
e-mail: katrina.hutchison@mq.edu.au

© Springer Science+Business Media Dordrecht 2017
T. Schramme, S. Edwards (eds.), *Handbook of the Philosophy of Medicine*,
DOI 10.1007/978-94-017-8688-1_40

relationship between an intervention and an outcome. However, epistemological critiques of EBM include reservations about whether EBM can "prove" causation, concerns about the rejection of mechanistic models of causation, challenges associated with applying the results of RCTs to individual patients, and lack of evidence regarding whether EBM has in fact benefitted patients and healthcare systems. The ethical justifications for EBM include its promise of better patient outcomes through better informed clinicians and the idea that public health policy based on EBM can support equity and minimize waste of resources. Ethical critiques of EBM note that despite its potential for reducing particular forms of bias, the research upon which EBM is based is often industry funded, creating conflicts of interest that are associated with new sources of bias. These include bias in the conduct of trials, the publication of results, and the choice of interventions for investigation. EBM also poses challenges for patient and clinician autonomy, especially where evidence-based clinical practice guidelines are enforced through targets or audits. In the face of these concerns, EBM is under pressure to reestablish its credibility. The chapter ends by identifying three current initiatives that seek to reinstate the aims of EBM to better inform healthcare decisions.

Introduction

Evidence-based medicine (EBM) is a formalized approach to using the results of research trials to inform the care of patients. It has been hugely influential in medical practice and medical education and upon health services more broadly. This chapter explains what EBM is and provides a brief account of the development of EBM since its introduction in the 1990s, before describing the epistemological and ethical foundations of EBM and current critiques of these. The chapter ends by noting suggestions for the future of EBM.

The term "evidence-based medicine" (EBM) was coined in 1980 to describe the appraisal and use of research results in the care of individual patients, as first proposed by the EBM Working Group at McMaster University. EBM sought to change the way that clinicians think about medical knowledge. The EBM Working Group (1992) described this change as a "paradigm shift" in what should count as evidence strong enough to inform medical practice. This shift heralded a move away from decisions based upon what were considered to be unsystematic clinical observations, reliance on mechanistic reasoning and pathophysiological principles, and deference to the views of experts. In contrast, EBM advocated decisions based upon the statistical analysis of the results of research trials.

Over time, EBM has had a major impact upon healthcare practice and policy, as a method for identifying and appraising the results of research studies and of synthesizing this information to guide clinical decision making. In one of the earliest papers by the EBM Working Group, EBM is described as a dramatic change "which involves using the medical literature more effectively in guiding medical practice" (EBM Working Group 1992, p. 2420).

More formal definitions of EBM emerged during the 1990s. One of the most significant of these was published in a 1995 editorial marking the launch of the first dedicated EBM journal:

> [E]vidence based medicine is rooted in five linked ideas: firstly, clinical decisions should be based on the best available scientific evidence; secondly, the clinical problem - rather than habits or protocols - should determine the type of evidence to be sought; thirdly, identifying the best evidence means using epidemiological and biostatistical ways of thinking; fourthly, conclusions derived from identifying and critically appraising evidence are useful only if put into action in managing patients or making health care decisions; and, finally, performance should be constantly evaluated. (Davidoff et al. 1995, p. 1085)

This comprehensive definition of EBM identifies the key notion of using the best available scientific evidence to address the clinical problems of individual patients. By specifying that the "best evidence" is derived from "epidemiological and biostatistical ways of thinking," this definition introduces the normative claim that some forms of evidence are to be preferred over others (Djulbegovic et al. 2009). The kind of evidence that is most highly valued within EBM is that produced from randomized controlled trials (RCTs) about the efficacy and safety of healthcare interventions (Sehon and Stanley 2003). There is a second normative claim in this definition, which is that clinical decisions should be based upon the best evidence as specified (Djulbegovic et al. 2009). Thus, EBM is defined, famously by Sackett et al., as "the conscientious, explicit, and judicious use of current best evidence in making decisions about the care of individual patients" (1996, p. 71).

The new approach of EBM was underpinned by four assumptions. The first of these assumptions makes claims about the unreliability of clinical experience and intuition compared with knowledge obtained from the systematic and unbiased collection of observations, such as occurs in high-quality research. The second assumption is that another traditional source of medical knowledge, derived from pathophysiological principles, is likewise unreliable. While understandings of basic disease mechanisms are useful to guide clinical practice, it was claimed that relying upon pathophysiological principles may lead to adverse events or inaccurate estimates about the efficacy of interventions. The third assumption underpinning EBM is that in order to critically appraise and correctly interpret research literature (i.e., identify and use the best evidence), it is necessary for clinicians to understand certain biostatistical "rules of evidence," understood in terms of the reliability of statistically identified associations in research. The final assumption is that EBM will lead to "superior patient care" (EBM Working Group 1992, p. 2421). Thus, EBM marked a change away from clinical experience, mechanistic based reasoning, and the uncritical or haphazard use of research results toward independent practice based upon the critical appraisal of research results and the use of probabilistic evidence about the efficacy of interventions.

There have been four separate models of EBM since the late 1980s (Charles et al. 2011; Wyer and Silva 2009). The first consisted of formally applying clinical research evidence to medical practice (EBM Working Group 1992). The second model, from the mid-1990s, advocated for decision making based upon patient preferences, research evidence, and clinical expertise in equal measure while explicitly recognizing the challenge of integrating research evidence with clinical expertise. Third, the prescriptive model of the early 2000s incorporated patient preferences with research evidence, together with information about the patient's clinical status; in this model, clinical expertise was seen as the overarching mechanism to combine these three elements. Just how this was to be achieved remained unclear. The most recent model of the mid- to late 2000s is called a model for evidence-based clinical care, applicable to healthcare practices beyond medicine. This model sees the inclusion of a fourth element, healthcare resources, to be considered along with patient values, research evidence, and clinical status. As with the previous model, clinical expertise must draw upon all of these elements in order to reach a considered decision.

Thus, EBM has evolved, from an intuitively attractive and almost unassailable initial proposal to use the best and latest research evidence to inform clinical decisions, into a much more specific and complex model prescribing the exercise of clinical expertise to reach a decision based upon patient values, the clinical status of the patient, and the availability of resources, as well as research evidence.

There are two main reasons as to why EBM emerged when it did. The first relates to growing recognition of the gap between research evidence and clinical practice, which resulted in "expensive, ineffective or harmful decision making" (Rosenberg and Donaldson 1995, p. 1122). This gap led to significant variations in practice, marked by the slow uptake of effective interventions, such as streptokinase for myocardial infarction, and the equally slow abandonment of harmful practices such as the use of anti-arrhythmic prophylaxis following myocardial infarctions (Djulbegovic et al. 2009; Howick et al. 2013). Clearly, it was problematic for practitioners to be putting their patients' lives at risk by being out of touch with new research evidence. The second reason may explain why clinicians had trouble keeping up with the literature: this period saw an explosion in the numbers of published papers. The increase in published research has been attributed, at least in part, to the 1962 Kefauver-Harris Amendments to the United States Federal Food, Drug and Cosmetic Act, which required that firms had to provide evidence of the effectiveness of their products. In addition, the tools of biomedical informatics facilitated literature searching, and the widespread use of computers allowed such searching to take place in the clinic rather than the library.

EBM promised a more reliable way of ascertaining the effectiveness of medical interventions than was possible using "the former paradigm" (EBM Working group 1992, p. 2421). EBM methods have the potential to reduce or eliminate bias and provide statistically significant evidence of efficacy even in the absence of an understanding of causal mechanisms. As well as the self-evident benefit of discriminating between ineffective or harmful interventions and safe and effective ones (Goodman 2003), EBM has a number of other advantages. EBM integrates research with clinical care, teaches clinicians how to critically appraise clinical trials, informs better use of resources by evaluating the clinical effectiveness of interventions, is broadly democratic in that most people can learn the skills of critical appraisal, and may foster better communication with patients (Rosenberg and Donald 1995).

EBM has had an enormous impact upon healthcare (Greenhalgh et al. 2014). First, EBM has led to a focus on research methodology leading to higher standards for research trials and publications. Well-known examples of these include the CONSORT Statement which is an evidence-based set of recommendations for reporting RCTs (Schulz et al. 2010), the GRADE approach for assessing the quality of evidence and the strength of recommendations (Guyatt et al. 2008), and the PRISMA Statement for reporting systematic reviews and meta-analyses (Moher et al. 2009). These and other EBM standards have been widely accepted and are used as benchmarks for assessing the quality of research. Second, EBM has led to the development of national and international organizations, such as the Cochrane Collaboration, undertaking systematic reviews, or those developing and updating evidence-based clinical practice guidelines (CPGs). Clinical practice guidelines have turned out to be the dominant mechanism by which research evidence is synthesized into a format that can be used by practitioners, as it is unfeasible for individual practitioners to perform their own systematic reviews. Third, EBM has dramatically increased the information literacy of clinicians (Wyer and Silva 2009). Finally, the methods of EBM have enabled clinicians and others to map the rapidly changing knowledge base, which is a prerequisite for knowledge translation.

The Epistemology of EBM

The central epistemological claim underlying EBM concerns what counts as good evidence for clinical decisions. Sackett et al. claimed that evidence from clinical experience alone (the "old paradigm") is biased, and therefore unreliable, and hence that systematic approaches to evidence should be preferred (1996). Several sources of bias were identified. First, doctors are likely to remember patients with good outcomes and hence consider their treatment effective. But the good outcomes may be unrelated to the treatment. For example, compliant patients, who return for follow-up, are more likely to get positive outcomes even if the treatment is ineffective. Second, most symptoms and signs tend to regress toward the mean over time irrespective of any intervention, but this can make any intervention administered in the interim seem effective. Third, efficacy may be overestimated in clinical care because of the placebo effect in the patient and the effect of the desire for success in both patient and doctor, biases which can only be eliminated by blinding within RCTs (Sackett 1989). Finally, even the most rigorous causal-inductive or mechanistic reasoning can be fallible (Djulbegovic et al. 2009; Howick et al. 2013).

In contrast, EBM uses a hierarchy of evidence, based on claims about reliability of knowledge obtained from different research methods. Evidence is graded into levels based upon certain methodological features of the research, specified in the hierarchy of evidence. Three central claims underpin the hierarchy. First, randomized controlled trials (RCTs) or systematic reviews of RCTs provide stronger evidence than observational studies. Second, comparative clinical trials (including RCTs and observational studies) offer stronger evidence than reasoning from pathophysiological principles (also described as mechanistic reasoning).

Third, comparative clinical studies offer stronger evidence than expert clinical opinions (Howick 2011). Thus, epidemiological evidence – whether in the form of RCTs or observational studies – is privileged over pathophysiological or mechanistic evidence, and both are privileged over the expertise or intuition of individual clinicians. The hierarchy has evolved over time, but its essential features remain largely unchanged: RCTs, or systematic reviews of RCTs, are at the top of the hierarchy as they are considered to be the most reliable and unbiased form of evidence. An early four-level hierarchy was published in 1979 (see Table 1: Canadian Task Force 1979, p. 1195). As with those that followed, the highest level of evidence ("best") derives from RCTs, while expert opinion is ranked fourth.

The most complex hierarchy evolved in the 2000s, developed by the Oxford Centre for Evidence-Based Medicine (OCEBM). This refers to the use of particular techniques for collating and synthesizing research results from multiple sources (known as systematic reviews) and specifies particular methodological features of trials that render them of greater or lesser quality (see Table 2 which is an adapted and simplified version of this hierarchy taken from the cited source).

Table 1 Levels of evidence (1979)

Level of evidence	Type of evidence
I	At least one properly randomized controlled trial
II-1	Well-designed cohort or case–control study, preferably from more than one center or research group
II-2	Evidence from studies comparing groups of patients between times or between places who did and did not receive the intervention under study
III	Opinions of respected authorities, based on clinical experience, descriptive studies, or reports of expert committees

Canadian Task Force (1979, p. 1195: Table created from text in original)

Table 2 Summary of OCEBM 2001 levels of evidence

Level of evidence	Type of evidence
1	1a. Systematic reviews of RCTs (with homogeneity)
	1b. High-quality RCTs (with narrow confidence intervals)
	1c. All or no trials
2	2a. Systematic reviews of cohort studies (with homogeneity)
	2b. Individual cohort study (including low-quality RCTs, e.g., <80 % follow-up)
	2c. "Outcomes" research; ecological studies
3	3a. Systematic reviews (with homogeneity) of case–control studies
	3b. Individual case–control study
4	Case series (and poor-quality cohort and case–control studies)
5	Expert opinion without explicit critical appraisal or based on physiology, bench research, or "first principles"

Adapted from the version of the 2001 OCEBM hierarchy (as cited in BJU 2010)

Table 3 Summary of OCEBM 2011 evidence hierarchy for treatment interventions

Level of evidence	Type of evidence
1	Systematic review of RCTs or n-of-1 trials
2	RCT or observational study with dramatic effect
3	Non-randomized controlled cohort/follow-up study
4	Case series, case–control studies or historically controlled studies
5	Mechanism-based reasoning

Adapted from OCEBM (2011)

The OCEBM has now simplified their hierarchy (see Table 3), which, apart from the addition of systematic reviews as level 1, otherwise closely resembles the original 1979 hierarchy.

The randomized controlled trial (RCT) is at the heart of EBM. RCTs aim to produce valid results by ruling out more confounding factors than other research methods. Observational studies are susceptible to at least three kinds of bias, including self-selection bias whereby patients who choose, or are chosen, to participate in the study differ in important ways from patients who are not chosen; allocation bias, in which those recruiting research participants systematically favor those with certain characteristics, such as likely compliance, which affect the outcomes; and performance bias which occurs when patients know they are taking an experimental intervention, and this knowledge affects their behavior and outcomes. RCTs seek to overcome these biases and any other potential confounding factors. Randomization prevents self-selection and allocation bias by allocating participants randomly to each arm of the trial, so that any unknown variables are likely to be distributed equally between the groups. A second feature of RCTs, blinding, addresses performance bias in patients as well as confounding factors generated by clinicians whose views about the experimental intervention may affect their assessments of the outcomes. Blinding involves concealing the allocation (e.g., to the active or control arm of the trial) from both patient and researcher/treating clinician. A third feature of RCTs is that they compare the intervention in question with a control which may be standard therapy or a placebo (usually justified only if no alternative effective therapy exists). Thus, in an ideal RCT, an adequate number of patients are randomly allocated to a blinded treatment, the effects of which are assessed by a clinician/researcher who is unaware as to whether the patient is receiving the intervention or the control. In an ideal RCT, in which bias has been reduced to the extent possible and which has an appropriate sample size, any significant effects noted in the trial can be attributed to the intervention itself rather than bias, chance, or any other confounding factors.

Epistemological Critiques of EBM

EBM has been subject to a number of epistemological criticisms. In this section several of the most prominent are discussed. These include concerns about the extent to which the epidemiological methods privileged by EBM can demonstrate causal relationships and related concerns about the discounting of pathophysiological evidence. Epidemiological research offers a very different type of causal understanding compared with pathophysiological research. Critics, however, point out that both have disadvantages; thus it is erroneous to exclude pathophysiological reasoning as a source of medical evidence. A further concern arises about how to apply the findings of RCTs, which generate probabilistic information about selected populations, to individual patients who share some (but not other) features with the trial population. Finally, there are concerns about judging the effectiveness of EBM. As it is not possible to randomize health systems either to use or not use EBM, the decision to practice EBM within a health system cannot be based on what EBM itself regards as the highest level of evidence.

One of the forms of evidence to which EBM ascribes a low value is pathophysiological evidence. Understanding the physiological underpinnings of disease should help to inform the development of effective treatments. When this works, it can lead to immediate, significant improvements in outcomes, as in the case of volumetric treatment of blood loss for hemorrhagic shock (Hardaway 2004). In contrast, however, this reasoning can lead to adverse outcomes when the mechanisms underlying mortality and morbidity are not fully understood. An oft-cited example is the increased mortality associated with prescription of anti-arrhythmia drugs following myocardial infarction. Despite preventing arrhythmias, which are mechanistically linked to mortality, these drugs did not reduce mortality but conversely increased it (Howick 2011, pp. 4–5).

One problem with mechanistic evidence is that it focuses on pathophysiological effects/pathways rather than patient outcomes. Thus, efficacy may be measured in terms of reduction of arrhythmias, or changes to other biological indicators, rather than in terms of significant patient end points (such as reduced mortality, alleviation of pain, or increased function) for which these are proxies. In contrast, because the biostatistical methods privileged by EBM tend to compare patient outcomes for two or more groups of patients, without necessarily referring to underlying mechanisms, they are able to identify effective or ineffective treatments even where the underlying causal mechanisms are unknown or not completely understood. However, this advantage of EBM is forfeited when RCTs have intermediate or surrogate end points, such as levels of HbA1C to reflect glycemic control in diabetes, rather than clinically relevant end points such as deaths from heart attacks.

The epistemological advantage of RCTs is their capacity to identify a causal relationship between a particular treatment and a patient outcome. This causal relationship is statistical and probabilistic. It is based upon statistically significant differences in outcomes occurring between groups that are otherwise identical aside from the intervention they receive. In such cases the difference in outcomes is attributed to the intervention because confounding factors are ruled out by the study design. However, the claim that all confounding factors are ruled out in high-quality RCTs has been challenged by a number of critics. While RCTs can rule out known confounders (such as age, sex, and known comorbidities) by equally distributing them across the arms of the trial or by performing baseline comparisons, it remains possible that unknown confounders are not equally distributed (Worrall 2007, 2011).

While it is correct that biostatistical methods, including well-designed RCTs, cannot infallibly demonstrate causal relationships between an intervention and an outcome, these concerns do not undermine the evidence hierarchies recommended by proponents of EBM, as the findings of well-designed RCTs are less likely to be confounded than those of observational studies or other non-randomized studies subject to self-selection, allocation, or preference bias. However, other forms of bias may affect the reliability of EBM, especially when the design and conduct of research are affected by conflicts of interest (see section on Ethical Critiques of EBM).

RCTs make claims about causation based upon tests of significance, which are used to determine whether any differences in outcomes between the control and treatment arms of a trial are due to chance or to the efficacy of the treatment. These tests report the likelihood of the result being due to chance (null hypothesis) as a probability. Conventionally a probability (P value) of 0.05 is used to indicate that a finding is significant rather than occurring by chance. However, statistical tests of significance may not always track important or relevant causal relationships. As Bradford Hill notes:

> [T]here are innumerable situations in which they [significance tests] are totally unnecessary – because the difference is grotesquely obvious, because it is negligible, or because, whether it be significant or not, it is too small to be of any practical importance. What is worse, the glitter of the t table diverts attention from the inadequacies of the fare. (1965, p. 299)

In addition, while a P value of 0.05 equates to a 95 % certainty that the findings are not an accident, on average, one in every twenty trials with a P value of 0.05 is likely to have a finding due to chance. This has prompted the claim that formal tests of significance cannot answer questions about causation (Bradford Hill 1965, p. 299).

The reliability of statistical analysis is a particular problem when it comes to subgroup analysis (Assmann et al. 2000). In a well-designed RCT with sufficiently large participant groups, known confounders are distributed equally between arms or can be adjusted for. However, this may not apply to subgroups within a trial, where the analysis is more likely to be affected by both known confounders (which may be unequally distributed within subgroups even if distributed equally in the trial at large) and unknown confounders which exert greater influence within the smaller sample size of subgroups. Members of subgroups are also unlikely to be allocated evenly across the arms of the trial, unless a modified randomization strategy involving blocking, stratification, or other techniques to balance the arms is used (Pocock and Simon 1975), while methods to control for known confounders are not always used (Assmann et al. 2000).

Even if epidemiological research is able to establish causal relationships or to demonstrate that such relationships are likely enough to safely proceed on the assumption that they pertain, the nature of these causal claims is philosophically puzzling. The measures of causal strength identified by epidemiologists are, mathematically speaking, calculations of the degree of association between two variables. In the absence of an extra ingredient, the *causal import* of such measures is unclear.

This is known as the "causal interpretation problem" (Broadbent 2013, p. 30). Researchers can establish (with a reasonable degree of certainty) that there is a causal relationship between the treatment and the outcome. However, the mechanism of causation cannot be explained by epidemiological studies, including the best designed RCTs, because these studies look at population level measures rather than the physiological effects of the intervention on individual patients. Thus, epidemiological causation is like a "black box" (Howick 2011, p. 124). In contrast, pathophysiological reasoning looks inside the black box at the mechanisms which determine how and why a treatment works.

Applying the results from RCTs to individual patients is also problematic. While RCTs are ideal for establishing that a treatment "works somewhere," they cannot establish whether a treatment "will work for us" in specific settings (Cartwright 2011, p. 1401). The situations where EBM is used are not necessarily similar in the relevant ways to the contexts where the RCTs were performed. There is no straightforward way of moving from the general probabilistic findings supported by RCTs to the particular knowledge required in clinical contexts, due to the complexity of causal connections and the challenge associated with working out how different factors are causally interacting to bring about the positive outcomes for some of the participants in the study (Cartwright 2011, p. 1401).

This problem has two parts: first, whether the target population (e.g., patients in a particular clinical context) is relevantly similar to the RCT populations and, second, whether the practical implementation of the intervention is relevantly similar to that of the RCT (Cartwright 2010). In order to resolve these problems, it is important to understand the mechanisms or causal capacities, which underlie and explain the regular connections between treatment and outcome that pertain in the RCT. Understanding the physiological underpinnings of treatment can provide a basis for identifying which patients will benefit from the application of a treatment that has been shown to work by RCTs and which patients for whom the treatment will not work (Cartwright 2011). However, the current conception of EBM excludes consideration of the causal model that informed the RCT, and information on the implementation conditions of the trial(s) may be incomplete.

A final epistemological concern regarding EBM is that there is no reliable evidence that EBM works. That is to say, it is not possible to randomize clinicians to either practice or not practice EBM and then compare patient outcomes in the two groups, nor is it possible to randomize health systems to implement or not EBM policies (Hayes 2002; Cohen et al. 2004). This criticism might seem unfair, but it is far from obvious what the overall impact of EBM is. Given the extent of change in healthcare and health research in the past 20 years, no meaningful historical comparison can be made. Furthermore, the costs associated with implementing EBM are significant, including the redesign of medical training and degree programs, the production of evidence-based guidelines, and provision of access to evidence for clinicians. Therefore, in order to represent value to health services, EBM should be significantly better than other alternatives.

Ethical Justifications for EBM

The ethical justifications for EBM are straightforward: EBM is grounded in widely shared assumptions about the value of health and the need to use the most effective means possible to protect health. Insofar as EBM is the most effective means, using it will lead to better health outcomes for patients (Gupta 2003). Thus, EBM is consistent with the ethical principles of beneficence and non-maleficence. In addition, at least some models of EBM incorporate patient values and preferences into decision making, thereby respecting patient autonomy. Finally, EBM has the potential to support equity in access to effective interventions and to minimize waste of health resources through the abandoning of ineffective or harmful interventions.

EBM is beneficence-based because it aims to ensure that the knowledge by which decisions are informed is the best (most reliable) possible. EBM thereby offers a scientific foundation for the implicit promise that the doctor does indeed know best about the effectiveness of possible treatment options. By using EBM, doctors are able to explain and justify their recommendations and to offer objective reasons for recommending one treatment rather than another. The implicit ethical claim of EBM is that it will lead to better patient outcomes than by using clinical expertise alone. This claim is supported by examples in the literature, such as that of the slow uptake of antenatal steroids for reducing the severity of lung disease in premature babies. By 1981, there was sufficient research evidence to demonstrate that the use of steroids significantly reduced infant mortality; however, this information had not been systematically collected or promulgated. As a result, steroids were not routinely used and research continued until 1995, leading to the preventable deaths of thousands of babies (Howick 2011, p. 163).

The use of EBM to identify and discard harmful or ineffective treatments meets the ethical requirement of non-maleficence. Using techniques of systematic review and meta-analysis, it is possible to discriminate between effective, ineffective, and harmful treatments. This information is essential for informing healthcare at the level of the individual patient and also for policy makers who may then decommission treatments that are harmful or ineffective. Treatments that had initial plausibility, such as the prophylactic use of anti-arrhythmic drugs in patients post-myocardial infarction or ligation of the internal mammary artery for angina, were later found to be harmful through the use of RCTs. EBM provides a systematic way of collecting and reviewing evidence, thereby increasing the likelihood that harmful or ineffective interventions will be identified and withdrawn.

Since the mid-1990s, models of EBM have included patients' values or preferences alongside research evidence. EBM proposes a transparent and open approach to decision making, in which evidence is used to inform the patient's choice about preferred treatment options. To be autonomous, decisions should be informed to the extent possible. Thus, EBM supports patient autonomy and informed consent, by its transparent approach to evidence. Yet just how patient preferences should be incorporated along with evidence and other relevant information into the decision process is unclear. One approach has been the development and use of patient decision aids to bring evidence into the consultation in ways that support patient autonomy (Edwards and Elwyn 2001).

Finally, EBM has implications for justice. EBM is committed to the rigorous evaluation of research evidence and applying the findings to all relevant patients. This approach has the potential to foster equity in access to medical treatment by mandating the same effective treatment for patients, irrespective of irrelevant features, such as race. Such an approach can reduce discrimination when efficacious treatments are given equally to all relevant patients. And there are examples of EBM reducing discrimination. An EBM guideline on hemodialysis, for example, significantly increased access to dialysis for African-American men, who, prior to its introduction, had a 60 % greater likelihood of receiving inadequate hemodialysis compared with whites. After the guideline was introduced, there was a 92 % increase in the proportion of African-American patients receiving adequate hemodialysis (Owen et al. 2002). As well as more equitable access at the level of individual patients, EBM has been used, for example, in the UK, to mandate the fair distribution of effective interventions through evidence-informed policy and allocation decisions at the population level. This can lead to more transparent and fairer purchasing decisions and address inequities in access caused by variable provision of interventions across geographical regions.

Ethical Critiques of EBM

Despite the clear ethical foundations of EBM, it has been subject to sustained ethical critique. Concerns fall into a number of areas. First, as discussed above, there is no strong evidence that EBM leads to better health outcomes than alternative approaches to medical decision making, making it uncertain as to whether or not EBM is beneficent. This concern is amplified by a series of related worries about the effects of EBM upon research and the reliability of research results. Somewhat ironically given bias-reducing claims about RCTs, several kinds of bias have been identified in the research upon which EBM is based, including in the conduct of trials, the publication of results, and the choice of interventions for investigation. There are also ethical questions about the effects of EBM on the treatment of participants in clinical trials and about the broader impact of EBM on the research agenda. A second set of concerns relates to the use of EBM in practice where it may be used to mandate or withhold treatment, often through the use of guidelines. Patient (and practitioner) autonomy may be marginalized if there are incentives or penalties linked to compliance with EBM guidelines. Finally, there are concerns about the broader societal effects of EBM, such as on health equity, and in entrenching particular kinds of medical authority at the expense of other forms of expertise.

Although EBM aims to promote the use of research methods that minimize bias, a number of biases have been identified that affect the reliability of research and thus may lead to EBM incorrectly identifying interventions as more effective and/or less harmful than they really are (Gupta 2003; Every-Palmer and Howick 2014). Some of these biases relate to the funding of clinical trials, while others arise from the nature of the underlying research questions. Conflicts of interest arising from the commercial funding of much of the research underpinning EBM are a major source of bias. There is now strong evidence that research funded by commercial sources is three to four times more likely to return positive findings (i.e., show that an intervention is effective) than research funded by noncommercial sources such as governments (Lexchin et al. 2003; De Vries and Lemmens 2006). This is problematic as it is estimated that the private for-profit sector funds 51 % of global research annually (Burke and Matlin 2008), with the suggestion that between two thirds and three quarters of published randomized controlled trials are industry funded (Every-Palmer and Howick 2014).

Bias may arise from manipulation of the study design to produce positive results, for example, by choosing a placebo or suboptimal dose of competitor drug as the comparator or by selecting participants with characteristics that favor the drug under investigation, rather than who reflect the target population for treatment. Outcomes may be selected to favor the trial drug, or statistical methods may be used to minimize or mask adverse events (Rogers and Ballantyne 2009). The trial may be too short to provide a meaningful estimate of efficacy for treatment of chronic conditions. Concealing adverse events has led to considerable preventable morbidity and mortality, resulting in a number of high-profile lawsuits and financial penalties. For example, Merck allegedly concealed evidence about the cardiac side effects of their blockbuster antiarthritic drug rofecoxib, leading to tens of thousands of excess cardiovascular events (Topol 2004), while DePuy Orthopedics (a subsidiary of Johnson & Johnson) used similar misinformation tactics in response to concerns raised about the safety of their metal-on-metal hip replacement prior to its eventual withdrawal from the market (Johnson and Rogers 2014).

A second kind of bias relates to the selective publication of research results. Funders own the results of research that they have sponsored, and they are under no obligation to publish these, especially if the findings are negative for the product under investigation. There are a number of publication practices that subvert the fair and transparent communication of research results. First, ghostwriting involves employees or subcontractors of the pharmaceutical industry drafting articles which are then published under the name of established academics (De Vries and Lemmens 2006). Links between the article and the funder may be difficult to identify, despite requirements by academic journals to disclose sources of funding and conflicts of interest. Negative results are suppressed, while positive results are published in results are published in strategic campaigns aimed at flooding the literature and creating a more optimistic record of research outcomes than warranted by the actual findings. For example, a campaign for the antidepressant sertraline involved 55 papers published between 1998 and 2001. These became a significant part of the evidence base about sertraline, drowning out other more critical results (Healy and Cattell 2003). Obtaining the raw data from commercial companies is extremely difficult, leading to initiatives which advocate for the registration of all clinical trials and the publication of all results, irrespective of funding source (AllTrials 2014).

A third kind of bias arises regarding the type of intervention under investigation, known as a technical bias (Gupta 2003). This favors familiar research methods and hence pushes research toward phenomena that we know how to investigate. For example, RCTs are ideally suited to pharmacological interventions, where it is possible to securely blind both participant and researcher through the production of identical-looking drugs (including placebos) for intervention and control groups. However, RCTs are far more difficult for complex interventions, especially those that involve physical modalities. Thus, the evidence base for surgery is much weaker than that for drugs, as it is difficult to mount surgical RCTs and, where the intervention is a change in surgical technique, rather than a new device, it may be difficult to secure funding as there is little potential for the commercialization of new surgical techniques. Likewise, there are far fewer RCTs of alternative and complementary therapies, and it is not clear whether at least some of the outcomes considered important to practitioners or patients are amenable to quantified assessment. Thus, technical bias leads to the skewing of the evidence base toward familiar interventions that are easy to investigate and quantify and away from complex interventions or those with qualitative outcomes. Commercial interests do not cause technical bias, but do amplify its impact.

Apart from introducing and amplifying bias and hence unreliability in research, commercial funding has other adverse effects, one of which is pressure to contain costs. This may lead either to outsourcing of research to contract research organizations (CROs) rather than academic teams within Western countries or to performing research in developing nations. CROs are under market pressures to be economical and produce results. This has led to concerns about the treatment of participants in research in the USA who make a living from serial enrollment in phase 1 pharmaceutical trials. Those involved as "guinea pigs" are often impoverished or indigent and lack protections if there are side effects or long-term consequences from their involvement in research (Elliott and Abadie 2008). Similar concerns about the exploitation of vulnerable populations arise when research is performed in resource-poor settings where participants may otherwise lack access to any healthcare and where the interventions under investigation address the diseases of affluent nations rather than those of most pressing concern within the nations hosting the research (Petryna 2007).

Concern about participants extends to vulnerable groups commonly excluded from research. This leads to an evidence base that is skewed toward the treatment of those represented among trial participants, who, in the latter part of the twentieth century, were predominantly white males (Rogers 2004). Women, ethnic minorities, and other groups perceived to be vulnerable, such as children and prisoners, were excluded from research for reasons including explicit protectionist policies of exclusion, practical considerations of research efficiency and cost, and false assumptions about the irrelevance of sex, gender, and racial differences (Rogers and Ballantyne 2009). Despite regulatory efforts to encourage the inclusion of women and minorities in research, distortions continue, with the persistent under-representation of women over the age of 65 in research and the overrepresentation of men in studies of heart disease and colorectal and lung cancer trials (Hutchins et al. 1999; Murthy et al. 2004). These practices lead to research results that are unable to answer questions about the safety and efficacy of clinical interventions for underserved groups. Issues associated with the exclusion of vulnerable groups from research are only partly explained by commercial interests. While companies may want to avoid the costs or risks associated with including members of these groups in trials, wider social norms and patterns of access to healthcare also play a significant role.

One final issue regarding the commercial funding of research concerns the research agenda, which, broadly understood, determines what research is conducted and therefore what results will be available to inform EBM. The research agenda reflects a mix of the interests of industry and the governments of predominantly high-income countries, with an ever-increasing role played by commercial research sponsors. This has led to a focus on patentable treatments that address the needs of affluent markets. The problem here is twofold: an emphasis on patentable treatments (e.g., drugs) at the expense of other potentially effective but less-profitable interventions such as non-patentable behavioral and environmental solutions to ill health and a focus on conditions prevalent in rich populations (Trouiller et al. 2002). For example, of 460 trials investigating treatment for osteoarthritis of the knee, 380 (82.6 %) evaluated drugs despite inadequate or absent evidence about the effectiveness of other kinds of interventions (Tallon et al. 2000).

These ethical concerns arise from placing RCTs at the top of the evidence hierarchy. By so doing, EBM has, inadvertently, encouraged commercial interests in research, leading to adverse effects such as distorting the research agenda, limiting methodological diversity, impoverishing the range of interventions under investigation, and introducing biases into clinical research. Taken together, these undermine both the capacity of EBM to provide answers for important and relevant questions about the clinical care of patients and the reliability of evidence about the effectiveness of interventions. In turn, these features call into question the extent to which EBM is indeed beneficent.

A second set of ethical concerns arises in the use of EBM. Clinicians tend to rely upon easily accessible forms of evidence such as formal summaries or clinical practice guidelines (CPGs), rather than performing their own systematic reviews. This raises a number of issues including the applicability of the evidence to the patient in question and the weight accorded to the evidence compared with other factors that might affect decision making such as patient preferences, availability of resources, practitioner responsibilities, or relevant policies.

First, as noted above, RCTs can provide strong evidence of efficacy, but the epistemological strength of a trial may be inversely related to its applicability. In reducing the number of variables in trials, participants are often limited to those with few or no comorbidities. In contrast, many patients in clinical settings have comorbidities, and thus, it can be unclear to what extent evidence from tightly controlled trials applies to them. This leads to a lack of evidence about which interventions are effective for populations routinely excluded from research, such as members of vulnerable groups or those with the poorest health due to comorbidities, leaving them with fewer treatment options than members of populations more likely to be included in trials (Rogers 2004). This injustice can be exacerbated when proof of efficacy is required to ensure access to treatment (Hope 1995).

Second, while it is widely accepted that patients should be able to exert their autonomy in making decisions about which healthcare interventions to accept and which to reject, patient autonomy may be compromised by rigid adherence to EBM. Use of evidence summaries or CPGs can lead to limited opportunities for exercising autonomy if patients are simply offered the choice of accepting or rejecting the evidence-mandated option. This point is particularly salient given that patient perspectives are largely excluded from the production of evidence through the use of researcher-defined populations, interventions, and end points. Interventions shown to be effective in RCTs may be unacceptable to patients because of the nature of side effects, cost, or inconvenience. Regarding guidelines, professionals and/or politicians choose the topics for guideline development; professional and/or economic interests dominate guideline recommendations; and guidelines are often used to direct rather than inform individual patient care. Thus, while at least some accounts of EBM propose using evidence to inform patient choices, this can be hard to achieve in practice when the evidence itself has been produced with little attention to what might matter for patients, and there are pressures to accept options that are statistically associated with better outcomes in RCTs.

As with patients, at least some practitioners feel that their autonomy and clinical judgment are undermined by overly directive CPGs or evidence summaries, sometimes referred to as "cookbook" medicine. Clinicians argue that following a guideline devalues or discounts their own knowledge of and expertise with their patients in favor of impersonally developed evidence-based recommendations. This is coupled with the fact that there is little information on how to integrate practitioner knowledge with EBM recommendations; and, in at least some practice settings, there may be penalties for not adhering to CPGs, which are used as tools to assess the quality of care. These concerns are amplified if practitioners do not trust the CPGs, either because they are seen as instruments of rationing rather than evidence about most effective care or because of commercial sponsorship of the guideline itself or the underlying research.

A third set of ethical issues relates to the broader societal effects of EBM. As EBM has become more widespread, it has been seen as a tool for rationalizing the provision of healthcare, appealing to the common sense notion that only healthcare known to be effective should be offered to patients. However, as noted above, not all potential recipients of healthcare are represented equally among research participants, and not all types of interventions are amenable to investigation through an RCT; thus, certain patient populations and interventions are likely to be neglected. In theory, this should not be a problem: EBM advocates the use of the best available evidence, and if this is from a cohort study rather than an RCT, then it is nonetheless the best evidence. But in practice, governments and insurers appeal to RCT evidence in decisions about the provision of some interventions rather than others and may justify their decisions on the grounds of justice in the allocation of resources (Gupta 2003). This takes on historic dimensions when new interventions, for which there is an evidence base, command funding previously allocated to older interventions that lack evidence as judged by EBM standards. A second societal effect of EBM relates to its impact upon medical authority. Those who perform evidence syntheses and who formulate guidelines acquire the power to direct healthcare spending and commission research in various ways, thereby further entrenching medical authority and in the process shifting it away from clinicians and toward epidemiologists (and commercial funders). This concentration of power into the hands of the few with a commitment to the assumptions of EBM further marginalizes others with potentially valuable contributions to setting the research agenda or determining research priorities (Gupta 2003).

These ethical critiques of EBM challenge claim about the value of EBM in patient care and draw attention to the unintentional consequences of favoring RCTs above other research methods. While some are contingent (it would be possible to have research that avoided the biases introduced as a result of commercial pressures), others identify central and ongoing tensions in the philosophy of EBM surrounding how to use evidence in clinical decisions.

The Future of EBM

Critical analysis of the challenges facing EBM has stimulated recent campaigns for an EBM "renaissance" and for changes to the ways trials are funded and reported. Meanwhile, the rise of personalized medicine poses both challenges and opportunities for EBM.

The EBM renaissance group was developed after a meeting between EBM critics and proponents in Oxford in late 2013, leading to a call for a return to "real" EBM. "Real" EBM designates a version of EBM in which the care of the patient is the highest priority and the use of evidence is individualized to meet patient needs (Greenhalgh et al. 2014). In order to achieve this, the focus of clinician training must shift away from following templates, rules, and guidelines toward enhancing the higher-level intuitive skills that are markers of true expertise; and publications (in journals and by guideline groups) must be better attuned to the needs of those who will be reading and using them. Finally, research must change to become more independent and free from conflicts of interest and broader in the scope of methods recognized as providing high-quality evidence.

Demand for a broader research agenda incorporating different research questions and methodologies challenges the current form of EBM, in which one dominant methodology, the RCT, bears the overwhelming burden of producing high-quality medical knowledge. Although the "renaissance group" retains the idea of gold standard systematic reviews (Greenhalgh et al. 2014), some of their recommendations for a broader research agenda seriously challenge current understandings of EBM, due to the considerable influence of evidence hierarchies on the funding and publication of research.

In recognition of the biases introduced by commercially funded research, especially selective publication of results, the AllTrials campaign calls for the prospective registration of all trials together with publication of a brief summary of the results within 12 months of completion of the trial and publication of full details about the trial's methods and results. AllTrials campaign documents and publications identify ways in which existing measures are failing, such as journals continuing to publish unregistered trials and the non-enforcement of FDA requirements for all trials located in the USA to be registered (AllTrials 2013; Goldacre 2013). AllTrials advocates for additional initiatives to improve the transparency of clinical trials and availability of data, including research contracts that do not allow companies to veto publication of the results, research ethics committees requiring publication of results as a condition of ethics approval, and treating the withholding of trial results as medical misconduct (AllTrials 2013, p. 5). All of these measures would, if implemented, go some way to addressing current shortcomings in the production of evidence.

The rise of personalized medicine poses challenges for EBM (Hamburg and Collins 2010). The notion of tailoring medical treatments to individual patients contrasts significantly with the epidemiological methods of EBM. Methods for deriving data from trials that might be useful for personalized medicine include stratified randomization, for example, randomization of cancer patients according to molecular information about their tumors. However, such stratification can reduce the effectiveness of blinding (Pocock and Simon 1975). The more strata that are introduced, the more challenging this issue becomes. A simpler form of "personalized" medical research is known as the n-of-1 trial. These are crossover trials with only one participant, in which the active and control arms are run sequentially to generate comparative data for individual patients. These trials can retain many of the advantages of well-designed RCTs (including the option of a placebo or active control and double blinding with some interventions), but rather than generating statistical data about a population, they generate personal data about the effectiveness and side effects of a treatment in an individual. In contexts where population level data is needed, multiple n-of-1 trials can be combined; in the future, combining the results from many such trials could be facilitated by sophisticated patient record-keeping systems (Lillie et al. 2011).

Conclusion

Since the early 1990s, EBM has changed the way that clinicians engage with the findings of medical research and apply these findings in the care of individual patients. EBM has influenced the priorities of researchers, policy makers, funders, and commercial entities involved in health research. A fundamental tenet of EBM is that certain forms of evidence, specifically that derived from well-designed RCTs and systematic reviews of RCTs, are the most reliable and should be privileged in the decision making of clinicians and policy makers. The evidence hierarchy has created incentives for researchers and funders to prefer RCTs over other research methods and encouraged clinicians and policy makers to eschew evidence deemed less reliable based on pathophysiological reasoning and expert opinion. Benefits of EBM include the generation of systems for publishing, retrieving, and summarizing data generated from health research, as well as improved uptake of at least some research findings about effective and ineffective treatment. Although there are both epistemological and ethical justifications for EBM, significant critiques have arisen from both these perspectives. While it is unlikely that the quest for better evidence about healthcare interventions will be abandoned, the exploitation of EBM by commercial interests, and the impact of EBM in narrowing the research agenda, may lead to a more or less radical restructuring of the EBM hierarchy and the way that research is performed and evaluated.

Definitions of Key Terms

Clinical practice guidelines (CPGs)	Are tools to support clinical decision making by providing recommendations based upon syntheses of evidence.
Confounders	Are any factors that influence the outcomes of a research trial, other than the intervention under investigation.
Efficacy	Is a measure of the clinically beneficial outcome resulting from an intervention as measured in a clinical trial.
Epidemiology	Is the study of the determinants and distribution of diseases in human populations, often using group comparisons.
Evidence hierarchy	Is a method of ranking evidence derived from different sources, based on the view that the most reliable evidence is generated by research methods, such as randomized controlled trials, that minimize bias.
Evidence-based medicine (EBM)	Refers to the use of the best available scientific evidence to inform the clinical care of patients.
Mechanistic reasoning	Is inferring the likely effects of a therapy based upon an understanding of the relevant physiological mechanisms.
Meta-analysis	Is a statistical method for combining the results of multiple clinical trials in order to identify relevant outcomes that are not reliably discernable within individual trials.
Pathophysiological principles	Are generalized rules based upon an understanding of the relevant physiological processes. They may inform mechanistic reasoning.
Randomized controlled trials (RCTs)	Are a type of experimental study designed to minimize bias by randomly allocating participants to either active (receiving the experimental intervention) or control (receiving the standard therapy or placebo) arms of the trial.
Rules of evidence	Are agreements about the reliability of statistically identified associations in research.

Statistical significance   Refers to the likelihood of an association being due to the efficacy of the treatment rather than chance. Conventionally, results are considered statistically significant if the probability of them occurring by chance is less than 5 %.

Systematic reviews   Are a summary of evidence on a particular clinical question, based upon all of the available research evidence and using pre-specified methods aimed at reducing bias.

Summary Points

- Evidence-based medicine is a highly influential approach to using the results of research, the "best evidence," to inform the clinical care of patients.
- EBM differs from previous approaches to medical evidence by relying upon statistical analyses to determine efficacy, rather than reasoning based upon pathophysiological principles or causal mechanisms.
- The major epistemological innovation of EBM is to change thinking about the reliability of different forms of evidence used to inform practice. In EBM hierarchies, results from randomized controlled trials are ranked as the most reliable form of evidence, while clinical experience is considered the least reliable form of medical evidence.
- The ethical foundation of EBM is that it promises better healthcare by reliably distinguishing effective from ineffective or harmful interventions.
- Weaknesses of EBM include the inability of RCTs to rule out all potential confounders, the probabilistic nature of the causal relationship between interventions and outcomes demonstrated by RCTs, the undervaluing of mechanistic reasoning, and the difficulty of applying the results of trials to individual patients.
- Ethical critiques of EBM identify the effects of conflicts of interest caused by the commercial funding of much of the research used to inform EBM, which can introduce bias; the effect of EBM on the research agenda, skewing it toward particular research methods and interventions; and effects on the autonomy of decision making in the clinical encounter.
- EBM may be strengthened by increasing the range of interventions for which evidence is sought, and the methods so used, and by freeing itself from the effects of conflicts of interest.

References

AllTrials (2013) Missing trial data – briefing notes. http://www.alltrials.net//wp-content/uploads/2013/01/Missing-trials-briefing-note.pdf. Accessed 20 Aug 2014

AllTrials (2014) http://www.alltrials.net/. Accessed 20 Aug 2014

Assmann SF, Pocock SJ, Enos LE et al (2000) Subgroup analysis and other (mis)uses of baseline data in clinical trials. Lancet 355:1064–1069

Bradford Hill A (1965) The environment and disease: association or causation? Proc R Soc Med 58 (5):295–300

Broadbent A (2013) Philosophy of epidemiology. Palgrave Macmillan, New York

Burke M, Matlin S (eds) (2008) Monitoring financial flows for health research 2008. Geneva: Global Forum for Health Research. http://www.globalforumhealth.org/filesupld/MFF08/MonitoringFinancialFlows2008.pdf

Canadian Task Force on the Periodic Health Examination (1979) The periodic health examination. Can Med Assoc J 121:1193–1254

Cartwright N (2010) What are randomised controlled trials good for? Philos Stud 147(1):59–70

Cartwright N (2011) A philosopher's view of the long road from RCTs to effectiveness. Lancet 377:1400–1401

Charles C, Gafni A, Freeman E (2011) The evidence-based medicine model of clinical practice: scientific teaching or belief-based preaching? J Eval Clin Pract 17(4):597–605

Cohen AM, Stavri PZ, Hersh WR (2004) A categorisation and analysis of the criticisms of evidence-based medicine. Int J Med Inform 73:35–43

Davidoff F, Haynes B, Sackett D et al (1995) Evidence-based medicine. BMJ 310 (6987):1085–1086

De Vries R, Lemmens T (2006) The social and cultural shaping of medical evidence: case studies from pharmaceutical research and obstetric science. Soc Sci Med 62(11):2694–2706

Djulbegovic B, Guyatt GH, Ashcroft RE (2009) Epistemologic inquiries in evidence-based medicine. Cancer Control 16(2):158–168

Edwards A, Elwyn E (eds) (2001) Evidence-based patient choice: inevitable or impossible? Oxford University Press, Oxford

Elliott C, Abadie R (2008) Exploiting a research underclass in phase 1 clinical trials. N Engl J Med 358(22):2316–2317

Every-Palmer S, Howick J (2014) How evidence-based medicine is failing due to biased trials and selective publication. J Eval Clin Pract. doi:10.1111/jep.12147

Evidence-Based Medicine Working Group (1992) Evidence-based medicine: a new approach to teaching the practice of medicine. JAMA 268(17):2420–2425

Goldacre B (2013) Are clinical trial data shared sufficiently today? No. BMJ 347:f1880

Goodman KW (2003) Ethics and evidence-based medicine: fallibility and responsibility in clinical science. Cambridge University Press, Cambridge

Greenhalgh T, Howick J, Maskrey N (2014) Evidence based medicine: a movement in crisis? BMJ 348:g3725

Gupta M (2003) A critical appraisal of evidence-based medicine: some ethical considerations. J Eval Clin Pract 9(2):111–121

Guyatt G, Oxman A, Vist G et al (2008) GRADE: an emerging consensus on rating quality of evidence and strength of recommendations. BMJ 336:924–926

Hamburg MA, Collins FS (2010) The path to personalised medicine. N Engl J Med 363(4):301–304

Hardaway RM (2004) Wound shock: a history of its study and treatment by military surgeons. Mil Med 169(4):265–269

Hayes RB (2002) What kind of evidence is it that evidence-based medicine advocates want health care providers and consumers to pay attention to? BMC Health Serv Res 2(3). doi:10.1186/1472-6963-2-3

Healy D, Cattell D (2003) Interface between authorship, industry and science in the domain of therapeutics. Br J Psychiatry 183:22–27

Hope T (1995) Evidence based medicine and ethics. J Med Ethics 21(5):259–260

Howick J (2011) The philosophy of evidence based medicine. Wiley Blackwell, Oxford

Howick J, Glasziou P, Aronson JK (2013) Problems with using mechanisms to solve the problem of extrapolation. Theor Med Bioeth 34(4):275–291

Hutchins LF, Unger JM, Crowley JJ et al (1999) Under representation of patients 65 years of age or older in cancer-treatment trials. N Engl J Med 341(27):2061–2067

Johnson J, Rogers W (2014) Joint issues – conflicts of interest, the ASR hip and suggestions for managing surgical conflicts of interest. BMC Med Ethics 15:63. doi:10.1186/1472-6939-15-63

Lexchin J, Bero LA, Djulbegovic B et al (2003) Pharmaceutical industry sponsorship and research outcome and quality. BMJ 326:1167–1170

Lillie EO, Patay B, Diamant J et al (2011) The n-of-1 clinical trial: the ultimate strategy for individualizing medicine? Pers Med 8(2):161–173

Moher D, Liberati A, Tetzlaff J et al (2009) Preferred reporting items for systematic reviews and meta-analyses: the PRISMA statement. BMJ 339:332–336

Murthy VH, Krumholz HM, Gross CP (2004) Participation in cancer clinical trials: race-, sex-, and age-based disparities. JAMA 291(22):2720–2726

OCEBM Levels of Evidence Working Group (2001/2010) Levels of evidence. Brit J Urol 105:155

OCEBM Levels of Evidence Working Group (2011) The Oxford 2011 levels of evidence. Oxford Centre for Evidence-Based Medicine. http://www.cebm.net/index.aspx?o=5653. Accessed 11 Aug 2014

Owen W, Szczech L, Frankenfield D (2002) Healthcare system interventions for inequality in quality: corrective action through evidence based medicine. J Natl Med Assoc 94:83S–91S

Petryna A (2007) Clinical trials offshored: on private sector science and public health. BioSocieties 2:21–40

Pocock SJ, Simon R (1975) Sequential treatment assignment with balancing for prognostic factors in the controlled clinical trial. Biometrics 31(1):103–115

Rogers WA (2004) Evidence-based medicine and justice: a framework for looking at the impact of EBM on vulnerable or disadvantaged groups. J Med Ethics 30:141–145

Rogers WA, Ballantyne AJ (2009) Justice in health research: what is the role of evidence-based medicine? Perspect Biol Med 52(2):188–202

Rosenberg W, Donald A (1995) Evidence based medicine: an approach to clinical problem-solving. BMJ 310(6987):1122–1126

Sackett DL (1989) Rules of evidence and clinical recommendations on the use of antithrombotic agents. Chest 95(2 Suppl):2S–4S

Sackett DL, Rosenberg WMC, Gray JAM et al (1996) Evidence based medicine: what it is and what it isn't. BMJ 312(7023):71–72

Schulz KF, Altman DG, Moher D (2010) CONSORT 2010 statement: updated guidelines for reporting parallel group randomized trials. Ann Intern Med 152(11):726–732

Sehon SR, Stanley DE (2003) A philosophical analysis of the evidence-based medicine debate. BMC Health Serv Res 3:1–10

Tallon D, Chard J, Dieppe P (2000) Relation between agendas of the research community and the research consumer. Lancet 355:2037–2040

Topol EJ (2004) Failing the public health – rofecoxib, merck, and the FDA. N Engl J Med 351 (17):1707–1709

Trouiller P, Olliaro P, Torreele E et al (2002) Drug development for neglected diseases: a deficient market and a public-health policy failure. Lancet 359(9324):2188–2194

Worrall J (2007) Why there's no cause to randomize. Br J Philos Sci 58:451–488

Worrall J (2011) Causality in medicine: getting back to the hill top. Prev Med 53:235–238

Wyer PC, Silva SA (2009) Where is the wisdom? I – a conceptual history of evidence-based medicine. J Eval Clin Pract 15(6):891–898

Randomized Trials and Observational Studies: The Current Philosophical Controversy

53

Jeremy Howick and Alexander Mebius

Contents

Abstract

The supposed superiority of randomized over non-randomized studies is used to justify claims about therapeutic effectiveness of medical interventions and also inclusion criteria for many systematic reviews of therapeutic interventions.

J. Howick (✉)
Nuffield Department of Primary Care Health Sciences, University of Oxford, Oxford, UK
e-mail: jeremy.howick@phc.ox.ac.uk

A. Mebius
Royal Institute of Technology (KTH), Stockholm, Sweden

Nuffield Department of Primary Care Health Sciences, University of Oxford, Oxford, UK
e-mail: alenik@kth.se; alexander.mebius@phc.ox.ac.uk

© Springer Science+Business Media Dordrecht 2017
T. Schramme, S. Edwards (eds.), *Handbook of the Philosophy of Medicine*,
DOI 10.1007/978-94-017-8688-1_45

However, the view that randomized trials provide better evidence has been challenged by philosophers of science. In addition, empirical evidence for average *differences* between randomized trials and observational studies (which we would expect if one method were superior) has proven difficult to find. This chapter reviews the controversy surrounding the relative merits of randomized trials and observational studies. It is concluded that while (well-conducted) observational can often provide the same level of evidential support as randomized trials, merits of (well-conducted) randomized trials warrant claims about their superiority, especially where results from the two methods are contradictory.

Introduction

A current and widely accepted view in medicine is that randomized studies are superior to non-randomized studies to support claims about therapeutic effectiveness (Higgins and Green 2008; Straus et al. 2011). This view is also sometimes used to as justification for excluding observational studies from systematic reviews (Higgins and Green 2008) and for making judgments about risk of bias in studies (Guyatt et al. 2008; OCEBM 2011). However, philosophers of science have criticized this view. For example, in the most widely cited critique of evidence-based medicine (EBM), John Worrall claims that randomization adds little epistemological value (Worrall 2002). Yet, more recently a systematic review concluded that there were no average differences between randomized trials and observational studies (which is contrary to what one would expect if one method were superior) (Anglemyer et al. 2014). The lack of average differences calls into question whether one method can be superior.

The aim of this chapter is to review current philosophical controversy. The following section begins with a brief description of the differences between randomized trials and observational studies and a warning about how to compare the two designs fairly (i.e., we must compare randomized trials and observational studies of similar *quality*). Section "A Note About Adequate Comparisons of Randomized Trials and Observational Studies" reviews some of the arguments that have been made against the view that randomized trials provide superior evidence, including some from Worrall (2002). The arguments for and against Worrall's view will not be reiterated here (but see Howick (2011) for an argument that Worrall sets up a straw man and La Caze et al. (2012) for an argument that Worrall's premise about the value of randomization is based on a misunderstanding). Section "Potential Versus Actual Benefits of Randomized Trials: The Elusive Search for Empirical Evidence That Randomized Trials and Observational Studies Provide Different Results" examines the implications of the recent systematic review that failed to detect an average difference between randomized trials and observational studies. Section "Internal Versus External Validity of Randomized Trials" reviews whether the external validity is more problematic for randomized trials than it is for observational studies. The chapter finishes with a brief review of some of the alleged practical advantages of observational studies (such as their ethical feasibility) and argues that many of these are exaggerated. It concludes that well-conducted observational studies will often provide similar results as randomized trials. However, in the cases where there are differences between randomized trials and observational studies, accepted benefits of randomized trials suggest that we should side with the randomized trial. Moreover, since it is not possible to know in advance whether the results from observational studies and randomized trials will differ, new interventions should be introduced in the context of well-conducted randomized trials.

Randomized Trials and Observational Studies

Observational Studies

In controlled observational studies, investigators compare people who are subject to an intervention with those who are not. The investigators neither allocate patients to receive the intervention nor administer the intervention. Instead, they compare records of patients who have received an intervention and been treated in routine practice with similar patients who did not receive the intervention. The main problems with observational studies are that they suffer from (i) self-selection bias (sometimes called patient preference bias, or confounding by indication), (ii) adherence bias, (iii) allocation bias, and (iv) performance bias. We will explain each of these in turn.

In one typical observational study, Petitti et al. (1987) compared the records of 2,656 women who took hormone (estrogen) replacement therapy (HRT) with 3,437 who did not and followed them for 10 or more years to measure rates of coronary heart disease (CHD) and overall mortality. They found that HRT users were only half as likely to die as those who did not use HRT. Stampfer and Colditz (1991) conducted a systematic review of all the available studies of the effects of HRT in preventing CHD, all but one of which were observational, and found that women taking HRT appeared to be, on average, half as likely to die as women who did not take HRT. They concluded that HRT could substantially reduce the risk for coronary heart disease. As a result, many thousands of women were given HRT to help prevent coronary heart disease. However, later randomized studies on the effect of HRT found that far from preventing coronary heart disease, stroke, and cancer, it appeared to increase the risks of developing these conditions (in addition to others including dementia) for quite a number of women (Rossouw et al. 2002). Why this apparent anomaly?

The observational studies of the effects of HRT, like all observational studies, suffered from the problem that people who choose to take HRT are likely to be very different in many ways from people who choose not to do so ("self-selection bias"). There might, for example, be significant differences in age; behavior, such as whether or not they smoked, how often they ate vegetables, and how much alcohol they drank; their working conditions; or where they lived. These differences could all affect how likely people are to contract CHD or cancer *independent* of whether or not they take HRT. In other words, the differences in the results might not be caused by the treatment, but are instead due to the better health of the women who chose to take HRT. Such differences between people in the experimental and control groups at the outset of a study and before the treatment is administered (the "baseline") are often referred to as "selection bias." Selection bias arising from patient choice is referred to as self-selection bias. Careful adjusting for baseline differences increases the quality of observational studies. At the same time, some differences will inevitably prove difficult to control for, because they are either unforeseen or information about them cannot be established. It can, for example, be difficult to obtain observational information about comorbidities, concomitant medication, and family history of disease.

Observational studies can also suffer from adherence bias. To see how, consider the following example. In a study of clofibrate versus placebo for treating coronary heart disease, researchers found that there was no difference in mortality between men treated with clofibrate and those in the placebo group (20 % in both groups). However, investigators found that patients who adhered to the treatment regime more strictly had a lower mortality (15 %) than those who did not (25 %) (Coronary Drug Project 1980). A systematic review confirms that adherence seems to be an independent factor that is directly correlated with positive outcomes (Boswell et al. 2012). This could be due to the fact that adherers are more hopeful or that adherence is typical among people who engage generally in more healthy behaviors. Since patients in an observational study choose to take the treatment, they could be more likely than an average patient in a trial to be an adherer, which could confound the study.

Another potential problem with observational studies is allocation bias, which arises because caregivers are in charge of deciding whether or not to prescribe a treatment. Caregivers could systematically favor certain sorts of patients. For example, if they thought the treatment was likely to be very effective, they might choose to give the treatment only to their sickest patients. Alternatively, if they were worried that the treatment had risky side effects that might be more serious for the sickest patients, they might choose to exclude this group.

Several confounding factors can also arise in observational studies because patients and caregivers know they are receiving treatment. Biases arising after the patient has received the treatment are often referred to as "performance biases." If patients believe they are taking a powerful therapy, whether or not the therapy is, in fact, powerful ("performance bias") and if patients know they are receiving the latest and best therapy, they might improve because of their beliefs and expectations and not because of the experimental therapy itself (Di Blasi et al. 2001). Similarly, investigator attitudes have been known to influence interpretation of rat (Rosenthal and Lawson 1964) and human behavior (Eisenach and Lindner 2004) and even to affect more "objective" measures such as blood cell counts (Berkson et al. 1939). Observational studies cannot generally deal with performance biases because (by definition) people taking the therapy know they are taking the therapy. These potentially serious issues warrant the worries with results from observational studies.

Randomized Trials

Randomized trials all involve comparing at least one experimental therapy with at least one control therapy. The control groups can either receive another treatment, a "placebo," or "no treatment." A placebo is a treatment capable of making people believe it is, or could be, the experimental treatment. It is often a sugar pill, although more sophisticated trials have also attempted to use a placebo that mimics the known side effects of the experimental treatment, to avoid patients becoming aware of whether they are in the experimental or control group (Howick 2011). "No treatment" controls are difficult to construct in practice. Participants are either left alone, in which case the investigators lose control over whether the "untreated group" choose to treat themselves with some other treatment, or they are closely monitored, although this is also known to have effects on the outcomes of the treatment or lack of it (Cocco 2009; McCarney et al. 2007).

Unlike in an observational study where patients choose whether to take the intervention themselves, participants in a randomized trial are randomly allocated to receive either an experimental intervention or a control. Simple random allocation is a process in which all participants have the same chance of being assigned to one of the study groups (Jadad 1998). Restricted randomization involves employing various strategies to ensure that the number of participants and various characteristics such as sex and age are similarly distributed between groups.

Strict randomization of participants to treatment and control groups reduces the risk of self-selection bias, adherence bias, and allocation bias, because neither participants nor caregivers can influence who receives the experimental intervention. However, unless the allocation sequence is concealed, randomization can be subverted, so in order for the potential benefits of randomization to be actualized, random allocation must be concealed. Violations of the assignment scheme are particularly dangerous when the investigators have a personal or financial interest in the new therapy appearing to be effective, because they can choose patients whom they think are more likely to benefit. Participants' knowledge of the group to which they are assigned can also corrupt the randomization process.

Randomized trials can also reduce the risk of performance bias. If the trial participants, caregivers (and perhaps also other groups involved in the trial), are blinded and do not know which participants receive the experimental intervention and which participants receive the control intervention, then performance biases can be ruled out. However, trials that are described as blinded in fact are rarely successfully blinded (Howick 2011). Participants who know they are receiving the "mere" control treatment could drop out of the trial or (which is bad for the validity of the trial but perhaps good for the participant) covertly seek other medication. This would tend to inflate the apparent benefits of the control treatment and reduce apparent benefits of the experimental treatment. Others may have read about potential side effects of the new treatment and therefore drop out of the experimental group.

Given that high-quality randomized trials can rule out more confounding factors than observational studies, it is unsurprising that even vociferous critics of the view that randomized trials provide better evidence acknowledge (including Worrall 2002) acknowledge the superiority of randomized trials. To be sure, Worrall claims that the *only* (and he insists, small) benefit of randomized trials is their ability to reduce "selection bias." This, however, is an understatement, since randomized trials but not observational studies can rule out various sources of performance bias as well.

Comparing Randomized Trials and Observational Studies

A Note About Adequate Comparisons of Randomized Trials and Observational Studies

Comparing "high-quality" or "well-conducted" (more on what this might mean below) randomized trials with shoddily conducted observational studies would not provide a fair basis for comparing the relative merits of the two study designs, nor would a comparison of a carefully controlled observational study with a large effect with a small, biased randomized trial. When comparing randomized trials with observational studies, it is therefore important to compare "high-quality" randomized trials with "high-quality" observational studies. But what does it mean for a study to be "high quality"? Following Worrall (2002), Howick (2011) argues that the quality is related to the extent to which the *effect size* revealed in the study can be taken to account for likely *confounding factors*. A confounding factor (or "confounder") is one that (a) potentially affects the outcome, (b) is unequally distributed between experimental and control groups, and (c) is unrelated to the experimental intervention. Each confounder provides an alternative explanation for the results of the study. For example, age and smoking status are likely confounders in many studies because age and smoking are independently correlated with many important outcomes measured in clinical trials. In other words (on Howick's account), an observational study whose effect size is much larger than the combined effect of potential confounders should provide enough evidence to warrant the use of that treatment in clinical practice (Glasziou et al. 2007). This account has been criticized by Broadbent (Broadbent 2013) who notes that even if the effect size is large, an observational study does not rule out common causes. This is a legitimate criticism; hence, we should add that in addition to demonstrating a large enough effect size to rule out confounding, an observational study needs to demonstrate that a common cause is an unlikely explanation for the association.

For example, an observational study showing that high doses of vitamin C made common cold symptoms disappear within 5 days supports the hypothesis that vitamin C cures the common cold, but does *not* rule out the plausible alternative hypothesis that the common cold symptoms go away without any treatment within 5 days. Henceforth in this chapter when referring to randomized trials or observational studies, we refer to examples of each that are high quality.

Philosophers of science (Borgerson 2009) as well as medical researchers (Altman 2002) have criticized randomized trials on the basis that many randomized trials are *not* high quality. For example, one particular randomized trial of treatments for sepsis suggested that using the monoclonal antibody to the endotoxin could cut mortality in half (Ziegler et al. 1991), but a subsequent trial, also randomized, but tenfold bigger, found that the same antibody could increase mortality (McCloskey et al. 1994). Many randomized trials are underpowered (Keen et al. 2005) and fail to successfully conceal or blind (Schulz et al. 1995; Wood et al. 2008; Schulz and Grimes 2002), which makes them susceptible to selection bias and allocation bias. Finally, they may also have effect sizes so small that statistically significant results can arise by chance (Sierevelt et al. 2007) or suffer from confounding from other sources that are not adequately explored (Smith and Ebrahim 2002; Barbui and Cipriani 2007). However, observational studies suffer from many of the same problems as randomized trials and perhaps more (Stroup et al. 2000). In order for the fact that many randomized trials are poorly conducted to count against the view that randomized trials provide better evidence than observational studies, one would have to show that randomized trials are *more likely* to suffer from bias than observational studies. The fact that some poorly conducted randomized trials should be interpreted with more suspicion than high-quality observational studies with large effects is well taken and also incorporated into common evidence-ranking schemes (Guyatt et al. 2008; OCEBM 2011).

Potential Versus Actual Benefits of Randomized Trials: The Elusive Search for Empirical Evidence That Randomized Trials and Observational Studies Provide Different Results

The above discussion illustrates that randomized trials have the potential to rule out numerous biases that threaten the validity of observational studies. However, empirical research supporting *actual* differences between the two study designs has proven hard to come by. A recent Cochrane Review summarized previous systematic reviews that compared results from observational and randomized trials (Anglemyer et al. 2014). The reviewers found that some randomized studies reported larger effect sizes than observational studies of the same treatment, while others had smaller, but often similar, effect sizes. On average Anglemyer et al. reported that there was no average difference between randomized controlled trials and observational studies. In their words: "there is little evidence for significant effect estimate difference between observational studies and RCTs, regardless of specific observational study design, heterogeneity, or inclusion of studies of pharmacological interventions" (Anglemyer et al. 2014, p. 2).

However, it is unclear whether Anglemyer et al.'s conclusion was acceptable. Specifically, one could challenge their decision to pool the results. The Cochrane Handbook cautions against pooling results if effect directions differ:

A systematic review need not contain any meta-analyses. . .particularly if there is inconsistency in the direction of effect, it may be misleading to quote an average value for the intervention effect. (Higgins and Green 2008, p. 279)

In fact a similar Cochrane Review chose not to pool and drew opposite conclusions. Odgaard-Jensen et al. compared trials in which randomization was adequately described with trials in which randomization was inadequately described. Their results were similar to those in the Anglemyer et al. review: some adequately randomized studies reported larger effect sizes than inadequately randomized studies, while others reported smaller, but again often similar, effect sizes (Odgaard-Jensen et al. 2011). However, instead of reporting an average result, Odgaard-Jensen et al. concluded that "results of controlled trials with adequate and inadequate/unclear concealment of allocation sometimes differed. . .However, it is not generally possible to predict the magnitude, or even the direction, of possible selection biases and consequent distortions of treatment effects from studies with non-random allocation or controlled trials with inadequate or unclear allocation concealment" (Odgaard-Jensen et al. 2011, p. 10).

We will not go into detail here about whether the decision to pool or not was correct (see Howick and Mebius 2014, for a more complete discussion). What we can conclude from the results of the Odgaard-Jensen et al. and Anglemyer et al. reviews is that (adequate) randomized trials often provide similar results to inadequately or non-randomized studies. This is not surprising if we consider that if a treatment has a real (and moderate) effect, the effects will tend to show up in both well-conducted observational studies and well-conducted randomized trials. However, in some cases results from randomized trials and observational studies *do* differ, and in these cases we need to know which studies to trust. Given the ability of randomized trials to rule out biases (something that even skeptics admit), then ceteris paribus it is safe to side with the results from the randomized trial. In fact this is what happens in practice. For example, observational studies suggest that high doses of vitamin C reduce the risk of cardiovascular disease (Knekt et al. 1994), homeopathy reduces the risk of depression (Oberai et al. 2013), and metformin reduces the risk of cancer among patients with diabetes (DeCensi et al. 2010). However, these results have been contradicted by randomized trials and therefore have not been accepted (Sesso et al. 2008; Adler et al. 2013; Stevens et al. 2012). Our challenge to philosophers of science who criticize the view that randomized trials provide better evidence than observational studies is simple. Let them provide just one single example where results from well-conducted randomized trials are different from results from observational studies and where they would side with the observational study.

More recently, and in a story that was widely reported in the news, a 2006 Cochrane Review of randomized trials suggested that neuraminidase inhibitors ("Tamiflu") reduced the risk of, and could cure, swine flu (Jefferson et al. 2006). On the basis of that review, many countries stockpiled billions of dollars' worth of the drugs. However, the authors of the review suspected that the manufacturer had not published all the relevant trials. After a hard-won fight and appeal to the Freedom of Information Act, the authors of the original review obtained access to all the trials, whether published or not, and updated the review, where they found little evidence of benefit and strong evidence of harms from neuraminidase inhibitors (Jefferson et al. 2014). At this stage the drug manufacturers suggested that the trials were unreliable because they tested the effects of the drugs in artificial (trial) conditions rather than "real world" (i.e., in an observational study) (Muthuri et al. 2014).

Internal Versus External Validity of Randomized Trials

Both Worrall (2002) and Cartwright (2007) argue that even if randomized trials have a higher degree of *internal validity* (the degree to which the study results of the study apply to the study population) than observational studies, they suffer from problems of external validity (the degree to which the study results apply to a "real world" or "target" population). Cartwright and Worrall are correct to draw our attention to the problem of external validity. Up to 90 % of potentially eligible participants are sometimes excluded from trials according to often poorly reported and even haphazard criteria (Mant 1999; Penston 2003; Zimmerman et al. 2002; Zetin and Hoepner 2007). For example, even the most effective antidepressants in adults have doubtful effects in children (Bylund and Reed 2007; Deupree et al. 2007). In another example taken from John Worrall (2007), the drug benoxaprofen (Oraflex™ in the USA and Opren™ in Europe) proved effective in trials in 18–65-year-olds, but killed a significant number of elderly patients when it was introduced into routine practice.

However, to infer from the problems with the external validity of randomized trials to any claim about the comparative benefits of randomized trials compared with observational studies is invalid. For one, if a study is not internally valid, then the issue of external validity is moot. Second, one would have to establish that observational studies have a *higher* degree of external validity than randomized trials to infer from the (alleged) relative lack of external validity of randomized trials. This assumption is taken for granted by Worrall and Cartwright and other philosophical critics of EBM, but they do not cite any evidence to support it. In fact scientists who actually do observational studies worry very much about the external validity of observational studies which themselves have inclusion criteria that can be very unrepresentative (Carlson and Morrison 2009). Doll and Hill's famous observational study of smokers, for example, was limited to doctors (who, at the time, were almost exclusively male). The people in this famous observational study were therefore very different from the general population. Moreover, many randomized trials ("pragmatic" trials) include almost all of the target population. For example, the GISSI-1 trial of thrombolysis for acute myocardial infarction recruited 90 % of patients admitted within 12 h of the event with a definite diagnosis and no contraindications (GISSI 1986): in other words, most of the people who would have been treated in practice. Third, neither Worrall nor Cartwright cites any empirical evidence that the alleged lack of representativeness of randomized trial populations is a real problem. Studies indicate that even if randomized trials appear to involve unrepresentative populations, the results generally apply to the target population (Vist et al. 2008).

Alleged (But Rarely Real) Relative Practical Advantages of Observational Studies

Numerous other alleged disadvantages of randomized trials are often used to challenge the view that randomized trials provide superior evidence. For example, it is often argued that randomized trials are sometimes unfeasible or unethical (McCulloch et al. 2002). This is true. For example, it would have required too large a sample size (and jumping through all but insurmountable ethical hurdles) to conduct a randomized trial that challenged Dr. Spock's advice to put babies to sleep on their stomachs. Hence, a number of very large observational studies were conducted that suggested (contrary to what Dr. Spock's mechanistic reasoning suggested) more babies who slept on their *backs* survived. However, it does not follow from the fact that randomized trials are sometimes unfeasible to the fact that they do not rule out more bias than observational studies *in cases where they are feasible*. Moreover, claims that randomized trials are unfeasible or unethical are often exaggerated. For instance, it is often claimed that randomized trials of surgical procedures are unfeasible (because surgeons have strong preferences) and unethical (because "control" or "sham" surgery usually involves incisions and anesthesia which are harmful). However, a recent systematic review identified 53 placebo-controlled trials of surgery, and in over half the "placebo" surgery was as good as the "real" surgery (Wartolowska et al. 2014). This result turns the ethical argument about randomized trials on its head: if the "placebo" surgery is as good as the "real" surgery, then it is arguably unethical to *not* conduct placebo-controlled randomized trials of surgical interventions. And given they have been done, they are also clearly feasible.

Another oft-heard argument is that industry interests influence results of randomized trials in various ways (Every-Palmer and Howick 2014). This is true. However, the very same industry influences also corrupt results from observational studies, mechanistic reasoning, and expert "consensus" statements (Jones et al. 2014). So again, one cannot infer from the fact that randomized trials are subject to influence from industry bias *by itself* to any claim about the relative merits of randomized trials. In fact one would suspect that it is easier for industry to introduce bias to observational studies and expert "consensus" statements. There is no need to go through the same regulatory processes to conduct an observational study, and these processes might provide some protection against nefarious influences of industry. Similarly, it is likely far cheaper to buy off a few experts at a consensus conference than to conduct a randomized trial.

Conclusion

Even critics of randomized trials admit that empirical studies show that well-conducted randomization and blinding can rule out bias, particularly selection bias (Worrall 2002). Given the benefits of (well-conducted) randomized trials over (well-conducted) observational studies, where there is any conflict between the results of randomized and observational studies, it seems reasonable to side with the randomized study and assume that its results are more reliable (Howick 2011). However, if the results of the two different types of study are consistent or homogenous, as is often the case, there is no reason *not* to accept evidence from observational studies (Mebius 2014). It is probably unsurprising that the results are often similar, because many truly effective treatments will reveal significant effects in both types of study. However, we cannot predict in advance whether results from randomized trials and observational studies will differ. Our challenge to philosophical critics of the view that well-conducted randomized trials provide better evidence than well-conducted observational studies is simple. Let them provide a single example where results from a well-conducted randomized trial differ from results in a well-conducted observational study and where they believe the observational study results lie closer to the truth. Until this challenge is met, new treatments should be introduced in the context of well-conducted randomized trials, and existing treatments should be evaluated by measuring their effects within well-conducted randomized trials.

Definitions of Key Terms

Observational studies	In controlled observational studies, investigators compare people who are subject to an intervention with those who are not. The investigators neither allocate patients to receive the intervention nor administer the intervention. Instead, they observe what happens to people who choose (or are chosen by their healthcare practitioners) to take an intervention (or not).
Randomized trials	Participants in a randomized trial are randomly allocated to receive either an experimental intervention or a control.
Systematic review	Systematic reviews aim to gather all evidence that fits pre-specified eligibility criteria to address a specific research question. They aim to minimize bias by using explicit and systematic methods (Higgins and Green 2008).
Internal validity	Internal validity is a property that reflects the extent to which the causal conclusion of a study is justified for the study population.
External validity	External validity is the property of a study that renders its conclusions generalizable to populations outside the study.

Summary Points

- Observational studies tend to suffer from problems that are believed to increase the risk of producing inflated results in randomized trials; randomized trials are believed to overcome these problems.
- Randomized trials may have a lower degree of external validity than observational studies.
- The alleged superiority of randomized trials has not led to statistically significant average differences between results of randomized trials and results of observational studies.
- Because of the potential for randomized trials to rule out a greater degree of bias than observational studies, it follows that, ceteris paribus, we should side with randomized trials in cases where results from observational studies and randomized trials differ.
- New treatments should be introduced in the context of randomized trials.

References

Adler UC, Krüger S, Teut M et al (2013) Homeopathy for depression: a randomized, partially double-blind, placebo-controlled, four-armed study (DEP-HOM). PLoS One 8:e74537

Altman DG (2002) Poor-quality medical research: what can journals do? JAMA J Am Med Assoc 287:2765–2767

Anglemyer A, Horvath HT, Bero L (2014) Healthcare outcomes assessed with observational study designs compared with those assessed in randomized trials. Cochrane Database Syst Rev 4: MR000034

Barbui C, Cipriani A (2007) Publication bias in systematic reviews. Arch Gen Psychiatry 64:868

Berkson J, Magath T, Hurn M (1939) The error of estimate of the blood cell count as made with the hemocytometer. Am J Physiol 128:309–323

Borgerson K (2009) Valuing evidence: bias and the evidence hierarchy of evidence-based medicine. Perspect Biol Med 52:218–233

Boswell K, Cook C, Burch S, Eaddy M, Cantrell R (2012) Associating medication adherence with improved outcomes: a systematic literature review. Am J Pharm Benefits 4:e97–e108

Broadbent A (2013) Jeremy Howick: the philosophy of evidence-based medicine. Philos Sci 80:165–168

Bylund DB, Reed AL (2007) Childhood and adolescent depression: why do children and adults respond differently to antidepressant drugs? Neurochem Int 51:246–253

Carlson MD, Morrison RS (2009) Study design, precision, and validity in observational studies. J Palliat Med 12:77–82

Cartwright N (2007) Are RCTs the gold standard? Biosocieties 2:11–20

Cocco G (2009) Erectile dysfunction after therapy with metoprolol: the Hawthorne effect. Cardiology 112:174–177

Coronary Drug Project (1980) Influence of adherence to treatment and response of cholesterol on mortality in the coronary drug project. N Engl J Med 303:1038–1041

DeCensi A, Puntoni M, Goodwin P et al (2010) Metformin and cancer risk in diabetic patients: a systematic review and meta-analysis. Cancer Prev Res 3:1451–1461

Deupree JD, Reed AL, Bylund DB (2007) Differential effects of the tricyclic antidepressant desipramine on the density of adrenergic receptors in juvenile and adult rats. J Pharmacol Exp Ther 321:770–776

Di Blasi Z, Harkness E, Ernst E, Georgiou A, Kleijnen J (2001) Influence of context effects on health outcomes: a systematic review. Lancet 357:757–762

Eisenach JC, Lindner MD (2004) Did experimenter bias conceal the efficacy of spinal opioids in previous studies with the spinal nerve ligation model of neuropathic pain? Anesthesiology 100:765–767

Every-Palmer S, Howick J (2014) How evidence-based medicine is failing due to biased trials and selective publication. J Eval Clin Pract 20:908–914

Glasziou P, Chalmers I, Rawlings M, McCulloch P (2007) When are randomised trials unnecessary? Picking signal from noise. Br Med J 334:349

Gruppo Italiano per lo Studio della Streptochinasi nell'Infarto Miocardico (GISSI) (1986) Effectiveness of intravenous thrombolytic treatment in acute myocardial infarction. Lancet 22:397–402

Guyatt GH, Oxman AD, Vist GE et al (2008) GRADE: an emerging consensus on rating quality of evidence and strength of recommendations. Br Med J 336:924–926

Higgins JJ, Green S (2008) The Cochrane handbook for systematic reviews of interventions. Version 5.1.0 [updated March 2011]. Wiley Blackwell, Chichester

Howick J (2011) The philosophy of evidence-based medicine. Wiley Blackwell/BMJ Books, Chichester

Howick J, Mebius A (2014). In search of justification for the unpredictability paradox. Trials 15:480

Jefferson T, Demichell V, Di Pietrantonj C, Jones M, Rivetti D (2006). Neuraminidase inhibitors for preventing and treating influenza in healthy adults. Cochrane Database Syst Rev 19(3)

Jadad A (1998) Randomized controlled trials. BMJ Books, London

Jefferson T, Jones MA, Doshi P et al (2014) Neuraminidase inhibitors for preventing and treating influenza in healthy adults and children. Cochrane Database Syst Rev 4:CD008965

Jones B, Howick J, Hopewell J, Liew SM (2014) Response to 'Position statement on ethics, equipoise and research on charged particle therapy'. J Med Ethics 40:576–577

Keen HI, Pile K, Hill CL (2005) The prevalence of underpowered randomized clinical trials in rheumatology. J Rheumatol 32:2083–2088

Knekt P, Reunanen A, Jarvinen R et al (1994) Antioxidant vitamin intake and coronary mortality in a longitudinal population study. Am J Epidemiol 139:1180–1189

La Caze A, Djulbegovic B, Senn S (2012) What does randomization achieve? Evid Based Med 17:1–3

Mant D (1999) Can randomised trials inform clinical decisions about individual patients? Lancet 35:743–746

McCarney R, Warner J, Iliffe S et al (2007) The Hawthorne effect: a randomised, controlled trial. BMC Med Res Methodol 7:30

McCloskey RV, Straube RC, Sanders C, Smith SM, Smith CR (1994) Treatment of septic shock with human monoclonal antibody HA-1A. A randomized, double-blind, placebo-controlled trial. Ann Intern Med 121:1–5

McCulloch P, Taylor I, Sasako M, Lovett B, Griffin D (2002) Randomised trials in surgery: problems and possible solutions. Br Med J 324:1448–1451

Mebius A (2014) Corroborating evidence-based medicine. J Eval Clin Pract 20:915–920

Muthuri SG, Venkatesan S, Myles PR et al (2014) Effectiveness of neuraminidase inhibitors in reducing mortality in patients admitted to hospital with influenza A H1N1pdm09 virus infection: a meta-analysis of individual participant data. Lancet Respir Med 2:395–404

Oberai P, Balachandran I, Janardhanan N et al (2013) Homoeopathic management in depressive episodes: a prospective, unicentric, non-comparative, open-label observational study. Indian J Res Homoeopath 7:116–125

OCEBM Levels of Evidence Working Group (2011) The Oxford 2011 levels of evidence. Oxford Centre for Evidence-Based Medicine. Available at: http://www.cebm.net/index.aspx?o=5653. Accessed 17 June 2011

Odgaard-Jensen J, Vist GE, Timmer A et al (2011) Randomisation to protect against selection bias in healthcare trials. Cochrane Database Syst Rev 4:MR000012

Penston J (2003) Fact and fiction in medical research: the large-scale randomised trial. The London Press, London

Petitti DB, Perlman JA, Sidney S (1987) Noncontraceptive estrogens and mortality: long-term follow-up of women in the Walnut Creek Study. Obstet Gynecol 70:289–293

Rosenthal R, Lawson R (1964) A longitudinal study of the effects of experimenter bias on the operant learning of laboratory rats. J Psychiatr Res 69:61–72

Rossouw JE, Anderson GL, Prentice RL et al (2002) Risks and benefits of estrogen plus progestin in healthy postmenopausal women: principal results From the Women's Health Initiative randomized controlled trial. JAMA J Am Med Assoc 288:321–333

Schulz KF, Grimes DA (2002) Blinding in randomised trials: hiding who got what. Lancet 359:696–700

Schulz KF, Chalmers I, Hayes RJ, Altman DG (1995) Empirical evidence of bias. Dimensions of methodological quality associated with estimates of treatment effects in controlled trials. JAMA J Am Med Assoc 273:408–412

Sesso HD, Buring JE, Christen WG et al (2008) Vitamins E and C in the prevention of cardiovascular disease in men: the physicians' health study II randomized controlled trial. JAMA J Am Med Assoc 300:2123–2133

Sierevelt IN, van Oldenrijk J, Poolman RW (2007) Is statistical significance clinically important? A guide to judge the clinical relevance of study findings. J Long Term Eff Med Implants 17:173–179

Smith GD, Ebrahim S (2002) Data dredging, bias, or confounding. Br Med J 325:1437–1438

Stampfer MJ, Colditz GA (1991) Estrogen replacement therapy and coronary heart disease: a quantitative assessment of the epidemiologic evidence. Prev Med 20:47–63

Stevens RJ, Ali R, Bankhead CR et al (2012) Cancer outcomes and all-cause mortality in adults allocated to metformin: systematic review and collaborative meta-analysis of randomised clinical trials. Diabetologia 55:2593–2603

Straus SE, Glasziou P, Richardson WS, Haynes RB (2011) Evidence-based medicine: how to practice and teach EBM, 4th edn. Churchill Livingston, Edinburgh

Stroup DF, Berlin JA, Morton SC et al (2000) Meta-analysis of observational studies in epidemiology: a proposal for reporting. Meta-analysis Of Observational Studies in Epidemiology (MOOSE) group. JAMA J Am Med 283:2008–2012

Vist GE, Bryant D, Somerville L, Birminghem T, Oxman AD (2008) Outcomes of patients who participate in randomized controlled trials compared to similar patients receiving similar interventions who do not participate. Cochrane Database Syst Rev 3:MR000009

Wartolowska K, Judge A, Collins G et al (2014) Use of placebo controls in the evaluation of surgery: systematic review. Br Med J 348:g3253

Wood L, Egger M, Gluud LL et al (2008) Empirical evidence of bias in treatment effect estimates in controlled trials with different interventions and outcomes: meta-epidemiological study. Br Med J 336:601–605

Worrall J (2002) What evidence in evidence-based medicine? Philos Sci 69:S316–S330

Worrall J (2007) Evidence in medicine. Philos Compass 2:981–1022

Zetin M, Hoepner CT (2007) Relevance of exclusion criteria in antidepressant clinical trials: a replication study. J Clin Psychopharmacol 27:295–301

Ziegler EJ, Fisher CJ Jr, Sprung CL et al (1991) Treatment of gram-negative bacteremia and septic shock with HA-1A human monoclonal antibody against endotoxin. A randomized, double-blind, placebo-controlled trial. N Engl J Med 324:429–436

Zimmerman M, Posternak MA, Chelminski I (2002) Symptom severity and exclusion from antidepressant efficacy trials. J Clin Psychopharmacol 22:610–614

Statistical Generalizations in Epidemiology: Philosophical Analysis

54

Federica Russo

Contents

Abstract

Epidemiology studies the variations in health in populations, according to a number of parameters. In this field, probability and statistics are used in order to provide a quantitative description and analysis of the variations in exposure and disease, as well as of the effects of possible preventatives. Thus, one goal of epidemiology is to establish statistical generalizations about health and disease in populations. Consequently, it is important to understand how statistical generalizations are established and what use one can make of them to establish medical knowledge or to design public health policies.

F. Russo (✉)
Department of Philosophy, Faculty of Humanities, University of Amsterdam, Amsterdam, The Netherlands
e-mail: f.russo@uva.nl

© Springer Science+Business Media Dordrecht 2017
T. Schramme, S. Edwards (eds.), *Handbook of the Philosophy of Medicine*,
DOI 10.1007/978-94-017-8688-1_39

887

Introduction: Epidemiology and Statistics

Epidemiology studies the *variation* in health in populations. This means several things. For instance, epidemiology studies how a disease is spread in a population (or across populations), according to different levels of exposures. Epidemiology also studies the association between different factors (biological or socio-economic) and different diseases, or whether certain treatments, interventions, or preventative factors are associated with decrease in the burden of disease in a population. These different aspects of epidemiological investigation into health and disease are captured by the definition of Miquel Porta (quoted in Saracci 2010, 10):

> [*Epidemiology is*] *the study of the occurrence and distribution of health-related states or events in specified populations, including the study of the determinants influencing such states, and the application of this knowledge to control health problems.*

Two aspects are immediately worth noting. The first is that epidemiology is interested in *populations*, i.e., groups of individuals, not primarily in *individual patients*. The second is that any epidemiological result is relative to some population of reference or relative to a comparison between specific populations.

Epidemiology also has a "composite" nature, as it blends theoretical instruments of medical research and of probability and statistics (Saracci 2010). Probability and statistics, in particular, are tools borrowed from demography and social science, thus also revealing the peculiar place of epidemiology in the realm of the sciences: it is right at the frontier between the social and the biomedical sciences. This is not just due to the kind of methods used in epidemiology (mainly, probabilistic and statistical approaches) but also for the *object* of study. In fact, epidemiology studies variations in health, according to factors that are biological, socio-economic, demographic, etc. This is also reflected in the various subfields within epidemiology: some areas, like social epidemiology, prioritize the study of health variations according socio-economic factors, while others, like molecular epidemiology, prioritize the study of health variations according to molecular (e.g., genetic) factors.

It is implicit in the definition of epidemiology given above that epidemiology prioritizes a *quantitative* description and analysis of health, as it studies exposure and disease with the tools of probability theory and statistics. This raises immediately two questions that are also shared by other germane scientific disciplines such as demography. First, to what extent, or under what conditions, do statistical analyses allow us to establish causal relations? Second, is it part of the objectives of epidemiology to formulate recommendations for policy? The first question is a perennial question in the philosophy of causality and in scientific method. While in epidemiology this issue has some peculiarities (to be discussed later), it also shares features and questions arising elsewhere. The second question ultimately has to do with the purported descriptive or normative character of a discipline. It is a debated issue whether it is part of any epidemiological study to aim to formulate policy recommendations or whether these should be formulated outside epidemiological studies. The formulation of policy recommendations is presented, in the definition of Porta reported above, as an integral part of epidemiology, although the relation between epidemiology and public health remains controversial (see, e.g., Jackson et al. 1999; Samet 2000).

In sum, it is a direct consequence of the meaning and definition of epidemiology to base empirical studies on the collection of data and on a statistical analysis of them. Epidemiology aims to establish *generic* claims about (variations in) health, and for that purpose probabilistic and statistical approaches are the preferred tools.

Statistical Generalizations

Statistical generalizations in epidemiology can be categorized according to their aim. *Descriptive* generalizations aim to provide a description of the variations in health and disease in a population. *Analytical* (or causal) generalizations also aim to identify those factors responsible for the observed variations. For instance, the European Centre for Disease Prevention and Control provides a report on development of measles and rubella in European countries for the period April 2014–March 2015 (ECDPC 2015). The reports include numbers about new reported cases, the countries most affected by the diseases, the percentage of the cases positively diagnosed by lab analyses, or about the percentage of vaccinated people. These types of report intend to provide a *description* of the health situation in a population. Although one might hypothesize that the revival of foci of infection might be due to a drop in vaccination, the *causal* character of such a generalization has to be established in further studies.

In order to understand the difference between descriptive and analytical generalizations, we need to introduce some technical terms used in epidemiology. *Prevalence* refers to the proportion of diseased individuals in a population, counted in a specific time and in a specific population. *Incidence* refers instead to the *new* cases reported in a given time lapse, and divided by the number of people who are at risk (but that do not have the disease). Prevalence and incidence are *descriptive* statistical concepts. Analytical generalizations also make use of the concept of *risk*, which is related (in way that is not always clear) to causality.

To begin with, epidemiology is interested in calculating, estimating, or analyzing different risks and odds. Risks and odds are associational measures that quantify the strength of association between two variables: a particular outcome (disease) and the presence of a factor (exposure).

For the purpose of this chapter, let us consider two variables E and D, denoting "exposure" and "disease," respectively, being binary or dichotomous, i.e., each has only two possible levels: exposed/unexposed and diseased/not diseased.

	D	
E	Diseased	Not diseased
Exposed	a	b
Unexposed	c	d

Here, $a + c$ is the marginal probability of disease, i.e., P(D), and $a + b$ is the marginal probability of exposure, i.e., P(E). Consequently, $b + d = P(\neg D)$ and $c + d = P(\neg E)$.

We can also organize observations in a contingency 2×2 table, having thus four cells.

	D	
E	Diseased	Not diseased
Exposed	n_{11}	n_{12}
	p_{11}	p_{12}
Unexposed	n_{21}	n_{22}
	p_{21}	p_{22}

The notation n_{ij} refers to the *number* of subjects observed in the corresponding cell, i.e., to the number of observations in the i-th row ($i = 1, 2$) and j-th column ($j = 1, 2$); the notation p_{ij} refers instead to the *proportion* of subjects observed in the corresponding cell, where $p_{ij} = n_{ij}/n$. With this data, we can compute relative risks, odds, and odds ratios and estimate probabilities.

The *relative risk* (RR) is defined as the ratio of risk in the exposed and unexposed group:

$$\frac{n_{11}/n}{n_{21}/n} = \frac{p_{11}}{p_{21}}$$

Thus, RR compares groups: the exposed and the unexposed. RR > 1.0 indicates that the risk of disease is increased when the risk factor (exposure) is present; RR < 1.0 indicates that the risk of disease is decreased when the risk factor is present, i.e., the factor is a protective factor or preventative.

The corresponding definition in terms of conditional probabilities is

$$\frac{P(D \mid E)}{P(D \mid \neg E)} = \frac{a/(a+b)}{c/(c+d)}$$

The *odds ratio* (OR) is another way to compare proportions in a 2×2 contingency table. OR is computed from odds, i.e., it is the ratio of the odds of disease in the exposed group and the odds of disease in the unexposed group:

$$OR = \frac{Odds_{ex}}{Odds_{unex}}$$

The odds of an outcome are equal to the probability that the outcome does occur, divided by the probability that the outcome does not occur. In a 2×2 contingency table, the probability of an outcome is equal to the number of times the outcome is observed divided by the total observations. Thus, we can write, for the odds of the exposure:

$$\text{Odds}_{ex} = \frac{n_{11}/(n_{11} + n_{12})}{n_{12}/(n_{11} + n_{12})} = \frac{n_{11}}{n_{12}}$$

where $n_{11}/(n_{11} + n_{12})$ is the probability that the disease occurs in the exposed group and $n_{12}/(n_{11} + n_{12})$ is the probability that the disease does not occur in the exposed group. We can express this in terms of conditional probabilities:

$$\text{Odds}_{ex} = \frac{P(D \mid E)}{P(\neg D \mid E)}$$

Similarly, for the odds of the unexposed:

$$\text{Odds}_{unex} = \frac{n_{21}/(n_{21} + n_{22})}{n_{22}/(n_{21} + n_{22})} = \frac{n_{21}}{n_{22}}$$

where $n_{21}/(n_{21} + n_{22})$ is the probability that the disease occurs in the unexposed group and $n_{22}/(n_{21} + n_{22})$ is the probability that disease does not occur in the unexposed group. We can express this again in terms of conditional probabilities:

$$\text{Odds}_{unex} = \frac{P(D \mid \neg E)}{P(\neg D \mid \neg E)}$$

OR can now be computed as

$$\frac{n_{11}/n_{21}}{n_{12}/n_{22}} = \frac{n_{11}n_{22}}{n_{12}n_{21}}$$

This is equivalent to

$$\frac{P(D \mid E)}{P(\neg D \mid E)} \times \frac{P(\neg D \mid \neg E)}{P(D \mid \neg E)}$$

It is also worth noting that there is a mathematical relation between odds and probabilities:

$$P = \frac{\text{Odds}}{1 + \text{Odds}}; \text{Odds} = \frac{P}{1 - P}$$

The interpretation of risks and odds raises at least two questions. One question concerns the fact that these measures make sense at the *generic* level, i.e., for groups of individuals, but *not* for individual patients. In other words, even if we can express risks and odds in terms of probabilities, this isn't convenient, as probabilities can be also taken to directly apply to the single case; however, in this context, this is a misleading interpretation. In fact, there isn't as yet a straightforward way to determine the *individual* risk of developing a disease, knowing the risk for the population. For instance, inherited mutations of genes *BRCA1* and *BRCA2* are associated with a high risk of developing breast cancer, but this does not imply that I *will* develop cancer (even if these mutations are found in my body). One reason for this is due to what philosophers called "the reference class problem," which refers to the difficulty of assigning an individual patient to the (most) correct reference class and thus making secured inferences about their health (see also Statistical Generalizations and Philosophy of Science). One hope of personalized medicine is precisely to measure biological characteristics of individuals so that more precise diagnostic and prognostic inferences as well as "patient-tailored" risk prediction and treatment can be made (for a discussion, see, e.g., Hayes et al. 2014).

Another question concerns the possible *causal* import of these measures. Admittedly, risks and odds are *associational* measures and cannot be given a direct, straightforward causal interpretation. However, it would be a mistake to totally dismiss it either. Risks and odds should be seen as part of our evidence base in order to formulate causal claims about health and disease. It should be noted that whether *risk* is a causal notion has not been settled yet. On the one hand, it is difficult to see how the notion of risk is completely devoid of *any* causal connotation, as information of risks is routinely used to design preventive interventions in public health. On the other hand, risk is clearly not coextensive with the term "cause," as it is widely agreed that claims about risks do not imply causation.

The causal interpretation is, in a sense, the core issue about statistical generalizations in epidemiology. This emerges also when considering generalizations not necessarily expressed in terms of risks and odds, but formulated as results of statistical modeling. In fact, not all epidemiological studies involve only two binary variables (diseased/not diseased; exposed/unexposed). Many of them analyze large datasets with numerous variables, not just dichotomous. Here, general methodological caveats apply about the choice of variables, the use of background knowledge, the quality of data, etc. All these apply to statistical modeling in *any* discipline (useful discussions can be found in Freedman (2005) and Russo (2009), among others).

In the following, the controversies concerning two issues, notably, (i) statistical tests and (ii) confounding and control, will be highlighted.

Statistical tests. Establishing statistical generalizations involves performing tests, and a typical argument is that results of these tests have to be *significant*. This means, to begin with, that tests concern *hypotheses*. These hypotheses come from a given research question. For instance, do statins reduce cholesterol level? Or, do calcium supplements help prevent osteophorosis in women aged 50 +?. Hypothesis testing is meant to compare the hypothesis with observations sampled from the population. In a statistical test, we can identify the following elements:

- *Null hypothesis*: there is no association between the two variables. E.g.: no association between statins and lower cholesterol levels.

- *Alternative hypothesis*: there is an association between the two variables. E.g.: there is an association between calcium supplements and osteoporoses in women aged 50+.

Hypotheses in epidemiology may concern, for instance, the differences or similarities in frequency of disease across populations, places, or time. They may also concern the variation in frequency of disease in relation to some specific factor.

Typically, attention is given to the conditions to *reject* the null hypothesis; these concern the test statistic and the significance level. The significance level is chosen on the basis of the amount of type I or type II error one is prepared to accept and on the basis of the problem at hand. A type I error means that the null hypothesis is rejected when in fact it is true, and a type II means that the null hypothesis is accepted when instead the alternative is true. Common test statistics are the z-test, the F-test, and the X^2-test. The specificities of these tests will not be discussed in this contribution. The null hypothesis is accepted or rejected at a given significance level (the *p-value*), which is usually set at 5 % (for a very lucid and accessible presentation of hypothesis testing, see, e.g., Freedman et al. 1998, Chaps. 26–29).

The logic behind hypothesis testing may appear intuitively very simple. However, tests of significance hide difficulties that concern their *interpretation*. David Freedman and his coauthors offer an inventory of these difficulties (Freedman et al. 1998, Chap. 29; Freedman 2005, 60ff). Let us examine some of these. Firstly, the word "significance" might be misleading. In fact, in the statistical jargon, "significant" is not synonymous with "important" or "relevant" but with "probably true," i.e., not due to chance. Secondly, the p-value of a test depends on the sample size and presupposes the quite strong assumption that the sample is *representative* of the population. Moreover, the threshold for significance is rather relative. Textbooks usually recommend rejecting the null hypothesis at 5 % or at 1 % level. Yet these levels are arbitrary. Freedman and coauthors, for instance, make the point that there isn't a real difference between two p-values, say one set at 5.1 % and the other at 4.9 % (Freedman et al. 1998, Chap. 29). Therefore, they recommend reporting the test used and the exact p-value; otherwise, "statistically significant" is too vague a statement.

The meaning and use of p-values have been often discussed in the literature because they are susceptible of multiple interpretations. Lagiou et al. (2005), for instance, discuss the interpretation of p-values specifically in the context of epidemiological research and point to two major difficulties: (i) the p-value is interpretable only when *one* comparison or *one* test is performed and (ii) the p-value itself does *not* convey information about the *strength* of the association. This second point is worth explaining in detail, as it is closely connected with the causal interpretation of statistical generalizations. Statistical hypotheses concern, in one way or another, *correlations* between variables. But the p-value does not give the chance of the null hypothesis being *true*. A small p-value has to be interpreted as evidence against the null hypothesis, in particular as suggesting that something beside chance is operating to make the difference. As Freedman and coauthors explain very clearly, a test of significance does *not* shed light on the causes of variations. Instead, significance tests merely test whether an observed variation is real (alternative hypothesis) or just chancy, that is, somehow an artifact of the dataset (see Freedman et al. 1998, Chap. 29).

The interpretation of probability is also worth mentioning. If we adopt a frequentist approach, what we test is not the probability of the hypothesis being true, but the probability of obtaining the observed sample *if* the hypothesis is true. This difference is subtle but fundamental. Under the frequentist interpretation, we cannot attach a probability value to a single case (for instance, a hypothesis). This is because probability expresses frequency of occurrence in finite or infinite sequences. Instead, if we adopt a Bayesian interpretation, we can attach a probability value to the single case and therefore have a meaningful way of expressing the probability of a particular hypothesis. For instance, if the hypothesis to be tested is about whether an unknown parameter θ lies in the interval (θ_1, θ_2) and confidence level for this test is 95 %, one may be tempted to interpret this as the probability of θ to lie in that interval. This interpretation, however, is not correct. Instead, this means that *if* we draw many samples of the same size and build the same interval around θ, *then* we can expect that 95 % of the confidence intervals will contain the unknown parameter. But this, notice, is not the same thing as asking what is the probability that a given parameter will lie in a given interval. For this reason Freedman and coauthors, discussing confidence intervals and the frequency interpretation, say that "chances are in the sampling procedure, not in the parameter" (Freedman et al. 1998, 347). Courgeau (2004) also provides a very lucid account of the meaning of hypothesis testing in a frequentist and in a Bayesian framework.

Confounding and control. Statisticians analyzing epidemiological (and other) data are well aware of the problem of confounding in establishing generalizations. Simply put, even if the statistical model attests to an association (or dependence or correlation) between two variables, this is no guarantee that the correlation corresponds to a causal relation. To begin with, correlations are symmetric. So, a priori, we cannot decide the direction in which causality is supposed to flow. But, in many occasions, we do have enough background knowledge – including temporal information about the occurrence of events – that allows us to *hypothesize* the direction of the causal relation. For instance, suppose we find a correlation, in a cohort study, about "lung cancer" and "yellow fingers," and suppose we know that individuals reported lung cancer events *after* yellow finger events. We might then be inclined to infer that having yellow fingers is a risk factor (or a cause?) of lung cancer. But once we include in the model a *third* variable, namely, "cigarette smoking," which is also temporally prior to lung cancer events, the correlation disappears. This is one (oversimplified and schematic) case where one variable (yellow fingers) confounds a causal relation (cigarette smoking → lung cancer). In this case, the solution is rather easy, as having yellow fingers is a mere "side effect" of cigarette smoking but has no proper causal role in this structure.

Some other cases are less easy to work out, even if "toy examples" rather than real epidemiological studies are analyzed. For instance, coffee drinking and heart disease are associated. This association, one might think, is explained away once cigarette smoking is introduced, as cigarette smoking is supposedly the cause of heart disease. However, cigarette smoking is *also* associated with coffee drinking. This complicates the analysis. On the one hand, coffee drinking may still have its own affect on heart disease (maybe positive, maybe negative). So, to properly understand variations in the outcome (heart disease), we have to individually control cigarette smoking and coffee drinking. On the other hand, the correlation between cigarette smoking and coffee drinking may be in need of further examination, for instance, introducing another explanatory factor, say stress, that explains it away. It may turn out that stress too is associated with, or even causally responsible for, heart disease. More generally, confounding and control constitute a challenge for epidemiology because diseases have, in many cases, *multiple* causes, rather than just one. The shift from "monocausal" models to "multifactorial" models has been a major advancement for epidemiology, both conceptually and methodologically (for a discussion, see Broadbent 2013).

Examples like this may easily turn into a conundrum to solve, but the real message to convey is the following. In *real* science, most often than not, we do *not* know which variables are confounded, which variables should be controlled for, and which other variables should be measured and included in the model. It is precisely the task of statistical modeling to analyze the relations among variables and to build a cogent story about their causal or noncausal role. In practice, statistics has been quite successful in developing methods for controlling variables at the level of study design (also called ex ante stratification) or after data collection (ex post stratification). It is not the goal of this contribution to provide a thorough presentation of methods for control, but rather to point to some of the theoretical issues involved.

Statistical Generalizations and Philosophy of Science

Statistical generalizations also raise philosophical issues, notably about their *status*. In fact, philosophers of science have long been interested in laws of nature because laws tell us how the world is, allow prediction about what will happen under specified circumstances, and are part of our explanations of phenomena. It didn't take long for philosophers to realize that laws of nature apply to *some* portions of reality, but not others. The quantum world is one example, but social and health contexts are no less controversial. While the debate on what makes an empirical generalization a lawful statement is not settled, it is also widely agreed that thermodynamics has laws, but not epidemiology. Thus, no matter how precisely we state a statistical generalization about vaccination habits and measles outbreaks or about smoking habits and cancer development, these are *not* laws. In the following, it will be discussed what good are statistical generalizations (in epidemiology) even if they are not laws.

In philosophy of science, Woodward (2003) put forward the idea that we should investigate what confers explanatory power to statements that are not lawful. His arguments mainly concern the kind of generalizations established in economics and social science, but it is easy to extend them to epidemiology. A note on terminology: it is necessary to adapt the statistical jargon used earlier to the philosophical argument presented next.

Woodward examines the status of empirical generalizations (i.e., statistical generalizations) and claims that these are *change-relating* relations. This characterization has important epistemological (and methodological) consequences, as also highlighted in Russo (2011). We can express empirical generalizations under the general form $Y = \beta X + \varepsilon$. It is worth noting that this "reduced" form is certainly general enough, even though it already encapsulates some hypotheses, for instance, that the relation between X and Y is linear. In many cases, this is certainly not the case. But for the present discussion, this is not central. A variational reading of this equation amounts to the following: variations in Y are due to variations in X. How much Y varies is quantified by the parameter β (and the errors ε indicate that the relation is stochastic rather than deterministic).

Two remarks are in order. First, a generalization is about *variations*. In epidemiology, we are interested in variations in the occurrence of disease, in exposure, in time, factors, etc. Second, implicit in that reading is also that there must be a variation *within* variables X and Y. If we study the relation between vaccination habits and measles outbreak, the dataset must contain observations about vaccination and *non*-vaccination and about occurrence and *non*-occurrence of measles. Some philosophers have expressed this idea emphasizing that causation is contrastive (see, e.g., Schaffer 2005; Northcott 2008). However, we are not to causation yet. All the equation $Y = \beta X + \varepsilon$ says is that there is a *joint variation* between X and Y.

Woodward (2003) famously explained that for change-relating relations to be causal, they also have to be *invariant*, notably invariant under interventions on the putative cause variable. Woodward is at pains to explain what that means using mainly examples from physics. The account, however, is meant to apply to socio-economic contexts too and, with some amendment, to epidemiology. Simply put, Woodward's account prescribes that *causal* generalizations are the ones that show invariant properties. This means that if we performed an intervention I on X and hold fixed any other possible factor influencing Y, Y should also vary. One peculiarity of this account concerns the meaning of I: interventions are manipulations on the putative cause variable X, such that they change *only* X, via X they change *only* Y, and they are uncorrelated with anything else in the model. Another peculiarity of this account is that it oscillates between providing a conceptual analysis of causation in terms of invariance under interventions and providing a methodology for testing whether empirical generalizations are (or are not) causal (for a discussion, see, e.g., Strevens 2007; Strevens 2008; Russo 2012). Some commentators pointed out that either way (i.e., whether the project belongs to the metaphysics or to the methodology of causation), it is ill suited to observational contexts, because the account hinges too heavily on *manipulations*. This is clearly the case of epidemiology, where the large majority of the empirical studies are observational, rather than experimental.

The account can regain generality and become applicable to non-experimental contexts using a "non-interventionist" notion of invariance. The hint comes from Woodward's analysis (Woodward 2003, p. 312), as he describes how invariance was tested in a 1959 study on smoking and lung cancer. At that time, the bio-chemical mechanisms of carcinogenesis were mainly unknown and empirical generalizations were established on the basis of large epidemiological studies, rather than on the results of lab experiments. Simply put, Woodward points out that, in the absence of interventions, we must check whether a correlation is stable (or invariant) across different subpopulations, for instance, men and women, different age groups, socio-economic status, different levels or types of smoking, etc. While Woodward calls this type of invariance *weak*, Russo (2014) argues that we should not create an opposition between strong and weak invariance, but rather understand how invariance tests are *implemented* in different modeling practices. After all, different implementations of invariance tests do share some common features, notably that they test the robustness and regularity of joint variations of variables and that they aim at establish *generic* claims. Both are important episte-mological points.

Concerning the first, its relevance has to do with what has also been called in the literature the "contrastive" character of causation, and that has been mentioned earlier: we need things to change and vary in order to establish which changes and variations are causal. The second is relevant because it has to do with the *scope* of generalizations. We need generalizations to be *generic*, namely, valid for the population as a whole, because this is the way they can contribute to building medical knowledge and to design public health interventions. It is worth noting that this does not exclude that case reports, which are essentially about single cases rather than populations, be important. Their role and use for medical knowledge and policy are different and fall beyond the scope of this contribution.

The problem of the Population of Reference

It is also worth drawing the attention to an issue that is simultaneously of theoretical and methodological relevance: the choice of the population of reference. Statistical studies in epidemiology and social science are all highly sensitive to the choice of the population of reference. This is key to extract a representative sample, to collect data, and to interpret the results of statistical analyses. Several issues are at stake.

One is the *scope* of statistical generalizations. If we establish generalizations about dengue disease using data collected from some regions in Brazil, are the results also valid for Indian regions where the disease is present? One might raise the point and argue that, clearly, regions in Brazil and India must be different in some respect, thus undermining the possibility of exporting the generalizations from Brazilian to Indian contexts. Suppose now we are interested in studying psycho-social risks related to stress and burnout at workplace in Belgium. *What* Belgium are we referring to? Only within Brussels capital region, we should pay attention to the composition of the sample: Walloon, Flemish, non-European immigrants, "eurocrats," etc., these are already *four* groups having distinct characteristics and yet composing *one* population; these four sub-populations might require quite different analyses or intragroup comparisons. Thus there is no single way in which we can define a population of reference. Sometimes it is from geographical parameters, some other times it is from ethnic or socio-economic factors or depending on exposure and occurrence of disease, or others.

The straightforward methodological consequence is that the choice of the population of reference has to be carefully pondered, using available background knowledge and, sometimes, preliminary analyses of data. In empirical studies, this choice is typically made *before* data are collected, but this does not exclude that the population of reference is refined in the course of empirical investigation, for instance, invariance or other tests may reveal further relevant sub-populations to be considered in the study.

The question of the population of reference is also directly related to the question of validity. In the methodological literature, validity received systematic discussions since the work of Cook and Campbell (1979), whose discussion refers to quasi-experimental models in social science. However, their considerations about validity are relevant to most statistical modeling practices, including in epidemiology, where discussions abound. In this context, validity refers to the confidence with which we draw conclusions from the study of correlations. *Statistical conclusion* validity refers to whether we gathered enough evidence and performed enough tests to infer that a given correlation is causal (or not causal). *Internal* validity refers to the confidence with which we can establish that the results apply to the chosen population of reference. *Construct* validity is about choosing the right "construct" for variables that cannot be measured directly, typically, "socio-economic status," or "education" but also self-rated health status or the like. Finally, *external* validity refers to the possibility of extending the results to *other* populations.

There is a vivid and vast debate raised by this taxonomy of validity; however, it will not be examined in detail here. It will suffice to mention that, in epidemiology, the debate often polarizes around an alleged dilemma: studies either have high internal validity or high external validity, but not both. This is important because, as the argument goes, we are not simply interested in establishing results at a "local" level but also to use them widely in public health interventions. Thus, if a vaccination program against dengue fever is successful for one population, we might want to try it out elsewhere. Conversely, if we can establish robust results about the obesity epidemic in children worldwide, it does not follow that we managed to identify factors that are specific to some population, rather than another. Broadly speaking, these are terms in which the debate is set.

It is worth noting, however, that validity is *not* an intrinsic property of studies, but of the *process* of carrying them out. The validity of results should be assessed with respect to the rigor used during the *whole* process of data collection, data analysis, interpretation of results, etc.

Questions about the choice of the population of reference and validity emerge when considering the hypothesis of "universal biological response,", which is usually made in randomized controlled trials (Victora et al. 2004). This means that we assume that individuals respond to treatments in a way that is similar enough. In turn, this presupposes that our bodies function in very, very similar ways. Victora et al. (2004) question this hypothesis saying that, while it may have plausibility if short causal paths are considered, individual responses are instead highly hetero-geneous when more complex causal paths are involved.

In addition to this line of argument, it is worth mentioning that individual responses may be different, even in short, simple causal pathways when *relevant* factors are considered. An interesting example in this respect is gender medicine, as it is trying, since some decades now, to spell out the mechanisms of health and disease involved in different genders. These may differ because of biological or socio-psycho-behavioral differences or because of the way male and female illnesses are understood. For instance, the phenomenon of wrong diagnoses of heart attacks in women has been widely documented; similarly, male breast cancer is poorly understood, and its mechanisms are largely extrapolated from studying females. Thus, gender ought not to be used *just* as a classificatory variable to use in a posteriori partitions of the population. Instead, the goal is to understand what is involved in different modes of being exposed, or of disease mechanism, or reacting to interventions.

An analogous argument holds for the use or "race" in epidemiological (and other social science) studies. Studying and understanding variations in exposure, disease, and interventions according to race may be important to capture *social and behavioral* factors. For instance, ethnic differences in hypertension and blood pressure have long been reported and documented. Surely, including data about race may also help explain differences in the biology of health and disease (see the hypothesis of universal biological response mentioned earlier), but clearly we should beware of not reviving value judgments from ethnic differences in health and disease.

Usefulness of Statistical Generalizations

Statistical generalizations, as discussed in previous sections, are sensitive to a number of methodological and philosophical caveats. At the methodological level, statistical generalizations are vulnerable to the problem of confounding, and, more generally, they do not automatically license causal inference. At the philosophical level, it is controversial to assign a clear status to statistical general-izations: they clearly aren't laws and yet they are essential to gain knowledge about health and disease. Thus, it is important to highlight the *usefulness* of statistical generalizations, in spite of all the caveats already discussed.

To begin with, statistical generalizations are useful to establish generic knowl-edge about health and disease. Epidemiology aims at providing a faithful descrip-tion and explanation of the variation of health and disease *in populations*, and, for this reason, statistical *generalizations* are vital. They are vital because it is on the basis of *generalizations* that we can design public health interventions.

Because of their generic character, statistical generalizations are also useful in that they provide *evidence of correlation*. Evidence of correlation complements evidence of production, or of mechanisms, in establishing causal claims in the medical sciences.

Statistical generalizations are also useful to make inferences about single cases. Claims about single cases are not deductively derived from the corresponding generic claims in any simple or direct way. Indeed, the relation between the generic and single-case level is complex. On the one hand, generalizations are not mere aggregates of single cases, and, conversely, single cases are not mere instantiations of generic relations. Russo and Williamson (2011) describe this complexity for the case of autopsies, showing how each level participates in establishing claims at the other level. Kleinberg (2013) develops a variant of the "connecting principle," originally proposed by Sober (1986), and explains, from a statistical point of view, how generalizations can be fruitfully used in making inferences to the single case.

Finally, with the rapid development and use of techniques for the analysis of *big* datasets, it is important to reflect upon the value of correlational claims. In epidemiology, data-intensive science offers an opportunity to explore the determinants of health and disease with unprecedented variety, volume, and velocity (the so-called three Vs). Scientists and philosophers alike are nonetheless cautious in declaring the advent of a revolution that will put an end to the conundrum of how to infer causation from correlation (see, e.g., Mooney et al. 2015; Alyass et al. 2015).

Definitions of Key Terms

Epidemiology	The study of variations of health and disease in populations according to biological and socio-economic factors.
Statistical generalization	Scientific statements expressing in a quantitative way facts about health and disease in a population, for instance, about risks or about the effectiveness of a drug or about an intervention.
Medical knowledge	The body of knowledge about health and disease that scientists gather together through epidemiological, laboratory, and other forms of studies.
Population of reference	The specific population being the object of an epidemiological study.
Confounding	Phenomenon occurring when a variable interferes while studying the correlation between two other variables.
Control	Any statistical technique to avoid or minimize confounding, for instance, conditioning on relevant variables or stratification.

Summary Points

- Epidemiology studies variations in health and in exposure in populations.
- Epidemiology uses probability and statistics to establish generalizations about exposure and disease about populations.
- Statistical generalizations are generic claims. While they lack the typical features of laws (of nature), they should be sufficiently invariant (or robust) to be used to establish medical knowledge or to design public health policies.
- Statistical generalizations in epidemiology are always established with respect to some population and reference class.
- An important methodological aspect in establishing statistical generalizations concerns controlling for possible confounding factors.

References

Alyass A, Turcotte M, Meyre D (2015) From big data analysis to personalized medicine for all: challenges and opportunities. BMC Med Genomics 8(1):33

Broadbent A (2013) Philosophy of epidemiology. Palgrave McMillan, New York

Cook TD, Campbell DT (1979) Quasi-experimentation design and analysis issues for field settings. Rand MacNally, Chicago

Courgeau D (2004) Probabilité, démographie et sciences sociales. Math Soc Sci 167:27–50

ECDPC (2015) Measles and rubella monitoring, April 2015 – reporting on April 2014 to March 2015 surveillance data and epidemic intelligence data to the end of April 2015. European Centre for Disease Prevention and Control. http://ecdc.europa.eu/en/publications/Publications/Measles-rubella-monitoring-second-quarter-2015.pdf

Freedman DA (2005) Statistical models: theory and practice. Cambridge University Press, Cambridge

Freedman D, Pisani R, Purves R (1998) Statistics, 1st edn. Norton, New York

Hayes DF, Markus HS, David Leslie R, Topol EJ (2014) Personalized medicine: risk prediction, targeted therapies and mobile health technology. BMC Med 12:37. doi:10.1186/1741-7015-12-37

Jackson LW, Lee NL, Samet JM (1999) Frequency of policy recommendations in epidemiologic publications. Am J Public Health 89(8):1206–11

Kleinberg S (2013) Causality, probability, and time. Cambridge University Press, New York

Lagiou P, Adam H-O, Trichopoulos D (2005) Causality in cancer epidemiology. Eur J Epidemiol 20:565–74

Mooney SJ, Westreich DJ, El-Sayed AM (2015) Commentary: epidemiology in the era of big data. Epidemiology 26(3):390–94. doi:10.1097/EDE.0000000000000274

Northcott R (2008) Causation and contrast classes. Phil Stud 139:111–23

Russo F (2009) Causality and causal modelling in the social sciences measuring variations. Methodos series. Springer, New York

Russo F (2011) Correlational data, causal hypotheses, and validity. J Gen Phil Sci 42(1):85–107

Russo F (2012) On empirical generalisations. In: Dieks D, Gonzalez WJ, Hartmann S, Stoeltzner M, Weber M (eds) Probabilities, laws, and structures. Springer, Berlin, pp 133–50

Russo F (2014) What invariance is and how to test for it. Int Stud Phil Sci 28(2):157–83. doi:10.1080/02698595.2014.932528

Russo F, Williamson J (2011) Generic vs. single-case causal knowledge. the case of autopsy. Eur J Phil Sci 1(1):47–69

Samet JM (2000) Epidemiology and policy: the pump handle meets the new millennium. Epidemiol Rev 22:145–154, http://epirev.oxfordjournals.org/content/22/1/145.full.pdf

Saracci R (2010) Epidemiology. A very short introduction. Oxford University Press, New York

Schaffer J (2005) Contrastive causation. Philos Rev 114(3):297–328

Sober E (1986) Causal factors, causal inference, causal explanation. Proc Aristotel Soc Suppl Vol 60:97–113

Strevens M (2007) Essay review of Woodward, making things happen. Philos Phenom Res 74:233–49

Strevens M (2008) Comments on Woodward, making things happen. Philos Phenom Res 77 (1):171–92

Victora CG, Habicht J-P, Bryce J (2004) Evidence-based public health: moving beyond randomized trials. Am J Public Health 94:400–405

Woodward J (2003) Making things happen: a theory of causal explanation. Oxford University Press, Oxford

Personalized Medicine: Conceptual, Ethical, and Empirical Challenges

55

Jan Schildmann and Jochen Vollmann

Contents

Abstract

The development of so-called personalized medicine (PM) has raised great hopes and expectations among researchers, patients, health-care providers, and politicians. This chapter explores firstly the terminology and conceptual premises of PM. In the second stage, there will be a brief review of the state of the art of PM and medical-technical challenges associated with this approach to medicine. The subsequent normative analysis will focus on two topics which have been given particular consideration in the philosophical and ethical debate around PM: (1) the relation between PM, autonomy, and responsibility of the individual and (2) the setting of priorities in light of the PM approach to research and practice.

J. Schildmann (✉) • J. Vollmann
Faculty of Medicine, Institute for Medical Ethics and History of Medicine, Ruhr-Universität Bochum, Bochum, Germany
e-mail: jan.schildmann@rub.de; jochen.vollmann@rub.de

© Springer Science+Business Media Dordrecht 2017
T. Schramme, S. Edwards (eds.), *Handbook of the Philosophy of Medicine*,
DOI 10.1007/978-94-017-8688-1_71

Introduction

Modern medicine has access to extensive genetic information about humans. The human genome was decoded in the international Human Genome Project, and technical progress in the field of sequencing technologies enables inexpensive analyses of the complete genome of an individual. Clinical medicine seeks to utilize these insights from molecular genetic research to treat patients more effectively. Knowledge about the individual genes of a patient in the field of medical diagnostics and treatment is being used to develop tailored treatments. One example involves situations in which doctors are able to determine whether or not a cancer drug will be effective against a specific tumor by identifying specific genetic biomarkers in a patient prior to starting treatment. This development which is often called "personalized medicine," "individualized medicine," or "targeted treatment" has raised great hopes and expectations among researchers, patients, health-care providers, and politicians (Collins 2010). At the same time "personalized medicine" (PM) has raised fears among others with regard to risks to informational privacy and solidarity within publicly financed health-care systems (Kollek and Lemke 2008). In recent years PM and its implications have been at the center of numerous ethical, legal, and social analyses. Given that the term PM is often used in a broad and underdetermined sense, it comes as little surprise that considerable parts of the interdisciplinary debate rest on various understandings of PM. Against this background this chapter aims firstly to shed some light on the terminology and conceptual premises of PM. In the second stage, there will be a brief review of the state of the art of PM and medical-technical challenges associated with this approach to medicine. Such analysis is important for any empirically informed, applied ethical analysis which aims to avoid discussions of scenarios which have little to do with current or expected implications of PM in practice (Fischer et al. 2015). The subsequent normative analysis will focus on two topics which have been given particular consideration in the philosophical and ethical debate around PM, namely, (1) the relation between PM, autonomy, and responsibility and (2) the setting of priorities in light of the PM approach to research and practice (Vollmann 2013).

Definition and Conceptual Aspects

The term "person" is usually understood to include psychosocial and evaluative aspects of the human being. Hence PM may be understood as a form of medicine taking into account multiple dimensions of the patient as person. However, most articles use the term as a label for strategies which are limited to biological features of individuals and according to which subgroups of patients can be stratified for the purposes of prevention, diagnosis, and treatment of disease. In recent years several study groups have sought to define PM by different methodological approaches. According to a "precising definition" by Schleidgen et al. (2013), based on the use of the term in research literature, PM is an approach to medicine which "seeks to improve tailoring and timing of preventive and therapeutic measures by utilizing biological information and biomarkers on the level of molecular disease pathways, genetics, proteomics as well as metabolomics" or, in a slightly adapted version, as an approach which "seeks to improve stratification and timing of health care by utilizing biological information and biomarkers on the level of molecular disease pathways, genetics, proteomics as well as metabolomics" (Schleidgen et al. 2013). The conceptual analysis of Langanke et al. (2012) points in a similar direction. These authors define "individualized medicine" as "research approaches and health care practices, if the biomarker-based prediction of (a) diseases and/or (b) the effectiveness of therapies by stratification is central" (Langanke et al. 2012). The considerable amount of work which has been invested into definitions of PM can be seen as a reaction to the notoriously vague usage of PM in the debate. This not only presents an obstacle to the discourse on the scientific as well as public level but also hinders the development of regulation and policy on issues which are related to PM. Furthermore, and relevantly from an ethical perspective, an underspecified use of the term PM may raise hopes and fears, which often enough reflect rather the goals of interest groups rather than an interest in a sincere discourse about facts and values relevant to the development of PM (Langanke et al. 2012; Schleidgen et al. 2013).

In contrast to the above definitions, the term "personalized medicine" alludes to a kind of medical care which focuses on the health situation and the particular needs of each individual person. This is incorrect and misleading in two ways. Firstly, the molecular genetic complexity of many illnesses makes the possibility of a treatment custom tailored to each individual person very improbable, while the extremely high efforts and costs of this approach do not appear feasible in the current health-care system. What the term connotes is, therefore, not *personalized* diagnosis and treatment, but at best diagnostic and therapeutic approaches which are targeted at specific patient subgroups – for example, groups which have the same tumor biomarkers (*stratified medicine*). Secondly, medical care focused on molecular genetic characteristics has nothing to do with medical care oriented to the individual patient. *Individualization* only takes place at the molecular genetic level, but not at the personal level between doctor and patient. In order to achieve a personal treatment, the "person" of the patient should be placed at the center of treatment, and this is exactly what so-called personalized medicine does not do (Hüsing 2010; Dabrock et al. 2012). A person is not only distinguished by biological traits but also by individual psychological and social characteristics and needs. Individuals have their own lifestyles, values, and preferences (Yurkiewicz 2010). Law and ethics emphasize the normative implications of the concept of personhood, as evident in ongoing debates about so-called personhood (Lampe 1998). As a consequence, the patient in the doctor-patient relationship is entitled to adequate education and information from the doctor and has the right to consent to or to refuse a treatment (Kohnen et al. 2013). The patient's self-determined decision must be respected, even if it goes against the doctor's advice and against a medical indication, precisely because we ascribe the person these rights (Vollmann 2008).

This ethical and anthropological understanding of the term "person" is expressed by many people in their wishes about modern medicine. Patients wish to be perceived by their doctors and by medical institutions as individual persons with wishes and normative preferences. In the citizens' report "High-Tech Medicine – What Kind of Health Care Do We Want?" of the German Federal Ministry of Education and Research (Bundesministerium für Bildung und Forschung, BMBF), citizens demand that medical and nursing staff should have better communication skills. Furthermore, alongside the specialist subjects, mental and interpersonal aspects in day-to-day patient care must play an equal role in medical and nursing education and training and in research. The importance of taking time for the patient should be rediscovered in modern medicine (BMBF 2011; Siegmund-Schultze 2011). This broader cultural understanding of the term "person" and the wishes of citizens for personal medical care are not considered in so-called PM. The term sounds appealing, but is misleading. The intention of the inappropriate use of the term "person," which is conveyed in numerous texts and images in advertising materials, is to achieve a positive image and wide acceptance in society. It is important to debunk this questionable advertising strategy because it abuses the concept of personhood, perceives patients primarily as carriers of molecular genetically determined traits, suggests a genetic determinism for medicine (Kerr and Cunningham-Burley 2000), and aims at setting specific priorities in research funding. The latter, in particular, requires a transparent and critical discussion, as well as democratic decision making.

State-of-the-Art and Empirical Challenges

PM, which will be understood in the following as approaches in medical research and clinical practice based on biological markers such as genetic mutations and which is used for prediction of diseases and/or the effectiveness of therapies, has gained considerable success in some fields of medicine. This is in particular the case for patient subgroups in oncology. However, it is also research in this medical field which demonstrates that the vision of a "targeted treatment" seems realistic only for a minority of patients in the near future. Among the reasons for this are the multitude of genetic variations associated with a disease, the interplay between environment and genetic makeup, and mechanisms of resistance as they can be observed in patients receiving targeted treatment (Browmann et al. 2014).

An important empirical challenge for PM is to translate the findings from genome-wide association studies (GWAS) into effective preventive, diagnostic, and therapeutic measures. In GWAS large volumes of genetic and clinical data are analyzed, for example, to identify associations between biomarker and certain diseases. Subsequently companion diagnostics, a combination of a test for a biological marker and a treatment for patients who carry the biomarker, are developed. One well-known example is the companion diagnostic of HER2 and the medication trastuzumab. The biomarker HER2 is prevalent in a proportion of women with breast cancer. Health research shows that while women who carry the HER2 biomarker have a worse prognosis, they benefit from trastuzumab. This antibody targets the HER2 receptor and improves health outcomes in this patient subgroup.

In recent years a high and still increasing number of biomarkers associated with diseases have been detected. However, little resources are invested in research to establish the validity and clinical utility of these markers (Ludwig 2012). The high number of biomarkers and substances targeting these biomarkers and the investments which are required to conduct prospective trials make it unlikely that all PM interventions can be assessed according to the established criteria of evidence-based clinical medicine. A further challenge is that the small number of patients with a specific marker will make it difficult to conduct trials with a large enough number of patients to be able to demonstrate statistically significant effects of a companion diagnostic. Against this background and based on the assumed possibility of translating biological concepts, identified in the context of PM, into clinical practice, it has been suggested that the usual cascade of clinical trials requested to prove the benefit of new substances may not be necessary to prove the benefit of PM interventions (Sleijfer et al. 2013). However, critiques point out that such demand is based on undue confidence in biological models and genetic determinism. According to this position, the clinical utility of companion diagnostics needs to be established according to the same standards of evidence-based medicine as this is true for other forms of medical treatment. Given the worldwide collaborations and other resources owned by pharmaceutical companies, it seems realistic that at least for a proportion of biomarkers and companion diagnostics, the standards of evidence-based medicine could be met if the industrial sector would be willing to set respective priorities (Browmann et al. 2014; Ludwig 2012; Schildmann et al. 2015).

The above sketch of the state-of-the-art and empirical challenges sheds light on the difficulties to prove the benefit of a particular intervention within PM. Moreover it is notable that the thresholds of evidence to determine benefit (and/or harm) are themselves the focus of scientific debate. What evidence is needed to accept PM interventions as being of more benefit than harm? Is deviation from established evidentiary standards justified in light of biological models which suggest that a certain treatment targets molecular markers which are associated with a certain disease? The answers to these questions differ, in part depending also on whether they come from the perspective of a clinician, a biomedical scientist, the pharmaceutical industry, or another interest group. Furthermore, empirical analysis can inform judgments on evidence. However, ultimately there will always be a normative component when making judgments about the evidentiary level required (Browmann et al. 2014; Strech and Tilburt 2008).

Autonomous Decision Making and Responsibility Within the Context of PM

The implications of PM with regard to patient autonomy and responsibility for health have been at the center of philosophical and ethical analysis. While a comprehensive review of the debate is beyond this chapter, the remit is to explore two frequently forwarded (and criticized) claims in this debate in more detail. The first claim is that by generating information about biomarkers associated with certain diseases and information about the effectiveness of particular treatment, PM will enable patients to make more autonomous decisions. The second claim is that the increase in knowledge about health risks associated with genetic makeup leads to obligations on the side of citizens to take more responsibility for their health. While there are links between the two claims, they will be presented and analyzed separately.

Making autonomous decisions in health care is clearly dependent on the information which is available to the patient prior to decision making. Accordingly, the ethical and legal doctrine of informed consent requires that competent patients are informed about health-related information at stake and subsequently can make decisions free from undue influence (Beauchamp and Childress 2012). In line with the account of autonomy underlying the doctrines of informed consent, one can speak about an improvement of autonomous decision making if one provides patients with more detailed health-related information. A patient with cancer can be described, for example, as making a more autonomous decision if she not only is informed about the diagnosis but also about a biomarker which is relevant for the responsiveness to a specific treatment. However, it should be noted that this account of autonomous decision making hinges on a number of premises. The first is to accept the linkage of autonomy solely with mental capabilities. As pointed out by Wabel in his analysis of different concepts of autonomy within the context of health care, such an understanding of autonomy omits to take into account that our ability to make decisions is affected by our physical experiences (Wabel 2015). Given the often intense consequences of illness on our body, Wabel suggests "embodied autonomy" as an alternative concept which takes into account the interdependence of physical experiences and decision making (Wabel 2015). Even if the more limited view that autonomous decision making is mainly linked with cognitive competences is accepted, the claim that provision of more information correlates with more autonomous decisions is open to challenges. Given the multitude and complexity of information generated in the context of PM and empirical findings which indicate that even many physicians have difficulties in understanding the clinical implications of this information (Hessling and Schicktanz 2012; Wäscher et al. 2013), it is an open question whether more information leads to more autonomous decision making by patients. Thirdly, the quality of health information generated in the context of PM needs to be taken into account when considering PM as a means to improve autonomous decision making. As pointed out in the preceding section, there is at present considerable evidentiary uncertainty with regard to the validity of many biological markers identified and their clinical utility. The combination of a high volume of information and lack of knowledge regarding the quality of generated data poses a challenge to the facilitation of informed autonomous decision making.

Following the admittedly brief and incomprehensive review of arguments for and against the claim that PM leads to more autonomous decision making, this section shall be concluded with some remarks on the often made link between PM and the call for persons' responsibility for health. The foundation of this claim is the view that the gain of knowledge about risks associated with biomarkers and the possibility to test for these biomarkers imply an obligation for the individual to acquire knowledge about such risks and to ensure a health-related behavior which is in line with any detected risks or predispositions. Such obligation may imply that one's care about one's own health will be taken into account when considering the premium for health insurance (Rohr and Schade 2000). While the argument will be explored here within the context of PM, it should be pointed out that it is not specific to the PM approach. After all most risk factors identified on a genetic level do not differ significantly from many other risk factors. This means that a claim to take responsibility for health against the background of a particular risk factor could be made with regard to a person who carries a genetic mutation posing her at risk to a specific disease as well as with regard to a person with risk factors such as smoking. However, and in line with the analysis of Langanke et al. (2013), the connection between an increase of health-related knowledge by PM and any claims for taking more responsibility for one's health hinges on presuppositions which often are not made explicit. First of all any demand for taking into account genetic risk dispositions with regard to health-related behavior requires sufficient evidence that a particular genetic (or other biological marker) causes a certain clinical manifestation. As pointed out above, such a clear link between biomarker and disease or other clinical manifestations is given in only a few cases. Furthermore, talk about responsibility of the individual for health within the context of any PM developments makes sense only if there is knowledge that a certain health-related behavior or other intervention affects the health of the patient (in a positive manner). It does not make sense, for example, to consider responsibility for health of the individual if it has been shown that a biomarker *causes* a certain disease regardless of the health-related behavior of the individual person. Finally, it will be a matter of public and also normative debate what can be appropriately expected from an individual with a certain biomarker-based risk constellation. As pointed out by Langanke et al. (2013), any demand for responsible health-care-related behavior of the individual in light of PM generated findings will require normative justifications. Even in cases of good evidence for biomarker-associated health risks and the availability of treatment, a society would need to make ethical decisions whether, and if so, on what grounds such knowledge would imply a demand for a specific health-care-related behavior.Responsibility

Priority Setting and Opportunity Costs

Personalized medicine is frequently used as a synonym for progress and the promise of modern medicine per se and often is presented in an uncritically positive way in research, business, and the media. Public research funding has declared personalized medicine to be a priority both at the national and European level (BMBF 2013; European Commission 2013), and large pharmaceutical and biotechnology companies invest substantial amounts of money in this research. Modern medicine is facing a new "revolution" due to new scientific insights and the close cooperation of research, clinics, and industry (Browmann et al. 2014; Hüsing 2010).

The high investment costs in research based on molecular genetic criteria raise the question of opportunity costs. This type of research ultimately provides stratified medical care that benefits subgroups of patients. Investments in this field have been made for more than a decade and, due to many open research questions, will continue to be made in the future (Rauprich 2010). Given the limited resources in the health-care sector, prioritization is required already at the research level regarding the extent of public resources that will flow into particular areas of the health-care system. A research priority in one area limits the remaining research funds for other medical speciality areas. With regard to the promotion of and funding the high costs of personalized medicine, this difficult normative and political decision is further exacerbated as at present there are only a relatively small number of patients who may benefit from these measures (Browman et al. 2011). That is why some clinical physicians are concerned that other important clinical and health-care areas, which might be beneficial for many patients, will be neglected due to the prioritized promotion of personalized medicine (Ludwig 2012). Based on previous experience, high profits can be expected from expensive cancer drugs for small patient groups (so-called niche busters), and, therefore, this approach continues to appear lucrative for the pharmaceutical industry without taking into account the health needs of the majority of patients in our health-care system.

Whereas in oncology, a small portion of patients have benefited from the innovations of personalized medicine, they have until now brought no benefit for patients in other socially and medically important disease groups. An example is the common disease type 2 diabetes: no molecular genetic descriptions of subgroups, biomarkers, and so on are superior to the usual preventive, diagnostic, and treatment options, and they do not improve the health situation of the patients affected (Schulze 2011). For such complex, multifactorial diseases, it seems unlikely that new molecular genetic insights will contribute to significant advances. Rather sociomedical care approaches and intensive public health research are needed to enable and support at-risk and affected people to adopt healthy behaviors as individuals. However, this research is seriously underfunded in our health-care system. Another example is the increasing importance of mental illness as a public health concern in our society. Mental illness and its treatment and prevention are of great significance for the patients affected, health insurance companies, and pension fund insurance companies who bear the cost for rehabilitation and for the labor market. The current care of these patients in our health-care system is under criticism due to excessively long sick-leave times, excessive waiting times for psychiatric and psychotherapy treatment and/or inpatient rehabilitation measures, and too frequent early retirements due to mental disorders. Investments are, therefore, required in research to develop new concepts for social-psychiatric prevention and treatment, for example, enabling effective prevention and early intervention at the workplace and improving the cooperation between, for example, the company doctor, primary care physician, psychiatrist, and hospital. This raises the issue of whether a society should respond to the increasing importance of mental illness primarily with high investments in molecular genetic research for "personalized treatment" or invest at least in equal measure in social-psychiatric and mental health research, which is allocated relatively little funding in current research policy.

Therefore, from a medical ethics perspective, the existing preference for molecular genetic medicine in personalized medicine in contrast to other research fields in the publically funded health-care system needs to be critically examined. In essence, all prioritization decisions are ethical decisions in which competing values must be weighed (Rauprich 2010). In doing so, transparency must prevail regarding who decides about what facts, which criteria are used, and on which arguments decisions are based. Therefore, it is ethically unacceptable that influential individual interests de facto determine medical research priorities and resource allocation in the publically funded health-care system; but this is exactly what is currently happening under the innocuous label of "personalized medicine." Cost-benefit assessments of the individual treatments – now often discussed – are also insufficient, since, on the basis of empirical data, they only allow statements about the medical benefits and the costs of the treatment area under investigation. In practice, the selection of the treatment area for research already frequently represents a setting of priorities within the overall spectrum of possible health-promoting measures without prior reflection on the norms involved. What is required for our health care in the future are transparent and democratically legitimized superordinate medical and research policy prioritizations.

Definition of Key Terms

Personalized medicine (synonyms: "individualized medicine," "stratified medicine")	An approach to preventive, diagnostic, and therapeutic measures in health care by which patient groups are stratified on the basis of biological markers.
Evidence-based medicine	An approach to medicine which advocates clinical decision making in medicine based on the strongest available evidence in health research such as randomized controlled trials and systematic reviews of controlled trials.

Summary Points

- "Personalized medicine" is an approach to medicine which makes use of biological marker to stratify patients into subgroups with the aim to improve prevention, diagnosis, and treatment.
- The term is misleading in two ways. Firstly, the molecular genetic complexity of many illnesses makes treatment custom tailored to each individual person very

improbable. Secondly, medical care focused on molecular genetic characteristics has nothing to do with medical care oriented on the individual patient.
- The frequently made ethical claims regarding PM as means to improve autonomous decision making and as a basis for an increase in health-related responsibility on the side of citizens or patients hinge on conceptual and empirical premises and cannot be supported without considerable qualifications.
- The high investment in research and structures necessary for PM and associated opportunity cost raises questions of justification on the spending of resources for a multidimensional approach to health care.

References

Beauchamp T, Childress J (2012) Principles of biomedical ethics, 7th edn. Oxford University Press, Oxford

Browman G, Hébert PC, Coutts J (2011) Personalized medicine: a windfall for science, but what about patients? Can Med Assoc J 183:E1277

Browmann G, Virani A, Vollmann J et al (2014) Improving the quality of 'personalized medicine' research and practice: through an ethical lens. Pers Med 11:413–423

Bundesministerium für Bildung und Forschung (2011) Bürgerreport: Hightech-Medizin – Welche Gesundheit wollen wir? Bürger-Dialog. Bundesministerium für Bildung und Forschung, Berlin

Bundesministerium für Bildung und Forschung (2013) Aktionsplan Individualisierte Medizin Ein neuer Weg in Forschung und Gesundheitsversorgung. http://www.gesundheitsforschung-bmbf.de/_media/BMBF_MASTER_Aktionsplan_IndiMed.pdf

Collins FS (2010) The language of life. DNA and the revolution in personalized medicine. HarperCollins, New York

Dabrock P, Braun M, Ried J (2012) Individualisierte Medizin: Ethische und gesellschaftliche Herausforderungen. Forum 27:209–213

European Commission (2013) Use of "-omics" technologies in the development of personalised medicine. http://ec.europa.eu/health/files/latest_news/2013-10_personalised_medicine_en.pdf. Accessed 26 June 2015

Fischer T, Dörr M, Haring R et al (2015) Alarming symptoms of a paradigm shift? An approach to bridge the gap between hypothetical ethics and the current status of individualised medicine research. In: Vollmann J, Sandow V, Wäscher S, Schildmann J (eds) The ethics of personalised medicine: critical perspectives. Ashgate, Farnham, pp 25–40

Hessling A, Schicktanz S (2012) What German experts expect from individualized medicine: problems of uncertainty and future complication in physician-patient interaction. Clin Ethics 7:86–93

Hüsing B (2010) Individualisierte Medizin – Potenziale und Handlungsbedarf. Z Evid Fortbild Qual Gesundhwes 104:727–731

Kerr A, Cunningham-Burley S (2000) On ambivalence and risk: reflexive modernity and the new human genetics. Sociology 34:283–304

Kohnen T, Schildmann J, Vollmann J (2013) Patients' self-determination in "personalized medicine": the case of whole genome sequencing and tissue banking in oncology. In: Braun M, Dabrock P (eds) "Individualised Medicine" between hype und hope. LIT, Münster, pp 97–110

Kollek R, Lemke T (eds) (2008) Der medizinische Blick in die Zukunft. Gesellschaftliche Implikationen prädiktiver Gentests. Campus Verlag, Frankfurt a. M

Lampe E-J (1998) Persönlichkeit, Persönlichkeitssphäre, Persönlichkeitsrecht. In: Lampe E-J (ed) Persönlichkeit, Familie, Eigentum: Grundrechte aus der Sicht der Sozial- und Verhaltenswissenschaften. Westdeutscher Verlag, Opladen, pp 73–102

Langanke M, Lieb W, Erdmann P et al (2012) Was ist Individualisierte Medizin? Zur terminologischen Justierung eines schillernden Begriffs. ZME 58:295–314

Langanke M, Fischer T, Erdmann P et al (2013) Gesundheitliche Eigenverantwortung im Kontext Individualisierter Medizin. Ethik Med 25:243–250

Ludwig W-D (2012) Möglichkeiten und Grenzen der stratifizierenden Medizin am Beispiel von prädiktiven Biomarkern und "zielgerichteten" medikamentösen Therapien in der Onkologie. Z Evid Fortbild Qual Gesundhwes 122:11–22

Rauprich O (2010) Rationierung unter den Bedingungen der Endlichkeit im Gesundheitswesen. In: Thomas G, Höfner M, Schaede S (eds) Endliches Leben Interdisziplinäre Zugänge zum Phänomen der Krankheit. Mohr Siebeck, Tübingen, pp 229–256

Rohr M, Schade D (2000) Selbstbestimmung und Eigenverantwortung im Gesundheitswesen – Ergebnisse des Workshops zu Forschungsbedarf im Bereich Medizin und Gesundheit, Arbeitsbericht Nr. 176. Akademie für Technikfolgenabschätzung in Baden-Württemberg, Stuttgart

Schildmann J (2015) 'Personalised medicine': multidisciplinary perspectives and in 'interdisciplinary recommendations on a framework for future research and practice'. In: Vollmann J, Sandow V, Wäscher S, Schildmann J et al (eds) The ethics of personalised medicine: critical perspectives. Ashgate Publishing, Farnham

Schleidgen S, Klinger C, Bertram T et al (2013) What is personalized medicine: sharpening a vague term based on a systematic literature review. BMC Med Ethics 14:55. doi:10.1186/1472-6939-14-55

Schulze M (2011) Programme of the international symposium: predictive genetic testing, risk communication and risk perception: Value of genetic. Information for diabetes risk prediction. Robert Koch Institut, Berlin

Siegmund-Schultze N (2011) Versorgung von Krebspatienten: Menschliche Zuwendung aufwerten. Dtsch Arztebl 108:A-932

Sleijfer S, Bogaerts J, Siu LL (2013) Designing transformative clinical trials in the cancer genome era. J Clin Oncol 31:1834–1841

Strech D, Tilburt J (2008) Value judgments in the analysis and synthesis of evidence. J Clin Epidemiol 61:521–524

Vollmann J (2008) Patientenselbstbestimmung und Selbstbestimmungsfähigkeit: Beiträge zur klinischen Ethik. Kohlhammer, Stuttgart

Vollmann J (2013) Persönlicher – besser – kostengünstiger? Kritische medizinethische Anfragen an die "personalisierte Medizin". Ethik in der Medizin 25:233–241. Parts of this publication form part of this article. With kind permission of Springer Science+Business Media

Wabel T (2015) Patient as person in personalised medicine. Autonomy, responsibility and the body. In: Vollmann J, Sandow V, Wäscher S, Schildmann J (eds) The ethics of personalised medicine: critical perspectives. Ashgate, Farnham, pp 53–64

Wäscher S, Schildmann J, Brall C et al (2013) Personalisierte Medizin in der Onkologie. Erste Ergebnisse einer qualitativen Interviewstudie zu Wahrnehmungen und Bewertungen onkologisch tätiger Ärzte. Ethik Med 25:205–214

Yurkiewicz S (2010) The prospects for personalized medicine. Hastings Cent Rep 40:14–18

Synthetic Biology and Its Envisioned Significance for Modern Medicine

56

Matthias Braun, Jens Ried, and Peter Dabrock

Contents

Abstract

Synthetic Biology (SB) is one of the leading branches within the current bundle of emerging biotechnologies. Following the hypothesis that the further development of SB will be negotiated at the interface of science and society, this chapter points out the current developments and challenges within SB by addressing the scientific as well as the societal issues.

Introduction

Synthetic Biology (SB) aims at designing and constructing new biological parts, devices, and systems as well as redesigning and modulating existing natural components with a strict focus on engineering principles. Nevertheless, up to now, there is no universally accepted definition of SB. Thus, this umbrella term covers quite disparate areas of work, including the group of "modulated

M. Braun (✉) • J. Ried • P. Dabrock
Department of Theology, Friedrich-Alexander-University Erlangen-Nuremberg, Erlangen, Germany
e-mail: matthias.braun@fau.de; jens.ried@fau.de; peter.dabrock@fau.de

© Springer Science+Business Media Dordrecht 2017
T. Schramme, S. Edwards (eds.), *Handbook of the Philosophy of Medicine*,
DOI 10.1007/978-94-017-8688-1_42

components", which elaborate and build (new) biological systems as well as the synthesis of extensive DNA strands.

Among other applications within the fields of agriculture or energy, SB substantially contributes to a so-called modern or biomarker-based medicine approach. Concrete examples are the development of novel and low-cost diagnostics and biosensors by engineering entire biological systems or DNA as nanomaterial. This material, if added to a sample of blood, urine, or water, is able to signal the presence of particular markers or pathogens. However, it is hitherto still open whether the promises and different approaches will come to the stage of concrete clinical use. Furthermore, the frame of SB is closely connected to different societal expectations, challenges, and fears. This chapter is premised by the hypothesis that the further development of SB will be negotiated at the interface of science and society. Thus, a detailed knowledge about the ethical and societal challenges is as necessary as taking note of the promising scientific progress within the field. On this account the chapter will map the field by drawing the picture of the scientific approaches and progresses and subsequently linking them with the different ethical and societal challenges.

Mapping the Diverse Field of Synthetic Biology

Synthetic Biology (SB) is supposed to be one of the leading branches within the current bundle of emerging biotechnologies (Nuffield Council on Bioethics 2012). Within the frame of SB different scientific disciplines such as physical and chemical sciences, biology, computer sciences, engineering, and biotechnological approaches are combined. This chapter maps the field of SB by firstly sketching out the overall approach of SB, secondly briefly elaborating the different pathways within SB, and thirdly plotting the current field of medical applications (see Fig. 1).

The underlying conceptual approach of SB is to gain a more in-depth and accurate understanding of biological systems. Therefore SB addresses a well-defined understanding of the organizational principles of biological organisms. By using a methodological framework of prediction, analysis, modulation, as well as by building new biological components (Kamm and Bashir 2014) SB tries to conceptualize and finally create new modularized biological systems. Thus, SB is perhaps more precisely understood if it is seen as a platform of different interacting biotechnological tools and newly modularized and constructed reagents (Cole 2014).

Within such a platform approach two different perspectives can be identified. On the one hand, there is much research activity within the so-called top-down approach to SB. This approach tries to progressively simplify cells by removing genes that are thought to be not necessary to sustain the essential properties of cellular life such as self-maintenance and self-reproduction (Purnick and Weiss 2009). The overall aim is to engineer a minimal cell, which is able to represent an organism by only comprising the lowest number of genes necessary to maintain basic cellular functions. On the other hand a so-called bottom-up approach equally

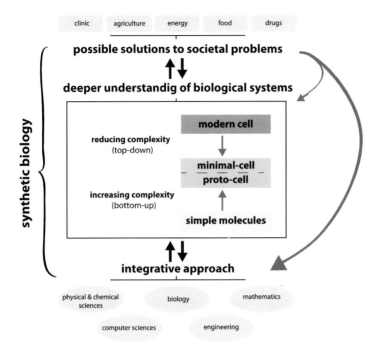

Fig. 1 Mapping the diverse field of synthetic biology. Own illustration according to Dzieciol and Mann 2012, Cole 2014, & Kamm and Bashir 2014

aims at building a certain kind of minimal cell but tries to sidestep the usage of complex cellular structures by starting with simple molecules or inorganic catalysts. This approach is also known as protocell biology (Dzieciol and Mann 2012). Protocell models, which are constructed by involving and combining simple membrane-bound and cell-like components, try to give an explanation how both a *prebiotic* – with regard to a more historical angle – and a *synthetic* cell – with regard to a more biotechnological perspective – can be designed and constructed. However, beyond these distinctions, there are many entanglements and conjunctions between these general approaches. Thus, one of the most popular, as well as critically discussed, experiments within SB, conducted by the group of Craig Venter, has been a mix of different methodological approaches and techniques (Gibson et al. 2010).

In the long term, the different disciplines and approaches within SB aim to offer a variety of diagnostic and therapeutic applications. With regard to a first scientific endeavor toward new achievements for a so-called modern medicine, SB focuses on the development of genetic circuits that link therapeutic activities to the detection of molecular disease signals. This first wave aims to pave the way to develop targeted therapeutics with increased efficacy and safety. Furthermore, first explorations indicate that synthetic control circuits may reduce the inherent tumorigenicity of stem cells (Schuldiner et al. 2003) and improve the efficiency of induced pluripotent stem cell reprogramming (Maherali et al. 2008). Novel genetic circuits, which are capable of guiding the ex vivo construction of complex tissues, may be built in the foreseeable future as researchers are continuing to unravel the SB behind cell fate decisions (Kueh and Rothenberg 2012). Up to now, the transition of these systems to concrete medical applications has been constrained by the limited availability of devices that are able to connect synthetic circuits with information in living systems (Chen et al. 2012). While the first wave of synthetic systems focused on the development of genetic circuits that encode dynamic behavior, cellular computational operations, and biological communication channels, in the second scientific wave the current focus of research focuses on implementing SB components in diverse fields of application (Ruder et al. 2011). Within this second wave SB is starting to tackle relevant medical challenges and provides new types of diagnostic and therapeutic tools for treating significant human pathologies (Weber and Fussenegger 2012; Aurand et al. 2012) or to develop new ways to combat the increasing incidence of antibiotic-resistant bacterial infections (Krom et al. 2015). Particular attention is paid to making a contribution toward the treatment of cancer or infectious diseases, as well as to approaches in vaccine development, microbiome engineering, cell therapy, and also regenerative medicine (Ruder et al. 2011). Beyond the first achievements within a synthetic version of the antimalarial compound artemisinin (Carothers 2013) there are several projects within SB, which sustainably aim at contributing to the fight against different communicable diseases such as the human immunodeficiency virus (Hansen et al. 2013; Rerks-Ngarm et al. 2009) or to enhance the hepatitis C virus vaccine (Liang 2013) development. One example within this field is the development of a vaccine-based approach to prevent diarrheal disease (Vohra and Blakey 2013). Up to now, there is a lot of infrastructure required to provide basic sanitation. Therefore the use of synthetic oral vaccines might offer a more rapid solution to a serious global childhood health issue by reducing the need for highly trained staff as well as the requirement for a sustained cold storage chain.

In envisioning and partly fulfilling such wide-ranging approaches SB can be seen as a paradigmatic case of the so-called emerging biotechnologies. The common feature of these technologies is that they intertwine innovative and cutting-edge scientific approaches with the societal desire for new possible solutions for current unsolved medical challenges. Thereby the developments envisioned by SB fit well into an environment of science governance in which research directions are set by scientific priorities as well as by societal challenges. Against this background, increased public funding is spent within the field (Pei et al. 2012).

Ethical, Legal, and Societal Challenges Within Synthetic Biology

Within the past years there have been different agendas and approaches in order to identify possible societal challenges within SB (Deutsche Forschungsgemeinschaft et al. 2009; Presidential Commission for the study of Bioethical Issues 2010; National Research Council and National Academy of Engineering 2013; OECD

2014). These reports mainly follow – with different accentuations – the idea of the existence of four major challenges (Schmidt et al. 2009). In the present article, the important issue of dealing with big data biology is added as a fifth challenge.

First, safety and security problems are pointed out (Deutscher Ethikrat 2014). Within this topic a frequently discussed issue is the problem of a possible misuse of the results and products of SB (Douglas and Savulescu 2010). Research results, which originally aim to increase the amount of scientific knowledge, can also be used for alternative purposes. Insofar as such information, reagents, and new technological approaches have the potential to be used both for beneficial as well as for harmful purposes, the work involved is designated as "dual use research" (World Health Organization 2010). More precisely for this range of possible use and misuse the term *Dual Use Research of Concern* (DURC) has gained international customary usage (World Health Organization 2013; Deutscher Ethikrat 2014). In order to face this problem, different measures and strategies have been developed. Many scientific organizations have elaborated and implemented codes of conduct as a kind of self-regulative setting of standards (Wilholt 2012) in order to influence the actions of the respective researchers. The crucial point for a high "quality" of these regulative effects is whether the codes of conduct contain rules of law in a strict sense, or are functioning more as a voluntary self-commitment (Qi and Arkin 2014). However, up to now, the existing laws are rated to sufficiently cover the current research action (Bar-Yam et al. 2012). Additionally, there are several points – especially with regard to the top-down approach – which need particular and ongoing awareness, particularly concerning the possible ecological effects. The aforementioned critical points are, first, the differences of the physiology of natural and synthetic organisms; second, the hitherto unknown alteration of synthetic organisms in different habitats; third, the possible evolution and adaptation of the produced synthetic organisms; and fourth, the possibility of microbes to take up free DNA from the environment or to exchange their genetic material with other organisms (Dana et al. 2012). Currently there are different approaches and endeavors to provide a foundation for a safer use of synthetic biology products such as the idea to work, for example, on synthetic bacteria that are isolated from natural ecosystems by a reliance in synthetic metabolites (Mandell et al. 2015).

Second, especially with regard to the protocell approach, ethical issues from a possible blurring of cultural concepts and distinctions such as "living versus non-living matters" or "natural versus artificial" have become subject to different explorations (Dabrock et al. 2013a). Notions and metaphors such as "creating life" or "playing God" can be understood as society's attempts of finding expressions for the present significance and effect of the technological development (Pearson et al. 2011). Especially the metaphor "playing God" shows that it was neither originally nor solely the frame of SB where such metaphors were originally coined. In fact, such metaphors have rather been used throughout long periods of time and then again as a heuristic marker in the discourse on scientific or new medical and biotechnical procedures (Dabrock 2009; Coady 2009; Dworkin 2000). In the following statement, the theologian Paul Tillich points out the main issue: "The significant thing, however, is not the replacement of one metaphor by another but the changed vision of reality, which such replacement expresses" (Tillich 1963, 15). Reformulated in a metaphor-theoretical way, the used metaphors are not only figures of speech but also forms that represent the individual and societal comprehension and constitution of reality. At this point the analyses of different metaphors used by science and society could indicate two different processes, which are caused by the emergence of new biotechnologies. On the one hand the capacity of biotechnologies may lead to profound transformations in the respective social, economic, or physical environments and therefore may have significant implications for the different shared ways of life. On the other hand, the generation of novel objects not found in nature may disturb and alter schemes of meaning and value and thereby gain potential for societal unease (Dabrock et al. 2013b).

Third, economic issues, especially in regard to questions of intellectual property (IP) and biocommercialization, have been discussed (Nuffield Council on Bioethics 2012). The conventional means through which medicinal products are developed and delivered to patients are IP-driven commercialization processes. The most common form of IP protection in biotechnology can be found in the form of patents and patent applications (Douglas and Stemerding 2013). Within such an IP-driven innovation process, two main implications with regard to the adaption of a SB approach for global health issues can be detected. The first is the possibly limited access to products that are marketed at prices that most people in "developing" or "under-developed" countries cannot afford. Second, there are only little incentives to develop drugs that will principally benefit people in those countries, since the potential users do not constitute an attractive market for pharmaceutical companies (Hollis 2013). Such a possible mismatch between access and availability need not, however, imply a break with current patent systems or intellectual property regimes. In fact, there are different approaches to develop further models, for example, alternative incentive strategies (van den Belt 2013). Open access has been seen as one of the considerable principles within such alternative strategies (van den Belt 2013): Scientists are allowed to benefit from using the developed and produced parts and components, which are available from the registry, for designing their own components and systems. In exchange, registry users are expected to share information and data on existing parts and new parts, thereby allowing the growth and improvement of this community resource (BioBricks Foundation 2013). However, the views among synthetic biologists on where to draw the line between public versus private ownership of parts and design principles differ significantly (Oye and Wellhausen 2009).

Fourth, the ethical and societal debate about dealing with emerging biotechnologies in general and SB in particular moves toward the question about who must and should be involved in making decisions pertaining to the stated questions (Pauwels 2009, 2013). Thus, it is not only at stake if the promises of SB will be fulfilled but likewise *how* and by *whom* they will and should be propelled. In other words, SB will become what scientists, innovators, regulators, funding agencies, civil society organizations, and others make of it. It could be used to foster public-value innovation or to stabilize and bolster existing power structures. The direction of this process will depend on which (group of) actors is involved and what kind of applications will, depending on which reasons, be in the focus. Furthermore the debate about the necessity and possibilities of public participation in science fits well into a science policy environment in which research directions are set less by disciplinary priorities and more by the need to address societal challenges (Carrier and Nordmann 2011). For that reason public participation in science is not only another "nice to have" item on the agenda of assessing emerging bio-technologies but will be decisive for the question of the future trajectory of SB. Furthermore the public engagement within science could be seen as a kind of bottleneck: Steady and consistent participation of society in SB would be a strong accelerator for the development of SB. On the other hand, if society decides to minimize their participation, it will be hardly possible for SB to set the envisioned and promised aims (Jones 2014). Recently, the modes of public participation in science have become subject to change: It is now easier than ever for nonprofes-sionally trained people to participate in the governance, regulation, and translation of science, as well as in some of the core activities of science itself (Prainsack 2014). At this point SB could possibly take a leading position in pushing this very development: It has perhaps never been that easy to participate in, as well to contribute to, science as in the so-called do-it-yourself biology ("biohackers") or in the International Genetically Engineered Machine (iGEM) competition. However, it still remains open which concrete concept of citizen science will gain a broader acceptance. The angle ranges from *citizens as data collectors* to *citizens as ancillary scientists* to *citizens as partners* up to *citizens as full-valued scientists* (Prainsack 2014).

Fifth, perhaps one the most challenging issues about the further contribution of SB within the field of modern medicine is big data. The recent development of SB demonstrates that the lines between SB and a so-called systems medicine approach are becoming more and more blurred – if there have ever been strict distinctions (Altaf-Ul-Amin et al. 2014). Thus, the more bioinformational perspective of systems biology and the more biotechnological approach of SB are becoming widely intertwined. In order to scrutinize how the different molecules and synthetic compo-nents could fit together, a massive set of data and backups about small molecules, proteins, and genes is needed. Up to now, there are enduring challenges for handling, processing, and moving this complex information as well as of the simulation clusters (Schadt et al. 2010). At this point the most puzzling problems are, on the one hand, the heterogeneity of the biological data caused by a wide range of experiments, which reveal many different and nonstandardized types of information (Marx 2013a). On the other hand, huge biological data and analysis volumes have to be stored via cloud computing while scientists are aware that there are risks of biohacking (Marx 2013b). Beneath these more technical challenges a so-called big data biology is also supposed to create a radical shift in how society thinks about research (Boyd and Crawford 2012). Therefore, big data biology reframes key questions about the constitution of knowledge, the processes of research, how societies can and should engage with information, the understanding and the categorization of reality, as well as challenges for the understanding of privacy issues (Dabrock 2012). The entanglement of these five points offers a sufficient and well-suited perspective to map the recent as well as the upcoming challenges within SB.

In connection to these intertwined five key aspects, the further development of SB is not only a question of the ongoing as well as predictable scientific progress, but it will also be determined by the societal estimation and appraisal of SB (Nuffield Council on Bioethics 2012). Therefore, the ethical and societal assessment of SB is challenged not only in terms of one or two of the outlined aspects, such as questions of biosafety and biosecurity (Douglas and Savulescu 2010) or intellectual property issues. Rather, SB has to be understood as a technological field at the interface of science and society, which is triggered by scientific progress as well as societal concerns, expectations, and unease. These societal hopes, fears, and expectations are linked to the general label of SB, even if the concrete formation of societal unease may differ with regard to the different fields of application, as well as to the different perspectives concerning, for example, protocell or the minimal cell approach. Apart from that, different agents, such as scientists, civil society organizations, and political decision-makers, have variable expectations toward SB (Jones 2014). Furthermore, the appraisal of and the attitude toward SB seems to also be strongly linked to the different fields of application (European Commission 2014). Up to now, it still remains unclear whether SB will be associated with the so-called red (medical application) or green (environmental application) biotechnology.

Definitions of Key Terms

Synthetic Biology	SB is an umbrella term covering quite disparate areas of work, which aim to design and construct new biological parts, devices, and systems as well as to redesign and modulate existing natural components with a strict focus on engineering principles.
Emerging Biotechnologies	Although emerging biotechnologies vary widely in nature and purpose, they jointly aim at bringing together a broad field of knowledge, a specific frame of research, and a more or less envisioned application of the respective techniques as well as the possible development of future products.
Citizen Science	Citizen Science is a term for all those endeavors which aim to scrutinize, observe, as well as improve public participation with science.
Big Data Biology	In systematically combining biological approaches, big data sets, and predictive elements big data biology reframes key questions about the constitution of knowledge, the processes of research, how societies can and should engage with information, the understanding and the categorization of reality, as well as challenges for the understanding of privacy issues.

Dual Use Research of Concern	Research results, which originally aim to increase the fund of scientific knowledge, can also be used for alternative purposes. Insofar as such information, reagents, and new technological approaches have the potential to be used both for beneficial as well as for harmful purposes, the work involved is designated as "dual use research."

Summary Points

- Synthetic Biology (SB) is a diverse field of research with different agendas and approaches integrating different disciplines and methods. SB aims to design and construct new biological parts, devices, and systems as well as to redesign and modulate existing natural components with a strict focus on engineering principles.
- In the long term, the different disciplines and approaches within SB aim to offer a variety of diagnostic and therapeutic applications. Therefore one of the basic endeavors of SB is the development of genetic circuits that link therapeutic activities to the detection of molecular disease signals in order to make them prospectively usable for medical applications.
- Regarding the societal impact of SB, five major challenges can be detected: first, biosafety and biosecurity issues; second, ethical issues from a possible blurring of cultural concepts and distinctions such as "living versus non-living" or "natural versus artificial"; third, economic issues, especially regarding questions of intellectual property (IP) and biocommercialization; fourth, the question about who must and should be involved in making decisions pertaining to further developments; fifth, and perhaps as one the most challenging issues about the further contribution of SB within the field of modern medicine, the issues of a so-called big-data-biology.
- Entangled with these five key aspects the further development of SB and its possible contribution to the development of medical applications is not only a question of the ongoing as well as predictable scientific progress but also a question of the determining force of societal estimation and appraisal of SB.

Acknowledgments This work is part of the MaxSynBio Consortium, which is jointly funded by the German Federal Ministry of Education and Research and the Max Planck Society.

References

Altaf-Ul-Amin M, Afendi FM, Kiboi SK, Kanaya S (2014) Systems biology in the context of big data and networks. BioMed Res Int. doi:10.1155/2014/428570
Aurand TC, Russell MS, March JC (2012) Synthetic signaling networks for therapeutic applications. Curr Opin Biotechnol 23(5):773–779
Bar-Yam S, Byers-Corbin J, Casagrande R, Eichler F, Lin A, Oesterreicher M, Regardh P, Turlington RD, Oye KA (2012) The regulation of synthetic biology. A guide to United States

and European Union regulations, rules and guidelines. SynBERC and iGEM Version 9.1, 10 Jan 2012 [Online]. Available: http://synberc.org/sites/default/files/Concise%20Guide%20to%20Synbio%20Regulation%20OYE%20Jan%202012_0.pdf. Accessed 29 Oct 2014

Biobricks Foundation (2013) Frequently asked questions [Online]. Available: https://biobricks.org/bpa/faq/#top. Accessed 31 Oct 2014

Boyd D, Crawford K (2012) Critical questions for big data. Inf Commun Soc 15(5):662–679

Carothers JM (2013) Design-driven, multi-use research agendas to enable applied synthetic biology for global health. Syst Synth Biol 7(3):79–86

Carrier M, Nordmann A (2011) Science in the context of application: methodological change, conceptual transformation, cultural reorientation. In: Carrier M, Nordmann A (eds) Science in the context of application. Springer, Dordrecht/New York, pp 1–11

Chen YY, Galloway KE, Smolke CD (2012) Synthetic biology: advancing biological frontiers by building synthetic systems. Genome Biol 13:240–250

Coady CAJ (2009) Playing God. In: Bostrom N, Savulescu J (eds) Human enhancement. Oxford University Press, Oxford, pp 155–180

Cole JA (2014) Synthetic biology: old wine in new bottles with an emerging language that ranges from the sublime to the ridiculous? FEMS Microbiol Lett 351:113–115

Dabrock P (2009) Playing God? Synthetic biology as a theological and ethical challenge. Syst Synth Biol 3:47–54

Dabrock P (2012) Privacy, data protection, and responsible government. Key issues and challenges in biobanking. Public Health Genomics 15:227–312

Dabrock P, Braun M, Ried J (2013a) From functional differentiation to (re-)hybridisation. The challenges of bio-objects in synthetic biology. In: Greif H, Weiss M (eds) Ethics – society – politics. De Gruyter, Berlin, pp 347–379

Dabrock P, Braun M, Ried J, Sonnewald U (2013b) A primer to 'bio-objects': new challenges at the interface of science, technology and society. Syst Synth Biol 7(1–2):1–6

Dana GV, Kuiken T, Rejeski D, Snow AA (2012) Synthetic biology: four steps to avoid a synthetic-biology disaster. Nature 483:29

Deutsche Forschungsgemeinschaft, Acatech, Deutsche Akademie Der Naturforscher Leopoldina (2009) Synthetic Biology Online. Available: http://www.dfg.de/download/pdf/dfg_im_profil/reden_stellungnahmen/2009/stellungnahme_synthetische_biologie.pdf. Accessed 27 Oct 2014

Deutscher Ethikrat (2014) Biosecurity – freedom and responsibility of research [Online]. Available: http://www.ethikrat.org/files/opinion-biosecurity.pdf. Accessed 27 Oct 2014

Douglas T, Savulescu J (2010) Synthetic biology and the ethics of knowledge. J Med Ethics 36:687–693

Douglas CMW, Stemerding D (2013) Governing synthetic biology for global health through responsible research and innovation. Syst Synth Biol 7:139–150

Dworkin R (2000) Sovereign virtue. The theory and practice of equality. Harvard University Press, Cambridge

Dzieciol A, Mann S (2012) Designs for life: protocells models in the laboratory. Chem Soc Rev 41:79–85

European Commission (2014): Special Eurobarometer 419: public perceptions of science, research and innovation [Online]. Available: http://ec.europa.eu/public_opinion/archives/ebs/ebs_419_en.pdf. Accessed 27 Oct 2014

Gibson DG, Glass JI, Lartigue C, Noskov VN, Chuang R-Y, Algire MA, Benders GA, Montague MG, Ma L, Moodie MM, Merryman C, Vashee S, Krishnakumar R, Assad-Garcia N, Andrews-Pfannkoch C, Denisova EA, Young L, Qi Z-Q, Segall-Shapiro TH, Calvey CH, Parmar PP, Hutchison CA, Smith HO, Venter JC (2010) Creation of a bacterial cell controlled by a chemically synthesized genome. Science 329(5987):52–56

Hansen SG, Ford JC, Lewis MS, Ventura AB, Hughes CM, Coyne-Johnson L, Whizin N, Oswald K, Shoemaker R, Swanson T, Legasse AW, Chiuchiolo MJ, Parks CL, Axthelm MK, Nelson JA, Jarvis MA, Piatak MJ, Lifson JD, Picker LJ (2013) Profound early control of highly pathogenic SIV by an effector memory T-cell vaccine. Nature 473(7348):523–527

Hollis A (2013) Synthetic biology: ensuring the greatest global value. Syst Synth Biol 7:99–105

Jones RAL (2014) Reflecting on public engagement and science policy. Public Underst Sci 23 (1):27–31

Kamm RD, Bashir R (2014) Creating living cellular machines. Ann Biomed Eng 42(2):445–459

Krom RJ, Bhargava P, Lobritz MA, Collins JJ (2015) Engineered phagemids for nonlytic, targeted antibacterial therapies. Nano Lett 15(7):4808–4813

Kueh H, Rothenberg E (2012) Regulatory gene network circuits underlying T cell development from multipotent progenitors. Wiley Interdiscip Rev Syst Biol Med 4:79–102

Liang TJ (2013) Current progress in development of hepatitis C virus vaccines. Nat Med 19 (7):869–878

Maherali N, Ahfeldt T, Rigamonti A, Utikal J, Cowan C, Hochedlinger K (2008) A high-efficiency system for the generation and study of human induced pluripotent stem cells. Cell Stem Cell 3:340–345

Mandell DJ, Lajoie MJ, Mee MT, Takeuchi R, Kuznetsov G, Norville JE, Gregg CJ, Stoddard BL, Church GM (2015) Biocontainment of genetically modified organisms by synthetic protein design. Nature 518(7537):55–60

Marx V (2013a) Biology: the big challenges of big data. Nature 498:255–260

Marx V (2013b) Genomics in the clouds. Nat Methods 10(10):941–954

National Research Council & National Academy Of Engineering (2013) Positioning synthetic biology to meet the challenges of the 21st century. Summary report of a six academies symposium series. The National Academies Press, Washington, DC

Nuffield Council on Bioethics (2012) Emerging biotechnologies: technology, choice and the public good [Online]. Available: http://nuffieldbioethics.org/wp-content/uploads/2014/07/Emerging_biotechnologies_full_report_web_0.pdf. Accessed 24 Oct 2014

OECD (2014) Emerging policy issues in synthetic biology [Online]. OECD Publishing. Available: http://dx.doi.org/10.1787/9789264208421-en. Accessed 30 Oct 2014

Oye KA, Wellhausen R (2009) The intellectual commons and property in synthetic biology. In: Schmidt M (ed) Synthetic biology. Springer, Berlin, pp 121–139

Pauwels E (2009) Review of quantitative and qualitative studies on U.S. public perceptions of synthetic biology. Syst Synth Biol 3:37–46

Pauwels E (2013) Public understanding of synthetic biology. BioScience 63(2):79–89

Pearson B, Snell S, Bye-Nagel K, Tonidandel S, Heyer LJ, Campbell AM (2011) Word selection affects perceptions of synthetic biology. J Biol Eng 5:9–11

Pei L, Gaisser S, Schmidt M (2012) Synthetic biology in the view of European public funding organisations. Public Underst Sci 21(2):149–162

Prainsack B (2014) Understanding participation: the 'citizen science' of genetics. In: Prainsack B, Schicktanz S (eds) Genetics as social practice. Ashgate, Farnham, pp 147–164

Presidential Commission for the Study of Bioethical Issues (2010) New directions the ethics of synthetic biology and emerging technologies Online. Available: http://bioethics.gov/sites/default/files/PCSBI-Synthetic-Biology-Report-12.16.10_0.pdf. Accessed 27 Oct 2014

Purnick PE, Weiss R (2009) The second wave of synthetic biology: from modules to systems. Nat Rev Mol Cell Biol 10:410–422

Qi LS, Arkin AP (2014) A versatile framework for microbial engineering using synthetic non-coding RNAs. Nat Rev Microbiol 12:341–453

Rerks-Ngarm S, Pitisuttithum P, Nitayaphan S, Kaewkungwal J, Chiu J, Paris R, Premsri N, Namwat C, De Souza M, Adams E, Benenson M, Gurunathan S, Tartaglia J, Mcneil JG, Francis DP, Stablein D, Birx DL, Chunsuttiwat S, Khamboonruang C, Thongcharoen P, Robb ML, Michael NL, Kunasol P, Kim JH (2009) Vaccination with ALVAC and AIDSVAX to prevent HIV-1 infection in Thailand. N Engl J Med 361(23):2209–2220

Ruder WC, Lu T, Collins JJ (2011) Synthetic biology moving into the clinic. Science 333:1248–1252

Schadt EE, Linderman MD, Sorenson J, Lee L, Nolan GP (2010) Computational solutions to large-scale data management and analysis. Nat Rev Genet 11:647–657

Schmidt M, Ganguli-Mitra A, Torgersen H, Kelle A, Deplazes A, Biller-Andorno N (2009) A priority paper for the societal and ethical aspects of synthetic biology. Syst Synth Biol 3:3–7

Schuldiner M, Itskovitz-Eldor J, Benvenisty N (2003) Selective ablation of human embryonic stem cells expressing a "suicide" gene. Stem Cells 21:257–265

Tillich P (1963) Systematic theology, volume three: life and the spirit history and the kingdom of God. University of Chicago Press, Chicago

van den Belt H (2013) Synthetic biology, patenting, health and global justice. Syst Synth Biol 7:87–98

Vohra P, Blakey G (2013) Easing the global burden of diarrhoeal disease – can synthetic biology help? Syst Synth Biol 7(3):73–78

Weber W, Fussenegger M (2012) Emerging biomedical applications of synthetic biology. Nat Rev Genet 13:21–35

Wilholt T (2012) Die Freiheit der Forschung. Begründungen und Begrenzungen. Suhrkamp, Frankfurt a.M

World Health Organization (2010) Responsible life sciences research for global health security. A guidance document [Online]. Geneva. Available: http://whqlibdoc.who.int/hq/2010/WHO_HSE_GAR_BDP_2010.2_eng.pdf. Accessed 29 Oct 2014

World Health Organization (2013) Informal consultation on dual use research of concern [Online]. Available: http://www.who.int/csr/durc/consultation/en. Accessed 29 Oct 2014

Complementary and Alternative Medicine (CAM) and Its Relationship to Western Medicine

57

Pekka Louhiala

Contents

Abstract

CAM is an acronym combining two terms, "complementary medicine" and "alternative medicine," both of which are recent. The definitions of CAM point out the diversity of phenomena behind the concept and list therapies currently belonging to the CAM field. A universal definition that would provide a demarcation line between CAM and the dominant system does not exist, and CAM is best understood as a residual category, defined by its exclusion from "official" or "medical school" medicine. Some CAM treatments are fundamentally incompatible with science, but some treatments, currently belonging to the CAM domain, will, sooner or later, be included in mainstream medicine, if their effectiveness can be demonstrated. CAM as a concept may be useful in

P. Louhiala (✉)
Department of Public Health, University of Helsinki, Finland
e-mail: pekka.louhiala@helsinki.fi

© Springer Science+Business Media Dordrecht 2017
T. Schramme, S. Edwards (eds.), *Handbook of the Philosophy of Medicine*,
DOI 10.1007/978-94-017-8688-1_47

927

describing a phenomenon from a sociological or political point of view, but from the scientific perspective there is only one medicine.

That is why there are, and always will be, pseudo-healers, wise women, homeopaths, and allopaths. (Tolstoy 2001, p. 518)

Introduction

CAM is an acronym combining two terms, "complementary medicine" and "alternative medicine," both of which are only a few decades old. "Alternative medicine" first appeared in medical journals in 1975 and "complementary medicine" in 1985. "Integrative medicine" was introduced in an English language journal in 1995, although it had appeared in German in an article 2 years earlier and in French already in 1951 (Louhiala and Puustinen 2012).

"Alternative medicine" as a term dates back to the alternative lifestyle movement that originated in the United States in the late 1960s (Issit 2009). "Complementary medicine" was adopted in Britain with the political objective of raising the question of whether medicine could include some of the alternative healing practices in its tool kit. "Integrative medicine" was introduced in order to suggest a deeper relationship between alternative treatments and medicine (Louhiala and Puustinen 2012).

In general, the "alternative movement" was part of a societal trend toward the rejection of science as a method of determining truths. Within the movement, it was also often asserted that "scientific medicine" (or "conventional medicine") is only one of a vast array of options in health care. The movement was ideologically close to the view that science is not necessarily more valid than pseudoscience.

All of the commonly used terms in the debate concerning medicine and its "alternatives" are problematic in one way or another, and often they describe both the phenomenon in question and the motives of the person using the term (Louhiala 2010).

Firstly, the nature of "alternative" in "alternative medicine" is anything but clear. Advocates of the term usually fail to define what they claim to offer an alternative to and on what grounds. In their rhetoric, medicine is presented as a monolithic and closed system that needs an alternative.

Secondly, choosing an alternative means that, in general, the other option is rejected. If we want, for example, to travel from London to Paris, there are several alternatives. One is fast, one is cheap, one is environment-friendly, etc. They all do, however, take us from London to Paris. There are also many ways to explore these alternatives scientifically. If a genuine "alternative" medicine existed, it should produce results that are similar to those of ordinary medicine, and a causal correlation between the treatment and the result should be demonstrable.

Thirdly, there are similar problems with all the other terms, too. If someone introduces herself as a practitioner of *complementary* medicine, is she not implicitly saying that she masters both ordinary medicine *and* some additional methods that do not belong to the toolbox of the majority of physicians? *Traditional* medicine can mean almost anything, and *official* or *school* medicine refers to medical education in a particular area and at a specific time. If *evidence-based* medicine is defined as "the conscientious, explicit and judicious use of current best evidence in making decisions about the medical care of individual patients," there is certainly not a physician alive who would not claim to practice it, as Mark Tonelli (1998) has remarked. And if *orthodoxy* in medicine were determined by the durability and degree of acceptance achieved by any particular medical idea, then humoral medicine would represent "orthodox Western medicine" *par excellence* (Bivins 2007). It certainly endured unchallenged far longer than biomedicine, which is less than 200 years old.

Some Historical Remarks

Various ideas and practices concerning health and illness have occurred throughout history, and they have often contradicted each other and offered alternative means with which to understand and alleviate illness and suffering. In the CAM rhetoric, it is not uncommon to claim that the practices marketed under these terms date back thousands of years (Larson 2007) or at least to the medical disputes of the eighteenth century. However, naming ancient ideas and practices as alternative, complementary, or integrative medicine is problematic, since none of the terms were in use prior to the 1970s (Louhiala and Puustinen 2012).

In order to have medical systems and practices that can properly be regarded as "alternative," one must have a recognized and at least relatively stable orthodoxy to which they oppose themselves. Such an orthodoxy emerged in the Western medical marketplace only in the nineteenth century, the "Paris School" being often identified as a starting point of modern scientific medicine (Bivins 2007).

The quacks of the eighteenth century did not present their medicines or therapies as "alternative" to those of orthodox physicians, apothecaries, or surgeons, but as better (Bivins 2007). They did not propose different medical systems nor different understandings of diseases, but argued that their remedies simply operated more effectively than their competitors. The common and dominating medical system was humoral medicine, which persisted in orthodox practice until the mid-nineteenth century. In fact, many "alternative" therapies of today have their roots in humoral medicine, although this is not the case with homeopathy.

In the early nineteenth century, there was no scientific medicine in the modern sense of the term. Closest to its idea came "allopathy," a term invented by Samuel Hahnemann, the German physician and founder of homeopathy. In Hahnemann's terminology, allopathy meant "treatment with opposites," while the basic principle of homeopathy was "like treats like" (*similia similibus curantur*). According to Roberta Bivins (2007), homeopathy made, along with mesmerism, strong claims to scientificity and was popular with the same educated consumers who also eagerly supported the natural sciences. Homeopathy's commercial and therapeutic successes forced major changes in ordinary medical practice. Sir John Forbes, a prominent physician of his time, noted in 1858 that "the favourable practical results obtained by the homoeopathists – or to speak more accurately, the wonderful powers possessed by the natural restorative agencies of the living body, demonstrated under their imaginary treatment – have led to several other practical results of value to the practitioners of ordinary medicine" (cited in Bivins 2007, 99).

The early homeopaths used the rhetoric of opposition to – and oppression by – medical orthodoxy to draw attention to the flaws of allopathic practice, which allowed them to build a strong identity. However, at the same time, they left homeopathy open to being grouped with all the other self-proclaimed "alternatives," some of which deserved respect, while others did not (Bivins 2007).

The origin of the notion of alternative medicine can be traced back to the late 1960s in the United States where, especially among college students, strong critique arose against a bourgeois lifestyle and values in the wake of the Vietnam War and the threat of a nuclear holocaust. Some authors pinpointed the heyday of this cultural phenomenon to the summer of 1968, when tens of thousands of youth drifted to San Francisco to join a spontaneous gathering that was named the hippie movement by the American press and was referred to the New Age by the proponents of this subculture (Issit 2009).

What started as a hippie or New Age movement with ideals of peace, freedom, and "planetary consciousness" soon lost its momentum and split into various diverse expressions of discontent for the mainstream American way of life and its values. One common denominator was the need to find alternatives to current housing, farming, food consumption, family structure, child-rearing, schooling, etc. Criticism of medical theory and practice can be seen as a part of this general development. After all, medicine in those days was male dominated and an increasingly technologically based activity, both of which were associated with the political and military power structure of the time.

The attempt to seek ways to meet the need for healing practices that were free of medical dominance led to the adoption of various indigenous healing systems, some of which were imported as side products of Eastern religions, especially Buddhism and Hinduism. Spiritual teachers of these religions had been imported to the United States ever since the late 1960s. Along with their cosmological views, they produced ideas on health, illness, and healing that were based on their general world view. In 1973, this development was boosted by President Nixon's visit in the People's Republic of China, where acupuncture was introduced to the West (although the practice itself had been known in Europe for centuries).

After this general development, there suddenly emerged a growing demand for nonmedical healing practices among the affluent, younger generation both in the United States and in Europe in the early 1970s. The rest of humankind relied, as they still do, on local indigenous healers and medical help, when available and affordable. Since there was no official training available with which to gain competence in these newly commercialized healing practices, self-appointed practitioners and trainers appeared who offered courses and diplomas in Eastern and other practices that were more or less adapted to Western taste. This situation not only led to competition between practitioners but also to competition with the medical establishment. This competition took place mainly in the media, which uncritically applied catchwords such as alternative, natural, soft, and holistic.

Current Definitions

In the light of the history of CAM and related terms, it is obvious that a universal definition that would provide a *demarcation line* between CAM and the "dominant system" cannot be reached.

The Committee on the Use of Complementary and Alternative Medicine of the American Public Board on Health Promotion and Disease Prevention (2005) defined CAM as

> . . . a broad domain of resources that encompasses health systems, modalities, and practices and their accompanying theories and beliefs, other than those intrinsic to the dominant health system of a particular society or culture in a given historical period. CAM includes such resources perceived by their users as associated with positive health outcomes. Boundaries within CAM and between the CAM domain and the domain of the dominant system are not always sharp or fixed.

The definition is an important description in pointing out the diversity of the phenomena behind the concept. This complexity also explains why the boundaries between the CAM domain and mainstream medicine are neither sharp nor constant.

Within the Cochrane Collaboration (a global independent network producing health information), an *operative* classification of CAM has been developed. It consists of a long list of therapies that the Cochrane Complementary Medicine Field classifies as complementary or alternative. The therapies are listed in alphabetical order, starting from açaí, acupressure, and acupuncture and ending with zinc supplements, Zishen Tongli Jianonang (a Chinese herbal medicine), and zone therapy (http://www.compmed.umm.edu/cochrane/CAM.asp). The authors of the list do not consider it to be exhaustive and point out that it is subject to expansion and elaboration over time. In fact, they question whether it is possible to arrive upon a definitive set of therapies that are universally agreed upon as CAM.

The above definitions aim to be neutral and descriptive, making no a priori claims about the ideological background or effectiveness of CAM therapies. The diverse nature of the therapies is acknowledged also among the representatives of CAM, but unsubstantiated claims about a shared ideology are often made in the literature. In an entry in the Encyclopedia of Applied Ethics, for example, it is claimed that CAM therapies "share a similar approach to treatment which differs fundamentally from that of orthodox medicine" (Whitelegg 1998). The author goes on to paint a black-and-white picture of the world as follows:

> . . .the biomedical perspective of practical exclusion of nonphysical factors as agents influencing either the cause or the progress of illness bases its treatment on rational and objective observation and evaluation with no interference from subjective influences. Complementary medicine, on the other hand, sees the patients and their problems as inextricably linked with their circumstances and their individual reactions to them and

their lifestyles, attitudes, and environments, and will consider body, mind, and spirit in its treatment.

Reflecting aspects from all the definitions above, Wolpe (2002) suggested that CAM is best understood as a "residual category," which means that it is defined by its exclusion from "official" or "medical school" medicine. "Alternative medicine" was defined along these lines in 1998 in a large study on national trends on the use of alternative medicine in the United States (Eisenberg et al. 1998):

> Alternative medical therapies, functionally defined as interventions neither taught widely in medical schools nor generally available in US hospitals...

In a thorough and critical article, Stephen Barrett (1998) accepted the category "alternative medicine" but suggested that, "to avoid confusion, 'alternative' methods should be classified as genuine, experimental, or questionable." In his terminology,

> *genuine* alternatives are comparable methods that have met science-based criteria for safety and effectiveness. *Experimental* alternatives are unproven but have a plausible rationale and are undergoing responsible investigation.... *Questionable* alternatives are groundless and lack a scientifically plausible rationale.... The archetype is homeopathy.

Barrett's classification is meaningful if the category "alternative medicine" is taken for granted. Some authors argue that such a category is not needed, and it is simpler and more useful to distinguish between *mechanisms not fully understood* and *mechanisms obviously absurd*. Hrobjartsson and Brorson (2002), for example, have written:

> If a postulated mechanism is absurd according to standard scientific position, there is a tendency to ascribe a prior probability of zero to a hypothesis about therapeutic effects, for example in the case of homeopathy... Other complementary/alternative therapies, for example acupuncture, are also based on theories foreign to conventional science, but are not obviously absurd: physiological responses caused by the insertion of needles on certain spots are not necessarily incompatible with standard scientific thinking. Therefore, the prior probability of acupuncture to have clinical effects exceeds zero....

Hrobjartsson and Brorson's view may, however, be too simple. The history of science provides plenty of examples of ideas that were originally dismissed as absurd and persisted as anomalies, only for new research to eventually provide sufficient support a mechanism to be proposed. The "standard scientific position" may be wrong and exclude the possibility of the maverick thinking that leads to paradigm shifts in science.

A political implication of the categorization by Hrobjartsson and Brorson would be that public money should not be invested in research on methods that are based on obviously absurd mechanisms. Although a preliminary clinical trial may not need to be expensive, it nevertheless implies an allocation of intellectual and economic resources. If the probability of getting positive results is very low, the enrollment of patients and the allocation of resources raise both ethical and socioeconomic problems.

CAM describes thus a *political* or *sociological* category, but it is also an example of a *buzzword*, which, according to Merriam-Webster Dictionary (2015), is "an important-sounding usually technical word or phrase often of little meaning used chiefly to impress laymen." The advocates of various forms of CAM are adept at using also other buzzwords and slogans like "natural," "soft," or "holistic," the meaning of which is vague (Louhiala and Puustinen 2012).

Natural, Soft, and Holistic

The three main concepts with which the advocates of alternative medicine have justified their products and treatments have been "natural," "soft," and "holistic." "Official medicine," on the other hand, has been considered "unnatural," "hard," and "fragmented."

To name and treat illnesses is a cultural phenomenon. In that sense, there are no treatments available in nature and all treatments are unnatural. As *Pneumococci* or HI viruses multiply in a patient's body, it is a fully natural phenomenon. When trying to interfere with their flourishing, we act against nature, no matter whether we use antibiotics, herbal remedies, or prayers. The often used claim by the proponents of CAM, that their methods act through strengthening the body rather than through killing the germs directly, does not change that fact. It only leaves the work to be done by the body rather than by antibiotic pills.

The problem with the term "soft" in this context is that it supposedly refers to the treatment used and not to the therapist in charge. In the light of the definitions of CAM, it is obvious that "softness" is by no means not a common factor between different CAM modalities. From the point of view of the patients, individual therapists of CAM as well as conventional medicine can be soft or hard in their practice.

The term "holistic" appears at least as often as "soft" in the rhetoric of CAM. The term is, again, offered as an antithesis to conventional medicine's alleged lack of a holistic feature. It seems to be an empty slogan that does not describe essential and common features of a multitude of treatments in the category CAM.

CAM Meets EBM

Evidence-based medicine (EBM) originated from the concern that numerous ineffective treatments had been adopted by mainstream medicine, and the randomized controlled trial (RCT) was viewed as the most reliable method by which to identify treatments that actually work.

The ideas behind EBM are old, but the concept was introduced to the wider medical community in 1992 as "a new approach to teaching the practice of medicine" and "a new paradigm for medical practice" (Evidence-Based Medicine Working Group 1992). According to the authors, EBM "de-emphasizes intuition, unsystematic clinical experience, and pathophysiologic rationale as sufficient grounds for clinical decision making and stresses the examination of evidence from clinical research." In particular, the 1992 paper instructed clinicians to search for studies with the question "Was the assignment of patients to treatments randomized?" The article was a bold program statement that divided the medical world into the old-fashioned pre-EBM and the revolutionary new EBM types of medicine.

A definition of EBM was formulated by the pioneers 4 years later: "Evidence-based medicine is the conscientious, explicit, and judicious use of current best evidence in making decisions about the care of individual patients" (Sackett et al. 1996). Despite its obvious vagueness, this has remained the most widely cited definition of EBM.

The story of the concept has been a success, although during all these years, it has not been clear what the phenomenon behind the three letters actually is. From the very beginning, critical voices were also heard, and already in 1998, a paper titled "The Rise and Fall of EBM" was published (Charlton and Miles 1998).

Many years and several definitions later, it is obvious that Timmermans and Mauck (2005) were right when they wrote that "The term [EBM] is loosely used and can refer to anything from conducting a statistical meta-analysis of accumulated research, to promoting randomized clinical trials, to supporting uniform reporting styles for research, to a personal orientation toward critical self-evaluation."

Despite the disagreements and confusions about the basic definitions of EBM, one aspect of the EBM program has been particularly essential since the introduction of the term in 1992, namely, the view of valid evidence: "[C]omparative clinical studies, preferably from randomised trials [RCTs], are deemed to provide better evidence than mechanistic reasoning and clinical experience" (Evidence-Based Medicine Working Group 1992).

CAM and EBM are often presented as opposites, at least by the representatives of mainstream medicine, who claim to practice EBM, but often fail to define what they exactly refer to. As we have seen, neither CAM nor EBM has been defined in a satisfactory way that would give us a demarcation line between CAM and non-CAM or EBM and non-EBM.

A more pragmatic approach can be taken, however, to explore the relationship between CAM and EBM at the level of medical practice (Louhiala and Hemilä 2014). Rather than opposites, they could be seen as concepts pointing at different directions. If CAM is understood to mean therapies that lie outside mainstream medicine and EBM is understood in the light of its main principle, the requirement to base treatments on RCTs, there are, in fact, evidence-based therapies that are currently listed as CAM (e.g., high-dose zinc acetate for common cold (Hemilä 2011) or vitamin C for patients with exercise-induced asthma (Hemilä 2013)).

The opposite of CAM is thus not EBM but "mainstream medicine," and some treatments obviously belong to the CAM domain for historical reasons and because of preconceptions within mainstream medicine.

Concluding Remarks

Many treatments currently classified as CAM are not credible from the scientific point of view, and there are good reasons for them to remain outside mainstream medicine. However, the fact that a specific treatment falls into the CAM domain does not prove that the treatment is ineffective.

Some CAM treatments, such as homeopathy, are fundamentally incompatible with science. It is extremely unlikely that such treatments will ever become part of mainstream medicine, even if some occasional research findings have been positive.

Publication bias and methodological flaws are far more plausible explanations for the positive results related to homeopathy than errors in basic theories of science.

On the other hand, it is likely that some treatments currently belonging to the CAM domain will, sooner or later, be included in mainstream medicine, if their effectiveness can be demonstrated.

CAM as a concept may be useful in describing a phenomenon from a sociological or political point of view, and people in a pluralistic society should be free to choose whatever treatments they like, also CAM. From the scientific point of view, however, there is only one medicine, and the alternativity of "alternative medicine," complementarity of "complementary medicine," and integrativity of "integrative medicine" are not based on any meaningful theoretical or practical line of division.

Definition of Key Terms

Complementary and alternative medicine (CAM)	Has been defined as a "broad domain of resources that encompasses health systems, modalities, and practices and their accompanying theories and beliefs, other than those intrinsic to the dominant health system." Another possibility is an operative definition listing therapies currently classified as complementary or alternative. These definitions overlap and do not provide a demarcation line between CAM and non-CAM.
Alternative medicine	Has also been defined functionally as "interventions neither taught widely in medical schools nor generally available in US hospitals." Reflecting this, it has been suggested that CAM is a residual category, defined by its exclusion from official medicine.

Summary Points

- CAM is an acronym combining two terms, "complementary medicine" and "alternative medicine," both of which are recent.
- Alternative medicine as a term dates back to the alternative lifestyle movement that originated in the United States in the late 1960s.
- All of the commonly used terms in the debate concerning medicine and its "alternatives" are problematic, and a universal definition that would provide a demarcation line between CAM and the "dominant system" cannot be reached.
- Rather than a scientific category, CAM describes a political or sociological category.
- CAM is also a buzzword, used to promote individual treatments.
- Many treatments currently classified as CAM are not credible from the scientific point of view.

- The fact that a specific treatment currently falls into the CAM domain does not prove that the treatment is ineffective.

References

This chapter builds partly upon, and contains small extracts from, Louhiala (2010), Louhiala and Puustinen (2012), and Louhiala and Hemilä (2014). The extracts are used with permission from the publishers and the co-authors

Barrett S (1998) "Alternative" medicine: more hype than hope. In: Humber JM, Almeder RF (eds) Alternative medicine and ethics. Human Press, Totowa, pp 1–42

Bivins R (2007) Alternative medicine – a history. Oxford University Press, Oxford

Charlton BG, Miles A (1998) The rise and fall of EBM. Q J Med 91:371–374

Committee on the Use of Complementary and Alternative Medicine by the American Public, Board on Health Promotion and Disease Prevention (2005) Complementary and alternative medicine in the United States. National Academy Press, Washington, DC, p 17

Eisenberg DM, Davis RB, Ettner SL et al (1998) Trends in alternative medicine use in the United States, 1990–1997: results of a follow-up national survey. JAMA 280:1569–1575

Evidence-Based Medicine Working Group (1992) Evidence-based medicine: a new approach to teaching the practice of medicine. JAMA 268:2420–2425

Hemilä H (2011) Zinc lozenges may shorten the duration of colds: a systematic review. Open Respir Med J 5:51–58

Hemilä H (2013) Vitamin C may alleviate exercise-induced bronchoconstriction: a meta-analysis. BMJ Open 3:e002416

Hrobjartsson A, Brorson S (2002) Interpreting results from randomized trials of complementary/alternative interventions: the role of trial quality and pre-trial beliefs. In: Callahan D (ed) The role of complementary & alternative medicine – accommodating pluralism. Georgetown University Press, Washington, DC, pp 107–121

Issit ML (2009) Hippies. Greenwood Press, Santa Barbara

Larson C (2007) Alternative medicine. Greenwood Publishing Company, Westport

Louhiala P (2010) There is no alternative medicine. Med Humanit 36:115–117

Louhiala P, Hemilä H (2014) Can CAM treatments be evidence-based? Focus Altern Complement Ther 19:84–89

Louhiala P, Puustinen R (2012) Alternative, complementary, integrative – conceptual problems in marketing healthcare ideologies and services. Focus Altern Complement Ther 17:156–159

Merriam Webster (2015) Definition of 'buzzword'. http://www.merriam-webster.com/dictionary/buzzword. Accessed 5 Mar 2015

Sackett DL, Rosenberg WMC, Gray JAM et al (1996) Evidence-based medicine: what it is and what it isn't. BMJ 312:71–72

Timmermans S, Mauck A (2005) The promises and pitfalls of evidence-based medicine. Health Aff 24:18–28

Tolstoy LN (2001) War and peace (transl. Louise and Aylmer Maude). Wordsworth Classics, London, London

Tonelli MR (1998) The philosophical limits of evidence-based medicine. Acad Med 73:1234–1240

Whitelegg M (1998) Alternative medicine. In: Chadwick R (ed) Encyclopedia of applied ethics, vol 1. Academic, San Diego

Wolpe PR (2002) Medical culture and CAM culture: science and ritual in the academic medical center. In: Callahan D (ed) The role of complementary & alternative medicine – accommodating pluralism. Georgetown University Press, Washington, DC, pp 163–171

Psychoanalysis as Science

58

Martin Hoffmann

Contents

Abstract

Psychoanalysis is one of the most prominent and most intensely discussed research programs of the twentieth century. One important debate in the philosophy of medicine centers around the question of whether or not psychoanalysis is a scientific research program. The paradigm case for the evaluation of this question is the theory of Sigmund Freud, who – in contrast to Carl G. Jung, Alfred Adler, and other proponents of psychoanalytic theory – regarded his theoretical efforts as a scientific project throughout his whole life. His project was continued by researchers in psychology and medicine, as well as

M. Hoffmann (✉)
Philosophisches Seminar, Universität Hamburg, Hamburg, Germany
e-mail: martin.hoffmann@uni-hamburg.de

© Springer Science+Business Media Dordrecht 2017
T. Schramme, S. Edwards (eds.), *Handbook of the Philosophy of Medicine*,
DOI 10.1007/978-94-017-8688-1_41

practitioners in clinical psychotherapy and psychiatry. In order to give a more elaborate answer to the question of the extent to which this project is judged to be successful in contemporary science, it is necessary to differentiate between psychoanalytic theory, psychodynamic therapy, and the research methodology applied in the Freudian tradition.

Even if Freud himself took psychoanalysis to be a scientific, validated theory, his own research methodology faces serious problems. From the perspective of contemporary science, it constitutes the most "unscientific" aspect of his whole conception, because it is generally seen as falling victim to the *post hoc ergo propter hoc* fallacy. It is therefore deemed inappropriate for producing any substantial scientific evidence. But – contrary to Popper's prominent critique – it cannot be denied that many claims of psychoanalytic theory are empirically testable and that since the 1950s, a remarkable body of evidence that fulfills scientific research standards has been generated with the aim of confirming the central theoretical claims of psychoanalysis and the efficacy of psychoanalytic therapy. Therefore, in a processual or methodological sense, today's psychoanalysis is without any doubt a scientific research program. But at the same time, it is an open question whether the scientific endeavor to confirm the central claims of psychoanalysis will turn out to be successful. The generally accepted theorems that form the common core of today's psychoanalytic theorizing are – in sharp contrast to Freud's original theory – rather carefully formulated and are not particularly specific. For this reason, the relevance of psychoanalysis for the further development of psychology and medicine and the question of the efficacy and effectiveness of an autonomous psychodynamic therapy are matters of a deep and ongoing controversy.

Introduction

Psychoanalysis is one of the most prominent and intensely discussed research programs of the twentieth century. One important debate in the philosophy of medicine concerns the methodological status of psychoanalysis as a research program. The central question of this debate is the following: is psychoanalysis a scientific research program or does it fail scientific standards? Although there are different theories which are called "psychoanalytic" (not just Sigmund Freud's theory but also Carl G. Jung's theory of archetypes and the collective unconscious, Alfred Adler's individual psychology, Melanie Klein's object relations theory, etc.), the debate concerning the scientific status of psychoanalysis centers primarily around Freud's theory. One historical reason for this is that Freud was the only proponent of psychoanalysis who saw himself as a scientist throughout his whole life and who characterized his theory as a scientific, or at least proto-scientific, project. Furthermore, it was virtually only the Freudian tradition that gave rise to a research program aimed at validating the central claims of psychoanalysis on the basis of scientific evidence and with the help of experimental methods (Hilgard 1952a, b; Kline 1981; Fisher and Greenberg 1996; Chiesa 2010).

The conception of psychoanalysis as a science was challenged primarily by two kinds of criticisms. One line of argument was that Freud fell victim to a "scientistic self-misunderstanding" ("szientistisches Selbstmißverständnis," Habermas 1968; see especially pp. 300–332). Habermas argued that Freud's project is not a branch of the natural sciences but – rightly understood – rather turns out to be a hermeneutics of the self or of consciousness in general. Other adherents of a philosophical reinterpretation of Freud's works localized him within the methodological framework of modern phenomenology and (post-) structuralism (Ricœur 1965). This line of argument is no threat for psychoanalysis as a science if one allows for an "interpretative pluralism" and admits that it is possible to use Freud's theory as a starting point for both a distinct project in the field of the hermeneutical philosophy of consciousness and, at the same time, for a scientific project. Leaving exegetic questions aside, this seems to be an entirely plausible assumption that holds for many theoretical projects (e.g., ancient atomism, which was a theoretical source for both philosophy of nature and modern chemistry). By contrast, the other criticism is far more threatening for the project of psychoanalysis as a science. It is also the origin of the controversy about the scientific status of psychoanalysis. The proponents of this criticism accused Freud of being the founder of a pseudoscience along with astrology, homeopathy, or Marx's historical materialism. They argued that Freud's theory is not a scientific theory, because it is not empirically testable (Karl Popper), that his research methodology is deeply misconstrued (Adolf Grünbaum), and that psychodynamic therapy is at best completely ineffective and at worst dangerous for people suffering from a mental crisis (Hans-Jürgen Eysenck). Defenders of psychoanalysis react to these far-reaching criticisms with certain revisions of the theory or with refutations of the arguments.

This paper reconstructs the core issues, positions, and arguments of this controversy. It takes Freud's theory as a starting point and begins with some remarks about his reasons for classifying his theoretical conception of human mental life as a scientific theory (section "Some Central Claims of Freudian Psychoanalysis"). It then examines further developments of psychoanalytic theorizing (section "Is Freudian Psychoanalytic Theory a Scientific Theory?"), Freudian research methodology (section "Is Freud's Research Methodology a Scientific Methodology?"), and psychodynamic therapy with respect to their scientific status (section "Is Psychodynamic/Psychoanalytic Therapy Scientifically Validated?: A Reflection on Three Stages of Psychotherapy Research"). Due to the absence of a universally accepted definition of the terms "psychoanalytic" and "psychodynamic," both expressions are used interchangeably.

Some Central Claims of Freudian Psychoanalysis

Sigmund Freud was educated in the scientific tradition: he studied medicine, worked in the laboratory of Ernst Brücke on the histology of the nervous system during his studies, collected practical experience as a physician in the areas of psychiatry and neurology, and acquired a lectureship in neuropathology in 1885. Ten years later he wrote a manuscript, later entitled *Project for a Scientific Psychology* (Entwurf einer Psychologie) by the editors, which opens with the words: "The intention of this project is to furnish us with a psychology which shall be a natural science: its aim, that is, is to represent psychical processes as quantitatively determined states of specifiable material particles and so to make them plain and void of contradictions ([Es ist die] Absicht, eine naturwissenschaftliche Psychologie zu liefern, d. h. psychische Vorgänge darzustellen als quantitativ bestimmte Zustände aufzeigbarer materieller Teile [und sie] damit anschaulich und widerspruchsfrei zu machen)" (Freud 1895, p. 387; the English translations of the quotes from Freud are taken from Strachey, 1966–1974). In this work, he tries to describe mental processes as shifts of quantums of energy within the nervous system. So in the years before 1900, he argued for a reductionist view of psychology as a field of natural science based on neurophysiological knowledge of the nervous system – which is a rather popular view in today's scientific psychology. In the following years he gave up this ambitious project, because he considered the neurophysiology of his time to be in a too rudimentary state of development in order to serve as a fruitful basis for his theoretical ideas. Nevertheless, during his entire lifetime he held the view that the psychoanalytic "hypothesis we have adopted of a psychical apparatus extended in space, expediently put together. . .has put us in a position to establish psychology on foundations similar to those of any other science, such, for instance, as physics ([u]nsere Annahme eines räumlich ausgedehnten, zweckmässig zusammengesetzten . . . psychischen Apparates . . . hat uns in den Stand gesetzt, die Psychologie auf einer ähnlichen Grundlage aufzurichten wie jede andere Naturwissenschaft, z. B. wie die Physik)" (Freud 1940, p. 126), as he wrote toward the end of his life in his work *An Outline of Psychoanalysis* (Abriß der Psychoanalyse).

According to Freud, the systematically conceptualized basic theory structure, the so-called metapsychology, is fundamental for the scientific character of psychoanalysis. The basic principles of his metapsychology are already outlined in his most famous book *The Interpretation of Dreams* (Die Traumdeutung 1900). The core of the theory consists (i) in a topography of the mental apparatus (first explicated as three mental subsystems of the Conscious, the Preconscious, and the Unconscious, subsequently superseded by the second topographic model of Id, Ego, and Superego); (ii) the dynamics of the mental apparatus, consisting of the unobservable mental forces that are causing human behavior (of special importance are the defense mechanisms such as repression, sublimation, and resistance); and (iii) the economic dimension of the mental system, explaining repression and other mental processes as shifts and exchanges of energy quantums between the different subsystems of the mental apparatus, directed from a higher level of "bound" energy to lower energy levels (see for a more detailed description of the general structure of Freud's metapsychology: Kitcher 1992, pp. 39–56). Freud defended the scientific status of the theory primarily with reference to its enormous explanatory power: psychologists, who merely theorize about conscious mental phenomena, can only provide fragmentary, scattered, and poor explanations of the complexity and diversity of human behavior. By contrast, it is the psychoanalytic assumption of the Unconscious that allows the causes of human actions, motives, and feelings to be explained in a comprehensive and unifying way (Freud 1940, pp. 80–81).

On the basis of this metapsychology, Freud developed more specific theory elements: a theory of personality and psychosexual development, a theory of psychopathology, and a method of psychotherapy, the psychoanalytic, long-term "talking therapy" with a duration of 300, 400, or more treatment sessions. He made an explicit statement about the cornerstones of psychoanalytic theory ("die Grundpfeiler der psychoanalytischen Theorie") in a paper published in 1923: "The assumption of unconscious psychical processes, the acknowledgement of the theory of resistance and repression, the assessment of sexuality and the Oedipus complex are the chief contents of psychoanalysis and the foundations of its theory, and anyone who does not accept them all should not be considered as a psychoanalyst (Die Annahme unbewußter seelischer Vorgänge, die Anerkennung der Lehre vom Widerstand und der Verdrängung, die Einschätzung der Sexualität und des Ödipus-Komplexes sind die Hauptinhalte der Psychoanalyse und die Grundlagen ihrer Theorie, und wer sie nicht alle gutzuheißen vermag, sollte sich nicht zu den Psychoanalytikern zählen)" (Freud 1923, p. 223). These different theory elements – this was one of his central ideas expressed in the quote – are not isolated from another but are deeply interdependent: the basic principles of metapsychology, the more specific theories, and the ideas about effective psychotherapy (compare section "Is Freud's Research Methodology a Scientific Methodology?" below). According to Freud, these elements have to be seen as a holistic framework for human mental life and mental disorder (see for an introduction to psychoanalysis Brenner 1973 and for a detailed account of the whole theory and its reception Köhler 2000).

Patricia Kitcher (1992) deserves credit for having worked out a detailed reconstruction of the embedding of Freud's theory in the research context of the psychiatry, neurology, and neurophysiology of his time. Kitcher convincingly argues that in the light of his historical background, Freud can be seen as the founder of an innovative "complete interdisciplinary science of mind" and his theory as a methodologically subtle and creative reaction to the groundbreaking developments of nineteenth-century neurology, psychiatry, and psychology. But even if this historical thesis is true and if we admit that Freud's theory was a proper part of science in his time, it may nevertheless be the case that psychoanalysis shares the fate of alchemy and astrology, which were branches of science until the sixteenth century, but subsequently became decoupled from the path of scientific progress and are now considered as pseudosciences by most scientists (Newman and Grafton 2001). The next section will investigate the systematic question of whether the further developments of psychoanalytic theory during the twentieth century justify ascribing to it the status of a scientific project in the context of current scientific research.

Is Freudian Psychoanalytic Theory a Scientific Theory?

Karl Popper's Argument Against the Scientific Status of Psychoanalysis

Karl R. Popper, one of the central figures of the philosophy of science in the twentieth century, formulated a far-reaching argument against the possibility of regarding psychoanalysis as a science. His main point was that psychoanalytic theory does not satisfy the demarcation criterion for science. In his book *Logic of Scientific Discovery*, first published as *Logik der Forschung* in German in 1935, he proposed the falsifiability of empirical theories as the decisive demarcation criterion for drawing a line between science and nonscience (Popper 1935). In contrast to the members of the Vienna Circle (e.g., Rudolf Carnap, Moritz Schlick, and Otto Neurath), who developed verificationism as a semantics and methodology for scientific theories, Popper argued that empirical theories are in fact not verifiable, because the method of induction (which is, according to the members of the Vienna Circle, an indispensable inferential tool for the confirmation of empirical theories) faces serious epistemological problems. As an alternative, Popper developed his falsificationism, which, he claims, is exclusively based on deductive inference. According to this view, empirical theories have to be falsifiable, which means it must be possible that the predictions of the theory conflict with observational data. "Every 'good' scientific theory is a prohibition: it forbids certain things to happen. The more a theory forbids the better it is" (Popper 1963, p. 36). Popper notes that already in 1919, when he became acquainted with Alfred Adler, he began to think about the question of what might be wrong with Marx's theory of history, Adler's individual psychology and Freud's psychoanalysis. He found that the problem of all of these theories is that they do not "forbid" anything to happen, i.e., that *every* course of events is compatible with and can be explained by these theories. This explanatory potential makes these theories attractive and suggestive and may also explain their great popularity. But due to their lack of falsifiability, their explanatory success is merely an illusion, because the theories cannot be tested against reality. "A theory which is not refutable by any conceivable event is non-scientific. Irrefutability is not a virtue of a theory (as people often think) but a vice" (ibid., p. 36). Therefore, according to Popper, psychoanalysis is not a branch of science but a form of psychological metaphysics.

Popper's argument was widely discussed and, in the end, turned out to be unsuccessful, because it faces two serious problems. The first problem lies in Popper's conception of falsifiability itself, which, in contemporary philosophy of science, is almost universally considered as inadequate for demarcating the line between science and nonscience. Popper conceptualizes falsifiability as a two-place relation with one theory in one place and observational evidence in the other. But, as Imre Lakatos convincingly showed, in order to determine the scientific status of a theory, we also have to take into account that scientific theories do not exist in isolation but partake in a scientific discourse along with competing theories and are diachronically embedded in a process of theoretical changes and reformulations. Lakatos developed a more sophisticated and adequate picture of the falsifiability of theories as a three-place relation between the observational evidence and two (or more) rival theories. Accordingly, falsifiability cannot be ascribed to single theories (as Popper claims for Freud's and Adler's theory) but has to take into account the embedding of a theory in a series of developing theories. Popper fails to take into account that these considerations are of crucial importance for evaluating the scientific status of a research program (Lakatos 1978). Furthermore, Popper's conception is a "single focus" approach to demarcation: he allows one and only one criterion for deciding the question of the theory's scientific status. By contrast, in contemporary philosophy of science, most people believe that the complex question of demarcating science and nonscience can only be answered (if at all) by a multi-criteria approach (Ruse 1982).

But Popper's argument fails for a second, even more serious reason. Popper does not present any case studies or any detailed reconstructions of Freud's theory. Other philosophers of science did so and found that psychoanalysis, e.g., Freud's theory of personality, his etiology of adult obsessional neurosis, and his theory of dreams, does in fact include falsifiable statements – which was already recognized by Freud himself (Grünbaum 1979). Furthermore, even if Popper were partially right and it would turn out that some of Freud's theories are not empirically testable in their existing formulation, it remains possible that they could be reformulated in a more precise way that makes them empirically testable.

Reactions to Popper: Establishing Psychoanalysis as a Scientific Project

During the 1940s and 1950s, several psychologists began working on the project of turning psychoanalysis into a scientific research program by looking for empirical evidence supporting it and by conducting experimental tests of psychoanalytic principles. The first person who coined the expression "psychoanalysis as science" was the Stanford psychologist Ernest R. Hilgard (1904–2001), who published a paper and a book with this title in 1952. His main idea was to collect and evaluate all of the experimental evidence available for psychoanalytic theory and psychoanalytic therapy at that time. His initial conclusions concerning the empirical validation of psychoanalysis (although they were refuted later on; see below) were quite euphoric: "[I]t has been possible to parallel many psychoanalytic phenomena in the laboratory. When this is done, the correspondence between predictions according to psychoanalytic theory and what is found is on the whole very satisfactory" (Hilgard 1952b, p. 42). Just a few years later, Ellis (1956) developed operational definitions of central terms of psychoanalytic theory (such as Id, Ego, Superego, phallic phase, libido, Oedipus complex, etc.) in order to enable a reformulation of the psychoanalytic principles in a way that makes transparent how they can be tied to an observational basis and which observable data confirm and which repudiate their existence. In the following years, the empirical methods became tremendously refined and improved, and a number of monographs were published that presented and collected empirical studies and conducted meta-analyses in order to test and validate the basic principles of psychoanalysis in a scientific way (Fisher and Greenberg 1977, 1996; Kline 1981). This development culminated in a book series edited by J. M. Masling, systematically collecting the *empirical studies of psychoanalytical theories* (first volume Masling 1983). So now there is in fact a remarkable body of observational and experimental data generated with the aim of proving the truth of the central claims of psychoanalytic theory.

Contemporary Developments

Nevertheless, it would be too hasty to consider psychoanalysis as a generally accepted and well-established field of scientific psychology today. At present, the issue whether psychoanalysis is satisfactorily confirmed with respect to its core concepts and principles or whether it is proven wrong in the end remains unsettled and is still the subject of highly controversial debates. This can be shown, for example, with reference to the controversial assessment of one of Freud's core ideas: in his introduction to a book about the empirical investigation of the neuronal bases of unconscious mental phenomena, James Uleman concludes that indeed the "psychoanalytic unconscious is, to most laypeople and those in the arts and humanities, the only unconscious," but "it does not provide an influential frame-work for understanding unconscious processes in academic or scientific circles" (Uleman 2005, pp. 4–5). On the other hand, there are approaches for integrating results from psychoanalytic theorizing about unconscious mental phenomena into the context of current scientific research in the neurosciences (Mancia 2006).

These and other highly controversial assessments of the scientific merits of psychoanalytic theory in contemporary discussions in scientific psychology and medicine primarily have two sources. The first is the complex shape and inhomo-geneity of the available empirical evidence. At present, certain assumptions of psychoanalytic theory are confirmed by empirical evidence, whereas others are either not sufficiently supported yet or are regarded as refuted – even by contem-porary psychoanalysts themselves. The latter holds not only for negligible assump-tions but also for some of Freud's most prominent claims: the existence of the Oedipus complex, traditionally seen as one of the core assumptions of his theory of the etiology of neuroses, is only confirmed by rather poor evidence (Kupfersmid 1995). The existence of the death drive, introduced as an antagonistic principle to the libido's "life drive," is currently considered to be clearly refuted in the light of modern evolutionary theory. However, defenders of Freud point out that Freud himself was very uncertain with respect to this element of his theory (introduced by him not until 1917 in rather tentative formulations) and insist that, although the idea of the death drive is wrong, "a number of lessons can be drawn" from it (Black 2011, p. 118). The empirical validation of the existence of repression and resis-tance, both generally regarded as centerpieces of psychoanalytic theory, is a matter of deep controversy (see the extensive discussion of an article by Erdelyi (2006) in the journal *Behavioral and Brain Sciences*). And finally the ideas of penis envy and the castration complex as well as the negligence of female psychosexual development are interpreted as a massive gender bias of Freud's theory (Gyler 2010).

At the same time, there are other psychoanalytic claims which are confirmed by empirical evidence and even by systematic experimentation. Westen (1998) has formulated five principles that he considers to be the core assumptions of current psychodynamic theory:

1. "[M]uch of mental life – including thoughts, feelings, and motives – is unconscious."
2. "[M]ental processes, including affective and motivational processes, operate in parallel so that, toward the same person or situation, individuals can have conflicting feelings that motivate them in opposing ways and often lead to compromise solutions."
3. "[S]table personality patterns begin to form in childhood, and childhood experiences play an important role in personality development."
4. "[M]ental representations of the self, others, and relationships guide people's interactions with others and influence the ways they become psychologically symptomatic."
5. "[P]ersonality development involves not only learning to regulate sexual and aggressive feelings but also moving from an immature, socially dependent state to a mature, interdependent one." (Westen 1998, pp. 334–335)

Westen reviews the evidence in favor of these principles and rates all of them as empirically confirmed to a satisfactory degree. He concludes: "Freud advanced several fundamental propositions, once highly controversial and unique to psychoanalysis, that have stood the test of time … This is probably the best any thinker could hope for in a rapidly developing discipline like ours 60 years after his death" (Westen 1998, p. 362). Of course one should agree with Westen that it would be illegitimate to identify contemporary psychoanalytic theory with Freud's theory and to regard the former as refuted if central claims of the latter are shown to be wrong. But even if it is taken for granted that all of the empirical evidence that Westen refers to is of high methodological quality and therefore entirely convincing, it remains a matter of controversy whether his five principles do in fact capture the essential claims of contemporary psychodynamic theory and if they are specific to it. A closer look at the principles shows that it would be very difficult to find anyone working in contemporary psychology and psychological medicine who questions the truth of principles (4) and (5). Moreover, the other three principles do not seem to be specific to proponents of psychodynamic theory. This holds especially for principle (1), because there are several different conceptions of the Unconscious – as much in current psychology as in the history of the sciences and humanities (see for more details Uleman 2005). In sum, Westen's principles seem to be rather cautiously formulated, and in part they consist in generally accepted psychological assumptions. For this reason, critics of Westen's approach might conclude that it is not too surprising that he is able to offer an attractive number of conclusive empirical evidence for their confirmation.

This discussion leads to the second source of the ongoing controversy regarding the scientific status of psychoanalytic theory. This controversy is not merely a matter of evaluating the quality of empirical evidence alone. Rather, it cannot be solved without answering another crucial question: what is the content specific to current psychoanalytic theory? Which set of assumptions does a proponent of this theory have to accept and which of these assumptions are only accepted by the proponents of the theory? This question cannot be decided on the basis of the available empirical evidence but is related to considerations about the essential theoretical content of the claims of psychoanalytic theorizing. Therefore, this is a highly controversial question even (and especially) between the proponents of psychodynamic theory. What many defenders of psychoanalysis say in favor of their position is that it fell victim to its own success in the sense that some of its claims, historically originating from Freud's theory and empirically well confirmed today, constitute common psychological and medical knowledge, which is accepted by nearly everyone. This might be true. But still the theoretical question remains whether these claims are strong enough to denote a theory core that is specific to psychoanalytic theory (as Westen and others seem to suggest). Only when this question is answered can the controversy about the scientific credibility of psychoanalytic theory be solved.

Is Freud's Research Methodology a Scientific Methodology?

While the scientific status of the content of Freudian theory is currently a matter of controversy, it is widely accepted that the research methodology Freud has introduced as the *via regia* for the empirical validation of psychoanalysis is, from a scientific point of view, the most problematic aspect of psychoanalytic thinking.

Freud himself only used interpretations of individual cases for the empirical confirmation of his theory. In current scientific methodology, this database, especially if used as the only empirical foundation, is generally considered to be poor evidence, because the selection of individual cases is a rather arbitrary process, and the great diversity of phenomena of human behavior and mental life allows for the confirmation of almost any hypothesis by only a small number of cases. Therefore, single case studies are seen as an appropriate heuristic method in theory development and in generating innovative hypotheses, but not as a source of providing evidence for rigorous theory checking.

Freud's way of selecting and interpreting his case studies is also prone to many distortions and biases. Most of the empirical data, cited in his *The Interpretation of Dreams* (1900) with the intention to confirm the basic principles of his metapsychology, are in fact interpretations of the dreams that he himself had during his self-analysis between 1897 and 1899. The other important sources of evidence – especially for the validation of his theory of psychopathology – are detailed analyses of individual patients. Wolpe and Rachman (1960) conducted a reanalysis of his perhaps most famous case study, the first psychoanalysis of a child (published by Freud in 1909 and entitled *Analysis of a Phobia in a five-year-old boy* (Analyse der Phobie eines fünfjährigen Knaben 1909)). Wolpe and Rachman's central criticism was that the study design violates fundamental standards of scientific objectivity: Freud saw the child only once during the treatment, and moreover, the therapy was conducted by the boy's father, whom Freud himself calls one of his "closest adherents." The emotional relation between the father and son, the partiality of the father with respect to Freud's theory, and the selection effects caused by the communication between the boy's father and Freud are all sources of systematic biases. The most important consequence is that a considerable proportion of the results must therefore be considered as a mere effect of suggestion or indoctrination during the therapy. Without any doubt, a patient in a mental crisis who expects help from the therapist (and in particular a 5-year-old boy in his relationship with his father) is predisposed to be influenced by the suggestions that lead him to accept the "truths" of psychoanalysis during the therapy.

Seven years after the publication of the *Analysis of a Phobia in a five-year-old boy*, in his *Introductory lectures on psychoanalysis* (Vorlesungen zur Einführung in die Psychoanalyse 1916/1917), Freud himself accepted that the problem of suggestion and indoctrination is the most important objection to his research method and he developed a counterargument to refute it. The decisive evidence for the truth of psychoanalytic theory consists, according to Freud, in the unique success of psychoanalytic therapy. This is now recognized, in contrast to, say, hypnosis, which Freud abandoned as a therapeutic method, because he considered it liable to suggestion. Consequently, Freud concluded that only psychoanalytic therapy yields a durable cure. His main argument to establish this conclusion is the so-called tally argument, which he presented in the last lecture of the *Introductory lectures* entitled "The analytic therapy" (Die analytische Therapie). It was reconstructed by Adolf Grünbaum (1984, pp. 135–141). This argument is based on two crucial premises:

1. Only psychoanalytic therapy provides the therapeutic option to not merely remove or shift the symptoms (as with other therapeutic procedures such as hypnosis) but to reveal the hidden (unconscious) causes of the patient's neurosis – even if these causes lie deep in the past of the patient's life.
2. Only this process of disclosure of the true causes of the mental problems to the patients can yield a durable cure from their neuroses (and not merely temporary improvements caused by shifts of certain symptoms and reactions).

From these premises Freud deduced the tally argument's main conclusion: every successful psychoanalytic therapy provides striking evidence for psychoanalytic theory, because the truth of psychoanalytic theory is the only explanation for the exclusive success of psychoanalytic therapy. This conclusion implies that a successful psychoanalytic therapy cannot be contaminated by suggestion or indoctrination. For in that case the therapy would merely remove the symptoms for a time and fail to reveal the true causes of the neurosis. But if the true causes of the neurosis remain unrevealed, no durable cure is possible.

Grünbaum criticizes this argument at length. He argues – against Popper – that his reconstruction of the argument shows the empirical testability of Freud's theory. In fact, there are several assumptions derivable from the tally argument's premises that are empirically testable, namely, (i) the only way to achieve a durable cure of a mental disorder is to reveal its true causes and (ii) psychoanalytic therapy is the only therapeutic method that can reveal a mental disorder's true causes. From (i) and (ii) follows (iii), psychoanalytic therapy alone provides a durable cure, which implies (iv), the occurrence of a spontaneous remission is empirically impossible (compare Freud 1909, p. 339), etc. Grünbaum's main point is that many of these assumptions are either not validated or are simply refuted by the available empirical data (Grünbaum 1984, pp. 141–176).

Even though Grünbaum's reconstruction and critique of the tally argument was criticized concerning certain exegetic respects (Esterton 1996), it is widely agreed that his main point is correct: Freud made the crucial mistake of an inadequate conflation of the empirical validation of causal claims of psychoanalytic theory with the empirical evaluation of the efficacy of psychoanalytic therapy (Greenwood 1996). Even the scientifically orientated psychoanalysts mostly admit that this methodological decision of Freud's is a pitfall for the scientific validation of psychoanalytic theory. The tally argument is usually interpreted as an instance of the *post hoc ergo propter hoc* fallacy, the mistake to derive a causal dependence from a temporal succession of events. This reasoning has certain established applications in medical practice – primarily the so-called *diagnosis ex juvantibus* (diagnosis on the basis of successful treatment). But even this special application is controversial and only admissible under restricted conditions: when the consequence is suddenly perceived after the preceding event and no alternative explanations for its occurrence are available (e.g., in the case of providing treacle in an acute hypoglycemia of a diabetic). None of these conditions are fulfilled in psychoanalysis. For this reason one has to conclude that Freud's research methodology fails to provide any conclusive scientific evidence for either psychoanalytic theory or psychodynamic therapy.

Is Psychodynamic/Psychoanalytic Therapy Scientifically Validated?: A Reflection on Three Stages of Psychotherapy Research

One lesson of the last section is that the areas of psychodynamic theory and psychodynamic therapy are considerably more independent from each other than Freud himself thought. This can be seen as good news for the project of the scientific validation of the methods of psychoanalytic therapy. The reason is that even if it turns out to be the case that the central claims of psychoanalytic theory have to be abandoned, psychoanalytic therapy might still be an effective method for the treatment of mental disorders. So the question about empirical evidence for the efficacy and effectiveness of psychoanalytic therapy arises.

First Stage: Clinical Studies and First Meta-Analyses

The progress of empirical research that has been carried out in order to confirm the efficacy and effectiveness of psychoanalytic therapy can be structured in three chronological stages. The first stage, beginning around the year 1950, is characterized by the first comparative experimental testing of different types of psychotherapy and by the attempt to integrate the results of these quite divergent clinical studies into several meta-analyses. In this early stage of psychotherapy research, most of the meta-analyses resulted in one of the following two results. A prominent example for the first result is the research of the psychologist Hans-Jürgen Eysenck, an influential theoretician of intelligence factor theory and defender of behavioral therapy. He conducted an oft-quoted meta-analysis of 24 effectiveness studies of psychotherapy and concluded that the recovery rate of neurotic patients after undergoing a psychoanalytic therapy is not higher than the rate of spontaneous remissions – in his own, somewhat polemic words: "[W]hen we discount the risk the patient runs of stopping treatment altogether, his chances of improvement under psychoanalysis are … slightly worse than his chances under a general practitioner or custodial treatment" (Eysenck 1952, p. 322). The second result, which is not necessarily contradicting Eysenck's verdict and can be found in many meta-analyses of that time, confirms the so-called dodo bird conjecture, named after the dodo bird in Lewis Caroll's *Alice in Wonderland* and its aphorism: "Everybody has won, and all must have prizes." The conjecture says that all types of psychotherapy (psychoanalytic therapy, behavioral therapy, and eclectic approaches) in the end show more or less equivalent outcomes – and if one type of therapy is shown to be superior in a given study, the result usually conforms with the preferences of the investigators (Luborsky et al. 1975). Sometimes this result is interpreted as a methodological artifact: most studies of that time did not reliably distinguish between different mental disorders. It could be that every type of therapy is effective only for some disorders and that the averaging evaluation of therapeutic success over all disorders merely levels out these differences. As a consequence, some psychoanalytically orientated psychotherapists recommended behavioral therapy for minor mental problems and psychodynamic therapy for the treatment of severe mental disorders (Pongratz 1973, p. 378). But there was no empirical evidence for this disorder-specific indication schema (and the current evidence seems to refute it, as shown below). From the present perspective, many of the clinical studies in that stage of research have to be criticized for their methodological deficiencies (subjective or obsolete diagnoses of the investigated mental disorders, unreliable measures of therapeutic success, failures in the statistical evaluations, selection biases in the meta-analyses), which undermine the credibility of the results.

Second Stage: Large-Scale Meta-Analyses

The second stage of psychotherapy research is characterized by the effort to overcome these methodological shortcomings with the help of more sophisticated statistical methods and larger samples of investigated subjects. During the 1980s, Grawe et al. (1994) began to plan and undertake one of these large-scale meta-analyses, which indicated a substantial advance in psychotherapy research. First, they conducted a careful survey of the entire available research literature including all clinical studies ever carried out for the evaluation of psychotherapy – from the beginning of psychotherapy research until 1983/1984. Initially, they found more than 3500 studies. After a criteria-based selection process, 897 of these studies were found to fulfill satisfactory methodological standards. (This means that Grawe et al. included nearly twice as many clinical studies as Smith et al. (1980), a far more influential meta-analysis in the English-speaking literature that includes 475 studies.) These 897 studies served as the data basis for their systematic comparative meta-analysis of more than 40 therapeutic techniques, sorted into three broad therapy types: humanistic therapies, cognitive-behavioral therapies, and psychodynamic therapies. In the area of psychodynamic therapy, they distinguished between nine different therapeutic methods, including classic long-term psychoanalysis, psychoanalytic short-term therapy, Adler's individual therapy, and Binswanger's "Daseinsanalyse." The scientifically best-evaluated methods were the psychoanalytic short-term therapy (29 studies) and psychodynamic therapy combined with medical treatment (13 studies). For the remaining 7 psychodynamic therapies, Grawe et al. found that only 28 studies fitted their criteria. So overall, until 1983, there were merely 70 studies that assessed the efficacy of psychodynamically orientated psychotherapies. By comparison, at the same time there were 452 studies that evaluated the efficacy of the different methods of cognitive-behavioral therapy. Another indicator for the relatively small effort to prove the efficacy of psychodynamic therapy is the fact that Grawe et al. did not find a single study that fulfilled their selection criteria and evaluated classic long-term psychoanalysis, favored by Freud himself. The only systematic and controlled study to evaluate long-term psychoanalysis is the famous and oft-quoted study of the Menninger foundation, which was initiated in 1954 and lasted for more than 20 years. The study was conducted by some of the most prominent psychoanalysts of that time (Otto Kernberg, Robert Wallerstein, Merton Gill, and others) and included 42 patients, all of them suffering from severe neuroses. One reason for the long duration of the study was the average duration of psychoanalytic treatment (of the 15 patients who finished the therapy) of almost 6 years; during this time each patient received 1017 treatments on average. It is a remarkable result that even in this extremely extensive study, undertaken by renowned psychoanalysts, it was in the end not possible to show that the long-term success of psychoanalysis is superior to an alternative psychotherapy with only one third of the treatment sessions (Wallerstein 1986, p. 515).

Grawe et al. (1994) did not include the Menninger study in their meta-analysis due to its methodological shortcomings, but they also conducted a direct comparison between the efficacy of the psychodynamic therapy type on the one hand and the two types of cognitive-behavioral therapy and humanistic therapy on the other hand. They selected the comparative studies and found that, in general, cognitive-behavioral therapy is significantly more effective than both psychodynamic therapies and humanistic therapies. A statistical effect size comparison of the 22 studies (with a total of 487 patients), which included a direct comparison, showed an averaged effect size of 0.83 for psychoanalytic psychotherapy and an averaged effect size of 1.23 for cognitive-behavioral therapy. Significance testing of this difference with the t-test for dependent samples showed that the difference is highly significant ($p < 0.0001$). Grawe et al. (1994, pp. 651–671) interpreted this result as strong evidence for both (i) the efficacy of psychodynamic therapy and also (ii) for the superiority of cognitive-behavioral therapy over the different methods of psychodynamic therapy.

Of course, Grawe and his colleagues' results provoked much criticism, especially from defenders of psychoanalytic therapy. Tschuschke et al. (1998) conducted a reanalysis of the 22 comparative studies from Grawe's meta-analysis. They undertook a systematized rating process by 12 independent psychotherapy researchers in order to evaluate the methodological quality of the studies. This expert rating showed the result that "only 5 or 8 of the 22 studies, respectively, could be accepted for a relatively fair comparison between the treatments under study" (Tschuschke et al. 1998, p. 430). They found all other studies to be either methodologically deficient or systematically biased. Surely, expert ratings have their own problems concerning the impartiality of and the criteria for the selection of the experts. But one systematic problem of many meta-analyses cannot be denied – regardless of how comprehensive their data base may be: the therapeutic interventions that are investigated in the multitude of the included studies (even if they are all summed up under the label of "psychodynamic therapy" or "psychoanalytic therapy") diverge considerably with respect to the dosage and realization of the treatment, the competence and practical experience of the therapist, and the duration of the therapy.

Third Stage: Comparative Psychotherapy Process-Outcome Research

In order to solve this methodological problem, which undoubtedly undermines the interpretability of the results, the third and current stage of psychotherapy research emerged, the so-called comparative psychotherapy process-outcome research. The aim of this branch of research is to empirically examine what exactly happens in the psychotherapeutic process, what the essential features of a certain method of psychotherapy are, and in which respect the properties of different methods and interventional practices diverge. Blagys and Hilsenroth (2000) conducted a study in order to isolate features that distinguish between cognitive-behavioral therapy on the one hand and psychodynamic-interpersonal therapy on the other. They did not only evaluate the theoretical literature on therapy but also generated a database in order to reveal information about the empirically perceived therapeutic processes that characterize the interventions usually labeled as psychoanalytic or psychodynamic therapy. They found seven features that reliably characterize the empirical practice of psychodynamic therapy in contrast to the methods of cognitive-behavioral therapy:

1. A "focus on affect and the expression of patients' emotions"
2. An "exploration of patients' attempts to avoid topics or to engage in activities that hinder the progress of therapy"
3. The "identification of patterns in patients' actions, thoughts, feelings, experiences, and relationships"
4. An "emphasis on past experiences"
5. A "focus on a patients' interpersonal experiences"
6. An "emphasis on the therapeutic relationship"
7. An "exploration of patients' wishes, dreams, or fantasies" (Blagys and Hilsenroth 2000, pp. 169–182)

On the basis of these criteria, it might become possible to define the core elements of psychodynamic treatment and to make clear comparisons between different therapy methods in order to isolate the most effective techniques. "In addition, future research on the relationship between process and outcome can aid in the determination of when and with whom the use of these techniques will be most effective" (Blagys and Hilsenroth 2000, p. 185). This project seems very promising, but it is in an early stage of its development. Presently there are no definite results concerning the efficacy of psychodynamic therapy on the basis of empirically validated process-outcome criteria that would be required for the project.

To sum up, the area of psychotherapy features a research situation that is similar to the stage of the empirical validation of the principles of psychodynamic theory (compare section "Contemporary Developments"). Again, one could question whether claims like Blagys and Hilsenroth's (2000) are strong enough to define a core of methods that can serve as the basis of an autonomous therapy method. Whereas some researchers work on the further development and validation of a specific psychodynamic psychotherapy (Shedler 2010), others regard this project as "confessional" and instead favor the strategy of integrating the most successful interventions from different therapy methods into a unified "professional" psychological psychotherapy (Grawe 1998). But there is no agreement on this matter. There is a great variety of diverging definitions and approaches in today's research on the efficacy of psychotherapy in general and psychodynamic therapy in particular (Levy and Ablon 2009).

Conclusion

This chapter has addressed the question of whether psychoanalysis is a science. Even if Freud himself thought of psychoanalysis as a scientific project, his own methodological conception of the validation of his theory faces serious problems, and given today's scientific standards, it probably has to be considered as the most "unscientific" aspect of his whole conception. His idea to construe the research methodology of psychoanalysis as deeply intertwined with its therapeutic methodology and his claim that therapeutic success is the most important validation for psychoanalytic theory are instances of the *post hoc ergo propter hoc* fallacy and therefore inappropriate for producing any substantial scientific evidence for psychoanalysis.

However, contrary to Popper's critique, it cannot be denied that many claims of the Freudian theory are empirically testable and that since the 1950s, a remarkable body of evidence that fulfills scientific research standards has been generated with the aim of proving the truth of psychoanalytic theory and of evaluating the efficacy of psychoanalytic therapy.

Nevertheless, in contemporary scientific medicine and psychology, it is highly controversial whether – and if so, to which degree – the attempt to confirm the central claims of psychoanalysis with scientific research methods will turn out to be successful. Again, Lakatos' terminology is helpful in order to adequately describe the state of the current discussions of the question about the scientific status of psychoanalysis. In his theory of research programs, Lakatos differentiates between the "hard core" of a research program, which is formed by the axioms, basic principles, and central theorems of the theory and its "protective belt," consisting of more specialized theory elements, paradigmatic heuristics and methods of experimental and observational research, ad hoc hypotheses, etc. (Lakatos 1978, pp. 47–90). Applying this terminology to psychoanalysis, its development during the twentieth century can be described as follows: in Freud's times, psychoanalysis was characterized by an ambitious "hard core" (complex and far-reaching theoretical principles formulated in Freud's extensive writings), but it lacked any substantial scientific validation. The observational and experimental research that has been carried out since the 1950s equipped psychoanalysis with a remarkable "protective belt" and turned it into an influential and well-known research paradigm in psychology, psychiatry, and clinical medicine. In this processual or methodological sense, today's psychoanalysis is a scientific research program. But at the same time, this process led to a significant thinning of the "hard core" of both the content of psychoanalytic theory and the methodology of psychodynamic therapy. The generally accepted theorems that form the common core of psychoanalytic theorizing today are rather cautiously formulated and are not particularly specific. For this reason, the progressiveness of this research program, its relevance for the further development of current psychology, and the philosophy of consciousness as well as the question of the efficacy and effectiveness of an autonomous psychoanalytic therapy remain highly controversial.

Definition of Key Terms

| Unconscious | A core concept of Freud's theory, introduced as an element of Freud's first topographic model of the mental apparatus, structuring the mind into three parts: the Conscious, the |

Preconscious, and the Unconscious. Freud was convinced that every instance of human behavior, motive, or feeling must have a mental cause. He regarded the Unconscious as the source of all of the "hidden" causes that have to be assumed as the basis of a comprehensive and unified explanation of any phenomena of human mental life.

Repression   A core concept of Freud's theory, introduced in order to describe the dynamics of human mental life. Mental content that is felt to be too awkward, displeasing, or painful to cope with is repressed in the Unconscious. These mental contents cause various mental phenomena (e.g., dreams or neurotic symptoms) that represent the repressed content in a deformed way to the Conscious.

Significance level   Statistical measure to specify the probability that a certain property, effect, or group difference measured in the study sample also exists in the overall population. A significance level of 5 % ($p = 0.05$) indicates that the investigated condition measured in the sample is also present in the overall population with a probability of 95 %. In other words, a probability of 5 % indicates that the study results do not represent a condition of the population but are merely due to a sampling error.

Effect size   Statistical measure to quantify the size or magnitude of a measured effect. This statistical measure is particularly relevant in psychotherapy outcome research, because the focus here is not only to show that the investigated treatment has an effect but also to show the magnitude of the effects. Significance levels are not helpful in this respect, because they do not contain any direct information about the magnitude of the measured effects or conditions. A metric that is often used for determining effect sizes is normalized with reference to standard deviations. So if an effect size of 1 is reported in order to quantify the success of a therapy, this means that the comparison between the average health status of the patients before and after the therapy showed a gain of one standard deviation.

Randomized con-   Study type which is currently regarded as the methodolog-
trolled trial (RCT)   ical "gold standard" in (clinical) psychology and medicine. In this field, RCTs are primarily used to conduct fair checks of the effectiveness and efficacy of innovative treatments. RCTs contain at least two subsamples, a treatment group, and one or more control groups. The treatment group receives the treatment under investigation, and the control group(s) receives either an alternative treatment or a placebo. The assignment of the participants to the different

	groups is carried out randomly as a statistical means for controlling the influence of distorting effects that are unknown to the researchers.
Meta-analysis	Complex statistical procedure for integrating the results of a multitude of single studies. The aim is to strengthen the validity of the results by considering as much information as possible, avoiding the effects of one-sidedness and balancing the methodological limitations of individual studies. The main problem of meta-analyses is the diversity of the included studies, which is a challenge for the applied statistical methods and may affect the interpretability of the results.
Post hoc ergo propter hoc fallacy	The fallacy to derive conclusions about causal dependencies from the mere temporal succession of events.

Summary Points

- Although there are different theories which are called "psychoanalytic" (not just Sigmund Freud's theory but also Carl G. Jung's theory of archetypes and the collective unconscious, Alfred Adler's individual psychology, Melanie Klein's object relations theory, etc.), the debate concerning the scientific status of psychoanalysis centers primarily around psychoanalytic theorizing in the Freudian tradition.
- The controversy about the scientific status of Freudian theory originated primarily from the fundamental criticism that psychoanalysis is a pseudoscience, along with astrology, homeopathy, or Marx's historical materialism.
- In order to provide an elaborate answer to the question to which extent the project of validating psychoanalysis with scientific methods is judged to be successful in contemporary science, it is necessary to differentiate between psychoanalytic theory, psychodynamic therapy, and the research methodology applied in the Freudian tradition.
- It is widely accepted that the research methodology Freud has introduced as the *via regia* for the empirical validation of psychoanalysis is, from a scientific point of view, the most problematic aspect of psychoanalytic thinking. It is generally seen as an instance of the *post hoc ergo propter hoc* fallacy and therefore as inappropriate for producing any substantial scientific evidence.
- However, since the 1950s, a remarkable body of evidence that fulfills scientific research standards has been generated with the aim of proving the central theoretical claims of psychoanalysis and the efficacy of psychoanalytic/psychodynamic therapy.
- The scientifically validated theorems that form the common core of today's psychoanalytic theory are – in sharp contrast to Freud's original theory – rather carefully formulated. It is generally seen as an open question whether these claims are strong enough to denote a theory core that is specific to psychoanalytic theory.

- The area of psychotherapy features a research situation that is similar to the stage of the empirical validation of psychoanalytic theory. Again, one could question whether the essential claims of current psychodynamic therapy are strong enough to define a core of methods that can serve as the basis of an autonomous therapy method.
- The progressiveness of psychoanalysis as a scientific research program, its relevance for the further development of current psychology and medicine, and the question of the efficacy and effectiveness of an autonomous psychoanalytic therapy remain highly controversial.

References

Black DM (2011) Why things matter. The place of values in science, psychoanalysis and religion. Routledge, Hove/New York

Blagys MD, Hilsenroth MJ (2000) Distinctive features of short-term psychodynamic-interpersonal psychotherapy: a review of the comparative psychotherapy process literature. Clin Psychol Sci Pract 7(2):167–188

Brenner C (1973) An elementary textbook of psychoanalysis. International Universities Press, New York

Chiesa M (2010) Research and psychoanalysis: still time to bridge the great divide? Psychoanal Psychol 27(2):99–114

Ellis A (1956) An operational reformulation of some of the basic principles of psychoanalysis. In: Feigl H, Scriven M (eds) The foundations of science and the concepts of psychology and psychoanalysis. University of Minnesota Press, Minneapolis, pp 131–154

Erdelyi MH (2006) The unified theory of repression. Behav Brain Sci 29:499–551

Esterson A (1996) Grünbaum's tally argument. Hist Hum Sci 9(1):43–57

Eysenck H-J (1952) The effects of psychotherapy: an evaluation. J Consult Psychol 16(5):319–324

Fisher S, Greenberg RP (1977) The scientific credibility of Freud's theories and therapy. Basic Books, New York

Fisher S, Greenberg RP (1996) Freud scientifically reappraised: testing the theories and therapy. Wiley, New York

Freud S (1895) Entwurf einer Psychologie (Project for a scientific psychology). Quoted from: Freud S (1987) Gesammelte Werke Nachtragsband. Fischer, Frankfurt am Main, pp 375–486

Freud S (1900) Die Traumdeutung (The interpretation of dreams). Quoted from: Freud S (1941) Gesammelte Werke, vols 2 & 3 (GW II & III). Imago Publishing Co, London

Freud S (1909) Analyse der Phobie eines fünfjährigen Knaben (Analysis of a Phobia in a five-year-old boy). Quoted from: GW VII, pp 241–377

Freud S (1916/1917) Vorlesungen zur Einführung in die Psychoanalyse (Introductory lectures on psychoanalysis). Quoted from: GW XI

Freud S (1923) "Psychoanalyse" und "Libidotheorie" (Two encyclopedia articles). Quoted from: GW XIII, pp 209–233

Freud S (1940) Abriß der Psychoanalyse (An outline of psychoanalysis). Internationale Zeitschrift für Psychoanalyse 25:7–67. Quoted from: GW XVII, pp 63–138

Grawe K (1998) Psychologische Therapie. Hogrefe, Göttingen

Grawe K, Donati R, Bernauer F (1994) Psychotherapie im Wandel. Von der Konfession zur Profession. Hogrefe, Göttingen

Greenwood JD (1996) Freud's 'tally' argument, placebo control treatments, and the evaluation of psychotherapy. Philos Sci 63(4):605–621

Grünbaum A (1979) Is Freudian psychoanalytic theory pseudo-scientific by Karl Popper's criterion of demarcation? Am Philos Q 16(2):131–141

Grünbaum A (1984) The foundations of psychoanalysis. University of California Press, Berkeley

Gyler L (2010) The gendered unconscious. Can gender discourses subvert psychoanalysis? Routledge, London/New York

Habermas J (1968) Erkenntnis und Interesse. Suhrkamp, Frankfurt am Main

Hilgard ER (1952a) Psychoanalysis as science. Eng Sci 16:11–17

Hilgard ER (1952b) Experimental approaches to psychoanalysis. In: Hilgard ER, Kubie LS, Pumpian-Mindlin E (eds) Psychoanalysis as science. Greenwood Press, Westport, pp 4–45

Kitcher P (1992) Freud's dream. A complete interdisciplinary science of mind. The MIT Press, Cambridge, MA/London

Kline P (1981) Fact and fantasy in Freudian theory, 2nd edn. Methuen, London/New York

Köhler T (2000) Das Werk Sigmund Freuds. Entstehung – Inhalt – Rezeption. Pabst Science Publishers, Lengerich/Berlin/Riga

Kupfersmid J (1995) Does the Oedipus complex exist? Psychother Theory Res Pract Train 32 (4):535–547

Lakatos I (1978) Falsification and the methodology of scientific research programmes. In: Worrall J, Currie G (eds) The methodology of scientific research programmes. Philosophical papers, vol 1. Cambridge University Press, Cambridge, pp 8–101

Levy RA, Ablon JS (2009) Evidence-based psychodynamic psychotherapy. Bridging the gap between science and practice. Humana Press, New York

Luborsky L, Singer B, Luborsky L (1975) Comparative studies of psychotherapy. Arch Gen Psychiatry 32:995–1008

Mancia M (2006) Psychoanalysis and neuroscience. Springer, Milan

Masling JM (ed) (1983) Empirical studies of psychoanalytical theories, vol 1. Analytic Press, Hillsdale

Newman WR, Grafton A (2001) Secrets of nature. Astrology and alchemy in early modern Europe. MIT Press, Cambrdige, MA/London

Pongratz LJ (1973) Lehrbuch der klinischen Psychologie. Psychologische Grundlagen der Psychotherapie. Hogrefe, Göttingen

Popper KR (1935) Logik der Forschung. Mohr Siebeck, Tübingen

Popper KR (1963) Conjectures and refutations: the growth of scientific knowledge. Basic Books, New York

Ricœur P (1965) De l'interpretation: essai sur Freud. Edition du Seuil, Paris

Ruse M (1982) Creation science is not science. Sci Technol Hum Values 7(40):72–78

Shedler J (2010) The efficacy of psychodynamic psychotherapy. Am Psychol 65(2):98–109

Smith ML, Glass GV, Miller TI (1980) The benefits of psychotherapy. Johns Hopkins University Press, Baltimore

Strachey J (1966–1974) Standard edition of the complete works of Sigmund Freud. Vol. I-XXIV. Vintage, London

Tschuschke V, Bänninger-Huber E, Faller H et al (1998) Psychotherapy research – how it should (not) be done. An expert reanalysis of comparative studies by Grawe et al. (1994). Psychother Psychosom Med Psychol 48(11):430–444

Uleman JS (2005) Introduction: becoming aware of the new unconscious. In: Hassin RR, Uleman JS, Bargh J (eds) The new unconscious. Oxford University Press, Oxford/New York, pp 3–15

Wallerstein RS (1986) Forty-two lives in treatment: a study in psychoanalysis and psychotherapy. Guilford Press, New York

Westen D (1998) The scientific legacy of Sigmund Freud: toward a psychodynamically informed psychological science. Psychol Bull 124(3):333–371

Wolpe J, Rachman S (1960) Psychoanalytic "evidence": a critique on Freud's case of Little Hans. J Nerv Ment Dis 130(8):135–148

Part VI

Nosology

WHO's Definition of Health: Philosophical Analysis

59

Jerome Bickenbach

Contents

Abstract

The notorious World Health Organization definition of health as "a state of complete physical, mental and social well-being and not merely the absence of disease or infirmity" has been roundly, and justifiably, criticized by philosophers more or less since it first appeared in 1948. Despite its obvious conceptual, and practical, limitations, it launched a highly productive debate about the nature of health in which two major strategies have dominated: a descriptive or naturalistic approach in which health is operationally defined in terms of normal functioning understood entirely in the language of the biological sciences and a normative approach which insists that health cannot be understood until the salient fact that health is a human good is explained. This debate has revealed a dilemma: any philosophically acceptable definition of health must make a place for our powerful intuitions that health is both intrinsically and instrumentally valuable. Yet, unless the notion is firmly grounded in the biological sciences and

J. Bickenbach (✉)
Human Functioning Sciences, Swiss Paraplegic Research, Nottwil, Switzerland
e-mail: jerome.bickenbach@paraplegie.ch

© Springer Science+Business Media Dordrecht 2017
T. Schramme, S. Edwards (eds.), *Handbook of the Philosophy of Medicine*,
DOI 10.1007/978-94-017-8688-1_48

susceptible to operationalization, it threatens to lose its scientific legitimacy. WHO has more recently and with far less fanfare, developed another definition of health "for measurement purposes" that recognizes the force of the dilemma and attempts, with debatable success, to address it.

Introduction

In the Constitution of the World Health Organization, approved in 1948, health is famously defined as "a state of complete physical, mental and social well-being and not merely the absence of disease or infirmity" (WHO 1948). The extreme breadth of the definition – "physical, mental and social well-being" – and its unrealistically high threshold of good health, "complete," made it tempting to dismiss the definition as an aspirational gesture emblematic of a new era of optimism in international public health. Yet, philosopher Daniel Callahan took it seriously in 1973 and roundly criticized the definition for fatal overreach, arguing that to define "health" in terms of "well-being" transforms human happiness into a medical outcome and social ills like injustice, economic scarcity, and discrimination into medical problems requiring medical solutions (Callahan 1973).

Despite these limitations, however, in retrospect the WHO definition has considerably enriched the philosophical debate over the nature of health. It set the stage for an important and ongoing dispute between normative accounts of health and far more restrictively biological or biostatistically grounded views. Although there has recently been a resurgence of the strongly normative, WHO-style definitions, ironically WHO itself has taken steps toward a more narrow view motivated by the need to develop a conceptualization suitable to "operationalize health for measurement purposes" (Salomon et al. 2003).

The current situation reflects a dilemma: any philosophically acceptable definition must make a place for our powerful intuitions that health is both intrinsically and instrumentally valuable. Yet, unless the notion is firmly grounded in the biological sciences and so susceptible to operationalization, it threatens to lose its scientific legitimacy. Specifically, without operationalization, scientists will be unable to compare, let alone measure, the difference in the health of two individuals, or the same individual before and after a health intervention, or by extension of the relative health of subpopulations of individuals. The capacity for ordinal, if not cardinal, comparisons of states of health is not merely a scientific desideratum; it is essential for any scientific or policy application of the notion, including in particular the assessment of the performance of clinical health care or public health systems. But if the cost of securing scientific legitimacy is to undercut the commonly held belief that health is a human good (indeed, a plausible human right), then the resulting conceptualization is philosophically objectionable for a different reason. The more recent WHO definition of health "for measurement purposes" was developed with recognition of this dilemma, but it arguably fails to address it adequately.

In this chapter, the philosophical evolution of WHO's contribution to the definition – or more accurately, the conceptualization – of health will be traced and its philosophical impact described. The original, 1948 definition, and its philosophical critique, is the starting point. The critique began a fruitful philosophical debate between two starkly different approaches to health conceptualization represented here by Christopher Boorse's biostatistical account and Lennart Nordenfelt's action-theoretical normative account. What arises out of this debate is a philosophical impasse in which both approaches fall short, for opposing reasons. After a review of a recent resurgence of normativism that so far seems only to have reprised the problems of WHO's original definition, this chapter turns to the current endpoint in the evolution of WHO's definition of health and its limitations.

WHO Definition of Health: A Philosophical Evolution

The 1948 WHO Definition and Its Philosophical Critique

The Preamble to the Constitution of the World Health Organization, adopted and signed immediately after World War II in 1946, and entered into force in 1948, set out principles governing the establishment of this first international organization devoted to human health:

> Health is a state of complete physical, mental and social well-being and not merely the absence of disease or infirmity.
> The enjoyment of the highest attainable standard of health is one of the fundamental rights of every human being without distinction of race, religion, political belief, economic or social condition.
> The health of all peoples is fundamental to the attainment of peace and security and is dependent upon the fullest co-operation of individuals and States.
> The achievement of any State in the promotion and protection of health is of value to all.
> (WHO 1948)

The first clause, whether it had been so intended or not, was quickly picked up as a definition of health. (Few noticed that it conflicted with the next principle inasmuch as the "highest attainable standard of health" suggests a flexible threshold of health, but the definition itself sets that threshold at "complete.") Implicit in the Preamble as a whole was a view attributed to sociologist HE Sigerist that health must be more than the absence of a problem; it must also be something positive (Sigerist 1941; Breslow 2006). Health is not merely an enjoyable state; it is something people seek out because it is both intrinsically and instrumentally valuable. The other innovation of the WHO definition – that health had mental and social dimensions – reflected the commonplace view that people are complex, biological, psychological, and social entities. Neither these two aspects of the definition were particularly controversial; it was the identification of health with human well-being that critics balked at.

In 1973, philosopher Daniel Callahan argued that the definition caters to a "cultural tendency" to define social problems as health problems, thereby blurring the lines of responsibility between the political order and the medical profession (Callahan 1973). Callahan noted, as others before him had (e.g., Wylie 1970), that the current rhetoric "medicalized" social problems because of a "grandiose" faith in science to cure sickness in all forms, biological, psychological, and social. This unbounded optimism, he insisted, was simply without empirical support. Neither is it plausible to suggest that all social evils are either caused by or examples of bad health: it is far more likely that political injustice and economic scarcity are the causes of these problems. Finally, transforming all human evils into health problems undermines human freedom and responsibility.

The ideological assumptions bound up in the WHO definition led philosophically to an abuse of language and common sense, Callahan concluded. Surely, the normativity of health can be preserved without insisting that it is the source of all human value. Health is undoubtedly a human good, but it is not the only human good. Some minimal level of health is probably essential to achieve any possibility of human happiness; yet, at the same time, some degree of ill-health is perfectly compatible with happiness, given that no one could hope to be in a state of "complete physical, mental, and social well-being."

To explain what might have gone wrong, Callahan observed that health is intuitively both a natural norm and an ethical ideal. Viewed as a norm, health is simply a matter of the heart, lungs, kidneys, and other body parts functioning up to a threshold of normality that can be established empirically and statistically. Yet, Callahan noted that thinking about health as a norm is unsatisfying because it does not address the obvious question why anyone would care about statistically normal functioning unless dipping below that threshold was unpleasant, inconvenient, painful, or generally a bad thing. Why too should society take any interest in subnormal bodily functioning unless, in the aggregate, it has socially adverse implications? There is no escaping the intuition that health is not merely the description of a state of biological affairs, matched against some statistically determined norm; it is also an ideal people take very seriously indeed. Health is a morally significant normal bodily functioning.

The philosophical challenge, however, is to do justice to both health as norm and as ideal. To insist that health describes a state of affairs, in principle reducible to biological and psychological functioning, and assessed in light of norms generated by population statistics (the basis for what came to be called descriptive theories of health) fails to capture intuitions about what makes health valuable; yet, accounts that focus on the normative significance of biological and psychological functioning (normative theories) fail for their part to provide a sound conceptual basis for the health sciences. The WHO 1948 definition thus became the starting point for an increased philosophical interest in the conceptualization of health. Whether motivated by a rejection of the WHO definition or an affirmation of its underlying insights, the subsequent philosophical literature took the definition as its starting point.

Normative and Descriptive Accounts of Health: Boorse and Nordenfelt

The most prominent advocate of the descriptive approach to health is Christopher Boorse who in a series of seminal articles in the mid 1970s mapped out what has come to be called the "biostatistical theory of health" (Boorse 1975, 1976, 1977). Initially, his concern was to reject normativism in health, especially in the characterization of mental health and in particular a rejection of the WHO definition. He did so in terms of the conceptual difference between a disease and an illness, the first being a biological state of pathology and the second a normative disvalued experience, roughly linked to pathology. Only the first is directly relevant to the conceptualization of health.

Boorse argued that biological functions can be fully described in terms of a hierarchy of goals ascribable to different levels of organisms: cells have metabolism functions, organs have body level functions such as blood circulation, whole organisms have eating and moving around functions, and all of these functions causally contribute to the species-typical goals of survival and reproduction. But this teleology need not be normatively understood since at the end of the day this is simply how organisms behave. So understood, the health of an organism is functional normality. The notion of a biological function is central to Boorse's approach (Boorse 1976), and philosophically it has drawn the most criticism from those who, in general terms, are otherwise quite sympathetic to Boorse's descriptivism (e.g., Engelhardt 1984; Caplan 1993; Beauchamp and Childress 2001).

All descriptivists concur that functional normality can be neutrally described, despite the fact that the state of functional normality tends to be judged as desirable. This is because the evaluation of normality is based on grounds and for reasons that are only tangentially relevant to individual biology or evolutionary theory. Thus, it is quite easy to imagine a "better" normal functioning than that which evolution has provided human beings; on the other hand, in some circumstances having a disease contributes to overall well-being (if, e.g., the disease would disqualify a person from military conscription). Describing and valuing are fundamentally different operations, and there is no reason to think they must be essentially linked in the conceptualization of health.

Pressed to explain the biological significance of "normal functioning," Boorse argued that normality is primarily a statistical construct guided by scientific assumptions about or hard evidence about species-typical functioning levels. Diseases are theoretical entities health scientists defined in terms of signs and symptoms of less-than-optimal functioning at some biological level – ultimately, reflecting the evolutionary imperative of species survival. Other descriptivist accounts have put more reliance that Boorse did on the power of evolutionary theory and homeostasis to account for normality in functioning (Bechtel 1985; Kovács 1998; Ananth 2008).

For Boorse's part, he acknowledged that functional normality was neither a necessary nor sufficient condition of health (red hair is not statistically normal, and there are diseases such as tooth decay that are nearly universal). But as an operationalization of disease (or more generally ill-health), functional normality is the most reliable indicator. Should the biological sciences devise a more sensitive indicator – perhaps one that incorporates epigenetic insights or some other more fundamental level of explanation – then scientists would turn to it. But, philosophically, the quality and reliability of the indicator of functional normality are irrelevant: at the bottom, the concept of health is in principle fully describable in normatively neutral terms. That health is universally valued and decrements in health caused by disease and injury universally disvalued are sociological facts that explain health-seeking behaviors, but they are conceptually independent of the nature of health and decrements of health.

Although on the first blush nothing could seem to be further from the WHO definition than Boorse's account (and such was his intention), in fact they are not incompatible in at least one respect: no advocate of the WHO definition would deny that health and mechanisms involve in impairing health are at the bottom biological phenomena. Arguably, the WHO definition only tells us the manner in which health is valuable to human beings – why it is individually and socially important – but leaves to biological scientists the description of states of health and ill-health. The normativist, in short, need not advocate the abandonment of the biological sciences or medical practice – he or she is merely interested in a different, but more salient, conceptual feature of health: why we value it.

Lennart Nordenfelt has been the leader in this second, normativist approach to health conceptualization, arguing that health cannot be understood philosophically unless and until it is clear why it is valuable. Health is not merely a biological norm, it is an ideal (Nordenfelt 1987, 1993). Health is about the capacity to act and to live a full life according to one's life plans. More formally, a person is healthy just in case he or she is in a bodily and mental state such that he or she has the ability to realize all his or her vital goals, in standard circumstances. A vital goal for an individual is one that is necessary for minimal happiness (understood robustly as a version of Aristotle's eudaimonia and not merely positive affect).

Nordenfelt took care to avoid some obvious traps of his theory. He took into account and sought to explain some apparent counterexamples, e.g., that people are often mistaken about what they believe will make them happy and that they can sincerely hold unrealizably vital goals or can, by pure luck, achieve minimal happiness despite utterly lacking the ability to do so. In particular, he recognized that a person may achieve minimal happiness with acceptable health, a level far below complete health. Like Boorse, in short, Nordenfelt begins with the WHO definition, but in his case he is more sympathetic to it and hoped to preserve it by crafting a philosophically sophisticated version that avoids obvious criticism.

But Nordenfelt was also keen to reject Boorse's biostatistical theory, not because he thought that health was not rooted in biology but because the mechanisms that limit individual health cannot be identified as diseases or injuries simply because they result in statistically abnormal levels of biological functioning at some level of the organism. That is not how medical theorists have identified diseases and other decrements of health, he insisted. Always in the forefront is the view that only abnormalities in functioning that also reduce the ability of the individual from realizing his or her vital goals, and so achieving minimal happiness, are decrements in health. Diseases are identified through the lens of vital goals in the first instances and only then in terms of biological abnormality of functioning.

Nordenfelt and normativists generally characterize their views as being holistic in the sense that health is intuitively attributed to individual persons and only metaphorically and by extension to cells and organs (or by aggregation to populations). And on this they have common intuitions on their side: "To be healthy is to function well. It is to feel strong and vital. It is to lack pain and disability. It is to be able to work, to be able to handle one's daily life and enjoy one's life." (Nordenfelt 1993, 83) A concern about cells, organs, and biological functions is the (perfectly legitimate) concern about the mechanisms behind the phenomena of health and disease. Scientists need to know about the bodily machinery to inform their health sciences. But conceptually, the biomedical sciences cannot explain why it is commonly understood that hearing or vision loss, pain, infections, or diseases like diabetes, spinal cord injury, or cancer matter very much to human being or why societies invest social resources into responding to these problems in living. Conceptually, the only way to explain these hard facts is an account of health that centers on what matters to people with respect to their bodily and mental functioning, and this must, in one way or another, analytically connect with human well-being.

Recent Resurgence of Interest in Normativism

The philosophical debate between Boorse and Nordenfelt and their defenders was at its height from the late 1970s to the early 1990s, primarily in the English-speaking philosophical world. It was also during this period that the WHO discovered that it could make good political use of its 1948 definition to further the cause of international public health. In a series of important declarations and other pronouncements during this period, WHO was able to transform its definition into a successful advocacy tool by highlighting an implicit theme of the definition: that health promotion is not exclusively a matter of developing more and more sophisticated medical diagnostic and prevention tools; it is also, and often more importantly, a matter of isolating the social determinants of ill-health across the population. As one of WHO leading advocates of the human right to health Jonathan Mann put it, the WHO definition "helped to move health thinking beyond a limited, biomedical and pathology-based perspective to the more positive domain of "well-being."" In addition, by explicitly including the mental and social dimensions of well-being, WHO radically expanded the scope of health and, by extension, the roles and responsibilities of health professionals and their relationship to the larger society (Mann et al. 1994; Kickbusch 2003).

Perhaps because of the lasting significance of the 1948 WHO definition in international public health, there has been a resurgence of interest in normative conceptualizations of health in recent years. Although some philosophers found some common ground in the two approaches (Schramme 2007), others, especially in the area of mental health, argued that the Boorsian natural function approach was unable to account for why mental illnesses are viewed as problematic (Varga 2011). Normativism seems to have won out. Unfortunately, the rejection of descriptivism has also led to normative accounts that lack the philosophical rigor of Nordenfelt's theory with the result that they have reprised some of the peculiarities of the WHO 1948 definition.

In 2011, Machteld Huber and colleagues proposed an "adaptation" of the WHO definition made necessary by the profound epidemiological shift in the worldwide burden of disease since 1948 from acute and communicable diseases to noncommunicable diseases, a shift made more dramatic by population aging and the fact that people are living longer with chronic diseases (Huber et al. 2011). These facts convinced the authors of the need to take into account the increasing importance, in public health, for individuals to adapt to environmental changes and to self-manage their chronic illnesses.

For a descriptivist, adaptation and self-management are irrelevant to the conceptualization of health and ill-health, although certainly significant to frame health intervention at clinical and population levels. If self-management, for example, helps to limit the range of potential comorbidities or functional consequences of a chronic condition such as high blood pressure, then interventions should properly focus on developing self-management skills. Chronic health conditions are by definition incurable – although their onset may be preventable – so addressing adaptation and self-management seems imminently sensible.

For a normativist, the importance of adaptation and self-management takes on a very different role in helping to explain the underlying human value that effective health interventions enhance. This focus leads Huber and colleagues to conclude that since an adequate level of capability to adapt and self-manage enhances one's well-being, it follows that health *is* the capability to adapt and self-manage. Moreover, since they are eager to affirm that "social health" is an essential component of health, they require a version of this self-management capability for the social sphere. For this purpose, they included in their account the capability "to participate in social activities including work."

The end result is a definition of health that falls victim to two substantial logical confusions (that normativist accounts tend to be prone to). The first is to conflate cause and effect: in our example, to confuse the impact of a plausible social determinant of health – for example, unemployment rates or some other force limiting the effectiveness of an individual to secure "social health" – with a component of the concept of health. Another more blatant example of this confusion at work can be found in the so-called Meikirch Model of Health in which good health is conceptualized as "individual potentials" – either biologically given or "personally acquired" – that produces a capacity that allows an individual to adequately or optimally respond to the "demands of life" in a context shaped by social and environmental determinants (Bircher and Kuruvill 2014). Personally acquired individual potentials are claimed to include "all of the physiological, mental, and social resources a person acquires during life" – that is to say, resources such as a good job, loving family relationships, educational attainment, and income level. Here again, plausible determinants of health are conflated with components of the concept of health.

The second logical error inherent in the Huber et al. definition is reductivism. For his part, Nordenfelt was careful to characterize the normative essence of health in very open and general terms, namely, as "a bodily and mental state sufficient for the ability to realize one's vital goals." Arguably, the ability to adapt and self-manage is part of that general ability, and indeed it may well be a necessary condition of the ability to realize vital goals. But it is very unlikely to be a sufficient condition for that general ability. If a person has a low level of self-esteem or personality characteristics that undermine his or her motivation to use highly developed skills to adapt and self-manage, then it is unlikely that this person would be able to realize his or her vital goals. Alternatively put, although it would be helpful to one's health to be able to adapt and self-manage, it is certainly imaginable that a person who was a terrible self-manager, by good luck, nonetheless enjoys full health. By reducing the normative essence of health to a single, albeit important, capability, the Huber et al. account is vulnerable to damning counterexamples.

Recent normativist accounts have also reprised what, to many critics, was the main problem with the WHO definition: an exaggeration of the importance of health as a human value. One recent normativist theory demonstrates this problem in stark terms. Building on Amartya Sen's influential capability theory (see, e.g., Sen 1999), Sridhar Venkatapuram has conceptualized health in terms of its potential as a "meta-capability" (Venkatapuram 2011). Incorporating but greatly expanding Nordenfelt's account of health, Venkatapuram has argued that health is both a necessary and sufficient capability to achieve all aspects of the good human life, well-being at its most expansively defined – a veritable *summum bonum*. The social impact of this normative inflation is noteworthy: Venkatapuram argues that the importance of health is such that a truly just society will be organized so as to effectively respond to every potential determinant of health so as to eliminate all forms of inequalities, physical or social, in the name of population health. This is health overreach on a grand level.

WHO's New Approach

The recent proliferation of normativist definitions of health reflects a continuation of the tradition which begun with the WHO definition in 1948, inspired by the insight that health is an aspect of human flourishing and so intrinsically a good thing for all to enjoy. What makes health a good thing and whether it is the only human good or just an especially or uniquely important one are open questions, and a normative theory will gain or lose credibility depending on how it addresses them. But though the WHO definition can be credited with the "normative turn" in conceptualizing health, recently as part of a multiyear project for health system performance assessment (WHO 2000), WHO has taken a step clearly in the direction of a descriptivist approach to health, a conceptualization of health "for measurement purposes."

Although informed by Boorsian descriptivism, WHO's more recent account of health was only possible because the development of WHO's *International Classification of Functioning, Disability and Health* (ICF) (WHO 2001). ICF is an epidemiological standard, a classification and coding system for health and disability data. Significantly, it is grounded in the notion of human "functioning," which parallels Boorse's own notion of "function" (Boorse 1976). ICF is a classification of domains of human functioning, discrete body functions (including mental functions), bodily structures, and the full range of simple to complex human behaviors, actions, and complex social patterns of behaviors and actions (such as being a sibling, being employed, participating in community activities). The ICF, in short, is a complete classification of human functioning for the purpose of operationalizing health.

The motivation for WHO's new definition of health is measurement, without which it is not possible to compare health over time between individuals, individuals over time, and across populations and over time (Salomon et al. 2003). Without meaningful measures of health, the goals of public health are unachievable: it would be impossible to know whether public health interventions changed health or reduced health inequalities across subpopulations. Without measurement there is no proper science of health. It has been a standard practice, at least in public health, to "measure" health states of populations in terms of standardized health indicators, such as incidence of chronic illnesses, infant mortality rates, or population survivorship rates (see examples in Goldsmith 1972; Bergner 1985; McDowell 2006). Indicators are, of course, proxy measures, and it was the goal of WHO to achieve a more robust measurement of health by means of an operational conceptualization of the notion. At the same time, the authors appreciate that little would be gained if the resulting conceptualization was too distant from the common notion of health and in particular our intuitions about health as a human value. Thus, the first step in the development of a new WHO definition of health, therefore, was to identify "consensus points" about the concept of health:

1. Health is a separate concept from well-being, and is of intrinsic value to human beings as well as being instrumental for other components of wellbeing;
2. Health is comprised of states or conditions of functioning of the human body and mind, and therefore any attempts to measure health must include measures of body and mind function; and
3. Health is an attribute of an individual person, although aggregate measures of health may be used to describe populations. (Salomon et al. 2003, 303)

It follows from these simple propositions that there is a clear, conceptual distinction between health and its determinants and consequences, a confusion that is the downfall of many normativist accounts of health. The distinction between determinant and concept follows straightforwardly from the first clause of the third consensus point, as does the core descriptivist premise that the language of health is that of the biological sciences. Income levels, employment rates, and social networks – all of these phenomena are likely determinants of a person's health, but for all of that, they are not attributes of an individual person and so not part of the concept of health.

The second consensus point is the essence of the new WHO account of health as "an intrinsic, multidimensional attribute of individuals" with universal, cross-population, and cross-cultural validity. The account is universal simply because it is grounded in states or conditions of functioning of the human body and mind. The ICF is a classification of these domains of functioning, decrements in which are impairments if the limitation is in a body function (or structure) or activity limitations and participation restrictions if the limitations is in what the person does or performs. The account, however, requires that these "states or conditions of functioning" refer to intrinsic capacities of an individual, rather than descriptions of what individuals do or perform in their actual environments. This is an important qualification, and as the philosophical plausibility of the WHO conception of health depends on it, it is worth developing the distinction between capacity and performance more fully.

As the model of functioning and disability embodied in the ICF makes clear, the nature, quality, and extent of what a person *does* (acts, executes, performs, behaves, and so on) often depend considerably on features of the environment in which the person acts. This is especially significant when the concern is to determine the state of a person's health, with limitations on what the person can do because of their intrinsic biological state. Thus, a person who has an impairment in hearing may in fact be able to hear with a hearing aid; similarly, a person with lower body muscle wastage may not be able to climb stairs in a public building because they are too steep but will be able in their own home where the stairs have been modified to accommodate this impairment. In short, to accurately assess a person's functioning in different domains – hearing, seeing, walking, climbing, grasping, carrying an object, and so on – it is important to discount the impact of the environment in which the person performs actions that depend on these functionings. Features of the physical and social environment may make it possible for the individual to perform better than he or she can intrinsically (when assistive technology or environmental modification facilitates performance); by the same token, other features may hinder performance. In either instance, to get at a person's health, the positive or negative effect of the individual's environment needs to be discounted. The result, in the ICF language, is the person's intrinsic functioning capacity.

But given the substantial number of bodily and person-level functionings that constitute the full repertoire of human functioning, it would be impractical to define health operationally in terms of all of these functionings. Though a practical rather than a conceptual issue, it is a measurement challenge that the WHO conception needs to resolve. Conceptually, the new WHO definition is completed by the three guiding principles quoted above, but as the point of the conceptualization is practical operationalization for measurement purposes, the authors are very much obliged to offer a solution to the challenge of identifying which human functionings are at the conceptual heart of the notion of health.

They approach this challenge by sketching out functioning domain selection guidelines: the domains of functioning sufficient for operationalizing the concept of health for measurement purposes should be those that have intuitive, clinical, and epidemiological significance; are classified in the ICF; are amendable to self-report, observation, or direct measurement; are cross-population comparable; and, finally, are "comprehensive enough to capture the most important aspects of health states that people value" (Ibid. 310).

This last criterion is not so much a measurement concern as a matter of face validity. When measuring health, it is important to measure what it is about health that makes health something perceived to be both intrinsically and instrumentally valuable. This should be taken as a gesture toward the normativist challenge, but it is not a complete answer to it. In effect, the new WHO definition of health turns the issue of the normative significance of health into a technical challenge, leaving unexplained why health matters to us. Given that the definition is held out to be cross-culturally universal as well as scientifically adequate, the failure to pinpoint the source of the value of health can fairly be seen as a significant failure of the WHO definition, at the conceptual level. Even if we are confident that the domains of functioning we select serve the purposes of scientific measurement, the resulting operationalization does not, on its own, give us an explanation why, in every culture, health is conceptually understood as a human good.

Conclusion

The 1948 WHO definition of health and the current, descriptivist WHO definition "for measurement purposes" reflected a persistent dilemma in the philosophical challenge of defining health. Any philosophically acceptable definition must take into account our powerful intuitions about the intrinsic and instrumental value of health. Health may not be the same as well-being or the summum bonum, but it is a component (or determinant) of human well-being and indisputably a human good and a central one at that (see Daniels 2008). Yet, unless the notion is firmly grounded in the biological sciences and understood as an attribute of the person, the concept resists operationalization and threatens to lose its scientific legitimacy. It is not just the World Health Organization that requires a notion of health in terms of which we can compare the health of an individual before and after a clinical intervention or a population of people before or after a health promotion or other public health intervention. As an unexplained, ineffable, indefinite, or inherently subjective phenomenon, the notion of health is not of particular use to us, nor would it have any useful input into how we structure our social institutions and systems to respond to actual human need. This is the philosophical challenge of defining health.

Definitions of Key Terms

Descriptive theory of health	A philosophical theory of health based on the premise that health is an attribute of an individual fully explainable in the language of the biological sciences.
Normative theory of health	A philosophical theory of health premised on the view that it is of the essence of health that it is an intrinsic and instrumental human good.
Operationalization of health	The process by which a conceptualization of health is transformed into a set of operations, procedures,

	or explicit criteria that define elements of health that can be measured in one manner or another.
Functioning	(In the International Classification of Functioning, Disability and Health, WHO 2001) a domain of health including specific body functions and structures and all human behaviors, movements, and actions, from the simplest individual movement or action to the most complex, socially constructed, action that constitute human activity.

Summary Points

- The 1948 Constitution of WHO defined health as "a state of complete physical, mental and social well-being and not merely the absence of disease or infirmity."
- Though strongly criticized, the WHO definition of health set the stage for an ongoing philosophical debate about the definition of health.
- The dominant theories of health emphasize either the biological and scientific core of the notion (descriptivist or "naturalistic" accounts) or the consensus that health is an intrinsic and instrumental human good (normativist accounts).
- Despite decades of high-quality philosophical debate about the concept of health, there remains a persistent dilemma: neither a descriptivist nor a normativist account of health is adequate, but these two approaches are in fundamental conflict.
- After two decades of relative inactivity in philosophical treatments of the concept of health, recently there has been a resurgence of interest in normativist definitions.
- It is essential for the scientific status of health sciences, and in particular for assessing the effectiveness of individual and population health intervention and comparing the health of individuals and populations, to use a conceptualization of health that is operationalizable for measurement.
- Although the 1948 WHO definition remains in use, WHO itself has based its own scientific work on a very different, basically descriptivist, account of health "for measurement purposes."
- The most recent WHO definition of health, although it gestures toward the normativist approach while being firmly descriptivist, nonetheless fails to adequately account for the common perception that health is both intrinsically and instrumentally valuable.

References

Ananth M (2008) In defense of an evolutionary concept of health nature, norms, and human biology. Ashgate, Aldershot
Beauchamp T, Childress J (2001) Principles of biomedical ethics, 5th edn. Oxford University Press, New York

Bechtel W (1985) In defense of a naturalistic concept of health. In: Humber J, Almedereds R (eds) Biomedical ethics review. Humana Press, Clifton, pp 131–170

Bergner M (1985) Measurement of health status. Med Care 23:696–703

Bircher J, Kuruvill S (2014) Defining health by addressing individual, social, and environmental determinants: new opportunities for health care and public health. J Public Health Policy 35:363–386

Boorse C (1975) On the distinction between disease and illness. Philos Public Aff 5:49–68

Boorse C (1976) Wright on functions. Philos Rev 85:70–86

Boorse C (1977) Health as a theoretical concept. Philos Sci 44:542–573

Breslow L (2006) Health measurement in the third era of health. Am J Public Health 96:17–19

Callahan D (1973) The WHO definition of 'health'. Stud Hastings Cent 1:77–87

Caplan A (1993) The concepts of health, illness, and disease. In: Bynum W, Porter R (eds) Companion encyclopedia of the history of medicine, vol I. Routledge, London, pp 233–248

Daniels N (2008) Just health: meeting health needs fairly. Cambridge University Press, New York

Engelhardt HT (1984) Clinical problems and the concept of disease. In: Nordenfelt L, Ingemar B, Lindahl B (eds) Health, disease, and causal explanations in medicine. Reidel Publishing Company, Dordrecht, pp 27–41

Goldsmith S (1972) The status of health status indicators. Health Serv Rep 87:212–220

Huber M, Knottnerus J, Green L, van der Horst H, Jadad A et al (2011) How should we define health? BMJ 343:d4163. doi:10.1136/bmj.d4163

Kickbusch I (2003) The contribution of the World Health Organization to a new public health and health promotion. Am J Public Health 93:383–388

Kovács J (1998) The concept of health and disease. Med Health Care Philos 1:33–48

Mann J, Gostin L, Gruskin S, Brennan T, Lazzarini Z, Fineberg H (1994) Health and human rights. Health Hum Rights 1:6–23

McDowell I (2006) Measuring health: a guide to rating scales and questionnaires, 3rd edn. Oxford University Press, New York

Nordenfelt L (1987) On the nature of health. An action-theoretic approach. Reidel Publishing Company, Dordrecht

Nordenfelt L (1993) Quality of life, health and happiness. Averbury, Aldershot

Salomon J, Mathers C, Chatterji S, Sadana R, Üstün TB et al (2003) Quantifying individual levels of health: definitions, concepts, and measurement issues. In: Murray CJL, Evans CJL (eds) Health systems performance assessment debates, methods and empiricism. World Health Organization, Geneva, pp 301–318

Schramme T (2007) A qualified defence of a naturalist theory of health. Med Health Care Philos 10:11–17

Sen A (1999) Development as freedom. Oxford University Press, Oxford

Sigerist HE (1941) Medicine and human welfare. Yale University Press, New Haven

Varga S (2011) Defining mental disorder. Exploring the 'natural function' approach. Philos Ethics Humanit Med 6:1

Venkatapuram S (2011) Health justice. Polity Press, Cambridge

WHO (1948) Constitution. World Health Organization, Geneva

WHO (2000) The world health report 2000: health systems: improving performance. World Health Organization, Geneva

WHO (2001) International classification of functioning, disability and health. World Health Organization, Geneva

Wylie C (1970) The definition and measurement of health and disease. Public Health Rep 85:100–104

Health as Notion in Public Health

60

Thomas Schramme

Contents

Abstract

Public health is a scientific and practical endeavor. It aims at preventing disease and promoting health in a population. Public health has a specific way to use the concept of health. It is positive in the sense that it facilitates the measurement of the health status of a population over and above the absence of disease. Health in public health is a gradual, not an absolute, notion. Public health also targets health risks or health dispositions, which should not be confused with intrinsic health statuses. This chapter also discusses the aspect of referring to health within a population, which poses some issues of measurement. Finally, it is discussed what normative issues are due to the specific understanding of health in public health.

T. Schramme (✉)
Department of Philosophy, University of Liverpool, Liverpool, UK
e-mail: t.schramme@liverpool.ac.uk

© Springer Science+Business Media Dordrecht 2017
T. Schramme, S. Edwards (eds.), *Handbook of the Philosophy of Medicine*,
DOI 10.1007/978-94-017-8688-1_49

Introduction

Modern societies are not only concerned with the health of individuals in terms of providing for curative medicine by a publicly funded system of health-care resources, professionals, and institutions. States also focus on preventing disease through measures such as provision of clean water, containment of contagious diseases, and screening programs to identify genetic dispositions. In addition, the idea of health promotion has gained more attention. The improvement of health conditions, especially for vulnerable and disadvantaged groups, has become a major political concern on a global scale (WHO 1986, 2010). Public health is the theory and practice of fulfilling this societal task of protecting the health of the population. From a philosophical perspective, it is important to ask what "health" means in public health. This issue is rarely discussed, maybe because it is thought to have a straightforward answer. But it will be seen that, on the contrary, the notion of health in public health is far from clear.

A first issue concerns whether health is understood as a negative or positive concept, that is, whether it is interpreted as the absence of disease or as something over and above such a minimal understanding. Public health indeed seems to include both these aspects, as can be seen in two definitions of public health. The first focuses on the negative aspects: "Public health is the prevention of disease and premature death through organized community effort" (Beauchamp 1995, p. 2210). The second definition states that public health is "the science and art of preventing disease, prolonging life and promoting health through organised efforts of society" (Faculty of Public Health of the Royal College of Physician of the United Kingdom, quoted in Nuffield Council on Bioethics 2007, p. 6). In this definition the idea of health promotion is explicitly mentioned. It is in relation to such advancement that the possible expansion of the concept of health over and above the absence of disease occurs.

A second issue concerns the emphasis of public health on the social determinants of health. It has been an important finding that the health status of individuals does not only depend on their internal condition, such as the well-functioning of their organs, but also, and maybe more importantly, on their living conditions. This was first mainly seen in relation to the physical environment, for instance, in regard to hygienic conditions or housing. In the last decades, the social determinants of health have been acknowledged to extend to far more factors, including working conditions, social relationships, and public safety. These more remote "causes of the causes," however, pose a theoretical problem, because being at (increased) risk of falling ill, for instance, because of a stressful and oppressive work atmosphere, is not the same as being in ill health. Conceptually, there is an important distinction between a particular health disposition and a status as being healthy. As will be seen, this distinction is related to the significant difference between a comparative and an absolute understanding of health. In focusing on healthy circumstances, public health is prone to confuse health dispositions and health statuses.

Third, public health is not only concerned with the health of individual citizens but with the health of populations. This raises conceptual issues concerning the object to which a certain health status is ascribed. Is it the aggregate sum of individuals in a particular population that makes up the group's health status or is a population deemed to be an entity in its own right that can also have a particular health status? To ascribe a certain level of health to populations does not only raise ontological questions concerning individualism versus collectivism but also practical problems of measurement.

Finally, the very fact that public health is not just a science, but a practice aiming at a common good (cf. Parmet 2009, p. 12), makes the concept of health in public health in a distinctive way a normative notion. Health is here obviously understood as a good, which should be protected and promoted. Indeed, it is usually seen as a moral concern if populations within a society, or globally, have different health statuses, not due to their own choices, but because of the social conditions they are living in. The conceptual problem here is one of a potential confusion between a scientific and possible value-neutral account of health in contrast to an interpretation of health in terms of political interests.

Negative Versus Positive Interpretations of Health

It is important to acknowledge that the concept of health is often used in a special sense in the theory and practice of public health. The relevant understanding of health is, in certain respects, discontinuous with the received view in general medicine. In medicine, health is commonly understood in a negative way, as the absence of disease or as medical normality. This is a minimal and absolute concept of health. A person is either healthy or not, there are no grades of health. In order to be regarded as healthy, it is merely necessary not to be in any pathological condition. To be sure, there are attempts to conceptualize health in a positive way, for instance, in the well-known formulation of the World Health Organization: "Health is a state of complete physical, mental and social well-being and not merely the absence of disease or infirmity." Yet, this definition has had no impact on medical theory or practice and has actually been criticized for its lack of distinction between well-being or happiness and medical health (Callahan 1973). In terms of Fig. 1 below, medicine is interested in the left side of the spectrum.

In public health, health is usually not seen in contrast to disease, but as a condition that can be present at a certain level, even where a person has a condition that is clinically subnormal. This makes sense insofar as people can cope with disease. Their well-being or welfare might not be affected by a medical condition, so they can be healthy despite having a pathological condition. Once such a gradual understanding is introduced, health can also be found at a higher level over and above the absence of disease. In this respect, persons who are either less likely to fall ill or who are fitter than others in terms of their organismic functioning have a higher grade of health.

In summary, conditions of persons can be understood in different ways. Health can mean the absence of disease, as in the common medical perspective. Health can also mean a point on a continuum, stretching from the absence of disease up to a

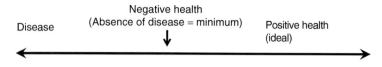

Fig. 1 Negative and positive health

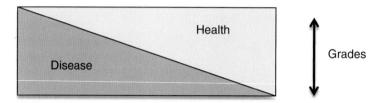

Fig. 2 Health grades

state of ideal health, as in Fig. 1. Health can finally be seen in combination with disease, in a more holistic fashion, which includes the life circumstances of persons. Here it also makes sense to talk about grades of health. This perspective can be seen in Fig. 2. Both ways of referring to grades of health, in terms of levels of quality and in terms of a holistic assessment, are found in public health. In fact, public health necessarily requires a gradual perspective, because otherwise there could be no comparisons of health statuses between individuals or populations. Also, to conceive of health in a holistic fashion naturally leads to an inclusion of social aspects of health, which is one of the distinctive theoretical and practical contributions of public health (cf. Arah 2009).

Positive health can be understood in relation to medically defined conditions, as superior or enhanced organismic functioning. The task of health promotion might be interpreted in this sense, for instance, when the lung capacity of people is increased. It might have been medically normal before, but enhanced via a public health intervention, such as incentivizing the use of bicycles. Another way to understand positive health in public health is in terms of welfare more generally, not just in relation to organismic functioning. Since in public health social determinants of health are seen in close relation to medical conditions, it is but a small step to a welfare notion of health (Venkatapuram 2011; cf. Holland 2014, p. 109 ff.). This is an interpretation of the notion of health that includes conditions that are internal and external to the person under the umbrella of health, such as being able to experience nature or to have occasions for recreation, which are not seen themselves as health conditions in medicine. Positive health here means to have superior or enhanced capabilities.

Promotion of health can therefore refer to the improvement of health over and above the absence of disease. It is focused on conditions of people. The practice of public health also includes the promotion of health in terms of advancing the awareness of the value of health. This is a focus on an abstract quality of conditions of people, the importance of health, not on the conditions itself. An understanding of health as welfare notion might at the same time make a straightforward case for health being of significant value, but also brush over important differences between welfare and organismic conditions. When health is understood as such an over-arching value and as a gradual, positive notion, we might tend to see any condition below the ideal as an impairment of welfare. It is therefore vital to always be clear about the understanding of the concept of health in public health contexts.

Intrinsic and Instrumental Health

Individuals can be healthy in the sense that they are not ill or do not have a disease. Here, their health status is intrinsic insofar as it is determined by their somatic and mental condition only. A person is either healthy or not healthy in this sense. Individuals can also be healthy in the sense that they are not likely to fall ill. A person who does not smoke and exercises regularly is healthy in this respect. Hence, it might be more fitting to say that they live a healthy life. Here, health is seen in its instrumental aspects, as a means to stay (intrinsically) healthy. This can be turned into a gradual standard: someone can be healthier than someone else or healthier than before. In addition, we can ascribe such instrumental healthiness to environments, not just conditions of people, as the circumstances causally have an impact on the ensuing physical and mental conditions of people. Clean air and nutritious food are healthy, whereas working in mines or being persecuted is not healthy.

The comparative perspective of public health therefore depends, up to a point, on the fact that people can have certain dispositions to fall ill. Yet health dispositions are not themselves health statuses, but propensities to fall ill. Even individuals who have a high propensity to develop a disease, say, because they are carriers of certain genes, are not therefore unhealthy in the absolute sense of the term. Intrinsic health and instrumental health therefore need to be kept apart (Boorse 1977, p. 553), though obviously both medicine and public health rely on assessments of instrumental health in their practice. Public health even has an understanding of instrumental health, which is not based on individual risk but on health dispositions within populations. Hence, individuals might have a worse status of instrumental health than others (in a particular respect, say, regarding respiratory capacity), in virtue of their membership in a particular targeted population, for instance, workers in a destitute area. Health risk, as in the individual case, is based on statistical findings and probabilistic theory (Parmet 2009, p. 17; Broadbent 2013, p. 129 ff.). When applied to populations, epidemiological findings also contribute to the assessment of health.

It is a mistake to confuse the intrinsic health status of individuals or populations with their internally or externally determined health dispositions or risks. This does not, of course, speak against researching on and politically discussing health risks. But it is wrong to say that risks themselves make us unhealthy in the intrinsic and absolute sense of the term (cf. John 2009). Conceptual confusion might lead to problematic decisions when developing public health policies.

Population Health: Aggregate or Distinctive Concept?

Usually, public health experts focus on particular socioeconomic groups, for instance, unemployed persons or single mothers. So when epidemiologists refer to population health, they usually mean the statistically aggregated sum of individual health traits or health statuses. The aggregation that leads to an account of population health depends on certain summary measures (e.g., Murray et al. 2002). Alternatively, but maybe more controversially, population health might be seen as a distinctive category, more than just the aggregate of individual health statuses (e.g., Arah 2009).

The particular way groups or populations are determined depends on the purpose of a study. Ultimately considerations in public health rely on hypotheses about social or socioeconomic determinants of health, or – to use another expression familiar to a public health perspective – the "causes of causes" (of health status). Hence, epidemiologists aim at findings about possible correlations between particular circumstantial aspects of citizens and their health conditions. In this respect, the population perspective is instrumental for understanding causes of individual disease that are of a social nature (e.g., Rose 1985).

Findings may be sought regarding socioeconomic aspects, such as income, educational background or gender, or behavioral aspects, such as lifestyle and diet. With these statistical correlations, it is possible to make comparisons between populations regarding their health, even on an international level. Obviously it is also possible to compare different policies in tackling possible inequalities. In more popular publications, public health scholars then end up with simple slogans, such as "inequality is bad for your health" (Daniels et al. 2001) or "uneducated people die younger," which only make sense from a population perspective. Such a collective perspective, it needs to be stressed, tends to ignore aspects on the individual level, for instance, individual responsibility for health status.

In order to distinguish grades of health, the perspective of public health needs measures of comparison. In what respect can a person (or group) be healthier than another? What may be the criteria for determining grades of health? This does not allow for a straightforward answer. In the definition of the WHO, for instance, the respective level of health is determined by a subjective state of well-being. This seems difficult to compare between persons or between different states of the same person, though there are now many efforts to turn even happiness into a quantifiable measure (Kahneman 1999). Also, it seems inadequate to call someone healthier merely because he feels better. We know that people can actually feel well and yet suffer from quite severe diseases, especially when they are symptomless. So the criteria for comparing health levels seem more likely to be measures that have to do with the organismic functions of human beings, such as lung capacity, metabolism, memory, or resilience. The more effective these mechanisms function, the more healthy is a person.

To be sure, these challenges regarding the measurement of levels of health are very difficult to surmount. This is because health is such a complex aggregation of different aspects. For instance, we can try to measure subjectively by assessing the individual quality of life in relation to health aspects or objectively by referring to clinical data and external circumstances of individuals (Coggon 2012, p. 20; Sen 2004). In addition, we can only compare people in certain respects; we can never say whether they are healthier than others tout court (Hausman 2012). Is someone with an irritable lung but a robust psyche less healthy than a marathon runner experiencing bullying at work? Such questions cannot be answered unless we focus on certain aspects of functioning. Public health usually works with only some particular health aspects, such as mental resilience or physical fitness. It also relies on proxies of these criteria, since they cannot easily be directly measured. Accordingly public health collects data, for instance, about frequency of visits to doctors or the number of days on sick leave. Finally, there is a more general problem of collecting data in epidemiology, because it often requires certain abstractions for purposes of generating statistical data. For instance, a common statistical measure for comparing health of certain groups is life expectancy. Obviously here it is not individual health that is measured and compared but a heavily modified proxy for health conditions. This can be particularly significant when politically aiming at certain health outcomes, for instance, when an attempt is made to introduce thresholds of enough health. Any threshold, such as "enough health," relies on a certain "currency," that is, an idea of what aspect of health should be targeted and up to which level it should be accessible for citizens.

Political Dimension of Health in Public Health

As we have seen, the fact that public health allows for grades of health opens the possibility to discuss health promotion in a way that includes enhancing health over and above the absence of disease. This is exactly the area where the worries about "healthism" begin. Health, understood in a positive sense, as in the definition of the WHO, does not have an internal normative stoppage point or threshold of adequate health. More health is always better than less. For egalitarians in the debate on health-care justice, more health might also be required for some groups as a matter of justice, because they are in worse health than other populations not due to their own fault. What is more, according to the public health perspective, improvement of health is not merely, and maybe not even primarily, a matter of improving the internal resources of a person, such as stamina and nutrition, but also of the social determinants of health, such as quality of work environment, access to leisurely activities, and so on. We can accordingly think of many ways to – if only indirectly – improve health dispositions of citizens by improving their living environment as well as changing their lifestyles. So the possible scope for public health interventions is very wide to say the least. If we now add the current value that is attached to health in many societies, we can see how this emphasis on health promotion opens the door for worries about paternalistic interventions, which are even more worrisome if interventions are due to state action and coercive legal measures. One way to avoid these problems would be to introduce a threshold of "enough" health, hence a sufficient grade of health that every citizen should be able to reach, without overreaching the target of adequate health promotion. But we have seen that it is far from trivial to determine and justify such a threshold.

One way forward is to explicitly acknowledge the political dimension of the notion of health in public health (Weinstock 2011). After all, health here is not simply a scientific notion. It is rather what might be called a functional notion, as its content is driven by public concerns about what we, as a political community, want to publicly secure for every citizen. What we regard as sufficient health within public health is therefore also influenced by theories and beliefs regarding social justice.

The health of the population is a common good. It is a public task to secure it. But it is not determined by the notion of health itself up to which level it ought to be safeguarded. This depends on issues that go far beyond conceptual issues. It is therefore important not to confuse normative aspects of the concept of health with the normative aspects of politically protecting and promoting population health. The fact that public health is both a scientific endeavor and a public policy practice makes it vulnerable to such confusion.

Conclusion

The notion of health within public health is of considerable theoretical and practical significance. There is no agreed definition to be found in the public health literature, yet it is implied that health is here understood as a gradable notion, not simply as the absence of disease. Measurement of health in certain respects and the focus on social determinants of health may lead to confusion of intrinsic and instrumental aspects of health. To have a statistically high liability or a high risk to fall ill is not the same as being in a status of ill health. Comparisons of health status – being healthier than someone else or than another population – are based on specific aspects of health and measurements that are usually proxies for health status. Again, being less healthy does not mean being in ill health. The gradual and the absolute notion of health need to be kept separate.

Public health, in its political purpose, aims at improving health within populations and often also at equalizing health statuses between socioeconomic groups. The value of health is rarely queried, but it needs to be seen in relation to other social values. However, when health becomes an all-encompassing notion via the focus on social and other determinants of health, there is a certain danger of supporting "healthism."

Definition of Key Terms

Collectivism	In the context of this chapter, collectivism is understood as a theoretical position to see society as more than just an assembly of individual

	persons. It may have a normative component, promoting the good of the public.
Grades of health	Health need not be understood as the absence of disease. People can then be deemed healthier than others and also in a certain level of health despite the presence of disease.
Healthism	The promotion of the value of health. Usually, the term is used in a pejorative way, meaning doing too much to promote health, especially using wrong means, such as social control to aim at population health.
Individualism	In the context of this chapter, individualism is understood as a theoretical position to see society as an assembly of individual persons.
Instrumental health	Disposition of a person to get a disease or to stay healthy; also statistically determined risk of health-related outcomes.
Intrinsic health	The health status of a person, either in absolute or gradual terms, but restricted to actual organismic functioning.
Population	In public health populations are statistical measures. They contain individuals combined according to a chosen characteristic, such as females living in a certain area.
Public health	The scientific and political endeavor of preventing disease and promoting health.
Social determinants of health	The aspects of the social environment, such as working conditions, housing, or security, which have an impact on people's health.

Summary Points

- Public health works with a specific notion of health.
- "Health" in public health is a gradable notion, not simply the absence of disease.
- Health dispositions and health risks are not the same as health statuses.
- The concept of health can also be applied to populations.
- The level of health within an individual or population needs to be specified in terms of particular aspects.
- Public health is concerned with environmental, especially social, determinants of health.
- Public health is a political practice as well as a scientific endeavor. In its practical role it promotes the value of health.
- The political aim of public health might lead to worries about supporting "healthism."

References

Arah OA (2009) On the relationship between individual and population health. Med Health Care Philos 12:235–244

Beauchamp DE (1995) Public health: philosophy. In: Post SG (ed) Encyclopedia of bioethics, 3rd edn. MacMillan Reference, New York, pp 2210–2215

Boorse C (1977) Health as a theoretical concept. Philos Sci 44(4):542–573

Broadbent A (2013) Philosophy of epidemiology. Macmillan Publishers, Houndmills

Callahan D (1973) The WHO definition of 'health'. Hast Cent Stud 1(3):77–87

Coggon J (2012) What makes health public? A critical evaluation of moral, legal, and political claims in public health. Cambridge University Press, Cambridge

Daniels N, Kennedy B, Kawachi I (2001) Is inequality bad for our health? Beacon, Boston

Hausman D (2012) Measuring or valuing population health: some conceptual problems. Public Health Ethics 5(3):229–239

Holland S (2014) Public health ethics, 2nd edn. Polity Press, Cambridge

John S (2009) Why 'health' is not a central category for public health policy. J Appl Philos 26 (2):129–143

Kahneman D (1999) Objective happiness. In: Kahneman D, Diener E, Schwarz N (eds) Well-being: the foundations of hedonic psychology. Russell Sage, New York, pp 3–25

Murray CJL, Salomon JA, Mathers CD, Lopez AD (eds) (2002) Summary measures of population health: concepts, ethics, measurement and applications. WHO, Geneva

Nuffield Council on Bioethics (2007) Public health: ethical issues. Cambridge Publishers, Cambridge

Parmet WE (2009) Populations, public health, and the law. Georgetown University Press, Washington, DC

Rose G (1985) Sick individuals and sick populations. Int J Epidemiol 14(1):32–38

Sen A (2004) Health achievement and equity: external and internal perspectives. In: Anand S, Peter F, Sen A (eds) Public health, ethics, and equity. Oxford University Press, Oxford, pp 263–268

Venkatapuram S (2011) Health justice: an argument from the capabilities approach. Polity Press, Cambridge

Weinstock D (2011) How should political philosophers think of health? J Med Philos 36:424–435

World Health Organisation (1986) The Ottawa charter for health promotion http://www.euro.who.int/__data/assets/pdf_file/0004/129532/Ottawa_Charter.pdf?ua=1

World Health Organisation (2010) Adelaide statement on health in all policies http://www.who.int/social_determinants/hiap_statement_who_sa_final.pdf

Identity Disorders: Philosophical Problems 61

Hugh Upton

Contents

Abstract

Any inquiry into identity disorders faces the difficulty that the ordinary understanding of personal identity is itself ambiguous and contentious. In what follows the concept of personal identity that has been of principal philosophical interest is distinguished and clarified, and ideas about the nature of the self are reviewed. The most influential approach to persons and their identity, deriving

H. Upton (✉)
College of Human and Health Sciences, Swansea University, Swansea, Wales, UK
e-mail: h.r.upton@swansea.ac.uk

© Springer Science+Business Media Dordrecht 2017
T. Schramme, S. Edwards (eds.), *Handbook of the Philosophy of Medicine*,
DOI 10.1007/978-94-017-8688-1_50

from the work of John Locke, is then set out as a basis for reflection on disorders. Varying degrees of disruption to the unity of consciousness are then considered, together with the effect of these on the conception of the self and its continuing identity. Finally, there is a discussion of dissociative identity disorder and of the way in which its conceptualization relates to its status as a disorder.

Introduction

One of the deep problems in philosophy arises from the combination of two very familiar ideas. The first is that the entire world, including ourselves, is one of continual change. The milk curdles, a tree blows down, the curtains fade, and you become fond of the music of Mahler. The second is that things stay the same. The curdled milk is the very milk that earlier someone forgot to put in the fridge, the tree is precisely the one in which we used to climb, those same curtains have been hanging there for years, and it is still you, not someone else, who now enjoys Mahler. It is assumed, then, that physical objects continue through time as the same things, even though they undergo changes in their properties. It is also assumed that each person persists through time as the same person, despite the many changes that naturally happen to people during their lives. In other words, persons retain a personal identity. Yet although this is seemingly a simple claim, it is one that has troubled philosophers for centuries (see Martin and Barresi 2003), raising many difficulties that need addressing before the matter of disorders of identity can be broached.

An example may help in bringing out the special significance of these underlying difficulties. Supposing, for contrast, that this inquiry concerned instead the philosophical issues relating to disorders of the liver, it would hardly be necessary to take account of the possibility that people's livers exist only as some kind of fiction. This, however, has been one conception of the self. Nor can the nature of the self simply be ignored in considering personal identity, since it is not possible to consider what constitutes the continuation of the same thing without some understanding of the kind of thing being referred to in the first place. Then, as further complications, there are different conceptions of what is meant by the identity of a person, and, under any chosen conception, there are different accounts of what mental and/or physical continuity would amount to a continuing identity. Some time must thus be spent in exploring these issues, for any obscurities and ambiguities in the understanding of identity will inevitably reappear in the conception of an identity disorder.

Conceptions of Identity and Identity Disorders

Personal Identity: Numerical and Narrative

The most familiar philosophical problem with personal identity (see Noonan 2003) is this: what is it that constitutes being the same person over time? It may be helpful to clarify the question, though, since an important ambiguity appears immediately.

For illustration, let us suppose that someone is asked: "Are you the same person that you were ten years ago?" After reflection on the events of the last 10 years, the reply might be: "No, I have changed a lot." Here, it should be noted that in saying "I have changed a lot," it is actually implied that something has remained constant: the "I" that has continued through the changes. It is this sense of "I" that has mainly preoccupied philosophical inquiry under the heading of "personal identity." To distinguish it from related areas of inquiry, it is often referred to as an example of "numerical identity," indicating the concern with one and only one person who continues as that person over a period of time.

It is important to be clear how this conception of personal identity differs from certain other matters that may be of related interest. Firstly, the sense of identity outlined here is plainly not that found in the expression "identical twins." This is a matter of qualitative identity, a situation of (nearly) indistinguishable properties rather than of there being just one person. Secondly, and more directly relevant, numerical identity is not what is typically referred to in talking of what gives meaning to people's lives, or how people see themselves, or how others see them. That is, it does not directly relate to those characteristics with which people might, as is often said, "identify themselves," such as being a scientist, having a deep commitment to socialism, or an allegiance to a football team. It is true that such characteristics are often referred to as forming part of a person's identity, but this concept (often called a narrative identity) is not that of numerical identity. To see this, it can be noted that although these characteristics are usually well entrenched, they are nevertheless aspects of a person that might change. As an example, someone who has for many years been an atheist might have become religious a month ago, telling her old friends that she is now a changed person; yet, her friends will still believe that they have known her for more than a month. Further, not only may people deliberately try to change these entrenched aspects of themselves, but their conception of success will be based on the assumption that the person will still be them, before and after the change. For example, suppose that after many years of unpleasant behavior, someone wishes to become a kinder person. In that case, this person's aim is not to disappear altogether and be replaced by someone kinder, but to continue living while becoming more kind. The question of (numerical) personal identity is thus: what is it that makes this continuing self the same one, despite changes even at the level of character or personality? Importantly, whatever it is, it is taken to be something beyond people's control. By contrast, people's narrative identity, involving those deep interests with which they identify ourselves, perhaps thereby giving a sense of unity to their lives, may to some extent be deliberately constructed.

It is worth noting one further point about this concept of numerical personal identity: it seems to be "all-or-nothing" rather than a matter of degree. That is, where numerical identity is concerned, someone is either precisely the same person as 10 years ago or not that person at all. Thus, it would make no sense to say that they were "rather identical" or "somewhat identical," expressions that appear to be in conflict with the linguistic role of this concept of identity. If ever there appears to be a reference to a degree of identity, there is usually an obvious way of resolving this into some other claim. To recall the earlier example, if twins are described as being "nearly identical," it is not being said that they are very nearly the same person but that they are very similar in appearance.

In what follows the focus will be on numerical rather than narrative identity, not least because of its central place in philosophical inquiry in this area. There is, though, another reason. While there are many problems that may arise with respect to people's narrative understanding of themselves, and while, were these problems to lead to seriously distressing and dysfunctional states for the subject, these states might be regarded as disorders, there would still be some doubt as to whether *identity* disorder would be the best way to characterize them. As an example, someone who had devoted many years of her life to being a writer might become depressed on coming to feel that she had "failed as an author"; yet although the role with which she had identified herself is one source of her problem, it might nevertheless be thought more appropriate to diagnose depression rather than an identity disorder. As another example, it might be felt that someone had developed a damagingly false narrative of himself, seeing himself as leading a life of great significance and entitlements, while regarding others as of no importance, to such an extent that it might prompt a diagnosis of narcissistic personality disorder. As with other personality disorders, this might be taken to involve "problems with one's identity or sense of self" (Butcher et al. 2015, p. 463) without it seeming appropriate to classify it as a disorder of identity. The risk, then, in taking problematic narrative identities as a basis for identity disorders is that the latter category would become too broad in its scope, going well beyond the central concern with the continuity of a single unified self.

Numerical Identity: Fact or Fiction?

Returning, then, to numerical identity, it is necessary to be aware of some of the different theoretical approaches within this conception of the self and personal identity, differences that may have a significant effect on the conception of disorders of identity (Fulford et al. 2006, pp. 761–763). The initial concern will be with just one fundamental distinction.

Firstly, there is the possibility of a realist conception of the self and its continuing personal identity. Underlying this conception is the belief that where people continue as the same person over time, this is in virtue of facts obtaining about them, perhaps simply some fact about a self or perhaps facts about their minds, bodies, or some combination of the two that constitute the self. It typically goes with the assumption that there is a truth to be discovered about personal identity. One particularly important implication of this conception is that it allows a distinction to be made between a person's identity and a person's *sense* of identity. Thus, a patient might be described as suffering a sense of alteration in identity, as reported in some schizophrenic patients (Oyebode 2008, p. 230), where it would be possible for this sense to be correctly contrasted by the clinicians with the fact that they have nevertheless been treating the same patient, before and since the onset of the disorder. Equally, on this realist conception, it is coherent to regard some conditions (perhaps those arising from dementia or severe amnesia) as providing legitimate grounds for uncertainty among observers regarding the current identity of the patient in front of them.

Secondly, there is what might be called an "anti-realist" position, connected in the history of western philosophy particularly with David Hume, which is skeptical of claims to there being a real self at all and thus, of course, skeptical of there being one with a continuing personal identity. On such a view there is no more to the self and its identity than a subjective awareness of the successive elements of a mental life, together with a (mistaken) supposition that they reflect facts about an actual self and its identity; a supposition induced, in Hume's opinion, by a sense of the resemblance between these elements (Hume 1739/1967, p. 254). Thus, although Hume was addressing the problem of numerical identity, and was proposing an account involving a process that simply happens to us, rather than being a deliberate construction on our part, he concluded that the self and its identity was a kind of fiction. On this basis, then, an "identity disorder" could not strictly be a disorder of the identity of the self (there being no self) but would presumably be a disorder of the mechanism for creating the illusion of an identity of a self. The result would thus be a disruption to the *sense* of having an identity but, since the sense of it is all there can be on this view, the contrast with a *real* identity (a possibility normally implied by this way of speaking) would in fact be lacking.

Self, Identity, and Psychiatry

Thus, one major philosophical issue is to what extent a realist account of the self and its identity can be defended against Hume's skepticism. This is too large a question to try to answer here. Instead, it can be noted that either the realist or the Humean (anti-realist) conception could constitute a framework for understanding references to the self and its disorders. It might of course be argued that the realist conception provides a better foundation for understanding abnormal states, if only because a disordered self sounds more serious than a disordered fictional self. Yet this need not be so: Hume was not denying the great psychological significance of a sense of personal identity, only questioning its basis. Anti-realism, then, does not in itself cast doubt on the seriousness of a disruption to one's sense of self and self-identity.

However, a second issue arises here. Even if the adequacy of anti-realism on this point were accepted, it might still be thought an advantage of a realist account that it usefully extends the conceptual framework beyond the subjective, in the way outlined above. Certainly, it provides the clearest framework for what might be regarded as identity disorders par excellence, those involving the loss not just of a sense of identity but of an actual identity; cases where those other than the sufferer might think that identity had been lost even while personhood continued. Valuable though this might be philosophically, however, some caution is needed, since this conceptual opportunity is not necessarily one that psychiatry will wish to take up. That is, even if realism regarding the self were to be accepted, it would not follow that the disorders will be conceptualized as disorders of the real self, rather than disorders in the sense of self. It is important, then, to have some awareness of both the identification and description of identity disorders to be found in psychiatry and abnormal psychology.

The current standard text for psychiatric classification is *DSM-5* or, to give its full title, the *Diagnostic and Statistical Manual of Mental Disorders* (American Psychiatric Association 2013). Here, the relevant general category is "dissociative disorders." These are described as involving "a disruption of and/or discontinuity in the normal integration of consciousness, memory, identity, emotion, perception, body representation, motor control, and behaviour" (p. 291). Of the three main examples of dissociative disorders, only one, "dissociative identity disorder" (DID), is explicitly called an identity disorder, and it will be discussed in detail later. The second, "dissociative amnesia," will also be discussed, on the grounds that although not labeled as such, it seems directly related to personal identity. On the other hand, the third, "depersonalization/derealization disorder," is arguably more directly related to a sense of self and only indirectly to identity, in that depersonalization involves, in various ways, a feeling of detachment from all or part of the self, sometimes involving an "out-of-body" experience.

By way of contrast, the slightly different taxonomy found in a well-known introduction to psychiatry, *Sims' Symptoms in the Mind* (Oyebode 2008), may be noted. Here, the relevant general classification is that of "disorders of the self," this being sub-divided on the basis of five aspects of a person's self-awareness: aware- ness of existing, of activity, of unity, of identity, and of the boundaries of the self (p. 222). Of these, disorders of identity are said to involve various kinds of discontinuity in the awareness of a continuing identity, though interestingly the category does not include DID, this being classified as a disorder in the awareness of unity rather than of identity. Of the three kinds of condition that it does include, the first (in extreme form) is a sense of having been "completely changed from being one person to another" (p. 230), a condition where even this description of the awareness involved seems deeply puzzling. To recall the opening discussion of numerical identity, if someone has a sense of having *changed into* someone else, this suggests also some sense of continuity between the two states; otherwise, there seems no reason to call it a change rather than simply a coming into existence. If that is correct, might this also be a sense of continuing identity, seemingly in conflict with the description of the condition? The other two kinds of identity disorder in *Sims* are a feeling of possession (included under dissociative identity disorder in *DSM-5*) and that of near death experiences (included, to some extent, under depersonalization in *DSM-5*).

In what follows, rather than attempting to resolve the realist/anti-realist debate, the possibility of greater objectivity mentioned earlier will be kept open by focusing on a realist account of numerical identity as the context for discussing identity disorders. Also, following what seems to be philosophically indicated, the scope will extend to issues of singularity, unity, and continuity of the self that go somewhat beyond the classification of disorders of identity found in *Sims* so as to include DID. Next, then, it is necessary to give some consideration to the nature of realist accounts of identity.

Are Persons Material Objects?

The issue of personal identity actually raises two questions at once: what exactly is a person and (whatever it is) what makes each of them the same one over time? One possibility is that persons are properly understood as no more than physical, human animals. Is it best, then, to focus on the body as the key to the self and its identity? Certainly, the body seems highly significant, since it is usually the means by which people immediately identify those known to them. Yet the fact that the appearance of the body is typically the way in which people identify each other does not necessarily mean that bodies are persons or are what make persons the same over time. Consider, for example, the use of fingerprints in forensic science. These aspects of the body may uniquely identify each person, but it does not follow that what makes people the same persons over time are their fingerprints. Further, even if bodies were taken to be persons, it must be remembered that the physical matter that constitutes the cells of the body changes completely over a period of a few years. So, if bodily continuity is what constitutes personal identity, the same problem would immediately arise as with objects such as tables, cars, and computers: how can they retain the same identity despite changes in the physical material that constitutes them? For example, if a car is gradually re-built with (some or all) new parts, will it be the same car?

One point about objects that seems to be unavoidable, and which might be unwelcome if transferred to persons, is that it seems unlikely that there is always a truth to be discovered that will settle the question of their identity. In the absence of such truths, it seems entirely appropriate that a decision may have to be made as to the identity of an object, perhaps for a specific purpose such as ensuring the legality of its description for sale. Here, although those who are making the decision will base their judgment on factual matters (on how much has changed or which parts), an assessment will also have to be made of the significance of these changes, something that is not a matter of fact but requires a value judgment. The idea that there may be only this kind of pragmatic or conventional answer may not seem philosophically troubling where objects are concerned, but it may well seem strange as an implication of a conception of personal identity.

Personal Identity and Mind Transfer

There may, of course, be reasons to reject such a reductive physicalist account of persons. It might be said that persons are "souls" (see Quinton 1975), perhaps something that animates a body and maybe survives its death. However, this will probably not help the inquiry much, since, particularly in a secular context, there is too much uncertainty about the supposed nature of souls. Unless it is simply another way of referring to the mind, talk of them will likely add to the obscurity rather than solve the problem in any informative way. This leaves the possibility that, although dependent upon bodies, what persons actually are resides in some way in their mental life. As mentioned at the outset, this too raises the familiar problem for identity, which is that changes occur precisely where continuity is sought. The mind, or at least its mental life, is something that changes all the time, as old experiences are forgotten and new sensations, ideas, dreams, hopes, and memories appear. Nevertheless, might a person be constituted by this succession? Or, if not the succession itself, might a person be the consciousness that has this succession of mental activity?

At this point, use can be made of an idea from Bernard Williams (1973), who provided an imaginary "test case" to aid reflection on the problems of what persons are and how they continue as the same ones. In brief, everyone is asked to consider this: if your mind was transferred to another body, and that body's mind transferred to yours, where would you be when you woke up after the operation? (As an alternative, this procedure may be imagined as a brain transplant, provided that it is remembered that it is the transfer of the mind that is really at issue in the example, not that of the brain.) Though Williams himself is skeptical about this answer, it is at least plausible that the person and their continuing identity would go with the mind into the new body, in virtue of the transfer of memories and other elements of mental life. Perhaps the friends of the subject would have to accept this too, after their initial puzzlement at the new appearance of the person who gives them a familiar greeting on their arrival at the bedside. In any event, this proposal will be taken as a cue for further inquiries.

John Locke on Persons and Identity

Perhaps the most influential philosophical account of personhood and personal identity derives from material included in the second edition of *An Essay Concerning Human Understanding* by John Locke (1694/1975). It is one that is consistent with the response to the mind transfer case just mentioned, in that it maintains that persons are to be understood in mental terms and that thus personal identity is the identity of a particular mental life.

For Locke, what defines a person is not that it is a certain kind of physical object but that it is a "thinking, intelligent being, that has reason and reflection" (1694/1975, p. 335). In particular, it must be self-aware, conscious of its own thoughts and perceptions, and capable of reflecting on its own experiences. It is an account with some important implications. For example, if the capacity for consciousness is essential to being a person, then the persistent vegetative state (PVS) victim who has no possibility of regaining consciousness would presumably have ceased to be one (see McMahan 2002, pp. 446–447). The requirement for self-awareness and reflection is also significant, since it would have to be accepted that babies would probably not meet this condition and thus would not count as persons. If so, it would follow that strictly, for Locke, adult persons were never babies, since their personal identity could not be shared with nonpersons. However, at least it may be accepted that there were babies who developed into adult human beings.

Turning, then, to the idea of identity, it will be useful to note that Locke uses the identity of animals by way of contrast with persons and personal identity. The identity of a particular cat, for example, will be a matter of the continuity of a specific cat's body. Given the physical changes that are bound to occur to it, this is not necessarily an entirely straightforward matter but, in any event, the account that will be needed here is one of the continuing identity of a physical object despite the occurrence of changes in that object. Then, since Locke includes human beings (or "man" as he says) under animals, what makes for the continuing identity of a particular human being (as opposed to a person) would in principle be just the same as what makes for the continuing identity of the cat: the continuation of a particular physical body despite the inevitable physical changes.

Locke saw the idea of personal identity in quite different terms. In setting it out, he drew upon one of the essential features of his conception of personhood, that of self-awareness. For Locke, what makes someone the same person over time is not the continuity of their body, or indeed of any substance, but a continuity that relates to a particular kind of self-awareness, that is, the present awareness of earlier experiences. Thus, Locke says, someone is the same person as far back (and no further) as the time of the occurrence of those experiences of which he or she now has memories (Locke 1694/1975, p. 335).

Whether or not it is ultimately accepted, there certainly seems to be something of value in this kind of account. There are also, though, complications that must be considered. Firstly, as Locke was well aware, there are always gaps in people's memories. These relate most obviously to times when they were asleep, but there are also those gaps relating to ordinary forgetfulness about periods in their waking life. However, the gaps are perhaps not too great a problem for Locke's account of identity; as he says, the same consciousness will extend back to remembered earlier experiences, despite any intervening gaps. Secondly, there may be uncertainties as to whether something is a genuine memory or not. If so, these will presumably result in uncertainty about how far back in time someone's identity actually extends. Thirdly, it seems difficult to accept that the natural loss of memories of early childhood will, in effect, reduce the lifespan of a person. However, a modified version of Locke's theory may help here, to the effect that you do not need to be able to recall every earlier experience now, so long as you can recall a time when you could recall them (Noonan 2003, pp. 55–56). In the context of this issue, it is also worth noting that Locke took personal identity to be a "forensic" concept, one that is concerned with the attribution of responsibility. Given that, it is possible to appreciate his reluctance to attribute continuing personal identity (and thus responsibility) to periods and actions that a person simply could not recall. Nevertheless, it does constitute a controversial aspect of Locke's theory. It can be explored further by returning to one of the clinical conditions mentioned earlier, that of memory loss.

Memory Loss and Identity

What should be said about the situation of someone in adult life who suffers serious loss of memory? One example of this might be the gradually worsening memory that is associated with dementia. Here, the discussion is complicated by the fact that the condition of its sufferers may raise questions about Locke's definition of personhood, since the capacity for "reason and reflection" will be a controversial requirement in this context. However, dementia has also been seen as raising questions specifically about the continuing personal identity of the sufferer. One practical manifestation of this (DeGrazia 2005) has been a question concerning the validity of an advance directive: if the earlier experience of writing it can no longer be recalled by the sufferer, is it correct to regard it as having been written by the same person who is now suffering from dementia?

By contrast, in cases of dissociative amnesia, there is no issue regarding loss of personhood but simply an inability to recollect experiences from before the onset of the condition, an inability that may persist for years, during which new experiences are retained in the normal way (Butcher et al. 2015, pp. 298–300). Here, on Locke's account, it would seem that the onset must mark the start of a new person, since the sufferer's current experiential memories go back as far as that time but not earlier. Yet this is bound to be a contentious claim. For one thing it may not accord with the judgment of the sufferer. For another we have to consider the reaction of those people who regard themselves (at least initially) as friends of the victim and call to see her. The face and body will be familiar to them but she, by contrast, will not recognize them. Are they meeting an old friend who has lost her memory, or have they lost their friend and are thus meeting a new person for the first time?

This dilemma brings us back to the question of whether there is a right answer here, a truth to be discovered about her identity. It might be argued instead that there is a decision to be made by the visitors, one that could reasonably go either way. Or, if not exactly a decision, perhaps a pragmatic acceptance of what turns out to seem the more appropriate response over a period of time. Thus, although they might initially be disposed to accept that their friend still exists (despite having forgotten them and everything that has happened earlier) they might simply find this belief impossible to sustain. More generally, as Derek Parfit (1987) has argued, whatever account of personal identity that is adopted, the assumption that there is a determinate answer to all puzzling cases may have to be abandoned.

Successive Selves and Multiple Selves

Having claimed that memory was the basis of personal identity, and having noted the facts of ordinary forgetfulness that result in gaps in memory, Locke discovered an intriguing possibility: he saw that in theory, there could be a succession of different persons in the same body. The form in which he envisaged this was one involving the alternation of "two distinct incommunicable consciousnesses acting the same Body, the one constantly by Day, the other by Night" (Locke 1694/1975,

p. 344). In such a case, where it can be assumed that there would also be two separate sequences of memories, Locke suggests that there would be two persons as distinct (as he puts it) as Socrates and Plato, regardless of the fact that they have a single body in common. In a similar vein, Jennifer Radden (2004) has suggested that even the cycles of bipolar mood disorders such as manic depression might constitute different selves. Perhaps, though, Locke's insight leads further still. If his conception is extended somewhat, so that it may include several more selves, together with the possibility of them existing concurrently rather than only successively, the outcome is the situation familiar from descriptions of dissociative identity disorder. Before reflecting on this condition, however, it is worth recalling some of the usual presuppositions about the unity of the mind and of the self and looking at the extent to which these might be questioned even without the radical possibility of the multiple personalities associated with DID.

The Unity of Consciousness

Just one thought existing in isolation seems to be inconceivable. It seems that thoughts, together with the other elements of a person's mental life, have to be understood as existing with others and as being related to them. However, for a plausible account of a unified self, there is a need for more than just this minimal condition of the relatedness of mental items. After all, the beliefs of different people may very easily be related; for example, one person's belief may be the negation of that of someone else. So an understanding of the self appears to presuppose some further requirement, one that brings thoughts into a closer relation and thus to form the sort of group that is regarded as being in (or perhaps constitutive of) a particular mind. There is a need, in other words, for some conception of the unity of each particular mind and of the distinction between one mind and another. Such a conception is part of a broader and very familiar idea of persons and their identity: that for each human being, there is just one mind and one person.

What then unifies a mind and separates it from other minds? It might naturally be said that these are achieved through its dependence on a particular brain. But even if it were to be accepted that this dependency of a mind on the physical brain is relevant to a general understanding of the mind, there are nevertheless other notions of unity that are important here. In particular, there are some that seem to need describing essentially in mental terms and which thus, arguably, relate more directly to the understanding of the unity of a person's mental life. Above all there is the idea of the unity of consciousness: that for each person there is a single consciousness that has a direct awareness of all that person's thoughts but no direct awareness of those of other minds. Admittedly, neither the ideas of the unity nor of the directness of the awareness are as clear as might be wished; yet the belief that, for each person, there is one continuing awareness of all that person's thoughts as they occur, and that this awareness cannot have the same relation to the thoughts of other people, seems entrenched in human experience.

Just how basic this is to the conception of a person is perhaps best revealed by the difficulties in attempting to abandon it. By way of illustration, schizophrenic patients may report a sense of "thought insertion," the feeling that some of the thoughts they are experiencing are, even at that time, not really their own but have been placed into their minds by others to whom the thoughts still really belong (Oyebode 2008, p. 167). It is a condition where, once again, an account of the symptoms is deeply puzzling, even considered as a delusional state. While a delusion of hearing voices, for example, seems at least to have a comprehensible description, there is by contrast a particular incoherence in supposing that a thought occurring in someone's mind is not now solely that person's own thought, whatever its source and however alien it might seem to the sufferer. This problem with the intelligibility of the symptoms makes it extremely difficult for non-sufferers to have any imaginative grasp of the feeling of an intrusion into the self that matches this description. To recall the earlier distinction, even if disruptions to real selves are left aside, it is a challenge to understand this kind of disruption even as one simply to the sense of self.

It is also worth mentioning two other features that seem important to the idea of a single mind and thus to the idea of a single person. Firstly, there is consistency of belief, to the effect that a person cannot knowingly hold inconsistent beliefs. It cannot be the case that someone genuinely believes some proposition P and also not -P, for example, that here and now it is both raining and not raining. This has implications from the third person point of view as well, in that inconsistent beliefs cannot properly be attributed to another in circumstances where the subject would be aware of the inconsistency. Secondly, there is the idea of a unified will, such that it is assumed that each person has a single "decision center" in the mind which can consider various options before deciding what to do. Thus, even if someone says "I was caught in two minds," what is normally meant is simply that one single decider was finding it difficult to choose between two options.

However, some bodily conditions raise problems for these ideas of unity. Two such conditions will be considered next as a way of exploring the degree of disunity that may be possible in what, at least arguably, remains one mind.

The Split Brain

The first condition derives from attempts to treat epilepsy by a surgical severing of the cerebral commissures, the nerve fibers linking the two cerebral hemispheres of the brain. As a result of this surgery, while there are still links lower down in the brain, the usual direct flow of information between the two hemispheres is lost. One intriguing result (Nagel 1979) was the absence of any immediately obvious effects on the behavior of the patients; only with carefully devised experiments were any effects eventually discovered. To take a single example of many, the right nostril, exclusively, would be exposed to a strong smelling substance, with the effect that the smell would be registered in the right hemisphere, as in normal cases. However, the patient would deny smelling anything, since the information reaching the right hemisphere could not reach the left, and the left is the one responsible for speech. In contrast to the denial, the patient would show the usual facial signs of detecting a strong smell. Also, from a selection of objects, while still denying smelling anything, the patient would point to the object related to the smell, this being done with the left hand, which was controlled by the well-informed right hemisphere.

On the assumption of the unacceptability in one person of beliefs known to be contradictory, these contrasting responses are problematic. After all, an implication of this assumption is that for any strong and obvious smell, either a person smells something, or they do not. The split brain case presents a challenge to this, in that there seems to be one person who at the same time both smells something and does not smell it. That is, while admittedly there are not two inconsistent statements of belief, there is nevertheless behavior normally clearly indicative of detecting the smell and behavior normally clearly indicative of not detecting the smell. It is thus hard to know how to describe the subject. If it is inappropriate to say that there are two minds here, then the case may at least show that a single functioning mind, and therefore a single self, can be less unified than is usually thought. Perhaps too it is suggestive of an inherent vagueness in our conception of minds. For example, Jonathan Glover (1989, p. 46) argues that these patients do have a divided consciousness but suggests that in counting minds we are dealing with something that has "fuzzy edges."

Alien Hand Syndrome

The second condition may also be found following brain surgery and typically involves one hand seemingly obstructing what someone has decided to do by means of the other hand. This condition is perhaps even more challenging, in that it seems to involve a conflict of decision-making, or of wills, rather than just the question of whether or not a person believes something. Thus, to take one example, a person may light a cigarette and attempt to smoke it, yet find that the other hand has extinguished it, where this extinguishing occurs without the usual feelings of indecision and change of mind that would normally explain such an action. Nevertheless, although the person is puzzled by the act, and feels thwarted by it, the movements of the "alien" hand can hardly be regarded as random. In fact, they appear typical of purposeful behavior, albeit behavior that is rejected as contrary to the person's will and, as it seems to the sufferer, is not owned by them (Gallagher and Vaever 2004). Much as with the split brain example, if the alien hand does not appear to warrant talk of two minds, or two persons, it does seem to challenge the usual conception of their unity. That is, if a person can feel both surprised and thwarted by a seemingly purposeful action, where this action involves his or her own body and has its source within it, this threatens at least the straightforward idea of a person as invariably having a single decision center and a unified will.

Dissociative Identity (Multiple Personality) Disorder

Two kinds of condition have thus been considered, each of which might be thought to cast some doubt on the unity of the mind, whether this is understood as relating to consistency among cognitive states or to the unanimity of the will. With those issues in mind, consideration can now be given to what is perhaps the best known disorder concerning identity, that of dissociative identity disorder (DID), a condition still sometimes called by its earlier name of multiple personality disorder. In *DSM-5* it is described as being "characterized by (a) the presence of two or more distinct personality states or an experience of possession and (b) recurrent episodes of amnesia" (American Psychiatric Association 2013, p. 291). Not surprisingly, the diagnosis is a controversial one in practice (Oyebode 2008, pp. 228–229), and how the condition is even to be conceptualized depends on some fundamental philosophical assumptions about the nature of human beings and persons.

One basis for a conception of DID would be the familiar belief that there can only be a single person per human being. Thus, in these cases, the assumption would be that the patient could only possibly be one person, though a person whose mind had suffered major disruptions. This would be the natural view if, for example, it was thought that persons actually *are* bodies and that our personal identity is constituted by the continuation of the same body. (Though here the precise structure of the body may be critical, since in the case of dicephalic conjoined twins, where much of the body though not the brain is shared, it seems clear that there are two persons.) Certainly, a "one-person" assumption links well with the problems of the split brain and alien hand syndrome just considered, where doubts may be raised about the degree of unity in what might nevertheless be regarded as still one mind and one person. On this approach DID might be taken as simply further evidence of just how great the disunity may be in a single person's mind.

Yet, as was mentioned earlier, there is the option of a more radical conceptualization, one that involves abandoning the belief in an invariable one-one relation between human being and person. Drawing upon Locke's account of personal identity, it seems possible that two or more minds, and thus two or more genuinely distinct persons, may coexist in a single human being. On this basis it could be said that cases of DID present, within one human being, an alternation between different persons, each of whom has his or her own distinct personal identity. Note that it could still be accepted that they all depend on the body for their existence; the claim would be that nevertheless each of them could be a distinct consciousness with distinct memories and thus constitute a distinct person. It is this possibility, to an extent foreseen by Locke, which makes his theory of personal identity particularly relevant to the understanding of DID. But is it a conception that can be accepted? Or, if not, is there a coherent way of understanding DID as a disruption to the mind of what is never more than a single person?

The well-known case of Miss Beauchamp may usefully be taken as an example of DID, one that began in 1898 and was documented at length by the American physician Morton Prince (1978). A few basic elements can be taken from his very long and detailed account, enough to enable consideration of the philosophical issues that arise from this kind of case. It involves three main personalities (labeled B1, B3, and B4) plus one (B2) of initially rather indeterminate status. The original patient, Christine Beauchamp (or B1) was a quiet, conscientious nurse who consulted Prince when suffering mental health problems after a traumatic incident at her hospital. B2 was not initially thought of as a different person but was just a name for B1's character when under hypnosis. B2 did however have considerable significance, since by the end of the case, when some kind of unity was achieved – initially under hypnosis – B2 came to be thought of as the real Miss Beauchamp, just in need of being "woken up" or brought out of hypnosis (Prince 1978, p. 519). B3, or "Sally," originally appeared when B1 was hypnotized but later appeared spontaneously, that is, without hypnosis. She was lively, carefree, and rather unkind, with a tendency to play tricks on B1. B4 (or the "Idiot," as Sally called her) appeared spontaneously one evening during a visit by Prince to see Christine Beauchamp. The first indication was a change in Miss Beauchamp's demeanor from extreme agitation to calm, which he later realized marked the emergence of a new personality. B4 had suffered amnesia with respect to the previous 6 years, since the traumatic incident, and was confused, rather silent, stubborn, and sometimes aggressive in nature.

Here, as with such cases in general, just one of the alternate persons (if that is what they were) would present themselves and be "in charge" at any one time. The question of the mutual awareness between them, however, was more problematic. The original Miss Beauchamp (B1) had no direct knowledge of B3 or B4, and thus there were simply gaps in her memory for those periods when either of the other two was conscious. Similarly, B4 knew nothing of B1 or B3 and also had memory gaps from those times when the other two were in charge. Most strange of all, though, was the situation of Sally (B3). She was not only aware of the existence of both B1 and B4 but was seemingly aware of B1's thoughts, even though denying ownership of them. Her situation thus involves two deeply puzzling issues (Radden 1996): an asymmetry of awareness between the alternating persons, and the idea, mentioned earlier, of a direct awareness of thoughts that are not your own.

For and Against the Idea of Distinct Persons

To return to the radical conception of DID, is the mental life of the various characters in the Miss Beauchamp case sufficiently distinct for them to count as different persons? Certainly, there do seem to be distinct histories and distinct memories. The histories may not have been very long relative to most lives, but then we do not normally set a minimum length for a life to qualify as that of a person. A more obscure issue, perhaps, is whether it matters that there is an earlier shared history, before the distinct strands appear. Here, there is no normal situation to which we can appeal for guidance, though the ideas explored by Derek Parfit by means of imaginary cases of fission may be relevant here (Parfit 1987). By contrast, J.L. Mackie (1985) drew attention to something more familiar, which is that

different interests and responsibilities are typically associated with different persons. Once allowance is made for the fact that a shared body means that some
interests are inevitably shared, Sally and B1, for example, do indeed seem to have
different interests. Likewise, it seems natural to hold Sally responsible for her
unkindness toward B1, much as would be done if they were quite evidently
different people. There are also different capacities: B1 knew French, for example,
while Sally did not. Further, B1 had no direct access to Sally's thoughts, a barrier
that is one of the crucial features of the usual conception of different minds and
different persons. However, matters are complicated here, as has been mentioned
earlier, since the direct access that Sally seems to have to the thoughts of B1 is
normally (as one aspect of the unity of consciousness) something that counts
strongly against the idea of two distinct persons. Yet the fact of the asymmetry,
that it is a one-way access between Sally and B1, may perhaps weaken the force of
this assumption.

Prince's Conception of the Case

Prince's own presuppositions are intimated by his rejection of the label "multiple
personality" for such cases in favor of "disintegrated personality" (Prince 1978,
p. 3). In his view there was one and only one real person, the real Miss Beauchamp,
to be recovered, and for this reason he thought it appropriate to try to achieve a
single unified consciousness. He was aware that this might be contentious, though,
and suggested three considerations in defense of his approach to the problem
(pp. 231–234). Firstly, he claimed that one of the multiples would be the one best
adapted to any environment and that this would be the real Miss Beauchamp.
Secondly, he claimed that any other self would be a "sick self," suffering from
such conditions as amnesia and poor motivation. Thirdly, he claimed that the real
person would be one that was not "artificial," not the product of "special
influences."

In response it should perhaps first be acknowledged that the concept of a person
is itself contestable (Braude 1991) and has to be applied with caution in a philosophical context. However, even with this proviso, it might be suggested that the
first of Prince's points seems clearly questionable as a test for genuine personhood.
The ability to adapt and cope successfully with various environments is clearly
important but that some (putative) persons are less able than others in this respect is
hardly grounds for denying their status as persons. After all, many people may be
badly adapted to life yet are unquestionably persons nonetheless. A similar
response seems appropriate to the second of Prince's considerations, regarding
the sick self: plainly, many people have cognitive and motivational difficulties
yet are as much persons as those who are better off in these respects.

The third consideration is rather different. If the splitting into multiples results
from a *special* event, does this in itself render the newcomers *artificial* and thus
disqualify them from being genuine persons? More generally, can the conception of
a "natural" person (see Lizza 1993) be relied upon or has this been undermined by

the reflections on the idea of personal identity discussed earlier? These issues are too complex to follow up in detail here, but the features regarded by Prince as relevant may be briefly considered. Of these, the concept of an event (such as a traumatic experience) as "special" is a difficult category to apply as it stands. It might be understood to mean "abnormal," but even then it would not be clear why an abnormal event would necessarily produce an "artificial" outcome, as opposed to one that was simply unusual. For example, if being born is a normal stage on the way to personhood, a caesarean birth could be regarded as abnormal, yet the resulting baby is not regarded as in any way artificial and nor is it doubted that it is (or will soon become) a person. Perhaps IVF provides an even clearer counter-example. It is a procedure that might reasonably be regarded as special, abnormal, even in some sense unnatural, and artificial, yet (when successful) persons are undoubtedly the eventual outcome. Thus, even if it were supposed that these descriptions applied to traumatic shock, or to any other supposed cause of multi-ples, it is not obvious that this would provide grounds for the denial of personhood.

Multiples as Real Persons

So far the usual assumption has been made: that if the existence of DID as a phenomenon is accepted, then it must be a disorder. To conclude, though, a different possibility may be considered. Suppose DID is conceived radically as involving genuine multiple persons in one human being, would this situation necessarily be in itself an illness? Arguably, there is no reason to see it in this way, since the appropriate question with respect to health would be whether any of the individual multiples were unwell. Though all of them might share a bodily illness, and any of them might have a mental illness, the mere fact of multiplicity does not seem obviously pathological. To say the least, the presence of multiples might sometimes be awkward, but then so are relations between people in different bodies. Further, if they were held to be genuine persons, the plan to unify them would be conceptually puzzling and (if it were possible to carry it out) open to moral objections. As for suppressing any one of them to enable another to flourish, this too raises obvious ethical issues (Saks and Behnke 2000, pp. 63–66). In fact, if they had problems as individuals or as a group, some form of counseling for each of them might be the most appropriate response.

In general, though, perhaps not surprisingly, there has been a reluctance to accept the possibility of genuine multiple persons in one body. The uncertainty of the whole issue is sometimes the reason for this, rather than any sense that it can be shown to be impossible. Kathleen Wilkes (1988, p. 128), for example, writes that perhaps our concept of a person has "fractured" in the face of DID; meaning, presumably, that we can no longer be sure how to apply it in this context. Yet, as Carol Rovane (1998) argues in her defense of the possibility, the reluctance may be no more than an understandably entrenched way of thinking about persons in general, while Saks and Behnke (2000) regards it as too soon to judge the issue. And it is worth noting that even if there are insufficient grounds for regarding them as different persons, it is not straightforward to think of them as fragments of a single person either: partly because they each have a reasonable degree of coherence in themselves and partly because, more generally, it is not clear whether we can make sense of the idea of a fragment of a person or indeed of a mind.

Definitions of Key Terms

Narrative identity	Someone's own conception of a meaningful personal history that gives a sense of unity to his or her self.
Numerical identity	This is what holds in virtue of some X being one and the same thing or person. It can hold over time despite changes to X's properties.
Qualitative identity	Being alike in virtue of having the same properties.

Summary Points

- The nature and importance of the distinction between numerical and narrative identity.
- The possibility of skepticism regarding the reality of the self.
- Is personal identity bodily identity?
- John Locke: the self as a thinking being and memory as the key to identity.
- That personal identity might be altered by amnesia.
- The significance of the unity of consciousness in the understanding of the self.
- The problem of split brains and alien hands for the unity of the self.
- Considering dissociative identity disorder from a Lockean standpoint suggests the possibility of genuine multiple persons.

References

American Psychiatric Association (2013) Diagnostic and statistical manual of mental disorders, fifth edition, DSM-5. American Psychiatric Publishing, Washington, DC
Braude SE (1991) First person plural: multiple personality and the philosophy of mind. Routledge, London
Butcher JN, Hooley JM, Mineka S (2015) Abnormal psychology. Pearson Education Limited, Harlow
DeGrazia D (2005) Human identity and bioethics. Cambridge University Press, Cambridge
Fulford KWM, Thornton T, Graham G (2006) Oxford textbook of philosophy and psychiatry. Oxford University Press, Oxford
Gallagher S, Vaever M (2004) Body: disorders of embodiment. In: Radden J (ed) The philosophy of psychiatry: a companion. Oxford University Press, Oxford, pp 118–132
Glover J (1989) I: the philosophy and psychology of personal identity. Penguin, Harmondsworth
Hume D (1739/1967) A treatise of human nature (ed: Selbey-Bigge LA). Clarendon, Oxford
Lizza JP (1993) Multiple personality and personal identity revisited. Br J Philos Sci 44:263–274

Locke J (1694/1975) An essay concerning human understanding (ed: Nidditch PH). Clarendon, Oxford

Mackie JL (1985) Multiple personality. In: Mackie JL (ed) Persons and values. Clarendon, Oxford

Martin R, Barresi J (2003) Personal identity and what matters in survival: an historical overview. In: Martin R, Barresi J (eds) Personal identity. Blackwell, Oxford, pp 1 74

McMahan J (2002) The ethics of killing: problems at the margins of life. Oxford University Press, Oxford

Nagel T (1979) Brain bisection and the unity of consciousness. In: Nagel T (ed) Mortal questions. Cambridge University Press, Cambridge, pp 147–164

Noonan HW (2003) Personal identity, 2nd edn. Routledge, London

Oyebode F (2008) Sims' symptoms in the mind. Saunders Elsevier, Philadelphia

Parfit D (1987) Reasons and persons. Clarendon, Oxford

Prince M (1978) The dissociation of a personality: the hunt for the real Miss Beauchamp. Oxford University Press, Oxford

Quinton A (1975) The soul. In: Perry J (ed) Personal identity. University of California Press, Berkeley/Los Angeles, pp 53–72

Radden J (1996) Divided minds and successive selves: ethical issues in disorders of identity and personality. MIT Press, Cambridge, MA

Radden J (2004) Identity: personal identity, characterization identity, and mental disorder. In: Radden J (ed) The philosophy of psychiatry: a companion. Oxford University Press, Oxford, pp 133–146

Rovane C (1998) The bounds of agency: an essay in revisionary metaphysics. Princeton University Press, Princeton

Saks ER, Behnke SH (2000) Jekyll on trial: multiple personality disorder & criminal law. New York University Press, New York

Wilkes KV (1988) Real people: personal identity without thought experiments. Clarendon, Oxford

Williams B (1973) The self and the future. In: Williams B (ed) Problems of the self. Cambridge University Press, Cambridge, pp 46–63

Personality Disorder: Philosophical Problems

62

Peter Zachar

Contents

Abstract

The concept of personality disorder was introduced in the twentieth century, emerging from a small collection of prior concepts such as constitution, temperament, self, character, and personality. Among the key events in the development of the concept are the introduction and subsequent rejection of degeneration theory, the work of Kurt Schneider, the DSM-III, and the recent proposals to dimensionalize personality disorder in DSM-5 and ICD-11. As the patchwork of ideas that belong to the domain of personality disorder are residues of its conceptual history, that history is herein used to guide an exploration of ongoing philosophical problems. Constitution and temperament raise the issue of the biological basis of personality and personality

P. Zachar (✉)
Department of Psychology, Auburn University Montgomery, Montgomery, AL, USA
e-mail: pzachar@aum.edu

© Springer Science+Business Media Dordrecht 2017
T. Schramme, S. Edwards (eds.), *Handbook of the Philosophy of Medicine*,
DOI 10.1007/978-94-017-8688-1_77

disorder. Recent work in behavioral genetics supports the hypothesis that personality has a genetic component but not that it is genetically determined. Surprisingly, the genetic component in personality may become more important in open societies where people can self-select into environments. Under the concept of self, the notions of causal explanation and self-continuity are important. Recent work on the psychometrics of latent variable modeling has given new life to traditional empiricist suspicions about reifying personality traits as causal entities. Longitudinal studies indicate that there is both continuity and variability in personality and personality disorder across the life span. Character is a concept drawn from moral theory and draws attention to the close association between some personality disorders and moral vices. In clinical settings, separating responsibility and blame is an important skill for working with patients diagnosed with a personality disorder. The concept of personality once referred to self-presentation but was gradually interiorized, leading to the problem of distinguishing surface versus deep features of personality. This chapter concludes with a survey of six different models regarding the nature of "disorder" in personality disorder.

Introduction: The Historical Development of Personality Disorder

The concept of personality disorder is a child of the twentieth century. Despite having similar names such as mania and melancholia, very few of the categories used in nineteenth-century psychiatry align with current concepts. Throughout the nineteenth century, the psychiatric landscape was expanded by the introduction of new diagnostic concepts. The most important new concepts for personality disorder were *manie sans délire*, monomania, moral insanity, and *folie lucide*. Encompassed under these new diagnoses were compulsions, impulsive acts, overvalued ideas, and rigid affective states – all in the absence of active psychosis. Although personality disorders could be included in this collection, only from our current historical vantage point is "personality" evident.

In the late nineteenth and early twentieth centuries, the psychological concept of personality was emerging out a collection of historically diverse concepts. According to Berrios (1996), these concepts include:

Constitution
Temperament
Self
Character
Personality

Theoreticians in different countries mixed and matched intellectual traditions in such a way that no simple story can be told of how these various strands led to our current conceptions. Indeed, the patchwork of ideas that constitute the concepts of personality and personality disorder are residues of this history.

Four Milestones: Degeneration, Schneider, DSM-III, and DSM-5

The kernel around which the concept of personality disorder developed was degeneration theory. Introduced in 1857 by Benedict Morel, degeneration came to be thought of as a process of de-evolution or a regression to a more primitive stage of development. Once initiated, a trajectory of degeneration was supposedly transmitted to offspring, with each new age group becoming increasingly degenerate. In literature, both Mr. Hyde and Count Dracula were late-nineteenth-century depictions of degeneration. The makeup for Mr. Hyde in the 1931 film starring Frederic March presented Hyde as a Neanderthal. This portrayal was closer to Robert Louis Stevenson's atavistic concept than is seeing Hyde as a manifestation of multiple personality disorder.

By the time Kurt Schneider published *Psychopathic Personalities* in 1923, degeneration was on the wane, somewhat. Both Schneider and Sigmund Freud had rejected it – although it remained influential in the eugenics movement throughout the 1930s, especially in *Nazi* Germany. It was not until the aftermath of World War II when many aspects of *Nazi* ideology were newly considered unacceptable that degeneration theory was abandoned.

Julius Koch's 1891 concept of psychopathic inferiority was formulated, in part, under the auspices of degeneration theory. The same is true of Emil Kraepelin's 1904 notion of the morbid personality. Schneider (1923/1950), however, explicitly claimed that the psychopathic personality was not a degenerate state. Nor was it even "psychopathic" in the current sense of the term. At that point in history, psychopathic was a synonym for "psychological pathology." Schneider viewed psychopathic personalities as statistical abnormalities – either an excess or deficit relative to the mean. When people suffer or they make others suffer because of these abnormalities, the personality can be considered disordered (i.e., psychopathic).

The notion of personality disorder as different in kind from both psychosis and neurosis (mood and anxiety disorders) was clearly articulated in Schneider's book. Soon thereafter the general term psychopathic personality/personality disorder became a center of gravity drawing into its orbit many phenomena that needed a home base in what was a rapidly changing psychiatric landscape. These phenomena included the various formes frustes (milder, incomplete forms) of other mental disorders such as schizoid and cyclothymic disturbances, substance abuse problems, and maladaptive stress reactions.

In the individualist culture of the USA, many psychiatric phenomena came to be considered personality like. Also in the USA, in the middle part of the twentieth century, the concept of personality disorder was augmented by psychoanalytic, neo-Freudian, ego-psychological, and object relation perspectives culminating in the introduction of borderline and narcissistic disorders (Kernberg 1975; Kohut 1971). Hervey Cleckley's (1941) work on psychopathy, which was descriptive rather than psychodynamic, was a parallel line of development.

The third edition of the *Diagnostic and Statistical Manual of Mental Disorders* (DSM-III), published in 1980, rivals Schneider's book in its historical importance.

The DSM-III gathered together a variety of personality disorder concepts used in American psychiatry and placed them into a single domain. These disorders were grouped into three clusters. The first cluster included paranoid, schizoid, and schizotypal personalities. The second included histrionic, narcissistic, antisocial, and borderline personalities. The third included avoidant, dependent, compulsive, and passive-aggressive personalities.

The DSM-III also highlighted the distinction between personality disorder and other psychiatric disorders by placing them on separate "axes." For instance, in a DSM-III diagnostic formulation, schizophrenia and depression were coded on axis I, while personality disorder was coded on axis II. After the introduction of axis II, personality disorder became a more distinct topic of specialization in psychiatry.

The stability that the domain of personality disorder has possessed since the publication of the DSM-III is increasingly fragile. The committee that developed the DSM-5 of 2013 hoped to introduce a new hybrid model of personality disorder composed of categories and a hierarchy of dimensions. This hybrid model requires that all cases of personality disorder have deficits in two or more dimensions of self and interpersonal functioning. These self and interpersonal dysfunctions are an amalgamation of borderline, narcissistic, and psychopathic features. In addition all cases of personality disorder have to possess one or more pathological personality traits. There are five broad trait dimensions (or *domains*) that can collectively be decomposed in 25 narrower facets. The domains are negative affectivity, detachment, antagonism, disinhibition, and psychoticism. Examples of facets are emotional lability and hostility for negative affectivity and risk taking for disinhibition.

The hybrid model reduces the number of personality disorder categories to six: borderline, narcissistic, antisocial, schizotypal, avoidant, and obsessive-compulsive. The retained categories are all identified by self and interpersonal deficits and profiles of pathological personality traits. Cases of personality disorder that do not fit one of the retained categories are also identified by self and interpersonal deficits and pathological personality traits, potentially making the categories peripheral.

This new model was controversial (Zachar et al. 2016). It was rejected for inclusion in the main text of the manual but was placed in section III of the book and titled *Alternative DSM-5 Model of Personality Disorders*. Its advocates treat it as being in competition with the old DSM categorical model, which was reprinted in section II of the DSM-5.

European and British psychiatrists have been less enthusiastic about the topic of personality disorder than Americans – although more recently the concept of dangerous and severe personality disorder has been important in the UK. The *International Classification of Diseases* (ICD) has mostly utilized the DSM personality disorder categories. The current plans for the ICD-11, however, are to replace all categories of personality disorder with a parsimonious model of five dimensions that will be rated for levels of severity (Tyrer 2014). The five proposed domains are negative emotional (affective), dissocial, disinhibited, anankastic, and detached. Presumably, the ICD approach will compete with the models in sections II and III of the DSM-5.

As might be expected from a conceptually complicated domain such as personality disorder, an exploration of the relevant philosophical problems could fill a handbook of its own. For this reason, selecting which problems to address is likely to provoke disagreement and second guessing. A useful map of the more perennial issues can be found in Berrios' list of the nineteenth-century concepts that preceded the current notion of personality disorder. In what follows, important philosophical and conceptual problems pertaining to constitution and temperament, self as substrate, self-continuity, character, and personality will be explored. In addition, this chapter will address the perennial problem of the nature of "disorder" in personality disorder.

Constitution and Temperament

Constitutional factors refer to innate features that are considered to be biological predispositions for psychiatric disorder. Temperament refers to affective and behavioral dispositions with a genetic component. Temperament in particular encompasses one of the oldest perspectives on psychological types – best exemplified by the humoral theory of Hippocrates and Galen. Their four temperaments were sanguine (extroverted and happy), choleric (energetic and irritable), melancholic (moody and reserved), and phlegmatic (thoughtful and calm).

Temperaments emerge early in life and are relatively stable over time, albeit expressed differently as people become psychologically complex (Kagan et al. 1994). Many different conceptualizations of temperament have been offered in the past 50 years. Among the temperaments considered important for psychopathology are negative affectivity, positive affectivity, and self-control.

According to Lee Anna Clark (2005), temperament is a predisposition for both personality and psychopathology. For instance, the temperament of negative affectivity is a common feature in the personality trait of neuroticism, borderline personality disorder, and major depressive disorder. As a common feature, it partly explains the tendency of neuroticism, borderline personality, and depression to co-occur. Each is also distinct. Neuroticism is a more complex phenomenon than negative affectivity because it also includes self-concepts, motivations, and coping styles. The borderline personality involves specific forms of self-concept, coping styles, etc. Both neuroticism and borderline personality can moderate the course of a depressive disorder.

An important philosophical issue with respect to temperament is its implications for the biological basis of personality and personality disorder. The behavioral genetics of the 1990s initiated a rebirth of biological models of personality as scientific evidence about the high heritabilities of personality traits accumulated (Bouchard and McGue 1990). For instance, even when reared apart, identical twins develop similar political attitudes and interests in religion. Later, the heritabilities of traits like neuroticism were used to argue that such traits are innate, universal features of human design selected for during evolution (Livesley et al. 1998; McCrae and Costa 1997).

Part of the difficulty in conceptualizing the genetic findings is a tendency to conflate high heritability with "highly inherited." They are not the same. Heritability is a technical statistical concept and not a simple proxy for "inherited." To illustrate, for mammals, being an oxygen breather has a heritability of zero, although it is a highly inherited, innate trait. Heritability is a numerical estimate of the percentage of the phenotypic variance that is due to genetic effects. Because all mammals are oxygen breathers, the variance of being an oxygen breather is zero. If the total phenotypic variance is zero, the percentage of that variance due to genetics must also be zero.

By the beginning of the twenty-first century, the optimism of the 1990s, at least among behavioral geneticists, was tempered by additional research (Johnson et al. 2009). As Turkheimer (1998) has pointed out, nearly every psychological trait studied is heritable. This is a strange finding because the ubiquity of heritability also includes time spent watching television and divorce. Time watching television cannot be a universal trait directly selected for during evolution as television was not available prior to the twentieth century. Nor can divorce be said to be inherited rather than acquired.

Additional research also showed that candidate genes for personality traits account for only a small percentage of the variance, and most of these findings do not reliably replicate across studies (McGue and Gottesman 2015). According to current views, there is a genetic basis for personality, but there is no such thing as a *gene for* a personality trait in the same way there is a *gene for* Huntington's disease. The genetic research supports the classical view that there is a genetic component to personality, but not the more modern view that personality is genetically *determined*.

The behavioral genetics of personality is also pertinent to the philosophical problem of freedom versus determinism. In an interesting and unexpected twist, allowing people freedom of choice may increase the extent to which personality traits are heritable in a population. In fact, as populations age, the heritabilities of traits can increase.

How can this be? In an open society, people are able to select the environments to which they are most often exposed. In doing so, they are likely to select environments that allow them to exercise their basic traits and talents (Scarr and McCartney 1983). For example, in the eighth century, people with intellectual interests had limited options. They could work in farming and agriculture, raise children, become a cleric, or practice the art of war. The paucity of available environments constrained the traits that could be developed. In contrast, modern people with intellectual interests have more options to self-select into environments where intellectual traits and abilities can be developed. With self-selection, the traits that are developed are aligned with individual dispositions, resulting in higher heritabilities.

If one's dispositions are maladaptive and the diversity of available environments is large, self-selection might not have such a healthy outcome for everyone. Consider the salesperson who spent a career needing to get along with customers and coworkers despite a disposition toward intense suspiciousness and mistrust. He gets along only with great difficulty and modest success. After retirement, he is freer to self-select into environments such as those that reinforce conspiracy theories, resentment, and black-and-white thinking. Over time, his suspiciousness can increasingly manifest as something more akin to a paranoid personality style.

The Self

The self with its long and rich philosophical history is a general topic rather than a specific concept. Concepts that fall under the general topic include self-consciousness, self-concept, self-esteem, identity, and personhood. For personality disorders, two key philosophical problems pertaining to the self are the self as substrate and self-continuity.

In the discussion that follows, both (categorical) types and (dimensional) traits will be mentioned. For this reason, some background information on types and traits will be helpful before proceeding.

The classification of personality disorder in psychiatry has tended to utilize types such as borderline, narcissistic, and psychopathic. One of the problems with types is that patients with complicated symptom presentations tend to meet diagnostic criteria for more than one type. For instance, they may be borderline and narcissistic. Generally speaking, mental health professionals believe it is more accurate to say that such patients have a single complicated personality disorder, not two comorbid disorders.

A second problem with types is that there is likely no single, privileged classification of types. Many different personality types exist, only a few of which are formally named. For instance, there were 11 types in the DSM-III. These 11 types do not comprehensively represent the domain of personality disorder as exemplified by the finding that most diagnoses of personality disorder using DSM categories are classified as personality disorder not otherwise specified.

Rather than expand the menu of types, many psychologists and psychiatrists believe that it would be better to develop a comprehensive model of the personality disorder domain with respect to pathological personality traits. Both the alternative DSM-5 model and the proposed ICD-11 model are trait oriented in this way. Ideally, a trait model would be empirically based, rather than founded only on clinical tradition. In addition, personality traits are almost always a matter of degree. For example, neuroticism and suspiciousness are traits on which everyone has a value from low to high. Traits therefore span across the normal and the abnormal. One of the attractions to such a "dimensional model" approach is that it could unify both normal and abnormal personality in a single domain.

Self as Substrate: Basic Issues

The self as substrate refers to the notion that the self is the possessor of psychological features such as perceiving, thinking, and emoting. According to René Descartes, just as length does not exist on its own but is a property of some material object, thoughts and emotions do not exist in on their own; rather, they are properties of the self.

An important contrast to this Cartesian view is that of John Locke who pointed out that "substrate" is inferred to explain why properties co-occur in a regular pattern, but as a concept the substrate is obscure, being little more than a name for "we know not what" supports these observable patterns. David Hume likewise denied that we have any experience of a self, viewing it instead as a speculative inference. Locke and Hume established an empiricist tradition which is wary of making inferences to hidden entities behind the appearances or more specifically wary about attributing metaphysical importance to inferred entities such as the self.

In the seventeenth century, the playwright Moliére mocked the pseudo-explanations used by the physicians of the day by having one of his characters explain the sleep-inducing properties of opium by claiming that opium has a *virtus dormitiva*. Roughly translated, *virtus dormitiva* means the "capacity to induce sleep." Moliére's mocking of the reification of technical phrases into causal entities is a favorite example of empiricists. An analogy in psychiatry would be to claim that a patient has unstable affect because of her borderline personality disorder.

The empiricist perspective has had a profound influence on philosophical thinking about personality traits – particularly the notion that hidden personality traits in the head are psychological causes of behavior. Consider the following:

Feeling tense and jittery
Having a quick temper
Being thin-skinned and readily insulted

In certain personality structures, these features regularly co-occur. One way to explain why they co-occur is to infer an underlying causal disposition – called neuroticism. In addition to explaining why these attributes co-occur, the explanatory construct of neuroticism allows us to make predictions about the presence of additional attributes such as feeling overwhelmed by daily stress.

However, one can ask – is the personality trait of neuroticism a psychological entity that causes people to both feel tense and be overwhelmed by daily stress or is it a general name referring to the regular co-occurrence of feeling tense and overwhelmed? According to the latter position, the name neuroticism is a place-holder for the various causes of these behaviors, but not a cause itself. If we knew what all those causal processes were, there would be no need to ever infer an additional causal process called "neuroticism."

Self as Substrate: Scientific Relevance

Some readers may question the relevance of armchair empiricist metaphysics, but similar considerations have recently gained renewed importance in the scientific study of personality disorder. Let me explain further.

As noted above, advocates for the dimensional approach have been seeking comprehensive, empirically based models of the domain of personality disorder. One of their strategies for doing so is the statistical technique of factor analysis.

Let us consider the 92 symptoms of the eleven DSM-III personality disorders as demarcating the domain of personality disorder. A factor analysis would examine the pattern of correlations between these symptoms and derive a small number of dimensions that statistically explain those correlations. Such dimensions are called latent variables because they are causes hidden in the correlation matrix. The five domain level traits of the alternative DSM-5 model are conceptualized as latent variables in this way.

The problem is that the interpretation of factors as causally potent latent variables may originate in metaphysical assumptions about the self. The important assumption in this case is that personality traits cause behavior. There are two reasons why these assumptions might not be justified in all cases.

First, the "factors" in these statistical models represent individual differences in a population, not causal processes inside the heads of individuals. As Borsboom et al. (2009) have shown, the mathematical requirements for taking individual difference factors derived from between-persons data and treating them as within-persons causal variables are rarely met.

Second, according to van der Maas et al. (2006), artificially constructed data sets in which the correlations between variables are a function of underlying common causes generate the appropriate factors using factor analytic models. However, these factors are also generated by data sets in which the variables are in direct causal relationship with themselves in the absence of underlying common causes (Cramer et al. 2010). For example, the neuroticism factor might be a concept that emerges from a reciprocal causal relationship between

Feeling tense and jittery
Feeling overwhelmed by daily stress

According to this perspective, the pattern named neuroticism refers to an interlocking network of causal relationships that maintains itself over time by means of feedback loops. Rather than *feeling overwhelmed by daily stress* being a surface indicator of a latent entity called neuroticism, it is a part of a pattern of activation in a causal network that we name neuroticism.

Self as Substrate: Situations Versus Traits

The psychologist Walter Mischel (1968) has argued that there is too much variability in behavior across situations to support inferences to causally important traits. If you want to explain why someone is suspicious at one time but not another, according to Mischel, the nature of the situation is a better place to look.

Social psychologists have also discovered that people are too quick to explain an individual's behavior with respect to internal states such as personality traits while ignoring situational influences (Nisbett and Wilson 1977). In some social psychological experiments, people resort to trait explanations even when they know that the situation is the primary causal factor (Jones and Harris 1967).

An example of erroneous trait explanation in psychiatry would be to see most behaviors of a person diagnosed with a personality disorder as expressions of that disorder. For instance, "She is in a bad mood today – there goes her borderline personality disorder again!" Besides the problem of propagating an overly simplistic casual theory, reducing a whole person to a diagnosis is dismissive. It is always prudent to augment explanations with respect to personal qualities by looking for situational influences.

In response to Mischel, advocates for studying personality traits claim that for any particular trait, people will differ on how important that trait is in their personality structure (Bem and Allen 1974). An individual can be suspicious without suspiciousness being a defining trait. Furthermore, for people for whom suspiciousness is central to their personality structure, there will still be variability across situations. To detect the consistency, it is important to aggregate situations and examine trends (Epstein 1979).

If treating personality traits as latent causal entities is justified, doing so requires experience and training. For example, Funder (1997) notes that shy people are often inaccurately judged to be aloof and cold. Shyness and aloofness share many of the same behaviors. Flawed inferences about traits are heightened once we develop conceptual expectations about what another person is like (e.g., she is aloof) and thereafter interpret behaviors in accordance with those concepts (i.e., "Eating lunch alone again? She is awfully aloof."). Rather than using behaviors to confirm trait inferences, it is important to actively differentiate manifestly similar traits by asking the person to report on their likes, dislikes, thoughts, emotions, and perceptions.

Self-Continuity

The problem of continuity versus change is one of the oldest in philosophy. What does it mean for something to change but still be the same thing versus becoming a different kind of thing? With respect to personality, change occurs between age 5 and age 30, between 30 and 55, and between 55 and 80. Some people change more than others.

Is the adult who as an adolescent expressed his shyness by spending most of his time reading alone in his bedroom expressing the same trait when at age 40 he rises early in the morning to have 2 hours of quiet reading? What if that same adult is sociable, interacts with people all day, and teaches courses on interpersonal skills?

Within our large behavioral repertoires, there will always be resemblances between what we were like in the past and what we are like now. Any observer makes a choice about which of these resemblances to call the same "trait." Such choices can be justified, but it is important to not minimize variation and change in order to preferentially see continuity over time.

As a general rule, clinical psychologists are reluctant to make attributions about pathological personality traits until someone reaches late adolescence or early adulthood. One reason for this reluctance is that young people are immature. The normal immaturities of children's and adolescents' personalities would likely be suggestive of personality disorder were they to occur in adults.

A second reason for this reluctance is that personality traits are less stable in our early years (Roberts et al. 2006). It makes sense to expect that if you get to know a

5-year-old girl very well but then you did not see her again until she is 30, you should expect to encounter someone you do really know. If, after getting to know her as an adult, you did not see her again until she was 55, you could reasonably anticipate meeting someone with whom you are familiar.

To an even greater extent, personality disorders are assumed to be fixed, with "inflexibility" being one of the features that make them maladaptive. For instance, the DSM-5 diagnostic criteria for personality disorder include:

An enduring pattern of inner experience and behavior.
The enduring pattern is inflexible and pervasive across a broad range of personal and social situations.
The pattern is stable and of long duration, and its onset can be traced back at least to adolescence or early adulthood.

More recent research, however, has shown that even for personality disorder, continuity versus change is not a simple matter. When personality disorder symptoms are evident in adolescence, if there are also other psychiatric difficulties such as mood, anxiety, and conduct problems, the personality disorder symptoms are more likely to be maintained into adulthood. Otherwise they decrease. This decrease may be correlated with maturation of normal personality traits.

What about the stability of adult personality configurations once diagnostic criteria for a personality disorder have been met? At the beginning of the twenty-first century, data from several longitudinal studies of personality disorder started to become available. According to Morey and Meyer (2012), the early indications were that even in severe cases, pathological symptoms decline over time, and personality disorders are less enduring than psychiatrists had assumed. However, as the time interval in these studies has increased, the picture has become more complicated. Even after a person no longer meets diagnostic criteria for a personality disorder, psychiatric distress and impairment are still evident; and remissions are also common.

An important argument for implementing a dimensional approach to personality disorder, claim Morey and Meyer, is that pathological personality traits such as affective instability and their associated functional impairments are more stable over time than are types such as borderline and narcissistic. The problem with types is that they include features that are stable (traits) and those that are more transient (states). In borderline personality disorder, for instance, affective instability seems to be more enduring, whereas frantic efforts to avoid abandonment are more situation bound.

Character

Prior to the nineteenth century, "character" was a term in moral theories that emphasized virtues and vices. So close was the association between moral theory and character traits that the term moral was often used to denote "psychological."

Considered as traits, virtues are stable dispositions. Examples include benevolence, fairness, and honesty. In the ideal exercise of virtue, a person's cognition, emotion, and action are coordinated. The virtuous person knows what is good, has good sentiments, and performs good acts.

In this tradition, Peter Goldie (2004) argues that character traits are concerned with a person's moral worth. He also believes that character traits are more important than personality traits because character traits can color all of the personality. For instance, someone can be outgoing, witty, and diligent, but these positive personality traits can be subservient to an all-consuming self-centeredness.

John Sadler (2013) has pointed out that many psychiatric disorders are vice laden, raising the problem of moral taint for diagnostic constructs. More specific to personality disorder, Louis Charland (2004) argues that some personality disorders are moral, not medical conditions. If so, then to have a certain type of personality disorder might be equivalent to being a certain type of bad person.

This problem is most evident for psychopathy and its DSM sibling called antisocial personality disorder in which all seven diagnostic criteria are morally tainted: *lawbreaker, deceitful, impulsive, continually fighting and assaulting others, recklessly disregarding others' safety, irresponsible,* and *lacking in remorse.* Although not our primary concern in this chapter, the concept of psychopathy may have as much relevance for moral philosophy as it does for personality disorder (Kiehl 2014; Schramme 2014).

Key features of borderline personality disorder, like impulsivity, are also associated with behaviors typically considered immoral such as infidelity. The diagnosis of narcissistic personality disorder is likewise vice laden as many of its clinical features parallel the seven deadly sins, e.g., "grandiosity" is *pride*, "enviousness of others" is *envy*, and "reacting to perceived insults with rage" is *anger*. Paranoid personality disorder and histrionic personality disorder also intersect with the moral realm. People who are paranoid display unjustified resentment and blaming of others. People who are histrionic exhibit a shallow self-centeredness.

This issue of moral taint is equally problematic for the alternative DSM-5 model because the self and interpersonal deficits that are required for *every* diagnosis of personality disorder are largely made up of borderline, narcissistic, and psychopathic features. These deficits include being unconcerned about the effect of one's behavior on others and cooperating predominately for personal gain.

Among the many issues falling under the problem of moral taint for the domain of personality disorder are:

Are personality disorders objective and value free, or must they be value laden?
If value laden, are the values moral values or nonmoral values?
Are failures of moral capacities pathological processes themselves or consequences of deficits in nonmoral capacities?
Under what conditions, if any, does a personality disorder either attenuate or increase responsibility for wrongful acts?

What implications do these philosophical issues have for clinical work? One worry is that emphasizing the moral dimension can mean that blame and stigmatization are increased if the people diagnosed with certain personality disorders are seen as being either born bad or irreparably bad.

Often, mental health professionals who work with drug and alcohol populations or in prison settings learn to expect deception and persistently insist that clients take responsibility for their actions. Their experience tells them that it would be naïve to hope for virtue rather than expect vice.

This confrontational strategy would seem to conflict with the empathic stance of the general psychotherapist who tries to understand the patient's perspective. However, the consequences of being empathic might not be positively uniform in a therapeutic sense. For instance, one way to achieve empathy is to view behaviors as reason responsive, meaning either (a) from the patient's perspective the behaviors are enacted for reasons or (b) we can understand the behavior with respect to reasons. But if behaviors are seen as being enacted for reasons, then the person is also seen as having a degree of control and responsibility – and therefore as being potentially blameworthy.

Hanna Pickard (2013) observes that the experience of being blamed often has a "sting" that can be anti-therapeutic. The sting, she argues, is related to an emotional form of blame in which one feels entitled to blame the other and believes that the other deserves the blame. Part of clinical training involves learning to manage emotional reactions that might interfere with the professional role. With such training, it is possible to hold patients responsible for their behaviors without engaging in emotional blame.

An important feature of the professional relationship is that it is limited to therapeutic contexts – and the limited nature of that relationship contributes to a clinician's ability to adopt attitudes that would be harder to maintain across all sectors of life. In this vein, clinicians should also be cautious about applying the concept of "personality disorder" outside of clinical settings as it might enhance blaming. Instead of the term "disorder," it is often possible to talk about immaturity instead.

Personality

Of all the concepts in our list, none has undergone a more fundamental transformation than the concept of personality. Our current notion of an individual's personality as those psychological features which (a) make her or him distinct from others and (b) the same over time is of recent origin. In both antiquity and the Medieval period, personality referred to self-presentation – or how we appear to others. In that sense, personality was a name for surface features. Psychological questions about internal features under the auspices of self, character, and soul became increasingly important in the modern era.

For example, Descartes wrote his *Meditations on First Philosophy* from the perspective of the experiencing "I." Half a century later, Locke wrote about "personality" as the awareness of a self-same I extending back in time in his *An Essay Concerning Human Understanding*. Still, the various conceptual strands were jumbled up. For Locke personality was similar to "personness," referring to a person's awareness of moral agency and responsibility across time.

According to Lombardo and Foschi (2003), it is against the backdrop a more spiritualist and speculative French tradition that the concept of personality began to evolve toward our present notions. A key aspect of this evolution was to understand personality as referring to the unity of the conscious self.

In late nineteenth-century France, with the arrival of positivism and its own suspicion of metaphysics, personality was naturalized. It became a descriptive concept for use in psychiatry and psychology. Among the contributors to this tradition were Eugène Azam, Théodule Ribot, and Pierre Janet – each emphasizing in some way alterations in self-consciousness as forms of *psychopathology*.

It is through William James' (1890) study of French thinking that the concept of personality gained a foothold in the USA. James' concept of personality is not well developed, but it seems to refer to a subjective awareness of self that can vary over time (echoing Locke).

In the first decades of the twentieth century, personality came to be preferred as a secular alternative to character because it lacked strong moral connotations. It was also a psychological alternative to the more biological concept of temperament.

The introduction of personality as a general topic under which the concepts discussed in this chapter were integrated was spearheaded by the psychologist Gordon Allport (1937) and others (Lewin 1935; Murray 1938; Stagner 1937). One of the most important features of Allport's work is that he advocated for the measurement of personality traits, but inspired by his time in Germany studying with William Stern, he also advocated for the importance of the qualitative study of individuals as historically unique (Nicholson 2003). Allport's worry was that restricting our scientific understanding of individuals to the measurement of traits was too shallow.

This tension in Allport's approach continues to exist today in psychiatry with respect to types versus traits. Types of personality disorder such as borderline were initially based on case studies and narratives – which represented a Germanic, qualitative approach to the study of personality. The rich intellectual traditions in the Germanic lands that influenced the concept of personality are too extensive to survey here. Among the various traditions that would need recounting are Immanuel Kant and his heirs, the organicist perspective, the influence of Wilhelm Dilthey, and the study of phenomenology.

Advocates for types state that constructs describing the integration of psychological processes in an individual patient are richer than dimensional profiles which tend to be lists of traits. In their view, coherent types offer bridges to deeper aspects of a personality, whereas dimensions are primarily research tools for identifying relationship among variables in a general population (Shedler et al. 2010). A trait profile might offer an overview of the personality to help initiate a diagnostic formulation, but it is largely a screening instrument.

In contrast, advocates for dimensional trait models believe that types are heuristics constructed from unsystematic clinical observation that lacks the validity of empirically derived dimensions (Livesley 2012). They allow that profiles need to be augmented with clinical conceptualizations, but in their view, the empirical grounding of traits should lead to better formulations in the long run.

Another manifestation of the contrast between surface versus deep features in psychiatry is the problem of nonconscious influences on behavior. The difficult conceptual issue, especially for scientific psychologists, is the notion of the dynamic unconscious in Sigmund Freud's sense. The Freudian unconscious encompasses impulses, emotions, and affect-tinged representations that are repressed, but that can influence behavior if the repression weakens. These influences are deeper because they were formed early in our development. In addition, because we lack awareness of them, we cannot moderate their influence as repression begins to fail.

The main philosophical problem of the metaphysics of self, i.e., the legitimacy of inferences to unobservable and unexperienced causal entities in the head, remains important. In the history of psychiatry, the unconscious is the ultimate latent variable. This problem is made thornier by the added complication of attributing intentionality and purpose in the absence of awareness. Here are some examples of such inferences:

Psychopaths seek to control others in order to avoid feelings of shame.
Paranoia is a defense against homosexual feelings.
Compulsive behaviors are strategies for undoing an imagined transgression.
Narcissistic grandiosity is rooted in fear of dependency on others

Irrespective of the validity of inferences about unconscious processes, algorithmically applying such attributions to all cases with a particular personality disorder diagnosis is best discouraged. As we saw earlier with the problem of being shy versus aloof, it is hard to appropriately name abstract psychological processes. The danger is that a fallacious version of confirmatory hypotheses testing can be used to transform inferences from behaviors to psychological processes into a conviction that whenever those behaviors occur, the inferred psychological processes are responsible (e.g., "Wow this guy is paranoid. Obviously pathologically unaware of his attractions to other men.").

What the contrast of deep versus shallow ultimately denotes is that the concept of personality helps us understand an individual by looking for patterns that are not immediately apparent. The concept of personality disorder seeks to inform us about patterns that have specific relevance for psychiatric settings and the professional problems of clinicians.

The "Disorder" in Personality Disorder

The problems discussed up to this point in this chapter largely pertain to the personality part of personality disorder. That leaves untouched the question of the nature of personality *disorder*. From its very inception, the concept of personality disorder was different from other psychiatric disorders. Unlike psychosis and many neurotic states, personality disorders are not usually considered afflictions. They are often understood to be ego-syntonic expressions of what someone is like.

An important problem with respect to the validity of personality *disorder* is that these diagnoses are applied to personality styles that people find disagreeable or unlikeable (Saulsman and Page 2004). Indeed, within clinical traditions that emphasize the importance of countertransference, unusually strong feelings toward a patient – including dislike – may be used as a diagnostic indicator of personality disorder.

To say that personality disorder is an appellation for clusters of disliked behaviors seems to make the concept thoroughly subjective. For this reason, it is helpful to have conceptual models that justify including personality in the domain of psychiatric disorder. Zachar and Krueger (2013) describe six different models.

The *vulnerability model* claims that personality disorders are disorders in the same way that essential hypertension is a disorder. Hypertension is a risk factor for heart disease and stroke. Personality disorders are risk factors for the development of other disorders such as depression, panic disorder, and substance abuse. One, however, can cogently argue that vulnerabilities are not disorders.

The *pathoplasticity model* holds that personality disorders are included in the psychiatric domain because they affect the course and outcome of other psychiatric disorders. People with personality disorder develop other psychiatric disorders earlier in life, experience more psychiatric disorders over their lifetimes, and have worse outcomes. Quite often, the diagnosis of a personality disorder is an indicator that a case may have a complicated symptom pattern.

The *spectrum model* claims that personality disorders and other psychiatric disorders share common genetic predispositions. Personality disorders are milder manifestations of those predispositions. The concept of a spectrum refers to the different ways and degrees of severity by which the predispositions can be expressed (Lenzenweger 2006). For instance, schizotypal, schizoid, and paranoid personality disorders have all been considered to be part of a schizophrenic spectrum.

According to the *decline-in-functioning model*, personality disorder symptoms are siblings to the psychological scars that appear in the wake of traumatic brain injury, severe emotional trauma, and severe psychiatric disorder. These "morbid changes" are associated with unambiguous declines in functioning. In cases of psychological scar, the aberrant causal history is known. For personality disorders, the causal history is less certain, but as they share the same pathological symptoms as seen in the trauma-induced cases, they are also considered disorders.

The *impairment-distress model* states that personality disorders are pathological by being directly associated with clinically significant distress or impairment in social, occupational, or other important areas of function. The earliest proponent of this model was Kurt Schneider who viewed personality disorders as statistically abnormal personalities that led to suffering on the part of their bearer. More recent proponents of this model emphasize both distress and impairment (Widiger and Sanderson 1995).

The *capacity failure model* asserts that personality disorders represent dysfunctions in normal, adaptive psychological capacities. These dysfunctions are the underlying pathological processes of any personality disorder. The difficulty with all capacity failure models is that they rely on speculative inferences about normal, healthy functioning.

Both Christopher Boorse (1975) and Jerome Wakefield (1992) advocate for some form of capacity failure model, with an important difference between them being that Wakefield holds that the term "disorder" should be applied only to those dysfunctions that are harmful to their bearer. Livesley's and Jang's (2000) application of Wakefield's harmful dysfunction model to personality disorder was an important inspiration for the self and interpersonal deficits that are part of the alternative DSM-5 model. According to them, these deficits represent failures to find adaptive solutions to universal life tasks.

There are multiple reasons why personality disorders are considered to be clinically relevant in psychiatry. Just as there is no single model of diseases that covers all the things we call disease (tuberculosis, cancer, systemic lupus, essential hypertension, etc.), no single model of disorder currently applies to everything that might be considered a personality disorder. From the standpoint of the medical model, a capacity failure approach may be the most preferable option, but a capacity failure model will need to be justified by auxiliary psychological and social concepts rather than being exclusively a biological or genetic model.

Conclusions

Many important philosophical problems in metaphysics, epistemology, and ethics are relevant to our understanding of personality disorder. Important problems in the philosophies of science, psychology, psychiatry, and medicine are relevant as well. In turn, the phenomena of personality disorder can enrich these philosophical domains. This chapter represents only a small sample of the wealth of material in the domain of personality disorder that is waiting to be explored in future interdisciplinary work.

Definition of Key Terms

Constitutional factors	Innate features that are considered to be biological predispositions for psychiatric disorder.
Dimensional model	A view of psychological and psychiatric traits that views them as being continuous with normality. In a dimensional model, anxiety would be an emotional state on which every person has a value from high to low. An anxiety disorder would occur when the amount of anxiety interferes with normal functioning. The contrast to dimensional model is a categorical model. In a categorical model, an anxiety *disorder* would be discontinuous from a state of normality. For example, posttraumatic stress can be seen as a qualitative change in the structure of one's psychological makeup that is different from excessive anxiety.

Neuroticism	A personality trait exemplified by frequent experiences of negative emotions and related thoughts and perceptions. Negative emotions include anxiety, anger, fear, and sadness. Feeling overwhelmed is another important feature of neuroticism. In contrast, the Freudian concept of neurosis refers to anxiety resulting from unresolved psychological conflict.
Personality disorder	Inflexible personality functioning associated with impairments in social and occupational functioning as a result of disturbances in identity, self-direction, empathy, or intimacy. The impairments are present by early adulthood and are usually chronic.
Psychopathology	A synonym for abnormal psychology, mental disorder, and psychiatric disorder. In the early twentieth century, psychiatric patients were also called psychopaths. Around mid-century, the term psychopath was narrowed to refer to a particular kind of personality disturbance featuring a lack of conscience, a failure to worry, and impulsivity.
Psychosis	A decline in functioning associated with an inability to adapt to the demands of everyday life, often accompanied with a distorted experience of reality. Excessive positive or negative emotions, cognitive disintegration, or misleading sensory experience and beliefs are most commonly associated with psychosis.
Temperament	Early emerging affective and behavioral dispositions with a genetic component.

Summary Points

- The concept of personality disorder was introduced in the twentieth century.
- Research in behavioral genetics supports the view that personality has an important biological component but not that it is biologically determined.
- In open societies in which people are free to self-select into environments, the variance in personality that is attributable to genetics increases.
- There are both philosophical and scientific reasons for viewing personality traits as coherent behavioral patterns (descriptively) rather than as causes of behavior.
- Personality and personality disorders are continuous over time, but with extensive variability.
- Many personality disorder diagnoses are described using moral terms for "vices." The challenge for clinicians is to hold patients appropriately responsible without engaging in emotional blame.

- The twentieth century's transformation of "personality" from something external to something internal introduced a problem about surface features versus deep features that continues to manifest in different ways.
- Personality disorders are psychiatrically relevant for many reasons, but currently there is no single reason that covers all phenomena included in the domain.

References

Allport GW (1937) Personality: a psychological interpretation. Henry Holt, Oxford
Bem DJ, Allen A (1974) On predicting some of the people some of the time: the search for cross-situational consistencies in behavior. Psychol Rev 81(6):506–520. doi:10.1037/h0037130
Berrios GE (1996) The history of mental symptoms. Cambridge University Press, Cambridge, UK
Boorse C (1975) On the distinction between disease and illness. Philos Public Affairs 5:49–68
Borsboom D, Kievit RA, Cervone D, Hood SB (2009) The two disciplines of scientific psychology, or: the disunity of psychology as a working hypothesis. In: Valsiner J, Molenaar PCM, Lyra MCDP, Chaudhary N, Valsiner J, Molenaar PCM, Lyra MCDP, Chaudhary N (eds) Dynamic process methodology in the social and developmental sciences. Springer Science + Business Media, New York, pp 67–97
Bouchard TJ, McGue M (1990) Genetic and rearing environmental influences on adult personality: an analysis of adopted twins reared apart. J Pers 58(1):263–292. doi:10.1111/j.1467-6494.1990.tb00916.x
Charland LC (2004) Moral treatment and the personality disorders. In: Radden J (ed) The philosophy of psychiatry: a companion. Oxford University Press, New York, pp 64–77
Clark LA (2005) Temperament as a unifying basis for personality and psychopathology. J Abnorm Psychol 114(4):505–521
Cleckley HM (1941) The mask of sanity; an attempt to reinterpret the so-called psychopathic personality. Mosby, St. Louis
Cramer AOJ, Waldrop LJ, van der Mass HLJ, Borsboom D (2010) Comorbidity: a network perspective. Behav Brain Sci 33(2–3):137–150
Epstein S (1979) The stability of behavior: I. On predicting most of the people much of the time. J Pers Soc Psychol 37(7):1097–1126. doi:10.1037/0022-3514.37.7.1097
Funder DC (1997) The personality puzzle. W. W. Norton, New York
Goldie P (2004) On personality. Routledge, London
Han L. J. van der Maas, Conor V. Dolan, Raoul P. P. P. Grasman, Jelte M. Wicherts, Hilde M. Huizenga, and Maartje E. J. Raijmakers (2006) A dynamical model of general intelligence: the positive manifold of intelligence by mutualism. Psychol Rev 113:842–861
James W (1890) The principles of psychology. Holt, New York
Johnson W, Turkheimer E, Gottesman II, Bouchard TJ Jr (2009) Beyond heritability: twin studies in behavioral research. Curr Dir Psychol Sci 18(4):217–220. doi:10.1111/j.1467-8721.2009.01639.x
Jones EE, Harris VA (1967) The attribution of attitudes. J Exp Soc Psychol 3(1):1–24
Kagan J, Snidman N, Arcus D, Reznick JS (1994) Galen's prophecy: temperament in human nature. Basic Books, New York
Kernberg OF (1975) Borderline conditions and pathological narcissism. Jason Aronson, New York
Kiehl KA (2014) The psychopath whisperer: the science of those without conscience. Crown Publishers/Random House, New York
Kohut H (1971) The analysis of the self: a systematic psychoanalytic approach to the treatment of narcissistic personality disorders. International Universities Press, New York
Lenzenweger MF (2006) Schizotaxia, schizotypy, and schizophrenia: Paul E. Meehl's blueprint for the experimental psychopathology and genetics of schizophrenia. J Abnorm Psychol 115:195–200

Lewin K (1935) A dynamic theory of personality. McGraw-Hill, New York

Livesley WJ (2012) Tradition versus empiricism in the current DSM-5 proposal for revising the classification of personality disorders. Crim Behav Ment Health 22:81–91

Livesley WJ, Jang KL (2000) Toward an empirically based classification of personality disorder. J Pers Disord 14(2):137–151. doi:10.1521/pedi.2000.14.2.137

Livesley WJ, Jang KL, Vernon PA (1998) Phenotypic and genetic structure of traits delineating personality disorder. Arch Gen Psychiatry 55:941–948

Lombardo GP, Foschi R (2003) The concept of personality in 19-th century French and 20-th century American psychology. Hist Psychol 6(2):123–142

McCrae RR, Costa PT Jr (1997) Personality trait structure as a human universal. Am Psychol 52:509–516

McGue M, Gottesman II (2015) Behavioral genetics. In: Cautin RL, Lilienfeld SO (eds) The encyclopedia of clinical psychology, vol I. Wiley, Hoboken, pp 341–351

Mischel W (1968) Personality and assessment. Wiley, New York

Morey LC, Meyer JK (2012) Course of personality disorder. In: Widiger TA, Widiger TA (eds) The Oxford handbook of personality disorders. Oxford University Press, New York, pp 275–295

Murray HA (1938) Explorations in personality. Oxford University Press, New York

Nicholson IAM (2003) Inventing personality: Gordon Allport and the science of selfhood. American Psychological Association, Washington, DC

Nisbett RE, Wilson TD (1977) Telling more than we can know: verbal reports on mental processes. Psychol Rev 84(3):231–259. doi:10.1037/0033-295X.84.3.231

Pickard H (2013) Responsibility without blame: philosophical reflections on clinical practice. In: Fulford K, Davies M, Graham G, Sadler JZ, Stanghellini G, Gipps R, Thornton T (eds) The Oxford handbook of philosophy and psychiatry. Oxford University Press, Oxford, pp 1134–1152

Roberts BW, Walton KE, Viechtbauer W (2006) Patterns of mean-level change in personality traits across the life course: a meta-analysis of longitudinal studies. Psychol Bull 132(1):1–25. doi:10.1037/0033-2909.132.1.1

Sadler JZ (2013) Vice and mental disorder. In: Fulford K, Davies M, Graham G, Sadler JZ, Stanghellini G, Gipps R, Thornton T (eds) The Oxford handbook of philosophy and psychiatry. Oxford University Press, Oxford, pp 451–479

Saulsman LM, Page AC (2004) The five-factor model and personality disorder empirical literature: a meta-analytic review. Clin Psychol Rev 23(8):1055–1085

Scarr S, McCartney K (1983) How people make their own environments: a theory of genotype→environment effects. Child Dev 54(2):424–435

Schneider K (1923/1950) Psychopathic personalities (trans: Hamilton MW). Cassell, London

Schramme T (2014) Being amoral: psychopathy and moral incapacity. MIT Press, Cambridge, MA

Shedler J, Beck A, Fonagy P, Gabbard GO, Gunderson J, Kernberg O, ... Westen D (2010) Personality disorders in DSM-5. Am J Psychiatry 167:1026–1028

Stagner R (1937) Psychology of personality. McGraw-Hill, New York

Turkheimer E (1998) Heritability and biological explanation. Psychol Rev 105(4):782–791. doi:10.1037/0033-295x.105.4.782-791

Tyrer P (2014) Time to choose—DSM-5, ICD-11 or both? Arch Psychiatry Psychother 16(3):5–8. doi:10.12740/APP/28380

Wakefield JC (1992) Disorder as harmful dysfunction: a conceptual critique of DSM-III-R's definition of mental disorder. Psychol Rev 99(2):232–247

Widiger TA, Sanderson CJ (1995) Toward a dimensional model of personality disorders. In: Livesley WJ (ed) The DSM-IV personality disorders. Guilford Press, New York, pp 433–458

Zachar P, Krueger RF (2013) Personality disorder and validity: a history of controversy. In: Fulford K, Davies M, Graham G, Sadler JZ, Stanghellini G, Gipps R, Thornton T (eds) The Oxford handbook of philosophy and psychiatry. Oxford University Press, Oxford, pp 889–910

Zachar P, Krueger RF, Kendler KS (2016) Personality disorder in the DSM-5: an oral history. Psychol Med, 46:1–10

Philosophical Implications of Changes in the Classification of Mental Disorders in DSM-5

63

Andreas Heinz, Eva Friedel, Hans-Peter Krüger, and Carolin Wackerhagen

Contents

Abstract

The new edition of the *Diagnostic and Statistical Manual for Mental Disorders* (DSM-5) by the American Psychiatric Association (Diagnostic and statistical manual of mental disorders, 5th edn. American Psychiatric Association, Washington, DC, 2013) has sparked considerable debate. Allen Frances (Saving normal: an insider's revolt against out-of-control psychiatric diagnosis, DSM-5, Big Pharma, and the medicalization of ordinary life, 1st edn. William Morrow, New York, 2013) and others (Heinz A, Friedel E, Der Nervenarzt 85:571–577, 2014) have argued that this revision may increase the risk to inadequately

A. Heinz (✉) • E. Friedel • C. Wackerhagen
Klinik für Psychiatrie und Psychotherapie Campus Charité Mitte, Charité-Universitätsmedizin Berlin, Berlin, Germany
e-mail: andreas.heinz@charite.de; eva.friedel@charite.de; Carolin.Wackerhagen@charite.de

H.-P. Krüger
Institut für Politische Philosophie und Philosophische Anthropologie, Universität Potsdam, Potsdam, Germany
e-mail: krueghp@uni-potsdam.de

T. Schramme, S. Edwards (eds.), *Handbook of the Philosophy of Medicine*,
DOI 10.1007/978-94-017-8688-1_76

pathologize socially unwanted behavior and to defocus psychiatric treatment. An undesirable result can be that more severely ill patients will not be adequately provided with services, while an abundance of problems of everyday life in modern societies receives a medical label. This may cause the ambivalent consequence that psychotherapeutic aid can be provided, but that social problems are individualized and isolated from their context instead of being open to social rather than medical or psychotherapeutic interventions. These concerns will be discussed with respect to three topics: firstly, it will be described how the general definition of mental disorders underwent a slight change with nevertheless considerable consequences; secondly, it will be exemplified how a loss of psychopathological traditions and a new definition of core symptoms in schizophrenia together with a lack of consideration of neurological disorders have widened the schizophrenia category to a degree that it may do more harm than good to patients; and thirdly, it will be discussed by way of example how the merging of the previously distinct categories of harmful substance use and substance dependence combines a diagnostically unreliable (harmful substance use) and a diagnostically reliable (substance dependence) clinical category resulting in a socially potentially abusive and poorly defined new category of "substance use disorders." It is argued that the underlying changes would have deserved a more profound discussion of their philosophical as well as social implications.

Introduction

The American Psychiatric Association revised its Diagnostic and statistical manual of mental disorders in 2013 (American Psyciatric Association, 2013). Unlike previous revisions, publishing DSM-5 sparked considerable debate. For example, Alan Frances (2013) critizised that the diagnostic manual fails to focus on the severely mentally ill and instead classifies a multitude of personal and social problems as disorders. Indeed, DSM-5 slightly altered its general definition of mental disorders and revised the required diagnostic criteria for several disorders, including schizophrenia and drug use as well as dependence, which is now relabeled as substance used disorders. In this essay, we discuss the philosophical and anthropological implications of these changes and some of their practical consequences.

Mental Disorders: How Slight Changes Can Have Profound Consequences

Throughout the history of psychiatry, there have been many attempts to define mental disorders. Karl Jaspers, whose work on "*General Psychopathology*" (1946) still has great influence on the field, already observed some 70 years ago that clinicians are interested in the definitions of specific disorders rather than general concepts of health and disease. In the discussion about mental disorders, philosophers used to have a rather profound impact. For example, Christopher Boorse (1976) suggested that mental disorders are defined by a substantial impairment of mental functions relevant for individual survival. As a consequence, the inability to roll your tongue is not a medical problem, because being able or unable to roll your tongue (in spite of being highly heritable) is generally irrelevant for the survival of human beings. On the other hand, being unable to swallow, for example, due to a stroke or some other neurological disease, impairs a function relevant for individual survival and hence fulfills a criterion for the presence of a disease, namely, the presence of a medically relevant dysfunction.

However, it has been suggested (Sartorius 2011; Heinz 2014) that the presence of a medical dysfunction is not sufficient to diagnose a mental disorder, but that it only represents one aspect (the disease criterion) of a mental malady and has to be accompanied by either personal suffering (the illness criterion) or social impairment (the sickness criterion) in order to be clinically relevant. There are indeed patients who hear voices, thus show a perceptual dysfunction, in this case a hallucination, that can generally be crucial for the survival of human beings and hence fulfills the disease criterion, but these subjects do neither suffer from their hallucinations nor do these perceptual dysfunctions impair their personal functioning in daily life. For example, one of our patients stated that his "voices should be left alone," because he would speculate at the stock exchange and these voices would give him valuable advice, which to date has never been to his disadvantage.

This example highlights the necessity to go beyond the "disease" criterion of mental maladies, which is rightfully defined as an impairment of a mental function generally relevant for survival (see Boorse 1976; Schramme 2000. NB: we disagree with Boorse 1976 and do not suggest that impaired reproduction is a valid criterion for a mental disorder; see Heinz 2014). It suggests to also consider the personal consequences of such dysfunctions for well-being, mainly discussed under the term "illness," as well as the implications for social inclusion and participation, which are generally discussed as the "sickness" aspect of a mental malady (Sartorius 2011). Indeed, medical philosophers such as Charles Culver and Bernard Gert (1982) emphasized that a mental malady is present if a dysfunction is harmful to the individual and either causes suffering or some other state that is undesirable to human beings. Also, Jerome Wakefield (2007) suggests that beyond the medical criterion of any given impairment, individual harm has to be present in order to diagnose a mental disorder. These considerations used to be reflected in the definition of mental disorders as described in DSM-IV, where the American Psychiatric Association stated that a mental disorder "is conceptualized as a clinically significant behavioral or psychological syndrome or pattern that occurs in an individual and that *is associated with* present distress (e.g., a painful symptom) or disability (i.e., impairment in one or more important areas of functioning) or with a significantly increased risk of suffering death, pain, disability, or an important loss of freedom. In addition, this syndrome or pattern must not be merely an expectable and culturally sanctioned response to a particular event, for example, the death of a loved one. Whatever its original cause, it must currently be considered a manifestation of a behavioral, psychological, or biological dysfunction in the individual. Neither deviant behavior (e.g., political, religious, or sexual) nor conflicts that are primarily between the individual and society are mental disorders unless the deviance or conflict is a symptom of a dysfunction in the individual, as described above" (American Psychiatric Association 2000).

Personal suffering, i.e., the illness experience, directly refers to the subjective side of any mental malady. Therefore, a person who suffers from acoustic hallucinations would rightfully be diagnosed with a mental malady because both the disease criterion (impairment of perception that can generally be relevant for survival) as well as the illness criterion (personal suffering) of a mental disorder are present. It has been suggested that a mental malady can also be diagnosed if a person does not personally suffer from his or her dysfunction, but is severely impaired in activities of daily living relevant for social inclusion and participation (the sickness criterion). For example, a patient suffering from Alzheimer's dementia with a clinically relevant dysfunction of memory (the disease criterion) should rightfully be diagnosed with a mental malady if the person is impaired in her ability to take care of herself (the sickness criterion), for example, because hygiene or nutrition is no longer possible, even if she is not aware of her impaired state and does not subjectively suffer from it, and thus, the illness criterion is not fulfilled. Likewise, an alcohol-dependent patient with a delirium during withdrawal will show symptoms fulfilling the disease criterion of a malady (e.g., disorientation and clouding of consciousness) and be absolutely unable to take care of himself with respect to basic activities of daily living (the sickness criterion), while due to a misperception of the current state, he may not subjectively suffer from his experience, may feel ill or in need for treatment, and hence would not fulfill the illness criterion. It is therefore suggested that the presence of medically relevant dysfunction has to be accompanied either by individual suffering or a profound impairment of social participation if a mental malady is rightfully to be diagnosed (see Fig. 1).

This necessity to combine medical, individual, and social aspects in order to diagnose a mental disorder is no longer upheld in the new version of DSM-5. Here, it is now stated that a mental disorder "is a syndrome characterized by clinically significant disturbance in an individual's cognition, emotion regulation, or behavior that reflects a dysfunction in the psychological, biological, or developmental process underlying mental functioning. Mental disorders are *usually* associated with significant distress or disability in social, occupational, or other important activities. An expectable or culturally approved response to a common stressor or loss, such as the death of a loved one, is not a mental disorder. Socially deviant behavior (e.g., political, religious, or sexual) and conflicts that are primarily between the individual and society are not mental disorders unless the deviance or conflict results from a dysfunction in the individual, as described above" (American Psychiatric Association 2013). The new definition thus only suggests that medically relevant dysfunctions are "usually" accompanied by the illness or sickness aspect of a mental malady. Hence, a mental disorder can now already be diagnosed if there are only symptoms relevant within the medical domain

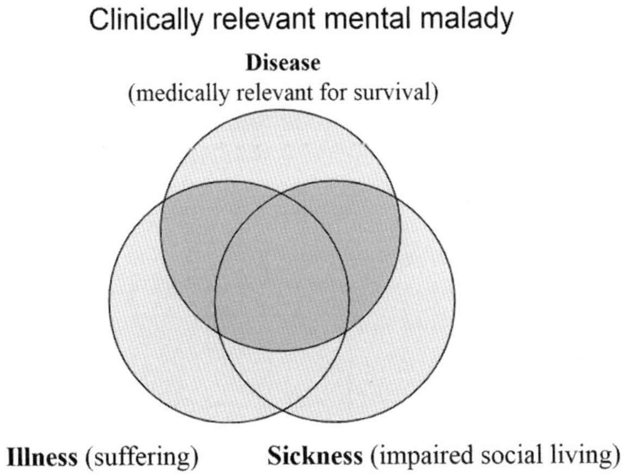

Clinically relevant mental malady

Disease
(medically relevant for survival)

Illness (suffering)   **Sickness** (impaired social living)

Fig. 1 It is suggested that a clinically relevant mental malady can be diagnosed if (1) medically relevant symptoms of a disease are present, defined as an impairment of functions generally relevant for human survival (disease criterion), plus either (2) such dysfunctions cause individual suffering (illness criterion) or (3) impair activities of daily living (hygiene, nutrition, etc.) and thus social participation (sickness criterion)

(the disease criterion of any disorder). This rather small change in wording has profound implications, because if taken seriously, it abolishes the necessary links between medical, social, and individual aspects of mental disorders and suggests that physicians and psychologists can diagnose a mental disorder solely on the basis of an impairment in one of the multifold functions that can be described in the cognitive or social realm. Accordingly, there is a concern that these changes in DSM-5 can lead to the pathologization of dysfunctions that do not cause subjective suffering or social impairment and thereby jeopardize a philosophically reflected, valid concept of mental disorders with rather profound social consequences.

Dropping Schneiderian First Rank Symptoms in Schizophrenia: The Development of a Dangerously Vague Category

In the 1940s, Kurt Schneider developed his concept of first-rank symptoms of schizophrenia. They include symptoms such as voices arguing or commenting on one's action, withdrawal, insertion or broadcasting of thoughts, made feelings, impulses, and volitional acts as well as delusional perception (Schneider 1942, see also Cutting 2015; Mellor 1970). Some of those symptoms describing alterations such as inserted thoughts have been called "bizarre delusions" in the American tradition, although alterations in the ownership or authorship of thoughts had never been considered a "delusion" in the German psychopathological tradition, because the term "delusion" was limited to a rigidly held, false belief concerning phenomena in the outside world (Spitzer 1988). Here, Schneider (1942) emphasized that psychiatrists tend to label a certain set of beliefs a delusion too easily, based on their feelings or observations of supposedly "bizarre" behavior of a person rather than investigating the truth content of such beliefs. Schneider therefore suggested to only rely on "delusional perceptions," i.e., the report of certain objective facts that can be assessed by both the examiner and the patient, which are imbued by a specific meaning for the individual patient that is incorrect, yet defended against all evidence by the delusional person. Reports of inserted thoughts, on the other hand, were considered to represent a deep disturbance of inner experience, which in the Kantian tradition (Kant 1986) involves a dysfunction of the "mineness" of thoughts (Mishara et al. 2014). Kant had suggested that perceptions and ideas are unified in consciousness by the act of a perception, the "I think," and that this act by itself is not subjected to a sensual perception (Kant 1986). Unifying procession of thoughts by an active act, which by itself is not represented in consciousness, is then apparently absent in "thoughts inserted by somebody else," which holds a paradoxical position: on the one hand, a person could not communicate that there are "alien" thoughts in her mind if they were to be completely inaccessible ("not her own"); on the other hand, these thoughts are phenomenologically distinct from common experience to a degree that they appear to be "alien" and "inserted" or "controlled" by an outside power ("not authored by the subject") (Sousa and Swiney 2011; Synofzik et al. 2013).

It has been suggested (Sass and Parnas 2003; Heinz et al. 2012) that thought insertion represents an impairment of fundamental aspects of a core self, i.e., a dysfunction of pre-reflective self-awareness. Self-awareness could only be impaired during split seconds or with respect to certain thoughts, because otherwise there would be no possibility for a person to contrast these "alien" thoughts to other ideations that also appear in a person's own stream of consciousness but are obviously not attributed to an outside author (Gallagher 2004; Heinz 2014).

There are two reasons why an impairment of thought authorship, as in the case of passivity phenomena (when thoughts appear to be inserted or controlled by an outside agent), is fundamental for our understanding of psychosis: on the one hand, they interfere with personal agency, thus severely altering a person's position in her "Mitwelt" (Plessner 1975); on the other hand, such first-rank symptoms focus on the articulation of psychotic experiences by the patients themselves instead of relying on the impressions of doctors and other experts with respect to incomprehensible or disorganized psychotic behavior.

With respect to the first aspect, impaired authorship of one's own thoughts may not directly interfere with the ability of a subject to survive in isolation; however, it severely interferes with human interactions and may render it impossible for other persons to know when a certain act carried out by a psychotic person is indeed based on her own considerations or when it results from inserted thoughts or commands of an outside agent that the psychotic person experiences to be controlled by Heinz (2014). With respect to the second aspect, a focus on symptoms reported by the patients themselves is particularly important in light of stigmatization and aggression to which patients with psychotic experiences are repeatedly exposed. For example, when Schneider developed his criteria, schizophrenia patients were subject to compulsory sterilization or even mass murder due to legislation and procedures enacted by the Nazi government and its psychiatric allies (Klee 2006). Schneider, though not actively resisting these Nazi policies, at least articulated a very cautious procedure toward the diagnosis of schizophrenia, which completely relies on symptoms reported by the patients instead of emphasizing the "impression" that the patient's behavior has on the examiner. As a consequence, disorganized speech or behavior is not a first-rank symptom, because diagnosis of such symptoms is much less reliable due to variation in the judgment of psychiatrists and psychologists.

Schneider (1942) indeed emphasized that expert-based ratings of behavior, i.e., of the "expression" of speech coherence or emotions by any person with psychotic experiences, always make an "impression" on the expert who rates them. If every "expression" is an "impression," rating of such symptoms can largely depend on prejudices and stereotypes that are shared by experts at a certain historical time (remember that Schneider wrote his comments during the Nazi rule). Again, one has to emphasize that even today, treatment of patients with psychotic experiences is often not up to humanitarian standards on a worldwide level. It may be wise to hear Schneider's warning to be cautious when diagnosing schizophrenia and to base this diagnosis mainly on reports of the patients, as impressions by experts are more prone to distortion than the report of inserted thoughts or commenting voices by the patients themselves. Schneider (1942) thus grounded the ability to reliably diagnose schizophrenia on the cooperation of the patients, which – decades before shared decision making or empowerment of patients has been discussed – at least gave some authority to the patients themselves, who have to trust the examiner in order to reveal their experiences.

DSM-5 now abolishes this specific focus on first-rank symptoms for the diagnosis of schizophrenia. While in DSM-IV, one of at least two criterion A symptoms ((1) delusions; (2) hallucinations; (3) disorganized speech; (4) grossly disorganized or catatonic behavior; and (5) negative symptoms, i.e., affective flattening, alogia, or avolition) would have been sufficient if delusions were "bizarre" or hallucinations were commentary or conversing voices; DSM-5 now only requires at least two criterion A symptoms *without any further specification* of the quality of delusions or hallucinations. This is done because a series of studies suggested that first-rank symptoms are not specific for schizophrenia but also appear in other mental conditions, for example, in affective disorders (Carpenter et al. 1973; Andreasen and Carpenter 1993; Shinn et al. 2013; Tandon et al. 2013; Oliva et al. 2014). However, this criticism appears to be controversial, because in the ICD-10, which is based on Schneider's nosological system, the presence of first-rank symptoms suffices to label affective disorders that represent in association with first-rank symptoms as "schizoaffective" (World Health Organization 1992). DSM also provides a schizoaffective category, but requires delusions or hallucinations to show in the course of a predominantly affective episode, during which affective symptoms are mainly absent, while in ICD-10, for the diagnosis of a schizoaffective disorder, affective and first-rank symptoms can be present *concurrently*. It is only by using DSM-IV criteria for affective disorders, which never incorporated the systematic approach of Schneider, that empirical studies can find first-rank symptoms in "purely" affective disorders. This can be deemed as an example of circular reasoning, in which the assumption that first-rank symptoms are not considered to be specific for schizophrenia is used to prove that they are not specific for schizophrenia (and schizoaffective disorders), while neglecting the fact that their presence (at least for Schneider) would be sufficient to diagnose a schizophrenia and schizophrenia spectrum disorder (ICD-10 F20). Disregarding the specific quality of delusions and hallucinations in the diagnostic process defocuses attention from patient's reports and emphasizes the power of the physician or psychologist to diagnose schizophrenia, even if patients do not report characteristic symptoms.

Medically, this may lead to misdiagnosis: there is a multitude of neurological disorders, including Lupus erythematodes or dopamine-associated psychosis in Parkinson's disease, which manifest with the new key symptoms of schizophrenia in DSM-5 (any kind of hallucinations or delusions). In our own experience, Schneiderian first-rank symptoms do not occur in all schizophrenia patients; however, they are rarely observed in neurological disorders that result in delusional or hallucinatory experiences and thus help to distinguish between schizophrenia and brain organic syndromes (Marneros 1988; Heinz et al. 1995). This line of argument is supported by a recent Cochrane review (Soares-Weiser et al. 2015): when reviewing studies that rely on expert ratings (e.g., using DSM criteria) to diagnose schizophrenia, first-rank symptoms correctly identified most (i.e., 75–95 %) of so-classified schizophrenia patients. Sensitivity of first-rank symptoms, on the other hand, was 60 %; thus, a rather large number of expert-classified patients will not receive a schizophrenia diagnosis. On the negative side, this may cause a delay in proper treatment and suggests that ICD-10 (World Health Organization 1992) is correct in not limiting schizophrenia diagnosis to the presence of first-rank symptoms. On the positive side, regarding first-rank symptoms to be specifically important for the diagnosis of schizophrenia can help to reconsider diagnosis in case of their absence and thus to detect subjects with primary neurological disorders (Marneros 1988; Heinz et al. 1995). From a neurological perspective, the decision to neglect specific psychotic experiences such as first-rank symptoms in the diagnostic process has been made without adequately recognizing the multitude of neurological disorders that can cause psychotic symptoms. Indeed, the presence of such neurological disorders is an exclusion criterion for the diagnosis of schizophrenia in DSM-5, as well as in ICD-10; however, due to budgetary limitations, adequate diagnosis of schizophrenia patients with respect to the multitude of potential neurological disorders that can cause any kind of hallucinations or delusions is not provided in the majority of countries worldwide to date.

Neglecting the diagnostic value of first-rank symptoms did not start with DSM-5; however, DSM-5 finally eliminates any specific focus on them (Tandon et al. 2013). Doing so on the basis of circular reasoning and disregard of neurological disorders appears to be questionable and can undermine the clinical utility of the schizophrenia category. The positive aspect of this development is the demand to reconsider the schizophrenia category altogether. Schneider, in the 1940s, stated that when first-rank symptoms are given, "in all modesty we *speak* of schizophrenia" (Schneider 1942). This statement clearly articulates two important aspects of

Schneider's approach: (1) the function of any diagnostic system for clinical communication rather than the reification of these entities and (2) the cautious approach that any physician should take toward labeling patients with a mental disorder. Both arguments have largely disappeared in the last decades. One consequence of the current neglect of first-rank symptoms in schizophrenia diagnosis may be the potential abolishment of the schizophrenia category altogether, which could be replaced by a label acceptable to patients and relatives as well as clinicians and by diagnostic categories that reflect the necessity to listen to patient's experiences and complaints, as Schneider did some 70 years ago.

Abolishing the Distinction Between Harmful Substance Use and Substance Dependence: How Merging of an Ill-Defined and a Well-Defined Category Can Result in a Fuzzy Concept Prone to Social Abuse

In DSM-5, substance use disorders are a new category that includes the previous categories of harmful substance use and substance dependence (American Psychiatric Association 2013; Hasin et al. 2013; Heinz and Friedel 2014, for a comparison see Table 1). The two concepts were merged because epidemiological studies suggested a gradual rather than a categorical distinction between harmful substance use and dependence (Rumpf and Kiefer 2011; Schacht et al. 2013). Moreover, merging these categories increases the number of substance use patients and therefore the necessity for adequate funding of addiction research. However, the "substance abuse" category was rather ill-defined, because it mainly focused on social problems associated with drug use such as interpersonal problems, impaired social functioning, and conflicts with law (Heinz and Friedel 2014) which depend upon socially and culturally diverse value judgments. For example, social problems increase if the drug is not legal in a given country – then considerable time is required to acquire the drug of abuse, and social consequences including conflicts in the family, job loss, and legal persecution can increase dramatically. Substance dependence, on the other hand, is quite well defined, as long as one keeps in mind Edwards' recommendation stating that tolerance, development, and withdrawal are at the core of the dependence concept (Edwards and Gross 1976). In this view, craving and reduced control are necessary, but additional diagnostic criteria, which should not be used in isolation, as any passion can lead to strong urges and reduced interest in other activities as well as excessive time spent, e.g., in groundbreaking research or other passionate activities (Plessner 2003). Merging the concepts of dependence and harmful use now results in a situation where legally banning alcohol consumption suffices to diagnose a substance use disorder in case a subject wants to consume the illegal drug. These considerations show that it may be quite dangerous to rely too much on diagnostic criteria that are largely depending upon legislation, particularly with respect to addictions.

In DSM-5, pathological gambling has now been classified along with substance-related addictions as an addictive behavior. While it has been agreed on that this

Table 1 A contrasting juxtaposition of DSM-IV and DSM-5 criteria for the diagnoses of harmful substance use and substance dependence and substance use disorder (Modified according to Heinz and Friedel (2014), Hasin et al. (2013))

	DSM IV Abuse		DSM IV Dependence		DSM-5 Substance use disorder	
Hazardous use	X		-		X	
Interpersonal problems related to use	X	≥ 1 criterion	-		X	
Impaired social functioning related to use	X		-		X	
Conflicts with law	X		-		-	
Wihtdrawel symptoms	-		X		X	
Tolerance	-		X		X	≥2 criteria
Increasing amounts consumed	-		X		X	
Unsuccessful attempt to quit	-		X	≥3 criteria	X	
Large amount of time spent for supply/consumption	-		X		X	
Physical/psychological problems related to use	-		X		X	
Narrowing activities on consume	-		X		X	
Craving	-		-		X	

may be useful (Heinz and Friedel 2014) there is an abundance of behaviors that have been suggested to fulfill criteria for behavioral addictions, starting from sex addiction to shopping addiction or even workaholism. While behavior of single cases may well fulfill criteria of behavioral addictions, and it may hence be helpful to classify such behavioral patterns as addictive, it must be cautioned that social pressures and demands can result in political abuse of such addiction categories. Imagine, for example, the power of a state to label an oppositional blogger as an "internet addicted" or the impact of some religious groups on standards of sexual behavior, which could result in an abundance of "sex addiction" diagnoses for behaviors that have just recently (i.e., since the 1960s) been accepted as individual rights of a person in an open society. Moreover, pressures on subjects to not only fulfill work requirements but also to take meticulous care of their own health may result in labeling passions that can interfere with a perfect work performance as addictions. Continuous pressure to perform in an age of omnipresent electronic devices for communication may thus be individualized as "workaholism" instead of being addressed on a social level. These considerations suggest that a wider discussion is required before more substance-related addictions beyond pathological gambling can be defined.

Conclusion

The current discussion about DSM-5 may miss some of the central points that are indeed worth considering. It is suggested in this chapter that not every psychological or social disorder is rightfully named a disease, but that, instead, the disease term should be limited to impairments relevant for survival or at least for the ability of a person to live with others in the "Mitwelt" (Plessner 1975). Moreover, a clinically relevant mental malady should not be diagnosed if only medical criteria for the presence of a disease are fulfilled, while there is no evidence for individual harm by such symptoms. A point in case are subjects reporting auditory hallucinations, which neither impair their social functioning (i.e., there is no presence of sickness) nor cause any individual suffering (i.e., the illness aspect of a mental malady is not present). It has been suggested (Wakefield 2007) that a mental malady with clinical relevance is not simply given if functions that are generally relevant for individual survival are impaired, as it is the case if there is a perceptual dysfunction resulting in a hallucination, but that in addition, such symptoms of a disease need to either cause suffering in the given individual or impair the person's social participation. This means that evidence for individual harm is required in addition to the presence of disease symptoms to diagnose a clinically relevant mental malady. In contrast to these considerations, in DSM-5 a mental disorder is already to be diagnosed if one out of a multitude of cognitive, affective, and behavioral dysfunctions is present, which do not even have to fulfill the criterion of impairing a function necessary for survival. This development can indeed result in a proliferation of mental disorders with the potential to pathologize socially unwanted behavior and to defocus support in the mental healthcare system from those who are severely ill to subjects suffering from everyday problems.

Furthermore, there is a concern that alterations in key criteria for psychosis may result in mislabeling a multitude of neurological disorders as schizophrenia, because the internal logic of previous schizophrenia classifications is misunderstood and lost in current discussions about key psychotic symptoms. Finally, merging the categories of substance abuse (harmful use) and dependence renders the diagnosis of substance use disorders prone to political interference and abuse. The concept of mental health and its impairment requires discussion on a broader level, including the participation of philosophically informed experts (Boorse 1976; Culver and Gert 1982; Schramme 2000), but also the participation of patients and their relatives in an open dialogue in international settings, as it had occurred and still happens with respect to the United Nations Convention on the Rights of

Persons with Disabilities and its implementation (United Nations 2006; UNBRK 2008; Müller et al. 2012).

Definition of Key Terms

Disease criterion

A medical dysfunction relevant for individual survival

DSM-5 substance use disorder

In DSM-5, all criteria of harmful substance use and substance dependence are joined under the term substance use disorders which are graded in mild (2–3 symptoms), moderate (3–5 symptoms), and severe (6 or more symptoms); social problems are treated equally with symptoms of reduced control, tolerance, and withdrawal.

Harmful substance use

In DSM-IV, harmful substance use is diagnosed if an individual has been using a psychoactive substance for at least 1 year, which was associated with problems in social functioning, hazardous situations, and conflicts with law or was continued although it led to interpersonal conflicts.

Illness criterion

Subjective experience of suffering due to a medical dysfunction

Mental disorder

While in DSM-IV a mental disorder is conceptualized as a behavioral or psychological syndrome *associated with* increased risk of death or pain, personal distress, or social impairment, DSM-5 defines a mental disorder as a clinically significant disturbance of the psychological, biological, or developmental process underlying mental functioning, which is *usually associated* with personal distress or social disabilities. In a philosophically reflected definition, mental disorders can be conceptualized as a medical dysfunction relevant for survival (disease criterion) which is either accompanied with personal suffering (illness criterion) or social impairment (sickness criterion).

Schneiderian first-rank symptoms

These include voices arguing or commenting on one's action, withdrawal, insertion or broadcasting of thought, made feelings,

	made impulses or volitional acts, and delusional perception.
Sickness criterion	Impairment of social (and/or occupational) functioning caused by a medical dysfunction
Substance dependence	In DSM-IV, substance dependence is narrowly tailored to reduced control of substance intake (in ICD-10 also craving) associated with tolerance development and withdrawal symptoms.

Summary Points

- From a philosophical perspective, a clinical relevant mental disorder can be defined as a medical dysfunction generally relevant for individual survival (the disease criterion), accompanied by personal suffering (the illness criterion) and/or social impairment (the sickness criterion).
- Reforms in DSM-5 have diminished the importance of personal suffering and social impairment as diagnostic criteria for mental disorders, which may cause a societally unfavorable distribution of therapeutic care.
- Schneiderian first-rank symptoms focus at the patient's own experience of disrupted personal agency as well as on "delusional perceptions," i.e., interpretations of objective facts that are held in spite of clear evidence to the contrary, which can be assessed by both the examiner and the patient. Relying on first-rank symptoms can be a protective mechanism against misdiagnosis of schizophrenia and stigmatization and can also be crucial for the distinction of schizophrenia from other neurological disorders that manifest with any kinds of hallucinations or delusions.
- Changes in DSM-5 have eliminated the particular importance of first-rank symptoms for the diagnosis of schizophrenia, which can undermine its clinical utility. On the positive side, these changes may open up a discussion to create a new label acceptable to patients, relatives, and clinicians.
- In DSM-5, categories of substance abuse (harmful use) and substance dependence were merged to substance use disorders, which, on the one hand, account for the gradual transition between substance use and dependence, but, on the other, by treating social problems as an equal criterion, make the category prone to political interference and abuse.

References

American Psychiatric Association (2000) Diagnostic and statistical manual of mental disorders, 4th edn (text rev.). American Psychiatric Association, Washington, DC

American Psychiatric Association (2013) Diagnostic and statistical manual of mental disorders, 5th edn. American Psychiatric Association, Washington, DC

Andreasen NC, Carpenter WT (1993) Diagnosis and classification of schizophrenia. Schizophr Bull 19:199–214

Boorse C (1976) What a theory of mental health should be. J Theory Soc Behav 6:61–84

Carpenter W, Strauss J, Muleh S (1973) Are there pathognomonic symptoms in schizophrenia? An empiric investigation of Schneider's first-rank symptoms. Arch Gen Psychiatry 28:847–852

Culver CM, Gert B (1982) Philosophy in medicine: conceptual and ethical issues in medicine and psychiatry. Oxford University Press, New York

Cutting J (2015) First rank symptoms of schizophrenia: their nature and origin. Hist Psychiatry 26:131–146

Edwards G, Gross MM (1976) Alcohol dependence: provisional description of a clinical syndrome. Br Med J 1:1058–1061

Frances AJ (2013) Saving normal: an insider's revolt against out-of-control psychiatric diagnosis, DSM-5, big pharma, and the medicalization of ordinary life, 1st edn. William Morrow, New York

Gallagher S (2004) Neurocognitive models of schizophrenia: a neurophenomenological critique. Psychopathology 37:8–19

Hasin DS, O'Brien CP, Auriacombe M, Borges G, Bucholz K, Budney A, … Grant BF (2013) DSM-5 criteria for substance use disorders: recommendations and rationale. Am J Psychiatry 170:834–851

Heinz A (2014) Der Begriff der psychischen Krankheit (Auflage: Originalausgabe). Suhrkamp Verlag, Berlin

Heinz A, Friedel E (2014) DSM-5: wichtige Änderungen im Bereich der Suchterkrankungen. Nervenarzt 85:571–577

Heinz A, Przuntek H, Winterer G, Pietzcker A (1995) Clinical aspects and follow-up of dopamine-induced psychoses in continuous dopaminergic therapy and their implications for the dopamine hypothesis of schizophrenic symptoms. Nervenarzt 66:662–669

Heinz A, Bermpohl F, Frank M (2012) Construction and interpretation of self-related function and dysfunction in intercultural psychiatry. Migr Ment Health 27(Suppl 2):S32–S43

Jaspers K (1946) Allgemeine Psychopathologie. Ein Leitfaden für Studierende, Ärzte und Psychologen, 4th edn. Springer, Berlin

Kant I (1986) Kritik der reinen Vernunft. Reclam, Philipp, jun. GmbH, Verlag, Stuttgart

Klee E (2006) Dokumente zur » Euthanasie « im NS-Staat, 6th edn. Fischer Taschenbuch Verlag, Frankfurt am Main

Marneros A (1988) Schizophrenic first-rank symptoms in organic mental disorders. Br J Psychiatry 152:625–628

Mellor CS (1970) First rank symptoms of schizophrenia. Br J Psychiatry 117:15–23

Mishara AL, Lysaker PH, Schwartz MA (2014) Self-disturbances in schizophrenia: history, phenomenology, and relevant findings from research on metacognition. Schizophr Bull 40:5–12

Müller DS, Walter H, Kunze H, Konrad N, Heinz A (2012) Zwangsbehandlungen unter Rechtsunsicherheit. Nervenarzt 83:1150–1155

Oliva F, Dalmotto M, Pirfo E, Furlan PM, Picci RL (2014) A comparison of thought and perception disorders in borderline personality disorder and schizophrenia: psychotic experiences as a reaction to impaired social functioning. BMC Psychiatry 14. doi:10.1186/s12888-014-0239-2

Plessner H (1975) Die Stufen des Organischen und der Mensch. Einleitung in die philosophische Anthropologie (3. Unveränd.). de Gruyter, Berlin

Plessner H (2003) Der kategorische Konjunktiv. Ein Versuch über die Leidenschaft. In: Gesammelte Schriften in zehn Bänden: VIII: Conditio humana. (Vol. 8, pp. 338–352). Frankfurt/M: suhrkamp taschenbuch wissenschaft.

Rumpf H-J, Kiefer F (2011) DSM-5: removal of the distinction between dependence and abuse and the opening for behavioural addictions. Sucht 57:45–48

Sartorius N (2011) Meta effects of classifying mental disorders. In: Regier DA, Narrow WE, Kuhl EA, Kupfer D (eds) The conceptual evolution of DSM 5. American Psychiatric Publishing, Arlington, pp 59–80

Sass LA, Parnas J (2003) Schizophrenia, consciousness, and the self. Schizophr Bull 29:427–444

Schacht JP, Anton RF, Myrick H (2013) Functional neuroimaging studies of alcohol cue reactivity: a quantitative meta-analysis and systematic review. Addict Biol 18:121–133

Schneider K (1942) Psychischer Befund und psychiatrische Diagnose. Thieme, Leipzig

Schramme T (2000) Patienten und Personen: Zum Begriff der psychischen Krankheit. FISCHER Taschenbuch, Frankfurt am Main

Shinn AK, Heckers S, Öngür D (2013) The special treatment of first rank auditory hallucinations and bizarre delusions in the diagnosis of schizophrenia. Schizophr Res 146:17–21

Soares-Weiser K, Maayan N, Bergman H, Davenport C, Kirkham AJ, Grabowski S, Adams CE (2015) First rank symptoms for schizophrenia (Cochrane Diagnostic Test Accuracy Review). Schizophr Bull sbv061

Sousa P, Swiney L (2011) Thought insertion: abnormal sense of thought agency or thought endorsement? Phenomenol Cogn Sci 12:637–654

Spitzer M (1988) Ichstörungen: in search of a theory. In: Spitzer M, Uehlein F, Oepen G (eds) Psychopathology and philosophy. Springer, Berlin/Heidelberg, pp 167–183

Synofzik M, Vosgerau G, Voss M (2013) The experience of agency: an interplay between prediction and postdiction. Front Psychol 4. doi:10.3389/fpsyg.2013.00127

Tandon R, Gaebel W, Barch DM, Bustillo J, Gur RE, Heckers S, . . . Carpenter W (2013) Definition and description of schizophrenia in the DSM-5. Schizophr Res 150:3–10

UNBRK (2008) aus un.org: Bundesgesetzblatt, Teil II, 35, Bonn. Gesetz zu dem Übereinkommen der Vereinten Nationen vom 13. Dezember 2006 über die Rechte von Menschen mit Behinderungen. Bonn. Retrieved from http://www.un.org/Depts/german/uebereinkommen/ar61106-dbgbl.pdf

United Nations (2006) Convention on the rights of persons with disabilities. http://www.un.org/disabilities/convention/conventionfull.shtml. Retrieved 6 May 2015

Wakefield JC (2007) The concept of mental disorder: diagnostic implications of the harmful dysfunction analysis. World Psychiatry 6:149–156

World Health Organization (1992) The ICD-10 classification of mental and behavioural disorders: clinical descriptions and diagnostic guidelines. World Health Organization, Geneva

Part VII

Health as a Social and Political Issue

Medicalization of Social Problems

64

Ashley Frawley

Contents

Abstract

Medicalization is a key concept in sociology, referring to the process by which an increasing array of personal and social phenomena come to be described and understood in medical terms. Concerned primarily with the ways by which social problems are described and defined, constructionist approaches to social problems have utilized medicalization to examine the ways that medical language has been used to describe an increasing array of social problems. Drivers of the proliferation of medical definitions have been identified as the expansion of expertise, the interests of pharmaceutical and biotech companies, and consumerism. Contextual factors include secularization, the growing power of medical and scientific knowledge, the decline of tradition, and the shift of political focus from production to consumption. Though benefits are generally recognized,

A. Frawley (✉)
Department of Public Health, Policy and Social Sciences, Swansea University, Swansea, UK
e-mail: a.frawley@swansea.ac.uk

© Springer Science+Business Media Dordrecht 2017
T. Schramme, S. Edwards (eds.), *Handbook of the Philosophy of Medicine*,
DOI 10.1007/978-94-017-8688-1_74

medicalization studies usually foreground the process's negative results. Studies utilizing both medicalization and constructionism are subject to general criticisms effecting either approach, including overstating the problem and theoretical inconsistencies.

Introduction

Medicalization is one of the few sociological coinages that have successfully permeated popular vocabularies. Literally meaning "to make medical," it refers to the process by which an increasing array of issues come to be described and understood in medical terms, often through the language of syndromes, diseases, and disorders (Gabe 2013). Its origins can be traced to the mid-twentieth century when many critics began to challenge what they perceived as the rising and potentially pernicious power of the medical profession and of psychiatry in particular. The term gained momentum in the 1970s, particularly through its links with understandings of social control, as social scientists began to describe apparent shifts in the means by which Anglo-American societies were defining and disciplining deviance. Since then, medicalization has been used to understand how a wide variety of phenomena have come to be considered medical issues including pregnancy, childbirth, alcoholism, obesity, sleep, educational underachievement, madness, drug addiction, and death.

The focus of medicalization has encompassed a wide variety of phenomena, which can be conceptualized as falling into two broad categories: (1) the medical redefinition of, and control over, hitherto unproblematic or at least common aspects of everyday life including pregnancy, birth, and death and (2) the medicalization of deviance or the process through which nonnormative or morally condemned attributes, beliefs, or behaviors come under medical jurisdiction (Mcgann and Conrad 2011). This chapter attempts to focus more acutely upon the latter category. In particular, it focuses on that form of deviance, or the transgression of social norms, that sociologists and other social scientists mostly espousing a social constructionist outlook study under the rubric of "social problems." From this perspective, the medicalization of social problems refers to the ways by which medical categories have come to be applied and increasingly accepted as one of the dominant means through which modern societies define and approach their problems. In other words, it is the process of defining "troubling conditions" as medical problems (Best 2008, p. 99).

After exploring the origins and definitions of medicalization and associated terminologies, this chapter moves to a consideration of the use of medicalization to understand social problems. Potential underlying drivers of the proliferation of medical definitions are considered as well as the consequences of this process for individuals and society. The final section considers general criticisms that have been launched against both medicalization and constructionist approaches to social problems that are relevant to studies combining the two.

Emergence of Medicalization Thesis

The twentieth century saw a rise in the stature of the medical profession, encouraging its gradual expansion into, and authority over, growing domains of individual and social life. Until the mid-twentieth century, this authority largely went unchallenged (Cockerham and Ritchley 1997). However, early analyses and critiques of medical power began to emerge as early as the 1950s. Talcott Parsons' notion of the "sick role" may be read as one of the first examinations of medicine as a form of social control for the way in which it defined, legitimated, and contained illness as a deviation from "wellness" as a social norm (Conrad 2007, p. 51). Though not necessarily employing the terminology of medicalization, theorists writing in the 1960s and early 1970s including Thomas Szasz (1961, 1970), Michel Foucault (1965), and Eliot Freidson (1970) began to forward critical analyses of the broadening scope of the medical profession, and psychiatry in particular, in its power to define and control deviance once considered in moral, religious, or criminal terms. For Thomas Szasz, the movement of "madness" into the realm of medicine effectively reified a social and moral category, unduly removing it from the cultural sphere and placing it in the realm of the biological. This transformation did not necessarily represent an enlightened progression toward more humane treatment of those once seen as witches or possessed, but rather served to obscure the social origins of human difference and distress.

At the same time, the growing feminist movement began to question the role of male doctors and a male-dominated health system in controlling women's bodies and reproductive health. Women began to expose and challenge the tendency for their experiences to be treated as forms of illness and deviations from an implied male norm (Nettleton 2013). Medicine was accused of attempting to discipline the "unruly" female body, and interventions into pregnancy and birth were criticized as unnecessary or even harmful interferences. Beginning in the late 1960s, organizations like the Boston Women's Collective and the Jane Collective variously encouraged women to take back control of their bodies, their sexuality, and their reproductive health.

Also exploring the growing power of medicine and its role in social control, Irving Zola drew attention to the ways by which medicine was "nudging aside, if not incorporating, the more traditional institutions of religion and law" in the regulation of everyday life (1972, p. 487). In one of the earliest explicit articulations of the medicalization thesis, he worried that not just childbirth, but nearly everything from "sex to food, from aspirins to clothes, from driving your car to riding the surf," had become associated with health and health risks, famously concluding that "I at least have finally been convinced that living is injurious to health" (Zola 1972, p. 498). While building his description of medicalization on earlier critiques of psychiatry, Zola thought this myopic focus on one form of medical knowledge was misplaced. Psychiatry had simply pushed to its logical conclusions the task long taken up by the medical profession as a whole: the control and containment of deviance and the disciplining of daily life.

Writing almost simultaneously with Zola, Ivan Illich argued the success of the medical profession had been overstated and that it often did more harm than good. Using instead the term "iatrogenesis," literally referring to harm "brought forth by the healer," he pointed to medicine's tendency to undermine people's capacity for self-care, paralyzing healthy responses to life processes and encouraging a dependence upon professionals. He also described the ways by which the side effects of medical interventions could sometimes outweigh the harm wrought by the initial condition. Indeed, Illich himself refused to have a large facial tumor removed since doing so could remove his ability to speak. His critique of modern medicine formed part of his broader questioning of the fruits of industrial progress and development. People would revolt, Illich argued, if medicine did not exist to tell people that their problems lay primarily in their bodies rather than the outside world (Sheaff 2005).

Thus, the medicalization thesis emerged from critiques of medical dominance and described the ways by which medicine's power was mobilized to control and discipline behaviors, bodies, and beliefs society deemed dangerous, unruly, or deviant. Although not always or initially using the terminology of medicalization, these early analyses all essentially drew attention to the growing use of medical language to describe human experiences and problems in the twentieth century.

Medicalization and Definitions

While many aspects of medicalization remain open to debate, it is clear that the key to the process lies in language or the way social phenomena are *defined* at a given time (Conrad 2013). Medicalization studies focus on the application of a medical framework, sometimes referred to as a medical model, to a wide range of phenomena previously considered the domain of religion, culture, criminality, or other nonmedical structures (Best 2008). While sometimes restricted to the explicit application of a diagnosis to new areas, in its broadest sense, medicalization refers to the process whereby individual and social life comes to be talked about and understood through the use of medical language *of any kind*. What is important is a definitional and rhetorical shift in the way that people talk about a given phenomenon from one sociohistorical moment to the next.

This means that although the profession of medicine is often pointed to as the source of medicalization, sometimes expressed through a critique of "medical imperialism," the medical profession itself need not play a key role. It is the power of medical language, rather than the medical profession itself, that is most significant and to which more recent critiques have pointed. There are numerous cases in which doctors have been uninvolved or even opposed to claims aiming to extend medical definitions to new domains. A famous example is the movement to define alcoholism as a disease which was led not by physicians but rather by individuals and groups associated with the Alcoholics Anonymous program and only loosely followed a strict biomedical model of disease (Best 2008). Indeed, there is some evidence that far from achieving unparalleled dominance, the medical profession is experiencing a process of deprofessionalization as other institutions challenge its authority. Deprofessionalization refers to a "decline in professional status and power resulting from a deterioration in those characteristics which distinguish professions from other occupations, especially the loss of autonomy over work and control over clients" (Cockerham and Ritchley 1997, p. 31). State regulation, managerial surveillance, suspicion toward doctors, the rise of litigation, the growth of alternative and complementary medicine, and the professionalization of other occupational groups including nurses have all been pointed to as sources of a decline in the medical profession's dominance (Furedi 2008). Thus, the expansion of medicalization is increasingly overseen by a wide variety of experts and professionals, advocacy groups, and even laypeople.

The growing use of medical language to understand new domains and new problems may be considered as part of a broader expansion of scientific knowledge in general into nearly all aspects of life. As Best (2008) describes, medical knowledge is merely a subcategory of the larger domain of scientific expertise. In the same way that medicine saw an expansion of authority due to prominent successes in the nineteenth and twentieth centuries, so too did staggering advancements made possible by science contribute to its cultural authority (Best 2008). This rise in the authority of science also oversaw or at least coincided with a decline in the ability for older structures like tradition and religion to lend meaning to everyday life and legitimacy to pronouncements. Although these structures have not entirely disappeared, it is difficult to argue that the voice of the priest and language of sin continue to hold the same power as they might have done even a century ago. At least in the West, audiences are more likely to be convinced by claims communicated in the language of diseases, syndromes, and disorders – "words that seem more grounded in medical, scientific classifications" (Best 2008, p. 97–98).

The increasing significance of science and new technologies has led to the coinage of biomedicalization as a terminology that more acutely grasps ways by which medicalization has developed and intensified in the twenty-first century. As Clarke and Shim (2011) describe, biomedicalization refers not only to medical control over phenomena but their actual transformation by technoscientific means. That is, the emphasis is shifting more toward scientific and technological interventions that actually change bodies and identities (Clarke and Shim 2011). These high-tech interventions often promise not only to treat or cure but also to enhance and optimize. While medicalization has continued, biomedicalization draws attention to the increased centrality of science and technology in the process. For instance, the past few decades have seen a revolution in genetics, which has led to claims that it will not be long before genetic markers will be found to underlie nearly all personal and social problems (Best 2008). As with medicalization, the biomedicalization of life encourages the view that it is biology that ultimately underlies almost every trouble and that it is toward biomedical advancements that one must turn if solutions are to be found.

In a similar way, psychologization has been suggested as a terminology that more acutely grasps the inclination within medicalization toward the discovery of new psychiatric categories and the expansion of old ones, so that more and more of individual and social life comes to be encompassed by psychiatric labels. It also captures the ways by which social problems are often conceptualized as stemming from problems at the emotional and psychological level. As Furedi (2008) describes, emotional and therapeutic terms like "stress, rage, trauma, low self-esteem, or addiction" increasingly offer up quasi-medical labels for interpreting virtually any human experience or issue. However, in spite of the potential specificity offered by terminologies like psychologization and biomedicalization – and indeed the many other "izations" that have since emerged (see Conrad 2013) – medicalization continues to be the most popular term utilized by social scientists and has developed to encapsulate many of these and other trends.

Finally, it is important to note that medicalization is not a straightforward process toward a foregone conclusion. Rather, the degree to which a phenomenon is considered an entirely medical category may not be total, and medicalization of a phenomenon may exist at many stages of cultural recognition and affirmation. It can also operate in reverse, a process referred to as "demedicalization." Some of the most oft-cited examples include the waning concern of medical professionals with masturbation and the declassification of homosexuality as a mental disorder (Mcgann and Conrad 2011). By the same token, categories can be "re-medicalized." Indeed, while homosexuality remains the most commonly cited example of a successful demedicalization campaign, it may be experiencing a process of re-medicalization through, for example, prominent associations with HIV/AIDS, discourses of genetically predetermined sexuality and searches for a "gay gene," and the introduction of "gender identity disorder" to the DSM (Conrad 2007). Although the overarching trend appears to be toward increasing medicalization, it is important to recognize that it is not a linear process toward a static end point (Gabe 2013).

Medicalization of Social Problems

The study of the medicalization of social problems has both contributed to and grown from broader medicalization debates discussed thus far. The first medicalization theorists were influenced by a variety of theoretical traditions; Zola and Freidson took inspiration from labeling theory and the then fledgling social constructionism, drawing attention to medicine's ability to define what illness is and to label as illness that which was not previously labeled (Busfield 2006). From the perspective of labeling theory, deviance does not exist within the people or actions themselves, but rather in the act of assigning a label. Similarly, social constructionism (also called constructivism) argues that ideas are not simple one-to-one reflections of objective reality, but are socially and historically conditioned. From infancy, people learn to assign names and categories to the world in order to understand it and from which they are able to attribute meaning to experiences (Best 2008). These names and categories in turn influence the ways by which people understand themselves and the world around them. Consider, for example, that although nearly every human society assigns gender classifications, the meanings that these classifications carry, and the implications for the identities and behaviors of the people to which they are attached, represent enormous cultural variation (Best 2008). Thus, what many may take for granted as a straightforward biological classification represents a complex process of meaning construction.

Although not all examinations of medicalization adopt a constructionist framework (Nettleton 2013), the thesis was adopted and extensively developed within the constructionist literature specifically pertaining to social problems beginning in the early 1980s. While social problems can be understood in a number of ways, the constructionist orientation adopts a subjectivist rather than objectivist orientation to their study. From an objectivist perspective, social problems are simply harmful conditions that affect society in some way (Goode and Ben-Yehuda 2009). By contrast, a subjectivist orientation views social problems in terms of people's subjective judgments about whether or not something is troubling (Best 2008). For instance, it may seem relatively uncomplicated that a condition such as racism or sexism should represent a problem for society. Rationales for defining these as problematic may rest on threats to well-being or violations of fairness or justice (Best 2008). However, such definitions seem less straightforward when one considers other imaginable foci for critiques of discrimination or unfairness that go unnoticed or unlabeled by society. As Best (2008) describes, while there is considerable evidence of discrimination based on height, which might also be considered unfair and detrimental to well-being, "heightism" as a social problem largely does not exist. If people do not think it is a problem, it will not become a social problem with the attendant societal recognition that both affirms it and seeks its amelioration.

As with medicalization, it is the definitional process that is key to understanding how social problems come into being. From this perspective, social problems are processes through which individuals and groups develop definitions and ways of understanding conditions they find problematic and work to bring these to the attention of the broader public, policymakers, and others they feel ought to recognize and respond to the issue. The medicalization of social problems therefore refers to the specific analysis of the convergence of these two processes, to the ways by which medical language has come to be bound up in definitional activities relating to social problems.

From at least the early twentieth century to the present day, many aspects of life once considered the product of bad people (volitional deviance) have come to be considered as illness, the product of sick people (unintentional deviance) (Cockerham and Ritchley 1997). The seven deadly sins have been recast in the language of personality disorder (Best 2008). Those responsible for adverse conditions are said not to require punishment so much as help; they do not require reform so much as treatment. Audiences are encouraged to act not on the basis of right and wrong, but on the basis of healthy and unhealthy. Children once classed as unruly, disruptive, or otherwise displaying undesirable behaviors are routinely labeled with disorders for which a variety of drug treatments are available (Cockerham and Ritchley 1997). Solutions to social problems like poverty, inequality, or unemployment are increasingly sought not in deep underlying economic structures, but through, for example, the provision of therapy or the close medical or other expert surveillance of behaviors and consumption habits of families and even pregnant women. It is worthwhile to mention, however, that the move of conceptualizations of social deviance from "badness" to "sickness" does not always entail blamelessness on the part of those classed as victims. Cultural appraisals of illness often reveal a great deal of ambivalence with regard to those labeled as ill – on the one hand describing them as victims and, on the other, as is sometimes the case with obesity and smoking as social problems, complicit in their own suffering.

Medicalization has arguably grown to become one of the leading means through which modern societies attempt to understand and address conditions they view as problematic (Best 2008). Its expansion is fostered both through the increased tendency to use the language of biology and medicine to understand social problems and the broadening of existing and new diagnostic categories, and particularly psychiatric categories, to encompass ever greater varieties of deviance (Conrad and Mcgann 2011). As with the expansion of the medicalization process in general, the success of this way of understanding social issues came at a time when advancements in science and medicine led to rising expectations that science would soon offer the answers to nearly all human problems, even those once considered solely moral, philosophical, or religious questions. Where these older belief systems seem to have atrophied, or at least lost their rhetorical power in the public sphere, the language of science seems to offer a value-neutral means of speaking to a diversity of audiences.

Note, however, that in the media and political arenas, where social problem claims mostly vie for attention, science operates differently to the way it (at least ideally) operates in other spheres. As Best (2008) describes, scientific developments are often slow and take a great deal of time to verify. By contrast, in social problem campaigns, uncertainty potentially undermines the credibility of claims-makers. Take, for example, the apparent tendency for particular foods and drinks to be associated on one occasion with health benefits and on another with health risks (coffee and wine being the most obvious examples). It is easy to see how this can lead to undermining the advice of dieticians if the facts seem to change from one day to the next. But studies must be repeated many times, mechanisms of causation identified, and alternative explanations invalidated before the latter can be definitively, if ever, put to rest. While conclusions may be drawn with a considerable degree of certainty in the physical sciences, this is less often the case in the biological sciences and least so in the social (Best 2008). However, in media claims-making about social issues, this ambiguity is often minimized.

Therefore, it may be more accurate to say that rather than "science" it is the rhetoric of science, or "scientism," that plays the greatest role in the medicalization of social problems. Scientism refers to the way that science can operate as a kind of secular religion by evoking a sense of ultimate truth, objectivity, and expert authority over personal and social matters (Freidson 1970). This is accomplished through the use of medical or technical language and models borrowed from the natural world in order to describe and understand human behavior and social life

(White 2009). With a bewildering array of potential social problems and limited space in newspapers, minutes in a television newscast, platforms in election campaigns, and now perhaps, characters in social media posts, it is essential that claims are effective in competing for attention and recognition among the cacophony of other competing claims. To do so, they must be compelling enough to move significant proportions of the population to act or at least not oppose the problem frame. Although performing many of the same functions, scientific and medical language has a greater potential to speak to, and avoid alienating, a far broader swathe of the public than moral, religious, or other nonscientific pronouncements.

Medical and scientific rhetoric also underpins the claims of particular classes of experts to assert authority and dominion over certain problems and their solutions. For example, through claims to specialized knowledge, psychiatrists were able to assert jurisdiction over a variety of deviant behaviors as symptoms of psychiatric disorders including juvenile delinquency, crime, homosexuality, and drug addiction (Best 2008). But specialisms and expertise need not come from medical training alone. It was not only psychiatrists, whose training placed them within the medical profession, but many others with more tenuous links to medicine including clinical psychologists, licensed social workers, and even those with little to no professional training (Best 2008). Professional "exes," survivors, and sufferers also steadily began to adopt the language of illness and disease to describe the problems they faced and to assert a special understanding over them. In addition to the previously cited example of the amateur campaigning for recognition of alcoholism as a medical condition by Alcoholics Anonymous, sufferers of contested conditions like myalgic encephalomyelitis (ME) and fibromyalgia have actively campaigned for medical recognition of their symptoms and have even been highly critical of doctors failing to recognize the medical origins of their difficulties (Furedi 2008). Collective action also played a key role in the movement of ADHD from a childhood condition to one diagnosed in adults. In these cases, diagnostic advocacy by laypeople who had largely self-diagnosed was decisive in legitimating new medical labels (Furedi 2008). In this way, the allusion of the early medicalization thesis to a "top-down" scapegoating of deviants has given way to a bottom-up movement, whereby an array of activists and citizen groups campaign for medical recognition (Furedi 2008).

Constructions of social problems benefit in a number of ways from adopting medical and scientific rhetoric. Most significantly, it allows advocates to eschew moral, aesthetic, or other overtly opinion- or value-based judgments in favor of an apparently value-free science that promises to act in the best interests of putative victims or populations as a whole. Medical claims, rooted as they are in the body, have the ability to bypass varied belief systems and political affiliations. Action is courted not on the basis of opinion, but on the basis of the true nature of (all) human beings, as uncovered by science. It thus encourages audiences to think about claims-makers' desired changes to bodies, behaviors, beliefs, or social policies not as moral injunctions, but as enhancements to personal health and well-being.

Causes and Contexts

Characterizations of the medicalization process have been subject to less debate than have its causes. While the thesis that "medical imperialism" ultimately underlies medicalization has waned, the expansion of expertise and professionalization of everyday life must not be entirely discounted. As the previous section described, the use of medical-scientific language is often a prelude to the assertion of authority and control over that domain by new or existing types of experts. By identifying new diseases and problems and offering expert solutions, many professions have created the needs they claim to satisfy, in turn justifying their existence and proliferation.

However, Peter Conrad has described a shift away from medicalization being primarily driven by physicians, social movements, and other interest groups toward a greater role played by pharmaceutical and biotech companies as well as consumers (Gabe 2013). In some countries, drug companies advertise new diseases and their cures direct to consumers who are encouraged to ask their doctors for specific drugs (Gabe 2013). Many parents actively seek out ADHD diagnosis and treatment for children who might otherwise have been labeled disruptive or unruly. Other parents fearing future discrimination suffered by short-statured children go to physicians seeking prescriptions for HGH (human growth hormone) (Conrad 2007). From this perspective, medicine has become a vehicle for broader projects of bodily enhancement and self-improvement, with consumers increasingly taking an active part. In some ways, this echoes earlier arguments made by Marxists and feminists that medicalization serves certain class and gender interests, but in this case those of large pharmaceutical and biotech companies (Gabe 2013).

Although perhaps instigated by professional or other interests, this does not entirely explain why, once the framework of health and illness was made available for making sense of daily life and social issues, it rapidly took off. Thus, medicalization studies have long rooted their analyses in more diffuse sociocultural processes rather than solely vested interests. Both Illich and Zola set their analyses against a backdrop of increasingly complex technological and bureaucratic structures, contexts that fostered the professionalization of everyday life and a reliance upon experts (Gabe 2013). Previous sections have described the ways by which additional forces such as secularization, the rise of science and technology, and the growing power of medical and scientific knowledge have all been bound up with the rise of medicalization. The institutional concern with health has also been suggested to have grown at a time when traditional politics and political affiliations were on the wane (Furedi 2008). The decline of a political focus on production and its succession by movements more concerned with consumption and lifestyles paved the way for ideals of health and well-being to pervade nearly all aspects of existence (O'Brien 1995). This expansion of the domain of health has meant that nearly any aspect of life and any social problem can be subsumed under its purview, from issues in interpersonal relationships to the structure of education and work. At the same time, health has come to be portrayed not as something one has, but something that must be promoted and actively pursued. As Wainwright (2008, p. 2) describes, health promotion has shifted the "clinical gaze from treatment of the sick to regulation of the well. What we eat, drink and smoke, who we sleep with, how we relate to family members and friends, and the demands of working life, have all become subjects of professional advice in the pursuit of that elusive end point: "wellbeing"."

These broader social and cultural developments offer an explanation for why medicalization "from below," that is, by consumers and other members of the lay public, has become such an important driver. According to Furedi (2008), a key moment occurred in the 1980s when contestation of medical labels gave way to their embrace and even promotion by groups who once fiercely opposed them. For instance, where feminists have traditionally contested the medicalization of women's experiences, more recently there has been less opposition to, and even outright support for, the increased application of diagnostic labels like postnatal depression (Furedi 2008). For some people, illness confers a positive sense of identity and meaning as well as structures of support and kinship. In the face of a decline in other identities and the shared systems of meaning from which they stemmed, and in an increasingly atomized world, illness arguably offers a rare common ground on which people can unite and share common experiences. It also provides an explanation of problem behavior and a means of dealing with it in a way that attracts sympathy rather than condemnation or disdain (Furedi 2008). This has led to a situation in which diagnoses are not simply passively received, but are rather actively sought out or even demanded.

The rise of medicalization is likely multicausal in nature, but it is important to understand that this process would not be so successful outside of a sociopolitical context hospitable to claims framing social problems in medical language. It is clear that modern society is one in which a variety of parties now routinely seek out medical and "quasi-medical" solutions to an expanding range of social problems (Conrad 2007, p. 14). In this way, "medicalization of all sorts of life problems is now a common part of our professional, consumer, and market culture" (Conrad 2007, p. 14).

Consequences

Medicalization is generally recognized to have both positive and negative effects (Mcgann and Conrad 2011). Moving people into the sick role increases the likelihood that they will seek help and that solutions to their difficulties will be more humane. For instance, diagnosis and treatment for ADHD is probably a more humane way of treating children who do not seem to "fit" into traditional school systems than punishment and constant reprimand. Medicalization can provide coherence to people's lives and assurance that people are not at fault for their putative transgressions (Mcgann and Conrad 2011). People once classed as deviants in need of punishment, segregation, or even eradication are re-classed as requiring help, compassion, and care. In spite of this, the medicalization thesis is usually forwarded as critique. Indeed, in Zola's early development of the concept, he described medicalization as an "insidious" phenomenon, despairing of the creeping pathologization of everyday life incurred through the attachment of medical labels (1972, p. 487). Thus, the concern is usually with "over-medicalization" rather than with a simple description of the movement of conceptualizations of phenomena from one category (nonmedical) to another (medical).

Medicalization theorists have long worried that medicalization encourages greater professionalization and disempowerment of ordinary people to deal with their problems. Both Illich and Zola worried that it increased people's reliance upon experts, granting undue authority to medical professionals over bodies, minds, and lives (Barker 2010). This professionalization of everyday life can transform previously mundane aspects of life into problems and everyday problems into subjects of professional knowledge and intervention, undermining existing means of living and coping. Moreover, social control is enacted through professional pronouncements on how to think and behave, allowing for its insidious expansion, its encroachment appearing unproblematic and therefore uncontested (Mcgann and Conrad 2011). Instead, as a "good citizen" one is simply expected to be "actively engaged with the advice of experts and lifestyle gurus, just as the recalcitrant citizen fails to adapt and adopt the identity and lifestyle moralities of psychology, health and medicine" (Back et al. 2012, p. 96).

The expansion of the sick role implied by medicalization also presents challenges to the moral autonomy of those classed as ill. Adoption of the sick role entails that the sick person is not responsible for his or her illness. While this potentially reduces stigma and culpability, it can also provide a "medical excuse" for deviance that diminishes individual responsibility for one's actions (Mcgann and Conrad 2011, p. 141). This acquires deeper significance as medical advancements, most notably in genetics and neuroscience, appear to locate the causes of various behaviors and dispositions ever deeper in human physiology, further deferring and displacing responsibility from the person to the body (Mcgann and Conrad 2011). The corollary of this can be a sort of "physiological determinism," which can encourage a fatalistic outlook and static vision of human potential. Further, the resultant construction of a human subject with a diminished capacity for rational action is one that also invites the increasing reliance upon experts.

In addition, the moral impulses that often guide social problem campaigns can be obscured through the use of medical and scientific language. Nazi Germany's early introduction of public smoking bans illustrates some of the ways that moral indignation and science can compound each other. Although Nazi tobacco epidemiology was among the most advanced in the world, smoking, like alcoholism, was antithetical to the ideology of racial hygiene (Cederström and Spicer 2015). Medical knowledge about harm and risk thus offered an underlying basis for moral judgments. In a similar way, while the apparent driver of contemporary debates about smoking has been ill-health and its associated economic costs, discussions are often underwritten by implicit moral indignation. While evidence of smoking's injuriousness to health may seem to straightforwardly lead to campaigns for its eradication, consider that many overtly risky behaviors are not widely considered de facto problematic including skydiving, mountain climbing, and other recreational activities that carry (or even court) high levels of risk.

Accepting a label is in some ways an admission of deviance. Although often not an admission that one is "bad" but merely "sick," there is nonetheless the implicit agreement that the condition is undesirable and, in many cases, needs to be rooted out. This implicit affirmation makes it difficult to propose alternative frameworks of meaning or otherwise challenge the medicalized frame. For example, the medical language of "obesity" guides campaigns primarily centered on threats to health and the economic costs of obesity-related illness. Even if the finger of blame is sometimes pointed at "obesogenic" environments and social structures, the focus of change is ultimately on the corpulent body. Medical language offers a guise of infallibility so that aesthetic and moral judgments about the social desirability of "fatness" seem irrelevant to the larger task of its eradication. However, even science requires moral judgment in terms of which questions are legitimately subject to scientific analysis, how questions are asked, results interpreted, and categories and classifications developed and decided. Indeed, body mass index (BMI) categories have been criticized for being culturally and aesthetically driven, particularly in terms of a lack of a significant relationship between the category "overweight" and adverse health outcomes (Best 2008). However, the language of science and measurement makes it difficult for alternative definitions of obesity, for example, a problem of discrimination, to compete against these medicalized definitions. Instead, the responsibility is placed upon those classed as deviant to change their behaviors and bodies (sometimes at great expense) rather than upon society at large.

Indeed, perhaps the most significant complaint forwarded by critics of medicalization is this tendency to deflect the focus of change from the social to the individual. By individualizing social problems, medicalization renders them apolitical, personal issues. For instance, the label of antisocial personality disorder is applied disproportionately to members of the lower social classes, often with experiences and histories heavily colored by poverty (Crews et al. 2007). Problems associated with poverty are therefore transformed into medical issues amenable to treatment rather than societal problems requiring political and/or economic solutions. Similarly, "female sexual dysfunction" locates within the female body issues that may well be rooted in broader cultural expectations associated with gender as well as problems within interpersonal relationships. Imbuing social problems with medical explanations also misses the opportunity to consider that phenomena classed as "deviant" may reflect rational adaptations to certain situations and contexts (Mcgann and Conrad 2011). It leads away from analysis of other potential explanations and encourages the view that even the most insoluble and perennial problems of society can at last be solved if only people would follow a given course of treatment, modify their behaviors, or otherwise learn to think and act in ways conducive to health.

Critical Perspectives

Particular case studies have been subject to a variety of critiques. However, the amalgamation of medicalization and a constructionist approach to social problems in particular has meant that such studies have been subject to many of the same general criticisms launched against both of these perspectives. In terms of medicalization, it has been argued that studies overstate the degree to which particular cases have been medicalized and understate constraints on the process. For instance, welfare states may have less incentive to medicalize social problems and encourage expensive drug treatments for their amelioration than may be the case elsewhere. Claims about social control may also overlook the considerable role played by laypeople in the medicalization process as well as the benefits afforded by application of a medical framework. For instance, redefining a problem as an appropriate object of medical attention can reduce guilt and social stigma, lend legitimacy to sufferers, and make it available for research and possibly prevention (Gabe 2013). Moreover, even if operating as a form of social control, it arguably exerts this in a far more benign way than other institutions like religion or the law.

On the other hand, the constructionist outlook that colors medicalization studies of social problems means they tend to bracket assumptions about a preexisting reality, "out there," that can be accurately grasped in language. But this leaves open the question of why constructionist conceptualizations of issues should be considered any more valid than the medical ones being bracketed. However, what constructionist studies may offer are alternative constructions of reality that foreground the role of social processes in scientific and medical discoveries. They also bring forward the social significance of labels and definitions attached to social issues at a given time. As Conrad (2013) describes, this may or may not lead to undermining the categories under scrutiny. Albeit most often operating as critique, in the same way that researchers study industrialization, medicalization can be studied as a social process without necessarily entailing a judgment about its detriment. Indeed, there are many cases in which medicalization has arguably been beneficial including epilepsy and, in many ways, childbirth (Conrad 2013).

It is also sometimes suggested that medicalization studies simply replace the medical model with a similarly functioning social model. That is, medicine's disproportionate focus on the body is replaced with one that roots more and more diseases in society. This can have the perverse effect of expanding the purview of medical interventions deeper into individual and social life. From this perspective, it is social scientists more than doctors who have been complicit in this expansion. By moving social factors like inequality into the etiology of disease, the threats posed by these conditions come to be understood primarily as health risks (O'Brien 1995). Social problems come to be understood as health problems whose primary connection to the social is through the latter's illness-inducing capacity. However, rather than searching out the causes of problems, social or, otherwise, constructionist studies tend to be more interested in the etiology of definitions (Conrad 1992). Nonetheless, medicalization studies have at least partially fostered critiques of medicine's narrow focus on the body and call to expand definitions of health to include social factors. While this has demonstrable benefits, there is a danger that the movement toward a more socially aware and humane medicine may produce one with an increasingly broad remit of control.

Conclusion

Since its emergence in the 1960s and 1970s, medicalization has become a key concept in sociology. Its application to studies of social problems has broadened understandings of the diverse ways by which contemporary societies make sense of the issues that face them. Increasingly, this has been through the medicalized language of health and well-being, illness and disease, syndromes and disorders, and treatments and cures. This shift has had a number of positive effects including more humane treatment of those once classed as bad, mad, or criminal, the removal of stigma, and the provision of systems of meaning and social support. On the other hand, it can produce a number of negative consequences, most notably in its capacity to depoliticize social problems by transforming them into personal and technical matters closed off from debate and alternative definitions. It can also erode moral autonomy and call into question human rationality, fueling reliance on expertise and the ongoing professionalization of everyday life. However, the expertise fueling medicalization has broadened and expanded so that it no longer stems primarily from the medical profession but to a wide variety of parties claiming specialized knowledge over medical and technical definitions of social problems and how they are to be resolved. Indeed, one of the key questions animating medicalization studies has been the shifting causes of medicalization in the face of an apparent decline in the authority of the medical profession. Rather than being a straightforward result of professional interest, it has been suggested that the proliferation of medicalized understandings of social problems can best be understood by studying the broader contexts into which these claims emerge (Conrad 2007). In particular, the decline of shared meaning systems once proffered by religion and tradition and the rise of medicine, science, and technology have made the latter pivotal in legitimating claims. Today, those wishing to draw attention to social problems are more likely to look not just to medicine but also to neuroscience, psychology, psychiatry, and epidemiology for support over the word of God or the strength of tradition. In many ways, this marks a clear progress, but when applied to human problems, the rhetoric of science can serve to obscure the moral, aesthetic, or other value-based impulses that ignite such campaigns in favor of what appear to be purely technocratic interventions on behalf of the common good.

Studies of the medicalization of social problems have been subject to many of the same criticisms launched against medicalization on the one hand and constructionist studies of social problems on the other. In spite of criticisms, the medicalization thesis remains a useful framework for understanding the changing ways by which modern societies have come to understand and approach social problems. One need only flip through the pages of a newspaper or scroll through popular social media websites to see that defining problems in medical terms continues to hold a strong grasp over the public imagination. Making problems social can be a dangerous and difficult task (Crews, et al. 2007). Solutions are often complex and difficult to communicate in a compelling way; sometimes they can be too radical for broad appeal or political expedience. Rendering them in medical language contains them and simplifies them and makes them seem less intractable and therefore treatable. But it is possible that some problems are unlikely to disappear even with the most advanced technological interventions; their solutions may lie in the deeper structures of society and may not be easily changed. Perhaps the biggest issue with medicalization is its tendency to deflect thinking from these deeper structures and from society as a whole, encouraging the view that nearly any problem is reducible to issues at the level of the individual body and mind.

Definitions of Key Terms

Medicalization	"[D]escribes a process by which non-medical problems become defined and treated as medical problems, usually in terms of illnesses or disorders" (Gabe 2013, p. 49).
Medical model	"A general framework for thinking about medical matters as diseases that require treatment" (Best 2008, p. 340).
Deviance	The violation of a social norm that may result in condemnation or punishment. Accounts of deviance can be subjective or objective. Objective accounts may consider the causes of deviant acts; subjective accounts consider how people and actions come to be defined as "deviant" (Goode 2011, p. 135).
Social problem	(1) Troubling conditions that affect society in some way (objectivist); (2) putative conditions defined as problematic by at least some individuals and groups in society (subjectivist).
Social construction	"The process by which people continually create – or construct – meaning" (Best 2008, p. 342).

Summary Points

- The medicalization of social problems refers to the process of applying medical definitions and descriptions to previously nonmedical issues.
- Medicalization is driven by a variety of professions, interest groups, and laypeople.
- Contextual factors fostering acceptance of medicalized social problems include secularization, growing power of medical and scientific knowledge, the decline of tradition, and the shift of political focus from production to consumption.
- Medicalizing social problems has benefits; it can remove social stigma, encourage people to seek help, and lead to more humane solutions.

- Medicalizing social problems has consequences; it can encourage reliance upon experts, undermine existing ways of coping, problematize notions of rationality and responsibility, close down other potential definitions, and lead to apolitical, individualized solutions.
- Studies have been criticized for overstating the consequences and scope of medicalization as well as the role of physicians in the process.
- Studies have been criticized for understating the benefits of medicalization and the role of laypeople in the process.
- Positing alternative social causes to medicalized social problems can ironically fuel medicalization as more and more aspects of social life come to be conceptualized as health risks.

References

Back L, Bennett A, Edles LD et al (2012) Cultural sociology. Wiley, Hoboken

Barker KK (2010) The social construction of illness: medicalization and contested illness. In: Bird CE, Conrad P, Fremont AM, Timmermans S (eds) Handbook of medical sociology. Vanderbilt University Press, Nashville, pp 147–162

Best J (2008) Social problems. Norton, New York

Busfield J (2006) Medicalisation. In: Scott J (ed) Sociology: the key concepts. Routledge, Abingdon, pp 99–103

Cederström C, Spicer A (2015) The wellness syndrome. Polity Press, Cambridge

Clarke A, Shim J (2011) Medicalization and biomedicalization revisited: technoscience and transformations of health, illness and american medicine. In: Pescosolido BA, Martin JK, McLeod JD, Rogers A (eds) Handbook of the sociology of health, illness, and healing: a blueprint for the 21st century. Springer, New York, pp 173–199

Cockerham WC, Ritchley FJ (1997) Dictionary of medical sociology. Greenwood Press, Westport

Conrad P (1992) Medicalization and social control. Annu Rev Sociol 18:209–232

Conrad P (2007) The medicalization of society. Johns Hopkins University Press, Baltimore

Conrad P (2013) Medicalization: changing contours, characteristics, and contexts. In: Cockerham WC (ed) Medical sociology on the move. Springer, New York, pp 195–214

Crews M, Moran P, Bhugra D (2007) Personality disorders and culture. In: Bhugra D, Bhui K (eds) Textbook of cultural psychiatry. Cambridge University Press, New York, pp 272–281

Foucault M (1965) Madness and civilization. Pantheon Books, New York

Freidson E (1970) Profession of medicine. Dodd, Mead, New York

Furedi F (2008) Medicalisation in a therapy culture. In: Wainwright D (ed) A sociology of health. Sage, London, pp 97–114

Gabe J (2013) Medicalization. In: Gabe J, Monaghan L (eds) Key concepts in medical sociology, 2nd edn. Sage, London, pp 49–53

Goode E, Ben-Yehuda N (2009) Moral panics: the social construction of deviance, 2nd edn. Wiley-Blackwell, Malden

Goode E, (2011) Deviance. In: Ritzer G, Ryan M (eds) The concise encyclopedia of sociology, 1st edn. Wiley-Blackwell, Malden, pp 135–136

Mcgann PJ, Conrad P (2011) The medicalization of deviance. In: Ritzer G, Ryan M (eds) The concise encyclopedia of sociology, 1st edn. Wiley-Blackwell, Malden, pp 141–142

Nettleton S (2013) The sociology of health and illness, 3rd edn. Polity Press, Cambridge

O'Brien M (1995) Health and lifestyle: a critical mess? Notes on the dedifferentiation of health. In: Bunton R, Nettleton S, Burrows R (eds) The sociology of health promotion: critical analyses of consumption lifestyle and risk. Routledge, London, pp 189–202

Sheaff M (2005) Sociology and health care. Open University Press, Maidenhead

Szasz T (1961) The myth of mental illness. Harper & Row, New York

Szasz T (1970) The manufacture of madness. Harper & Row, New York

Wainwright D (2008) The changing face of medical sociology. In: Wainwright D (ed) A sociology of health. Sage, London, pp 1–18

White K (2009) An introduction to the sociology of health and illness, 2nd edn. Sage, London

Zola IK (1972) Medicine as an institution of social control. Soc Rev 20:487–504

Changing Human Nature: The Ethical Challenge of Biotechnological Interventions on Humans

65

Jan-Christoph Heilinger, Oliver Müller, and Matthew Sample

Contents

Abstract

There is currently a prolific ethical debate about biotechnological interventions into human beings and the potential to alter the human organism, its functioning,, or genetic makeup. This article presents how such interventions can be seen as a challenge to concepts of "human nature" and reviews the different understandings

J.-C. Heilinger (✉)
University of Munich, Munich Center for Ethics, Munich, Germany
e-mail: heilinger@lmu.de

O. Müller
University of Freiburg, Department of Philosophy and BrainLinks-BrainTools, Freiburg, Germany
e-mail: oliver.mueller@philosophie.uni-freiburg.de

M. Sample
University of Washington, Department of Philosophy, Seattle, WA, USA
e-mail: sample@uw.edu

© Springer Science+Business Media Dordrecht 2017
T. Schramme, S. Edwards (eds.), *Handbook of the Philosophy of Medicine*,
DOI 10.1007/978-94-017-8688-1_52

of this notion. Representative of this debate is the ethical concern about "human enhancement interventions" that aim to improve human functioning beyond what can be considered as healthy or normal. The different ethical stances toward enhancement are presented.

Introduction

One of the consequences of the "biotechnological revolution" is that "human nature" is increasingly claimed as a central topic of bioethical reflection. It is widely assumed that some of the currently available and emerging biomedical and biotechnological interventions into the human organism may alter human nature and our understanding of it, respectively. In order to understand and assess this assumption it will be necessary to specify which interventions into the human organism may have an altering effect on human nature (section "Medical and Biotechnological Interventions as a Challenge for Conceptions of Human Nature"). Next, it is important to be clear about how to understand human nature in the first place, seeing as it is a complex term with a long philosophical history. This conceptual investigation requires two steps. It is important, firstly, to identify the metaethical and conceptual problems, gaining an awareness of the intricate relation between human nature and normativity. Secondly, it is necessary to distinguish the main conceptions of human nature as they are employed in bioethical debate (section "Human Nature in Bioethics: Conceptions and Implications"). On this basis, the normative function of arguments that draw on concepts of human nature can be analyzed more precisely. Specifically, within the current bioethical debate, the different conceptions of human nature support three main positions: bioconservative, bioliberal, and transhumanist. Each position represents a certain set of attitudes toward biotechnological interventions and bioethical (and biopolitical) agendas. This is particularly evident in the debate about human enhancement interventions (section "The Ethical Debate on Enhancement: An Exemplary Clash of Views About Human Nature"). As will become clear, the debate about conceptions of human nature is ongoing, and the dispute between the different positions is not settled yet.

Medical and Biotechnological Interventions as a Challenge for Conceptions of Human Nature

Human nature has been a subject of debate for a broad range of biomedical and biotechnological interventions. These interventions can be assembled into four general groups based on their mode of action: genetic, surgical, pharmaceutical, and prosthetic. While each group presents unique ethical challenges, the worry that humans are changing human nature often occurs as a technology pushes the boundary between therapy and enhancement or when a technology intervenes on a culturally significant part of the body (e.g., our genes or our brain).

Genetic interventions, here, refers to the set of technologies and procedures that center on the genetic material of humans or human cells. Notable examples include both indirect gene selection, such as preimplantation genetic diagnosis (PGD) and selective abortions, as well as more active interventions that directly modify genetic material, such as germline enhancement, gene therapy, and the creation of human-to-animal chimeras. Though the characteristics of an adult human are not fully determined by genetic endowment, the mere possibility of removing certain genes from the population or promoting the proliferation of a culturally desirable gene has incited scholars to weigh the importance of an unengineered genome (Habermas 2003).

Surgical interventions typically do not trigger the same concerns about tinkering with humanity's genetic "essence." But to the extent that they alter the body and its typical function or introduce foreign tissue into a person, they too can seem threatening to our nature. Cosmetic surgery, transplantation, xenotransplantation, body modification such as tongue splitting, and voluntary amputation of healthy limbs are some of the more striking examples. Taking a particular case, xenotransplants might provide much-needed organs for society, but the creation of adult human chimeras may problematically blur the line between human and nonhuman animals (Robert and Baylis 2003).

Psychopharmaceutical interventions aim to change an individual's cognitive or emotional state by acting on the brain. Their therapeutic and off-label use has been discussed extensively in the bioethics literature (see, e.g., Elliott 1998). Antidepressants, for instance, are marketed for a range of mood disorders beyond depression. Modafinil and other stimulants, though intended to treat narcolepsy and attention deficit disorders, are often perceived as multipurpose "steroids" for the mind. By aiming to change the brain via chemical rather than cognitive means, psychopharmacology tends to challenge many deep-seated cultural intuitions regarding authenticity and self-control. The concept of human nature, however, becomes increasingly relevant as ethical debate is confronted with a future in which the nontherapeutic ("cosmetic") use of psychopharmaceuticals is commonplace (Parens 2000).

Prosthetic interventions, lastly, augment the human form with additional "hardware," often involving both structural support and complex circuitry. Therapeutically, prosthetics can replace missing limbs, restore neural function, and support muscles weakened by age. To this end, engineers and scientists have developed a range of smart prosthetics, brain-computer interfaces ("neuroprosthetics") that reconnect the motor cortex to a limb or a muscle, and robotic exoskeletons. But even in therapeutic contexts, scholars have focused on the potential for these technologies to stretch current conceptual categories. Deep brain stimulators, for example, may be able to replace cognitive functions lost as a result of brain disease or damage; it is an open question whether or not a brain composed of both tissue and machine constitutes an unprecedented way of being (Schermer 2009).

Human Nature in Bioethics: Conceptions and Implications

If biomedical technologies seem to intervene in our nature in ways that might change our understanding of "human nature," then this intuition presupposes, on the one hand, that we have a solid knowledge of what human nature is, including the implication that shifts in the conceptions of human nature are or should be of ethical concern. On the other hand, attempts to bring "human nature" – a concept that has played most often no important role in the major theories of medical ethics – into the bioethical debate may be seen as an effective strategy to introduce specific – and neglected – normative frameworks into the debate. Although the question "what is 'human nature'?" has been part of ethical reflection since the ancient Greeks, in a sense it is true that ethical theories have systematically tended to avoid drawing on concepts of human nature at least since Kant; the term "human nature" was considered either too vague or metaphysically ballasted. This is one of the reasons why the concept of "personhood" made its career in ethical theories. However, the biotechnological revolution entails a certain discomfort in view of the constraints that are carried with the concept of the person – and forces bioethicists to rethink the relevance of "human nature" for an adequate ethical evaluation of new technologies.

Such concern for "anthropological" issues includes two interconnected questions, both the classical philosophical question "what actually is 'human nature'?" and the ethical question "what kind of normative framework (which set of values) follows from a robust concept of human nature?" Obviously, these questions lead to conceptual and methodological problems, which will be mentioned briefly (section "Conceptual and Meta-Ethical Aspects"). In distinguishing the main arguments that draw on specific concepts of "human nature" within a bioethical argument, one can group them into a highly schematic "pool" of prominent positions (section "A "Pool" of Prominent Positions").

Conceptual and Metaethical Aspects

Among the wide range of conceptual problems that arise when referring to "human nature," there are two aspects of particular importance for bioethical debate: firstly, the conceptual and semantic problems regarding the notion of "nature" generally; secondly, the problems of drawing normative conclusions from a description of human nature that are often discussed under the label "naturalistic fallacy."

Firstly, the term "human nature" carries an intricate ambiguity: Nature can mean not only "essence," in some cases, but also can refer to concepts or background theories of "naturalness." Ambitious philosophical approaches try to combine "essence" and "naturalness" systematically (as prominent "classical" position Scheler 1928/2007), but in bioethical contexts one often finds a certain focus on the mere "naturalness" of human beings – and this changes both the perspective on "human nature" and the reflection on the normative implications (see Birnbacher 2014 for a discussion). But often "personhood" is invoked to capture the "essence" of human nature (Singer 1979 may count as a prominent and controversial example). The specific qualities and capabilities of persons – such as self-consciousness, rationality, responsibility, etc. – then count as the core aspects that should be included in an ethical reflection or even foundation. Given the focus on "natural-ness," however, one tends to discuss aspects that are not necessarily covered by the concept of a person. Unsurprisingly, naturalness could be conceptualized in very different ways, from reductionist positions that accept only the biological nature of homo sapiens to Aristotelian approaches that are based on a natural striving for certain goods to theories of embodiment that include the vulnerability and fragility of human existence to metaphysical theories of a God-given "pure" nature – to name but a few distinctive positions.

Secondly, on a metaethical level it has to be discussed whether justifying a norm or value by reference to a concept of human nature is plausible. David Hume was right to raise awareness for the is-ought gap in ethical theories because there is indeed a certain temptation to step in an unreflective way from a descriptive "is" to a normative and prescriptive "ought." This, however, could be a severe methodolog-ical problem when dealing with human nature in ethics (Hume 1739/2011). It is rather easy to claim that human nature or a certain aspect of human nature should be preserved or should be the benchmark for a value. But it is difficult to substantiate these kinds of intuitions and provide good reasons for the normativity of human nature or parts thereof. So, Hume's formulation of the is-ought problem as well as Moore's "naturalistic fallacy" and his "argument of the open question" raise con-cerns about the problematic relation between natural and moral properties (Moore 1903/1971). Yet the charge of committing a naturalistic fallacy can be abused, too. Stipulating, for example, that natural human fragility or vulnerability has some moral significance or even moral value is not necessarily based on that fallacy. Nor is referring to a normatively charged Aristotelian understanding of nature per se fallacious. The role of human nature stands or falls by the normative framework that explicates certain values – which, however, always has to avoid simplistic inferences of norms from its understanding of human nature.

A "Pool" of Prominent Positions

During recent decades, different conceptions of human nature have been employed to evaluate the ethical implications of biomedical interventions. The following "pool" of prominent positions tries to categorize the main concepts and arguments. These positions are ideal types, with a focus on select examples; they stand for a range of partly overlapping variants that cannot be fully spelled out here. The present focus will be on conceptions of human nature that are promoted as alternatives or additions to normative conceptions of "personhood." Consequently, the long West-ern tradition of humans as persons or of defining humans as *animal rationale* is missing in the following compilation. While the demand for "informed consent" with its underlying understanding of a human being as a rational, autonomous agent could count as the most prominent example for a bioethical principle that is based on a conception of human nature in this respect, too, drawing on human nature in the bioethical debate usually goes beyond a mere guarantee of such rational, informed consent in difficult decisions.

Human Nature as Pure and Untouched by Culture and Technology

In some contexts human nature is understood in an essentialist way which is based on the conviction that there is a "pure" human nature before all culture and technology. This is Rousseau's idea of an "authentic" nature that becomes subverted by technology ("L'Homme naît naturellement bon, c'est la société qui le corrompt."). More prominent in the debate are conceptions that understand human nature as somehow "given" and "untouched" before technological interventions. Leon R. Kass is a well-known proponent of this position. In his book *Life, Liberty and the Defense of Dignity* he understands medical technologies as challenging human nature as such: "Human nature itself lies on the operation table, ready for alteration, for eugenic and neurophysic 'enhancement' for wholesale redesign. In leading laboratories, academic and industrial, new creators are confidently amassing their powers and quietly honing their skills, while on the street their evangelists are zealously prophesying a posthuman future. For anyone who cares about preserving our humanity, the time has come to pay attention." (Kass 2002, p. 4). Kass underlines that his reference to human nature means more than referring to the concept of a person (and a "liberal" framework, respectively): "The account of human dignity we seek goes beyond the said dignity of 'persons' to reflect and embrace the worthiness of embodied human life, and therewith of our natural desires and passions, our natural origins and attachments, our sentiments and aversions, our loves and longings... It is a life that will use our awareness of need, limitation and mortality to craft a way of being that has engagement, depth, beauty, virtue and meaning – not despite our embodiment but because of it." (ibid., pp. 17–18) It is typical that such an understanding of human nature perceives technology as a threat. With their potential changes, new biotechnologies undermine this concept of human nature and consequently put "human dignity" in danger. Kass' human nature has a pretechnological status; it is understood as something that is technologically untouched and has to be treated as a "given" – by God or nature itself. This "givenness" has a normative dimension insofar as Kass and others argue to restrict biotechnological interventions. Speaking of the untouched status of human nature implicates that it is "fixed." In this respect, Kass' position is close to approaches that refer to the "biostatistical" normalcy of human nature (see section "Biological Conceptions of Human Nature").

Kass explicitly uses religious and Judeo-Christian intuitions about human nature, but one can find the idea of human nature as "untouched" in texts by secular authors as well. A famous example is Jürgen Habermas, who speaks of "das Gewachsene" or "das Gewordene" ("the grown," cf. Habermas 2001, p. 80). Habermas' notion is, albeit on a different foundation, quite close to the idea of the "untouched" as he contrasts "das Gewachsene"/"Gewordene" with "das Gemachte" ("the made"/"the produced"/"the fabricated"). Habermas explicitly refers to the Aristotelian distinction between nature and technology. In doing so, Habermas bases his theory on the presupposition that human nature and technology could be thought of as separated and that there are at least some important pretechnological elements of human nature. Consequently, the "Gewachsene" has normative implications; in the Habermasian sense it should be respected as something valuable per se that is not at our unrestricted disposal.

Human Nature as Contingent

Some authors assert that humans should strive to accept natural bodily differences that they might call disabilities or imperfections. By this reasoning, one should hesitate to promote medical interventions that promise to remove such differences, like selective abortions or genetic enhancements. Garland-Thomson (2012) is a useful example of these positions; she calls for a "conservation" of disability as a natural and valuable part of the quite diverse human condition. For her, "honoring the 'is' rather than the 'ought'" of human nature is based on a conviction that differences coming along with disability and imperfection are valuable. The existence of bodily differences, she argues, is not a liability that needs to be tolerated and protected but is rather a source of narrative, ethical, and epistemic resources. The empirical understanding of the world, for instance, might be impoverished if society erased individuals who cultivate alternative sensory modalities.

Sandel (2009) fits within this framework of valuing difference and disability. He claims that an "openness to the unbidden," a recognition that we humans are not in complete control of our lives, is crucial for healthy parent–child relationships and encourages kindness and generosity toward the less-fortunate in society. Similarly, Parens (1995) stresses that human "fragility" is a source of diversity and meaning for us. For these authors, the existence of disability or imperfection is a resource for humanity, a chance to appreciate good fortune and to exercise virtuous behavior toward others. Medical technologies that promise to remove human vulnerability, with their "Promethean striving," can represent the opposite attitude, the expectation that individuals master their own fates such that virtuous behavior is not necessary.

Though these authors avoid subjecting themselves to the charge of committing a naturalistic fallacy, their arguments do rely on some factual claim about human nature; their prescriptions for acceptance presuppose that human nature is essentially contingent and entails some inescapable tendency toward difference and disability. As Garland-Thomson emphasizes, the human body transforms as it ages, pulling even the most able-bodied into a radically different mode of being. And it is this inevitability, she notes, that makes disability a "generative" concept. To the extent that society has the biotechnological or medical means necessary to erase such bodily differences and prevent economic or biological misfortune, arguments based on the capriciousness of fate might seem less compelling, and the value of accepting the "unbidden" might wane (see section "Human Nature as Flawed" for an elaboration of this line of thought).

Aristotelian Understandings of Human Nature

Several positions in the debate stand in an Aristotelian tradition: as more or less "essentialist" these positions tend to understand human nature as striving for a good life. In her contribution to "Human dignity and Bioethics" (one of the essays commissioned by the President's Council of Bioethics), Martha C. Nussbaum underlines that we humans have to include more aspects of human nature than only rationality. This is perfectly in line with the approaches of human nature that try to complement the concept of personhood: "In general, when we select a political conception of the person we ought to choose one that does not exalt rationality as the single good thing and that does not denigrate forms of need and striving that are parts of our animality. Indeed, it is crucial to situate rationality squarely within animality, and to insist that it is one capacity of a type of animal who is also characterized by growth, maturity, and decline, and by a wide range of disabilities, some more common and some less common. There is dignity not only in rationality but in human need itself and in the varied forms of striving that emerge from human need." (Nussbaum 2008, p. 363) On this basic assumption about human nature, Nussbaum developed a "capabilities approach" that tries to list the main capabilities of human beings, based on a series of dimensions of the essence of human nature (such as being able to live to the end of a human life of normal length, have good health, have adequate shelter, form a conception of the good, and engage in critical reflection about the planning of one's life).

Nussbaum's view is only one example for an Aristotelian approach to human nature. Foot (2001) and Thompson (1995) are others. The latter introduced "Aristotelian categoricals" in the debate that should help to describe human nature in a nonreductionist way. Typical for such positions is the idea that the "human flourishing" should be respected. In contrast to "human nature as untouched," more sophisticated Aristotelian positions do not perceive biotechnological interventions as per se against human nature because the concepts of human flourishing and of human capabilities allow the integration of biomedical techniques into the "good life." This is a political question as Nussbaum points out: "It means that the respectful government promotes health capabilities, not healthy functioning. That is, it should make sure that all citizens have adequate health insurance and access to good medical facilities... In short, respecting human dignity requires informing people about their choices, restricting dangerous choices for children, but permitting adults to make a full range of choices, including unhealthy ones – with the proviso that competitive sports need to set reasonably safety conditions so that unwilling participants are not dragooned into taking a health risk that they don't want to take." (Nussbaum 2008, p. 370). The capability approach and its conclusions, however, are not paternalistic. Buchanan (2009), in discussing the President's Council for Bioethics, notes that arguments based on human nature can be interpreted as either a form of normative essentialism or an assertion about the good life. Strengthening the capabilities means strengthening the responsibility to lead a good life – hence to fulfill the intrinsic goodness of human nature.

Biological Conceptions of Human Nature

Human nature can also be understood in terms of the characteristics of the human species, as disclosed by biological and other scientific investigation. Fukuyama (2003) defines human nature as "the sum of the behavior and characteristics that are typical of the human species, arising from genetic rather than environmental factors." In drawing on a population-based understanding of our nature, Fukuyama follows current scientific categorizations of the human species. According to these "biologically respectable" understandings, a species is more like a particular individual with relative properties than a "kind" with some definable essence; unlike a chemical element, a species has no intrinsic properties and refers to a population that comes into existence, can change over time, and may even comprise members that are genetically different (Lewens 2012). Authors differ, however, in what they choose to draw from this scientific insight.

Fukuyama, for example, takes the complex features that are shared by members of the population to justify an account of human rights. He suggests that biotechnological alteration of the species risks upsetting "Factor X," his term for a multicausal human quality that justifies basic rights, gives humans a common form, and grounds liberal social structures. For Fukuyama, then, the cost of altering our nature is nothing less than endangering "human dignity." But for practical reasons some do not follow Fukuyama to this conclusion. Daniels (2009), for example, who also advocates a biostatistical understanding of human nature, stresses that population-scale interventions are highly unlikely, given the current and near-future state of medical technology. And if we humans are unable to actually change human nature, then the associated ethical worries are merely hypothetical.

Simultaneously, other authors deny that a biological understanding of human nature can contribute to ethical debates. Buchanan (2009) highlights the fact that if humans have a nature, it likely consists of both desirable and undesirable characteristics. It is an empirical question, he argues, whether specific interventions on human biology will inevitably disrupt the desirable tendencies. Thus, the question of altering our nature can seem too broad to be helpful. Along these lines, Lewens (2012) and Buchanan (2009) both stress the fact that invocations of human nature – biologically understood – often disguise normative commitments in seemingly descriptive scientific language. In this way, they highlight the possibility for nature-based arguments to preempt discussions of value by relying on the cultural authority of science or by relying on the naturalistic fallacy.

The *Homo Faber* View of Human Nature

In the philosophy of technology there is a certain consensus that human beings are "by nature artificial" and because of their natural disposition "technicians" (cf. Plessner 1928/1975). What is called human nature is the nature of *homo faber* who is constantly transforming the world and, in doing so, himself. In this context, technology is often compared to language. Technology is then a way of self-exploration and self-understanding (cf. Cassirer 1930/2004). Human nature is not thinkable without technology. There is no pretechnological human nature. This assumption is widely spread in the debate although it is not often made explicit. A controversial exception is Andy Clark, who argues explicitly that human beings always tend to transform themselves technologically. Human nature cannot be understood unless we think of it as being technologically shaped; Rousseau's "pure" human nature simply does not exist. To encapsulate his position he coined the expression of human beings as "natural-born cyborgs," creatures in transition.

Clark's main work "is the story of that transition and of its roots in some of the most basic characteristic facts about human nature. For human beings, I want to convince you, are natural-born cyborgs... What makes us distinctively human is our capacity to continually restructure and rebuild our own mental circuitry, courtesy of an empowering web of culture, education, technology, and artifacts." (Clark 2003, pp. 3, 10) This *homo faber* position includes openness for any transformation of human nature. Yet it is no "transhumanist" or "posthumanist" position (see below) because it does not call for overcoming human nature as it is.

Biotechnological interventions may allow misuse, but as human nature is per se and always technologically transformed, humans only have to be careful, not abstinent: "And we do need to be cautious, for to recognize the deeply transformative nature of our biotechnological unions is at once to see that not all such unions will be for the better. But if I am right – if it is our basic human nature to annex, exploit, and incorporate nonbiological stuff deep into our mental profiles – then the question is not whether we go that route, but in what ways we actively sculpt and shape it. By seeing ourselves as we truly are, we increase the chances that our future biotechnological unions will be good ones." (Clark 2003, p. 198) Normatively, this position promotes openness to biomedical interventions and is insofar close to a bioliberal attitude in general. Consequently, the *homo faber* view is unable to develop concrete advice about *which* biotechnological transformation may be worthwhile or not, because of the imprecision of its underlying concept of human nature.

Human Nature as Flawed

The vision of humans as *homo faber*, as natural technicians, takes on a different meaning when it is placed within a narrative of progress. Transhumanism has provided one such narrative in the recent bioethical literature. Bostrom (2003) asserts that the transhumanist sees human nature as "as a work-in-progress, a half-baked beginning that we can learn to remold in desirable ways." (p. 493) Senescence, limited memory, and vulnerability to disease may be part of the human condition, as it exists, but the transhumanist does not afford this fact any special significance, as do the authors (in section "Human Nature as Pure and Untouched by Culture and Technology" and section "Human Nature as Contingent"). Transhumanists see humanity's undesirable characteristics as flaws waiting to be fixed via technoscientific or even social interventions. Accordingly, Bostrom and Sandberg (2009) suggest the use of an "evolutionary heuristic" to sort out which traits are well suited for the modern world from those which are only holdovers from humanity's hunter-gatherer past, such as metabolic constraints on cognitive capacity or immune activation. In this way, transhumanists hope to plan a deliberate transition to the "posthuman."

By calling for the redesign of human nature, the transhumanist perspective does more than merely imply that tool use and self-modification is part of our nature. Beyond the invocation of *homo faber*, transhumanist literature presents a theme of progressive change, a persistent yearning for a better nature. It is an impulse in keeping with H.G. Wells' vision for the dawning twentieth century; he asks, "why should things cease with man?" (Wells 1902). Like Wells, transhumanists stress both the promise and inevitability of "posthumanity." The implication of "posthuman" is not that humanity will completely disappear but that the particularities of our current nature, especially the negative ones, are transient (Birnbacher 2009). The transhumanist understanding of human nature, thus, can be interpreted as a negative point; human nature is not what it could (and perhaps should) be. This idea will be explicated further in the next section.

The Ethical Debate on Enhancement: An Exemplary Clash of Views About Human Nature

In the current ethical debate about the legitimacy of altering human nature, the variety of views presented above becomes visible. As indicated above, the constellation of positions regarding human nature resists easy categorization as "pro-" and "anti-" biotechnology. Even when scholars agree on a feature or a definition of human nature, they can leverage that understanding to justify radically different attitudes toward biotechnological or biomedical interventions. Biostatistical or biological understandings of human nature, as mentioned above, have been used to both forbid alteration of human nature and – somewhat paradoxically – to dismiss the very possibility of such alteration. This flexibility in the argumentative use of human nature demands that we carefully disentangle the subtly different ways in which scholars ground their conclusions. One can, nevertheless, place scholars within a broader framework based on their general attitude toward changing human nature, whether enthusiastic, worried, or otherwise. This last section is devoted to that task.

The debate on human enhancement can be understood as a forceful and significant clash of different concepts of human nature. For a decade or so there has been a thriving international debate on the legitimacy of enhancement technologies, on biotechnological interventions "beyond therapy." Typical arguments in this debate refer to justice, fairness, individual responsibility, etc. It is evident that beside these normative concepts human nature is seen as relevant for the ethical evaluation (Heilinger 2014). And it is characteristic for this debate that different concepts of human nature are subsumed in the named broader frameworks that "bundle" different concepts of human nature.

One such general framework has emerged organically within the bioethics literature and deserves consideration here. One can distinguish three main views with regard to such alterations: a bioconservative, a bioliberal, and a transhumanist one. Each of these views draws on different understandings of human nature in order to reach ethical conclusions about the legitimacy of enhancement interventions. These views are distinguished by whether human nature is to be seen as fixed or malleable and as intrinsically or instrumentally valuable. The three views pertain to the use of the various technologies that aim at altering human nature, including therapies, but become particularly visible in the debate about human enhancement interventions.

Those who see alterations of human nature as morally problematic and highlight the dangers of technology are often called bioconservatives. In stressing the importance of preserving human nature as it is, they often cite an "untouched" human nature that is fixed and intrinsically valuable. Those who are willing to endorse changes in human nature if it is conducive to a greater good are often labeled transhumanists or posthumanists, since they wish to expand the current boundaries of human existence. This position tends to stress the malleability of human nature, as a means to achieve other instrinsically valuable states. Between these two extremes, one can find bioliberals, who do not deny that changes in human nature occur and that some of them may be very worthwhile, while holding that human nature may have both some intrinsic and instrumental value. These three views will be briefly presented.

Still exemplary for the bioconservative position is the influential report "Beyond Therapy. Biotechnology and the Pursuit of Happiness" (2003) by the former President's Council on Bioethics (which Barack Obama ended when he came into office). In this text the negative consequences of attempting to alter human nature are vividly illustrated, sometimes with a clearly evident religious background. The authors of this report – among them Leon Kass, Francis Fukuyama, and Michael Sandel – direct attention first and foremost to several "essential sources of concern." Kass' concept of human nature that is explicated in this context was mentioned above (section "Human Nature as Pure and Untouched by Culture and Technology"). It is one possible background assumption about human nature which may lead to a bioconservative position that can be described as reacting to certain "dangers." There is (1) the danger of lacking humility and "respect for the given" when playing God and trying to alter human nature with its intrinsic value, (2) the danger that unnatural means will threaten the dignity of the naturally human way of activity, because the valued process of effort, success, and merit is cut short, (3) the danger that individuals will lose their personal identity and individuality when undergoing alterations of their human nature and (4) the danger that the pursuit of perfection in some domains of human existence may, when it accompanies alterations of human nature, ultimately lead to an impoverished life, not a flourishing one. On the basis of these concerns, the bioconservative position tries to find arguments against enhancement technologies, referring to the aforementioned dangers and the supposed threat to human nature.

As mentioned above (section "Human Nature as Flawed"), trans- or posthumanists fully endorse the options provided by using biotechnologies to enhance human beings. Transhumanists see themselves as "extending the liberal democratic humanist tradition to a defense of our right to control our own bodies and minds, even if our choices make us something other than 'human'" (Hughes 2004, p. xv). Even if, in the end, humans will turn into transhuman beings, this is not to be regretted. Quite to the contrary, humans should strive to bring about beings that are capable to reach these higher states of mind.

Transhumans can be understood to be still human beings, but those humans that are already on their way to becoming posthuman. Bostrom, for example, argues that some distinctively posthuman modes of being are intrinsically valuable, even though they are not only gradually but substantially different from standard human modes. Hence it could be very good for human beings to become posthuman. By a posthuman, he understands a being that has at least one "posthuman capacity," understood as "a general central capacity greatly exceeding the maximum attainable by any current human being without recourse to new technological means" (Bostrom 2008, our emphasis). These capacities are, following Bostrom, a healthy life span, cognition, or emotion.

The posthumanist argument for alterations of human nature shifts the burden of proof from those who want to strive for posthuman capacities to those who want to deny persons the pursuit of those capacities. If there are means available to improve the human lot in realizing obvious, widely shared goods – like living longer, healthier lives, becoming smarter, or emotionally better off – those who are opposing such changes stand in need to justify their opposition. One should not hold back because of concern for some abstract idea of the nature of human beings. What matters is that lives go well, not that they match some disputed idea of a fixed human nature, or so transhumanists argue.

Between bioconservatives and transhumanists one can identify bioliberals as holding an intermediate position. Despite all differences, these intermediate positions share the conviction that there are no principled objections against alterations of human nature. They hold this view either because they doubt the existence of something fixed that can be called human nature or because they doubt that human nature is intrinsically valuable and must hence never be altered. Instead, they are willing to consider alterations on a case-by-case basis. Buchanan has rightly pointed out that the dispute in the ethical debate about human enhancement is not so much between those who object to and those who promote enhancements (contra- and proenhancement) but between those who fundamentally object to enhancements (antienhancement) and those who do not share this general objection (anti-antienhancement). Those being anti-antienhancement hence are not obliged to promote or call for enhancements. Their position is determined rather by a willingness to consider enhancement interventions if they meet certain other criteria (Buchanan 2011).

The bioliberal ethical assessment of possible interventions draws the main attention not to "anthropological" arguments about human nature. Instead, it focuses on assessments of risks and benefits and considerations about justice. Furthermore, as liberals they hold the individual, informed, and autonomous decision for or against some intervention with a potentially human nature–altering effect particularly important.

Conclusion

The understanding of human nature and its ethical implications in the context of medical, biotechnological, and enhancement interventions in the human organism is a widely debated topic in contemporary philosophy of medicine and bioethics. A lot of academic attention has been paid to the challenge to phrase in philosophical and secular terms the widely shared intuition that there are some limits to what we may ethically do with the biological underpinnings of our human existence. But the debate is not settled yet. Transhumanists often seem overly optimistic about the possibility of improving the human lot while neglecting dangers associated with it. Bioconservatives often seem overly pessimistic and sometimes endorse religiously motivated views or intuitions that are difficult to justify in secular terms. This makes the bioliberal view attractive, at least prima facie. However, being generally open to allow for alterations of human nature is rather the statement of the problem and offers no solution yet. Hence, no single approach presented above can claim to have provided a solution to the challenge yet, but the bioliberal view, when it integrates both the concern and the promises connected to human enhancements, should, it seems, be pursued further in order to determine a wise way of dealing with the novel technologies.

Definition of Key Terms

Human nature	A complex, multivalent concept used to, among other things, justify various and sometimes contradictory attitudes toward biotechnological interventions on humans
Human enhancement interventions	Biological, technical, or medical interventions in the healthy human organism that aim to improve the human organism or its functioning beyond a level of normalcy
Biotechnologies	Intentional biological, technical, or medical interventions on living organisms
Bioconservatives	Those holding that human enhancements are morally prohibited, since they alter human nature
Bioliberals	Those holding that some forms of human enhancements may be morally acceptable, even if they come along with changes of human nature
Transhumanists	Those holding that human enhancements are morally desirable, because they help overcoming some limitations of human nature

Summary Points

- Biotechnological interventions that have the potential to alter human nature can be genetic, surgical, psychopharmacological, or prosthetic.
- The notion "human nature" plays a complex and disputed role in contemporary bioethics. It has to be employed carefully, due to its possibly normative content.
- The concept of human nature is contested, and there are different attempts to spell it out: some contrast human nature with culture; others understand it as consisting essentially in culture. Some define an ultimate and fixed essence of human existence, while others stress the contingency of human traits.

- Normatively, these views can support diverse evaluations of human nature as perfect and in need of protection on the one hand and of human nature as flawed and worthy of improvements on the other.
- With regard to the ethical debate about human enhancement interventions, three prominent attitudes are evident. Bioconservative views clash with bioliberal or even transhumanist views over whether enhancement interventions that may change human nature are morally problematic, acceptable, or desirable.

References

Birnbacher D (2009) Posthumanity, transhumanism and human nature. In: Chadwick R, Gordijn B (eds) Medical enhancement and posthumanity. Springer, Dordrecht, pp 95–106

Birnbacher D (2014) Naturalness. Is the "natural" preferable to the "artificial"? (trans: Carus D). University Press of America, Lanham

Bostrom N (2003) Human genetic enhancements: a transhumanist perspective. J Value Inq 37 (4):493–506

Bostrom N (2008) Why I want to be a posthuman when I grow up. In: Gordijn B, Chadwick R (eds) Medical enhancement and posthumanity. Springer Netherlands, Berlin, pp 107–136

Bostrom N, Sandberg A (2009) The wisdom of nature: an evolutionary heuristic for human enhancement. In: Human enhancement. Oxford University Press, Oxford, pp 375–416

Buchanan A (2009) Human nature and enhancement. Bioethics 23(3):141–150

Buchanan A (2011) Beyond humanity? The ethics of biomedical enhancement. Oxford University Press, Oxford

Cassirer E (2004) Form und Technik. In: Gesammelte Werke, vol 17. Felix Meiner Verlag, Hamburg, pp 139–183

Clark A (2003) Natural-born cyborgs. Minds, technologies, and the future of human intelligence. Oxford University Press, Oxford

Daniels N (2009) Can anyone really be talking about ethically modifying human nature. In: Savulescu J, Bostrom N (eds) Human enhancement. Oxford University Press, Oxford, pp 25–42

Elliott C (1998) The tyranny of happiness: ethics and cosmetic psychopharmacology. In: Parens E (ed) Enhancing human traits: ethical and social implications. Georgetown University Press, Washington, DC, pp 177–188

Foot P (2001) Natural goodness. Clarendon, Oxford

Fukuyama F (2003) Our posthuman future: consequences of the biotechnology revolution. Macmillan, Picador, New York, NY

Garland-Thomson R (2012) The case for conserving disability. J Bioeth Inq 9(3):339–355

Habermas J (2001) Die Zukunft der menschlichen Natur. Suhrkamp, Frankfurt am Main

Habermas J (2003) The future of human nature (trans: Beister H, Rehg W). Polity Press, Cambridge, UK

Heilinger J-C (2014) Anthropological arguments in the ethical debate about human enhancement. Hum Mente J Philos Stud 26(2014):95–116

Hughes J (2004) Citizen Cyborg. Why democratic societies must respond to the redesigned human of the future. Westview, Cambridge, MA

Hume D (1739/2011) A treatise of human nature. Oxford University Press, Oxford

Kass L (2002) Life, Liberty and the Defense of Dignity: The Challenge for Bioethics. Encounter Books, New York

Lewens T (2012) Human nature: the very idea. Philos Technol 25(4):459–474

Moore E (1903/1971) Principia ethica. Cambridge University Press, Cambridge

Nussbaum M (2008) Human dignity and political entitlements. In: Human dignity and bioethics: essays commissioned by the President's Council on Bioethics, President's Council of Bioethics, Washington, DC

Parens E (1995) The goodness of fragility: on the prospect of genetic technologies aimed at the enhancement of human capacities. Kennedy Inst Ethics J 5(2):141–153

Parens E (2000) Enhancing human traits: ethical and social implications. Georgetown University Press, Washington, DC

Plessner H (1975) Die Stufen des Organischen und der Mensch. Einleitung in die philosophische Anthropologie. De Gruyter, Berlin/New York

President's Council on Bioethics (2003) Beyond therapy. Biotechnology and the pursuit of happiness. Dana Press, New York

Robert JS, Baylis F (2003) Crossing species boundaries. Am J Bioeth 3(3):1–13

Sandel MJ (2009) The case against perfection. Harvard University Press, Cambridge, MA

Scheler M (2007) Die Stellung des Menschen im Kosmos. In: Gesammelte Werke, vol 9. Bouvier, Bonn, pp 7–71

Schermer M (2009) The mind and the machine: on the conceptual and moral implications of brain-machine interaction. Nanoethics 3:217–230

Singer P (1979) Practical ethics. Cambridge University Press, Cambridge

Thompson M (1995) The representation of life. In: Hursthouse R, Lawrence G, Quinn W (eds) Virtues and reasons. Oxford University Press, Oxford, pp 247–297

Wells H (1902) The discovery of the future. Nature 65(1684):326–331

Social Determinants of Health

66

Sridhar Venkatapuram

Contents

Abstract

This chapter discusses social determinants of health, an area of research and health policy initially coming out of epidemiology. Two categories of philosophical issues are presented including epistemological issues related to casual explanations as well as ethical issues related to health inequalities and social justice. In pursuing better explanations of causation and distribution of disease, social epidemiology expands the scope of causal chain outward beyond factors on or within the body as well as upward in terms of nested spaces such as family, neighborhood, region, country, and global system. New thinking about the ethical value of health and well-being and the causal role of social factors in producing inequalities in health raise questions of social justice and require drawing on disciplines such as political philosophy that evaluate conceptions of a good or just society.

S. Venkatapuram (✉)
Global Health and Social Medicine, King's College London, London, UK
e-mail: Sridhar.venkatapuram@kcl.ac.uk

© Springer Science+Business Media Dordrecht 2017
T. Schramme, S. Edwards (eds.), *Handbook of the Philosophy of Medicine*,
DOI 10.1007/978-94-017-8688-1_72

Introduction

"Social determinants of health" (SDH) is a phrase that has emerged from the discipline of epidemiology, the science that identifies the determinants and distribution of morbidity and mortality. However, while epidemiological and related literature use the phrase "social determinants of health," in actuality, the language refers to the social determinants of disease, disability, illness, mortality, and other such negatively valued states of biological and mental functioning. Some chapters in the present book as well as other authors discuss how the concept of health is contested and in flux (Nordenfelt et al. 2001; Blaxter 2010; Cribb 2005; Venkatapuram 2011). And, indeed, there have been important advances recently in our knowledge about various dimensions of "positive health" (e.g., well-being, longevity, resilience, happiness, life satisfaction) (Huppert et al. 2005; Diener et al. 1999; Ryan and Deci 2001). Nevertheless, despite being directly relevant, the debates on conceptions of health as well as research on positive health are going to be set aside in the following discussion. Unless stated otherwise, SDH from here on refers to the social determinants of states of ill-health and premature mortality because that is what is most often meant.

There is a long history of identifying the role of the social environment in the causal pathways to disease and mortality. It was central to the epidemiological work of Louis-René Villermé and Rudolph Virchow in the nineteenth century (Virchow and Rather 1985; Julia and Valleron 2011). And it was very much a visible part of community and social medicine that began to flourish in the mid-twentieth century (Trostle 2004). However, as epidemiology developed into a distinct and sophisticated scientific discipline in the twentieth century in the United States, its research paradigm or scope was increasingly narrowed down to individual-level factors (Krieger 1994). That is, disease was understood to be caused by the independent or interactive result of individual-level factors such as individual biology, behaviors, and harmful proximate exposures to the body.

In contrast, contemporary social epidemiology harnesses state-of-the-art epidemiological tools and methodologies combined with sociological analysis to explicitly identify supra-individual social phenomena that affect both the causation and distribution of ill-health across individuals and social groups, within and across countries, and over time (Marmot and Wilkinson 1999; Berkman et al. 2014; Krieger 2011). One the of many interesting aspects of SDH research is that while the vast majority of epidemiological research is undertaken and published in the United States, much of the SDH research has been done by researchers outside the United States, mainly in Europe (Braveman et al. 2011). The explicit focal points of social epidemiological research – social phenomenon as causes and inequalities in health across social groups – are the initial entry points for philosophical investigations that are both intellectually challenging and have profound real-world implications.

The present chapter will first introduce social epidemiology and some of its insights and then discuss the implications for the philosophy of epidemiology. The subsequent sections discuss the social justice implications of SDH, and then the chapter concludes.

Social Epidemiology

The science of epidemiology is the informational engine of medicine, public health, health research, and policy. Despite the foundational role it has in these fields, epidemiologists themselves consider it to be a relatively new discipline and still in an early stage of development (Rothman et al. 2008, p. v). While there has been enormous growth starting in the 1960s in research outputs as well as in the understanding of epidemiological concepts, there are still some strong disagreements about fundamental concepts. One of the central controversies is whether epidemiology should include research on social determinants (Rothman et al. 1998; Zielhuis and Kiemeney 2001; Susser 1999; Krieger 2011). To put it simply, the debate is about whether epidemiology is and should be a natural science or a social science. Including the study of social determinants would make epidemiology more like a social science. And, in the opinion of some epidemiologists, this would make epidemiology less objective, authoritative, and scientific (Rothman et al. 1998; Zielhuis and Kiemeney 2001; Marmot 1976).

A common view understands scientific research and moral reasoning as belonging to two separate spheres, and scientific research is often treated as factual and objective inputs into the sphere of moral reasoning ("evidence-based policy"). In line with such a view, some epidemiologists see themselves as pure natural scientists discovering natural facts about biological processes, which then become inputs into the separate sphere of moral reasoning regarding which health policies to pursue through social action. Contrary to such a view which upholds a strong fact-value distinction, a "science is social" perspective recognizes scientific research as occurring within a social context. Whether in epidemiology or other scientific fields, social values and intellectual virtues of individuals are recognized as influencing scientific practice starting from which questions are researched, how hypotheses are framed, the scope of observations, how data and hypotheses are adjusted, how causal inferences are made, how findings are disseminated, and so forth. The conflict between these two perspectives on what science is and how it should be done is real and cannot be overstated. It is at the center of the acrimonious debates occurring within epidemiology for well over a decade. For a good reflection of the debates, see the article by Zielhuis et al. and commentaries in the same journal issue (Zielhuis and Kiemeney 2001).

What initiated and sustains this debate about the type of science epidemiology should be is that social epidemiologists have been producing a growing base of significant findings. Among the many productive insights from social epidemiology over the last four decades, one discovery has been particularly revolutionary. Initially discovered by the researchers of the Whitehall studies in the late 1970s, epidemiologists have been producing compelling evidence that health outcomes (e.g., life expectancy, mortality rates, obesity, cognitive development, etc.) are distributed along a stepwise, social gradient; each socioeconomic class – defined by income, occupational grade, educational attainment, etc. – has worse health outcomes than the one above it (Kawachi et al. 2002; Macintyre 1997; Marmot et al. 1997). Health and disease are not simply divided between the haves and have-nots; there is a health/illness gradient from top to bottom of the social hierarchy within all societies. Such a stepwise gradient in health outcomes suggests a "dose-response" pathway between social determinants related to social hierarchy/inequality and health outcomes. Research also shows that the steeper the socioeconomic gradient (i.e., the more social inequality there is in a society), the lower the health of the entire population overall. Everyone in a given society is worse off in the domain of health and many other life domains than they could be otherwise – if there was less social inequality (Wilkinson and Pickett 2009; Deaton 2003).

Prior to the identification of the health gradient, social epidemiology was mainly focused on including social, economic, and cultural factors in the individual-level exposure category and seeing if there was a causal inference to be made with disease. The remarkable findings on the social distribution patterns of ill-health across groups now motivate research that seeks to explain both causation of disease in individuals and distribution across social groups. That is, unlike most epidemiological studies that try to identify risks or what causes a disease in one individual rather than other, post-gradient social epidemiology aims to identify what causes a disease in certain individuals and differing amounts of that disease in different social groups.

Researchers have so far identified a whole range of social determinants (discrete factors and pathways) to ill-health throughout the entire life cycle, starting from the social conditions surrounding the mother while the child is still in utero all the way to the quality of social relationships in old age. To be clear, health care is still recognized as being crucial to treating or mitigating ill-health, but social epidemiologists argue that the more influential *causal* determinants of health and disease include such things as early infant care and stimulation, safe and secure employment, housing conditions, discrimination, self-respect, personal relationships, community cohesion, and income inequality (Marmot and Wilkinson 1999; Berkman et al. 2014). And along with the rapid growth in knowledge about discrete social factors and pathways, a variety of explanatory theories have been proposed. While keeping in mind that most social epidemiological research so far has been done in high-income countries, Mackenbach presents a good review of the extant theories (Mackenbach 2012). The World Health Organization's Commission on the Social Determinants of Health presented an explanatory model for all societies and human beings (Commission on Social Determinants of Health 2008). More recently, a Lancet commission considered the transnational social factors that affect health and health inequalities (Ottersen et al. 2011).

Philosophy of Epidemiology

For most of the twentieth century, SDH were largely thought of in terms of material deprivations affecting the poor or as an additional factor to the proximate individual-level causal factors of biology, behavior, and exposures to harmful agents. However, in light of the many research findings and the identification of the social gradient in health in every society and across societies, SDH are now argued to be more dominant than proximate factors; SDH, in fact, shape the proximate causes. And where one stands on the social gradient determines the types and levels of harmful exposures and protective factors in pathways to ill-health and mortality. The significance of this is that social epidemiology has the potential to produce a more general explanatory paradigm for epidemiology than the currently prevailing explanatory paradigm that focuses only on individual-level factors.

In philosophical terms, both the epistemology of causation of ill-health and the ontology of causal factors have been affected. The methods used to acquire knowledge, the causal processes we acquire knowledge about, and the qualities of the things being observed are now more expansive than before. On the one hand, we now know that the number of links in the causal chain from exposures to the onset of ill-health is larger than previously thought. We are confident of this finding even though the specific causal links and processes are just beginning to be more specified. On the other hand, multilevel analysis has opened up new dimensions in the causal chain beyond individual-level exposures. Such multilevel analysis attempts to identify the independent and interactive effects on the causal chain by determinants operating at various social levels (Kawachi et al. 2002; Subramanian and Kawachi 2004). These supra-individual levels can be that of the family, work environment, neighborhood, state, region, country, and so forth.

Such analysis of the impact of phenomena at multiple levels on individual biological functioning has motivated the use of the metaphor of "Chinese boxes" (Susser and Susser 1996a, b). Though it has limitations, the metaphor helps to visualize an etiological model of ill-health where different levels of determinants are nested within each other with the individual's biological processes in the center. The metaphor is particularly helpful in illuminating the tension between discounting the effects of determinants at each level as it becomes more distal from the individual and at the same time recognizing that each distal level significantly defines and/or constrains the determinants operating at levels nested within. This opening-up of epidemiological analysis outward and upward to include supra-individual social phenomena or contexts that influence individual biological functioning has been labeled "macro-epidemiology"(Rockett 1999). However, to put things into perspective, exponentially more resources are being channeled into research identifying determinants going in the other direction, at the molecular level. In facing persistent limitations to effective or complete knowledge of the causation of chronic diseases, there is great optimism that genetic "risk factors" are the missing pieces of the "causal pie" or the hidden links in the "web of causation" of individual impairments and mortality. The continued focus on individual-level factors and the more concerted effort to dig deeper down into the biological makeup of the individual are referred to as "micro-epidemiology" (Rockett 1999).

What is currently at play in the field of epidemiology is whether micro-epidemiology, the dominant explanatory paradigm during the second half of the twentieth century, can continue to survive as a general theory of epidemiology in the twenty-first century. In order for micro-epidemiology to survive, it must at least be able to integrate macroanalysis. The productivity of SDH research over the last few decades compels both intellectually and ethically pursuing further SDH research and the construction of an explanatory paradigm with less blind spots or "slippage." As it now stands, the individual-level multifactorial framework, whether metaphorically described as the web of causation or a causal pie, does not recognize "nonnatural" determinants of disease and mortality. The model allocates relative responsibility for the causation of ill-health across three categories of determinants consisting of individual biological factors, individual behaviors, and proximate exposures to harmful substances. While the model does not limit the number of different links in the web of causation or pieces in the causal pie, the directions of interactions, or of timescales, all determinants must come from within the three categories. Such a causal model clearly excludes social phenomena that influence the three proximate categories of causal factors.

For example, individual biological endowments, the category that seems to be the most natural of the causal factors, in fact, can be significantly affected by social factors. Prior to an individual's birth, social phenomena can profoundly affect an individual's parents' sexual behavior, reproduction, and the quality of pregnancy, which then directly determine an individual's biological endowments and functioning (Posner 1992; Bauman 2003; Barker 2001). So, all three categories in the micro-epidemiology model can clearly be subject to social influence. Furthermore, by only recognizing individual-level factors, the model only recognizes individual variations and, therefore, cannot recognize or evaluate the distribution of health outcomes across social groups within a population or explain differences across populations.

The inability of micro-epidemiology's explanatory framework to recognize the influences of social phenomena on the three individual-level "natural" causal categories yields incomplete explanations. Alternatively, we can say that such explanations are useful only for specific kinds of causal determinants and pathways. Indeed, many effective health interventions have been based on such individual-level analyses. However, only when the causal links beyond individual-level factors – the causes of proximate causes – are allowed into the frame are we able to perceive other types of proximate natural and social causes as well as social distribution patterns (Rose 1985). If micro-epidemiology cannot integrate macroanalysis, a new general theory or explanatory paradigm for epidemiology must be found that can account for the independent and interactive effects of determinants that work at the molecular level all the way up to the global social environment (March and Susser 2006).

Health Inequality and Ethics

The link between SDH and social group inequalities in health raises ethical questions in the follow way. The interest in identifying inequalities in health across social groups for their own sake as well as to identify the social determinants of such inequalities both directly intersect concern for social ethics and justice. Any practical policy deliberations striving to identify the right social response to ill-health in individuals or groups unavoidably confront ethical questions. Health policies are profoundly political because they distribute significant and diverse benefits and burdens across individuals and groups. In contemporary health policy debates, ethical ideas are often used to justify how limited resources are distributed across individuals and groups or for constraining individual rights. But just beyond these familiar and immediate policy questions about distribution of resources or individual liberties, there exist more fundamental questions and "wicked" problems regarding how and why there should be social interventions to address ill-health in the first place. What is it about health or ill-health that compels a social response or makes it a concern for social justice? Is it the types of causes of ill-health, the absolute levels of health achievements, their relative inequalities, or the consequences of ill-health that must be addressed as a matter of social justice? There are good reasons to believe that all of these multiple dimensions of health should matter for realizing social equity and justice (Sen 2002). Even so, how do we then morally evaluate the different dimensions of the types of causes, levels of ill-health, and consequences of ill-health in relation to each other? Which dimension should social action address first, second, and so on? Furthermore, how does the understanding of what matters about these different dimensions change when the moral concern for individuals is supplemented by concern for groups?

SDH research complicates these numerous and difficult ethical questions even further by showing how improving absolute and/or relative health inequalities requires making changes to a range of basic social practices and institutions. In light of SDH research, the scope of social intervention to address health concerns has now become much larger than just providing health care or addressing individual-level material causal factors. In fact, SDH research explodes the scope of social intervention to encompass all social environments as it strives to identify and address any and all possible social determinants of impairments and mortality. While some social determinants are such things as the social bases of autonomy, freedom, dignity, or respect, interventions to transform such determinants could mean redistributing economic resources and opportunities, material goods, as well as choices and duties of individuals and institutions. What this means is that addressing inequalities in the realm of individual or group health achievements will have to manipulate or, indeed, create inequalities in other realms of individual lives and societal functioning.

In the language of distributive justice debates, mitigating or manipulating social determinants of ill-health and mortality means that there must be a redistribution of some valued goods or "things" in different social spheres. While SDH research has provided information on some social bases of causal pathways to impairments and mortality, the literature has given little attention to the possible consequences in other non-health social spheres that would follow from transforming such causal pathways. It is often implicit in the SDH literature that the logical social response to the identification of social determinants of ill-health is to transform them. Ideally, transforming or redistributing a particular social determinant will improve health achievements which, in turn, will create even more positive social determinants. For example, engendering the social bases of dignity through creating opportunities for income and wealth could improve health achievements. Individuals who take advantage of those opportunities could in turn create more opportunities for income and wealth and thus, also, more social bases of dignity for themselves and others. Where such a virtuous circle does not exist, however, what sort of criteria shall we use to evaluate if, when, and how trade-offs are made between improving absolute levels and relative inequalities in health functioning, and how things function or are distributed in other social realms?

In conjunction with evaluating such multiple dimensions such as causes, distribution, and consequences of ill-health, the identification of SDH means that reasoning about the right social response to health concerns must occur across multiple disciplines. Multidisciplinary reasoning is necessary in order to both identify the variety of social bases of the causal factors of ill-health and identify the potential non-health consequences in other social realms of possible interventions addressing SDH. It is important to identify how addressing various kinds of SDH will affect their respective social spheres because avoiding ill-health is only one among other goals valued by individuals and societies (Preda and Voigt 2015).

When standing within the health sector, it seems self-evident that the primary goals of health interventions are to transform the causes, levels, and consequences of ill-health. All things being equal, it may be a good thing to lessen health inequalities. Yet, as is now made more obvious by SDH research, health policies must also be cross-sector social policies. Thus, determining the right social response will require reasoning about how the moral concern for the multiple dimensions of health of individuals and groups relates to the right and just functioning of a variety of social spheres. Ideally, a general theory of social justice would provide a clear framework which would help guide social action by identifying why and how to address health concerns in relation to pursuing other social goals. However, there is no general theory of social justice that is commonly accepted within a society or across societies.

Social Justice Theory

Throughout the nineteenth and most of twentieth centuries, the dominant conception of social justice in liberal societies was framed by the philosophy of utilitarianism. Simplifying greatly, an action or society was considered to be just if it produced the greatest happiness or welfare for the greatest number of individuals. However, since the 1970s, due to the profound critiques of utilitarianism and a meaningful alternative proposed by the philosopher John Rawls, debates on alternative conceptions of social and, indeed, global justice are flourishing again (Kymlicka 2002). Utilitarian thought, however, continues to profoundly shape public policy making around the world and particularly public health policy.

All liberal theories of social justice begin from the premise of the individual as the primary unit of analysis or moral agent, and that every individual has equal moral worth. The equal moral worth of individuals is seen to arise from the capacity of human beings to reason and thereby conceive and purse a plan of life. Equal moral worth and the freedom to conceive and pursue one's life plans are seen as interrelated concepts. From this common starting point, different theories go on to articulate what that means for how society must treat the individual. This central question of how individuals should be treated by society has been transformed into the question of what should be distributed to individuals. The reason why treatment has turned into distribution is because social contract theories have had profound influence on liberal conceptions of social justice, of which John Rawls's theory is the most recent (Rawls and Kelly 2001; Rawls 1971). Such influence has meant that liberal social justice, or how society should justly treat its members, is predominantly understood as being a conception of how to distribute the benefits and burdens of social cooperation fairly across individuals (Brighouse and Robeyns 2010).

In reviewing the range of alternative theories, Amartya Sen has argued that the various modern conceptions of liberal social justice can be understood to differ most fundamentally according to the "thing" that is valued and how the theory distributes that thing across individuals (Sen 1992). Among the range of different theories of social justice, the things to be distributed include welfare (preferences, objective welfare), resources (income, primary goods, personal and impersonal resources, negative liberties), or capabilities (basic capabilities, ten central human capabilities). Underlying both the identification of the things and the distribution schemes is the profound concern for inequality. Each of the different theories provides reasoning as to how the equal moral worth of individuals allows or disallows inequalities in different aspects of lives of individuals thought to be relevant to social justice. Importantly, what has come to be accepted is that equal respect and concern for every individual does not necessarily mean the distribution of things equally to individuals (Daniels 1996; Sen 1992; Clayton and Williams 2002).

Despite the resurgence of philosophizing about social justice over the past five decades, only within the last two decades have the concerns for health, health inequalities, and SDH been given significant attention by social justice philosophers. One explanation may be that the philosophers like most others also thought ill-health was caused by the natural lottery of biology, personal behaviors, and proximate exposures. SDH shifts both the causal story and the moral responsibility of ill-health from the individual and nature squarely onto social institutions and choices. Various philosophers have sought to rise to the challenge of developing a theory of social justice or health justice that takes account of SDH (Sen 1999; Daniels 2008; Powers and Faden 2008; Venkatapuram 2011; Weinstock 2015). The comparative evaluation of these theories is just beginning.

Conclusion

This chapter has outlined two kinds of philosophical issues raised by SDH. One set relates to the philosophy of science and epidemiology, and the other relates to social justice theorizing. Given the emerging nature of the debates, the chapter aimed to present an introduction to the major philosophical issues rather than specific issues. It was argued that the starting points of the study of the social and the concern for inequality in the SDH research lead immediately to a rich and complex set of philosophical questions that are only just beginning to be given concerted attention. There is much to be done.

Definitions of Key Terms

Social determinants of health	The causes of the proximate causes of disease.
Health gradient/social gradient in health	Health outcomes follow the social gradient. The higher the social position of individuals and groups, the better the health outcomes.
Multilevel analysis of health determinants	Analysis of factors that operate at different social levels such as family, neighborhood, state, country, etc.
Distributive justice	An area of social justice philosophy that identifies and values things related to human well-being and rules for their distribution.

Summary Points

- Social determinants of health are causes of the causes on or within the body that causes disease.
- These factors challenge the existing scope, methodologies, and purpose of the science of epidemiology.
- These factors raise questions about inequality and social justice.
- Philosophical reasoning is needed both to improve the science of epidemiology and to identify the appropriate social responses.

Acknowledgements I would like to thank John Wiley and Sons for permission to draw on an article published in Bioethics journal titled Epidemiology and Social Justice in Light of Social Determinants of Health.

References

Barker DJP (2001) A new model for the origins of chronic disease. Med Health Care Philos Eur J 4:31–35

Bauman Z (2003) Liquid love: on the frailty of human bonds. Polity Press/Distributed in the USA by Blackwell Pub, Cambridge, UK/Malden

Berkman LF, Kawachi I, Glymour MM (2014) Social epidemiology. Oxford University Press, Oxford

Blaxter M (2010) Health. Polity, Cambridge

Braveman P, Egerter S, Williams DR (2011) The social determinants of health: coming of age. Annu Rev Public Health 32:381–398

Brighouse H, Robeyns I (eds) (2010) Measuring justice: primary goods and capabilities. Cambridge University Press, Cambridge

Clayton M, Williams A (2002) The ideal of equality. Palgrave, Basingstoke

Commission on Social Determinants of Health (2008) Closing the gap in a generation: health equity through action on the social determinants of health. Final report of the Commission on Social Determinants of Health. World Health Organization, Geneva

Cribb A (2005) Health and the good society: setting healthcare ethics in social context. Clarendon, Oxford

Daniels N (1996) Equality of what: welfare, resources, or capabilities? In: Justice and justification: reflective equilibrium in theory and practice. Cambridge University Press, Cambridge, UK/New York

Daniels N (2008) Just health: meeting health needs fairly. Cambridge University Press, Cambridge/New York

Deaton A (2003) Health, inequality, and economic development. J Econ Lit 41:113–158

Diener E, Suh EM, Lucas RE, Smith HL (1999) Subjective well-being: three decades of progress. Psychol Bull 125:276–302

Huppert FA, Baylis N, Keverne B (2005) The science of well-being. Oxford University Press, Oxford

Julia C, Valleron AJ (2011) Louis-Rene Villerme (1782–1863), a pioneer in social epidemiology: re-analysis of his data on comparative mortality in Paris in the early 19th century. J Epidemiol Community Health 65:666–670

Kawachi I, Subramanian SV, Almeida-Filho N (2002) A glossary for health inequalities. J Epidemiol Community Health 56:647–652

Krieger N (1994) Epidemiology and the web of causation: has anyone seen the spider? Soc Sci Med 39:887–903

Krieger N (2011) Epidemiology and the people's health: theory and context. Oxford University Press, New York

Kymlicka W (2002) Contemporary political philosophy: an introduction. Oxford University Press, Oxford/New York

Macintyre S (1997) The Black Report and beyond: what are the issues? Soc Sci Med 44:723–745

Mackenbach JP (2012) The persistence of health inequalities in modern welfare states: the explanation of a paradox. Soc Sci Med 75:761–769

March D, Susser E (2006) The eco- in eco-epidemiology. Int J Epidemiol 35:1379–1383

Marmot M (1976) Facts, opinions and affaires du coeur. Am J Epidemiol 103:519–526

Marmot MG, Wilkinson RG (1999) Social determinants of health. Oxford University Press, Oxford/New York

Marmot M, Ryff CD, Bumpass LL, Shipley M, Marks NF (1997) Social inequalities in health: next questions and converging evidence. Soc Sci Med 44:901–910

Nordenfelt L, Khushf G, Fulford KWM (2001) Health, science, and ordinary language. Rodopi, Amsterdam

Ottersen OP, Frenk J, Horton R (2011) The Lancet-University of Oslo Commission on global governance for health, in collaboration with the Harvard Global Health Institute. Lancet 378:1612–1613

Posner RA (1992) Sex and reason. Harvard University Press, Cambridge, MA/London

Powers M, Faden RR (2008) Social justice: the moral foundations of public health and health policy. Oxford University Press, New York/Oxford

Preda A, Voigt K (2015) The social determinants of health: why should we care? Am J Bioeth 15:25–36

Rawls J (1971) A theory of justice. Harvard University Press, Cambridge

Rawls J, Kelly E (2001) Justice as fairness: a restatement. Harvard University Press, Cambridge, MA

Rockett IRH (1999) Population and health: an introduction to epidemiology. Population Reference Bureau, Washington, DC

Rose G (1985) Sick individuals and sick populations. Int J Epidemiol 14:32–38

Rothman KJ, Adami HO, Trichopoulos D (1998) Should the mission of epidemiology include the eradication of poverty? Lancet 352:810–813

Rothman KJ, Greenland S, Lash TL (2008) Modern epidemiology. Wolters Kluwer Health/
    Lippincott Williams & Wilkins, Philadelphia
Ryan RM, Deci EL (2001) On happiness and human potentials: a review of research on hedonic and
    eudaimonic well-being. Annu Rev Psychol 52:141–166
Sen A (1992) Inequality reexamined. Harvard University Press, Cambridge
Sen A (1999) Development as freedom. Knopf, New York
Sen A (2002) Why health equity? Health Econ 11:659–666
Subramanian SV, Kawachi I (2004) Income inequality and health: what have we learned so far?
    Epidemiol Rev 26:78–91
Susser M (1999) Should the epidemiologist be a social scientist or a molecular biologist? Int J
    Epidemiol 28:S1019–S1022
Susser M, Susser E (1996a) Choosing a future for epidemiology: I. Eras and paradigms. Am J
    Public Health 86:668–673
Susser M, Susser E (1996b) Choosing a future for epidemiology: II. From black box to Chinese
    boxes and eco-epidemiology. Am J Public Health 86:674–677
Trostle JA (2004) Epidemiology and culture. Cambridge University Press, Cambridge,
    UK/New York
Venkatapuram S (2011) Health justice. An argument from the capabilities approach. Polity Press,
    Cambridge
Virchow RLK, Rather LJ (1985) Collected essays on public health and epidemiology. Science
    History Publications, Canton
Weinstock DM (2015) Health justice after the social determinants of health revolution. Social
    Theory Health 13:437–453
Wilkinson RG, Pickett K (2009) The spirit level: why more equal societies almost always do better.
    Allen Lane, London
Zielhuis G, Kiemeney L (2001) Social epidemiology? No way. Int J Epidemiol 30:43–44

Further Reading

A popular and accessible overview of the science of SDH is presented in Wilkinson R, Marmot MG
    (1998) Social determinants of health: the solid facts. Centre for Urban Health/World Health
    Organization/Regional Office for Europe, Copenhagen. For an economist's view on SDH across
    time and geography seen Deaton AA (2013) The great escape: health, wealth, and the origins of
    inequality, Princeton University. The journals of Public Health Ethics, Bioethics and Interna-
    tional Journal of Epidemiology are good sources for the most recent literature on the issues
    presented.

Health Promotion in Public Health: Philosophical Analysis

Peter Allmark

Contents

Abstract

Health promotion can reasonably be viewed as a major element in public health work. The latter was defined around a century ago as "the science and art of preventing disease, prolonging life and promoting health through the organized efforts of society." Health promotion involves (i) health education, such as advertising; (ii) illness prevention, such as screening; and (iii) legislation, such as banning smoking in public places. Although it has older roots, it is largely a phenomenon of the mid-twentieth century and beyond. Three factors stimulated

P. Allmark (✉)
Centre for Health and Social Care Research, Sheffield Hallam University, Sheffield, UK
e-mail: p.allmark@shu.ac.uk

© Springer Science+Business Media Dordrecht 2017
T. Schramme, S. Edwards (eds.), *Handbook of the Philosophy of Medicine*,
DOI 10.1007/978-94-017-8688-1_53

its development. The first was the development of epidemiology and in particular the work showing the link between smoking and illness followed by success in reducing smoking in the population. The second was the increased cost of health care in its standard form of illness treatment. And the third was a concern that despite improvements in health and, in the UK, the inception of a National Health Service, the inequality in health status between rich and poor remained and even grew. The philosophical questions concerning health promotion fall into three categories: the philosophy of science, ethics, and political philosophy.

Introduction

This chapter sets out the major areas of philosophical interest and controversy in the practice of health promotion and, by extension, of public health. It begins with the definition and delineation of the central concepts before setting out their historical roots. The rest of the chapter is concerned with the main task. The areas of philosophical interest it discusses concern the philosophy of science, ethics, and political philosophy.

Definition and Delineation

In the *Bangkok Charter for Health Promotion in a Globalized World*, the World Health Organization (WHO) defines health promotion as

> the process of enabling people to increase control over their health and its determinants, and thereby improve their health. It is a core function of public health and contributes to the work of tackling communicable and non-communicable diseases and other threats to health. (p. 1)

Note that this situates health promotion as a subset or "core function" of public health. In turn, public health work is defined in the Acheson Report as "the science and art of preventing disease, prolonging life, and promoting health through the organised efforts of society" (Winslow 1920). Commonly, public health work is divided into the three categories:

- Health improvement – for example, by improving housing stock or encouraging healthy lifestyles
- Improving services – for example, by reducing waiting lists
- Health protection – for example, by reducing environmental health hazards or planning for pandemics (Griffiths et al. 2005)

Acheson's definition needs an additional limitation, which is that the "organized efforts" must in some way be directed at preventing disease and so on. Without that limitation, almost any activity could constitute public health work; for example, a television station showing a good comedy might improve the nation's health, but this is not part of its intention and as such it is not public health work. The WHO definition of health promotion also looks broad, and it would arguably seem to cover all three categories of public health work. Indeed, a widely used three-way categorization of health promotion activity seems to cover similar areas to that given of public health work:

- Health education – such as putting health messages in public places
- Illness prevention – such as screening and vaccination
- Legislation – such as banning environmental tobacco smoke in public places (Doxiadis 1987)

The distinction between public health and health promotion is only of import where it is used, say, to mark out areas of responsibility for different groups of professionals. In itself, not too much rests on it philosophically. As such, philosophical problems relating to health promotion will most likely relate also to public health. From here on, therefore, this chapter will use both terms with little distinction between them.

Roots of Health Promotion

The idea that one can affect people's health by altering factors in their behavior or in the environment is ancient. Aristotle talks of the virtuous agent indulging in pleasures only to the extent that they are "conducive to health and vigour" (Aristotle 2000, 1119a). The Greeks also were aware of a distinction in the activity of health carers between prevention and cure (Kleisiaris et al. 2014). And both the Romans and Greeks were aware of the possibility of biological warfare through, say, poisoning a water supply (Roffey et al. 2002). In the Victorian era, Dr. Snow's using of epidemiological research to advocate closing of the Broad Street pump in London's Soho area to combat an outbreak of cholera is an early and often cited example of the involvement of health professionals in health promotion (Smith and Ebrahim 2001). However, the idea of the systematic involvement of health professionals is probably best seen as a postwar phenomenon.

A central driver in this development was Doll and Bradford Hill's research showing the strong link between smoking and lung cancer (in 1950) and subsequently between smoking and heart disease (in 1954). The results were "compelling and unexpected" (Richmond 2005); a widespread social activity that was not obviously noxious (in the way that excessive drinking or drug-taking is) was shown nonetheless to be seriously harmful to the population's health. It took some time for the research to affect public behavior, but as it did so health improved; thus was manifest the possibility of preventing illness through population behavior change. And the search for other health-affecting behavior that could be altered began in earnest.

Alongside this, at least two other drivers can be detected. The first relates to the cost of health care. Maynard coins the term the "Nye Bevan fallacy" to indicate the idea that as a nation spends more on health care, so the health of its population improves, and over time the demand for and cost of health care fall (Maynard and Sheldon 2001).

It is Bevan's fallacy as it was one of the beliefs that lay behind the setting up of the UK National Health Service in 1947 (when Aneurin Bevan was the Health Secretary). Green and Kreuter suggest health promotion came to the fore in the 1960s in what they term the era of cost containment (Green and Kreuter 1991). Governments recognized that health care was increasingly expensive. The problem seemed to be that control of contagious diseases led to the emergence of other diseases (the so-called diseases of affluence) such as cancer and heart disease. Often these could be traced to people's behavior. Thus, in 1976 a UK Government paper, produced under the direction of the then Health Secretary David Owen, says,

> Much ill-health in Britain today arises from over-indulgence and unwise behaviour. Not surprisingly, the greatest potential and perhaps the greatest problem for preventive medicine now lies in changing behaviour and attitudes to health. The individual can do much to help himself, his family and the community by accepting more direct responsibility for his own health and wellbeing. (Department of Health and Social Security 1977, p.39)

This theme of personal responsibility is repeated in Government documents and beyond throughout the 1980s.

At the same time, a second and quite distinct driver of health promotion emerged; this was associated more with the political left where the personal responsibility driver was associated with the political right. This driver is related to health inequality. The Black Report into health inequality was commissioned under a Labour Government and was famously ignored when it was published under a new Conservative Government in 1978 (Black et al. 1982). It was followed by other reports showing the same phenomenon, most recently, the Marmot Review (Marmot 2010). This phenomenon is that in relatively prosperous Western countries, the so-called diseases of affluence fall disproportionately on the poorest. In fact, the phenomenon can be generalized further: in any society with wealth inequalities, there will be health inequalities; whatever harms people in such a society will harm the poor most. For those concerned to reduce health inequality, health promotion was seen as a potential tool. Thus, both political right and left saw value in health promotion: the right emphasizing personal responsibility and the left social determinants of health such as poor housing and education.

The critics of health promotion were primarily from the political libertarian right. This critique is considered below in the sections on the philosophical issues associated with health promotion. These issues are discussed under three broad headings: philosophy of science, ethics, and political philosophy. Each section is discrete such that readers can skip, say, the philosophy of science if their interest is in ethics or political philosophy.

Philosophy of Science

One of the central questions in philosophy of science is whether and if so how scientific method delivers knowledge. Health promotion is grounded in epidemiology, the science concerned with patterns of health and illness in the population.

For example, epidemiology showed that lung cancer was linked to smoking. The job then for practitioners of health promotion is to find interventions that successfully reduce smoking in the population, such as health education and bans on smoking in public places. As with other health interventions, these should be judged for effectiveness using the principles of evidence-based medicine, for example, and, in particular, by a randomized controlled trial (RCT). If shown to be successful, the intervention should then be further judged for cost-effectiveness before being implemented. Thus, while health promotion begins with epidemiology, it also uses social sciences such as those relating to education and psychology. This picture could be said to mirror other areas of health care. For example, the treatment of cancer is grounded in the biology of cancer and oncology but also in the sciences of pharmacology, surgery, and radiation, which tell us how it might be treated, and of statistics, which tells us how these treatments might be tested. And both are then subject to evaluation by the science of health economics.

Despite this similarity in the structure of science and practice between cancer treatment and health promotion, it is notable that there is a difference in what might be termed the hardness of the sciences involved. In the case of cancer treatment, almost all the science involved is hard, natural science. There is room for social science, particularly in relation to health economics and also to the question of compliance with treatment, but at the core is natural science.

With health promotion, almost the opposite applies. In epidemiology, the data are often woolly and unreliable, for example, people are inclined to lie or deceive themselves about their intake of tobacco, alcohol, and food (Smith and Ebrahim 2001). Furthermore, the data for epidemiology are situated in society, which is an open system. An open system is one in which there are interactions between the internal elements and the outside environment. For example, if you seek to isolate smoking as a cause of lung cancer, you are faced with numerous problems of confounders; compared to nonsmokers, smokers might live in more polluted areas, have different diets, drink more coffee, and so on. Any one of these, or a combination, might be the true cause of lung cancer rather than smoking. Davey-Smith and Ebrahim (2001, p. 5) suggest that statistical adjustment in population studies for a few potential confounders "fails to recognise the complexity of the reasons why people differ with regard to particular and general characteristics of their lives." A recent example is hormone replacement therapy (HRT) which was repeatedly shown to be cardioprotective in epidemiological studies but which randomized controlled trials (RCTs) have shown to be the reverse (hence, Davey-Smith and Ebrahim ask "Is this the death of observational epidemiology?"). By contrast, research in oncology is largely done in a relatively closed environment, such as in cellular research or animal models.

One response to the HRT example is to suggest that health promotion needs to be more like the rest of evidence-based medicine, adopting the RCT as the gold standard for evaluating interventions. This is problematic. Open systems tend to be resistant to control. Indeed, one criticism of RCTs in standard medical treatment is that they show only that a treatment works (or not) in carefully controlled situations, not in the open environment in which they will actually be given.

An alternative to RCTs is to embrace methods that are designed for open systems, such as logic models (Allmark et al. 2013; Davies et al. 2006; Murphy et al. 1998). The work of philosophical realists, such as Pawson, has been influential in the development of methodology for open systems (Pawson and Tilley 1997; Pawson 2013). To the extent that health promotion takes on this approach, it is set apart from the more empiricist RCT-focused methods in other parts of health care. However, there is a case for introducing realist methods more widely: RCTs produce results that are often not replicated in practice perhaps because the control involved in them renders them inapplicable to the real world (Craig et al. 2012).

Ethics

The most widely discussed ethical issue in health promotion concerns the balance of liberty against intervention; this is covered in the next section under the heading of "Political Philosophy." This section discusses two related issues that appear in the literature and which are more tightly focused on specific health promotion strategies. The first concerns hidden harms in treatment and, the second, the problem of treating populations rather than individuals.

Hidden Harms

Skrabanek, a central libertarian critic of health promotion, asks "Why is preventive medicine exempted from ethical constraints?" (Skrabanek 1990). His question is prompted in part by the perception that health promotion interventions are judged only to be of potential benefit and hence are not tested rigorously for harm. Unfortunately, health promotion can harm. Allmark et al. looked at how public health education initiatives relating to smoking had been evaluated between 1992 and 2004 (Allmark et al. 2010). They found that the evaluation was done purely on behavior, namely, whether people stopped smoking or did not take it up; if so, the initiative was judged successful. However, in their own separate research, they examined people who had shown signs of lung cancer but had been late to present to health-care professionals. At that time, the UK had a poor record of late presentation with lung cancer. In qualitative interviews, patients reported a number of ways in which information they had gathered from health education had influenced their late presentation. For example, ex-smokers reported being told and believing that their risk of lung cancer would revert to that of a nonsmoker if they gave up; nonsmokers believed they could not get lung cancer; and smokers believed they could get lung cancer but that nothing could be done if they did. All these beliefs are false, had developed in the light of health education, and had influenced late presentation. Clearly the harm done to these few individuals might be outweighed by massive health benefits to those persuaded to behave differently, but for any other treatment such harm would be looked for in evaluation – hence Skrabanek's question. Allmark et al.'s (2010) finding is supported in a review of unintended harm associated with public health interventions (Allen-Scott et al. 2014).

Treating Populations

The previous example might be characterized as a concern about utilitarian reasoning; that harm to a few is justified by good to many. The concern carries over into the notion of treating whole populations rather than individuals. A particular example is Rose's population strategy (Rose 2001). Rose points out that "a large number of people at a small risk may give rise to more cases of disease than the small number who are at high risk" (p. 431). Thus, the most effective health promotion intervention will target the whole population and try to get everyone to, say, reduce their fat intake, even those whose intake does not put them at high risk of coronary heart disease. In this way, the whole Poisson (bell curve) distribution curve will shift to the left; those at high risk will be at lower risk; those at low risk will be at virtually no risk. There are at least two criticisms of this. The first is that risk may sometimes rise at the low end. For example, those who reduce their alcohol, fat, and BMI levels beyond a certain point may increase their risk of illness (Adams and White 2005). The second is that it is wrong to ask people to change their behavior when it is not high-risk behavior: if a man drinks 21 units of alcohol per week, which is not associated with risk to health, one should not ask him to reduce it for the sake of a population goal. Similar questions of balancing individual good against that of the population arise in other areas of health promotion such as vaccination, fluoridation of the water supply, and screening (Nuffield Council on Bioethics 2007).

Political Philosophy

Libertarianism

The central philosophical debates in health promotion and public health have been in the area of political philosophy and, in particular, the legitimate role of the state or government. Broadly the division is between those who view the role to be to protect citizens' liberty, largely through protecting the operation of the free market, and those who view the role as greater than this, perhaps to create the conditions in which citizens can flourish. This division is in turn based upon a difference in view between those who believe that individual flourishing is best assured through individual liberty and those who believe more is required, such as the provision of a minimum level of external goods. In 2004, the UK Department of Health characterized the discussion in the following way:

> While there were many notable successful public efforts ... too often work to tackle longstanding, intractable or emerging problems was increasingly caught up in a sterile

national debate . . . that created a false dichotomy between those proposing a heavy handed nanny state on one hand, and those supporting inactivity bordering on neglect in the name of individual freedom on the other. (Department of Health 2004) (Paragraph 6 of Executive Summary)

Arguably, however, there were few on the "nanny state" side while the "bordering on neglect" side set the agenda; discussions tended to be either statements of or responses to libertarian criticism of health promotion. Critics of health promotion largely emanate from the political right, especially the libertarian element. The right-wing think-tank the Social Affairs Unit and the pro-smoking lobby group FOREST were both involved in documents and campaigns against health promotion. Well-known right-wing authors are James Le Fanu and Petr Skrabanek (Skrabanek 1990, 1992; Le Fanu 2011). A small left-wing group in the UK also criticized health promotion. Their origins were in the Revolutionary Communist Party but are now linked to the Institute of Ideas, in London, and the Spiked website. Its key representative in this area is Michael Fitzpatrick, a London GP and author (Fitzpatrick 2001). It too has a libertarian agenda. However, Fitzpatrick also argues that health promotion is being used as a Trojan horse for equality and socialism but that it is ineffective in that role.

The starting point for the libertarian critique of health promotion is Mill's Liberty (or Harm) Principle:

the sole end for which mankind are warranted, individually or collectively, in interfering with the liberty of action of any of their number, is self-protection. That the only purpose for which power can be rightfully exercised over any member of a civilized community, against his will, is to prevent harm to others. His own good, either physical or moral, is not sufficient warrant. He cannot rightfully be compelled to do or forbear because it will be better for him to do so, because it will make him happier, because, in the opinion of others, to do so would be wise, or even right. . . The only part of the conduct of anyone, for which he is amenable to society, is that which concerns others. In the part which merely concerns himself, his independence is, of right, absolute. Over himself, over his own body and mind, the individual is sovereign. (Mill 1972, p.78)

This powerful and compelling principle seems to have important implications for health promotion. The most obvious are in relation to legislation, the third category of health promotion in Doxiadis's list (see above). Some health promotion legislation prevents individuals from harming others, that relating to infection, pollution, and work safety, for example. But much seems to be there to prevent individuals harming themselves; examples include legislation against taking recreational drugs and enforcing the wearing of seat belts and crash helmets. Some legislation rests between these; the ban on environmental tobacco smoke was defended for its effect both on the health of passive smokers and also on smokers themselves.

One response to this has been to say that many self-harming activities do in fact harm others. Motorcyclists without crash helmets endanger their own lives but also endanger those who witness or attend the accidents, their families who endure the outcome, and the carers who look after the survivors. The small infringement of liberty is justified to avoid this overwhelming harm, particularly if one factors in also the cost of treating survivors. Feinberg in a work that follows Mill's Principle through to a number of conclusions about the role of the State considers the crash helmet issue in detail (Feinberg 1986). The problem lies in part with the loose nature of the terms employed in the discussion, particularly harm. Feinberg warns against taking an overgenerous definition of harm such that bans become justified if, for example, they harm people by offending or upsetting them. As a consistent libertarian, he finds it hard to conclude in favour of the ban although he expresses unease (see also Dworkin 1988).

However, consistent libertarianism is a minority view, particularly outside the USA, and is based in part at least on a misreading of Mill (Crisp 1997; Nuffield Council on Bioethics 2007). Arguably it has had undue influence on health promotion discussion, perhaps in part due to the influence of the tobacco industry. A consistent libertarian will find all state-funded health promotion objectionable as it involves coercing people to spend money (via taxes) on a product they do not choose. But such a libertarian will also find government health spending in general objectionable for the same reasons. For a libertarian, individuals should be free to harm themselves but also must make their own decisions about preparing for the consequences; if they do not insure themselves for health care, they will not get it when they become ill. Anyone who believes the government should provide some level of health care is not a full-blown libertarian. And once health-care provision is accepted, there seems no reason to believe the government might justifiably also have a role in protecting the health of the population.

Autonomy and Positive and Negative Liberty

For non-libertarians, then, the question is not whether some kind of state interference in the population health is justified but rather how much and of what type. Broadly, the scope of opinion ranges from the Liberal (Seedhouse 1997) to the communitarian and Aristotelian (Allmark 2005; Buchanan 2006; Eriksson and Lindström 2008). Liberals are committed to something like Mill's view of the good life for human beings being constituted in "experiments in living" through which an individual finds happiness. The State should ensure that such experiments are possible but should interfere little in them. By contrast, communitarians have what is sometimes termed a "thick" view of the good. This is that the good life for all human beings has a large amount that is shared both as and between individuals. In other words, most people need similar things to live well and all need to do so as part of a well-functioning community. In order to achieve this, State interference to some degree is justified. Applied to health promotion, this means that Liberals would tend to disallow State control or limitation of self-harming activities and communitarians and Aristotelians to allow it to some degree. The stewardship model of the state adopted by the Nuffield Council on Bioethics discussed below probably errs on the side of the communitarian.

One way of addressing the issue of limiting or trying to alter people's unhealthy choices has been to raise doubts about the idea of liberty and, in particular, the notion of autonomy, or self-rule (Allmark 2008; Cheung and Yam 2005; Dworkin 1988;

Lindley 1986; May 1994; Mcknight 1993; O'Neill 2001). Some people's self-harming decisions can be badly informed; Mill finds it acceptable to, for example, prevent someone from taking a route that he does not know is dangerous because a bridge might collapse. Once that person is informed, however, should the decision be left to him? This might depend on his state of mind; if suffering a psychosis he believes he can fly over the gap, again it would be reasonable to prevent him. What if he wants to die? What if he wants to impress his friends with his bravery (or foolhardiness) in stepping right up to the edge? Some authors say that the respect due to people's free choices should be proportional to the extent to which those choices are truly their own; they should be unencumbered by excessive emotion (as when a heartbroken teenager wants to harm himself) and by undue influences from others (as when someone refuses a medical treatment to comply with his parents' but not his own religious beliefs). On such an account, banning recreational drugs or enforcing crash helmets is justified on the basis that these are the right choices for individuals which they would make if they were fully rational, or fully themselves, unencumbered by emotions and other influences.

Isaiah Berlin calls this an "inner citadel" view of people, the idea that inside the person who is actually thinking and choosing is their true self, what they would be if fully unencumbered (Berlin 1969). He uses this notion in a contrast between what he terms positive and negative liberty. Negative liberty is what people are or should be allowed to do without interference. Positive liberty is more like self-determination, free of controlling influences that manipulate, pressure, or misinform you to have the desires you do (Christman 1991). Berlin accepts that positive liberty is part of being free; it is no good being able to make a wide range of choices if the choice you actually make is the product of others' manipulation of you. However, he sees danger in the idea. Berlin has in mind examples from politics such as Marx's concept of false consciousness; this is roughly the idea that the nonrevolutionary beliefs most working class people actually have do not reflect the beliefs they would have once enlightened by Marxism. The political outcome of this is that governments may oppress people's real choices on behalf of their hypothetical ideal ones.

The implication for health promotion philosophy is that caution should be exercised in any use of the idea of a divided self as the justification for the inhibition of negative liberty, such as bans of self-harming activities or the use of techniques to "bring out" positive liberty. It seems unlikely there is an easy solution here. Berlin is not opposed to positive liberty, but he is aware of its dangers. Helping people to overcome alcohol or drug addiction looks like health promotion that promotes positive liberty without compromising negative liberty. By contrast, some notions of so-called empowerment, such as that whereby people are judged to be empowered only once they make the right choices, are more questionable (Allmark and Tod 2006).

Nudge

The recent turn to the use of behavioral intervention techniques (or "nudge") presents related issues (Department of Health 2010). Psychological study shows that people's choice-making is often nonrational, that in decision making, people often use heuristics that bypass reasoning. For example, people opt for the status quo, or follow the herd, or overly discount the future in favour of the present (Thaler and Sunstein 2009). How we choose, therefore, is often more a product of our environment than our reasoning. Advertisers and sellers make use of this notion of choice architecture in manipulating consumers; a supermarket plays fairly fast music to encourage rapid buying, and has a bakery to put out the scents that make people hungry, for example. This being so, the proponents of nudge suggest that the same techniques could be used for more beneficial ends, such as encouraging people to save more for their pensions, to pay their tax on time, and to eat more fruits and vegetables. This is something that has been taken up in a number of Western countries, with some success (see examples on the website of the Behavioural Insights Team). The concern of course is whether using unethical methods for a good end is nonetheless unethical. For instance, if we view health promotion interventions as akin to health treatments, then it looks as though these are being undertaken without informed consent, something usually considered objectionable except in emergencies. The Lords Committee set up to look at nudges suggested two questions by which to judge the acceptability of a nudge style intervention (Science and Technology Select Committee 2011):

(i) Is it visible in principle? Earlier it was noted that supermarkets sometimes introduce smells, such as coffee or baking, to increase customers' spending. Although usually unnoticed, it is not hidden. In the same way, environmental changes designed to encourage people to, say, take the stairs or buy more vegetables are not hidden. If an intervention is visible in principle, it is less worrying than one that is not, such as subliminal advertising (if such a thing exists).

(ii) Is it proportionate? This question is one asked of all health-care interventions and is usually answered in terms of risk of harm versus chance of benefit set against cost. However, there is an additional issue here which is whether the bypassing or manipulation of people's choice is proportionate to the gain made. The Nuffield ladder (discussed below) offers a tool that can be used in making this judgment.

To these two questions, Allmark and Tod (2014, p. 114) add:

(iii) "Is the end unequivocal or disputed? The ends sought through some nudges are unequivocal; no reasonable person would prefer environments in which, say, they were more likely to insert their credit card in the wrong way, or forget to turn off the gas when leaving home. Where this is so, it counts in favour of the nudge. Other ends are disputed. Some who smoke, drink or overeat might object to being manipulated towards not doing so. Other ends may be highly disputed; it seems unlikely that all young people would value the avoidance of drug taking, binge drinking and unsafe sex. The more disputed the ends, the less justified the nudge."

(iv) "Is choice-architectural design required? Doors must have handles; pension schemes must have default contribution levels; supermarkets have to put their shelves in some order; organ donation schemes have to be opt-out or opt-in. In contrast, there is no requirement to have posters informing youngsters that drug-taking is a minority pursuit, or that binge drinking exposes you to danger and ridicule. Where choice-architectural design is required it seems reasonable that the design would favour choices all or most people would prefer to make. Where there is no immediate need to change choice architecture this would seem to require a slightly higher level of justification. For example, building new housing that is naturally warm seems perfectly acceptable whilst insulating the house of someone who stoically prefers to be cold does not."

These questions are useful once it is accepted that the State has a justifiable role in public health; however, the problem of consent remains – nudges, and other health promotion interventions, look like health measures that are undertaken without the informed consent of those who receive them and, as such, seem to be unethical.

Stewardship

This issue is addressed by the Nuffield Council on Bioethics in its report "Public health: ethical issues" (Nuffield Council on Bioethics 2007). The principle it suggests is that consent is only required for interventions where health or other risks are involved. Advertisers do not seek consent before putting up posters; supermarkets do not seek consent before baking bread or playing background music. Similarly, if the State is justified in intervening to affect public health, then explicit consent is required only when the interventions are intrusive or risky. O'Neill says that

> An adequate ethics of public health needs to set aside debates about informed consent and to consider the permissible limits of just compulsion for various types of public good. (O'Neill 2004, p. 1133)

As to what these permissible limits are, the Nuffield report advocates a stewardship model of the state in which it has a responsibility to look after the important needs of its citizens. One of those needs is health. The report also discusses the types of public health intervention a steward state might undertake from, at one end, low-level provision of information to, at the other, complete enforcement of behavior by law. It develops a tool called the Nuffield Intervention Ladder (Nuffield Council on Bioethics 2007; see Fig. 1).

This is a simple and useful device although it is noteworthy that some types of nudge policy, akin to the smells in supermarkets, do not fall into any of the categories. The device also says nothing about how to decide when a State is justified in stepping up the ladder from no intervention to quite restrictive intervention. However, the Nuffield report provides principles and examples that the policy maker might find useful.

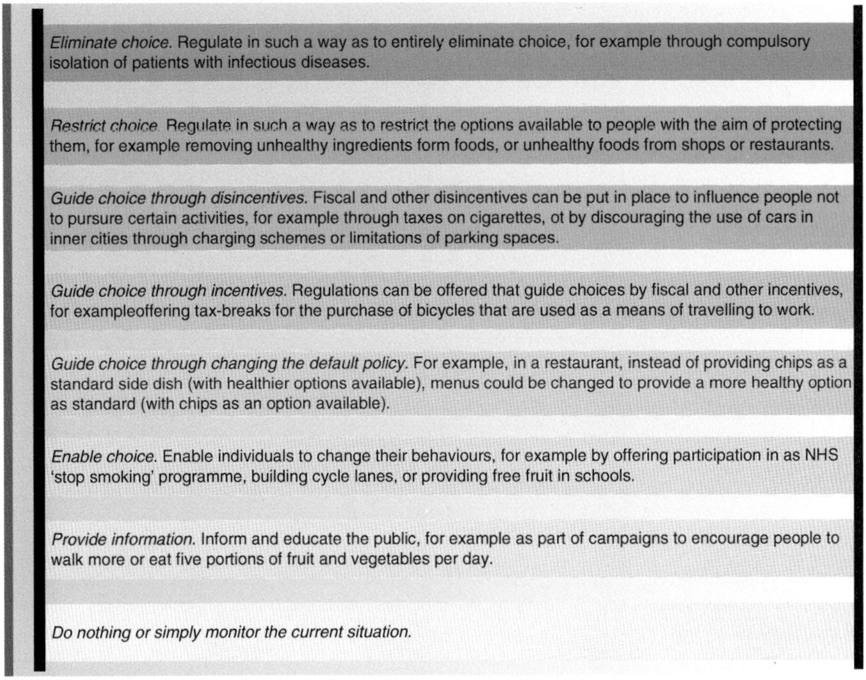

Eliminate choice. Regulate in such a way as to entirely eliminate choice, for example through compulsory isolation of patients with infectious diseases.

Restrict choice. Regulate in such a way as to restrict the options available to people with the aim of protecting them, for example removing unhealthy ingredients form foods, or unhealthy foods from shops or restaurants.

Guide choice through disincentives. Fiscal and other disincentives can be put in place to influence people not to pursure certain activities, for example through taxes on cigarettes, ot by discouraging the use of cars in inner cities through charging schemes or limitations of parking spaces.

Guide choice through incentives. Regulations can be offered that guide choices by fiscal and other incentives, for exampleoffering tax-breaks for the purchase of bicycles that are used as a means of travelling to work.

Guide choice through changing the default policy. For example, in a restaurant, instead of providing chips as a standard side dish (with healthier options available), menus could be changed to provide a more healthy option as standard (with chips as an option available).

Enable choice. Enable individuals to change their behaviours, for example by offering participation in as NHS 'stop smoking' programme, building cycle lanes, or providing free fruit in schools.

Provide information. Inform and educate the public, for example as part of campaigns to encourage people to walk more or eat five portions of fruit and vegetables per day.

Do nothing or simply monitor the current situation.

Fig. 1 The Nuffield Intervention Ladder. Source: Nuffield Council on Bioethics (2007) [with permission]

Inequality

In a section above, it was noted that the observation of health inequality was a root of the development of health promotion as an area of health practice. The hope was that, for example, education in healthy lifestyle would reduce the impact of lifestyle illnesses on those groups who suffered most, particularly the poor. Unfortunately this has not happened, and, as the Marmot Review shows, health inequality in the UK is increasing (as it is in other Western nations) (Marmot 2010). Two philosophical questions arise:

1. Why should we be concerned with health inequality at all? The thought here is that provided health is improving to all sections of the population, it is not of concern that it improves for some faster than others (Le Fanu 2011). There are at least two lines of response to this. The first is empirical: it might be suggested that health inequality has negative effects on wider social well-being. This thesis is suggested and backed up by a large range of statistics in relation to various types of inequality by Wilkinson and Pickett (2008). There may also be a concern about connectedness; infectious illness, in particular, if allowed to take hold in some sections of society, will eventually pass on. The second line

Table 1 Alternative ten tips for better health

Ten tips for better health	Alternative ten tips for better health
Don't smoke. If you can, stop. If you can't, cut down	Don't be poor. If you can, stop. If you can't, try not to be poor for long
Follow a balanced diet with plenty of fruits and vegetables	Don't have poor parents
Keep physically active	Own a car
Manage stress by, for example, talking things through and making time to relax	Don't work in a stressful, low-paid manual job
If you drink alcohol, do so in moderation	Don't live in damp, low-quality housing
Cover up in the sun, and protect children from sunburn	Be able to afford to go on a foreign holiday and sunbathe
Practice safer sex	Practice not losing your job and don't become unemployed
Take up cancer screening opportunities	Take up all benefits you are entitled to if you are unemployed, retired, or sick or disabled
Be safe on the roads: follow the highway code	Don't live next to a busy major road or near a polluting factory
Learn the first aid ABC – airways, breathing, circulation	Learn how to fill in the complex housing benefit/ asylum application forms before you become homeless and destitute

Raphael (2000, p. 362) [with permission]

of response is philosophical and is essentially that it is unjust for health to be unevenly distributed in this way; health and health care is an important human good and its distribution is at least to some extent within human control; it is therefore a matter of justice how it is distributed. Such an argument might draw on the capability approach to justice of Sen (2010) and Nussbaum (2011); see, for example, Venkatapuram (2011).

2. Is health promotion the right way to tackle health inequality? One problem with health promotion interventions is that they may even increase health inequality. Typically, well-off and educated people gain most from, for example, health education initiatives. One response to this is to invoke the social model of health. This locates the primary determinants of health in social and environmental factors rather than individual behavior. It was amusingly illustrated in a table that compares the behavior-focused recommendations from a UK Government report with some suggested alternatives based on social determinants of health (Raphael 2000) (Table 1).

The practical problem is that it is easier to address individuals' behavior rather than social issues such as those in the right-hand column. Thus, despite homage paid to the social model of health and to health inequality, much health promotion still ends up being about trying to get poor people to behave differently rather than to stop being poor. If health promotion is to succeed in tackling social determinants of health, it needs a stronger remit. This leads us to the issue of the scope of health promotion.

Scope

Consider first the well-known WHO definition of health taken from its 1946 constitution:

> Health is a state of complete physical, social and mental well-being, and not merely the absence of disease or infirmity. WHO

Then, add to this the social model of health illustrated in Dahlgren and Whitehead's famous image – see Fig. 2 (Dahlgren and Whitehead 1993).

In the light of these, it seems difficult to imagine life-enhancing measures that a State or others might undertake which could not also be described as health promotion. The provision of schools, the improvement of transport and the housing stock, and improvements in wages, couldn't these all be described as health promotion measures? Some health bodies have funded the provision of information about welfare rights and benefits as a health promotion measure, for example (Allmark et al. 2013). The UK has recently (2014) seen much of the budget for public health moved from the health service to the local government; would local government be justified in spending this money on, say, improving the condition of weather-damaged roads? In this way, health promotion may become wide and nebulous to the point of meaningless.

By contrast, Seedhouse perceives the danger that the remit of health promotion could become wide and oppressive; it could become what he terms well-being promotion (Seedhouse 1997). The broad range of factors that might improve our

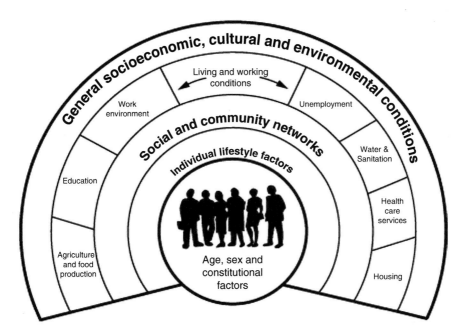

Fig. 2 The Social Model of Health. Source: Dahlgren and Whitehead (1993) [with permission]

health ranges from social equality to healthy walks in the country; is all this to be deemed suitable grounds for health promotion intervention? Seedhouse's concern is that of a Liberal faced with a communitarian or Aristotelian agenda discussed earlier. Communitarians are likely to be untroubled by the State's involvement in promoting the well-being of its population; Liberals are likely to view it as either wrong in principle or likely to fail in practice. As this chapter has attempted to demonstrate, the issue of the role of the State is at the core of much of the controversy in health promotion.

Definition of Key Terms

The definitions offered here are brief and cover only their use in relation to this chapter. Clearly, for example, there is much more that could be said in defining Aristotelian philosophy.

Aristotelian – Aristotle's ethical and political philosophy has two points of importance for this chapter. First, he views the human good (also called inter alia happiness, flourishing, eudaimonia) as having many shared elements across all people; for example, a life of intemperance or of inactivity is not good for anyone even if that is what they desire. This is sometimes called a thick view of the good and is contrasted with liberal and libertarian "thin" views of the good, which emphasize the differences between people in what constitutes a flourishing life and the role of choice in allowing people freedom to discover what works best for them. Second, he views the state's purpose as to enable human flourishing. This is liable to give it a far more interventionist role than is acceptable from a liberal or libertarian viewpoint.

Communitarian – This emphasizes the role of the community in human flourishing. It grew up in opposition to liberal (and now libertarian) viewpoints; where these see human flourishing as consisting in the autonomous actions of individuals, communitarians see it as existing where individuals are part of a flourishing community. It resembles Aristotelianism in this because Aristotle too sees people as essentially social and therefore flourishing also as having a major social element. However, some Aristotelians have distanced themselves from elements of the philosophy.

Liberal – This has been called "the most confusing term in the world" (Chang 2014, p. 68); but, for the purpose of this chapter, liberal views can be seen as moderate libertarianism. Liberals have a thin view of the good, emphasizing people's own experiments in living as the basis for their flourishing. The State has some role in this, for example, in the education of children; what should be the extent of this role is a matter of debate within liberalism.

Libertarian – Libertarian views in the context of this chapter are the antithesis of Aristotelian ones. Libertarians see the human good as comprised primarily in the freedom of people to act as they wish without interference. The State has at most a minimal role, to protect this freedom. It has no role, for example, in enforcing or encouraging certain behavior for people's own good or in protecting them from their, perhaps foolish, decisions.

Health promotion and public health – See definitions in the chapter, under the heading "Definition and Delineation."

Summary Points

The philosophical questions concerning health promotion fall into three categories: the philosophy of science, ethics, and political philosophy.

(A) *Philosophy of Science*

The complexity of roots of causation in public health makes it resistant to scientific inquiry of an empiricist or positivist nature and more amenable to something like a realist approach, using, for example, logic modeling.

(B) *Ethics*

Hidden harms: There are concerns about the quality of evidence behind health promotion, and in particular that potential harmful effects are ignored in its evaluation.

Treating populations: Health promotion is often focused on the health of the population rather than of individuals; this can give rise to ethical concerns when treatment is based more on the health of the population than of an individual person such as in vaccination and mass medication.

(C) *Political Philosophy*

Libertarianism: Much health promotion appears to violate Mill's Harm (or Liberty) Principle that "the only purpose for which power can be rightfully exercised over any member of a civilized community, against his will, is to prevent harm to others. His own good . . . is not sufficient warrant" (*On Liberty* 1.9).

Autonomy and positive and negative liberty: It might be said that a decision is autonomous only to the extent that it is consistent with the individual's personality or is rational to some degree. The danger of this argument is that it can be used to justify preventing people from doing what they want on the basis that if only they were, say, fully rational, they would not want to do so.

Nudge: Advertisers have long exploited nonrational and environmental factors to bypass our reason and get us to buy. The idea of nudge is to use the same techniques for social good, such as promoting healthy behavior. There are concerns as to whether this is acceptable given that it bypasses consent and involves manipulating people.

Stewardship: In response to libertarianism, it has been suggested that the State should have a stewardship role in which it takes some responsibility for the important needs of its citizens, including health and health care. In order to help judge what level of health promotion intervention the state should take in response to a health issue, the Council offers a tool, the Nuffield Intervention Ladder.

Inequality: Health inequality is one driver of health promotion policy. Two philosophical questions arise. (1) Why is health inequality a health problem? (2) Is health promotion the right tool to tackle health inequality?

Scope: There are two concerns about the scope of health promotion. (1) The first is that almost all social action that is aimed at improving some element in society could be deemed health promotion, for example, improving the roads. (2) Might not health promotion become well-being promotion? To some extent, those concerned about the second question are more likely to be of liberal or libertarian ilk.

References

Adams J, White M (2005) When the population approach to prevention puts the health of individuals at risk. Int J Epidemiol 34(1):40–43

Allen-Scott L, Hatfield J, McIntyre L (2014) A scoping review of unintended harm associated with public health interventions: towards a typology and an understanding of underlying factors. Int J Public Health 59(1):3–14

Allmark P (2005) Health, happiness and health promotion. J Appl Philos 22(1):1–15

Allmark P (2008) An Aristotelian account of autonomy. The J Values Inq 42(1):41–53

Allmark P, Tod A (2006) How should public health professionals engage with lay epidemiology? J Med Ethics 32(8):460–463

Allmark P, Tod A (2014) Can a nudge keep you warm? Using nudges to reduce excess winter deaths: insight from the Keeping Warm in Later Life Project (KWILLT). J Public Health 36(1):111–116

Allmark P, Tod A, Abbott J (2010) The evaluation of public health education initiatives on smoking and lung cancer: an ethical critique. In: Peckham S, Hann A (eds) Public health ethics and practice. Policy Press, Bristol, pp 65–82

Allmark P, Baxter S, Goyder E et al (2013) Assessing the health benefits of advice services: using research evidence and logic model methods to explore complex pathways. Health Soc Care Community 21(1):59–68

Aristotle (2000) In: Crisp R (ed) Nicomachean ethics. Cambridge Univ Press, Cambridge

Berlin I (1969) Four essays on liberty. Oxford University Press, Oxford

Black D, Morris J, Smith C, Townsend P (1982) The black report. Pelican, London

Buchanan D (2006) Perspective: a new ethic for health promotion: reflections on a philosophy of health education for the 21st century. Health Educ Behav 33(3):290–304

Chang H-J (2014) Economics: a user's guide. Pelican, Harmondsworth

Cheung P, Yam B (2005) Patient autonomy in physical restraint. J Clin Nurs 14(3A):34–40

Christman J (1991) Liberalism and individual positive freedom. Ethics 101(2):343–359

Craig P, Cooper C, Gunnell D et al (2012) Using natural experiments to evaluate population health interventions: new Medical Research Council guidance. J Epidemiol Community Health 66 (12):1182–1186

Crisp R (1997) Mill on utilitarianism. Routledge, London

Dahlgren G, Whitehead M (1993) Tackling inequalities in health: what can we learn from what has been tried? Working paper prepared for The King's Fund International Seminar on Tackling Inequalities in Health, September 1993, Ditchley Park, Oxfordshire. The King's Fund, London. Accessible In: Dahlgren G, Whitehead M (2007). European strategies for tackling social inequities in health: levelling up Part 2. WHO Regional office for Europe, Copenhagen. http://www.euro.who.int/__data/assets/pdf_file/0018/103824/E89384.pdf

Davies M, Macdowall W, Black N, Raine R (2006) Health promotion theory. Open University Press, Maidenhead

Department of Health (2004) Choosing health: making healthy choices easier. London. Available via http://webarchive.nationalarchives.gov.uk/+/www.dh.gov.uk/en/Publicationsandstatistics/ Publications/PublicationsPolicyAndGuidance/Browsable/DH_4880358

Department of Health (2010) Healthy lives, healthy people: our strategy for public health in England. Department of Health. Available via http://www.dh.gov.uk/en/index.htm

Department of Health and Social Security (1977) Prevention and health: everybody's business. Department of Health, London

Doxiadis S (1987) Ethical dilemmas in health promotion. Wiley, New York

Dworkin G (1988) The theory and practice of autonomy. Cambridge University Press, Cambridge

Eriksson M, Lindström B (2008) A salutogenic interpretation of the Ottawa charter. Health Promot Int 23(2):190–199

Feinberg J (1986) The moral limits of the criminal law: volume 3: harm to self. Oxford University Press, New York

Fitzpatrick M (2001) The tyranny of health: doctors and the regulation of lifestyle. Routledge, London

Green L, Kreuter M (1991) Health promotion planning: an educational and environmental approach, 2nd edn. Mayfield, Mountain View

Griffiths S, Jewell T, Donnelly P (2005) Public health in practice: the three domains of public health. Public Health 119:907–913

Kleisiaris C, Sfakianakis C, Papathanasiou I (2014) Health care practices in ancient Greece: the Hippocratic ideal. J Med Ethics Hist Med 7:3–7

Le Fanu J (2011) The rise & fall of modern medicine, 2nd edn. Abacus, London

Lindley R (1986) Autonomy. Macmillan, London

Marmot M (2010) Fair society, healthy lives: strategic review of health inequalities in England post 2010. Department of Health, London, Available via www.marmotreview.org

May T (1994) The concept of autonomy. Am Philos Q 31(2):133–144

Maynard A, Sheldon T (2001) Limits to demand for health care [Letter]. BMJ (Br Med J) 322:734

Mcknight C (1993) Autonomy and the akratic patient. J Med Ethics 19(4):206–210

Mill JS (1972) On liberty. Dent, London

Murphy M, Black N, Lamping D et al (1998) Consensus development methods, and their use in clinical guideline development. Health Technol Assess 2(3):1–88

Nuffield Council on Bioethics (2007) Public health: ethical issues. Nuffield, London, Available via http://nuffieldbioethics.org/

Nussbaum M (2011) Creating capabilities: the human development approach. Belknap/Harvard University Press, Cambridge, MA

O'Neill O (2001) Autonomy and trust in bioethics. Cambridge University Press, Cambridge

O'Neill O (2004) Informed consent and public health. Philos Trans R Soc London Ser B-Biol Sci 359(1447):1133–1136

Pawson R (2013) The science of evaluation. Sage, London

Pawson R, Tilley N (1997) Realistic evaluation. Sage, London

Raphael D (2000) The question of evidence in health promotion. Health Promot Int 14(4):355–367

Richmond C (2005) Sir Richard Doll obituary: epidemiologist who showed that smoking caused cancer and heart disease. BMJ (Br Med J) 331:295

Roffey R, Tegnell A, Elgh F (2002) Biological warfare in a historical perspective. Clin Microbiol Infect 8(8):450–454

Rose G (2001) Sick individuals and sick populations. Int J Epidemiol 30(3):427–432

Science and Technology Select Committee (2011) Behaviour change. House of Lords, London, Available via http://www.publications.parliament.uk/pa/ld201012/ldselect/ldsctech/179/179. pdf

Seedhouse D (1997) Health promotion: philosophy, prejudice and practice. Wiley, Chichester

Sen A (2010) The idea of justice. Penguin, Harmondsworth

Skrabanek P (1990) Why is preventive medicine exempted from ethical constraints? J Med Ethics 16(4):187–190

Skrabanek P (1992) Smoking and statistical overkill. Lancet 340(8829):1208–1209

Smith GD, Ebrahim S (2001) Epidemiology – is it time to call it a day? Int J Epidemiol 30(1):1–11

Thaler R, Sunstein C (2009) Nudge: improving decisions about health, wealth and happiness. Penguin, Harmondsworth

Venkatapuram S (2011) Health justice: an argument from the capabilities approach. Polity, Cambridge

Wilkinson R, Pickett K (2008) The spirit level: why more equal societies almost always do better. Allen Lane/The Penguin Press, Harmondsworth

Winslow C (1920) The untilled fields of public health. Science 51(1306):23–33

Psychopathy: Morally Incapacitated Persons

Heidi Maibom

Contents

Abstract

After describing the disorder of psychopathy, I examine the theories and the evidence concerning the psychopaths' deficient moral capacities. I first examine whether or not psychopaths can pass tests of moral knowledge. Most of the evidence suggests that they can. If there is a lack of moral understanding, then it has to be due to an incapacity that affects not their declarative knowledge of moral

H. Maibom (✉)
University of Cincinnati, Cincinnati, OH, USA
e-mail: heidimaibom@gmail.com

© Springer Science+Business Media Dordrecht 2017
T. Schramme, S. Edwards (eds.), *Handbook of the Philosophy of Medicine*,
DOI 10.1007/978-94-017-8688-1_56

norms, but their deeper understanding of them. I then examine two suggestions: it is their deficient practical reason or their stunted emotions that are at fault. The evidence supports both explanations. I conclude with an overview of the debate concerning whether they are morally or legally responsible for their actions.

Introduction

The psychopath lacks a conscience, regards others as mere means to his selfish and unscrupulous ends, experiences no empathy for others and no regret at his harmful actions, and is incapable of seeing his or others' actions as wrong or right, good or bad. These and other equally sensational claims surround psychopathy. This has led to a spirited philosophical debate about whether psychopaths even understand right and wrong or good and bad, what role their emotional and rational deficits play in such understanding, and whether they are morally or legally responsible. But what does the evidence actually show about this intriguing disorder? Below, I give an outline of the current debates and present the evidence from psychology and neuroscience as it stands.

What Is Psychopathy?

Psychopathy is a mental disorder characterized by deficient emotionality, interpersonal dysfunction, behavioral disinhibition, and antisocial behavior. Between 1 % and 2 % of the population suffer from psychopathy. Males are disproportionately affected, with an estimated four males for each female sufferer. Having psychopathy is one of the best predictors of criminal offending and reoffending; psychopaths are three times as likely as other offenders to recidivate. The average North American psychopath will have four convictions for violent crime by the age of 40. Since the prison population is estimated to contain around 20 % psychopaths, roughly 90 % of all psychopaths are either incarcerated, on probation, or on parole (Kiehl and Lushing 2014). Consequently, most of the research on psychopathy is conducted with male criminals. Two of the most common measures of psychopathy are *The Psychopathy Checklist-Revised* and *Levenson's Self-Report Psychopathy Scale*. The former is more commonly used in forensic settings, whereas the latter is an easier measure to use outside such settings.

Psychopathy is a dimensional construct, meaning that there is a relatively arbitrary cutoff point, above which someone is classified as a psychopath and below which he is not. However, the individual who does not make the cut will share many of the features of the psychopath. There is some debate about the ideal cutoff on the various scales. There is also debate about whether psychopathy should be regarded as a mental disorder at all or whether it should be thought of as an adaptation characterizing a subgroup of human beings (Hare 2004).

Deficient Affect

According to Robert Hare (2004), psychopaths have shallow affect, lack remorse, guilt, and empathy. Hervey Cleckley (1976) thought they had no shame and David Lykken (1957) that they lacked fear. Shallow affect describes an inability to experience the full range or depth of normal emotions. Whereas people normally recognize emotional words quicker than nonemotional words, psychopaths do not. They are sometimes confused about whether an event is positive or negative, and although they sometimes engage in dramatic displays of emotion, particularly anger, they often appear cold and unemotional (Hare 2004). Psychopaths trivialize the harms they do, which is one reason they are thought to lack empathy or sympathy. They tend to blame others for their own actions or failings, rarely take responsibility, and appear to experience little, or no, guilt or remorse. The prospect of pain or punishment seems not to deter them. Psychopaths do not experience stress, anxiety, or fear in the types of situations where people normally feel them, or when they do, these emotional reactions do not affect them as they would others (Lykken 1957).

Relating to Others

Psychopaths tend to think that they are better than other people and consequently that their needs and desires have priority. They do not shy away from manipulating others to get what they want whether by flattery, deception, or coercion. They are often fanciful liars, seemingly taking great pleasure in telling tall tales about their experiences and accomplishments. When caught in a lie, they appear unfazed. Psychopaths may be quite charming, but usually in rather superficial and shallow ways. Although they may speak authoritatively about technical matters, they typically do not possess the relevant knowledge although they have a certain ability to mimic experts. Psychopaths are known for having many short-term marital relationships and not to put much stock in being faithful to their lovers.

Psychopathic Lifestyle

Psychopaths commonly engage in irresponsible and impulsive behavior. For instance, they may leave infants unattended while going on a weekend bender, fail to show up at work or simply quit because they are bored, bludgeon a shop attendant to avoid paying for beer, or force a woman to have sex with them because the opportunity suddenly arises. They tend not to plan ahead, and when they do, their goals are often unrealistic. They crave stimulation, and so drug and alcohol addiction are quite common in psychopaths. They also prefer to live off others compared to making their own way.

Antisociality

Psychopaths engage in antisocial and harmful conduct mostly from an early age. They may torture defenseless animals, such a puppies, coerce other children to perform sexual acts, steal from others, frame others for their misconduct, and so on. This conduct continues or worsens in adolescence. Their criminal conduct tends to be extremely diverse compared to other criminals, and they are more likely to reoffend than are other criminals and to violate conditional release or escape from prison.

Psychopathic Subtypes

Some people argue that psychopathy is composed of clinically distinct subtypes. People distinguish between the primary, low-anxious, or callous-unemotional psychopath and the secondary, high-anxious psychopath. Many regard secondary psychopathy as a sort of hodgepodge category, which likely contains many distinct types of antisocial and emotionally dysregulated individuals. Primary psychopaths are characterized predominantly by deficient affect and a callous interpersonal style of relating to others. Many now assume that there is a genetic component to psychopathy (Blair et al. 2005), though most assume that psychopathy is a result of an interaction between genetic predisposition and a problematic early environment, often characterized by neglect or violence (Porter 1996). Deficient affect is typically used to explain why psychopaths have few qualms about harming others. But interestingly, evidence suggests that secondary psychopaths, who have relatively spared affective abilities, are more violent than primary psychopaths (Hicks et al. 2004).

Judging Right and Wrong, Good and Bad

Do psychopaths *understand* moral categories? Can they comprehend right and wrong? Are they capable of seeing their own or other people's actions as good or bad? Psychopaths can certainly *say* that it is wrong to lie, steal, murder, etc. But although the legal stance is that psychopaths have sufficient understanding of right and wrong to be held responsible for their actions, moral philosophers have long questioned whether psychopaths *really* understand right and wrong. Recently, James Blair's (1995) study of psychopaths' performance on the moral-conventional distinction has been thought to show that psychopaths lack moral understanding. As we shall see, however, the evidence is much more complex and perplexing.

The better known tests of moral competence are the Kohlberg moral stages test and Turiel's moral-conventional distinction. Kohlberg's stages are meant to measure reasoning about wrongs and rights, ranging from the so-called preconventional to postconventional. Preconventional reasoning concerns mainly how to avoid morally motivated aggression from others, such as punishment of wrongs. At the conventional stage, people come to appreciate the importance of meeting the expectations of others, upholding the law, and fulfilling one's social obligations. At the most advanced postconventional stage, individuals' reasoning about moral rights and wrongs issue from an autonomous internalized conscience which may or may not accord with society's principles and which focuses on the application of abstract and universal moral principles. Perhaps surprisingly, one study of psychopaths' performance on the moral stages shows their performance to be superior (Link et al. 1977) and another that any deficient performance is accounted for by differences in IQ (O'Kane et al. 1996).

Turiel's moral-conventional distinction is a largely instrumental measure of moral competence, although he thinks morality mainly concerns harms, rights, and justice. The degree to which a transgression is thought to be serious, impermissible, and subject to change by authority is a mark of its being moral or conventional. Moral transgressions are judged to be more serious, less permissible, and less subject to change by a relevant authority than conventional transgressions. Blair's well-known experiment shows that psychopaths do not make a distinction between moral and conventional norms on any of these dimensions (Blair 1995). However, Blair himself failed to replicate the result (Blair 1997). Others found that psychopaths perform as well as controls on all moral transgressions except accidents (Young et al. 2012), rate moral transgressions as severe as controls do (Harenski et al. 2010), and judge actions to be wrong even if there are no rules prohibiting them (Aharoni et al. 2012).

Because both Kohlberg's and Turiel's moral tests represent disputed conceptualizations of the moral realm, other tests have been proposed. For instance, the Moral Foundations Questionnaire reflects Jonathan Haidt's more eclectic view of the moral domain. In two studies – one conducted with criminal psychopaths and another with a subclinical population with psychopathic tendencies – psychopaths were found to perform as well as nonpsychopaths on measures relating to authority, in-group loyalty, and purity. Where they were lacking in both studies were in their harm and fairness ratings; here, they performed significantly below the norm (Aharoni et al. 2011; Glen et al. 2009b). The results, however, contrast with those of other studies testing psychopaths' tendencies to make welfare justifications. Although Blair (1995) found that his psychopathic subjects made fewer welfare justifications than his other subjects, he and others have failed to replicate this result (Blair 1997; Aharoni et al. 2012).

Other areas of moral competence are thought to be affected in psychopaths, for instance their judgments concerning the permissible tradeoff between the good of the many and the harm done to the one. Here, too, the evidence is mixed. A couple of studies find increased tendency to judge that the one should be sacrificed to save the many particularly in low-anxious psychopaths (Bartels and Pizarro 2011; Koenigs et al. 2012), whereas others do not (Glen et al. 2009a; Cima et al. 2010) (for more detail, see section "Reason and Emotion").

When it comes to the behavioral data, then the findings are again mixed. Some show intact performance, some do not, but often there are more of the former than the latter. Some of the more promising studies suggesting a moral deficit are Abigail

Marsh's, and they indicate that psychopaths think it slightly less wrong to cause fear in others than nonpsychopaths do (Marsh and Cardinale 2012). Such results, however, are pretty bland compared to the rather sensational literature on psychopaths' amorality! If so many studies of psychopaths' ability to make moral judgments show that they perform as well as nonpsychopaths, why should we think that they are not able to make moral judgments?

Here is a diagnosis of the problem. Most philosophers believe that if you judge that harming others is wrong, you are thereby motivated not to harm others. This is also known as internalism about moral judgment and motivation. If this idea is right, we can use lack of motivation as a sign of lack of the corresponding judgment. Someone who regularly abuses and hurts others is very unlikely to actually believe that it is wrong to abuse or hurt others. This seems to be the case with psychopaths. Psychopaths *say* that harming others is wrong, and they justify harm norms in terms of victim welfare. Nonetheless, they are involved in an awful lot of harm (see section "What Is Psychopathy?"). This suggests that there is something about right and wrong that these individuals fail to grasp! The suspicion is intensified by the observation that psychopaths don't evince the right kind of guilt or remorse about the harm that they have caused. So whereas it is possible to imagine someone who acts against her better judgment more often than others do, it is hard to imagine that she would experience neither guilt nor remorse as a consequence. But this is exactly what the psychopath fails to do. The conclusion appears ineluctable: psychopaths are not motivated to do right and not to do wrong like others are. If they are not, then they cannot really believe that what they are doing is wrong, when they do wrong. Consequently, psychopaths do not have the ability to *truly* judge that something is right or wrong; they cannot make *true* moral judgments.

Some philosophers object to this way of thinking about morality. They think that judgments of right and wrong are independent of any motivation to act in accordance with such judgments (Brink 1989). That is not to say that they do not agree that people are *typically* motivated to act in accordance with their moral judgments, only that there is no need to doubt that someone makes a true moral judgment if he or she appears unmotivated to act in accordance with it at the same time. Some people argue that the curious constellation of relatively intact declarative moral knowledge and immoral conduct in the psychopath provides evidence in favor of such externalism about moral motivation (Aharoni et al. 2012).

Affect and Reason in Moral Judgment

If psychopaths are not able to make true moral judgments, the most obvious interpretation of their deficit is that they fail to *understand* moral demands or restrictions. There is therefore something deficient about the way that they think or reason. Others retort that psychopaths do not have any obvious reasoning deficits, wherefore it must be their lack of emotion that causes the problem. Both positions have empirical support.

Deficient Practical Reason

The balance of evidence concerning intelligence – as measured by standard intelligence tests – suggests that psychopaths have as high, or higher, intelligence as matched controls (Salekin 2006). This finding is important as low IQ is correlated with deficient performance on tests of moral aptitude and with criminality generally. Since psychopaths do not appear to suffer from obvious rational impairments, some conclude that reasoning impairments cannot be responsible for their problems telling right from wrong (Nichols 2004). That is too quick. Although psychologists and social scientists often think of reason purely as theoretical reason, the sort of reasoning ability that is relevant for most philosophers when it comes to morality is *practical*. And here psychopaths have demonstrated deficits.

In this debate, the centrality of reason to morality is typically pitched in terms of Immanuel Kant (1785/1993), whose work has had a profound impact on theories of morality. Kant thought that what he called pure practical reason must be the driving force behind categorical judgments of right and wrong. Think of practical reason as decision-making. Practically rational agents subject their reasoning to the so-called categorical imperative. Its most famous forms include the injunction not to make exception to oneself when reasoning about the permissibility of performing an action and not to use others merely as means to an end. To be able to reason in this way, however, requires being able to comprehend what it is to have ends in the first place. Psychopaths, some argue, are incapable of comprehending what an end is (Duff 1977; Kennett 2002). Others argue that while psychopaths may comprehend the notion of ends, their ability to reason practically is so impaired that they are unlikely to consider to the moral value of many of their actions (Maibom 2005).

Psychopaths do, in fact, have decision-making deficits. This is abundantly evident in the anecdotal evidence. Hare (1993), for instance, tells the story of a psychopath who decided to bludgeon a shop attendant so that he didn't have to pay for a six-pack of beers. He was going to a party and did not want to show up empty-handed, but had forgotten his wallet at home. Instead of going back to retrieve it, he assaulted the attendant who subsequently suffered severe brain damage. Psychopaths often decide to represent themselves in court – take Ted Bundy, for instance – often with disastrous consequences to themselves. The long checkered criminal record of the average psychopath also suggests a lack of long-term planning.

It is not just anecdotal evidence that suggests that psychopaths have difficulties making good decisions. There is good experimental evidence too. Psychopaths have extensive attention and inhibition deficits. When it comes to attention, psychopaths are relatively insensitive to contextual and other information that is not the focus of their attention (Hiatt and Newman 2006). They focus narrowly and exclusively on what they are attending to and are comparatively blind to other, potentially relevant features of the situation. Whereas people generally attend to multiple features of objects, actions, and situations, psychopaths typically attend to only a subclass of those. Part of the problem is that they have difficulties shifting attention from one feature of the situation to another in response to relevant contextual cues (Hiatt and Newman 2006).

Psychopaths are also relatively insensitive to punishment. If asked to navigate a maze where at each choice point, 1 of 4 choices is reinforced with an electrical shock, psychopaths are as likely to choose the option associated with shock as they are to choose the other options. Needless to say, that contrasts with the choices of ordinary people (Lykken 1957). Psychopaths are not altogether insensitive to punishment, pain, or fear of punishment. They do as well as nonpsychopaths on simple negative reinforcement tasks. It is specifically when avoiding punishment interferes with their standing pursuit of a goal that psychopaths have problems (Hiatt and Newman 2006). However, if given clear information about the reward-punishment contingencies of a task or when forced to pause before each new choice, these problems disappear.

Although psychopaths can learn simple reward-punishment contingencies, as we have seen, once they learn to respond in a certain way, they have difficulties adjusting once their behavior is no longer adaptive. For instance, switching the reward-punishment contingencies in an experiment leads to reduced performance by psychopaths. Ordinary subjects adjust relatively easily, learning to respond to previously punished stimuli and to cease to respond to previously rewarded stimuli; psychopaths do not (Newman and Kosson 1986; Blair et al. 2001).

What does this have to do with one's ability to understand right and wrong or good and bad? According to Kant, such judgments are permissibility judgments and form part of our decision-making ability. One rule of decision-making is that if you want to achieve or possess something, you must also want to do what it takes. Philosophers talk of willing the necessary means to one's ends. But the rule or rules that specifically concern an actions' moral status are about the very structure of decision-making. What is permissible for one agent in her situation is permissible for another agent in the same situation. We can understand the situation broadly so as to consist in not only the environmental features but also the role the agent plays in that situation. For instance, what is permissible for a policeman qua policeman need not be permissible for a chimney sweeper qua chimney sweeper. A policeman can arrest somebody, for instance. However, what is permissible for one policeman is also permissible for another policeman assuming that the two situations are sufficiently similar. This rule is known as the categorical imperative. When you apply it, you think something like this: "could I will that anyone in my situation do what I am considering doing?"

It is easy to see that such thinking immediately rules out acts like cutting in line and making false promises. Someone who cuts in line expects to get where he or she is going faster. However, this will only be true if *other* people do not cut in line. To consistently will to cut in line, the agent must both will that she cuts in line and that nobody else does. But if she applies the categorical imperative to her proposed action, she sees that she must will at one and the same time that anybody in her position cuts in line and that nobody *other than herself* does so. That is inconsistent. False promising leads to other problems. Let us say that I get you to lend me money by promising that I will pay you back next month. I know, however, that my finances are not going to be any better next month or the month after that, etc., and so I will not be able to pay you back. To go through with this action, I will have to intend that anyone in need of money can falsely promise to pay them back. To make this act of lying successful, I am relying on the practice that people keep their promises. However, if no one were to keep their promises, the very practice that I am relying on would cease to exist. So I would be willing an action that depends on a practice whose very existence my action would undermine. That is not consistent either.

Another version of the categorical imperatives states that we should never only use others only as a means to our ends but also always regard them as ends in themselves. Other agents are not ours to use *merely* for our own projects. This idea seems to underlie our practice of seeking consent for various activities involving others, e.g., sexual intercourse. Clearly, psychopaths do not adhere to either of these principles. They appear to play little or no role in their reasoning. In fact, the modus operandi of psychopaths is one that relies on others adhering to moral and social rules and they do what they please. Whereas psychopaths are simply outraged by being treated badly by others and sometimes go on about it at considerable length, they tend trivialize their own bad behavior (Hare 1993). They also regard others as mere means to their ends; they are extraordinarily manipulative and exploitative.

Some argue that psychopaths do not understand what ends are or the reasons they generate (Kennett 2002). Now to understand what having an end involves, you must understand that if you want to achieve something, you must also want what is necessary and sufficient to achieving that something and that is within your power. You must also be careful that you do not foil your own achievement by adopting a course of action that will ultimately prevent you from obtaining your goal. If this understanding also involves a comprehension of the demands of the various formulations of the categorical imperative, it is easy to see how this would go over the head of most psychopaths. Others argue that since psychopaths' reasoning deficits are, in the end, relatively subtle and context-specific, we don't have evidence that they have *no* conception of ends. However, we do know that if their attention is focused on something they want, they tend not to pay a lot of attention to other features of the situation, presumably including the moral features of it (Maibom 2005). They are unlikely to subject their decision-making to the categorical imperative in any of its formulations and thus to notice how their false promising or lying conceptually undercuts the very intentions they adopt in their actions.

Deficient Emotion

It is now more popular to think that the *real* problem with psychopaths is their deficient emotionality: their lack of guilt, remorse, empathy, and so on. The idea here is that true moral judgment is infused with affect. Take that affect away, and all we are left with are hollowed out thoughts or empty words. To understand this idea, think about the difference between so-called conventional norms and moral norms. We adhere to a number of relatively arbitrary conventions because doing so makes things run more smoothly. In England and many of its former colonies, you drive on the left side of the road; mostly you drive on the right side in the rest of the world.

The decision of what side to drive on is not driven by deeper or more profound concerns. There are two options; you choose one and stick to it. Of course, once the convention holds, individuals cannot choose, willy-nilly, which side to drive on. But coming to England, you are not morally outraged by this practice, though it might be the cause of some concern when crossing the road. Contrast this with prohibitions against harming others. Such norms are near universal – although who may be harmed and under what circumstances vary considerably – and are not arbitrary in the way which side of the road to drive on is. Violations of such norms often give rise to considerable outrage. Take, for instance, the practice of family members killing rape victims in parts of the world. Contemplating such acts, and the people who perform them, typically causes a strong emotional reaction we might describe as anger or outrage. For sentimentalists the ability to experience such emotional reactions – whether they be anger, guilt, shame, sadness, and so on – in response to agents performing certain kinds of actions is necessary for, or a constituent part of, our understanding such actions as being right or wrong, good or bad.

David Hume said that when he considered people and their actions, he did not see goodness or badness there, but only inside his own chest, as it were. What he meant was that an action or agent's goodness or badness rests on how it or she makes us feel. He talked broadly of the sense of approbation for judgments of right or good and the sense of disapprobation for judgments of wrong or bad. Hume thought that our basic propensity to feel with our fellow human beings was foundational to all our moral sentiments. In other words, the basic ability to empathize with another is the source of all the other sentiments one experiences in reaction to what people do to others. It is easy to see why this idea is appealing. Why do we think it is wrong to harm others? Because when we contemplate such harm, we feel some of the pain of the victim in our own bodies by means of the empathic affective reaction. This basic propensity, then, gives rise to other, more recognizable moral emotions, such as anger at injustice.

Lack of empathy or sympathy is understandably the top candidate for the affective deficit that is responsible for psychopaths failing to understand moral right and wrong. Various suggestions have been made as to how lack of empathy leads to the full-scale moral deficits psychopaths seem to have. It has been suggested that psychopaths are born with a deficient violence inhibition mechanism, which prevents them from developing empathy, moral emotions, and moral understanding (Blair 1995). This idea takes its departure from the evidence that psychopaths have deficient physiological responses to others' pain and distress. Another proposal has it that moral judgment has two components: one which involves knowledge of norms and another which involves the capacity to have concern for the well-being of others (Nichols 2004). Psychopaths may have the former, but lack the latter. Without concern for others, psychopaths are unable to make *true* moral judgments. They know, in a discursive sense, what is right or wrong. However, they fail to appreciate the wrongness of wrong because they lack the ability to experience the requisite emotional reaction to such wrong. Or so the story goes, at any rate.

Lack of empathy is one of the diagnostic criteria for psychopathy, but what exactly does it come to? As defined in the *PCL-R*, lack of empathy may mean anything from lack of concern for the well-being or rights of others to deficient ability to imagine being in their position. It may even include the inability to relate to others emotionally as other agents or a failure to appreciate the reality of other agents as agents. On the background of this characterization, it is rather extraordinary that so many studies of empathy in psychopaths show no deficits. One of the most used tests of empathy is the Interpersonal Reactivity Index. Four studies show intact performance on the empathic concern component (Shamay-Tsoory et al. 2010; Domes et al. 2013; Lishner et al. 2012; von Borries et al. 2012), and another study only has secondary or high-anxious psychopaths underperforming, but not primary or low-anxious psychopaths (Mullins-Nelson et al. 2006). Two studies also show psychopaths experience normal personal distress (Shamay-Tsoory et al. 2010; von Borries et al. 2012). Furthermore, studies showing pictures of people in distress elicit ratings of unpleasantness similar to those of ordinary subjects (Herpertz et al. 2001; Birbaumer et al. 2005; Levenston et al. 2000). Considering how psychopaths act, this is rather puzzling.

Physiological measures and, to some degree, brain scans are more revealing and support the common assumption that psychopaths *do* have empathy deficits. Although the evidence is still somewhat mixed, more studies suggest that psychopaths have reduced skin conductance and attenuated fear-potentiated startle to others in distress compared to nonpsychopaths that do not (Herpertz et al. 2001; Birbaumer et al. 2005; Patrick et al. 1994; Verona et al. 2013). Skin conductance measures arousal. Increased skin conductance is associated with stress, fear, anxiety, and pain. It would appear that others' pain and distress cause a generalized stress response in observers. This is not true of psychopaths, however. Fear-potentiated startle indicates that the organism is on high alert, ready to initiate defensive action. It would therefore seem that psychopaths do not regard others' pain and suffering as a threat, but that normal people do.

The fMRI data is also suggestive, but more mixed. Psychopaths have reduced orbitofrontal cortex and ventromedial prefrontal cortex activation compared to nonpsychopaths in response to pain or distress in others (Decety et al. 2013a, b, 2014). However, the evidence is mixed when it comes to the activation of the areas most consistently associated with empathy: the anterior insula (AI), the anterior cingulate cortex (ACC), and the inferior frontal gyrus (IFG). When specifically asked to empathize with a person experiencing social rejection, for instance, psychopaths show intact activation in all these areas. However, if given no instructions, they activate these areas less than nonpsychopaths do (Meffert et al. 2013). This suggests that psychopaths *are* capable of empathizing with others, but they tend not to do so spontaneously. The idea that there might be intact empathic capacity in psychopaths after all is also supported by studies by Jean Decety and his group. If a psychopath is shown a picture of a person in a painful situation and asked to imagine that this is happening to himself, he has intact activation in AI, ACC, and IFG. If, on the other hand, he is asked to imagine it happening to someone else, he does not (Decety et al. 2013a). The same discrepancy in activation to explicit instructions to feel with and imagine-self in pain and no instructions or imagine-other in pain is evident in the amygdala. The two first sets of instructions are associated with intact activation, the latter ones with deficient activation compared to controls (Meffert et al. 2013; Decety et al. 2013a). Again, it does seem as if the psychopath is capable of intact empathic responding to pictures of people in pain; he just has to imagine that it is himself who is in pain. This speaks less to a pervasive empathy deficit than to a more selective impairment in spontaneous empathizing with others.

Other researchers have alternative explanations of the morally relevant emotional deficits in psychopaths. Jesse Prinz, for instance, suggests that their behavioral inhibition system is impaired, and this expresses itself in the lack of emotions that are supposed to inhibit actions, such as fear and sadness (Prinz 2007). As we have seen, it is plausible that deficient fear is at the core of psychopaths' deficient affective response to others' pain and distress. It also explains the range of risky behaviors psychopaths regularly engage in. Prinz's account may link up less elegantly to moral concerns than theories that focus on deficient concern for the well-being of others. Fear is rarely regarded as a morally relevant emotion by philosophers, who instead tend to focus on such emotions as resentment or guilt (Greenspan 1995; Strawson 1962; Wallace 1996). Interestingly, at least one test of guilt in psychopaths found that primary or low-anxious psychopaths reported as much guilt as nonpsychopaths; only secondary or high-anxious psychopaths reported less guilt than controls (Mullins-Nelson et al. 2006).

Even if psychopaths do not altogether lack emotional reactions to the types of situations that typically give rise to moral affect in nonpsychopaths, they clearly have deficient emotional responses to them. It is therefore easy to see how such a deficit would impair their ability to make true moral judgments. When they see harm done to another, for instance, they are not gripped with the fear and horror that ordinary people are, and so the wrongness of the act may seem like a relatively superficial property of that act, like what clothes the agent was wearing or what knife was being used. Extend this general line of thinking to all other types of moral transgression – though probably not those committed toward the psychopath himself – and it should be clear what a sentimentalist picture of the psychopaths' moral deficit might look like.

Reason and Emotion

Some philosophers have taken a more ecumenical approach to moral judgment, arguing that some moral judgments are more based in reason, others more based in emotion (Greene et al. 2001). Much of the literature on so-called utilitarian versus deontological judgment reflects this idea. Utilitarianism and deontology constitute two philosophical theories about morality. For utilitarians the basic good is happiness, and the more happiness is created by an action, the better it is. Moral agents can either calculate the foreseeable happiness that their actions will produce before they act (act utilitarianism) or they may adopt general rules, which typically have happiness-maximizing effects (rule utilitarianism). Typically, the happiness of the many will outweigh the happiness of the few. One need not only focus on maximizing happiness; one can also be concerned with minimizing suffering. If the latter, the best act would be the one that causes the least amount of suffering. By contrast, deontological moral theory rests on the idea that people have certain inviolable rights that no amount of optimizing happiness elsewhere can trump. There are certain things that are simply wrong, no matter how good the consequences. For instance, we may not kill an innocent person even if doing so would save many other innocent people. Killing (the innocent) is simply wrong and is therefore absolutely impermissible. The rightness or wrongness of an action rests in the kind of action that it is, not in its good or bad consequences. For instance, an action is wrong if it violates basic rights that a person has in virtue of being an agent or if it violates the categorical imperative (see above).

Most people have both utilitarian and deontological intuitions, though perhaps not at the same time. These intuitions are often brought out in moral dilemmas. Imagine that you are hiking next to a rail track. You reach an interchange. You look up the track and spot an out-of-control trolley bearing down the tracks. You look in the other direction and see hikers on both tracks. However, whereas one set of tracks only has one hiker on it, the other has six. The rails are set so that the trolley will go down the track with six hikers on it, almost certainly killing all of them. Should you pull the switch at the interchange, thereby causing the train to go down the track with just the one hiker on it, almost certainly killing her? Most people think it would be ok for you to do so. After all, you are saving six people even if you cause one to die. This thinking seems to be based on the utilitarian-sounding principle that it is better to sacrifice the few to save the many. But this principle does not hold in other situations. Imagine that you are a doctor at a hospital. You have in your care six patients in urgent need of organ transplants: liver, heart, kidneys, and lungs. You also have a routine meeting with a healthy patient. If you put that patient down, you can harvest his organs and thereby save six of your other patients. Should you kill your one patient to save six of your other patients? Most people say such an act would be impermissible. It seems just plain wrong to kill a healthy person even if doing so might save the lives of six others. Whatever the principle is here, it sounds more deontological. There is something wrong in the act of killing the patient itself, no matter what its positive consequences. However, the two situations seem similar: they both involve sacrificing the one to save the many.

Joshua Greene and colleagues (2001) scanned the brains of people while they were making decisions about moral dilemmas of the sort discussed above. They found that when people make deontological decisions – typically refusing to sacrifice the one to save the many – they engage more emotional areas of the brain than when they make utilitarian ones – roughly sacrificing the one to save the many. Greene concludes that deontological reasoning is based in affect. This is surprising since deontological reasoning is associated with Kant, who was a rationalist. The problem with affect, though, is that it often skews our opinions.

Consequently, we should be very skeptical about our deontological intuitions. There is considerable debate both about the appropriateness of labeling the decisions utilitarian or deontological and about whether deontological reasoning really is as affect laden as Greene seems to think. However that may be, some studies suggest that psychopaths make more utilitarian judgments than do controls. This has caused some people to argue that utilitarianism is associated with not caring much for people (Bartels and Pizarro 2011). This is certainly a bit of an odd conclusion, since utilitarian reasoning is based on a concern for others' well-being.

As before, the evidence is not as clean as one would hope. Where one study shows impaired performance (Bartels and Pizarro 2011), another shows that psychopaths make as many utilitarian-type judgments as do nonpsychopaths (Glen et al. 2009b). It is sometimes thought that the difference comes out most clearly in so-called personal dilemmas, where sacrificing the one involves physical contact with the victim (pushing, smothering, and so on). People with damage to their prefrontal cortex make more utilitarian-type judgments on such dilemmas (Koenigs et al. 2007), and such patients are often compared with psychopaths because of their partially overlapping symptomatology. However, at least one study shows no tendency of psychopaths to make more utilitarian-type judgments on this restricted range of moral dilemmas (Cima et al. 2010). Another study shows that only low-anxious psychopaths make more utilitarian judgments on personal moral dilemmas compared to controls, whereas high-anxious psychopaths perform at norm (Koenigs et al. 2012). This latter study does support the idea that affect backs deontological-type reasoning, but the results from other studies are so mixed that it would be premature to conclude anything very definite about the affective-moral capacities of psychopaths. There is also the added difficulty that even if low-anxious psychopaths make more utilitarian judgments on personal moral dilemmas, this hardly shows that they have a moral *deficit*. For perhaps they are making the *right* decision, they just happen not to be swayed by morally irrelevant affect.

Are Psychopaths Responsible?

The question of whether psychopaths are responsible for their actions is typically addressed either in moral or legal terms. Although legal responsibility typically tracks moral responsibility, the two can come apart, as in cases of strict liability. So, someone may not be morally responsible, yet be legally responsible. Someone may be morally responsible for something and not legally responsible because there are no laws prohibiting the kind of behavior. Concerns about psychopaths' standing as responsible agents derive from two sources: their emotional and rational deficits. Whether or not theorists think psychopaths are responsible for their actions comes down to how pervasive they think their deficits are in the areas that most affect understanding right and wrong.

Legal Responsibility

Historically, psychopaths have not been exempted from legal responsibility. This is largely due to the fact that they are aware of what they are doing when they commit a wrong, they know it is wrong, and they are able to control their actions. Furthermore, they do not suffer from delusions or hallucinations of the sort that usually exculpate other mentally ill defendants. They appear neither cognitively nor volitionally impaired in ways relevant to criminal responsibility. A number of philosophers (Maibom 2008), psychopathy researchers (Hare 1993; Cleckley 1976), and legal theorists (Reznek 1997) argue that they are therefore legally responsible, whereas others maintain that psychopaths do not have sufficient understanding of right and wrong to be held responsible (Duff 1977) or at least not fully responsible (Glannon 1997).

In order to be held legally responsible for a wrongdoing, a person must have what is called "a guilty mind," or *mens rea*. She must understand, or be capable of understanding, what she is doing and she must know, or be capable of knowing, that what she is doing is wrong. There is little argument that psychopaths know what they are doing. The question is whether they know that what they are doing is wrong. The law distinguishes between two types of wrong: *malum prohibitum* and *malum in se*. *Malum prohibitum* is a legally enforced conventional wrong, such as double-parking or nude bathing. *Malum in se*, on the other hand, refers to something that is wrong in itself – i.e., something that has a deeper justification outside its being legally culpable – such as murder, rape, or theft. It seems, therefore, in order to have *mens rea* of murder, say, one must be capable of a deeper understanding of right and wrong.

As we have seen, there are some reasons to think that psychopaths may lack a deeper understanding of right and wrong, either because they have deficient rational capacities or deficient or absent affectivity. Accordingly, there are philosophers who maintain that psychopaths are no more responsible for their wrongdoings than other people who suffer from mental disorder (Duff 1977; Wallace 1996; Glannon 1997). We noted before that psychopaths have both deficient practical reason or deficient affective responses to the pain and distress of others. It should be stressed, however, that such capacities are impaired, not absent.

Those who argue that psychopaths have sufficient moral knowledge to be legally responsible typically focus on the fact that their deficits appear to be just that: deficits not inabilities. They have enough understanding to appreciate the wrongness of their actions – namely, that they are causing pain and disability to others, that they are acting against their wishes, and so on – so that they can be held legally responsible for them. This is the view of two more prominent psychopathy researchers, Hervey Cleckley and Robert Hare. Others argue that there is a fundamental difference between the moral disability experienced by people judged to be insane and psychopaths. Whereas the former have lacunae in an overall intact moral capacity, what seems to characterize psychopaths is a distinct *lack* of moral concern. We excuse the insane for committing wrongs often because had their mistaken beliefs been right, their action would have been justified (Reznek 1997). By contrast, psychopaths' "mistake" is to think of others as having value only to the extent that they can help further their own goals, and to believe that the suffering of others comes second to their own interests. In a way, their mistake is to think that nothing that they do is impermissible. That is tantamount to being immoral or bad. And thus, it is only if you think that one cannot be bad without being mad that you will be convinced that psychopaths are not legally responsible because they are insane (Maibom 2008).

Another way to argue that psychopaths are not legally responsible would be to focus on their volition. Are they really capable of controlling their actions in the way the law requires? This line of argument is typically not explored because of the difficulty of showing that a defendant could not have done otherwise.

Moral Responsibility

Many consider legal responsibility to depend on moral responsibility, so that only if someone is morally responsible, can she also be legally responsible. Theories of moral responsibility are rather diverse. They typically all require either a capacity for practical rationality and/or for affective resonance or reactivity to others and their plight. As such, most of what was discussed above can be applied here. Typically, the debate is put in terms of whether psychopaths are responsive to moral *reasons*. This raises the difficult issues of what reasons for actions are and what counts as being responsive to them. A reason for you not to run to work is that you are going to show up all sweaty and put your colleagues off. For that to count as a reason for you, you must also want to not put off your colleagues. Moral reasons are somewhat different from such simple practical reasons in that they are supposed to give you reasons to act or refrain from acting no matter what your desires or plans are. Let's say the only way for you to get the job you want is to arrange the early demise of another candidate who has just been offered the job. The fact that you would have to kill another to get the job is reason enough for you not to do it period. In less extreme cases, the fact that you will hurt someone's feelings at least counts against the action that you are contemplating even if you end up performing it anyway. Psychopaths act in rather disorganized ways – even so-called successful psychopaths are typically found in community settings such as short-term work centers – that raise questions even about their ability to act in their own best interests. It is therefore understandable how they might be thought to not really grasp the nature of reasons (Kennett 2002).

As always the debate is about whether the deficits psychopaths have in the area of practical reasoning are sufficient to make it the case that they do not understand the nature of reasons. Whereas as a number of philosophers argue that they fail to understand the nature of reasons (Kennett 2002; Duff 1977), others argue that it is questionable that psychopaths are *that* deficient in their reasoning (cf. Maibom 2005). What is often definitive in this debate is how thick a reading one gives of "reasons." Those who think that psychopaths do not understand reasons tend to have rather thick notions of what such understanding consists in. A thinner notion characterizes the thoughts of those who think psychopaths have the ability to comprehend the nature of reasons. The worry about the thicker notion, of course, is that many people other than psychopaths may also fail to understand the nature of reasons, rendering a potentially large number of people incapable of being morally responsible for their actions.

Not all ways of fleshing out the ability to be responsive to reasons are in terms of cognitive or rational capacities. Some argue that to understand moral reasons, we must be capable of understanding that other people's preferences are reason-giving *for us*. But such an understanding flows from our ability to empathize with them, some say (Shoemaker 2015). In a similar vein, it has been argued that without empathy we cannot appreciate the value of other people's goals and projects and therefore they cannot move us (Deigh 1995). Others maintain that the capacity to feel concern for others is foundational to moral judgments (Nichols 2004), yet others that sadness and (moral) anger are (Prinz 2007). And since psychopaths are deficient in these areas, these thinkers conclude that they are not morally responsible for their actions. Lastly, one could argue that psychopaths are undermotivated to do what is right and refrain from doing what is wrong. Again, one can reference either their practical reasoning deficits or their deficient emotions. This possibility is relatively underexplored.

Conclusion

It is evident that psychopaths have a very different attitude to moral and legal demands on their actions than ordinary people do. They frequently engage in immoral or illegal activities, and they demonstrate a curious lack of empathy for their victims and guilt or remorse for their actions. They have deficits in a number of areas that theorists have identified as central to moral capacities, such as practical reason or emotion. Such deficits may account for their deficient or lacking moral sense. Whether they also render them exempt from moral and legal responsibility depends on what is required for such responsibility and how pervasive you understand these deficits to be.

Definitions of Key Terms

Practical reason	The capacity for decision-making.
Moral understanding	Understanding that, and possibly why, certain acts are right/wrong, good/bad.
Moral judgment	The determination of the moral quality of an agent or an action; can be a thought or a verbal act.
Utilitarianism	The theory that the ultimate moral good is happiness and the ultimate moral evil is suffering. Thus, we ought to strive to increase happiness and reduce suffering. It is the total amount of happiness and suffering that counts. The moral value of our actions lie in the *consequences* they produce.

Deontology	The idea that certain actions are permissible or impermissible in virtue of the sorts of actions that they are, not due to their good or bad consequences.
Welfare justification	A justification of why some act is morally wrong that refers to the harm, suffering, or reduced welfare of the subject that is the patient of that action.
Purity	Concern with purity is one of Jonathan Haidt's moral domains. Purity concerns are very prominent in many religious cultures, where certain animals (pigs), certain people (women menstruating, untouchables), or certain actions (masturbating) are impure. The justification of why purity violations are wrong is not that there is harm involved. One may substitute "pure" for "natural" to get a sense of how the category is most commonly applied in the West.
Internalism about moral judgment	In its conceptual variant, it holds that it is part of our concept of what it is to judge that something is wrong (or: right) that you are also motivated not to (or: to) perform it. In its empirical form, it claims that as psychological matter of fact, if you judge an act to be wrong, you are thereby also motivated not to perform it.
Moral motivation	Motivation to act in accordance with what is thought to be right/good or to avoid doing what is thought to be wrong/bad.
Externalism about moral judgment	The opposite of internalism. Either it is not part of the concept of a moral judgment that if you make it, you are thereby motivated to act in accordance with it, or it is not an empirical fact about human psychology that if you make a moral judgment, you are thereby motivated to act in accordance with it.

Summary Points

- Psychopaths can distinguish between right/good and wrong/bad actions.
- Psychopaths are capable of giving moral justifications.

- Psychopaths do not react to pain and suffering in others as ordinary people do.
- Psychopaths have impaired ability to make good decisions.
- Psychopaths may lack a deeper understanding of right/wrong, good/bad due to their practical reasoning deficits and/or their impaired emotionality.
- It is debatable whether psychopaths' deficits are sufficient to make them not responsible for their actions, legally or morally.

References

Aharoni E, Atanenko O, Kiehl K (2011) Disparities in the moral intuitions of offenders: the role of psychopathy. J Res Pers 45:322–327

Aharoni E, Sinnott-Armstrong W, Kiehl K (2012) Can psychopathic offender discern moral wrong? A new look at the moral/conventional distinction. J Abnorm Psychol 121:484–497

Bartels D, Pizarro D (2011) The mismeasure of morals: antisocial personality traits predict utilitarian responses to moral dilemmas. Cognition 121:154–161

Birbaumer N, Veit R, Lotze M et al (2005) Deficient fear conditioning in psychopathy. Arch Gen Psychiatry 62:799–805

Blair RJR (1995) A cognitive developmental approach to morality: investigating the psychopath. Cognition 57:1–29

Blair RJR (1997) Moral reasoning and the child with psychopathic tendencies. Personal Individ Differ 22:731–739

Blair RJR, Colledge E, Mitchell D (2001) Somatic markers and response reversal: is there orbitofrontal cortex dysfunction in boys with psychopathic tendencies? J Abnorm Child Psychol 29:499–511

Blair RJR, Mitchell D, Blair K (2005) The psychopath: emotion and the brain. Blackwell, Oxford

Brink D (1989) Moral realism and the foundations of ethics. Cambridge University Press, Cambridge

Cima M, Tonnaer F, Hauser MD (2010) Psychopaths know right from wrong but don't care. Soc Cogn Affect Neurosci 5:59–67

Cleckley H (1976) The mask of sanity, 5th edn. Mosby, St. Louis

Decety J, Chen C, Harenski C et al (2013a) An fMRI study of affective perspective taking in individuals with psychopathy: imagining another in pain does not evoke empathy. Front Hum Neurosci 7:489. doi:10.3389/ fnhum.2013.00489

Decety J, Skelly L, Kiehl K (2013b) Brain responses to empathy-eliciting scenarios involving pain in incarcerated individuals with psychopathy. JAMA Psychiatry 70:638–645

Decety J, Skelly L, Yoder K et al (2014) Neural processing of dynamic emotional facial expressions in psychopaths. Soc Neurosci 9:36–49

Deigh J (1995) Empathy and universalizability. Ethics 105:743–763

Domes G, Hollerbach P, Vohs K, Mokros A, Habermeyer E (2013) Emotional empathy and psychopathy in offenders: an experimental study. J Personal Disord 27:67–84

Duff RA (1977) Psychopathy and moral understanding. Am Philos Q 14:189–200

Glannon W (1997) Psychopathy and responsibility. J Appl Philos 14:263–275

Glen A, Iyer R, Graham J et al (2009a) Are all type of morality compromised in psychopathy? J Personal Disord 23:384–398

Glen A, Raine A, Schug A, Young L, Hauser M (2009b) Increased DLPFC activity during moral decision making in psychopathy. Mol Psychiatry 14:909–911

Greene JD, Sommerville RB, Nystrom LE et al (2001) An fMRI investigation of emotional involvement in moral judgment. Science 293:2105–2108

Greenspan PS (1995) Practical guilt: moral dilemmas, emotions, and social norms. Oxford University Press, New York

Harenski CL, Harenski KL, Shane MS, Kiehl KA (2010) J Abnorm Psychol 119:864–874

Hare R (1993) Without conscience: the disturbing world of psychopaths among us. Pocket Books, New York

Hare R (2004) The Hare psychopathy checklist-revised. Multi-Health System, Toronto

Herpertz SC, Werth U, Lukas G et al (2001) Emotion in criminal offenders with psychopathy and borderline personality disorder. Arch Gen Psychiatry 58:737–745

Hiatt KD, Newman JP (2006) Understanding psychopathy: the cognitive side. In: Patrick CJ (ed) Handbook of psychopathy. Guilford Press, New York, pp 334–352

Hicks B, Markon K, Patrick C et al (2004) Identifying psychopathy subtypes on the basis of personality structure. Psychol Assess 16:276–288

Kant I (1785/1993) Grounding for the metaphysics of morals. (trans, Ellington J). Hackett Publishing, Indianapolis

Kennett J (2002) Autism, empathy and moral agency. Philos Q 52:340–357

Kiehl KA, Lushing J (2014) Psychopathy. Scholarpedia 9:30835

Koenigs M, Young L, Adolphs R et al (2007) Damage to the prefrontal cortex increases utilitarian moral judgments. Nature 446:908–911

Koenigs M, Kruepke M, Zeier J et al (2012) Utilitarian moral judgment in psychopathy. Soc Cogn Affect Neurosci 7:708–714

Levenston G, Patrick C, Bradley M et al (2000) The psychopath as observer: emotion and attention in picture processing. J Abnorm Psychol 109:373–385

Link NF, Scherer SE, Byrne PN (1977) Moral judgment and moral conduct in the psychopath. Can Psychiatr Assoc J 22:341–346

Lishner DA, Vitacco MJ, Hong PY, Mosley J, Miska K, Stocks EL (2012) Evaluating the relation between psychopathy and affective empathy: two preliminary studies. Int J Offender Therapy Comp Criminol 56:1161–1181

Lykken DT (1957) A study of anxiety in the psychopathic personality. J Abnorm Soc Psychol 55:6–10

Maibom HL (2005) Moral unreason: the case of psychopathy. Mind Lang 20:237–257

Maibom HL (2008) The mad, the bad, and the psychopath. Neuroethics 1:167–184

Marsh A, Cardinale E (2012) Psychopathy and fear: specific impairments in judging behaviors that frighten others. Emotion 12:892–898

Meffert H, Gazzola V, den Boer JA et al (2013) Reduced spontaneous but relatively normal deliberate vicarious representations in psychopathy. Brain 136:2550–2562

Mullins-Nelson JL, Salekin RT, Leistico A-MR (2006) Psychopathy, empathy, and perspective taking ability in a community sample: implications for the successful psychopath concept. Int J Forensic Ment Health 5:133–149

Newman J, Kosson D (1986) Passive avoidance learning in psychopathic and non-psychopathic offenders. J Abnorm Psychol 96:257–263

Nichols S (2004) Sentimental rules: on the nature and foundation of moral judgment. Oxford University Press, New York

O'Kane A, Fawcett D, Blackburn R (1996) Psychopathy and moral reasoning: comparison of two classifications. Personal Individ Differ 20:505–514

Patrick C, Cuthbert B, Lang P (1994) Emotion in the criminal psychopath: fear image processing. J Abnorm Psychol 103:523–534

Porter S (1996) Without conscience or without active conscience: the etiology of psychopath revisited. Aggress Violent Behav 1:179–189

Prinz JJ (2007) The emotional construction of morals. Oxford University Press, New York

Reznek L (1997) Evil or ill: justifying the insanity defence. Routledge, London

Salekin RT (2006) Psychopathy in children and adolescents: key issues in conceptualization and assessment. In: Patrick C (ed) Handbook of psychopathy. Guilford Press, New York, pp 389–415

Shamay-Tsoory S, Harari H, Aharon-Perez J et al (2010) The role of orbitofrontal cortex in affective theory of mind deficits in criminal offenders with psychopathic tendencies. Cortex 46:668–677

Shoemaker D (2015) Responsibility from the margins. Oxford University Press, Oxford

Strawson PF (1962) Freedom and resentment. Proc Br Acad 48:1–25

Verona E, Bresin K, Patrick C (2013) Revisiting psychopathy in women: Cleckley/Hare conceptions and affective response. J Abnorm Psychol 122:1088–1093

von Borries AKL, Volman I, de Bruijn ERA et al (2012) Psychopaths lack the autonomic avoidance of social threat: relation to instrumental aggression. Psychiatry Res 200:761–766

Wallace RJ (1996) Responsibility and the moral sentiments. Harvard University Press, Cambridge, MA

Young L, Koenigs M, Kruepke M et al (2012) Psychopathy increases perceived moral permissibility of accidents. J Abnorm Psychol 121:659–667

Index

© Springer Science+Business Media Dordrecht 2017
T. Schramme, S. Edwards (eds.), *Handbook of the Philosophy of Medicine*,
DOI 10.1007/978-94-017-8688-1

Printed by Printforce, the Netherlands